# The Youth Labor
# Market Problem

A National Bureau
of Economic Research
Conference Report

# The Youth Labor Market Problem: Its Nature, Causes, and Consequences

Edited by **Richard B. Freeman and David A. Wise**

The University of Chicago Press
*Chicago and London*

RICHARD B. FREEMAN is professor of economics at Harvard University and director of the NBER's program in labor studies. DAVID A. WISE is Stanbough Professor of Political Economy at the John F. Kennedy School of Government and an NBER research associate.

This material results in part from tax-supported research (U.S. Department of Labor contract no. J-9-M-8-0043).

Figures 15.1 and 15.2 are reproduced from the U.K. *Department of Employment Gazette* for August 1978.

The University of Chicago Press, Chicago 60637
The University of Chicago Press, Ltd., London

**Library of Congress Cataloging in Publication Data**

Main entry under title:

The Youth labor market problem.

(A National Bureau of Economic Research conference report)
Includes indexes.
1. Youth—Employment—Congresses.  I. Freeman,
Richard Barry, 1943-    .  II. Wise, David A.
III. Series.
HD6273.Y656      331.3'412      81-11438
ISBN 0-226-26161-1                      AACR2

Since this volume is a record of conference proceedings, it has been exempted from the rules governing critical review of manuscripts by the Board of Directors of the National Bureau (resolution adopted 6 July 1948, as revised 21 November 1949 and 20 April 1968).

# Contents

# 1 The Youth Labor Market Problem: Its Nature, Causes, and Consequences

Richard B. Freeman and David A. Wise

Youths and young adults have traditionally worked less than older persons. While some youths work less than adults because they are devoting a major portion of their time to schooling or to leisure activities, others work less because they have great difficulty obtaining jobs or because they are in the midst of switching their primary activity from schooling to employment, a process that involves considerable searching and job changing before settling into more or less permanent employment.

In recent years, as large numbers of youths have entered the job market, and because some groups of young persons have lower employment rates than comparable groups in the past, there has been rising concern about the operation of the youth labor market. Youth unemployment has become a major issue, as evidenced by congressional legislation such as the Youth Employment and Demonstration Projects Act of 1977.

Under the auspices of the National Bureau of Economic Research (NBER), economists from several universities have been engaged in extensive investigation of the nature of youth employment, the causes of changes in youth employment rates over time, the causes of individual differences in employment experiences, and the consequences of youth unemployment. This chapter represents a distillation of the findings of that work. We will summarize briefly the principal results of the NBER analysis and then describe the nature of these results in greater detail.

## 1.1 Dimensions of the Youth Employment Problem

1. One of the most important lessons of our analysis is that standard published statistics may not adequately measure the dimensions of youth

Richard B. Freeman is professor of economics at Harvard University and director of the NBER's program in labor studies. David A. Wise is Stanbough Professor of Political Economy at the John F. Kennedy School of Government and an NBER research associate.

employment and joblessness. First, different sources of employment information lead to widely differing estimates of the number of employed youths. The Current Population Survey (CPS), which provides the official government statistics, reports a smaller number of youths employed than do other government-financed surveys.

Second, the traditional distinction between being unemployed (out of work and looking for a job) and being out of the labor force (out of work and not looking for a job) appears less clear for young persons than for older workers. Many youths are on the borderline between seeking work and not seeking work, and switch frequently from one group to the other. Some youths who are out of the labor force may in fact desire to work but have simply given up looking. On the other hand, some youths who are classified as unemployed may not be seeking work as actively as unemployed adults. In addition, many youths who are classified as unemployed are also in school full time, an activity that many would consider as productive as work. While for all age groups the difference between unemployment and being out of the labor force is ambiguous, the ambiguity is especially great for youths.

2. Constant references to *the* youth employment problem, as if all or the majority of young persons had difficulty obtaining jobs, appear to misinterpret the nature of the difficulty. Youth joblessness is in fact concentrated, by and large, among a small group who lack work for extended periods of time. Over half of the male teenage unemployment is, for example, among those who are out of work for over six months, a group constituting less than 10% of the youth labor force and only 7% of the youth population. The concentration of joblessness among a small group means that lack of employment is a major problem for that group, but also that most youths have little difficulty obtaining work.

3. The youths who make up the relatively small group that is chronically without work have distinct characteristics. They are disproportionately black; disproportionately high school dropouts, and disproportionately residents of poverty areas. Over time, the percentage of black youths with jobs has fallen while the proportion of white youths with jobs has not, implying a deterioration in the employment chances of black youths. Despite the extremely high rate of unemployment among black youths, though, the fact is that since there are many more whites than blacks in the population, most unemployment in even this chronic group is accounted for by whites.

While the employment rate of black youths has fallen sharply over the past decade, the wages of young blacks have risen relative to those of white youths. By the mid-1970s the wage rates of black and white youths with comparable levels of education were approximately equal.

## 1.2    The Causes of Youth Employment Problems

4. One of the most important determinants of youth employment is the strength of the economy as a whole. When the aggregate level of economic activity and the level of adult employment is high, youth employment is also high. Quantitatively, the employment of youths appears to be one of the most highly sensitive variables in the labor market, rising substantially during boom periods and falling substantially during less active periods.

Another frequently mentioned determinant of youth employment is the proportion of youths in the population. According to our analysis, however, while the increase in the relative number of young people in recent years has adversely affected youth employment, its primary impact has been to depress youth wages relative to adult wages.

A third important determinant of youth employment is the minimum wage; our evidence confirms previous findings that by making youth labor more expensive, increases in the minimum wage reduce youth employment.

5. At any given time, youths with certain background characteristics tend to have lower employment rates than youths with other characteristics. Some of the characteristics associated with lower employment appear to be unrelated to wages. Youths from poor families frequently tend to be employed less often than youngsters from wealthier families, although once employed both groups earn about the same wages. As noted earlier, blacks are employed less often than whites, but earn about the same wages when employed. The sizable increase in black youth wage rates may have contributed to the relative deterioration in employment of black youths.

6. Some forms of preparation during high school are related to subsequent labor market experiences of youths while others are not. Vocational training in high school shows little, if any, relationship to labor market success, even among youths who obtain no further education after high school. Academic performance in high school, on the other hand, is positively related to both employment and wages after graduation and entry into the labor force. And most important and possibly surprising, youths who work in high school work much longer per year when they enter the labor force full time than teenagers who do not work while in high school, and they earn more per hour as well.

## 1.3    The Consequences of Youth Employment and Unemployment

7. Much of the recent discussion about youth unemployment is focused on the fear that lack of work during one's youth will contribute substantially to unemployment later in life. This fear appears to be

greatly exaggerated. We have found that unemployment immediately following the completion of school has virtually no effect on employment three or four years later. Indeed, initial wage rates have almost no effect on later wage rates. However, early unemployment has a sizable negative effect on later wage rates.

8. While the precise links have yet to be established, the changing employment situation of young black persons has been associated with other widespread social developments: increases in youth crime, drug use, violence in schools, and youth suicide, suggesting that the consequences and correlates of the problem go beyond standard economic issues. The finding that youth unemployment is concentrated among a small group of youths in itself suggests that this group may also have other social problems.

In short, this NBER volume has found that many commonly held views about the youth employment problems are erroneous and that many critical aspects of the problems have been inadequately understood: youth unemployment, rather than being widespread among a large proportion of youths, is in fact concentrated among a small group; the nature of youth employment and unemployment differs substantially from that of adult employment and unemployment; and youth unemployment generally does not have the major long-term consequences on later employment that some have feared, though it does affect later wages.

## 1.4   The Nature of the Youth Employment Problem

A few basic statistics will motivate and provide background for our subsequent discussion. Employment and unemployment rates for selected years by race, sex, and age are shown in table 1.1 (Freeman and Medoff, chapter 3).
These data show divergent levels and trends in the percentages of youths with jobs and the percentage unemployed; they describe the primary characteristics of the youth labor market.

Although youth unemployment is sometimes perceived and portrayed as a crisis of youth in general, these data do not support this interpretation. The employment rate of white male youths has changed only modestly in the past two decades; indeed, the trend has been upward since the mid-1960s. The percentage of white females employed has also risen substantially, even in the 1970s.

On the other hand, since 1954 the percentage of black youths with jobs has fallen dramatically and there has been a correspondingly large increase in the black unemployment rate. This disturbing trend is even more troublesome in light of the fact that it is a relatively recent one. In 1954, approximately equal percentages of black and white youths were employed. Since that time, unemployment rates for black youths have

Table 1.1                Employment and Unemployment Rates 1954–77

|  | White | | | | Black and other | | | |
|---|---|---|---|---|---|---|---|---|
|  | 1954 | 1964 | 1969 | 1977 | 1954 | 1964 | 1969 | 1977 |
| Men | | | | | | | | |
| Percentage Employed | | | | | | | | |
| Age: 16–17 | 40.6 | 36.5 | 42.7 | 44.3 | 40.4 | 27.6 | 28.4 | 18.9 |
| 18–19 | 61.3 | 57.7 | 61.8 | 65.2 | 66.5 | 51.8 | 51.1 | 36.9 |
| 20–24 | 77.9 | 79.3 | 78.8 | 80.5 | 75.9 | 78.1 | 77.3 | 61.2 |
| 25–54 | 93.8 | 94.4 | 95.1 | 91.3 | 86.4 | 87.8 | 89.7 | 81.7 |
| Percentage of Labor Force Unemployed | | | | | | | | |
| Age: 16–17 | 14.0 | 16.1 | 12.5 | 17.6 | 13.4 | 25.9 | 24.7 | 38.7 |
| 18–19 | 13.0 | 13.4 | 7.9 | 13.0 | 14.7 | 23.1 | 19.0 | 36.1 |
| 20–24 | 9.8 | 7.4 | 4.6 | 9.3 | 16.9 | 12.6 | 8.4 | 21.7 |
| 25–54 | 3.9 | 2.8 | 1.5 | 3.9 | 9.5 | 6.6 | 2.8 | 7.8 |
| Women | | | | | | | | |
| Percentage Employed | | | | | | | | |
| Age: 16–17 | 25.8 | 25.3 | 30.3 | 37.5 | 19.8 | 12.5 | 16.9 | 12.5 |
| 18–19 | 47.2 | 43.0 | 49.2 | 54.3 | 29.9 | 32.9 | 33.9 | 28.0 |
| 20–24 | 41.6 | 45.3 | 53.3 | 61.4 | 43.1 | 43.7 | 51.5 | 45.4 |
| 25–54 | 40.1 | 41.0 | 46.2 | 54.1 | 49.0 | 52.7 | 56.3 | 57.4 |
| Percentage of Labor Force Unemployed | | | | | | | | |
| Age: 16–17 | 12.0 | 17.1 | 13.8 | 18.2 | 19.1 | 36.5 | 31.2 | 44.7 |
| 18–19 | 9.4 | 13.2 | 10.0 | 14.2 | 21.6 | 29.2 | 25.7 | 37.4 |
| 20–24 | 6.4 | 7.1 | 5.5 | 9.3 | 13.2 | 18.3 | 12.0 | 23.6 |
| 25–54 | 5.0 | 4.3 | 3.2 | 5.8 | 8.3 | 8.4 | 5.0 | 9.8 |

risen and their employment position has deteriorated greatly. As can be seen in the figures of table 1.1, the unemployed proportion of black youths has increased relative to black adults as well as relative to white youths. (In 1954, the unemployment rate of black youths was about 1.5 times the rate for black adults; by 1977, the youth rate was almost 4 times the adult rate.)

Thus, to the extent that trends in the data signify a deterioration in the employment of youths, that deterioration is concentrated among black youngsters. Nonetheless, because a much greater proportion of the population is white, the vast majority of unemployed youths are white.

What the numbers in the table above do not reveal is that almost half of the teenagers classified as unemployed are also in school. The unemployment of a young person in school, most would agree, represents less loss to society than that of an adult seeking full-time work.

The Bureau of Labor Statistics defines unemployment as the ratio of persons looking for work to the number employed plus the number looking. According to this (BLS) definition, 18% of male teenagers aged 16 to 19 were unemployed in October 1976. Since most full-time students are not included in the youth labor force, however, this figure overstates the fraction of young persons who are ready to work but have no productive way to spend their time. Just 4.9% of teenagers are both unemployed and not in school. On the other hand, the unemployment data ignore youths who are not in the labor force. In October 1976, 9% of male teenagers 16 to 19 years old were either unemployed or out of the labor force and not in school. Moreover, only 70% of the out-of-school teenagers (many of whom were high school dropouts) held jobs according to the Current Population Survey data.[1]

Whichever groups are considered, unemployment is concentrated among those with the lowest levels of education. Among out-of-school teenagers, for example, persons with less than 12 years of school account for 58% of the unemployed. Unemployment rates are much higher among high school dropouts than among high school graduates. Moreover, unemployment is also concentrated among relatively few persons: those unemployed for very long periods. If we add up all periods of unemployment for male teenagers, for example, we find that 54% of the total is composed of persons who are unemployed for more than six months of the year. Even more striking, 10% of all teenagers account for more than half of total teenage unemployment (Feldstein and Ellwood, chapter 2; Clark and Summers, chapter 7). The majority of young persons move in and out of the labor force and obtain jobs with ease; many youths either experience no unemployment at all between transitions or are unemployed only for very short spells. However, the concentration of unemployment among a small fraction of youths has presumably higher social costs than if unemployment were evenly distributed among all youths.

In short, the data suggest that most teenagers do not have substantial employment difficulties, but that for a minority of youths, there are long periods without work that constitute severe problems. This group is composed in large part of high school dropouts and contains black youths in numbers disproportionate to their representation in the population.

It is commonly believed that young persons have much more difficulty in finding jobs than their adult counterparts. Measured by the lengths of spells of unemployment, the evidence does not support this view. The average duration of periods of unemployment for teenagers is about the same as the average for adults.[2] However, many spells of teenage unemployment end not when a job is found, but when the young person drops out of the labor force. Teenagers average as much as five months between loss of a job and attainment of a new job (Clark and Summers, chapter 7). (The volatility of the youth labor force, with persons frequently entering and leaving the officially measured labor force, raises questions about the adequacy of the data in distinguishing between the two states.)

Unemployment rates can be broken down into two components: the rate at which persons change jobs or switch from out of the labor force into the labor force, multiplied by the rate at which the changers or switchers are unemployed. Analysis of these two components of unemployment shows that young persons are unemployed more than adults because they change jobs or situations more often than adults, not because they have a greater chance of unemployment given a change in status.

About one-fourth of young men aged 18 to 24 change jobs in a year, compared to less than one-tenth of men aged 35 to 54. The differential proportion of job changers by age is itself largely attributable, according to Mincer and Leighton's calculations, to differences in seniority by age. Low-seniority workers, of necessity primarily young workers, change jobs frequently, while high-seniority workers, of necessity primarily older workers, change less frequently and are as a result less likely to be unemployed. One of the key factors behind the high rate of youth joblessness is the high mobility and short job tenure of the young (Mincer and Leighton, chapter 8).

Finally, we emphasize that the interpretation of all these data is complicated by uncertainty about the accuracy of their magnitudes. Recent large-scale surveys that interview young persons themselves rather than resident adults in a household as is common in the widely used Current Population Survey, reveal higher rates of employment and different rates of unemployment than do the official government statistics.

For example, for October 1972, employment rates for out-of-school male high school graduates, based on the National Center for Educational Statistics study of the high school class of 1972, were 88% for whites and 78% for blacks (Meyer and Wise, chapter 9). The comparable Current Population Survey data, the basis for official Bureau of Labor statistics numbers, implied substantially lower unemployment rates of 82% and 68% respectively. Similar differences arise in comparing the Current Population Survey rates with those based on the National Longitudinal Survey of Young Men. A large portion of the difference among the various rates can be attributed to who answers the survey questions in each case. Youths report more employment activity for themselves than is reported by the household member most likely to respond to government population surveys, a youth's mother. The differences in reports are larger for in-school youths with full-time jobs (Freeman and Medoff, chapter 4). It is important to remember that until the discrepancy in survey results is completely resolved and the "correct" rate of youth employment determined, there will be ambiguity about the causes and consequences of the problem.

## 1.5   The Consequences: Market Determinants of Youth Employment

Whether a youth is employed or not depends partly on the strength of the economy and on broad demographic conditions, and partly on individual characteristics of the youth himself. The aggregate determinants are those that influence the average level of youth employment at a given time; the individual influences are those that determine differences among individuals at a given time. We shall discuss the broader influences on the average youth employment rate in this section, and individual differences in the next section.

The most important aggregate determinant is the level of economic activity. There is strong evidence that when the economy is strong, youths as well as adult workers are better off. A widely used indicator of the level of aggregate economic activity is the unemployment rate for adult males. Young persons living in areas where the local unemployment rate is high have more spells of unemployment than comparable youths in areas with strong economies (Mincer and Leighton, chapter 8).

Analysis of differences among metropolitan areas, based on 1970 Census data, indicates that an increase in the adult male unemployment rate is associated with disproportionately large decreases in the proportion of youths who are employed. When the adult unemployment rate rises by one percentage point, the proportion of youths who are employed drops by the following percentage amounts (Freeman, chapter 5):

| All Young Men | | Out-of-school Young Men | |
|---|---|---|---|
| Aged: 16 to 17 | 5% | Aged: 16 to 17 | 5% |
| 18 to 19 | 2% | 18 to 19 | 3% |
| 20 to 24 | 3% | 20 to 24 | 3% |

Evidence based on changes in adult unemployment over time confirms these findings. The time series data show that a one percentage point increase in the adult male unemployment rate is associated with a 5% decrease in the proportion of young men aged 16 to 19 who are employed.[3] Thus youth employment is highly sensitive to cyclical movements in the economy.

A second indicator of aggregate economic activity, the growth rate of personal income, also shows a substantial positive relationship to youth employment, according to our comparative analysis of metropolitan areas. If these indicators reflect aggregate demand, then demand forces have a substantial effect on youth employment.

Two other measures of aggregate economic conditions are also strongly related to youth employment. One is the "industrial mix" in the area where the young person lives, and the other is the average income level in the area. Based on comparisons across metropolitan areas, youth employment is higher in those areas with a large number of industries that traditionally employ many young workers. Some of these industries have large numbers of jobs that do not require extensive training; other industries may simply have developed production processes, and organized their work forces, in such a way that large numbers of young persons are accommodated. The "industrial mix" has an approximately equal effect on the employment of teenagers aged 16 to 19 as the effect of aggregate economic activity (as measured by the adult unemployment rate), but has smaller effects on those aged 20 to 24 (Freeman, chapter 5).

In addition, the extent of poverty in an area affects the employment chances of youths. Those areas with greater proportions of families living in poverty, and those youths living in officially designated poverty areas, tend to have lower rates of youth employment (Rees and Gray, chapter 13; Freeman, chapter 5). This is true even among areas with similar levels of adult unemployment, personal income growth rates, and industrial mix. Thus some characteristics of youths, or of the demand for young workers in poor areas, are not captured by these other geographic characteristics.

Another frequently mentioned aggregate determinant of the percentage of youths who are employed is the proportion of the total population who are young. Over the past decade and a half, this proportion has increased dramatically. It is argued that production technologies and institutional arrangements may make the economy slow to adapt to large changes in the relative numbers of younger versus older workers, thereby increasing unemployment and reducing the number of youths who work.

Our evidence suggests that while there may be some such effects, especially for 16 to 17 year olds, the large increase in the number of the youths relative to adults in the labor force has affected wage rates more than employment. The fact that during the period of rapid increase in the youth proportion of the population the fraction of youths employed did *not* fall casts doubt on the importance of the number of young persons as a major determinant of their employment.

The large increases in the youth labor force in the summer months without a corresponding increase in youth unemployment also bring into question the effect of the proportion of youths in the population on their employment rate. During the summer months, the labor market absorbs large numbers of teenagers. Although teenage labor force participation has been almost 40% higher in July than the annual average, in July the teenage unemployment rate has been somewhat lower than the annual average (Clark and Summers, chapter 7).

Evidence from geographic areas with different proportions of young persons, however, suggests that a one-percentage-point increase in the proportion of the population that is young may lead to a noticeable reduction in the employment rate of 16 to 17 year olds, but not those aged 18 to 19, or those aged 20 to 24. Additional evidence based on movements over time in the employment of youths suggests that increases in the relative number of youths are, in general, associated with declines in the employment ratio of most youth groups (Wachter and Kim, chapter 6), though not by enough to dominate the other factors contributing to youth employment.

Perhaps the greatest effect of the increasing proportions of youths in the population has been a decrease in youth wages relative to adult wages, rather than a decrease in youth employment. The earnings of black and white male youths, as a percentage of earnings of adult males, are shown in the tabulation below for 1967 and 1977 and for selected age groups (Wachter and Kim, chapter 6).

| Age | White | | Black and Other | |
|-----|-------|------|-----------------|------|
|     | 1967  | 1977 | 1967            | 1977 |
| 18  | 54    | 49   | 44              | 44   |
| 20  | 66    | 58   | 63              | 52   |
| 22  | 79    | 63   | 59              | 54   |
| 24  | 87    | 75   | 60              | 63   |

The earnings of young white men in all age groups declined rather dramatically relative to adult wages between 1967 and 1977. On the other hand, the earnings of black youths have not changed much, on average, relative to adult earnings. Thus the market adjustment to larger numbers of youths has been reflected to some extent in a relative decline in youth wages. Indeed, for white youths, wages may have been the primary equilibrating mechanism, allowing the employment rate to be maintained in the face of large increases in the relative number of youths in the population. Traditional supply-and-demand analysis suggests that whenever the supply of any group of workers increases relative to the demand for them, the larger numbers will be employed only at a lower wage rate. In contrast to the decline in the white youth wage rates relative to adult wages, the wages of black youths—both male and female—rose relative to the wages of white youths. At the same time, black youths were finding it increasingly difficult to find jobs. It is likely that the change in the relative wages of the two groups contributed to the deterioration in black versus white employment.

There is also a wide body of evidence showing that the employment of both white and black youths is handicapped by the minimum wage, presumably because the minimum wage is higher than employers are willing to pay some youths. Since the number of young persons looking for jobs can change when the minimum wage changes, the minimum wage has a more systematic effect on employment than on unemployment of the young. Some results suggest larger effects on employment for 16 to 17 year olds, and for black youths in general, than for other groups (Wachter and Kim, chapter 6). Both the evidence on the relationship between youth employment and youth wage rates and the evidence on the effect of the minimum wage are consistent with evidence from the United Kingdom, where youth employment appears to be quite sensitive to the level of youth wages (Layard, chapter 15). The downward trend in youth wages relative to adult wages in the U.S. may, however, have been a more important determinant of youth employment in the 1970s than changes in the legal minimum. In addition, although most discussions of the minimum wage focus on its likely effects on youth employment and wages, it is also possible, in theory, for the minimum wage to shorten the duration of teenage jobs and thus increase the frequency with which youths change jobs (Hall, chapter 14).

Though some headway has been made in determining the causes of changes in youth employment experiences, it is important to stress that major questions remain unanswered, in particular the differential pattern of change between white and black youths.

## 1.6   The Causes: Individual Determinants and Correlates of Youth Employment and Wages

We now turn to individual characteristics that contribute to differences in employment experience among youths. These are attributes that influence the experience of one youngster relative to another at a given time. It is important to realize from the start that most of the variation in employment and wages among individuals cannot be explained by differences among them that we can observe and measure, such as education or family income. Most of the variation is due to factors, such as individual tastes, opportunities, or chance, that we are unable to explain. Nonetheless, the effect of some characteristics is very substantial. The most important determinants of youth employment and wages follow.

### 1.6.1   Education

As we have already emphasized, high school dropouts are employed fewer weeks per year on average than high school graduates. More generally, out-of-school youths of any age with education below the average for their age group are employed noticeably less than other out-of-school youths in that age group (Rees and Gray, chapter 13).

Particular educational experiences may also affect employment and wages. Much public discussion and policy have centered on the potential influence of job training on later ability to find and do jobs. Yet we have found that vocational training in high school is virtually unrelated to subsequent employment and wage rates, even for persons who obtain no further education after leaving high school. Academic performance, on the other hand, seems to be positively related both to the number of weeks per year that youths are employed and to their wage rates after entering the labor force full time (Meyer and Wise, chapter 9).

In addition, there is a very strong relationship between hours worked while in high school and later employment and wage rates, with persons who work during high school employed many more weeks per year and having higher wage rates when they enter the labor force full time than those who do not work in high school (ibid.). We have not as yet differentiated adequately between two possible explanations for these relationships: that working in high school reflects an underlying commitment and ability to perform well in the market, that the work experience itself enhances these characteristics, or most likely, that both of these situations interact. The relationship suggests, however, that high school work experience may hold significant potential for enhancement of later work experience and at the same time raises the possibility that unemployment among in-school youths, while different from that of out-of-school youths, may result in lost preparation for future work.

### 1.6.2  Family Background

It is widely accepted that early family experiences are likely to affect later employment as well as the educational attainment of youths. We have no knowledge of the early family experiences of youths, but we do have access to measures of some family characteristics such as income. We have found that such measures are related to both school and labor force experiences, but the relationships are not entirely what we expected. For all youths, family background, as measured by parents' income, shows little relationship to employment. Thus family income apparently has little to do with the inclination of youths to seek employment or with their ability to find jobs, although it may affect inclination *and* ability to find work in an offsetting way. However, youths whose brothers and sisters have jobs are more likely to have jobs themselves (Rees and Gray, chapter 13). This finding is subject to several interpretations. It may reflect local labor market conditions or characteristics common to all family members, or it could mean that employed siblings help other youths in the family to secure jobs.

Though children from wealthier families seem to be no more successful in finding jobs than those from poorer families, we have found that youngsters from wealthier families obtain jobs that pay more per hour (Meyer and Wise, chapter 9). The reasons for this pattern have yet to be determined.

We have also found that youths in female-headed households and in households on welfare tend to have fewer jobs than youths from other families, though the differences are not sizable. Again, while this result is not surprising, it is not clear why this relationship occurs. Youths in families where the adult heads are less likely to have jobs may themselves be less likely to seek employment. On the other hand, youngsters from such families may simply have fewer job opportunities. Here too, however, once a youth is employed, family characteristics are not related to wage rates. It is possible, of course, that those who are the most productive on the job are also the most likely to seek employment and the most likely to be hired.

### 1.6.3    Race

As noted earlier, black youths have noticeably lower chances of working than white youths, although the magnitude of black/white differences in employment differ by survey; in some surveys the differences are modest for high school graduates. In contrast, black and white youth wages tend to be quite similar for all educational levels, so that employed young blacks earn about as much as employed young whites. One reason for the downward trend in black youth employment has been a marked increase in the school attendance of young blacks. The increase in black schooling, however, explains only a small proportion of the black/white differences in employment that have arisen since 1954.

We find it implausible to explain the decreased employment in terms of discrimination of the traditional type, particularly in view of increased legal and other pressures placed on discriminators. Perhaps other factors having to do with the social conditions in inner city slums have worsened and have contributed to the weakened employment situation of blacks. No empirically verified explanation presently exists.

## 1.7    The Consequences

Many persons have expressed the fear that periods of unemployment early in one's working career could have substantial adverse effects on employment in future years. We have found that these fears are largely unfounded, and that the evidence has often been misinterpreted to imply that there are large effects. In fact, there is little evidence that time spent out of work early in a youngster's career leads to recurring unemployment (Meyer and Wise, chapter 9; Ellwood, chapter 10). Rather, the cost of not working is the reduction in wages persons suffer later because they failed to accumulate work experience, something employers reward. That early unemployment has little effect on later unemployment does *not* mean that young men and women who have unusually low levels of employment early in their working lives are unlikely to work less in later years. Young men who do not enroll in college and spend some time unemployed their first year out of school, for example, are twice as likely to experience unemployment again than are their peers who escaped early unemployment (Ellwood, chapter 10). But this effect is due almost entirely to persistence of individual differences such as education, academic ability, and motivation. The existence of such characteristics creates a positive correlation between time worked in one year and that worked in the next and subsequent years. To isolate the effect of unemployment itself on future unemployment, it is necessary to control for these individual differences. Once individual differences are controlled for, so that persons can be compared only on the basis of early work experience, there is little relationship between employment experience after high school and employment four years later.

This conclusion holds for widely differing groups of young men and probably for young women as well. It is supported by evidence on young men who do not enroll in college, including high school dropouts, who were followed in the National Longitudinal Survey of Young Men (ibid.). It is also supported by evidence on a large national sample of high school graduates surveyed as part of the National Longitudinal Study of the High School Class of 1972 (Meyer and Wise, chapter 9). Comparable evidence based on young women in the National Longitudinal Survey of Young Women supports this conclusion as well (Corcoran, chapter 11). This does not mean, of course, that we should be unconcerned that some persons will always tend to have poorer labor force experience than others. But it does mean that initial employment in itself does not increase or decrease employment over the long run. Thus, for example, simply creating jobs for persons right after high school should not be expected to increase the number of weeks that they will be employed four years later.

Since wage rates increase with experience, there is, however, a cost to not working today. Individuals who are unemployed in their youth obtain lower wages in subsequent years because they have accrued fewer years of experience. The effect for high school graduates three or four years later appears to be modest, and it is somewhat less for women than for men (Meyer and Wise, chapter 9; Corcoran, chapter 11). Evidence for young men with less than fourteen years' education showed considerably higher estimates of the effects of early experience on wage rates three or four years later, upwards of 15% per year out of work (Ellwood, chapter 10). All of this evidence is consistent with previous research findings on the relationship between earnings and experience. In short, unemployment does not by itself foster later unemployment, but the effect of unemployment is felt in lower future wages, and this effect may be quite substantial.

Not only is there little effect of early employment on subsequent employment, but initial wage rates in themselves have little effect on subsequent wage rates. Once persistent individual differences are controlled for, there is virtually no relationship between wage rates early in a person's labor force experience and wages earned several years later (Meyer and Wise, chapter 9). After allowing for individual characteristics, a low paying job one year will not by itself lead to a low paying job three or four years later, according to our findings. Thus the fear that a low-level job one year—as indicated by a low wage rate—will harm one's chances of obtaining a better job in later years appears to be unfounded.

These findings are distinct from the observation that unemployment varies according to occupational characteristics. Young persons working in occupations with high initial wages but slow wage growth, and in occupations whose work force is highly mobile across industries also have higher rates of unemployment (Brown, chapter 12).

## 1.8 Conclusions

The NBER research has illuminated several aspects of youth employment and unemployment. We have found that severe employment problems are concentrated among a small proportion of youths with distinctive characteristics but that for the vast majority of youths lack of employment is not a severe problem. Thus the youth unemployment crisis should be thought of as one specific to only a small proportion of youths, not as a general problem. Black youths are less likely to be employed than white youths, but once employed the two groups have similar wage rates; this rough equality is a recent development. While work experience and academic performance in school have been found to be related to employment and wages, vocational training in school has not. Aggregate economic activity has been found to be a major determinant of the level of youth employment.

Early employment experience has virtually no effect on later employment after controlling for persistent characteristics of individuals, such as education. Similarly, wages earned upon entry into the labor force have no effect themselves on wage rates earned a few years later. But not working in earlier years has a negative effect on subsequent wages because wage increases are related to experience.

Finally, we have found large differences between employment and unemployment rates based on Current Population Survey data—the traditional source for such information—and evidence based on two other recent large-scale surveys. This uncertainty not only leads to questions about the basic magnitude of youth employment and unemployment but complicates analysis of youth employment experiences as well.

# Notes

1. Feldstein and Ellwood (chapter 2); based on data from October, 1976 (Current Population Survey). Wachter and Kim (chapter 6) give comparable figures using annual averages, including summer months, for 1978.

2. Mincer and Leighton (chapter 8) find duration to be longer for adults than young persons in their analysis.

3. Clark and Summers (chapter 7). A comparable estimate for nonwhites in this age group is over 6%. Estimates obtained from a separate time series analysis are also consistent with this general order of magnitude (Wachter and Kim, chapter 6).

# 2 Teenage Unemployment: What is the Problem?

Martin Feldstein and David T. Ellwood

An individual is officially classified as unemployed if he is not working and is seeking a full-time or part-time job.[1] In recent years, 50% of the unemployed were less than 25 years old. Teenagers alone accounted for half of this youth unemployment or 25% of total unemployment. In 1978, an average of 1.56 million teenagers were classified as unemployed, implying an average unemployment rate of 16.3% of the teenage labor force.[2]

It is clear therefore that teenagers account for a large share of the high unemployment rate in the United States. But how much of this teenage unemployment represents a serious economic or social problem? How many of these unemployed are students or others seeking part-time work? How much of all teenage unemployment represents very short spells of unemployment of those who move from job to job and how much represents really long-term unemployment of those who cannot find a job or at least any job that they regard as acceptable? Among those who are not officially classified as unemployed but are neither working nor in school, how many should really be regarded as "unemployed but too discouraged to look" and how many should be classified as just "not currently interested in working"? And even among those who are officially classified as unemployed, how many are unemployed by the official definition but not really interested in work at the current time?

Martin Feldstein is president of the National Bureau of Economic Research and professor of economics at Harvard University. David T. Ellwood is an assistant professor at the John F. Kennedy School of Government at Harvard University and a faculty research fellow at the National Bureau of Economic Research. This study was prepared as a background paper for the NBER Project on Youth Joblessness and Employment. We are grateful for comments on our earlier draft, especially the suggestions of Jacob Mincer, Linda Leighton, and Lawrence Summers. The views expressed are those of the authors and should not be attributed to any organization.

17

To shed light on these questions, we have analyzed the detailed information on youth employment and unemployment that is collected in the Department of Labor's monthly Current Population Survey. We have not relied on the published summaries of this survey but have examined and tabulated the basic records on more than 5,000 individual teenage boys about whom information was obtained in the Current Population Surveys of March 1976 and a similar size sample in October 1976. Analyzing the raw data provides the very important advantage of permitting us to examine a variety of special subgroups that cannot be studied with the published summaries.

In particular, we decided quite early in our study to limit our attention to male teenagers who are not enrolled in school.[3] We believe that the problems and experience of the in-school and out-of-school groups of unemployed teenagers are very different and must be studied separately.[4] Since, as we show below, half of the male unemployed teenagers are still in school, looking at both groups together can obscure much that is important. Moreover, the social and economic problems of unemployment may be of greater significance for the out-of-school group than for those who are still in school. Limiting our analysis to boys also reflects a view that the problems and experiences of the boys are likely to differ substantially from those of girls of the same age and therefore that the two should be studied separately.

Even with the study limited to out-of-school young men, we have a sample of 1,451 individuals in October 1976. This is large enough to make statistically reliable estimates of unemployment and employment rates for most major groups.[5] In some cases, however, for example when nonwhites are classified by family income, the sample becomes too small to permit estimates to be made with great confidence. In these cases, as in others where a larger sample is desirable, it would be useful in the future to pool data from several monthly surveys.

Since our analysis refers primarily to the unemployment experienced in October 1976 and, in some cases, during the preceding year, it is useful to describe briefly the state of the labor market during that period. In October 1976, the overall unemployment rate for the population as a whole was a relatively high 7.2 percent. Unemployment had been falling from a peak rate of 9.1 percent in June 1975. The mean durations of unemployment were therefore very long; the 14.2 week mean duration of unemployment for all the unemployed in the October 1976 survey was roughly 25% longer than the average duration of 11.5 weeks that prevailed in the years from 1960 through 1975. Our study should therefore be seen as an analysis of the experience of out-of-school young men during a time in which the labor market was depressed but improving. This should be remembered in interpreting any of our findings, a warning that will not be repeated. It would clearly be interesting to repeat our analysis for a year like 1974 when the unemployment rate for all persons was only 5.6% as well as for 1979 when those data became available.[6]

Our finding may be summarized very briefly:

Unemployment is not a serious problem for the vast majority of teenage boys. Less than 5% of teenage boys are unemployed, out of school, and looking for full-time work. Many out-of-school teenagers are neither working nor looking for work and most of these report no desire to work. Virtually all teenagers who are out of work live at home. Among those who do seek work, unemployment spells tend to be quite short; over half end within one month when these boys find work or stop looking for work. Nonetheless, much of the total amount of unemployment is the result of quite long spells among a small portion of those who experience unemployment during the year.

Although nonwhites have considerably higher unemployment rates than whites, the overwhelming majority of the teenage unemployed are white. Approximately half of the difference between the unemployment rates of whites and blacks can be accounted for by other demographic and economic differences.

There is a small group of relatively poorly educated teenagers for whom unemployment does seem to be a serious and persistent problem. This group suffers much of the teenage unemployment. Although their unemployment rate improves markedly as they move into their twenties, it remains very high relative to the unemployment rate of better educated and more able young men.

1. *More than 90% of all male teenagers are either in school, working, or both. Most unemployed teenagers are either in school or seeking only part-time work. Only 5% of teenage boys are unemployed, out of school, and looking for full-time work.*

Although the unemployment rate among teenage boys was 18.3% in October 1976, this figure is easily misinterpreted for two reasons. First, since most teenagers are in school and neither working nor looking for work, the labor force size on which this unemployment rate is calculated is only a fraction of the teenage population. The unemployed therefore represent a much smaller percentage of the teenage population than they do of the teenage labor force. Second, more than half of the *unemployed* teenagers are actually enrolled in school and generally interested only in some form of part-time work.

It is reasonable to classify mature men into the "employed" and "not employed" and to regard the situation of the first group as satisfactory from a social and economic standpoint and that of the second group as unsatisfactory. This is clearly inappropriate for teenagers. The "satisfactory" group for teenagers includes those in school as well as those at work and therefore more than 90% of this age group, almost the same as the "satisfactory status" rate for mature males. Less than 5% of teenage boys are unemployed, out of school, and looking for full-time work. The problem of unemployment affects only a very small fraction of teenagers.

The detailed statistics on which these statements are based are presented in table 2.1. Nearly 70% of male teenagers are enrolled in school in October 1976. Among the teenage boys who are officially classified as unemployed, more than half (52.7%) are enrolled in school. There are only 79,000 boys who are out of school and seeking full-time work.[7] Of course, the fact that half the teenage unemployed are in school does not mean that the unemployment rate among out-of-school teenage boys is half of the unemployment rate for all teenage boys. The two rates are in fact quite similar: 18.3% overall and 18.9% among out-of-school boys.

It is also clear that the experience of 16 and 17 year olds is very different from that of 18 and 19 year olds. While 90% of the younger boys are in school, only 48% of the older boys are. Among the 16 and 17 year olds who are classified as unemployed, nearly 80% are in school and less than 25% are seeking full-time work. In contrast, among the 18 and 19 year olds who are classified as unemployed, only 29% are in school and more than 75% are seeking full-time work. Only 1.8% of the 16 and 17 years olds are out of school, unemployed, and seeking full time work. We are reminded that the official unemployment rate once included the experience of 14 and 15 year olds but that the age limit was raised to reflect the growing school enrollment of this group. It may again be time to raise the age threshold for official labor force participation. Excluding 16 and 17 year olds, with their official unemployment rate of more than 20%, would reduce the overall unemployment rate for men of all ages from 7.2% to 6.9%.

These comments should not be taken as minimizing the importance of unemployment for some young people. The figures do show however that only a very small fraction of teenagers are unemployed and that only 46% of the unemployed are both not in school and looking for full-time employment. Less than 5% of teenage boys are out of school, without work, and seeking full-time employment.

2. *Most spells of teenage unemployment are quite short and most teenage jobseekers have relatively little trouble in finding work. The bulk of unemployment is experienced by a relatively small group of teenagers with long spells of unemployment.*

Short spells are characteristic of most out-of-school male teenagers who become unemployed. In October 1976, 45.5% of the unemployed in this group had been unemployed for four weeks or less. The survey also found that 16.2% of the unemployed in this group had been unemployed for between five and eight weeks. Only 10.7% of all the unemployed in the survey had been unemployed for as long as twenty-six weeks. Because those who find work relatively quickly are less likely to be counted in the distribution of unemployed, these figures actually overstate the

**Table 2.1**     **Activities of Male Teenagers (March 1976)**

| | 16-17 | | 18-19 | | 16-19 | |
|---|---|---|---|---|---|---|
| | Population | Percentage of population | Population | Percentage of population | Population | Percentage of population |
| *In school* | | | | | | |
| Employed | 1,307,233 | 31.1 | 731,300 | 18.5 | 2,038,533 | 25.0 |
| Unemployed | 317,419 | 7.5 | 126,620 | 3.2 | 444,039 | 5.4 |
| Full time | 22,000 | 0.5 | 28,399 | 0.7 | 50,399 | 0.6 |
| Part time | 295,419 | 7.0 | 98,221 | 2.5 | 393,640 | 4.8 |
| Not in labor force | 2,174,278 | 51.8 | 1,048,669 | 26.5 | 3,222,947 | 39.5 |
| Total population | 3,798,930 | 90.4 | 1,906,589 | 48.3 | 5,705,519 | 69.9 |
| *Not in school* | | | | | | |
| Employed | 209,259 | 5.0 | 1,506,038 | 38.1 | 1,715,297 | 21.0 |
| Unemployed | 82,454 | 2.0 | 316,251 | 8.0 | 398,705 | 4.9 |
| Full time | 74,949 | 1.8 | 304,355 | 7.7 | 379,304 | 4.7 |
| Part time | 7,505 | 0.2 | 11,896 | 0.3 | 19,401 | 0.2 |
| Not in labor force | 105,996 | 2.5 | 226,980 | 5.7 | 332,976 | 4.1 |
| Total population | 397,709 | 9.6 | 2,049,269 | 51.7 | 2,446,978 | 30.1 |
| Total civilian population | 4,196,639 | 100.0 | 3,955,858 | 100.0 | 8,152,497 | 100.0 |

SOURCE: Tabulations of the October 1976 Current Population Survey.

fraction of longer spells. In fact, considerably more than one-half of all the teenage boys who become unemployed are no longer so within just one month.[8]

The experience of young people during the summer also implies that finding employment is not difficult for most young people. Although detailed data is not available by sex and the level of school attainment, the published figures permit us to trace the overall experience of teenagers of both sexes on a month-by-month basis.[9] In March 1976, 3.8 million 16 to 19 year olds were in the full-time labor force. This rose to 7.0 million in June, 8.3 million in July, and 7.5 million in August before dropping back to approximately 4 million for the rest of the year. Of the 4.5 million extra entrants into the full-time labor force between March and July, 4.0 million or 89% were working in July. Although the number of unemployed rose between the spring and summer, the unemployment rate actually fell sharply from 22.6% in March to 16.3% in July and 15.3% in August. It is clear that this comparatively able group of teenage boys and girls had relatively little difficulty finding work.

The labor market's ability to increase teenage employment by more than 100% between May and July is certainly remarkable. Employers clearly anticipate a seasonal increase in the supply of teenagers and organize production to take advantage of their availability. We are struck by the contrast between this experience and the claim that much of the current high teenage unemployment rate is due to the demographic shift that increased teenagers from 7% of the labor force in 1958 to 10% today. If production can adjust so rapidly to the seasonal shift in the demographic composition of the labor force, it would be surprising if it could not adjust to the much slower change in demography over the past two decades. This leads us to believe that too much weight has generally been given to the demographic explanation for the rising teenage unemployment rate.

While most teenagers have little problem with unemployment, teenage unemployment is concentrated in a group that experiences long periods of unemployment. Table 2.2 presents information on the distribution of unemployment in 1975 based on the responses of the out-of-school group in the March 1976 Current Population Survey.[10] Table 2.2 reveals that in 1975 nearly two-thirds of these teenagers experienced no unemployment at all. Another 13% were unemployed for a total of less than two months. Only one teenager in twelve was out of work for a total of more than twenty-six weeks during the year, but this high unemployment group accounted for 52% of all the weeks of unemployment among these teenagers. Thus about half of all unemployment among male out-of-school teenagers in a year is concentrated in a group of roughly 250,000 boys.

Table 2.2    **Distribution of Population and Total Unemployment
by Weeks Unemployed in the Previous Year**

| Weeks unemployed last year | Percentage of population | Percentage of those with some unemployment | Percentage of all unemployment in the year |
|---|---|---|---|
| None | 63.7 | 0.0 | 0.0 |
| 1–4 | 8.5 | 23.5 | 3.8 |
| 5–8 | 4.9 | 13.5 | 5.0 |
| 9–13 | 5.2 | 14.4 | 9.3 |
| 14–26 | 9.3 | 25.7 | 31.3 |
| 26+ | 8.3 | 22.9 | 50.7 |

SOURCE: Tabulations of the March 1976 Current Population Survey. All figures refer to male teenagers whose major activity in March 1976 was not classified as attending school.

3. *Many of the teenagers who are out-of-school and out-of-work are not officially classified as "unemployed." Most of this "out of the labor force" group show relatively little interest in finding work. For many of them, there is relatively little pressure or incentive to find work.*

More than 45% of the out-of-school but not employed teenage boys are officially classified as out of the labor force rather than unemployed.[11] This means they reported engaging in no work-seeking activity during the previous four weeks, including such things as asking friends or looking in the newspaper. The evidence that we present later in this section indicates that only a relatively small proportion of these young men would really like to work.

Kim Clark and Lawrence Summers[12] have shown that a substantial fraction of all measured spells of unemployment end with the individual leaving the labor force. They argue that the distinction between youngsters who are out of work and seeking a job and those who are out of work but not seeking employment is questionable and suggest further that most persons without work might be regarded as unemployed. According to this interpretation current unemployment figures understate the magnitude of the problem. While we agree that the distinction between the unemployed and those out of the labor force may be poorly captured in the data, our evidence suggests that the vast majority of those out of the labor force cannot reasonably be classified as "unemployed" with its implication of active interest in finding work. Indeed, it is quite possible that current unemployment figures overstate the problem since many unemployed move frequently to the out-of-the-labor-force status in which few report a desire for work.

Our interpretation of this evidence reflects our conclusion that the young men who are out of the labor force are *not* "discouraged workers" who have stopped looking because they believe no work is available. We have reached this conclusion after analyzing the data about the out-of-the-labor-force group that was collected in the March 1976 survey. These data are of two types: (1) questions about the individual's interest in working and beliefs about job availability,[13] and (2) evidence on the financial incentives and pressures to seek work.

When the out-of-school teenagers who had not done anything to look for work during the past four weeks were asked, "Do you want a job now?", only 37% answered yes.[14] Forty-six percent said no and 17% said they did not know.[15]

Among the out-of-the-labor-force group, only 18% said they wanted a job but believed there was no work or couldn't find any, and 2.8% said that the prospective employers thought they were too young. Thus no more than 21% of those in the out-of-the-labor-force group desire employment but believe that search would not result in finding a job. In 63% of the cases, the individual just did not want a job. An additional 7.1% said they did not look because they were attending school even though school was not given as their major activity.

We believe that much of the high unemployment and nonemployment rates among the out-of-school young men reflect the lack of pressure or incentive to find work. Although unemployment insurance is relatively unimportant for this age group,[16] the family acts as an alternative source of income when young people are not working.[17] More than 87% of the unemployed in this group live with parents (80.5%) or other relatives (7.0%). Only 7.5% live alone or with a family of their own. Among the group that is not in the labor force, 97% live with parents (89.6%) or other relatives (7.4%). While the unemployed teenagers come disproportionately from lower income families, nearly two-thirds of the unemployed were in families with incomes above $10,000 in 1976 and 22% were in families with incomes over $20,000.

4. *The problem of unemployment and nonemployment is concentrated in a group with little education. The unemployment and nonemployment rates in this group drop sharply as its members move into their early twenties. Nevertheless, the rates remain very high among those who do not complete high school.*

Since unemployment is concentrated in a group of teenagers with relatively little schooling, it is worth emphasizing that nearly 70% of 16 to 19 year old males are still in school. The out-of-school group whose unemployment we are studying therefore left school before two-thirds of those in their age cohort. Moreover, for our out-of school group, unemployment rates are much higher among those who did not complete high school (twelve years of education). Table 2.3 shows that these school dropouts accounted for 57.5% of the unemployed and 58.0% of the nonemployed. They had an unemployment rate of 28.2% and a nonemployment rate of 42.1%. The rates for nonwhite dropouts were even higher.

**Table 2.3**          **Education and Unemployment**

| | Years of schooling | | | |
| | Less than 12 years | 12 years | More than 12 years | All |
|---|---|---|---|---|
| *Percentage distribution of* | | | | |
| Population | 41.2 | 53.8 | 5.1 | 100.0 |
| Labor force | 38.4 | 56.9 | 4.7 | 100.0 |
| Unemployed | 57.5 | 40.2 | 2.3 | 100.0 |
| Nonemployed | 58.0 | 37.3 | 4.7 | 100.0 |
| *Unemployment rates* | | | | |
| Whites | .264 | .105 | .069 | .163 |
| Nonwhites | .412 | .396 | .513 | .406 |
| All | .282 | .133 | .093 | .189 |
| *Nonemployment rates* | | | | |
| Whites | .386 | .171 | .216 | .259 |
| Nonwhites | .618 | .501 | .796 | .571 |
| All | .421 | .208 | .277 | .299 |

SOURCE: Tabulations of the October 1976 Current Population Survey. All figures relate to teenage boys who were not enrolled in school at the time of the survey.

Table 2.4 compares the unemployment rates of teenagers with the unemployment rates of 20 to 24 year olds at each level of education. Among those with less than twelve years of education, the unemployment rate drops from 0.282 to 0.175, a drop of 38%. The decreases for the two groups with more years of schooling is relatively smaller (a 20% decline for both groups), but the final unemployment rates are substantially lower. Among 20 to 24 year olds, those who did not complete high school have nearly twice the unemployment rate of those who did. Note that the unemployment rate for all 20 to 24 year olds (0.110) is actually 42% lower than the teenage rate, reflecting the change in the mix of the labor force to those with more education and lower unemployment rates as well as the decline in rates within each demographic group.

**Table 2.4**          **Unemployment Rates by Age and Education**

| Years of schooling | Age and race | | | | | |
| | Age | | Whites | | Nonwhites | |
| | 16–19 | 20–24 | 16–19 | 20–24 | 16–19 | 20–24 |
|---|---|---|---|---|---|---|
| Less than 12 years | .282 | .175 | .264 | .151 | .412 | .276 |
| 12 years | .133 | .106 | .105 | .098 | .396 | .168 |
| More than 12 years | .093 | .074 | .069 | .063 | .513 | .184 |
| All | .189 | .110 | .163 | .097 | .406 | .207 |

SOURCE: Tabulations of the October 1976 Current Population Survey. All figures relate to males who were not enrolled in school at the time of the survey.

A similar pattern is seen for each race group. Among those with less than twelve years of education, the white unemployment rate drops by 43% and the nonwhite unemployment rate drops by 33%. For the groups with more education, the gains are relatively greater for nonwhites but the sample is too small to regard these differences as statistically significant.

Table 2.5 presents comparable figures for nonemployment. It will again be seen that the rates for the lowest education group improve substantially with time but still remain quite high. Once again, the total rate declines by more than the decline at each education level because the out-of-school population changes to include a higher proportion of young men with more education.

Although these two tables show that there is a substantial improvement in the condition of the poorly educated teenagers as they age, the figures should also serve as a warning that the problem of high unemployment and nonemployment among the low-education group does not fully correct itself as these problem teenagers get older.

5. *Nonwhites have considerably higher rates of unemployment and nonemployment than do whites. However, since nonwhites are a relatively small fraction of the teenage population, they account for only a small portion of unemployment and nonemployment. Lowering the unemployment rate of the nonwhite group to the rate of the white group would eliminate less than 60,000 unemployed teenagers in the whole country and would only lower the unemployment rate for all out-of-school male teenagers from 19% to 16%.*

Nonwhite teenagers suffer very high rates of unemployment and nonemployment. Forty percent were unemployed in October 1976; nearly 60% were without work. While these figures clearly show a serious employment problem for nonwhite teenagers, it should be remembered that since the bulk of teenagers are white, the bulk of the out-of-school teenage unemployed are also white.

**Table 2.5**    **Nonemployment Rates by Age and Education**

| Years of schooling | Age | | Age and race | | | |
| | | | Whites | | Nonwhites | |
| | 16–19 | 20–24 | 16–19 | 20–24 | 16–19 | 20–24 |
| --- | --- | --- | --- | --- | --- | --- |
| Less than 12 years | .421 | .264 | .386 | .215 | .618 | .436 |
| 12 years | .208 | .147 | .171 | .129 | .501 | .286 |
| More than 12 years | .277 | .112 | .216 | .101 | .796 | .235 |
| All | .299 | .162 | .259 | .137 | .571 | .330 |

Source: Tabulations of the October 1976 Current Population Survey. All figures relate to males who were not enrolled in school at the time of the survey.

Table 2.6 summarizes the racial composition of unemployment and nonemployment among out-of-school male teenagers. Since nonwhites constitute only 12.7% of the 2.45 million boys in this group, they account for only a small fraction of the overall unemployment and nonemployment despite their relatively high unemployment and nonemployment rates. In October 1976, whites represented 77% of the unemployed, 76% of the not employed, and 14% of those not in the labor force. Even among those out of work for twenty-three weeks or more, whites accounted for 77%.

By using the March 1976 survey, it is possible to obtain additional information on the relative magnitudes of white and nonwhite unemployment. (This requires using the "major activity" criteria of classifying an individual's "school" status; this decreases the in-school population and raises the share of whites in the unemployed from 77% to 81%.) The March survey figures indicate that whites accounted for 79% of those who experienced at least twenty-six weeks of unemployment in 1975 and 80% of the weeks of unemployment in that year. The March survey also provides evidence on unemployment in the central cities of Standard Metropolitan Statistical Areas. Because nonwhites constituted 24.3% of the male teenage out-of-school labor force in the central cities of Standard Metropolitan Statistical Areas (in comparison to 24.2% nationally), they accounted for a larger share of total unemployment in central cities. But even there, nonwhites represented only 36% of the unemployed. Whites accounted for 64% of the unemployment in the central cities and 84% outside the SMSAs.[18] Even among families with incomes of less than $10,000, whites accounted for 70% of the unemployment nationally and 50% in central cities. The stereotyped image of an unemployed teenager

**Table 2.6**    **Unemployment Experience of White and Nonwhite Out-of-school Male Teenagers**

|  | Number of persons | | Proportion of persons | | Unemployment and non-employment rates | |
|---|---|---|---|---|---|---|
|  | White | Nonwhite | White | Nonwhite | White | Nonwhite |
| Unemployed[a] | 307,214 | 91,491 | 77.1 | 22.9 | .163[a] | .406 |
| Not employed[b] | 553,382 | 178,299 | 75.6 | 24.4 | .259[b] | .571 |
| Not in labor force[b] | 246,168 | 86,808 | 73.9 | 26.1 | .115[b] | .278 |
| Long term unemployed (more than 13 weeks in the current spell) | 81,619 | 23,973 | 77.3 | 22.7 | N/A | N/A |

SOURCE: Tabulations of the October 1976 Current Population Survey. All figures relate to teenage boys who were not enrolled in school at the time of the survey.

[a]Rate as a percentage of labor force.

[b]Rate as a percentage of population.

as a black central city resident represents less than 15% of the unemployed.

The figures in table 2.6 imply that reducing the nonwhite unemployment rate from 40.6% to the 16.2% that prevailed among whites would cut nonwhite unemployment from 91,491 to 36,732, a reduction of 54,759. This accounts for only 13.4% of the total of 408,705 unemployed male out-of-school teenagers. Reducing the nonwhite unemployment rate to the white rate would therefore only lower the total unemployment rate from 18.9% to 16.3.

Again, we want to stress that we are not minimizing the importance of the high rates of unemployment and nonemployment among the nonwhite teenagers. With 57% not employed, there is clearly a serious employment problem among nonwhite out-of-school teenagers. It is important, however, to recognize that the vast majority of employed and nonemployed teenagers are white. Reducing the unemployment rate of nonwhite teenagers to the corresponding rate for whites would eliminate less than 15% of all the current unemployment among teenage boys who are not in school.

6. *Approximately half of the difference between the unemployment rates of white and nonwhites can be accounted for by other demographic and economic differences. Among the very low income households, the unemployment rates of whites and nonwhites are similar. Rising family income appears to be associated with a much greater fall in the unemployment rate for whites than for nonwhites.*

We have examined how unemployment rates differ within each race by schooling, family income, and age. More specifically, we have divided the population into forty-eight non-overlapping groups based on all interactions among these three factors. Thus one group contains only those 17 year olds with exactly twelve years of schooling who live in a family whose income (excluding that of the teenagers) is between $10,000 and $20,000. Each group is further divided into whites and nonwhites, and the unemployment rate is calculated for each subgroup. On the basis of this detailed information, we can calculate how much of the white/nonwhite difference in unemployment rates is due to differences between the rates in each of the forty-eight demographic groups and how much is due to differences in the demographic composition of the white and nonwhite groups.[19] The results are summarized in the first two columns of table 2.7.

The actual unemployment rate for white, male, teenage boys who are out of school is 16.3%; the corresponding rate for nonwhites is 40.6%. If nonwhites had the same demographic composition as whites but retained their annual unemployment rates in each demographic group, their overall unemployment rate would fall from 40.6% to 27.9%. This is shown in table 2.7 as the unemployment rate based on "white weights and nonwhite rates." These figures imply that the differences in the demographic

Table 2.7    **Demographically Adjusted Unemployment and Nonemployment Rates of Whites and Nonwhites**

|  | Unemployment rates | | Nonemployment rates | |
|---|---|---|---|---|
|  | White weights | Nonwhite weights | White weights | Nonwhite weights |
| White | .163 | .210 | .259 | .325 |
| Nonwhite | .279 | .406 | .469 | .571 |

SOURCE: Tabulations of the October 1976 Current Population Survey. All figures refer to out-of-school male teenagers.

composition of the two race groups accounts for 12.7 percentage points of the 24.3 percentage point difference in the overall unemployment rates, i.e., for more than 50% of the difference between the races.

Table 2.7 also shows the implications of reversing this procedure and calculating the unemployment rate that whites would have if they retained their actual unemployment rate in each demographic group but had the same demographic composition as the nonwhites. With the nonwhite demographic weights, the white unemployment rate would rise from 16.3% to 21.0%, an increase of 4.7 percentage points or only about 20% of the difference between the observed unemployment rates.

Similar calculations for nonemployment rates are also presented in table 2.7. The first type of adjustment, i.e., using the white demographic composition, results in a decrease in the nonwhite nonemployment rate from 31.2 percentage points to 21.0 percentage points, a reduction of 33%. Similarly, applying nonwhite weights to white unemployment rates raises the white nonemployment rate from 25.9% to 32.5%, and accounts for only 21% of the race difference in nonemployment rates.

In short, a limited set of demographic factors can account for a substantial part of the racial difference in unemployment rates and a smaller part of the difference in nonemployment rates. Changing the demographic weights is more important for the nonwhite population than for whites.

We have extended our analysis of the relationship between race and unemployment by examining the unemployment rates of white and non-white teenagers in families at different income levels.[20] Two interesting conclusions emerge from this analysis. First, among low income families there is relatively little difference in the unemployment rates of whites and nonwhites. More precisely, in families with incomes below $10,000 (excluding any income of the teenager) white out-of-school boys had an unemployment rate of 0.26 while nonwhites had a rate of 0.30. Similarly, the nonemployment rates for whites was 0.39 while that for nonwhites was 0.45.

Our second finding is that rising family income appears to be associated with a much greater fall in unemployment rates for whites than for nonwhites. Among white teenagers, the unemployment rate drops from

0.26 in families with incomes below $10,000 to 0.14 in families with incomes of $10,000 to $20,000. The nonwhites show no decline at all; the unemployment rate actually rises slightly from 0.30 to 0.33. The same lack of improvement with income is seen in the nonemployment rates of nonwhites; while the white nonemployment rate drops from 0.39 to 0.22, the nonwhite rates rises from 0.45 to 0.54. Only when family incomes rise to more than $20,000 does the experience of whites and nonwhites become similar. The unemployment rates for this income group are 0.26 and 0.18 for whites and nonwhites respectively while the corresponding nonemployment rates are 0.24 and 0.25.

The poor employment of middle-income nonwhites remains a puzzle to us. Our sample is too small to pursue this by further disaggregation, but we believe that much could be learned by pooling samples in order to explore whether this apparent difference between middle-income whites and nonwhites was just due to chance in our sample and, if not, whether it can be explained by such factors as location or education.

## Conclusion

It is our conclusion that unemployment is not a serious problem for the vast majority of teenage boys. School is the predominant activity of the young. For many of the out-of-school but not employed group, the data provide evidence of weak labor force attachment and little incentive or pressure to find work. Most youngsters who do seek work remain unemployed only a short time.

Nonwhites suffer disproportionately high unemployment rates, but whites still represent the vast majority of unemployed young people. Nearly half of the differences in white and nonwhite unemployment rates are attributable to demographic differences in age, schooling, and family income. Unemployment rates of whites and nonwhites appear to be much more similar at the high and low ends of the income distribution than in the middle. The mystery is the middle-class nonwhite teenagers who suffer far more unemployment than their white counterparts.

There is a small group of relatively poorly educated young men for whom teenage unemployment is a serious problem. High school dropouts suffer over half of the teenage unemployment and these persons show only a slow improvement as they reach their twenties.

In considering these findings, it should be borne in mind that the results reported in this paper are based on samples for 1976 only. As we noted above, we have repeated the analysis by examining data from 1975 and 1977 and found quite similar results. It would nevertheless be useful to extend these calculations to other years in which economic conditions were substantially different from 1975 through 1977.

This paper is not the place to discuss the implications of our evidence for appropriate policies to deal with youth unemployment. It is appropriate, however, to conclude with a few words of caution. Since we have emphasized that the real problem of teenage unemployment is currently concentrated in the relatively small group that experiences long periods of unemployment, it may be tempting to believe that the problem could be solved by a program of targeted job creation. The 250,000 boys with long periods of unemployment who currently account for more than half of the year's unemployment among out-of-school teenage boys could in principle be hired at a cost of $3 billion even if they were paid more than twice the minimum wage. The primary danger in such an approach is that the provision of relatively attractive public sector jobs could induce a very much larger number of boys to seek such positions. This could detour many of those who have little or no problem with unemployment away from more productive jobs or from additional schooling. The challenge to public policy is thus to create opportunities for employment and on-the-job training for those who would otherwise experience long periods of nonemployment without providing adverse incentives to the vast majority of young people.[21]

# Notes

1. Individuals who are on layoff from a job to which they expect to be recalled are also classified as unemployed even if they are not actively seeking work.

2. The unemployment rate for a demographic group is calculated as the percentage of the members of the corresponding labor force who are currently classified as unemployed. The labor force is defined as everyone in that demographic group who is either employed or unemployed. An individual may be both attending school and in the labor force if he or she is working part time or full time or is looking for such work.

3. In the earlier version of this paper, we focused on the male teenagers who do not report attending school as their "major activity." An individual may be enrolled but also working. For most purposes, the two methods of classification give similar results but we were convinced by subsequent comment and analysis that classifying by enrollment is more appropriate, especially for 16 and 17 year olds.

4. We are of course aware that remaining in school represents an economic decision and should in principle be regarded as endogenous to the problem we are studying. It would be interesting to extend the current analysis to examine the relation between work availability and the decision to remain in school.

5. In estimating unemployment and employment rates, a sample of 100 yields a standard error of no more than 0.005. Appendix table 2.A.1 presents selected sample sizes. Table 2.A.2 presents the standard errors for probabilities based on selected sample sizes.

6. We have repeated the analysis for the two other recent years for which data are available, 1975 and 1977. The results are quite similar to those for 1976 reported in the text of this paper.

7. Recall that we classify as "in school" anyone who is enrolled, whether or not school is his major activity. If we use the "major activity" basis of classification instead, the number of out-of-school boys who are seeking full-time work is essentially unchanged at 394,000. The total unemployed and out-of-school group (seeking part-time or full-time work) is 399,000 based on "enrollment" and 416,000 based on "major activity."

8. Clark and Summers report that 70% of spells end in one month; some of these spells end with the teenagers leaving the labor force. See Kim B. Clark and Lawrence Summers, "The Dynamics of Youth Unemployment," chapter 7 of the present volume.

9. These figures come from the *1977 Handbook of Labor Statistics* (U.S. Department of Labor, 1978).

10. The March survey is used for these calculations because information on unemployment in the previous year is not collected in October.

11. An individual is classified as out of the labor force if he is neither employed nor seeking work. The figures in table 2.1 indicate that there were 333,000 teenage boys who were not in the labor force in October 1976. By comparison there were 399,000 unemployed boys. The out-of-the-labor force group thus accounted for more than 45% of those who were out of school but not working.

12. Kim B. Clark and Lawrence Summers, chapter 7 of this volume.

13. These questions are asked only of a random subsample of the out-of-the-labor-force group. Some of this information is available for March and not for October.

14. The question in the CPS may be answered by one adult in the household for all persons in the household. The questions about a teenager are typically answered by his mother although the group that is out of school and out of work may be more likely than usual to be present at the interview.

15. Although the sample of individuals who were asked this question was so small that these percentages cannot be regarded as precise estimates of the true percentages for *all* teenagers who were out of the labor force, there are enough observations to assert that there is less than one chance in ten of observing an estimated "yes" response rate as low as 37% if the "true" fraction of potential "yes" responses is even 50% or higher. (Evidence for October 1976 further supports this conclusion since an even lower fraction of the out-of-the-labor-force group expressed interest in working.)

16. Data on the receipt of unemployment benefits were collected in a special May 1976 survey. Only 10% of unemployed male teenagers not in school received unemployment benefits.

17. It would be very interesting to have more data on the way in which a young person's unemployment affects his family's cash and in-kind gifts to him and his expected contribution to the overall family budget.

18. Among the 370,273 unemployed whites, 97,701 lived in central cities of SMSAs. For nonwhites, the corresponding figures are 88,964 and 55,781.

19. Although the number of observations in each of the forty-eight cells is small, the standard error of the mean depends essentially on the total number of observations. Similar results are obtained with the data for the March Survey.

20. We use the March 1976 survey to obtain more detailed income information.

21. See the discussion of such policies in Martin Feldstein, "*Lowering the Permanent Rate of Unemployment*," Joint Economic Committee, U.S. Congress (Government Printing Office: Washington, 1973) and Martin Feldstein, "Economics of the New Unemployment," *The Public Interest* (1973).

**Table 2.A.1**    **Selected Sample Sizes of Males Not Enrolled in School (October 1976)**

| October | 16–19 | | 20–24 | |
|---|---|---|---|---|
| | White | Nonwhite | White | Nonwhite |
| *All education levels* | | | | |
| Population | 1250 | 201 | 3460 | 461 |
| Labor force | 1106 | 154 | 3305 | 396 |
| *Under 12 years education* | | | | |
| Population | 507 | 97 | 654 | 166 |
| Labor force | 421 | 68 | 604 | 132 |
| *12 years education* | | | | |
| Population | 680 | 96 | 1757 | 202 |
| Labor force | 632 | 82 | 1696 | 167 |
| *Over 12 years education* | | | | |
| Population | 63 | 8 | 1049 | 93 |
| Labor force | 53 | 4 | 1005 | 88 |

**Table 2.A.2**    **Table of Standard Errors for Probabilities**

| Sample Size | Estimated probability of rate | | | | |
|---|---|---|---|---|---|
| | .1 or .9 | .2 or .8 | .3 or .7 | .4 or .6 | .5 or .5 |
| 10 | .10 | .13 | .15 | .16 | .17 |
| 25 | .06 | .08 | .09 | .10 | .10 |
| 50 | .04 | .06 | .07 | .07 | .07 |
| 100 | .03 | .04 | .05 | .05 | .05 |
| 250 | .02 | .03 | .03 | .03 | .03 |
| 500 | .01 | .02 | .02 | .02 | .02 |
| 1000 | .01 | .01 | .01 | .01 | .01 |

# 3 The Youth Labor Market Problem in the United States: An Overview

Richard B. Freeman and James L. Medoff

The unemployed young person has replaced the unemployed breadwinner as the focus of much concern about joblessness in the United States and other countries. In part, the upsurge of interest reflects a major demographic development of the 1960s and 1970s—the increased proportion of young persons in the population—which has raised the youth share of the unemployed. In part, it also reflects an upward trend in rates of joblessness among some groups of young persons, most notably blacks, relative to the population as a whole. Considerable social concern has also been expressed about the correlates of youth joblessness—crime, violence in schools, illegitimate births, and suicide, among others—and about potential long-term consequences in the form of a "lost generation" of young workers. What are the quantitative dimensions of the youth joblessness problem in the United States? In what ways is youth unemployment similar or dissimilar to adult unemployment? How concentrated is the problem among minorities? To what extent is the lack of employment associated with other major social problems? What questions and topics must be addressed if we are to understand the nature of the youth labor market problem?

This chapter examines these questions with information from various sources. It presents an overview of the nature of the youth labor market problem in the U.S., sets out the principal patterns in the data, and develops the questions to which they give rise. Section 3.1 focuses on job market phenomena as depicted in Current Population Survey (CPS) and related data. It shows that the problem of high and increasing joblessness

James L. Medoff is an associate professor in the department of economics at Harvard University. The authors have benefited from the research assistance of Kathy Coons, Jon Fay, Wayne Gray, Jennie Hay, Alison Hopfield, David Mandelbaum, Elizabeth Philipp, Anne Preston, and Martin VanDenburgh.

is concentrated among black youths and the less educated, that it is intimately associated with movements into and out of the labor force, and that the youth labor market problem has wage as well as employment dimensions. Section 3.2 examines a number of major national problems—crime, violence in schools, illegitimate births, and suicide—which may be related to youth joblessness. Regardless of how one views the job market difficulties of the young, the interrelation between employment problems and other social ills clearly merits serious attention. The second section also considers briefly the research questions to which the quantitative analysis directs attention.

### 3.1 Quantitative Dimensions of Job Market Problems: Current Population Survey Evidence

There are several ways in which to measure the labor market position of young workers: through indicators of the amount of labor, the type of jobs held, rates of pay, and so on. Each of these measures has both advantages and disadvantages for analysis, highlighting some aspects of the position of the young while neglecting other aspects. The most widely used indicator, the rate of unemployment, provides a measure of the divergence between supply and demand at a point in time but has the disadvantage of being highly dependent on the self-reported job search of persons. Labor force participation rates offer evidence on the available supply of labor but suffer from the same problem. Because the young move into and out of the work force more frequently than members of many other groups, the distinction between being in the labor force and unemployed or being out of the labor force is tenuous, making these rates potentially misleading indicators of the position of the young. The ratio of employment to population is a "harder" statistic as it reflects "objective" numbers: employment can be measured with establishment as well as household survey data. The disadvantage of the employment to population ratio is that it fails to indicate the extent to which economic constraints prevent individuals from carrying out their desired activities.

With respect to other indicators, measures of the wage and type of job held by young persons are not as easy to interpret as the comparable measures for older workers because the young seek employment for differing reasons: to obtain short-term cash or for longer-run career purposes. To the extent that wages for jobs that offer good future prospects are lower than those for other jobs, the usual measure of the value of employment, wages, can be misleading. Therefore, for at least some purposes, it is important to obtain information on several characteristics of youth jobs, such as their permanent or temporary status, whether they have a future, and the extent of learning involved, as well as wage rates.

The various indicators of the position of youths in the labor market are, it should be stressed, interrelated. Decreases in the wages of the young are likely to increase employment, increased participation due to exogenous supply shifts will lower wages, and so forth. For this reason, and because of the multifaceted nature of the employment relation, a variety of indicators of the youth labor market are examined in this section. The amount of labor is measured by the rate of unemployment, the labor force participation rate, and the employment to population ratio, with particular attention given to the last statistic. Characteristics of jobs are measured by the broad industry and occupation of workers, which are associated with diverse employment characteristics, and by wages.

In addition to different indicators of labor market position, there are also several different surveys of persons which provide information on the young. The most widely used survey is the Current Population Survey of the U.S. Bureau of the Census, which obtains information by a random sample of over 50,000 households. Two other surveys that provide information on young workers are the National Longitudinal Survey of Young Men (NLS) and the National Longitudinal Survey of the High School Class of 1972 (NLS72). These surveys follow individuals over time, whereas the CPS is primarily a cross-sectional survey. In another study, we examine in detail the difference between the CPS and the longitudinal surveys.[1] Since the differences we find are fairly substantial, they should be considered in interpreting the CPS data used in this chapter.

### 3.1.1   Amount of Labor

Young workers have traditionally had higher rates of unemployment, lower rates of labor force participation, and lower employment to population ratios than other workers. While some of these differences reflect enrollment in school, even youths who are out of school have long exhibited lower rates of work. Figures 3.1–3.3 graph the pattern of utilization rates over the postwar period for all young men, young men who are not enrolled in school, and young women, by specified age groups. They also graph the utilization rates that are predicted for each of these youth groups by a regression of that group's actual rates on the rates of "prime age" males, aged 35–44, for the postwar period. The patterns of actual rates over time reveal general trends in the utilization of youth labor, while deviations between actual and predicted rates provide some indication of how youth rates have moved relative to prime-age male rates (see the appendix for the regressions used to create figure 3.1).

Figures 3.1–3.3 highlight various important aspects of the employment problem in the United States for young persons. First, youth unemployment has trended upward both relative to adult rates and absolutely. The pattern of residuals from the regressions reveals a distinct upward trend

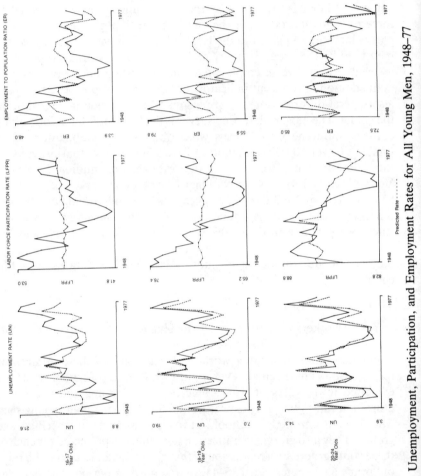

**Fig. 3.1** Unemployment, Participation, and Employment Rates for All Young Men, 1948–77

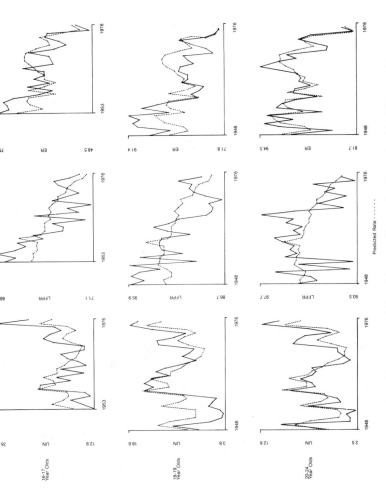

**Fig. 3.2** Unemployment, Participation, and Employment Rates for Out-of-school Young Men, 1948–76

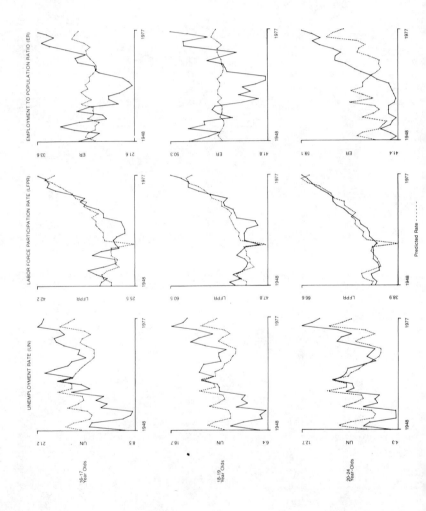

in youth rates relative to prime-age male rates, particularly in the 1970s. Among all 16–17 year old men, for example, actual rates of unemployment average about three to four percentage points above the rates predicted in the 1970s compared to three to four percentage points below those predicted in the 1950s. Moreover, for the period 1948 to 1977, addition of a simple time trend to a regression of the rate of unemployment of either young men or young women of specified ages on the rate of unemployment of 35 to 44 year old men yields the following established trend coefficients (standard errors):

| | Coefficients (standard error) of time trend: | |
| Age: | Male | Female |
| --- | --- | --- |
| 16–17 | .31 (.02) | .34 (.03) |
| 18–19 | .17 (.02) | .32 (.02) |
| 20–24 | .10 (.02) | .18 (.01) |

However, in contrast to the clear picture of change in unemployment rates, figures 3.1–3.3 tell a more mixed and uneven story about trends in participation rates and employment ratios. Among all young men (figure 3.1), participation rates fall through the early 1960s for 16–17 year olds and through the late 1960s for 18–19 year olds, and then rise through the 1970s. Similarly, employment to population ratios show an upward trend after the early 1960s for the 16–17 and 18–19 age groups, and are consistently above those predicted for all three age groups after the early 1970s, which runs counter to the picture of marked deterioration found in the unemployment data.

The situation for out-of-school young men (figure 3.2), on the other hand, shows a more definite pattern of deterioration. Participation rates reveal an overall downward trend, without the consistently strong increases found for all young men during the 1970s. Similarly, employment to population ratios for the out-of-school group show a continuing downward trend through the 1970s, and, in contrast to those of all young men, are frequently below those predicted during the 1970s, particularly for the 16–17 and 18–19 age groups. As far as can be told from these graphs, utilization of *all* young men did not worsen markedly in the 1970's, while that of the out-of-school group did.

The measures of the labor market position of all young women in figure 3.3 show even greater divergences between the pattern of utilization as indicated by unemployment rates and the pattern as indicated by participation rates and employment ratios. Unemployment of young women rises both absolutely and relative to the unemployment rate of prime age men. However, employment ratios and participation rates also rise both absolutely and relative to the rates for prime-age males, implying more, rather than less, utilization of teenage and young women workers.

In sum, while the rate of unemployment among the young shows a deterioration relative to older male workers, the employment to population ratios and labor force participation ratios tell a different story, particularly for women. Overall, the data raise doubts as to the existence of a "job crisis" for all young workers.

### 3.1.2   Black Youth Joblessness

The absence of a definite deterioration in the employment of all young workers does not mean, however, that there is no youth employment crisis, but rather that the problem may be localized. Data on the employment, unemployment, and labor force participation rates of young workers by race from the Current Population Survey show a striking deterioration in the utilization of young blacks, which can be viewed as the essence of the youth employment problem in the United States. This claim is documented by the evidence on the overall magnitudes of employment and joblessness among white youths and among black and other youths from the early 1950s to the 1970s given in table 3.1. First, the employment to population ratios given in line 1 for young men show a marked drop for blacks compared to the rough stability for whites. Among 16–17 and 18–19 year old black men, the ratios drop sharply from 1954 to 1964, stabilize in the late 1960s, and then drop sharply in the 1970s recession. Among 20–24 year old black men, the ratios hold steady until the 1970s, but then drop noticeably. Regressions linking the black employment ratios to those for comparably aged whites and a time trend make clear the extent of deterioration. The estimated trend coefficients (standard errors) are: $-1.04$ (.05), $-1.06$ (.09), and $-.39$ (.12), for 16–17, 18–19, and 20–24 year olds respectively.[2] As a result of the downward trend in utilization, the ratio of black to white employment rates drops from rough equality in the early 1950s to .43 (16–17 year olds), .57 (18–19 year olds), and .78 (20–24 year olds) by 1977.

The decline in the employment to population rate for young black men has two components: a marked rise in the fraction out of the labor force (line 2), which contrasts with stable fractions for young whites; and an increase in the fraction in the labor force lacking jobs (line 3), which also occurs among whites, although to a much lesser extent. The relative importance of the two adverse developments can be gauged by decomposing the identity that links the employment ($E$) to population ($P$) ratio to the labor force participation rate ($L$) and to the unemployment rate ($U \equiv L - E/P$):

(1)             $$E/P \equiv (L/P)\,(1 - U/L);$$

or in log differential form:

(2)             $$d\ln E/P \equiv d\ln L/P + d\ln (1 - U/L).$$

**Table 3.1**    Dimensions of the Minority Youth Employment Problem 1954–77[a]

| | Black and other male | | | | White male | | | | Black and other female | | | | White female | | | |
|---|---|---|---|---|---|---|---|---|---|---|---|---|---|---|---|---|
| | 1954 | 1964 | 1969 | 1977 | 1954 | 1964 | 1969 | 1977 | 1954 | 1964 | 1969 | 1977 | 1954 | 1964 | 1969 | 1977 |
| **1. Percent with job** | | | | | | | | | | | | | | | | |
| Age: 16–17 | 40.4 | 27.6 | 28.4 | 18.9 | 40.5 | 36.5 | 42.7 | 44.3 | 19.8 | 12.4 | 16.8 | 12.5 | 25.8 | 23.6 | 30.3 | 37.5 |
| 18–19 | 66.9 | 51.7 | 51.2 | 36.9 | 61.2 | 57.7 | 61.1 | 65.2 | 29.6 | 32.9 | 33.7 | 28.0 | 47.2 | 43.1 | 49.1 | 54.3 |
| 20–24 | 75.7 | 78.1 | 77.3 | 61.2 | 77.9 | 79.4 | 78.8 | 78.7 | 43.1 | 43.8 | 51.6 | 45.4 | 41.6 | 45.3 | 53.3 | 61.4 |
| **2. Percent in labor force** | | | | | | | | | | | | | | | | |
| Age: 16–17 | 46.7 | 37.3 | 37.7 | 30.8 | 47.1 | 43.5 | 48.8 | 53.8 | 24.5 | 19.5 | 24.4 | 22.6 | 29.3 | 28.5 | 35.2 | 45.8 |
| 18–19 | 78.4 | 67.2 | 63.2 | 57.8 | 70.4 | 66.6 | 66.3 | 74.9 | 37.7 | 46.5 | 45.4 | 44.8 | 52.1 | 49.6 | 54.6 | 63.3 |
| 20–24 | 91.1 | 89.4 | 84.4 | 78.2 | 86.4 | 85.7 | 82.6 | 86.8 | 49.6 | 53.6 | 58.6 | 59.4 | 44.4 | 48.8 | 56.4 | 67.7 |
| **3. Percent of labor force unemployed** | | | | | | | | | | | | | | | | |
| Age: 16–17 | 13.4 | 25.9 | 24.7 | 38.7 | 14.0 | 16.1 | 12.5 | 17.6 | 19.1 | 36.5 | 31.2 | 44.7 | 12.0 | 17.1 | 13.8 | 18.2 |
| 18–19 | 14.7 | 23.1 | 19.0 | 36.1 | 13.0 | 13.4 | 7.9 | 13.0 | 21.6 | 29.2 | 25.7 | 37.4 | 9.4 | 13.2 | 10.0 | 14.2 |
| 20–24 | 16.9 | 12.6 | 8.4 | 21.7 | 9.8 | 7.4 | 4.6 | 9.3 | 13.2 | 18.3 | 12.0 | 23.6 | 6.4 | 7.1 | 5.5 | 9.3 |
| **4. Percent without work experience** | | | | | | | | | | | | | | | | |
| Age: 16–19 | | (c) | 32.7 | 55.3[b] | | (c) | 24.5 | 37.6[b] | | (c) | 60.0 | 68.7[b] | | (c) | 38.7 | 36.4[b] |
| 20–24 | | 9.7 | 12.8 | 20.8[b] | | 7.2 | 9.8 | 7.2[b] | | 34.2 | 30.3 | 39.8[b] | | 34.4 | 25.9 | 21.5[b] |

[a]Lines 1, 2, and 3 are based on figures from U.S. Department of Labor, *Employment and Training Report of the President, 1978*, tables A–4 and A–14 (pp. 187–88 and pp. 202–4). Line 4 is based on figures from U.S. Department of Labor, Special Labor Force Reports *Work Experience of the Population: 1976* (table A–8, p. 20), 1969 (table A–8, p. A–15), 1964 (table A–8, p. A–11).

[b]Data are for 1976.

[c]In 1964, 49.6% of nonwhite males, 41.6% of white males, 63.5% of nonwhite females, and 56.1% of white females aged 14–19 had no work experience.

For the period 1954–1977, equation (2) yields the following decomposition of the secular change in the employment to population ratio for young black men in the three stated age groups:[3]

|  | Age groups: | | |
|---|---|---|---|
|  | 16–17 | 18–19 | 20–24 |
| $d\ln E/P$ | −.76 | −.59 | −.21 |
| $d\ln L/P$ | −.41 | −.30 | −.14 |
| $d\ln (1 − U/L)$ | −.35 | −.29 | −.07 |

The drop in labor force participation is, according to these statistics, as or more important a factor in the falling employment ratio than is the increased rate of unemployment. This implies that changes in unemployment rates *understate* the extent of the unemployment problem facing young blacks and that the behavior of nonparticipants is critical to understanding the black youth unemployment problem.

Line 4 of table 3.1 examines the lack of employment for blacks from a different perspective: in terms of the fraction of young persons who obtain *no* work experience over a year. In contrast to the employment, labor force, and unemployment figures, which are based on monthly surveys of activity during a given week, these figures are obtained from a retrospective question (on the March CPS) about activity over an entire year. What stands out is the marked increase in the proportion of blacks without work for a whole year: from 10% of 20–24 year old blacks in 1964 to 21% of this group in 1976, whch contrasts to the rough stability in the proportion of white men aged 20–24 without work experience.

Lines 5–8 present comparable figures for black and white women. While the employment to population ratios and labor force participation rates for young black women do not trend downward in absolute terms, they drop sharply *relative* to the rates for white women. In 1954, the ratio of black and other to white female employment rates was .77 for 16–17 year olds, .63 for 18–19 year olds, and 1.04 for 20–24 year olds. By 1977, the increased employment of white women brought the ratios down to .33, .52, and .74 respectively.

The marked deterioration in the relative employment of young black workers shown in 3.1 constitutes one of the major puzzles about the youth labor market in the United States and thus one of the prime questions for future research: Why has the utilization of young black workers declined relative to that of young white workers?

The striking difference in the labor force participation rates of 16–24 year old blacks and whites in the 1970s, which accounts for much of the difference in employment to population ratios, is examined further in table 3.2 which gives the percentage distribution of black and white young persons by various exclusive labor market categories from 1976 to 1973. Three basic differences between blacks and whites stand out in the

**Table 3.2**　　　　**Labor Market Status: May 1976, 1977, 1978[a]**

| Age and status | All young persons | | | | | | Out-of-school young persons | |
| --- | --- | --- | --- | --- | --- | --- | --- | --- |
| | May 1976 | | May 1977 | | May 1978 | | May 1978 | |
| | Black | White | Black | White | Black | White | Black | White |
| *16–17* | | | | | | | | |
| Working | 12.4 | 36.7 | 11.4 | 38.8 | 12.0 | 41.9 | 32.7 | 64.4 |
| Not working | 87.6 | 63.3 | 88.6 | 61.2 | 88.0 | 58.1 | 67.3 | 35.6 |
| With jobs | 0.7 | 1.6 | 0.1 | 1.5 | 1.0 | 1.7 | 4.3 | 2.6 |
| Without jobs | 86.9 | 61.7 | 88.4 | 59.7 | 86.9 | 56.4 | 63.0 | 33.1 |
| Have looked | 17.3 | 13.3 | 18.1 | 13.9 | 16.2 | 13.1 | 26.5 | 13.2 |
| Available for work | | | | | | | | |
| and looking[c] | 10.7 | 8.3 | 9.7 | 7.8 | 11.0 | 7.8 | 23.8 | 12.1 |
| Not looking actively | 0.6 | 0.3 | 0.5 | 0.4 | 0.7 | 0.2 | 2.8 | 0.4 |
| Not available for work[d] | 6.0 | 4.7 | 7.8 | 5.8 | 4.6 | 5.1 | 0.0 | 0.7 |
| Not in labor force | 69.6 | 48.4 | 70.4 | 45.8 | 70.7 | 43.3 | 36.4 | 19.9 |
| *18–19* | | | | | | | | |
| Working | 26.1 | 56.5 | 25.1 | 56.6 | 29.4 | 58.9 | 42.3 | 74.5 |
| Not working | 73.9 | 43.5 | 74.9 | 43.4 | 70.6 | 41.1 | 57.7 | 25.5 |
| With jobs[b] | 1.2 | 2.7 | 1.3 | 2.9 | 1.6 | 2.3 | 2.4 | 2.4 |
| Without jobs | 72.6 | 40.8 | 73.6 | 40.5 | 68.9 | 38.8 | 55.3 | 23.1 |
| Have looked | 20.5 | 12.3 | 23.6 | 12.3 | 23.5 | 11.0 | 28.0 | 8.0 |
| Available for work | | | | | | | | |
| and looking[c] | 15.7 | 8.0 | 17.2 | 7.8 | 19.9 | 6.8 | 26.1 | 7.5 |
| Not looking actively | 0.6 | 0.2 | 0.7 | 0.4 | 1.2 | 0.3 | 1.5 | 0.3 |
| Not available for work[d] | 4.2 | 4.0 | 5.8 | 4.1 | 2.4 | 4.0 | 4.4 | 0.2 |
| Not in labor force | 52.2 | 28.6 | 50.0 | 28.2 | 45.4 | 27.8 | 27.2 | 15.1 |
| *20–24* | | | | | | | | |
| Working | 51.4 | 64.7 | 48.7 | 66.9 | 50.3 | 68.9 | 57.3 | 75.9 |
| Not working | 48.6 | 35.3 | 51.3 | 33.1 | 49.7 | 31.1 | 42.7 | 24.1 |
| With jobs[b] | 3.0 | 3.7 | 4.0 | 3.2 | 3.8 | 3.4 | 4.5 | 3.5 |
| Without jobs | 45.6 | 31.6 | 47.3 | 29.8 | 45.9 | 27.7 | 38.2 | 20.7 |
| Have looked | 15.5 | 8.5 | 17.2 | 8.1 | 15.5 | 6.7 | 15.2 | 5.3 |
| Available for work | | | | | | | | |
| and looking[c] | 13.6 | 6.7 | 15.1 | 5.8 | 13.7 | 4.9 | 14.5 | 4.9 |
| Not looking actively | 0.4 | 0.2 | 0.6 | 0.1 | 0.2 | 0.1 | 0.1 | 0.1 |
| Not available for work[d] | 1.5 | 1.6 | 1.5 | 2.2 | 1.5 | 1.7 | 0.5 | 0.3 |
| Not in labor force | 30.1 | 23.1 | 30.1 | 21.7 | 30.4 | 21.0 | 23.0 | 15.3 |

[a]Based on weighted counts with the appropriate Current Population Surveys.

[b]Includes employed workers not working because of illness, vacation, bad weather, or labor dispute and unemployed workers on temporary or indefinite layoff or about to start a new job.

[c]Includes job losers, job quitters, workers who left school, and those wanting temporary work.

[d]Includes people who already have jobs and those unavailable because of school or temporary illness.

table. The first is the sizable differential in the proportion of young persons working: in each age group the proportion of whites working exceeds that of blacks by more than 10 percentage points. Second is the extent to which differentials are associated with differences in the fraction not in the labor force, as opposed to unemployed. In 1978, for instance, 90% of the 29.9 percentage point gap in the fraction working among 16–17 year olds is due to the fraction not in the work force; 60% of the 29.5 point gap among 18–19 year olds and 51% of the 18.6 point gap among 20–24 year olds are also associated with persons not in the labor force. The possibility that the labor force participation differences between young blacks and whites are due to differential propensities to enroll in school is, it should be stressed, rejected by the data. As can be seen in the last two columns of table 3.2, even larger differences are found between blacks and whites out of school than are found in the overall population.

The differential patterns and trends in the employment of young blacks and whites are examined further in table 3.3, which presents the employment, labor force, and unemployment rates of out-of-school high school graduates and dropouts. Lines 1 and 2 deal with all 16–24 year old male high school graduates or dropouts while lines 3 and 4 treat males and females who either graduated or dropped out in the given year. The figures in lines 1 and 2 show that the percentages of black male high school graduates or dropouts with jobs are much lower than the percentages for comparable young white men and that, after a modest decline from 1964 to 1969, the differentials grew sharply between 1969 and 1976, when black labor participation rates fell and unemployment rates rose. Lines 3 and 4 tell a similar story for persons in the relevant graduating class or dropout population. The magnitudes of some of the differences in 1976 are startling, to say the least. According to the CPS survey only 39% of black high school graduates in the class of 1976 who were not enrolled in college were employed in October 1976 compared to 73% of their white peers; the black participation rate was 16 points below that for whites; and the unemployment rate was nearly three times as high for blacks. Among dropouts only 20% of black youths compared to 50% of white youths were employed, with a 23 point difference in participation rates and a twofold differential in unemployment rates.

Because a sizable proportion of black/white differences in youth employment results from differences in labor force behavior, it is important to examine with the Current Population Survey the position of individuals who are not participants in the labor force. Table 3.4 records the percentage of 16–19 and 20–24 year old nonparticipants who are in and out of school, the percentage of these groups who report that they do or do not want a job in the survey week, and their activity or reason for not seeking employment. For men, the data suggest that most nonpartici-

**Table 3.3**         **Employment of High School Graduates and Dropouts 1960–76[a]**

| Age and status | Black and other | | | White | | | |
|---|---|---|---|---|---|---|---|
| | 1964 | 1969 | 1976 | 1960 | 1964 | 1969 | 1976 |
| 1. All male high school graduates not enrolled in college 16–24[a] | | | | | | | |
| a. Percent with a job | 75.8 | 81.6 | 67.3 | | 86.5 | 88.1 | 87.0 |
| b. Percent in labor force | 93.3 | 91.5 | 86.1 | | 94.9 | 93.8 | 95.4 |
| c. Percent of labor force unemployed | 18.8 | 11.3 | 22.0 | | 8.9 | 6.0 | 8.9 |
| 2. Male high school dropouts 16–24[b] | | | | | | | |
| a. Percent with a job | 70.3 | 72.7 | 50.4 | | 76.1 | 74.7 | 71.1 |
| b. Percent in labor force | 85.8 | 83.0 | 73.6 | | 88.1 | 83.7 | 88.5 |
| c. Percent of labor force unemployed | 18.1 | 12.4 | 31.5 | | 13.6 | 10.8 | 19.7 |
| 3. Male and female high school graduates in reported year not enrolled in college | | | | | | | |
| a. Percent with a job | 52.3 | 50.0 | 39.0 | 67.0 | 64.6 | 73.4 | 72.9 |
| b. Percent in labor force | 81.1 | 72.6 | 70.3 | 77.0 | 77.5 | 80.2 | 85.9 |
| c. Percent of labor force unemployed | 35.6 | 31.2 | 44.5 | 13.0 | 16.7 | 8.5 | 15.1 |
| 4. Male and female school dropouts in reported year | | | | | | | |
| a. Percent with a job | 49.3 | 49.3 | 19.7 | 48.7 | 39.2 | 51.4 | 50.2 |
| b. Percent in labor force | 63.4 | 62.7 | 46.2 | 59.7 | 52.8 | 60.9 | 69.2 |
| c. Percent of labor force unemployed | 22.2 | 21.3 | 57.3 | 18.4 | 25.7 | 15.5 | 27.4 |

[a]All figures are taken from *Employment of High School Graduates and Dropouts*, 1960 (table 2, p. 465, table A, p. A–5); 1964 (table 1, p. 639, table 4, p. 642); 1969 (table 2 and table 3, p. 38); 1976 (table 3, p. A–13, table K, p. A–18).
[b]1964 and 1969 figures in lines 1 and 2 include male graduates aged 16–21 only.

pants, including those out of school, do not in fact want a job in the survey week, but does not elucidate the reasons why they are not seeking work. Two-thirds of 16–19 year old out-of-school male nonparticipants do not want a job for "other" (unknown) reasons while half of 20–24 year old out-of-school male nonparticipants are also reported as not wanting a job for "other" reasons. Among 16–19 year old out-of-school women, the proportion who do not want a job for "other" reasons is about one-third. Among 20–24 year olds, however, it is clear that choice of household activities causes people to be out of the labor force.

The figures in columns 5 and 6 of the table show a much higher proportion of out-of-the-labor force blacks wanting a job but "discouraged" because they think they cannot get a job or for "other" reasons. Thirty-six percent of out-of-school 16–24 year old black nonparticipants

Table 3.4     Distribution of Nonparticipants in the Labor Force, by School Status and Desire for Work, 1977[a]

| | All races | | | | Both sexes | |
| | Male workers | | Female workers | | White | Black and other |
| Status | 16–19 | 20–24 | 16–19 | 20–24 | 16–24 | 16–24 |
|---|---|---|---|---|---|---|
| Total out of labor force | 100.0 | 100.0 | 100.0 | 100.0 | 100.0 | 100.0 |
| In school | 80.8 | 71.0 | 67.6 | 23.5 | 58.9 | 60.3 |
| want a job now | 21.4 | 15.7 | 19.6 | 16.2 | 18.3 | 23.6 |
| do not want a job now | 78.6 | 84.3 | 80.4 | 83.8 | 81.7 | 76.4 |
| Out of school | 19.2 | 29.0 | 32.4 | 76.5 | 41.1 | 39.7 |
| want a job now but | 27.1 | 34.7 | 22.5 | 18.8 | 18.7 | 35.6 |
| ill, disabled | 1.3 | 6.3 | .9 | .9 | 1.4 | 1.3 |
| think cannot get job | 11.3 | 12.3 | 6.9 | 3.6 | 4.8 | 11.6 |
| household responsibility | — | — | 7.7 | 9.3 | 5.5 | 12.9 |
| other reasons | 14.5 | 16.2 | 7.0 | 4.9 | 7.1 | 9.9 |
| do not want a job now | 73.0 | 65.5 | 77.5 | 81.2 | 81.3 | 64.2 |
| ill, disabled | 3.8 | 15.7 | 1.5 | 2.4 | 3.3 | 3.6 |
| keeping house | 2.5 | 1.0 | 43.9 | 71.4 | 53.2 | 35.3 |
| other | 66.8 | 48.8 | 32.2 | 7.4 | 24.8 | 25.1 |

[a]U.S. Department of Labor, *Employment and Earnings*, vol. 25, no. 1 Survey, 1978, table 39, p. 167 and table 40, p. 168. Columns may not add because of rounding.

desire a job compared to 19% of their white peers. While defining samples as including women as well as men keeping house the main reason for not wanting a job, one-quarter of both black and white groups do not want a job for "other" reasons.

The sizable differences in labor force participation rates between young blacks and whites, the declining rate of participation among young blacks, and the lack of information about unenrolled nonparticipants direct attention to a second major research question, the answer to which is needed in order to understand the youth labor market problem in the United States: What are the out-of-the-labor force youths doing and why have they left the work force?

While much of the difference between the employment of young black and white workers is associated with differences in labor force participation, there are also sizable interracial differences in the proportion of young persons available for work and looking for work, particularly in the older age groups. According to table 3.2, 17.2% of 18–19 year old blacks, for example, were available and looking in 1977 compared to 7.8% of 18–19 year old whites, while 15.1% of 20–24 year old blacks were looking compared to 5.8% of 20–24 year old whites.

What are the direct causes of this differential in unemployment? Table 3.5 presents data on the proportion of black and white labor force unemployed for several "direct" reasons: loss of job, quitting, and entrance into the labor force, with this last group being divided between reentrants, defined as those who previously worked at a full-time job lasting two weeks or longer but who were out of the labor force prior to beginning to look for work, and new entrants, defined as persons who never worked at a full-time job lasting two weeks or longer. The figures direct attention to two factors in the high unemployment rate of black youngsters: difficulty in obtaining an initial job upon entry to the work force, which is the prime cause of black/white differences among 16–17 year olds and 18–19 year olds; and loss of jobs, which explains the bulk of differences among 20–24 year olds.

The differences in the proportions of black and white teenagers who are unemployed entrants are remarkable. In 1969, 11.4 of the 13.9 percentage point difference between the unemployment rates of 16–17 year old blacks and whites was attributable to entrants; 5.5 points of the 12.8 percentage point differential between 18–19 year olds was also due to entrants. In 1978, the relevant differences were 28.8 of 30.2 points for 16–17 year olds, and 26.0 of 29.0 points for 18–19 year olds. By contrast, differential rates of job leaving had very little impact on the overall differential in unemployment rates, and rates of job loss had only a slight effect on the difference in unemployment rates by race among 16–17 year olds and a moderate effect on the differences in unemployment rates by race among 18–19 year olds.

Table 3.5          Direct Cause of Youth Unemployment, 1969–78[a]

| | Black | | | White | | |
|---|---|---|---|---|---|---|
| Age and status | 1969 | 1975 | 1978 | 1969 | 1975 | 1978 |
| *16–17* | | | | | | |
| Total unemployment rate | 24.6 | 42.4 | 44.0 | 10.7 | 17.7 | 13.8 |
| losers | 2.7 | 5.6 | 3.4 | 1.4 | 3.3 | 1.5 |
| leavers | 2.4 | 1.8 | 0.8 | 1.0 | 1.4 | 1.3 |
| total entrants | 19.6 | 35.1 | 39.8 | 8.2 | 13.0 | 11.0 |
| reentrants | 7.7 | 19.5 | 11.9 | 3.5 | 5.0 | 4.2 |
| new entrants | 11.9 | 15.6 | 28.0 | 4.7 | 8.0 | 6.8 |
| *18–19* | | | | | | |
| Total unemployment rate | 18.5 | 36.7 | 38.0 | 5.7 | 15.9 | 9.0 |
| losers | 5.4 | 13.1 | 4.8 | 1.9 | 7.2 | 2.7 |
| leavers | 4.5 | 0.7 | 2.7 | 0.7 | 1.3 | 1.9 |
| total entrants | 8.6 | 22.9 | 30.5 | 3.1 | 7.4 | 4.5 |
| reentrants | 8.1 | 14.1 | 17.8 | 2.5 | 4.8 | 2.9 |
| new entrants | .05 | 8.8 | 12.7 | 0.6 | 2.6 | 1.6 |
| *20–24* | | | | | | |
| Total unemployment rate | 7.1 | 28.3 | 18.8 | 4.4 | 13.6 | 6.6 |
| losers | 2.5 | 18.0 | 8.7 | 1.6 | 8.7 | 3.1 |
| leavers | 2.7 | 1.7 | 2.2 | 1.0 | 1.0 | 1.2 |
| total entrants | 2.0 | 8.7 | 7.9 | 1.7 | 4.0 | 2.3 |
| reentrants | 1.5 | 5.8 | 5.1 | 1.5 | 3.6 | 1.8 |
| new entrants | 0.5 | 2.9 | 2.9 | 0.2 | 0.4 | 0.5 |

[a]Weighted counts from the appropriate May CPS tapes.

The high proportion of young black labor force participants in the entrant and unemployed categories could be due to one of two factors: an especially large number of black entrants or an especially high rate of unemployment among entrants. That the problem is largely one of inability to find a job upon entry rather than a high reentry rate can be seen by comparing black and total entry rates, defined as the proportion of persons who have entered the labor force in a month relative to the number in the labor force. For blacks, Clark and Summers,[4] using CPS data, report a rate of flow out of the labor force into the labor force of .19, which, given a ratio of labor force participants to nonparticipants of about 1 to 1 for the group, yields an entry force of .19. For all men, Clark and Summers report a rate of flow from out of the labor force into the labor force of .21 which, at a ratio of labor force nonparticipants of about 2 to 3 gives an entry rate of .14 ( = .21 × 2/3). The 5 percentage point differential in entry rates falls far short of the 10 to 25 point differential in rates of unemployment among new entrants in table 3.5. More direct evidence from Clark and Summers on the probability that new entrants obtain jobs immediately upon entry confirms the interpretation of table 3.5 in terms of the difficulty that blacks have in finding jobs. According to their data, 51% of blacks compared to 36% of whites move from the labor force to unemployment rather than employment.[5] Compilation of data from the NLS reveals the same pattern of flows, although the estimates vary somewhat from those derived from the CPS.

Finally, it is important to note that the increased rate of unemployment among young blacks from 1969 to 1978 can be attributed to increased unemployment among new entrants and increased unemployment due to losses of jobs:

| Age | Change in unemployment | Change in losers rate | Change in entrants rate |
|---|---|---|---|
| 16–17 | 19.4 | 0.7 | 20.2 |
| 18–19 | 19.5 | − 0.6 | 21.9 |
| 20–24 | 11.7 | 6.2 | 5.9 |

In short, the evidence on direct causes of unemployment suggests that, for teenagers, failure to obtain a job rapidly upon entrance into the market and (for 20–24 year olds) a high job loss rate constitute major labor market problems, raising additional questions regarding the nature of the youth labor market: Why do young blacks have greater problems in finding a first job than young whites? Why are young blacks laid off more frequently than young whites?

### 3.1.3   Characteristics of Employment

The labor market position of workers depends not only on whether they hold a job or not but also on the type of job and rate of pay. In this section we will compare the industrial and occupational distribution of young male workers to that of all male workers, the percentage of young workers with part-time as opposed to full-time positions to the same percentage for all workers, and the earnings of young workers to the earnings of all workers. The data show that the young are concentrated in a different set of jobs from other workers, are especially likely to work part-time, and have experienced sizable declines in relative earnings in the period studied.

Evidence on the industrial and occupational position of young and all male workers is given in table 3.6, which records percentages employed in one-digit industries and occupations from the decennial Censuses of Population, and in table 3.7, which presents similar percentages from Current Population Surveys. The divergence between the employment distributions of young and all workers is summarized with an Index of Structural Differences (ISD), defined as the sum of the absolute values of the percentage point differences between the groups. Formally, if $\alpha_{ij}$ is the percentage of workers in age group $i$ in the $j$th category and $\alpha._{j}$ is the percentage of all workers in the category, the index is defined for the age group $i$ as $\sum_{j} |\alpha_{ij} - \alpha._{j}|$.

**Table 3.6**  The Industrial and Occupational Distribution of the Employment of Young and All Male Workers Census of Population (1950–70)[a]

| Industry or occupation | 1950 | | | | 1960 | | | | 1970 | | | |
|---|---|---|---|---|---|---|---|---|---|---|---|---|
| | 16–17 | 18–19 | 20–24 | Total[b] | 16–17 | 18–19 | 20–24 | Total | 16–17 | 18–19 | 20–24 | Total |
| **Industries** | | | | | | | | | | | | |
| Agriculture | 39.2 | 24.5 | 15.0 | 15.9 | 18.1 | 11.8 | 7.4 | 9.0 | 8.8 | 5.7 | 3.8 | 5.3 |
| Mining | .5 | 1.5 | 2.3 | 2.2 | .2 | .8 | 1.2 | 1.4 | .2 | .7 | 1.1 | 1.2 |
| Construction | 4.0 | 6.6 | 8.0 | 8.2 | 3.5 | 6.9 | 8.4 | 8.4 | 3.5 | 6.5 | 8.4 | 9.1 |
| Manufacturing | 15.0 | 26.5 | 30.0 | 27.0 | 15.5 | 25.5 | 32.6 | 30.2 | 13.1 | 24.7 | 31.0 | 29.7 |
| Transp., etc. | 2.4 | 5.1 | 8.9 | 9.2 | 1.9 | 3.8 | 6.6 | 8.5 | 2.0 | 4.8 | 7.7 | 8.6 |
| Trade | 23.7 | 22.0 | 18.8 | 17.1 | 40.5 | 29.3 | 19.6 | 17.0 | 52.5 | 37.0 | 21.3 | 18.9 |
| Finance | .5 | 1.6 | 2.0 | 2.8 | .8 | 1.7 | 2.8 | 3.4 | 1.1 | 1.7 | 3.7 | 4.0 |
| Bus and repair | 1.8 | 2.5 | 3.4 | 3.0 | 2.9 | 3.5 | 3.3 | 2.9 | 3.8 | 3.9 | 3.9 | 3.6 |
| Pers. service | 2.9 | 2.6 | 2.4 | 2.9 | 4.3 | 2.8 | 2.1 | 2.5 | 3.6 | 2.2 | 1.8 | 2.1 |
| Ent. and rec. | 4.4 | 2.0 | 1.2 | 1.0 | 3.5 | 1.6 | .9 | .8 | 3.2 | 1.7 | 1.1 | .9 |
| Prof. and rel. | 1.6 | 2.4 | 3.5 | 4.8 | 3.6 | 5.4 | 6.8 | 6.9 | 7.2 | 9.2 | 12.1 | 10.4 |
| Public admin. | .4 | .9 | 3.2 | 4.6 | .4 | 1.3 | 3.3 | 5.3 | 1.0 | 1.9 | 4.2 | 6.1 |
| Not reported | 3.4 | 1.7 | 1.4 | 1.3 | 4.7 | 5.7 | 5.1 | 3.6 | | | | |
| Index of structural differences | 68.9 | 29.5 | 10.8 | | 75.3 | 35.5 | 12.3 | | 82.1 | 39.3 | 11.6 | |

Occupations

| Occupations | | | | | | | | | | | | |
|---|---|---|---|---|---|---|---|---|---|---|---|---|
| Prof. tech. and kindred | .5 | 2.1 | 5.5 | 7.3 | 1.3 | 3.3 | 9.3 | 10.3 | 1.7 | 4.2 | 14.5 | 14.4 |
| Farmers and managers | 2.7 | 3.6 | 5.6 | 10.4 | 1.8 | 1.7 | 2.0 | 5.5 | .4 | .5 | .9 | 2.8 |
| Managers ex farmers | .5 | 1.2 | 3.4 | 10.5 | .5 | 1.3 | 3.8 | 10.6 | .7 | 1.6 | 4.9 | 11.2 |
| Clerical | 4.8 | 9.4 | 9.4 | 6.5 | 7.8 | 11.3 | 10.3 | 7.0 | 7.9 | 11.4 | 11.3 | 7.6 |
| Sales | 10.7 | 7.5 | 6.9 | 6.4 | 13.8 | 7.8 | 6.2 | 6.9 | 9.3 | 6.7 | 6.2 | 6.9 |
| Craftsmen and foremen | 3.4 | 8.1 | 14.9 | 18.7 | 4.6 | 10.1 | 15.4 | 19.5 | 5.6 | 12.4 | 18.5 | 21.2 |
| Operatives | 15.9 | 25.8 | 28.1 | 20.1 | 18.5 | 26.0 | 26.5 | 19.9 | 18.1 | 26.7 | 24.1 | 19.5 |
| Private household | .2 | .1 | .1 | .2 | .5 | .2 | .1 | .1 | .3 | .1 | .1 | .1 |
| Service ex priv. | 9.7 | 6.0 | 4.6 | 5.9 | 11.5 | 8.0 | 5.6 | 6.0 | 24.8 | 14.1 | 8.1 | 8.0 |
| Farm laborers | 35.7 | 20.0 | 8.6 | 4.9 | 14.7 | 8.8 | 4.4 | 2.7 | 7.0 | 4.1 | 2.1 | 1.7 |
| Laborers ex farm and mine | 13.0 | 14.5 | 11.5 | 8.1 | 19.1 | 14.2 | 9.4 | 6.9 | 24.1 | 18.1 | 9.3 | 6.6 |
| Not reported | 2.6 | 1.7 | 1.3 | 1.1 | 5.8 | 7.3 | 6.6 | 4.6 | | | | |
| Index of structural differences | | 89.5 | 63.3 | 37.4 | | 76.9 | 56.3 | 30.6 | | 85.1 | 62.1 | 23.3 |

[a]*U.S. Census of the Population,* "Industrial Characteristics," 1950, Table 3; 1960, Tables 2, 4; 1970, Tables 32, 34. "Occupational Characteristics," 1950, Table 6; 1960, Tables 2, 6; 1970, Tables 39, 40.

**Table 3.7**   The Industrial and Occupational Distribution of the Employment of Young and All Male Workers; Current Population Survey: May 1969, 1973, 1978[a]

| Industries | 1969 | | | | 1973 | | | | 1978 | | | |
|---|---|---|---|---|---|---|---|---|---|---|---|---|
| | 16-17 | 18-19 | 20-24 | Total[b] | 16-17 | 18-19 | 20-24 | Total[b] | 16-17 | 18-19 | 20-24 | Total[b] |
| Agriculture | 8.7 | 4.9 | 2.9 | 2.6 | 6.8 | 4.4 | 3.1 | 2.5 | 6.5 | 5.0 | 3.5 | 2.6 |
| Mining | .1 | .7 | .7 | 1.1 | .1 | .8 | 1.1 | 1.2 | .2 | 1.0 | 1.5 | 1.4 |
| Construction | 4.5 | 7.8 | 8.7 | 9.2 | 5.2 | 11.7 | 11.7 | 9.7 | 5.0 | 11.2 | 13.1 | 9.4 |
| Manufacturing | 11.5 | 24.5 | 37.9 | 35.2 | 12.0 | 24.6 | 29.2 | 31.6 | 10.7 | 19.7 | 28.0 | 29.2 |
| Transportation, etc. | 2.3 | 4.7 | 8.0 | 9.1 | 1.9 | 3.9 | 7.5 | 8.8 | 2.5 | 3.8 | 6.9 | 9.1 |
| Trade | 46.9 | 35.7 | 17.5 | 16.7 | 49.1 | 35.4 | 22.4 | 18.5 | 52.2 | 38.1 | 24.2 | 19.4 |
| Finance | 1.1 | 1.9 | 3.2 | 3.8 | 1.2 | 1.7 | 3.8 | 4.3 | 1.1 | 1.6 | 3.2 | 4.1 |
| Bus. & repair | 4.6 | 4.5 | 3.2 | 2.9 | 3.7 | 4.2 | 4.0 | 3.1 | 3.4 | 5.8 | 5.3 | 3.8 |
| Personal service | 8.2 | 2.5 | 1.8 | 1.9 | 7.5 | 2.3 | 1.5 | 1.7 | 7.6 | 3.3 | 1.7 | 1.7 |
| Ent. & rep. | 4.5 | 2.11 | 1.1 | .0 | 3.8 | 1.9 | .9 | 6.9 | 4.1 | 2.2 | .9 | 1.1 |
| Prof. & rel. | 6.2 | 8.8 | 10.5 | 9.6 | 7.8 | 8.0 | 10.5 | 10.7 | 5.6 | 6.3 | 8.6 | 11.6 |
| Public admin. | 1.5 | 1.9 | 4.5 | 7.0 | .9 | 1.0 | 4.2 | 7.0 | 1.2 | 2.1 | 3.0 | 6.6 |
| Index of structural differences | 92.1 | 47.0 | 11.7 | | 85.8 | 43.7 | 15.0 | | 89.7 | 52.8 | 21.0 | |

|  | 1969 | | 1973 | | 1978 | |
| Occupations | 16–19 | Total | 16–19 | Total | 16–19 | Total |
|---|---|---|---|---|---|---|
| Professional, tech, kindred | 2.8 | 14.4 | 2.0 | 13.4 | 1.6 | 15.2 |
| Farmers & managers | (c) | .08 | (c) | .05 | (c) | .1 |
| Managers ex. farmers | 1.1 | 11.4 | 1.2 | 12.2 | 1.3 | 12.7 |
| Clerical | 6.0 | 8.0 | 7.4 | 7.3 | 6.6 | 6.9 |
| Sales | 6.0 | 5.5 | 5.6 | 5.8 | 5.4 | 5.8 |
| Craftsmen & foremen | 7.5 | 21.2 | 10.8 | 21.9 | 10.5 | 21.2 |
| Operatives ex. transport | 25.5 | 22.1 | 20.3 | 14.1 | 16.5 | 12.4 |
| Private household | .2 | .06 | .2 | .05 | .4 | (c) |
| Service ex private HH | 16.1 | 7.1 | 20.8 | 8.8 | 22.7 | 9.2 |
| Farm laborers | 5.9 | 1.8 | 4.4 | 1.8 | 4.1 | 1.7 |
| Laborers ex farm & mine | 24.3 | 8.1 | 23.3 | 8.3 | 26.0 | 8.6 |
| Transport operatives | (c) | 8.1 | 4.1 | 6.3 | 5.1 | 6.2 |
| Index of structural differences | 70.9 | | 72.0 | | 75.4 | |

aTabulations are from the appropriate May Current Population Surveys, excluding the self-employed.

bMales 16 years and older.

cLess than .05 percent.

The industry employment figures reveal an enormous difference between the sectors of employment of 16–17 year old men and all male workers, a sizable difference between the industries hiring 18–19 year olds and all men, but only a modest difference between the industrial distribution of 20–24 year olds and all men. Both the Census data and the CPS data show 16–17 year olds to be largely concentrated in trade and substantially underrepresented in manufacturing, among other sectors. From 1950 to 1970 the employment of 16–17 year olds as well as of other men in agriculture dropped sharply. Men in the next age bracket, 18–19 year olds, are also relatively overrepresented in trade but much less so than 16–17 year olds. The 18–19 year olds tend to find a relatively large number of jobs in manufacturing. Overall, the ISD is reduced by about 50% as the group increases in age from 16–17 to 18–19. In contrast to teenage groups, the industrial distribution of 20–24 year olds closely mirrors that of all male workers, suggesting that when they reach their twenties the young are beginning to enter what may be called adult job markets. From 1973 to 1978, however, the ISD grew for 20–24 year olds as well as for the teenagers.

Divergences in job distributions are considerably greater along occupational dimensions, with 16–17 year olds highly concentrated in laborer and service jobs and 18–19 year olds in laborer, service, operative, craft, and clerical jobs. For 20–24 year olds, the divergences are smaller and appear to have fallen from 1950 to 1970.

Whether the marked difference in the industrial and occupational distribution of employment of teenagers and all male workers does, in fact, reflect differences in job markets depends on the link between the jobs obtained by teenagers and adult jobs. The wide divergences shown in tables 3.6 and 3.7 are, at the least, suggestive of significant differences between the teenage and adult job markets.

The data on part-time versus full-time work given in table 3.8 lend some support to the separate market interpretation of the divergences in job distributions. According to the table, nearly half of teenage workers and three-fourths of those aged 16–17 are either employed part time or are on part-time schedules. By contrast, the proportions of all workers employed part time and on part-time schedules are much smaller. Over 40% of unemployed teenagers are seeking part-time jobs compared to about 20% of all unemployed workers. To the extent that the markets for full-time and part-time workers are at least reasonably separable, these figures support the contention that there are substantive differences between the youth, especially teen, and adult job markets.

### 3.1.4 Wages

On the price side of the youth labor market, two major developments stand out: a sharp drop in the relative earnings of young workers in the

**Table 3.8**     **The Distribution of Youth and All Workers by Part-time Job Status: 1977[a]**

| Age and sex | Percentage of employed working part-time[b] | Percentage of unemployed seeking part-time work | Percentage on part-time schedules[c] |
|---|---|---|---|
| Civilian labor force, both sexes | | | |
| All ages | 14.4 | 20.7 | — |
| 16–19 | 45.5 | 43.9 | — |
| Nonagricultural male employees | — | — | |
| All ages | | | 7.6 |
| 16–17 | | | 74.5 |
| 18–24 | | | 15.3 |
| Nonagricultural female employees | — | — | |
| All ages | | | 27.4 |
| 16–17 | | | 82.6 |
| 18–24 | | | 23.2 |

[a]U.S. Department of Labor, *Handbook of Labor Statistics, 1978*, tables 21, 22, pp. 87–93.
[b]Includes voluntary part-time; persons on part-time schedules for economic reasons were counted as full-time employees.
[c]Includes persons who wanted only part-time work.

period under study and an increase in the earnings of young blacks compared to young white workers. Columns 1–3 of table 3.9 document the marked fall in the relative earnings of the young in terms of the ratio of usual weekly earnings of full-time white men aged 16–24 to the usual weekly earnings of full-time white men 25 and older. These data are taken from the May Current Population Survey, which provides a continuous series of rates of pay from 1967 to the present. The data show drops in the rates of earnings for each age group of 10 points on average. Corroboratory information on the annual earnings of year-round and full-time workers from the March CPS reveals similar patterns of change: a twist in the age-earnings profile against young workers.[6] Because a fairly sizable number of young persons are employed part time, columns 4–6 of the table record the ratio of the earnings of part-time young white men to the earnings of full-time older workers. All but two of these earnings ratios drop, though by a smaller margin than the ratios for full-time workers, presumably because of their initially low levels. If the full-time and part-time workers are treated as a single group, the deterioration in the earnings position of the young becomes even more marked. This is because the proportion of 16–24 year old out-of-school men working part time doubled over the period covered from 8% in 1965 to 16% in 1977, exacerbating the drop in relative earnings.

**Table 3.9  Percentages of the Median Usual Weekly Earnings of Out-of-school Men to Workers Aged 25 and Older, by Race: 1967–77[a]**

| Age | Earnings of full-time young white men/ Earnings of full-time white men, age 25+ | | Change in earnings ratios | Earnings of part-time young white men/ Earnings of full-time white men, age 25+ | | Change in earnings ratios | Earnings of full-time young nonwhite men/ Earnings of full-time white men, age 25+ | | Change in earnings ratios |
|---|---|---|---|---|---|---|---|---|---|
| | 1967 | 1977 | 1967–77 | 1967 | 1977 | 1967–77 | 1967[b] | 1977 | 1967–77 |
| 16 | .38 | .34 | −.04 | .19 | .14 | −.05 | .33 | .32 | −.01 |
| 17 | .49 | .39 | −.10 | .21 | .19 | −.02 | .39 | .32 | −.07 |
| 18 | .54 | .49 | −.05 | .22 | .20 | −.02 | .44 | .44 | .00 |
| 19 | .61 | .52 | −.09 | .22 | .24 | .02 | .42 | .43 | −.01 |
| 20 | .66 | .58 | −.08 | .35 | .26 | −.09 | .63 | .52 | −.11 |
| 21 | .73 | .61 | −.12 | .22 | .23 | .01 | .57 | .50 | −.07 |
| 22 | .79 | .63 | −.16 | .41 | .24 | −.17 | .59 | .54 | −.05 |
| 23 | .84 | .71 | −.13 | .38 | .32 | −.06 | .59 | .54 | −.05 |
| 24 | .87 | .75 | −.12 | .37 | .26 | −.11 | .60 | .63 | −.03 |

[a]U.S. Department of Labor, unpublished tabulations from May 1967 and May 1977 Current Population Surveys. 1967 refers to voluntary part-time unless out of school; 1977 refers to all part-time workers.
[b]No whites in 1967.

Finally, the last three columns in table 3.9 reveal a pattern of change in the earnings of young blacks relative to full-time white male workers aged 25 and older which is of a smaller magnitude than those obtained for young white men, indicating of an improvement in the earnings of young blacks vis-à-vis young whites. This contrasts with the worsened employment record of young blacks relative to young whites, possibly indicating movement along a relative demand schedule. It may be that the increase in the relative earnings of blacks is attributable to an outward shift in the demand schedule for blacks relative to whites due to the passage of the Civil Rights Act of 1964.

### 3.1.5 Summary

The evidence in this section from the Current Population Survey on the labor market position of young workers has yielded several findings regarding the changing market for the young. We have found that the unemployment rate of all young workers deteriorated relative to older workers; that, by contrast, the employment to population ratio did not decline, except for young men not enrolled in school; that all indicators of employment—unemployment rates, labor force participation rates, and employment to population ratios—showed a worsened labor market position for young blacks while, by contrast, their relative earnings position improved; that a large proportion of the drop in black employment is associated with nonparticipation in the work force, about which relatively little is known; that much of black unemployment is due to problems in finding a first job and to job loss; that the occupational and industrial distribution of teenage employment diverges sharply from that of adult males, suggesting a reasonably distinct job market, while the distribution of jobs of 20–24 year old men is quite similar to that of all men; that relatively many teenagers are part-time employees; and that the relative earnings of young workers dropped sharply in the period studied.

### 3.2 Associated Social Problems

Two basic aspects of the concern about youth unemployment are fear that high rates of joblessness among the young will have long-term consequences for their economic well-being, and fear that youth unemployment is associated, perhaps causally, with social problems such as youth crime, drug abuse and the like. The potential long-term economic effects of being unemployed during youth are examined by Ellwood,[8] Corcoran, and Meyer and Wise. The immediate social problems that may be linked to youth joblessness are analyzed in this section.

## 3.2.1  The Social Problems

Figures from a variety of sources seem to indicate a growing malaise among young people in the U.S. during the past two decades. In this section, we briefly present the data available on youth crime, violence in school, illegitimate births, and youth suicide rates.

### Youth Crime

Table 3.10 demonstrates that youth arrest rates for both violent crimes and property crimes have risen dramatically since the mid-1950s. It is interesting to note not only the absolute increase in the rate of crime, but also the increase in the youth (under 21 years of age) rate relative to that of the entire population. In all cases reported in table 3.10, the youth rate was lower than that of the entire population in 1950 but surpassed that rate in all categories in 1975.

Table 3.11 demonstrates that the increase in youth arrests is found for blacks as well as whites. In addition, the arrest rates for blacks are consistently much higher than those for whites.

### Violence in School

Table 3.12 shows the sharp increase in violence in schools from 1964 to 1968, and table 3.13 shows the striking increase in school violence from 1970 to 1973. The increase in assaults is especially dramatic in both periods. Over the same periods, school enrollment rose only modestly and thus cannot account for such striking increases.

**Table 3.10**     **Annual Arrests per Thousand Population of Relevant Age: 1950–75[a]**

| Category | 1950 | 1955 | 1965 | 1970 | 1975 |
|---|---|---|---|---|---|
| All arrests | | | | | |
| all ages | 5.3 | 11.3 | 26.0 | 32.3 | 37.6 |
| under 21[b] | 2.1 | 5.0 | 20.0 | 31.9 | 42.7 |
| Violent crimes[c] | | | | | |
| all ages | .6 | .3 | .8 | 1.2 | 1.7 |
| under 21 | .3 | .2 | .6 | 1.2 | 1.9 |
| Property crimes[d] | | | | | |
| all ages | .9 | .9 | 3.5 | 5.1 | 7.2 |
| under 21 | .8 | 1.5 | 6.0 | 8.8 | 12.9 |

[a]Number of arrests from U.S. Federal Bureau of Investigation, *Uniform Crime Reports for the United States* XXI (1950) 2:110–11, XXVI (1955):113–14, XXVI (1965):114, XLI (1970):128, LXVI (1975):190.

Population figures from U.S. Bureau of the Census, *Statistical Abstract of the United States* 72 (1951):10; 77 (1956):26; 87 (1966):8; 97 (1976):27. Data unavailable for 1960.

[b]1950 population aged 20 estimated as one-fifth the population aged 20 to 24.

[c]Includes murder, nonnegligent homicide, rape, robbery, and aggravated assault; includes negligent homicide in 1950.

[d]Includes burglary, larceny and auto theft.

Table 3.11       **Annual Arrests per Thousand Population
                  of Relevant Age, by Race: 1965–75**[a]

| Category | Whites | | | Blacks[b] | | |
|---|---|---|---|---|---|---|
| | 1965 | 1970 | 1975 | 1965 | 1970 | 1975 |
| All arrests | | | | | | |
| all ages | 18.9 | 24.6 | 29.9 | 65.3 | 74.8 | 79.1 |
| under 18 | 12.2 | 18.4 | 27.3 | 27.8 | 38.9 | 45.4 |
| Violent crimes[c] | | | | | | |
| all ages | .3 | .5 | .9 | 3.0 | 5.1 | 6.3 |
| under 18 | .1 | .3 | .6 | 1.5 | 2.9 | 4.0 |
| Property crimes[d] | | | | | | |
| all ages | 2.5 | 3.6 | 5.4 | 9.0 | 14.2 | 17.6 |
| under 18 | 4.0 | 5.3 | 9.0 | 11.0 | 15.6 | 19.6 |

[a]Number of arrests from Uniform Crime Reports XXXVI (1965):117–18: XLI (1970):131, 132; XLVI (1975):192–93. Population figures from same source as table 3.10.
[b]All nonwhites in 1965.
[c]Includes murder, rape, robbery, and aggravated assault.
[d]Includes burglary, larceny, and auto theft.

## Other Social Problems

Two more problems, the rate of births to unmarried young women and the rate of suicides among young persons, are not signs of juvenile delinquency nor necessarily of juvenile degeneracy, but are still causes of great social concern. Table 3.14 demonstrates two important trends in the rate of illegitimate births to young women. First, the fertility rates for

Table 3.12       **Percentage Increases in Crimes in Schools
                  in 110 Urban School Districts (1964–68)**[a]

| Category | Cases | | Percentage increase |
|---|---|---|---|
| | 1964 | 1968 | |
| Homicide | 15 | 26 | 73 |
| Forcible rape | 51 | 81 | 61 |
| Robbery | 396 | 1,508 | 376 |
| Aggravated assault | 475 | 680 | 43 |
| Burglary, larceny | 7,604 | 14,102 | 85 |
| Weapons offenses | 419 | 1,089 | 136 |
| Narcotics | 73 | 854 | 1,069 |
| Drunkenness | 370 | 1,035 | 179 |
| Crimes by nonstudents | 142 | 3,894 | 2,600 |
| Vandalism incidents | 186,184 | 250,549 | 35 |
| Assault on teachers | 25 | 1,081 | 7,100 |
| Assault on students | 1,601 | 4,267 | 167 |
| Other | 4,796 | 8,824 | 84 |

[a]Senate Subcommittee on Juvenile Delinquency Survey, 1970, reported in J. M. Tien, *Crime/Environment Targets*.

**Table 3.13**    **Percentage Increases in Crime in Schools in 516 School Districts (1970–73)[a]**

| Category | Percentage increase |
|---|---|
| Homicide | 18.5 |
| Rape and Attempted Rape | 40.1 |
| Robbery | 36.7 |
| Assault on Students | 85.3 |
| Assault on Teachers | 77.4 |
| Burglary of School Buildings | 11.8 |
| Drug and Alcohol Offenses on School Property | 37.5 |
| Weapons Confiscated | 54.4 |

[a]*Our Nation's Schools . . . ,* Preliminary Report of the Senate Subcommittee to Investigate Juvenile Delinquency, 1975.

both white and nonwhite unmarried women between the ages of 15 and 19 have increased in the past two decades. The rate for white women has increased steadily, while that for nonwhite women fell through 1965, jumped sharply between 1965 and 1970, and has been falling since. Second, the difference in fertility rates has remained relatively constant over time—a difference of about 70 births per thousand each year. These trends may indicate a serious social problem, especially if these women are very young. These mothers are usually either out of school when they become pregnant or are forced to leave during their pregnancies. Many are unable to work or go to school after their children are born because they have no one who can care for the child.

Table 3.15 shows two major trends in the rate of suicides among young persons. First, although the suicide rate has stayed relatively constant for the population as a whole during the past two and a half decades, the suicide rate for young persons has risen dramatically. In 1970, for example, the suicide rate for 20–24 year olds, both white and nonwhite, rose above that of the population as a whole. Second, the suicide rate for 20–24 year olds is consistently higher than that for 15–19 year olds.

**Table 3.14**    **Fertility Rates for Unmarried Teenage Women: 1955–76[a]**

| Year | Births per 1,000 unmarried women | |
|---|---|---|
| | White | Nonwhite |
| 1955 | 6.0 | 77.6 |
| 1960 | 6.6 | 76.5 |
| 1965 | 7.9 | 75.8 |
| 1970 | 10.9 | 90.8 |
| 1975 | 12.1 | 88.1 |
| 1976 | 12.4 | 84.6 |

[a]National Center for Health Statistics.

Table 3.15    Suicides per 100,000 Population, 1950–76[a]

|       | Nonwhite | | White | | |
|-------|------|------|------|------|------------|
| Year  | 15–19 | 20–24 | 15–19 | 20–24 | Population |
| 1950  | 1.9  | 4.9  | 2.8  | 6.4  | 11.4 |
| 1955  | 2.4  | 5.8  | 2.7  | 5.5  | 10.2 |
| 1960  | 2.4  | 4.5  | 3.8  | 7.4  | 10.6 |
| 1965  | 3.9  | 8.3  | 4.1  | 9.0  | 11.1 |
| 1970  | 4.2  | 12.0 | 6.2  | 12.0 | 11.6 |
| 1975  | 4.6  | 14.4 | 8.1  | 16.9 | 12.7 |
| 1976  | 5.4  | 13.8 | 7.7  | 16.8 | 12.5 |

[a]National Center for Health Statistics.

### 3.2.2   Relationships to Labor Market Problems

The preceding social statistics reveal substantial changes in several important social indicators regarding youth. While cause and effect are very difficult to untangle, the increases in youth crime, violence in schools, illegitimacy, and suicide are probably linked, at least to some extent, to the labor market problems of the young. The relationship between youth labor force experiences and social problems may be causal. On the other hand, the labor market problems and the social problems may both be indicators of underlying changes in the values and environment of young persons.

Many of the studies that examine the social correlates of youth labor market difficulties have focused on the problem of youth crime. The major works that study the relationship between unemployment and youth crime fall roughly into three categories: the subculture approach, the cost-benefit approach, and the institutional approach.

The subculture approach maintains that youth crime is principally the result of a peer group subculture: young people band together in social groups whose values differ from those of adult society. Many of the youth groups value violence, destruction, theft, and individual escapism via drugs. They engage in these activities for social prestige rather than monetary gain. This view is well articulated both by Cohen in his studies of youth peer groups and by Howard and Ohlin. Cohen emphasizes the wide differences between the values of youth and the values of adults, and he stresses the importance of these values in determining behavior. Cohen believes that a lack of guidance from and contact with parents may be a reason for rejection of adult values on the part of youth. Emotional instability in family relationships, broken families, working mothers, and teachers are held responsible, in part, for delinquency. According to this approach, high adult unemployment will tend to reduce juvenile delinquency since unemployed parents will have more time to spend with their children. Proponents of this theory also argue that a decline in youth unemployment will lead to a decline in youth crime. Subculturists assume that employment requires steady, disciplined contact between youths and their elders, thus decreasing the strength of peer subculture attachments and values.

The second group of theories on the relationship between delinquency and economic conditions emphasizes the role of cost and benefit calculations for the potential delinquent. These theorists argue that crime, like other human activities, can be viewed as having certain monetary costs and benefits associated with it. The individual chooses crime because he perceives that the benefits of crime outweigh the costs. The cost-benefit theorists, unlike the subculturists, believe that the decisions to engage in crime is an individual decision rather than a group one. The conditions that determine the costs and benefits are externally influenced but are subject to the tastes and perceptions of the individual. This approach emphasizes the pecuniary aspect of crime rather than its social deviancy. Hence, the theory offers a better explanation of crimes of property such as theft, larceny, robbery, prostitution, and drug dealing, than of violent crimes such as rape and murder, which rarely involve direct pecuniary benefits.

The foremost proponents of the cost-benefit approach, Becker, Fleisher and Ehrlich, believe that the amount of youth crime is affected primarily by the expected costs of crime, taking into account the likelihood of arrest and conviction, injury, and so on; the expected benefits of crime, based on the demand for stolen goods; and tastes, such as a desire for the thrill of crime, and the strength of the need for additional income. As youth unemployment increases, the ability to generate income legally is reduced. In order to maintain a minimum income level, a youth may decide to earn money illegally. Thus cost-benefit theorists believe that as youth unemployment increases, youth crime (especially property crimes) will also increase.

The institutional approach reflects a more complex concept of the behavior of youths than do the previous two. The theory is based on direct observation of small groups of youths rather than upon aggregate data. The institutional approach shares the emphasis of the cost-benefit approach in distinguishing between various types of crime and in emphasizing the monetary incentives behind much of youth crime. This theory, however, stresses the fact that many criminal activities are virtually indistinguishable from legitimate careers, and may be perceived as such by youths. "Selling dope," "taking numbers," "pimping," and other illegal activities, when engaged in regularly, can provide a steady income. Like legitimate jobs, they have peak hours and off hours on a daily or weekly basis, they require a period of training before earnings can be maximized, and they operate by a standard system of norms and procedures. Adherents to this approach predict that, contrary to the results of the cost-benefit approach, an increase in youth unemployment will be associated with a fall in youth crime. Institutionalists predict that youths will view those crimes that generate a steady income as forms of regular employment. Thus, in response to an employment survey, a youth may report himself as employed because he works at a regular job, even if the job is illegal. A youth may also choose to report himself as employed if he is earning a good income illegally in order to justify a level of consumption that greatly exceeds what he could spend from other sources of income. He may also fear that if he is categorized as unemployed, he will be forced to join unemployment programs that would compromise his ability to earn income from illegal activities. For these reasons, a youth who is engaged in illegal activities may be recorded as employed. Thus, as participation in criminal activities rises, the unemployment rate may actually fall, implying an inverse relation between unemployment and crime. On the other hand, the youth engaging in crime may report himself as being out of the labor force—neither working nor seeking work.

Table 3.16 briefly summarizes some of the major studies done in support of the alternative theories of youth crime. The techniques and variables used vary dramatically across studies, and the empirical research has often produced contradictory results.

The evidence from all three viewpoints seems to point to crime as an alternative for youths who cannot find jobs, but the statistics reveal little more. Most studies relate measures of criminal activity to measures of unemployment and other variables but the selection of variables and research techniques differs considerably. Some studies use youth arrests, some use all arrests, and some include nonproperty crime while others do not. Most studies examine the link between crime and youth unemployment but some use general unemployment and one uses overall business activity. Some use different age groups while others lump age groups together. The income level in an area seems to have a strong effect on crime, yet many studies include no income variable. The descriptive studies center only on ghetto youths, although they may operate quite differently from those middle-class youths whose monetary incentives for crime may not be so strong. Statistics on crime are weak because they fluctuate with the budgets made available for law enforcement as much as with the amount of crime. Also, those who are arrested may be innocent, while many other criminals are never caught.

Another issue that is not touched on in any of the empirical studies is the importance of school enrollment for teenagers below college age and the effect of teenage unemployment on enrollment. If youths have difficulty finding jobs they may just stay on in school rather than join the labor market legally or illegally.

**Table 3.16**     Summary of Empirical Research on the Relationship between Unemployment and Crime.

| Authors | Method and sample | Results and conclusions |
|---|---|---|
| *Subculture*<br>Glaser and Rice | Estimated correlations between age specific arrest data from an FBI national sample and both age specific and total unemployment rates from 1932 to 1950. Also studied municipal arrest data from Chicago, Cincinnati and Boston for selected years between 1980 and 1952. | Glaser and Rice found a significant negative correlation between crime and both unemployment figures for youths under age 18. For adults aged 19–34, there was a significant positive relationship, and for adults over age 35, the correlation was significant negative. The municipal data indicated a significant positive relationship between the unemployment rate and property crime arrests for persons aged 25 and older. |
| *Cost-benefit*<br>Fleisher | Fleisher performed extensive regression analysis on: (1) the municipal data used by Glaser and Rice; (2) the national sample also used by Glaser and Rice; (3) cross-sectional data from Chicago for 1958; and (4) data from 101 cities from FBI police agency reports. | With these four data sets, Fleisher derived the following results (respectively): (1) controlling for income, race, etc., unemployment had a uniformly positive effect on arrest rates; (2) there was a positive relationship between crime and unemployment for all age groups except those below age 16; (3) unemployment positively affected delinquency; and (4) unemployment had a significant positive effect on delinquency for the lowest income group. |

| | | |
|---|---|---|
| Ehrlich | Examined the effect of the unemployment rate for 14–24 year old urban males on their decision to engage in unlawful activities. Controlled for probability of apprehension, time served by offenders, income, education, and per capita public expenditure on crime control. | Results on unemployment were generally inconsistent and insignificant. Income, race, and time served in prison have strong effects. The labor force participation rate for 14–24 year olds has a significant positive effect on auto theft and larceny. |
| Cook | Studied recidivism rates among 327 men paroled from Massachusetts institutions for felons. | Cook found a positive correlation between short job tenure (which he used as a proxy for job dissatisfaction) and recidivism. He reasoned that it is not a lack of jobs *per se* that encourages criminal activity but rather a lack of interesting or well-paying jobs. |
| *Institutional* | | |
| Bullock | Interviewed 304 black and 268 Chicano teenagers in Watts and East Los Angeles in 1971. | Illegal activities constitute the single greatest source of market income for young men in central cities. The principal activity is drug dealing. |
| Friedlander | Interviewed 25 black teenagers in Harlem in 1968. | Criminal activity serves as an alternative occupation for a person in the ghetto with few skills and little education. |
| Liebow | Studied low-income black men in a Washington, D.C. ghetto. | The legitimate jobs available to youths who have little education are perceived as dull, degrading, and low paying, and as not offering an improved future. |

Finally, what difference does the status of the youth—whether he is living at home under parental support, living alone, or supporting his own family—make in his desire for legal or illegal employment? Evidence from descriptive studies seems to indicate that the greater the degree to which he must support himself and/or others, the more desperately he will need an income and the more vigorously he will pursue an occupation—legal or illegal.

Although more research is clearly required, it appears that youth labor market problems are linked to youth crime in a complex manner. Less work has been done on the relationship between youth labor market problems and the other social ills examined earlier. However, the evidence that does exist suggests that there is some link between labor market problems and social problems.

The evidence already cited on violent crimes would seem to be relevant to the more specific problem of violence in schools. In particular, the subculture theory provides a plausible theory linking youth unemployment and violent behavior. A link between youth problems in the labor market and rising illegitimacy rates has been examined by the National Advisory Council on Economic Opportunity. The council cites a number of indications that putting off marriage because of poor job prospects or unemployment contributes to the high rates of illegitimate births among the poor. Finally, both the National Advisory Council and Fleisher have found a positive correlation between suicide and unemployment, although the reason for this relationship is unclear for young persons.

These studies are both interesting and suggestive, but they by no means provide conclusive evidence on the nature of the relationship between youth labor market difficulties and social ills. As mentioned above, the relationship may be causal, or both the labor market problems and the social problems may be symptoms of a serious underlying change in the attitudes and environment of American youths. Clearly more investigations concerning this topic should be undertaken.

### 3.2.3   Future Research

The review of the literature above indicates that there is no clear answer to the question of how youth unemployment is related to other social problems. Increases in rates of delinquency may be due to many other causes including a decline in the number of two-parent families, peer pressure, a lack of good education for many youths, and various social factors. In order to determine the magnitudes of these effects on delinquency relative to the effect of poor labor market experience, new types of data must be collected, and a large amount of research must be done.

We recommend, for example, that questions be included in surveys of youth labor force activity which ask what the unemployed and nonparticipants do. Of those students who attend school, ask what they do in the afternoons; of those who do not attend school, ask probing questions about how they spend their time. Questions asking a youth what he does do should be much more informative than questions that tend to rule out what he does not do (i.e., "Did you work over forty hours in the past week at a job?") Also, more detailed questions about the types of jobs held by those who are employed might lead us to a better understanding of what youths are doing. Questions on the perceived permanence of a specific job could indicate youth attachment to that job. Questions on the amount and nature of training, and on the likelihood of promotion within the firm could indicate, more objectively than the previous questions, what future the youth can expect from his job.

# Notes

1. See Freeman and Medoff, "Why Does the Rate of Youth Labor Force Activity Differ across Surveys?," chapter 4 of this volume.
2. Data for these regressions were taken from *Employment and Training Report of the President, 1978*, pp. 187–88, 213–14.
3. Data for these calculations were taken from *Employment and Training Report of the President, 1978*, pp. 188, 214.
4. From Clark and Summers, "The Dynamics of Youth Unemployment," chapter 7 of this volume.
5. See Clark and Summers, chapter 7 of this volume.
6. See Freeman, "The Effect of Demographic Factors on Age-Earnings Profiles" for substantiation of this fact.
7. See Ellwood, "Teenage Unemployment: Permanent Scars or Temporary Blemishes?," chapter 10 of this volume; Corcoran, this volume; Meyer and Wise, this volume.

# References

Bullock, P. 1973. *Aspirations vs opportunity: careers in the inner city.* Ann Arbor: Institute of Labor and Industrial Relations, University of Michigan, Wayne State.

Becker, G. "Crime and Punishment." U.S. Department of Labor. 1978. *Employment and training report of the president, 1978.* Washington, D.C.: GPO.

Cloward, R. and L. Ohlin. 1973. *Delinquency and opportunity.* Glencoe, Illinois: The Free Press.

Cohen, A. 1960. *Delinquent boys.* Glencoe, Illinois: The Free Press.

Cook, P. 1975. The correctional carrot: better jobs for parolees. *Policy Analysis* 1:11–54.

Ehrlich, I. 1973. Participation in illegitimate activities: a theoretical and empirical investigation. *Journal of Political Economy* 3:521–65.

Fleisher, B. 1966. *The economics of delinquency*. Chicago: Quadrangle Books.

Ford, G. and U.S. Department of Labor. 1977. *Employment and training report of the president, 1977*, Washington, D.C. GPO.

Freeman, R. B. 1978. The effect of demographic factors on age-earnings profiles. *The Journal of Human Resources* 3:289–319.

Friedlander, S. 1972. *Unemployment in the urban core: an analysis of thirty cities with policy recommendations*. New York: Praeger Publishers.

Glaser, D. and K. Rice. 1959. Crime, age, and unemployment. *American Sociological Review* 5:679–86.

Henry, A. F. and J. F. Short. 1954. *Suicide and homicide*. Glencoe, Illinois: The Free Press.

Liebow, E. 1967. *Tally's corner: a study of negro streetcorner men*. Boston: Little, Brown and Co.

National Advisory Council on Economic Opportunity. 1979. The human cost of unemployment. In their *11th Annual Report*, Washington, D.C. Pp. 21–23.

Ogburn, W. F. and D. S. Thomas. 1922. The influence of the business cycle on certain social conditions. *Journal of the American Statistical Association* September: 305–50.

U.S. Bureau of the Census. *U.S. census of the population, 1950*. Volume 4, Special Report Part 1, chapters B and D. Washington, D.C.: GPO.

U.S. Bureau of the Census. *U.S. census of the population, 1960*. Subject Report PC(2) 7A and 7F. Washington, D.C.: GPO.

U.S. Bureau of the Census. *U.S. census of the population, 1970*. Subject Report PC(2) 7A and 7B. Washington, D.C.: GPO.

U.S. Bureau of Labor Statistics. 1978. *Employment and earnings*, Vol. 25, no. 1. Washington, D.C.: GPO.

U.S. Bureau of Labor Statistics. 1966, 1970. *Employment, high school graduates and dropouts*. Special Labor Force Reports #54 and #121. Washington, D.C.: GPO.

U.S. Bureau of Labor Statistics. 1961. *Employment of June 1960 high school graduates*. Special Labor Force Report #15. Washington, D.C.: GPO.

U.S. Bureau of Labor Statistics. 1977, 1979. *Handbook of labor statistics 1977 and 1978*. Bulletins 1966 and 2000. Washington, D.C.: GPO.

U.S. Bureau of Labor Statistics. 1977. *Students, graduates and dropouts in the labor market, October 1976*. Special Labor Force Report #200. Washington, D.C.: GPO.

U.S. Bureau of Labor Statistics. 1966, 1971, 1977. *Work experience of the population*. Special Labor Force Reports #62, 127 and 201. Washington, D.C.: GPO.

# Appendix

The data graphed in figures 3.1–3.3 are from the *Employment and Training Report of the President, 1978*, table A-4, pp. 186–87, and table A-19, p. 212. The predicted values in figures 3.1–3.3 were generated by the following regressions of youth rates on prime age male rates.

Regression Results Used to Create Figure 3.1

| Regression Number | Estimated Coefficients (Standard Errors) | | |
|---|---|---|---|
| 1. | $ERMK = -85.85 + 1.34\ PER$ <br> (44.50) (0.47) | SEE = | 3.25 |
| | | $R^2$ = | .20 |
| 2. | $ERMT = -85.32 + 1.55\ PER$ <br> (50.10) (0.53) | SEE = | 3.65 |
| | | $R^2$ = | .21 |
| 3. | $ERMYM = -85.15 + 1.74\ PER$ <br> (23.10) (0.25) | SEE = | 1.69 |
| | | $R^2$ = | .63 |
| 4. | $LFPRMK = 81.32 - 0.34\ PLFPR$ <br> (65.20) (0.67) | SEE = | 3.05 |
| | | $R^2$ = | -.03 |
| 5. | $LFPRMT = -1.08 + 0.73\ PLFPR$ <br> (73.30) (0.75) | SEE = | 3.42 |
| | | $R^2$ = | .00 |
| 6. | $LFPRMYM = -32.92 + 1.22\ PLFPR$ <br> (31.10) (0.32) | SEE = | 1.45 |
| | | $R^2$ = | .32 |
| 7. | $UNMK = 10.14 + 1.69\ PUNR$ <br> (1.73) (0.54) | SEE = | 2.95 |
| | | $R^2$ = | .23 |
| 8. | $UNMT = 4.80 + 2.65\ PUNR$ <br> (1.01) (0.32) | SEE = | 1.72 |
| | | $R^2$ = | .71 |
| 9. | $UNMYM = 1.13 + 2.33\ PUNR$ <br> (0.67) (0.21) | SEE = | 1.14 |
| | | $R^2$ = | .81 |

Regression Results Used to Create Figure 3.2

| Regression Number | Estimated Coefficients (Standard Errors) | | |
|---|---|---|---|
| 1. | $ERMKO = -260.70 + 3.43\ PER$ <br> (78.30) (0.83) | SEE = | 5.07 |
| | | $R^2$ = | .41 |

2.    $\text{ERMTO} = -178.30 + 2.75 \text{ PER}$    $\text{SEE} = 4.07$
      $(58.40)\ (0.62)$    $R^2 = .40$

3.    $\text{ERMYMO} = -109.50 + 2.11 \text{ PER}$    $\text{SEE} = 1.79$
      $(25.60)\ (0.27)$    $R^2 = .68$

4.    $\text{LFPRMKO} = -266.8 + 3.55 \text{ PLFPR}$    $\text{SEE} = 3.83$
      $(90.50)\ (0.93)$    $R^2 = .37$

5.    $\text{LFPRMTO} = -88.55 + 1.85 \text{ PLFPR}$    $\text{SEE} = 2.26$
      $(51.70)\ (0.53)$    $R^2 = .28$

6.    $\text{LFPRMYMO} = 21.97 + 0.76 \text{ PLFPR}$    $\text{SEE} = 0.99$
      $(22.60)\ (0.23)$    $R^2 = .26$

7.    $\text{UNMKO} = 11.30 + 2.89 \text{ PUNR}$    $\text{SEE} = 4.60$
      $(2.97)\ (0.93)$    $R^2 = .27$

8.    $\text{UNMTO} = 3.46 + 2.54 \text{ PUNR}$    $\text{SEE} = 3.52$
      $(2.06)\ (0.65)$    $R^2 = .34$

9.    $\text{UNMYMO} = 0.69 + 1.94 \text{ PUNR}$    $\text{SEE} = 1.80$
      $(1.06)\ (0.33)$    $R^2 = .54$

Regression Results Used to Create Figure 3.3

| Regression Number | Estimated Coefficients (Standard Errors) | |
| --- | --- | --- |
| 1. | $\text{ERFK} = 86.72 - 0.63 \text{ PER}$ $(45.40)\ (0.48)$ | $\text{SEE} = 3.31$ $R^2 = .02$ |
| 2. | $\text{ERFT} = 63.09 - 0.18 \text{ PER}$ $(31.20)\ (0.33)$ | $\text{SEE} = 2.28$ $R^2 = -.02$ |
| 3. | $\text{ERFYM} = 245.30 - 2.10 \text{ PER}$ $(72.20)\ (0.77)$ | $\text{SEE} = 5.26$ $R^2 = .18$ |
| 4. | $\text{LFPRFK} = 462.70 - 4.43 \text{ PLFPR}$ $(51.90)\ (0.53)$ | $\text{SEE} = 2.42$ $R^2 = .70$ |
| 5. | $\text{LFPRFT} = 361.00 - 3.17 \text{ PLFPR}$ $(30.10)\ (0.31)$ | $\text{SEE} = 1.41$ $R^2 = .78$ |
| 6. | $\text{LFPRFYM} = 843.50 - 8.14 \text{ PLFPR}$ $(43.80)\ (0.45)$ | $\text{SEE} = 2.05$ $R^2 = .92$ |
| 7. | $\text{UNFK} = 11.58 + 1.36 \text{ PUNR}$ $(1.93)\ (0.61)$ | $\text{SEE} = 10.91$ $R^2 = .12$ |
| 8. | $\text{UNFT} = 8.72 + 1.29 \text{ PUNR}$ $(1.76)\ (0.55)$ | $\text{SEE} = 3.00$ $R^2 = .13$ |
| 9. | $\text{UNFYM} = 3.78 + 1.33 \text{ PUNR}$ $(0.98)\ (0.31)$ | $\text{SEE} = 1.67$ $R^2 = .38$ |

Means (Standard Deviations) of Dependent Variables

| ERMK | 40.58 | (3.56) | LFPRMYMO | 95.62 | (1.13) |
| ERMT | 61.14 | (4.03) | UNMKO | 16.80 | (8.67) |

| | | | | | | |
|---|---|---|---|---|---|---|
| ERMYM | 78.98 | (2.73) | UNMTO | 11.08 | (4.25) |
| LFPRMK | 47.83 | (2.96) | UNMYMO | 6.54 | (2.62) |
| LFPRMT | 70.11 | (3.36) | ERFK | 27.21 | (3.30) |
| LFPRMYM | 86.02 | (1.73) | ERFT | 46.03 | (2.21) |
| UNMK | 15.26 | (3.31) | ERFYM | 47.35 | (5.73) |
| UNMT | 12.61 | (3.11) | LFPRFK | 32.34 | (4.35) |
| UNMYM | 8.18 | (2.56) | LFPRFT | 52.72 | (2.96) |
| ERMKO | 52.23 | (24.12) | LFPRFYM | 51.45 | (7.04) |
| ERMTO | 81.37 | (5.17) | UNFK | 15.67 | (3.46) |
| ERMYMO | 89.39 | (3.10) | UNFT | 12.61 | (3.17) |
| LFPRMKO | 65.24 | (29.63) | UNFYM | 7.79 | (2.08) |
| LFPRMTO | 91.47 | (2.63) | | | |
| LFPRMYMO | 95.62 | (1.13) | | | |
| UNMKO | 16.80 | (8.67) | | | |

## Definitions of Variables

*Independent Variables*

PER:     employment to population rates for prime-age males.
PLFPR:   labor force participation rate for prime-age males.
PUNR:    unemployment rate for prime-age males.

*Dependent Variables*

ERMK:     employment to population ratio for 16–17 year old males.

ERMT:     employment to population ratio for 18–19 year old males.

ERMYM:    employment to population ratio for 20–24 year old males.

LFPRMK:   labor force participation rates for 16–17 year old males.

LFPRMTN:  labor force participation rates for 18–19 year old males.

LFPRMYM:  labor force participation rates for 20–24 year old males.

UNMK:     unemployment rate for 16–17 year old males.

UNMT:     unemployment rate for 18–19 year old males.

UNMYM:    unemployment rate for 20–24 year old males.

ERMKO:    employment to population ratio for 16–17 year old out-of-school males.

ERMTO:    employment to population ratio for 18–19 year old out-of-school males.

ERMYMO:   employment to population ratio for 20–24 year old out-of-school males.

LFPRMKO:  labor force participation rate for 16–17 year old out-of-school males.

LFPRMTO:      labor force participation rate for 18–19 year old out-of-school males.

LFPRMYMO:    labor force participation rate for 20–24 year old out-of-school males.

UNMKO:        unemployment rate for 16–17 year old out-of-school males.

UNMTO:        unemployment rate for 18–19 year old out-of-school males.

UNMYMO:       unemployment rate for 20–24 year old out-of-school males.

ERFK:         employment to population ratio for 16–17 year old females.

ERFT:         employment to population ratio for 18–19 year old females.

ERFYM:        employment to population ratio for 20–24 year old females.

LFPRFK:       labor force participation rate for 16–17 year old females.

LFPRFT:       labor force participation rate for 18–19 year old females.

LFPRFYM:      labor force participation rate for 20–24 year old females.

UNFK:         unemployment rate for 16–17 year old females.

UNFT:         unemployment rate for 18–19 year old females.

UNFYM:        unemployment rate for 20–24 year old females.

# 4 Why Does the Rate of Youth Labor Force Activity Differ across Surveys?

Richard B. Freeman and James L. Medoff

One prerequisite for analysis of the economic problem of youths is a set of sound estimates of the employment and labor force status of the young. Yet existing estimates of the extent of labor market involvement and the extent of work activity of the young based on the monthly Current Population Survey (CPS), the source of official government figures on this subject, and from special longitudinal surveys of the young, notably the National Longitudinal Survey of Young Men (NLS) and the National Longitudinal Survey of the High School Class of 1972 (NLS72), give strikingly different pictures of the labor market for young men.[1] Labor force participation rates, employment to population ratios, and weeks worked are noticeably higher in both longitudinal surveys than in the CPS. Unemployment rates differ significantly but are neither higher nor lower consistently across surveys.

The differences in the recorded activity rates constitute a major problem in evaluating the magnitude and nature of the labor force problem for young men. If the CPS data are incorrect and understate the employment to population ratio for young individuals, standard discussions of youth employment problems are exaggerated. If the longitudinal data are incorrect, studies that use the longitudinal surveys to ascertain the causes and effects of the youth employment problem may be invalid. What explains the large differences in rates of male youth labor force activity found in the different surveys? Can the observed differences be traced to specific differences in survey procedures or questions?

The purpose of this chapter is to answer these questions by providing a detailed quantitative analysis of the divergences between the rates of

We are extremely grateful to M. Borus, K. Coons, J. Fay, W. Gray, S. Hills, R. Lerman, D. Mandelbaum, E. Phillipp, M. Van Denburgh, and H. Woltman for their assistance in helping us address this question.

labor force activity for male youths indicated by these surveys. Section 4.1 describes the three surveys providing the youth labor force information on which we focus: the CPS, NLS, and NLS72. Section 4.2 compares the labor force participation rates, ratios of employment to population, rates of unemployment, and rates of school enrollment given by the surveys. Section 4.3 uses a matched mother-son sample drawn from the NLS and other information to examine three potential causes of survey differences: (1) the fact that youths report their own activity in the NLS and NLS72 while parents or other adults typically report the activities of youths in the CPS; (2) differences in the samples studied; and (3) differences in the survey methods employed. In the fourth section, some suggestions for further investigations of alternative measures of the employment of young persons are offered.

Our analysis indicates that there are significant differences between rates of activity for young males calculated with surveys in which young people respond for themselves and those calculated with surveys in which they are unlikely to do so. Of particular importance is the fact that the responses of young male self-respondents imply a significantly higher employment to population ratio than is implied by the responses of proxy respondents. The person questioned about the activity of young men appears to be a major determinant of the responses obtained, which raises important questions about current ways of obtaining information about the youth joblessness problem.

### 4.1 Survey Procedures and Questions

In this section we will compare the questions asked and survey methods employed in the CPS, NLS, and NLS72. Each of the surveys seeks information about labor force activity, weeks worked in the previous year, and enrollment in school. While the questions are reasonably similar across surveys, the survey methods, in particular the relative importance of proxy versus self-response, differ. These differences must be understood if the large disparities in the picture of the youth labor market given by the surveys are to be explained.

The CPS[2] interviews approximately 56,000 households (47,000 before July 1975) using a stratified sample. Part of the sample is changed each month to avoid problems of noncooperation when a person is interviewed for many months in a row. The method of rotation of the sample is such that a group will be interviewed for four consecutive months one year, deleted from the CPS for eight months and then interviewed in the same four months of the following year. As a result, 75% of the sample is common from month to month and 50% is common from year to year. Each month, during the calendar week containing the nineteenth day, interviewers contact some "responsible person" in each of the sample households. Personal visits are used to obtain 90% or more of the responses during the first and fifth months that the household is in the sample and about 50 to 60% in the second month; in other months more than 75% of the responses come from telephone interviews. Roughly half of the households in any month are interviewed by phone. Though the questions are asked for every individual in the household, it is important to understand that *young individuals usually do not respond for themselves*. This is because one "responsible person" in the family, usually not a teen,[3] answers for every household member.

Tabulated results from the CPS are derived by using responses to calculate a "composite estimate" of the status of individuals by taking the unweighted mean of two separate estimates: the "actual" value for the current month and a figure obtained by adding to the preceding month's composite estimate the change in the actual value of each item between the preceding month and the present month based on the part of the sample that is common to both months. By using raw data for most of our analysis we have taken into account the possible bias caused by this procedure.

To determine the labor force status of an individual, the CPS asks a standard set of interrelated questions that are designed to classify a person as a member of one of three categories: employed, unemployed, and out of the labor force. Figure 4.1 gives this set of questions from the CPS survey.

To determine weeks worked over the previous year the CPS asks (in its March questionnaire only):

In 19__ how many weeks did _____ work either full time or part time not counting work around the house? Include paid vacation and paid sick leave.

The CPS has two questions regarding enrollment in school. Each October the CPS asks:

Is _____ attending or enrolled in school?

In each month, the major activity question

What was _____ doing most of last week?

provides information on attendance at school (see question 19 in figure 4.1).

The National Longitudinal Survey[5] is a survey that covers about 5,000 persons in several specified age groups: young men aged 14 to 24 in 1966 (more accurately, as of April 1, 1966); young women aged 14 to 24 in 1968; women between the ages of 30 and 44 in 1966; and men 45 to 59 in 1966. The original samples were chosen through a multistage probability sampling procedure. To ensure that reliable information on blacks could

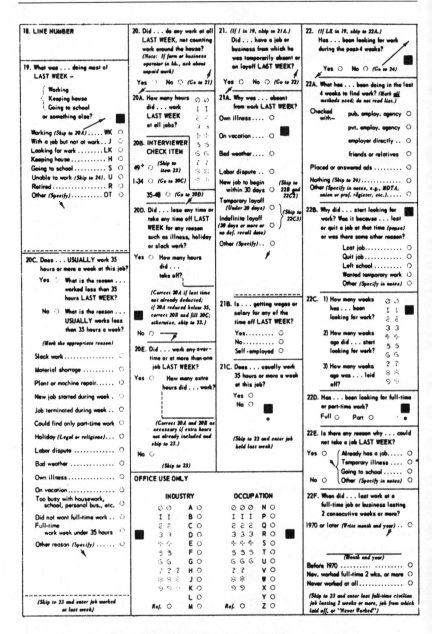

**Fig. 4.1**    The CPS Labor Force Questions[4]

be derived from the surveys, this group was oversampled. The NLS interviews the same persons repeatedly as they age over a ten-year period. In-person interviews were conducted from 1966 to 1971, telephone interviews were generally employed in 1973 and 1975, and no interviews were conducted in 1972 and 1974.

The weeks-worked question in the NLS varies only slightly from that in the CPS:

> In how many different weeks did you work either full- or part-time in the last 12 months, (not counting work around the house)? Count any week where you did any work at all. . . . (Include paid vacations and paid sick leave.)

The NLS asks two questions to ascertain the enrollment status of individuals. At one point it inquires:

> Are you attending or enrolled in regular school?

At another point it asks a question regarding the major activity of the individual to which one answer is "going to school."

The NLS and CPS surveys are reasonably similar. Both are administered by experienced CPS interviewers. Both use the standard set of CPS labor force questions to determine whether a person is employed or out of the labor force. The NLS differs from the CPS, however, in that each individual in the NLS describes his/her own labor force experience rather than having it described by someone else in the household and in that the NLS is part of a larger battery of labor force questions.[6]

The NLS72 is a very different survey.[7] It was based on a stratified national probability sample of 1,200 high schools (later slightly amended) from which eighteen persons per school in the class of 1972 were selected for the survey. An initial base-year survey of students was administered followed by several "follow-up" questionnaires designed to track each individual's progress over time. Most of the information was obtained by mail, with between one-quarter and one-third of the respondents interviewed by telephone. The response rate to the NLS72 was extremely high, with 95.5 percent of an initial base group of 23,457 students responding to either the base-year or first follow-up questionnaires and with a large percentage responding to ensuing follow-up surveys.

To obtain information on the individual's labor force status in October 1972, the interviewer asked:

> Now please think back to about a year ago. Did you hold a job of any kind during the *month of October 1972?*
>
> Yes, same job as in October 1973                                         1
>
> Yes, but different job than in October 1973                              2
>
> No                                                                                                3

What were the reasons you were not working during the *month of October 1972?* (Circle one number on each line.)

|  | Applies to me | Does not apply to me |
|---|---|---|
| Did not want to work | 1 | 2 |
| On temporary layoff from work or waiting to report to work | 1 | 2 |
| Was full-time homemaker | 1 | 2 |
| Going to school | 1 | 2 |
| Not enough job openings available | 1 | 2 |
| Union restrictions | 1 | 2 |
| Would have required moving | 1 | 2 |
| Required work experience I did not have | 1 | 2 |
| Jobs available offered little opportunity for career development | 1 | 2 |
| Health problems or physical handicap | 1 | 2 |
| Could not arrange child care | 1 | 2 |
| Other family responsibilities (including pregnancy) | 1 | 2 |
| Waiting to enter or in armed forces | 1 | 2 |
| Not educationally qualified for types of work available | 1 | 2 |

Did you look for work during October 1972?

Yes     1
No      2

To obtain information on the weeks worked by the individual in the year, the following question was asked:

Each part of this question refers to the entire 52-week period *from October 1972 to October 1973.*

About how many different weeks did you work altogether during this period? (Count all weeks in which you did any work at all or were on paid vacation.) _____ Number of weeks

To ascertain the enrollment status of the former high school seniors in October 1972 (a period for which comparable CPS data on the high school class of 1972 is available), the students were asked (in 1973):

Now please think back a year to the Fall of 1972. Were you taking classes or courses at any school during *the month of October 1972?*

Yes     1
No      2

To summarize, the CPS and NLS use roughly the same set of questions but employ survey methods that differ in a number of potentially important respects. It seems that the primary difference in interview procedures is that individuals self-report activity in the NLS but are often reported for by proxy respondents in the CPS. The CPS and NLS72 differ in more fundamental ways, both in terms of questions and survey procedures. The NLS and NLS72 have one basic similarity: each seeks self-responses as opposed to proxy responses.

### 4.2 Estimates of Differences in Youth Activity among Surveys

This section will document the basic "fact" under study: the strikingly different rates of labor force activity reported for young males in the NLS and NLS72 from those in the CPS. Our study reveals generally large differences in employment to population ratios, labor force participation rates, and weeks worked, and occasionally substantial differences in unemployment rates. Basically, both the NLS and NLS72 show greater work activity among male youths than does the CPS.

### 4.2.1 CPS vs. NLS

First, we will examine differences in the patterns of labor force and school activity for young males indicated by the CPS and the NLS. Table 4.1 compares the percentage of young persons in school, employment to population ratios, labor force participation rates, unemployment rates, and weeks worked, as defined by the Bureau of Labor Statistics, for males in the civilian, noninstitutional population aged 16–17, 18–19, and 20–24 as indicated by the two surveys. The NLS figures are based on weighted counts of individuals interviewed in the 1966–71 surveys, with the number of respondents as given in the table. In addition to the NLS sampling weights, a second set of weights was applied to people of different ages to correct for a problem with reporting on the age of NLS respondents. Because NLS codes the age of respondents as of April 1 and interviews the respondents primarily in November,[8] there is a seven-month lag between the reported age and the time of the employment status question. This lag means that the age variable for roughly seven-twelfths of the sample must be increased by one year between the time their age is recorded and the time their labor market status is ascertained. In light of this problem, we applied different weights to people of different recorded ages in the NLS (unless otherwise stated). These weights were chosen so that we could derive NLS figures for "X-Y" year olds that are comparable to CPS figures for "X-Y" year olds. For example, in constructing an NLS average for 16–17 year olds, we attached to 15 year olds a weight of seven-twelfths (the probability of their having turned 16 by the interview date), to 16 year olds (all of whom would be either 16 or 17) a weight of one, and to 17 year olds a weight of five-twelfths (the probability of their not having turned 18 by the interview date). The final weight applied to a respondent in the NLS was the product of this weight and the individual's sampling weight.

The CPS data are obtained from published documents, with enrollment figures relating to November, and weeks-worked information covering the calendar year. Because of the timing of the surveys, the NLS figures do not refer to the same time periods. While most of the NLS interviews occur in November, some take place in the surrounding months. Also, while the NLS weeks-worked question covers the preceding twelve months, the CPS question relates to the calendar year, creating a divergence of one to two months. While these slight differences in timing may have some effects, there is typically not wide enough variation in rates of activity across CPS surveys in the relevant months to suggest any major problems in comparison. We did, however, attach different weights to those of different ages (eleven-twelfths or one-twelfth using the method described above) for the NLS weeks-worked data because CPS weeks-worked and age questions are asked in March while the NLS age pertains to April of the preceding year.

The figures in table 4.1 reveal five differences between the NLS and CPS descriptions of youth activity.

First, and most important, the NLS indicates a much higher proportion of young males employed than does the CPS. The employment to population ratios diverge by 9.7 to 11.2 points among 16–17 years olds, by 4.6 to 10.0 points among 18–19 year olds, and by 3.5 to 6.4 points among 20–24 year olds. Since individuals either have a job or do not, the employment to populations ratio is a more straightforward measure than is the unemployment rate. Thus the difference in the reported levels is striking.

Second, rates of unemployment also differ between the surveys, with the NLS showing typically higher rates among the youngest males and generally lower rates among the older males. The unemployment rates for 16–17 year olds diverge by 4.2 to 8.6 points; those for 18–19 year olds by − 0.5 to 3.9 points; those for 20–24 year olds by − 1.2 to 0.2 points.

Third, the higher employment to population ratios and differing rates of unemployment translate into even larger differences in labor force participation rates (LFPRs) between the surveys although the differences narrow with age. For 16–17 year old males, the NLS LFPRs are 14.3 to 18.3 points above the CPS LFPRs; for 18–19 year old males, the NLS LFPRs are 8.1 to 11.1 points higher; and for 20–24 year old males, the NLS rates dominate by 2.7 to 5.9 points.

Fourth, consistent with the employment to population ratio evidence, the evidence on weeks worked in the previous year also shows diver-

**Table 4.1**    Comparison of Rates of School and Labor Force Activity for Young Men, 1966–71: NLS vs. CPS

| Year | No. in NLS sample[a] | Percent in school[b] | | Emp/Pop[c] | | LFPR[c] | | Unemployment[c] | | Weeks worked[d] | |
|---|---|---|---|---|---|---|---|---|---|---|---|
| | | NLS | CPS | NLS | CPS | NLS | CPS | NLS | CPS | NLS | CPS |
| **16–17 year olds** | | | | | | Total males | | | | | |
| 1966 | | 89.8 | 89.9 | 47.6 | 36.4 | 59.2 | 40.9 | 19.7 | 11.1 | 18.8 | 14.7 |
| 1967 | | 90.2 | 91.0 | 44.9 | 35.2 | 56.3 | 42.0 | 20.3 | 16.1 | 20.4 | 15.5 |
| **18–19 year olds** | | | | | | | | | | | |
| 1966 | 1519 | 61.8 | 57.8 | 63.5 | 54.2 | 71.0 | 59.9 | 10.5 | 9.6 | 29.2 | 24.4 |
| 1967 | 1622 | 63.0 | 56.3 | 62.3 | 52.3 | 70.5 | 59.5 | 11.6 | 12.1 | 29.3 | 24.8 |
| 1968 | 1619 | 59.0 | 60.4 | 64.2 | 54.3 | 70.3 | 59.8 | 8.7 | 9.2 | 30.0 | 25.2 |
| 1969 | 1621 | 59.6 | 59.4 | 60.9 | 56.3 | 70.0 | 61.9 | 13.1 | 9.2 | 29.8 | 30.4 |
| **20–24 year olds** | | | | | | | | | | | |
| 1966 | 2056 | 30.1 | 29.2 | 83.6 | 79.5 | 86.3 | 83.1 | 3.1 | 4.3 | 38.8 | 37.7 |
| 1967 | 1976 | 31.9 | 30.6 | 82.1 | 77.8 | 85.4 | 81.7 | 3.8 | 4.8 | 38.6 | 35.1 |
| 1968 | 1909 | 33.5 | 30.5 | 80.3 | 76.8 | 83.2 | 80.4 | 3.5 | 4.4 | 39.0 | 34.6 |
| 1969 | 1970 | 31.1 | 32.0 | 80.4 | 76.9 | 84.7 | 80.8 | 5.1 | 4.9 | 38.0 | 33.9 |
| 1970 | 2283 | 29.2 | 29.3 | 77.9 | 74.3 | 84.9 | 82.2 | 8.3 | 9.5 | 41.6 | 33.5 |
| 1971 | 2600 | 28.7 | 29.2 | 79.9 | 73.5 | 87.4 | 81.5 | 8.6 | 9.8 | 37.3 | 33.2 |

[a]The numbers in this column are unweighted counts of the observations used in generating the relevant row estimates. Thus, for example, the sixteen- to seventeen-year-old figures include all males who were fifteen to seventeen years old in April of the given year. The NLS numbers in all other columns are based on counts weighted in accordance with age. (See pages 81–82 for a discussion of the weighting procedure.)

[b]U.S. Bureau of the Census, *Current Population Reports*, Series P-20, "School Enrollment," October 1966–71, numbers 167, 190, 206, 222, 241. Table: "Enrollment Status of the Population 3 to 34 Years Old, by Age, Race, Sex, and Selected Educational Characteristics, for the United States."

[c]U.S. Bureau of Labor Statistics, *Employment and Earnings*, December 1966–71. Table: "Employment Status of the Noninstitutional Population by Age, Sex, and Color."

[d]U.S. Bureau of Labor Statistics, *Work Experience of the Population*, Special Labor Force Reports 91, 107, 115, 127, 141, 162. Table: "Age: Persons with Work Experience, by Sex."

gences, with the CPS indicating that young males work fewer weeks than is indicated by the NLS.

Fifth, although the NLS and CPS report strikingly different patterns of work activity, they report similar proportions of young men in school.

And sixth, differences in reported labor force activity tend to be less for older males than for younger.

### 4.2.2   Racial Differences

Does the pattern of higher rates of work activity in the NLS than in the CPS hold for nonwhite males as well as for all young men? To what extent does the magnitude of white/nonwhite difference in work activity differ between the surveys?

Table 4.2 contains the basic data needed to answer these questions: rates of activity disaggregated by race. The figures in the table show that the pattern of work activity rates higher in the NLS than in the CPS is found among nonwhite males as well as among white males. More importantly, comparison of the rates of activity of nonwhite and white young men estimated with the two surveys reveals a general pattern of much smaller absolute differences in employment to population ratios between nonwhite and white male youths in the NLS than in the CPS, especially for younger men (see table 4.3).

If the NLS figures are correct and the CPS figures incorrect, the differences in employment to population ratios for nonwhite young men and for white young men are much smaller than is generally believed. Alternatively, if the CPS figures are correct and the NLS figures incorrect, studies of the causes and effects of nonwhite/white differences in employment using the NLS tapes are questionable.

Inspection of other variables in table 4.2 reveals that while the CPS yields white labor force participation rates that are higher in five out of nine cases compared with the corresponding nonwhite rates, the NLS gives nonwhite participation rates that are typically above the comparable white rate. White/nonwhite differences in percentages in school are larger in the NLS than in the CPS, while differences in unemployment rates tend to be somewhat smaller in the NLS than in the CPS, at least for younger men, as shown in table 4.4.

### 4.2.3   School Status

How do the differences in work activity between the NLS and CPS vary with regard to the school status of the young? Given the differences by age group presented in table 4.2, one would expect greater divergences among those whose major activity is reported as being in school than among those whose activity is not being in school. Table 4.5 presents evidence for the 16–21 year old group of males for whom the Census

**Table 4.2**      **Comparison of Rates of School and Labor Force Activity for Young Men by Race, 1966–1971: NLS vs. CPS**

| | No. in NLS[a] sample | Percent in School[b] | | Emp/Pop[c] | | LFPR[c] | | Unemployment[c] | |
|---|---|---|---|---|---|---|---|---|---|
| | | NLS | CPS | NLS | CPS | NLS | CPS | NLS | CPS |
| | | | | White males | | | | | |
| **16–17 year olds** | | | | | | | | | |
| 1966 | 1310 | 90.7 | 90.3 | 48.4 | NA[e] | 59.4 | NA | 18.6 | NA |
| 1967 | 1319 | 91.7 | 91.4 | 45.6 | 36.7 | 56.1 | 42.8 | 18.7 | 14.4 |
| **18–19 year olds** | | | | | | | | | |
| 1966 | 1093 | 63.3 | 59.0 | 64.1 | NA | 70.6 | NA | 9.1 | NA |
| 1967 | 1099 | 64.3 | 57.2 | 62.8 | 56.7 | 70.0 | 63.4 | 10.3 | 10.6 |
| 1968 | 1085 | 60.0 | 61.5 | 64.6 | 55.7 | 70.2 | 60.2 | 7.9 | 7.5 |
| 1969 | 1103 | 62.0 | 60.9 | 61.2 | 56.8 | 69.9 | 61.4 | 12.5 | 7.6 |
| **20–24 year olds** | | | | | | | | | |
| 1966 | 1570 | 32.2 | 31.6 | 83.1 | NA | 85.8 | NA | 3.1 | NA |
| 1967 | 1496 | 33.9 | 32.2 | 81.8 | 78.0 | 84.5 | 81.2 | 3.2 | 4.0 |
| 1968 | 1410 | 35.4 | 32.5 | 79.7 | 76.5 | 82.6 | 79.8 | 3.4 | 4.1 |
| 1969 | 1402 | 32.8 | 33.6 | 80.8 | 76.7 | 84.6 | 80.3 | 4.6 | 4.5 |
| 1970 | 1619 | 30.6 | 30.9 | 78.2 | 75.0 | 84.5 | 82.2 | 7.4 | 8.8 |
| 1971 | 1869 | 30.0 | 30.3 | 80.5 | 74.1 | 87.5 | 81.8 | 8.0 | 9.3 |
| | | | | Nonwhite males | | | | | |
| **16–17 year olds** | | | | | | | | | |
| 1966 | 656 | 84.9 | 87.2 | 43.0 | NA | 58.2 | NA | 26.2 | NA |
| 1967 | 657 | 84.4 | 88.0 | 40.6 | 26.2 | 57.8 | 36.7 | 29.8 | 28.8 |
| **18–19 year olds** | | | | | | | | | |
| 1966 | 426 | 49.8 | 49.1 | 58.5 | NA | 74.0 | NA | 20.9 | NA |
| 1967 | 523 | 54.4 | 50.5 | 59.7 | 47.0 | 74.0 | 60.1 | 19.4 | 21.7 |
| 1968 | 534 | 53.3 | 53.5 | 61.7 | 45.6 | 71.3 | 57.2 | 13.5 | 20.3 |
| 1969 | 518 | 43.5 | 49.8 | 59.0 | 52.6 | 70.9 | 65.1 | 16.9 | 19.0 |
| **20–24 year olds** | | | | | | | | | |
| 1966 | 486 | 15.3 | 12.3 | 89.9 | NA | 90.1 | NA | 3.5 | NA |
| 1967 | 480 | 16.2 | 18.9 | 84.8 | 76.9 | 91.9 | 85.7 | 7.8 | 10.3 |
| 1968 | 499 | 18.5 | 16.3 | 84.6 | 79.0 | 87.9 | 84.7 | 3.7 | 6.7 |
| 1969 | 568 | 18.1 | 20.5 | 78.1 | 78.2 | 85.5 | 84.7 | 8.7 | 7.7 |
| 1970 | 664 | 18.9 | 18.1 | 75.1 | 69.0 | 87.9 | 81.2 | 14.6 | 15.0 |
| 1971 | 731 | 19.1 | 21.7 | 75.3 | 69.5 | 86.7 | 79.9 | 13.2 | 13.0 |

[a],[b],[c],[d]See corresponding notes in table 4.1.
[e]Not available.

**Table 4.3**    Difference in Employment to Population Ratios
for Young White Males versus Young Nonwhite Males
from table 4.2 (White Minus Nonwhite)

|                    | 1967  | 1968  | 1969  | 1970 | 1971 |
|--------------------|-------|-------|-------|------|------|
| 16–17 year olds    |       |       |       |      |      |
| CPS                | 10.5  | —     | —     | —    | —    |
| NLS                | 5.0   | —     | —     | —    | —    |
| 18–19 year olds    |       |       |       |      |      |
| CPS                | 6.2   | 10.0  | 4.2   | —    | —    |
| NLS                | 3.1   | 2.9   | 2.1   | —    | —    |
| 20–24 year olds    |       |       |       |      |      |
| CPS                | 1.1   | −2.5  | −1.4  | 6.0  | 4.6  |
| NLS                | −3.0  | −4.9  | 2.7   | 3.1  | 5.2  |

publishes data on work activity by school status which is consistent with this expectation. The table shows three things.

First, NLS/CPS differences between the employment to population ratios and labor force participation rates for young men are greater for those youths whose major activity is school than for others. Employment to population figures differ by 10.9 to 12.3 points for the in-school young men compared to 4.8 to 10.6 points for other young men.

Second, mean weeks worked for 16–21 year old males are higher by 4.1 to 7.1 weeks in the NLS than in the CPS for those sample members whose major activity is school, and by about 2.6 to 3.4 weeks for the other sample members.

Third, the direction of differences between the unemployment rates calculated from young men with the NLS and those calculated with the CPS depends critically on the major activity of persons. For 16–21 year old males whose major activity is other than being in school, the NLS

**Table 4.4**    Differences in Unemployment Rates for Young White Males
Versus Young Nonwhite Males from table 4.2 (Nonwhite Minus White)

|                    | 1967  | 1968  | 1969  | 1970 | 1971 |
|--------------------|-------|-------|-------|------|------|
| 16–17 year olds    |       |       |       |      |      |
| CPS                | 14.4  | —     | —     | —    | —    |
| NLS                | 11.1  | —     | —     | —    | —    |
| 18–19 year olds    |       |       |       |      |      |
| CPS                | 11.1  | 12.8  | 11.4  | —    | —    |
| NLS                | 9.1   | 5.6   | 4.4   | —    | —    |
| 20–24 year olds    |       |       |       |      |      |
| CPS                | 6.3   | 2.6   | 3.2   | 6.2  | 3.7  |
| NLS                | 4.6   | 0.3   | 4.1   | 7.2  | 5.2  |

**Table 4.5**        **Comparison of Rates of School and Labor Force Activity for Young Men, by Major Activity, 1967, 16–21 Year Olds: NLS vs. CPS**

| | No. in NLS[a] sample | Major activity[b] NLS CPS | Emp/Pop[c] NLS CPS | LFPR[c] NLS CPS | Unemployment[c] NLS CPS | Weeks worked[d] NLS CPS |
|---|---|---|---|---|---|---|
| | | | **Total Males** | | | |
| Major activity: school | 2284 | 65.2  64.7 | 42.8  31.7 | 52.7  36.5 | 18.8  13.1 | 21.5  17.1 |
| Major activity: other | 1248 | 34.8  35.3 | 87.8  82.1 | 92.8  91.3 | 5.3  10.2 | 37.1  33.7 |
| | | | **White males** | | | |
| Major activity: school | 1657 | 66.3  66.1 | 43.9  33.0 | 52.9  37.5 | 17.0  11.9 | 22.0  17.9 |
| Major activity: other | 786 | 33.7  33.9 | 88.6  83.8 | 92.5  91.6 | 4.2  8.5 | 38.0  34.6 |
| | | | **Nonwhite males** | | | |
| Major activity: school | 627 | 57.5  55.8 | 33.9  21.6 | 51.0  28.8 | 33.7  25.2 | 17.4  10.3 |
| Major activity: other | 462 | 42.5  44.2 | 83.7  73.1 | 94.2  90.1 | 11.1  18.9 | 32.4  29.8 |

[a],[b],[c],[d]See corresponding notes in table 4.1.

shows much lower rates of unemployment than the CPS. For those males whose major activity was school, however, the NLS shows much higher rates of unemployment than the CPS.

Overall, the greater differences in work activity or desired work activity for those in school suggest that many of the differences between surveys occur among those who are going to school and are thus most likely to have a more marginal commitment to the work force.

### 4.2.4   CPS vs. NLS72

Table 4.6 compares the October 1972 rates of work activity for young males indicated by the National Longitudinal Survey of the Class of 1972 with the rates for young men indicated by the CPS study of graduates and dropouts in the class of 1972. The principal finding in the table is that NLS72, like the NLS, reports higher employment to population ratios among young males not enrolled in school than does the CPS, somewhat smaller differences in employment to population ratios between nonwhite and white young men, and much smaller rates of unemployment for both white and nonwhite male youths. With respect to labor market activity, the figures based on the NLS72 differ from the figures based on the CPS data in the same direction as the NLS-based estimates differ from the CPS-based estimates.

Table 4.6          Comparison of School and Labor Force Activity for Young Men,
                   by Race, October 1972: NLS 72 vs. CPS Survey
                   of the High School Class of 1972

|  | White youths | | Nonwhite youths | |
|---|---|---|---|---|
|  | NLS72[a] | CPS[b] | NLS72[a] | CPS[b] |
| 1. Percent enrolled in school[c] | 57.6 | 52.8[d] | 46.7 | 52.5[d] |
| 2. Percent not enrolled | 42.4 | 47.2 | 53.3 | 47.5 |
| 3. Percent employed of not enrolled | 88.0 | 81.5 | 78.4 | 68.0 |
| 4. Percent in labor force of not enrolled | 92.9 | 91.6 | 90.2 | 88.0 |
| 5. Percent unemployed of not enrolled youth | 5.3 | 11.0 | 13.0 | 22.7 |

[a]Meyer and Wise, "High School Preparation and Early Labor Force Participation," chapter 9 of the present volume, table 9.1.

[b]U.S. Department of Labor, Bureau of Labor Statistics, *Employment of High School Graduates and Dropouts: October 1972*, Special Labor Force Report 155. Table 1: College Enrollment and Labor Force Status of 1972 High School Graduates, October 1972, p. 27.

[c]Full- and part-time students.

[d]Enrolled in college.

## 4.3   What Explains the Difference?

There are three major potential sources of differences between the youth activity rates reported in the CPS and those reported in the longitudinal surveys.

First, the surveys could yield different results because of differences among respondents—the fact that in the longitudinal surveys youths report their own activity, whereas in the CPS proxy respondents report what youths do. Young men report themselves doing relatively more work than proxies report them doing. The male youths may tend to exaggerate their work time or they may actually hold jobs unknown to other household members. Whatever the cause, at least some of the CPS/NLS and CPS/NLS72 differences could reflect "respondent bias."

Second, the surveys could yield different results because of the differences in the population covered. The longitudinal surveys may be subject to selectivity bias because of the unwillingness of some young men to participate, particularly as time proceeds. If the male youths who do not participate have a lower probability of being employed than those who do, the longitudinal surveys would yield higher employment to population ratios than the CPS.

Third, the differences in work activity estimates across surveys could also be due to differences in the way in which the surveys are conducted. For instance, differences in the extent of reliance on telephone versus in-person interviews or differences in the number of times that an individual is interviewed in a given year could affect the responses yielded by the various surveys.

This section attempts to ascertain the relative importance of each of these three potentially relevant factors. The main finding is that a very substantial portion of the CPS/NLS differences in the estimated probability that a teenage male is employed seems to be explicable by the fact that the CPS relies primarily on proxy responses while the NLS does not.

### 4.3.1   Respondent Bias

The most direct way of evaluating the extent to which "proxy-respondent bias" contributes to the CPS and longitudinal survey differences in rates of school and labor force activity among young males is to compare the self-reported labor force activity of young men with the activity reported for them by other household members. If some of the differences in results with the CPS and longitudinal surveys are due to respondent bias, then we would expect to find males giving self-responses that indicate more employment than do the proxy-responses given by their parents. The information needed for this type of experiment was collected in the NLS; to save on sampling cost, the survey queried more than one member of a substantial number of families. In particular, both mothers and sons were asked about the work activity and enrollment of the sons. Thus with these data it was possible to develop a matched sample for comparing the activity reported by a young man with the activity ascribed to him by his mother, the most likely proxy respondent. We used the family record numbers on the tapes to create a matched file of this nature; it contains information on 1,541 mother-son pairs in 1966, 1,094 pairs in 1968, and 734 pairs in 1970. While the mothers were not asked the labor force status of their sons at a given time, they were asked, "In all how many weeks did _____ work either full or part time (not counting work around the house)?" which is comparable to the weeks worked question on the young men's survey.

### 4.3.2   Weeks Worked Comparisons

A comparison with NLS data of the weeks worked by a group of young men as reported by their mothers and by themselves must be done carefully because of modest differences in the time period to which the relevant questions relate. As indicated in table 4.7, mature women were asked about the activity of their sons over a calendar year while their sons were asked about their own activity over a slightly different period, one covering the twelve months prior to the survey. If, as seems reasonable, youth work activity increases over time, the one-month difference in the period covered should, if anything, lead to *higher* rates of activity reported by mothers than by sons, as the mothers' reference period is one month or more later in time than the sons'. Since this potential problem is likely to reduce the estimated impact of respondent bias, we ignore it in the ensuing analysis.[9]

**Table 4.7**

| Respondents | Approximate month of year interviewed | Weeks worked of young men relates to |
|---|---|---|
| Mature women | May 1967 | 1966 (Jan. '66–Dec. '66) |
| Young men | Nov. 1966 | Past 12 months (approximately Dec. '65–Nov. '66) |
| Mature women | May 1969 | 1968 (Jan. '68–Dec. '68) |
| Young men | Nov. 1969 | Past 12 months (approximately Dec. '68–Nov. '69) |

Table 4.8 presents the basic results of the comparison of self-reported and mother-reported weeks worked of young men on the matched file. Only those observations for which data were available from both mother and son were used. Line 1 records the number of sons in the sample. The second line gives the distribution of weeks worked reported by mothers and sons, including a "missing" category. The mean weeks worked for all responses and for mother-son pairs with no missing values is given in line 3.

What stands out in the table is the markedly lower rates of work activity among young men indicated by the mother proxy responses than by the son self-responses; the differences in mean weeks worked vary from 4.2 to 6.5 weeks depending on the year and age group (or from 14 to 27% of the mean of sons' self-reported weeks worked). For 16–17 year olds, the figures differ by 5.6 to 6.5 weeks, for 18–19 year olds and 20–24 year olds they differ by 4.2 to 6.4 weeks.

To what extent can the differences in weeks worked between mothers and sons explain the differences in weeks worked between the NLS and CPS? Table 4.9 presents the data from tables 4.6 and 4.8 that can answer this question.

According to these calculations, the difference in mother-son reporting could easily explain the divergence in weeks worked reported between the NLS and the CPS and indeed tends to "overexplain" the differences. The anomalous overexplanation could be rationalized by the fact that the mother/son differences in table 4.8 relate only to those males *living at home*, while the CPS/NLS differences in table 4.1 relate to *all* males. According to the respondent bias hypothesis, differences between the CPS and NLS arise when a proxy reports a young male's status on the CPS and the individual reports his status on the NLS. For males not living in their parents' home, we would expect smaller differences in rates of activity between the surveys than are found for young men living at home. One would expect that overexplanation would be more prevalent for older males in the sample since they are less likely to live at home. Indeed, our results show that for 20–24 year old males, roughly half of whom reside outside their parents' home, the overexplanation is substantially larger than for the younger males.

This argument suggests that we should tabulate weeks worked for 20–24 year old males who are unmarried heads of households and for those who are not heads of households and use the resultant figures to reestimate the effect of respondent bias on the CPS/NLS difference. The former group will presumably give self-responses in both the CPS and NLS. The latter group will tend to have the mother as proxy respondent

**Table 4.8**    **Comparison of Weeks Worked Reported by Sons and Mothers: National Longitudinal Survey 1966 and 1968[a]**

| Age: | 16–17 | | 18–19 | | 20–24 | |
|---|---|---|---|---|---|---|
| | 1966 | | 1966 | | 1966 | |
| Respondent: | Mother | Son | Mother | Son | Mother | Son |
| 1. Sample size (sons)[b] | 1250 | 1250 | 430 | 430 | 152 | 152 |
| 2. Distribution of weeks worked | | | | | | |
| missing | 16.5 | 0.3 | 8.2 | 0.0 | 11.7 | 0.0 |
| 0 | 36.3 | 27.9 | 14.8 | 7.0 | 11.3 | 4.2 |
| 1–13 | 25.2 | 27.4 | 33.6 | 24.6 | 28.9 | 23.9 |
| 14–26 | 8.8 | 17.9 | 15.3 | 23.6 | 11.7 | 19.2 |
| 27–39 | 2.2 | 6.7 | 6.1 | 10.2 | 4.8 | 11.7 |
| 40–47 | 1.6 | 3.4 | 2.2 | 5.7 | 4.2 | 7.7 |
| 48–49 | 0.2 | 1.7 | 1.9 | 3.3 | 2.0 | 4.8 |
| 50–52 | 9.2 | 14.7 | 17.8 | 25.6 | 25.3 | 28.5 |
| 3. Mean weeks worked (with observations missing relevant information deleted) | 12.1 | 17.7 | 21.2 | 27.6 | 26.4 | 30.6 |
| Age: | 16–17 | | 18–19 | | 20–24 | |
| | 1968 | | 1968 | | 1968 | |
| Respondent: | Mother | Son | Mother | Son | Mother | Son |
| 1. Sample size (sons)[b] | 603 | 603 | 619 | 619 | 282 | 282 |
| 2. Distribution of weeks worked | | | | | | |
| missing | 3.4 | 3.0 | 3.1 | 7.0 | 5.3 | 11.8 |
| 0 | 30.5 | 13.4 | 15.6 | 8.4 | 14.2 | 5.4 |
| 1–13 | 28.2 | 29.1 | 30.9 | 23.0 | 20.4 | 14.7 |
| 14–26 | 14.4 | 16.5 | 15.1 | 16.1 | 17.6 | 15.6 |
| 27–39 | 3.7 | 7.6 | 9.3 | 8.1 | 5.9 | 9.0 |
| 40–47 | 2.3 | 7.5 | 3.5 | 8.0 | 4.1 | 9.1 |
| 48–49 | 0.3 | 3.3 | 1.3 | 4.8 | 2.3 | 3.8 |
| 50–52 | 17.2 | 19.6 | 21.2 | 24.6 | 30.3 | 30.6 |
| 3. Mean weeks worked (with observations missing relevant information deleted) | 17.5 | 24.0 | 22.9 | 28.4 | 27.4 | 33.1 |

[a]The NLS estimates presented in this table are weighted averages. The weighting scheme that makes the NLS figures more comparable to those from the CPS, is described on pp. 81–82.

[b]The sample sizes given are before weighting for age. For example, the sample of sixteen- to seventeen-year-olds includes all those males aged fifteen to seventeen in April of the given year.

**Table 4.9**    **Comparison of Differences in Mean Weeks Worked as Reported by the NLS and the CPS and by the NLS Mother-Son Matched File**

|  | (1) Difference in mean weeks worked (NLS–CPS) | (2) Difference in mean weeks worked (Sons–Mothers) |
|---|---|---|
| 16–17 year olds | | |
| 1966 | 4.1 | 5.6 |
| 18–19 year olds | | |
| 1966 | 4.8 | 6.4 |
| 1968 | 4.8 | 5.5 |
| average | 4.8 | 6.0 |
| 20–24 year olds | | |
| 1966 | 1.1 | 4.2 |
| 1968 | 4.4 | 5.7 |
| average | 2.8 | 5.0 |

for the CPS. In the tabulation below NLS observations have been weighted (using the weighting procedure described on pages 81–82) so that NLS interviewee ages are comparable to those in the CPS. However, the Census weeks-worked figures relate to the preceding calendar year (January 1968–December 1968) while the NLS figures relate to the twelve months prior to interview (approximately December 1967–November 1968). Thus there is one month difference in the time span to which the question pertains. Resolution of this problem has been ignored in the tabulation:

|  | Mean weeks worked from Dec. '67–Nov. '68; 1968 NLS 20-24 year old males | Mean weeks worked in 1968: March 1969 CPS 20–24 year old males | Difference in mean weeks worked |
|---|---|---|---|
| Unmarried heads | 41.1 | 37.3 | 3.8 |
| Not heads | 33.9 | 28.8 | 5.1 |

As expected, the difference for unmarried heads is much smaller than that for young men who are not heads.

### 4.3.3   Matrix of Responses

Analysis of the differences in responses between mothers and sons is pursued further in table 4.10 which cross-classifies the weeks worked by the son as reported by the mother with the son's weeks worked as reported by the son. Each element in the matrix gives the percentage of mother-son pairs reporting a given pair of weeks-worked values. If there were perfect agreement between mothers and sons, all of the elements of

**Table 4.10 Comparison of Weeks Worked Reported by Mothers and Their Sons; 1966 NLS Data for Males Aged 16–24[a]**

| | | | Percent of mothers reporting weeks worked | | | | | | | | |
|---|---|---|---|---|---|---|---|---|---|---|---|
| | Weeks worked | Number of sons reporting | 0 | 1–13 | 14–26 | 27–39 | 40–47 | 48–49 | 50–52 | Missing | Total |
| Percent of | 0 | 327 | 63.0 | 11.0 | 2.8 | .3 | .3 | .3 | .9 | 21.4 | 100.0 |
| sons | 1–13 | 405 | 30.4 | 40.5 | 8.4 | 1.0 | — | — | 3.5 | 16.3 | 100.0 |
| reporting | 14–26 | 295 | 16.3 | 38.3 | 17.3 | 5.4 | 2.4 | .3 | 7.5 | 12.5 | 100.0 |
| weeks | 27–39 | 121 | 19.0 | 28.1 | 17.4 | 8.3 | 3.3 | — | 12.4 | 11.6 | 100.0 |
| worked | 40–47 | 67 | 14.9 | 28.4 | 14.9 | 7.5 | 9.0 | 1.5 | 13.4 | 10.4 | 100.0 |
| | 48–49 | 36 | 2.3 | 13.9 | 13.9 | 5.6 | 5.6 | 8.3 | 41.7 | 8.3 | 100.0 |
| | 50–52 | 287 | 13.2 | 16.4 | 11.5 | 4.2 | 3.5 | 2.1 | 41.5 | 7.7 | 100.0 |
| | Total | 1,541 | 29.2 | 27.3 | 10.6 | 3.2 | 1.9 | .8 | 12.8 | 14.2 | 100.0 |
| | Missing | 3 | 33.3 | 66.7 | — | — | — | — | — | — | 100.0 |

[a]As of April 1, 1966.

the matrix would fall along the main diagonal and would equal 100. (If there were no relation between the weeks worked reported by mothers and sons, all columns would be identical.) While there is a definite concentration at or near the diagonals, a very large proportion of the sample lies off the diagonal: only 63% of mothers whose sons self-report working 0 weeks last year also report their sons as working 0 weeks; only 41.5% of mothers whose sons report themselves as working 52 weeks report their sons in that category, and so forth.

The divergences provide evidence of potentially large response bias and measurement error in the weeks-worked data, which supports the respondent bias hypothesis. In addition, the divergences suggest the value of a detailed analysis of why some mother-son pairs are in agreement and others are not, a question we address to some extent later in this section.

### 4.3.4 Employment Activity of Heads vs. Others

If respondent bias is the major cause of the differences in the labor force activity rates of young males implied by the NLS and CPS, one would expect only negligible survey differences for young males who are themselves unmarried heads of households. The activity of these persons in the CPS is more likely to be reported by the individual himself than by others, making the results from the CPS more likely to be consistent with those from the NLS.

To test this implication of the respondent bias hypothesis, the rates for 1969 of labor force activity of 20–24 year old males who are unmarried heads of households and those who are not heads of households were tabulated with the NLS and CPS tapes. The results of the calculations, shown in table 4.11, yield a striking conclusion: for 20–24 year old unmarried heads of households there are *no effective differences* in the ratio of employment to population or in the rate of labor force participation, whereas for comparable individuals who are not heads there are sizable differences. It appears that the bulk of the differentials reported earlier is attributable to those whose status is self-reported in the NLS but likely to be reported by the mother in the CPS.

In sum, there appears to be considerable support in the data for the hypothesis that much of the NLS/CPS difference shown in section I is attributable to respondent bias.

### 4.3.5 Differences in Samples and Methods

Since detailed information on persons designated to be included in the NLS or in the CPS who were not represented is missing, it is difficult to assess accurately the importance of sample differences in explaining the observed differences in the employment experience of young men. However, an examination of the NLS and CPS sampling procedures and

**Table 4.11    Comparison of Labor Force Rates by Household Status of Men Aged 20–24[a]**

|  | National Longitudinal Survey Fall 1968 | Current Population Survey March 1969 | Difference between NLS Fall '68 and CPS March '69 |
|---|---|---|---|
| **Unmarried heads** | | | |
| Employment/Population | 82.7 | 83.0 | −0.3 |
| Labor force participation | 83.9 | 84.9 | −1.0 |
| Unemployment (UNE) | 3.2 | 4.3 | −1.1 |
| Out of labor force; major activity is being in school | 9.7 | 9.3 | 0.4 |
| **Not Heads** | | | |
| Employment/Population | 66.1 | 61.0 | 5.1 |
| Labor force participation | 68.3 | 63.0 | 5.3 |
| Unemployment | 4.7 | 5.5 | −0.8 |
| Out of labor force; major activity is being in school | 22.1 | 26.2 | −4.1 |

[a]Although the NLS observations were weighted in accordance with age to facilitate comparability between the CPS and the NLS estimates (see pages 81 and 82), there is still a difference between the two sets of figures. Both sets of data refer to the survey week. The NLS, however, takes place in November while the CPS is administered in March. Thus there is approximately a four-month difference in the period referred to by the NLS and the CPS under analysis. The figures in the table were based on weighted counts with the CPS March 1969 microdata and NLS microdata.

the characteristics of their samples yields some insights into the possible magnitude of sample survey bias.

We will examine first the sampling procedures. One major difference between the CPS and NLS methods is that the former uses a one-stage screening procedure to obtain households for surveying, whereas the latter uses a two-stage procedure. During the first stage of the NLS process, each of the four NLS samples (young men aged 14–24, young women aged 14–24, women aged 30–44, and men aged 45–59) was designated to represent the civilian noninstitutional population of the United States. An initial group of 42,000 households from the primary sampling units of the Census was selected by the NLS; a sample of this size was drawn so that no age/sex/color group would be underrepresented. The 42,000 households were screened by interviews conducted in March and April of 1966, and adequate numbers of each age/sex/color group were identified for each of the four NLS samples.

In the fall of 1966, however, a second stage of screening was undertaken to insure that during the months since April the sample size for young men had not become inadequate because of the mobility of male youths. From these two screenings, 5,713 young men were designated to be interviewed; of these 5,225 were actually interviewed, giving a noninterview rate of 8.6%.[10] By contrast the noninterview rate on the CPS was considerably lower, ranging from 4.1 to 4.4% annually in the 1974–76 period.[11]

If the employment to population ratio for noninterviewees (those designated to be interviewed who were not) in the NLS is less than for interviewees,[12] and if the employment to population ratio for young males in noninterviewee CPS familes is less than for young men in the interviewee families by the same amount, the differential noninterviewee rates in the NLS and the CPS that were observed would cause the estimated NLS employment to population ratio to be higher than the estimated CPS ratio; this would explain part of the difference in employment to population ratios between the NLS and CPS. If, because the CPS is based on proxy as opposed to self-responses, the employment to population ratio for young males in noninterviewee CPS families is closer to the rate in interviewee families than the NLS noninterviewee rate is to the NLS interviewee rate, then the higher NLS noninterviewee rate might account for an even larger proportion of the NLS/CPS young male employment to population ratio differential. In the absence of information on the employment of noninterviewees, only the crudest estimates of the magnitude of the effects can be made.

The calculations that can be made do, however, indicate that noninterviewee bias most likely cannot explain a major fraction of the observed differences in the NLS and CPS employment to population ratios for young men. Under the totally unrealistic assumption that absolutely none of the NLS noninterviewees worked and the assumption that young men in noninterviewee CPS families have the same employment to population ratio as do those in interviewee CPS families, there are still substantial differences in the NLS and CPS young male employment to population ratios to be explained: a 7.1 percentage point differential for 16–17 year olds in 1966 and a 3.8 percentage point differential for 18–19 year olds in the same year. Under the seemingly more realistic assumption that the NLS noninterviewees worked only half as much as the NLS interviewees, the comparable differentials are 9.1 and 6.6 percentage points. Thus noninterviewee bias could only account for a part of the 11.2 and 9.3 percentage point differentials for 16–17 and 18–19 year old males in 1966 shown in table 4.1.

In the NLS72, 21,350 of 23,451 students responded to the first follow-up survey, giving a noninterview rate of 9.0%, which is comparable to the NLS rate.[13] As argued above in the discussion of sample bias with the NLS, this noninterview rate could also explain some, but certainly not all of the differences between the surveys.

An alternative method for assessing important sample differences is to compare the nonwork characteristics of the samples. The NLS two-stage screening process described above was specifically designed to compensate for the high mobility of young men. It seems that young men who passed through this double screen would be more stable than those selected through a single screening process (such as that found in the CPS). If the NLS sample does have a larger fraction of young persons with stable characteristics, then we would expect some of the estimated differences in employment to population ratios to be attributable to characteristics of the sample respondents.

Information on the household status of individuals in the NLS and CPS suggests that the surveys' samples include similar fractions of high-propensity-to-work individuals. In the CPS 46% of 20–24 year old men are heads of households; in the NLS 48% of the comparable group are heads, a negligible 2 percentage point difference. If the CPS heads/others difference in employment to popular ratios given in table 4.11 is assumed valid, the 2 percentage point difference in the relative importance of heads and others implies a .57 ( = 28.3 × .02) point NLS/CPS differential in the overall ratios. If the NLS heads/others difference in employment to population ratios given in table 4.11 is used, the 2 percentage point difference translates into a .47 ( = 23.6 × .02) point differential. By contrast, the difference in the employment to population ratio for others in the table predicts about a 3.0 point differential no matter which estimate of the ratio of others to others plus heads is used. Thus sample differences appear to account for a relatively tiny fraction of the NLS/CPS difference in employment to population ratios.

There are two other potentially important differences in the way the NLS and CPS surveys are carried out. These involve the rotation pattern and the method of interview.

Under the CPS, a respondent will appear in a survey for four months, be dropped for eight months, interviewed for another four months, and then be dropped permanently. During any month, one-eighth of the sample will be interviewed for the first time, one-eighth for the second time, and so on. Under the NLS, the same young male sample group is interviewed once each year for the duration of the survey.

The other difference concerns interview technique. The CPS used primarily telephone interviews to collect its data. The NLS data on young persons (for the time periods discussed in this study) were gathered using face-to-face interviews almost exclusively.

It is likely that these two differences in survey methods will lead to a difference in the employment to population ratios observed between the NLS and CPS. This contention is supported by analyses of the National Crime Survey (NCS) currently being conducted by R. Lerman and H. Woltman.[14]

The NCS surveys 14,000 households each month. A total of 72,000 households are selected for interview over a three-year period. They are interviewed one month, left out of the sample for five months, interviewed again, left out for another five months, and so on for the three-year period.

There are two other important characteristics of the NCS. First, more than 90% of the survey responses are self-reported, which makes the NCS similar to the NLS and NLS72. Second, about 80% of the NCS interviews are personal interviews, in contrast to the CPS in which the majority of interviews are done by telephone. Therefore, the most important differences between the NCS and the CPS are that the NCS is self-response as opposed to proxy response, is based primarily on personal rather than telephone interviews, and uses a rotation pattern under which sample members are never surveyed two months in a row. In all these respects, the NCS methodology is similar to the NLS methodology.

In analyzing the NCS data, Lerman looks separately at young persons as categorized by age, race, and sex. His age groups are 16-17 year olds, 18–19 year olds, 20–21 year olds, and 22–24 year olds. Lerman's tabulations reveal that the employment to population ratios among young males (especially nonwhites) based on the NCS are significantly higher than those derived with the CPS. However, the Lerman employment to population rates for young females show substantially smaller differences than those observed for males. In fact, for Lerman's largest group of females (white females aged 22–24), the CPS employment to population ratio is higher than it is with the NCS. These findings suggest somewhat different patterns of response bias for women than for men.

Woltman examined samples of people who were coming into the NCS or CPS for the first time. He limited his sample to incoming survey members in an effort to control for potential differences in rates caused by differences in the surveys' rotations and in the extent to which the surveys rely upon telephone and personal interviews. This could be accomplished since in both surveys the first interview conducted with a sample member is done in person.

Woltman did his calculations for two age groups (16–19 year olds and 20–24 year olds) but did not cross-classify individuals by age, race, or sex. He found virtually identical employment to population ratios for each age group for new members of the NCS and new members of the CPS. Part of Woltman's result can be explained by the fact that he, unlike Lerman and us, did not focus just on young males, since, according to Lerman's analyses, there appear to be much smaller and even differently signed differentials for young females. Nevertheless, it is unlikely that this fact can fully explain the Woltman findings. This leads us to believe that the nature of a survey's rotation pattern and its reliance on personal versus telephone interviews affect the estimates that it obtains of the employment to population ratios for young males. The numbers derived by Lerman and Woltman do not appear to refute our belief that the *key* factor causing differences in the employment to population ratios among young males estimates with various surveys is whether or not the surveys relied on self-responses as opposed to proxy responses. They do, however, underscore the need for more data collection and analysis concerning the issue at hand.

## 4.4   Future Research

The finding that many of the cross-survey differences in reported male youth work activity depend on the way in which these surveys are conducted raises many important questions. What factors explain the differences in the responses that young males give concerning their work activity and the responses that proxies give about the work activity of these youths? What additional research is needed to confirm or refute the respondent bias hypothesis? How can we discover whether young persons or their parents provide more accurate information on actual activity? What should be done to improve our data base?

### 4.4.1   Why Responses Differ

There are two basic reasons for expecting differences between self-reported work activity and proxy-reported work activity: first, differences in knowledge of the facts; second, differences in the accuracy of reporting a given set of facts, possibly for reasons of self-esteem.

The NLS matched mother-son file can be used to analyze the factors that affect the mother's report of son's weeks worked. To do this, we ran regressions of the son's weeks worked as reported by his mother in 1966 on the seemingly relevant and available characteristics of the son, his mother, and their household. The estimated coefficients for 1966 of the most complete equation fit and the mean and standard deviation of each of the model's variables are given in table 4.12. These figures indicate several interesting results.

First, the coefficient relating the young males' weeks worked reported by mothers to the weeks worked reported by sons is markedly less than 1. While increases in sons' reported weeks worked raise mothers' reported weeks worked, the effect is just .6 weeks for every 1 week increase reported by sons. Thus the absolute difference in weeks worked grows with weeks worked.

Second, the race of the family affects the number of weeks worked the mother reports for her son. The mother tends to report a much smaller number of weeks worked for the son if the family is nonwhite. The − 2.8 weeks effect of race is a 15% difference in weeks worked at the mean of the sample.

Table 4.12    Factors Affecting Number of Weeks Worked for Son as Reported by Mother, 1966 NLS Data for Males Aged 16–24[a] (N = 474)

| Independent variables: | Mean (S.D.) | Coefficient[c] (Standard error) |
|---|---|---|
| | Dependent variable: son's weeks worked in 1966 reported by mother[b] | |
| Reported by son | | |
| son's weeks worked | 25.10 | .576 |
| | (18.73) | (.040) |
| Son's enrollment status | .723 | −2.634 |
| (in school = 1) | (.448) | (1.754) |
| Son's usual hours worked per week | 28.52 | .076 |
| | (17.49) | (.043) |
| Son's hourly wage in | 1.370 | −.541 |
| current or last job | (.853) | (.946) |
| Son's age[a] | 17.41 | .207 |
| | (1.680) | (.461) |
| Son's race | .418 | −2.827 |
| (nonwhite = 1) | (.494) | (1.587) |
| Reported by mother | | |
| Mother's weeks worked | 24.22 | .008 |
| | (23.33) | (.052) |
| Mother's usual hours worked | 22.16 | .031 |
| per week | (19.79) | (.060) |
| Mother's education | 10.12 | .096 |
| | (2.737) | (.285) |
| Number in household | 5.97 | −.367 |
| | (2.517) | (.300) |
| 1966 family income | 8.659 | .000 |
| (in thousands of dollars) | (6.008) | (.000) |
| $R^2$ | | .393 |

[a]As of April 1, 1966.
[b]The mean (S.D.) of the dependent variable is 19.61 (18.75).
[c]A constant was included in the regression estimated.

Third, the son's enrollment status has a large negative (though insignificant) effect on his mother's proxy response: if the son is enrolled in school the mother's reported response will be much smaller than if he is not enrolled.

Fourth, the mean of the son's reported usual weekly hours worked is large (28.5), indicating that our typical young male labor force member with a job is working more than just a couple of hours a day; the estimated coefficient of this variable is positive (but insignificant).

In contrast, family income has no partial relationship to the number of weeks worked reported by a mother for her son. Neither do a mother's educational background, her current labor market status, and the size of her household seem to be partially related to her proxy response.

Overall, the principal finding is that the divergence between self- and proxy responses appears to be larger for youths whose attachment to the labor force is weaker, while, except for race, the demographic characteristics of individuals do not greatly affect the divergence.

### 4.4.2  Improving the Data Base

The cross-survey differences in rates of young male work activity reported in this study suggest that the magnitude, not to mention the nature, of youth joblessness is known with less certainty than is currently believed. If the estimates from relevant surveys other than the CPS are correct, more young males hold jobs than is reported in government statistics, and some aspects of the youth joblessness problem are exaggerated. If the CPS data are correct, analyses of youth joblessness based on the longitudinal surveys could be seriously flawed. Because valid scientific analysis and policy prescription requires data that deal accurately with the issue at hand, improving our information about what youths in our society are actually doing should be a top priority for those concerned with the youth unemployment problem. In this section we offer some suggestions about ways in which improvements might be made.

First, it is important to obtain better estimates of the extent to which respondent bias affects estimates of the work activity of the young. While useful, our analyses of the matched mother-son NLS sample suffer from various problems, as described earlier, and should be corroborated (or disproved) with actual CPS-derived data. We recommend that the Bureau of the Census survey youths whose families are included in the CPS and compare the youths' self-reported work activity to that reported by proxy respondents. If such a study substantiates our findings, it will be necessary to devise new methods of obtaining information about youth work activities, either through new questions designed to elicit more accurate information about the employment of the young or through CPS supplements answered by the young (and other relevant individuals) themselves. Whatever approach is taken, the Bureau of the Census should undertake a major analysis of the respondent bias problem as it relates to youths.

Second, a substantial effort should be devoted to determining whether self-reported or proxy-reported youth work activity rates are the more accurate. This can be done by requesting information about the putative employer of the youth and verifying the reported job with the employer. Such an analysis would go far beyond what we have been able to do in this study and significantly improve our knowledge of basic labor force activity. Thus we recommend that the Bureau of the Census request names of employers from young persons, particularly those reporting employment when a proxy respondent does not report the youth as having a job, and attempt to verify the position of the youth.

Third, we believe that serious attention should be given to the development of entirely new questions and concepts for analysis of the activity of youths (and others who are not typically heads of households). The current set of CPS questions were developed in large measure to determine the employment status of adult heads of households and are not well suited to an understanding of the economic problems of youths. Current CPS questions provide very little information on the activities of jobless persons who are out of school, and essentially define their status negatively: they are not employed and not in school. What is needed is a set of questions evaluating what these people do with their time, possibly oriented in part toward whether their current activity is likely to increase or decrease their chances for employment in ensuing periods. We recommend that the Bureau of the Census experiment with new sets of questions to find out what persons are doing who are out of school and not employed. Such questions should seek to determine the way in which time is allocated by the young (and others in this state) among unpaid work in the home, part-time school, "loafing," and so forth. It is difficult to understand the problems faced by the not-employed, not-enrolled young person when we have so little information about what he is doing. What is needed, we wish to stress, is not additional questions designed to differentiate discouraged from other young workers on the basis of possible work plans, but rather *objective* information on what people actually do when they are not employed and not in school.

Basically, we believe that to deal adequately with new economic problems such as youth joblessness we need new data. The payoff from obtaining more information about what teenagers are really doing and why they are really doing it will most likely be extremely high.

# Notes

1. The divergence between youth labor market conditions as depicted in the NLS and the CPS was noted in the important study by Borus, Mott and Nestel. An earlier but much less complete discussion of the phenomenon is found in Parnes.

2. For an in-depth discussion of the CPS see Hanson.

3. This information was gathered in a telephone conversation with Paul Flaim of the Bureau of Labor Statistics.

4. U.S. Bureau of Labor Statistics, *BLS Handbook of Methods*, Bulletin 1910.

5. For an in-depth discussion of the NLS, see Ohio State University.

6. Another difference, pointed out by Borus et al., exists between the 1966 CPS and NLS. The NLS adopted changes in the definitions of employment and unemployment in 1966 which were not adopted by the CPS until 1967.

7. For a discussion of the NLS72 survey, see U.S. Department of Health, Education and Welfare.

8. This information was gathered in a telephone conversation with Gilbert Nestel of Ohio State University.

9. Another possible source of discrepancy exists because mothers are interviewed about their son's activity from four to six months after the end of the reference period. Sons, however, are interviewed immediately after the reference period. The direction of the bias introduced by this discrepancy is unclear.

10. These data were calculated with NLS tapes.

11. See Hanson, p. 23 for a discussion.

12. See Borus et al., p. 18 for more information.

13. These figures were derived from data in Levinsohn et al.

14. This discussion is based on telephone conversations with Robert Lerman and Henry Woltman and on a memorandum by Woltman.

# References

Borus, M. E., F. L. Mott, and G. Nestel. 1978. Counting youth: A comparison of youth labor force statistics in the current population survey and the national longitudinal surveys. *Conference Report on Youth Unemployment: Its Measurement and Meaning*: 15–34. Washington, D.C.: U.S. Department of Labor; Office of the Assistant Secretary for Policy, Evaluation and Research; and the Employment and Training Administration.

Hanson, R. H. 1978. *The current population survey: Design and methodology*. Washington, D.C.: U.S. Department of the Census, Technical Paper #40.

Levinsohn, J. R. et al. 1978. *National longitudinal study base year, first second and third followup data file users manual*. Washington D.C.: National Center for Education Statistics.

Ohio State University, College of Administrative Science, Center for Human Resources Research, 1977. *The national longitudinal surveys handbook*.

Parnes, H. S. et al. 1970. *Career thresholds*. Manpower Research Monograph vol. I, no. 16, appendix E. Washington, D.C.: GPO.

U.S. Bureau of the Census, 1967–72. *Current population reports*. Series P-20, "School Enrollment," October 1966–October 1971. Washington, D.C.: GPO.

U.S. Bureau of the Census. 1966–71. National longitudinal surveys, survey of work experience of males 14–24. Forms LGT-201, 211, 221, 231, 241, 251. Washington, D.C.: GPO.

U.S. Bureau of Labor Statistics. 1976. *BLS handbook of methods*. Bulletin 1910. Washington, D.C.: GPO.

U.S. Bureau of Labor Statistics. 1966–71. *Employment and earnings*. December 1966–71. Washington, D.C.: GPO.

U.S. Bureau of Labor Statistics. 1972. *Employment of high school graduates and dropouts: October 1972*. Special Labor Force Report 155. Washington D.C.: GPO.

U.S. Bureau of Labor Statistics. 1966–71. *Work experience of the population*. Special Labor Force Reports 91, 107, 115, 127, 141, 162. Washington, D.C.: GPO.

U.S. Department of Health, Education, and Welfare, Office of Education. 1973. *National longitudinal study of the high school class of 1972. Final report*. Washington, D.C.: GPO.

Woltman, H. 1979. Memorandum for Tom Walsh, comparison of youth employment estimates from the CPS and the NCS. Washington, D.C.: U.S. Bureau of the Census, Statistical Methods Division.

## Comment     Paul O. Flaim

The existence of some differences between the findings from the Current Population Survey (CPS) and those from the National Longitudinal Survey (NLS) with regard to the rates of labor force activity and unemployment of youths has been known for some years. While the dimensions of these differences had perhaps not been clearly defined until recently, they were most usefully quantified and discussed in a 1978 paper by Borus, Mott, and Nestel.[1] What Freeman and Medoff set out to do was to dissect these differences and try to attribute their causes to various factors.

Their conclusions, if I may cite them at the outset, are as follows: (1) A larger proportion of youths are found to be employed in the NLS than in the CPS; (2) Although the rates of unemployment are not materially different in the two surveys, the discrepancies in terms of employment are sufficiently large to call into question our knowledge of the magnitude and nature of the youth employment problem: (3) In order to shed more light on this question, the Bureau of the Census should undertake special methodological studies and add further questions to the CPS questionnaire.

It is hard to argue against the desirability of the proposed methodological studies or against the collection of additional information on the labor force status of youths. After all, even the National Commission on Employment and Unemployment Statistics has recently recommended the regular collection of some additional data on youths through the CPS.[2] However, before mounting any large and costly studies based on the measurement differences discussed in the Freeman-Medoff chapter, we ought to ask ourselves whether these differences are truly as important as they seem.

Paul O. Flaim is an official of the Bureau of Labor Statistics. However, these comments reflect his views and not necessarily those of the Bureau of Labor Statistics.

Using data for 1967—which are also fairly representative of the NLS/CPS differences in other years—the findings from the two surveys in terms of the labor force status of male youths are summarized in table C4.1.

As shown, there are no systematic differences between the two surveys in terms of the incidence of unemployment for young men, with the CPS jobless rate being slightly higher than the NLS rate for some groups and slightly lower for others. In terms of employment, however, there is a clear pattern of systematic differences, with the employment-population ratios considerably higher as measured in the NLS than in the CPS. But let us look a little closer at these differences.

What we see is that as the age of youths increases and as their attachment to the job market becomes firmer, the NLS/CPS differences in employment-population ratios become smaller and smaller, both in absolute as well as relative terms. And here it might be pointed out that the rapid growth in the attachment of youths to the job market as they age can be confirmed not only in terms of the age related rise in employment-population ratios, but also in terms of a similar rise in the number of hours worked each week. Data for 1978 (which are also representative of the workweek pattern for youths in other years) are given in table C4.2.

Clearly, the widest NLS/CPS differences in the measurements of youth employment turn up for the 16 and 17 year olds, those who, as shown above, are most likely to work only part time. As youths age and move into jobs which take up much more of their time, and which thus acquire more meaning as part of their lives, the measurements of their employment status as derived from the NLS and the CPS become much more similar. True, the NLS turns up more employed youths than does the CPS even in the 20–24 age group, with the respective employment-population ratios being 81.8 vs. 78.0% for white males and 84.8 vs. 76.9% for black males. But how consequential are these differences? Are they of such magnitude that they might possibly affect any decisions concerning youth employment policies? I cannot see how.

**Table C4.1**

| Age, sex, and race | | Employment/population ratios | | Unemployment rates | |
|---|---|---|---|---|---|
| | | NLS | CPS | NLS | CPS |
| White males: | 16–17 years | 45.6 | 36.7 | 18.7 | 14.4 |
| | 18–19 years | 62.8 | 56.7 | 10.3 | 10.6 |
| | 20–24 years | 81.8 | 78.0 | 3.2 | 4.0 |
| Nonwhite males: | 16–17 years | 40.6 | 26.2 | 29.8 | 28.8 |
| | 18–19 years | 59.7 | 47.0 | 19.4 | 21.7 |
| | 20–24 years | 84.8 | 76.9 | 7.8 | 10.3 |

**Table C4.2**

|  |  | Weekly hours |
|---|---|---|
| White males: | 16–17 years | 22.7 |
|  | 18–19 years | 34.7 |
|  | 20–24 years | 39.9 |
| Nonwhite males: | 16–17 years | 21.9 |
|  | 18–19 years | 30.5 |
|  | 20–24 years | 37.8 |

Decisions about youth employment policies have generally been made on the basis of the unemployment rates for youths, rather than on the basis of some normative value concerning employment ratios. And, as already noted, the unemployment rates from the NLS and the CPS are not that dissimilar. This is not to suggest that we should not be concerned with the NLS/CPS differences, but simply that we should put them in the proper perspective.

As to the reasons for these differences, Freeman and Medoff (and Borus et al. before them) point rather convincingly to the fact that the NLS data were obtained through personal interviews with the youths whose work activity was actually being measured, while the CPS data for youths are most often obtained from other members of the households, and generally from the mothers of the youths in question. In logical pursuit of this line, Freeman and Medoff turned to the data from the Longitudinal Survey of the High School Class of 1972 (NLS72) and found strong evidence that mothers tend to report less employment activity for their sons than is reported by the sons themselves.

However, we should still not jump to the conclusion that mothers are biased when it comes to reporting the employment of their children. There is, I think, a better explanation. My hypothesis is that the parent/youth differences in the reporting of the youth's employment arise simply from different perceptions as to what constitutes having "worked" or having held "a job," particularly when the employment in question is of very marginal nature. For example, a 16 year old who earns, say, $10 in a given week through lawn-mowing or baby-sitting tasks may attribute considerable importance to such work and would probably report it to an interviewer. On the other hand, the mother of such a teenager may not view such tasks as worth mentioning.

It must be kept in mind that in the typical CPS interviewing sequence the mother would first be queried about her husband's job with the ABC corporation and then, if applicable, about her own job with the XYZ corporation. Her mind having been focused upon such jobs, it is quite possible—and understandable—that she would then view the casual lawnmoving and baby-sitting jobs of her son or daughter as not worth reporting.[3]

There are, admittedly, situations in which the parents may simply not have adequate knowledge of the employment status of their children. This situation is most likely to arise when youths are temporarily away at school and when their labor force status in the CPS is determined on the basis of data obtained from their parents as part of the interiews conducted in their home town. In such instances—and they are clearly numerous—the parents may simply not know whether their sons or daughters worked (or looked for work) during the reference period.

Table C4.3 shows several hypothetical situations where, either because of different perceptions or different levels of knowledge, the reporting of a youth's employment status could vary significantly depending on whether the pertinent questions are addressed to the youth or to his parents.

What the table illustrates is that the employment status of youths is very often not a matter of black and white but a gray area where the dichotomy between "working" and "not working" is not that obvious. It is thus not surprising that parents might draw the line differently from their children in considering what constitutes a job, or what is worth mentioning as a job.

It should also be emphasized that the work activity questions asked in the CPS are not always identical to those asked in the NLS, and we know that only a slight difference in the wording of such questions can affect the answers. In determining how many weeks a person worked during the previous year, the annual question in the CPS has been: "In [year x] how many weeks did _____ work either full time or part time not counting work around the house? Include paid vacation and sick pay leave." In the NLS, the youths were asked about the number of weeks during the year in which they did "any work at all." It is not surprising that the NLS question, which includes this additional phrase, might result in the reporting of more weeks of employment than would a question which does not contain such a phrase.

There are other features of the CPS which are very dissimilar relative to the NLS and which might contribute to the differences discussed in the Freeman-Medoff chapter. As mentioned in the chapter, the reporting of employment and of job-seeking activity in the CPS tends to be significantly higher in the households being visited for the first time than in those whose members are being interviewed for the second, third, or fourth time. While this "rotation group bias" has never been satisfactorily explained, we know it is particularly large in the case of persons whose labor force activity, as reported in the first-month interview, is somewhat marginal. To cite an extreme example, the average number of women reported as looking for part-time work is generally about one-fourth higher in the first monthly interview than in the third one.[4]

While the rotation group bias in the CPS data for youths may not be that large, it tends generally in the same direction. As shown in table

**Table C4.3    Possible Reasons for Differences between Parents and Youths in Reporting of Youths' Labor Force Status**

| Hypothetical situation | Perception of situation and probable reporting by youth | Perception of situation and probable reporting by parent |
|---|---|---|
| 1. Boy mowing lawns; girl baby-sitting; both working only a few hours per week. | Income from tasks very important to youth; tasks likely to be reported as employment. | Parent may not consider such occasional tasks as a "job" and may not report as employment, particularly in a retrospective survey. |
| 2. Youth away at college; working part time in library. | Would probably report employment but is treated as resident of parents' household for CPS purposes. | Parents likely to answer "don't know" when asked what youth did last week, and youth is not classified as employed. |
| 3. Youth away at college; looking for part time job. | Would probably report job-seeking efforts but is treated as resident of parents household. | Parents may not know of job-seeking efforts and youth would not be reported as unemployed. |
| 4. Youth residing at home; making sporadic efforts to find casual work. | Would probably report job-seeking efforts. | Parents may not consider such sporadic efforts to find casual work worth mentioning as a job-seeking activity. |

C4.4, the employment-population ratios and unemployment rates based on the first interview are generally higher than those based on the entire survey. Thus NLS/CPS comparisons would yield smaller differences if based on first-month data from the CPS. Alternatively, they would also probably be much smaller if the NLS data were collected through repeated monthly interviews as in the CPS.

Conclusion

Given the rather marginal nature of the labor force activity of many youths and the different ways in which the data on their labor force status is collected and computed in the NLS and the CPS, it is not surprising to find some differences between the findings from the two surveys. Freeman and Medoff shed very useful light on these differences and on the processes that may lead up to them. They recognize as well that these differences are most apparent where labor market attachment is most tenuous. Their suggestions for further research on the topic and for a sharpening of the labor force questions relative to youths are quite valid and in line with suggestions made by the National Commission on Employment and Unemployment Statistics. I do not think, however, that the differences are of such weight as to warrant any large-scale methodological studies. Moreover, since the employment status of many youths is not easily defined, I doubt whether the NLS/CPS differences could ever be satisfactorily reconciled, even through a special survey designed specifically for that purpose.

**Notes**

1. Michael E. Borus, Frank L. Mott, and Gilbert Nestel, "Counting Youth: A Comparison of Youth Labor Force Statistics in the Current Population Survey and the National Longitudinal Surveys," in *"Conference Report on Youth Unemployment: Its Measurement and Meaning,"* U.S. Department of Labor, 1978.

2. *Counting the Labor Force*, final report of the National Commission on Employment and Unemployment Statistics, 1979.

3. In the spring of 1979, an observer of the CPS interviewing process noted the following situation. A mother who was asked about the labor force status of her young son reported that he had not done any work during the previous week, that he did not have a job from which he was temporarily absent, etc. After the interview was completed, it turned out that the son was about to go off to play the drums in a cafe where he performed with a small group three nights a week. Obviously, this mother did not regard such activity as the equivalent of "working" or "having a job."

4. *The Current Population Survey Design and Methodology*, Technical Paper 40, U.S. Department of Commerce, Bureau of the Census, 1978. (see particularly table VIII-4, page 84).

**Table C4.4** Comparisons of employment-population ratios and unemployment rates from CPS as derived from data from first-month households and as derived from entire sample. Annual averages for 1977.

| Age, sex, and race | | Employment-population ratios | | | Unemployment rates | | |
|---|---|---|---|---|---|---|---|
| | | First-month households (1) | Entire sample (2) | Difference (1)–(2) | First-month households (3) | Entire sample (4) | Difference (3)–(4) |
| **Males** | | | | | | | |
| White | 16 to 24 | 68.5 | 67.5 | 1.0 | 12.5 | 11.5 | 1.0 |
| | 16–17 | 48.2 | 44.3 | 3.9 | 18.6 | 17.6 | 1.0 |
| | 18–19 | 66.8 | 65.2 | 1.6 | 13.6 | 13.0 | 0.6 |
| | 20–21 | 72.0 | 72.8 | –0.8 | 12.2 | 10.7 | 1.5 |
| | 22–24 | 82.8 | 82.9 | –0.1 | 8.9 | 8.3 | 0.6 |
| Black and other: | 16 to 24 | 47.1 | 44.2 | 2.9 | 27.7 | 27.2 | 0.5 |
| | 16–17 | 25.5 | 19.0 | 6.5 | 34.9 | 38.7 | –3.8 |
| | 18–19 | 41.5 | 36.9 | 4.6 | 35.7 | 36.1 | –0.4 |
| | 20–21 | 56.5 | 52.8 | 3.7 | 23.4 | 26.0 | –2.6 |
| | 22–24 | 65.2 | 67.7 | –2.5 | 22.3 | 18.7 | 3.6 |
| **Females** | | | | | | | |
| White: | 16 to 24 | 56.4 | 54.4 | 2.0 | 13.2 | 11.9 | 1.3 |
| | 16–17 | 40.2 | 37.5 | 2.7 | 19.9 | 18.2 | 1.7 |
| | 18–19 | 56.8 | 54.3 | 2.5 | 15.5 | 14.2 | 1.3 |
| | 20–21 | 61.4 | 60.2 | 1.2 | 10.9 | 10.1 | 0.8 |
| | 22–24 | 64.0 | 62.3 | 1.7 | 9.8 | 8.7 | 1.1 |
| Black and other: | 16 to 24 | 35.3 | 33.6 | 1.7 | 34.8 | 29.1 | 5.7 |
| | 16–17 | 15.3 | 12.5 | 2.8 | 51.3 | 44.7 | 6.6 |
| | 18–19 | 29.3 | 28.0 | 1.3 | 43.5 | 37.4 | 6.1 |
| | 20–21 | 39.8 | 38.2 | 1.6 | 34.5 | 29.3 | 5.2 |
| | 22–24 | 51.8 | 50.6 | 1.2 | 24.2 | 20.2 | 4.0 |

# Comment     Stephen M. Hills

As Freeman and Medoff note, the discrepancy between CPS and NLS estimates of labor force statistics is not a new research topic. Their research extends comparisons to a greater number of years than was the case in the most recent study by Borus, Mott and Nestel. Borus et al. were reluctant to make comparisons for more recent years because of the decreasing degree of representativeness of the NLS caused by attrition. Nevertheless, the same pattern of responses is shown in the Freeman/Medoff data for later years of the NLS (1968–71) and for earlier years when attrition was not a problem (1966–67).

Freeman and Medoff seek to improve our understanding of the discrepancies in several ways. First, they adjust the data from the NLS for slight differences in age that result because of the timing of the sample screening. Borus et al. did not adjust their data for age and furthermore did not break down comparisons by as many age categories as have Freeman and Medoff. The important result that emerges in table 4.1 is not only the large discrepancy in employment to population ratios which is the focus of the paper. The table also shows very large discrepancies in the degree of unemployment reported for 16 and 17 year olds. The discrepancy in unemployment does not appear to be that great in the earlier study by Borus et al., both because the data are not adjusted for age and because they are reported for 16–19 year olds as a total group.

Second, Freeman and Medoff seek to extend the comparisons of labor force statistics by utilizing a second longitudinal data set, the NLS72. This attempt to generalize was, in my opinion, not very successful because of important differences in methods used to obtain employment status. Respondents in the NLS72 were asked to recall whether or not they were looking for work during the month of October, 1972, but the date at which they were asked to recall this information was twelve months later. The intervening time period should result in a serious underreporting for rates of unemployment. To determine whether a respondent was employed, the questionnaire simply asks if a job was held at any time during the month of October, 1972. Since CPS employment status is based on a survey *week* one would need to divide the number of weeks employed in October by 4.3 (the number of weeks in the month) and average this ratio for all respondents to obtain an estimate of the employment to population ratio that was at all comparable with the CPS. The employment to population ratio now reported is an overestimate since the time period on which it is based is approximately four times longer than the time period for the CPS.

Stephen M. Hills is assistant professor of labor and human resources and associate project director of the National Longitudinal Surveys at Ohio State University.

Third, Freeman and Medoff focus on the differences in CPS reports and NLS reports for work experience across a twelve-month period of time. In this area the authors have significantly extended our understanding of the *potential* causes of differences in estimates of survey week status. The data do not permit a direct experiment, however, to determine the sources of bias that may exist in survey week status. We must *infer* this from the experiment which is performed on data for work experience. Nevertheless, the inference is strong that proxy respondents could account for much of the discrepancy in labor force statistics, and the authors present a convincing set of comparative data to support their case.

The focus of the chapter is therefore on the discrepancy between mean weeks of work experience reported in the March supplement of the CPS and in the work experience sections of the NLS. Mothers underreport the weeks of work experience for their sons by about six weeks, regardless of age category or year for which comparisons are made. There are undoubtedly systematic differences in underreporting which the authors examine through a mother/son matrix of responses and a multivariate analysis. Still more can be done simply by examining in slightly different fashion the distribution contained in table 4.8.

We can establish as a hypothesis that what we observe is a systematic underreporting of specific kinds of work that young people are doing. It is quite likely that adults may ignore particular kinds of work that teenagers do as trivial—baby sitting, distributing advertising pamphlets, working a few hours each week at the grocery store. Teenagers themselves may consider these jobs important enough to report even though they do not spend much time working at them or earn much money from them. The discrepancy between reports of the mother and the son may be due both to a problem of recall and to a different evaluation of what "work" really is.

If we reexamine the distributions of table 4.8, we can see that most of the discrepancy in mean weeks worked flows from the "missing" category, the zero category, or the 1–13 week category. If we assume that the missing category is proportionately distributed across the other categories of each distribution, we find for 1966 that mothers report 74% of their sons working 0–13 weeks whereas only 55% of the sons report that they worked only that amount for the year. For 18–19 year olds the figures are "mother's report," 63%, "son's report," 32%. Finally, for 20–24 year olds, the figures are 46% and 28%. If we recalculate the distributions, looking only at the portion of the sample that was reporting 14–52 weeks, the picture looks quite similar for both the mother's and the son's reports. If anything, there is some tendency in these instances for mothers to overrepresent the number of sons in the fifty-two week category, shifting the distribution upwards somewhat. Results of the recalculation are shown in table C4.5.

The conclusion that can then be drawn is this: disproportionate numbers of mothers report zero weeks of work when they really do not know what kinds of jobs their sons have. Likewise, others report 1–13 weeks (perhaps a summer job) when the son reports that he was working more consistently throughout the year.

The NLS also contains a report of the kind of work that the son was doing, both reported by the mother and by the son. Thus it is possible to examine the kinds of work being underreported by the mother when there are serious discrepancies between her report and the son's. Freeman and Medoff do not deal with this issue directly and therefore it must be considered as a possibility for future research.

A critique of the Freeman/Medoff chapter also requires comment on the policy interpretations that could be attributed to their findings. The traditional philosophy underlying the gathering of labor force statistics has been to ask a consistent set of questions that are as unambiguous as possible and hope that respondents interpret them in approximately the same manner. The concept of "work" is not terribly ambiguous for the prime-age worker with a steady, paid job. For younger workers the concepts of both "work" and "looking for work" become much more ambiguous. Yet we make normative judgments about whether or not "the youth joblessness problem is exaggerated" based on these data.

It seems clear that if the source of discrepancy between CPS and NLS data is due to proxy respondents, we should have more faith in the data obtained from young people themselves, regardless of the meaning they attach to the concepts of "work" or "looking for work." Furthermore, if we accept their responses as more reliable, two conclusions flow from the Freeman/Medoff chapter and each should have equal emphasis. In the late 1960s young men were working more than the CPS estimates indicated, even though we don't know much about the kinds of jobs that were missed by the CPS. Very young men, particularly those aged 16 and 17, were also looking for work in greater numbers than the CPS estimates would have indicated. This latter issue, which was first raised in the

**Table C4.5**          **Distribution of Weeks Worked If 14–52 Weeks Were Reported**

|  | Age | 16–17 | | 18–19 | | 20–24 | |
|---|---|---|---|---|---|---|---|
|  |  | Mother | Son | Mother | Son | Mother | Son |
| Weeks | 14–26 | 40 | 40 | 35 | 34 | 24 | 27 |
| worked | 27–39 | 10 | 15 | 14 | 15 | 10 | 16 |
|  | 40–47 | 7 | 8 | 5 | 8 | 9 | 11 |
|  | 48–49 | 1 | 4 | 4 | 5 | 4 | 7 |
|  | 50–52 | 42 | 33 | 41 | 37 | 52 | 40 |

mid-sixties, has again become relevant with the publication of preliminary figures on employment status for youths, drawn from the newest
extension of the NLS.

The newest comparisons with the CPS are for youths aged 16–21. They
provide support for the arguments made by Freeman and Medoff by
showing that for out-of-school youths, the CPS and NLS estimates of
labor force participation, unemployment and employment to population
ratios are relatively close. For in-school youths who are the most likely to
be living at home, however, the discrepancies can be extremely large.
NLS in-school employment/population ratios range from five percentage
points higher than the CPS for white females to almost nine percentage
points higher for black males. NLS estimates of the unemployment rate
for in-school youths are five percentage points higher than the CPS for
white males (the minimum discrepancy), but exceed the CPS by a startling twenty-four percentage points for black females.[1] The largest differences between the March 1979 CPS and the NLS occurred for females,
both white and black, and for black males. Given the importance of labor
force statistics for policy purposes, this most recent information only
underscores Freeman and Medoff's call for immediate attention to the
way in which we gather data on the labor market activities of youth.

## Note

1. Richard Santos, "The Employment Status of Youth," chapter 2 in *Research on Youth
Employment and Employability Development—Findings of the National Longitudinal Sur-
vey of Young Americans, 1979*, Youth Knowledge Development Report 2.7, table 2.7
(Washington, D.C.: U.S. Government Printing Office, May 1980), p. 34.

# 5 Economic Determinants of Geographic and Individual Variation in the Labor Market Position of Young Persons

Richard B. Freeman

Relatively high and increasing rates of joblessness and decreasing earnings for young persons relative to older persons constituted one of the major labor market problems in the United States and other countries in the 1970s. Several hypotheses have been offered to explain the deteriorated economic position of young persons. Some cite macroeconomic factors and the general weakening of the job market; others emphasize the role of the minimum wage and related market rigidities; yet others have stressed the demographic changes of the period, which took the form of sizable increases in the relative number of young workers. While the issue is one of change over time, the available time series, though useful, lack sufficient variation to provide strong tests of the competing hypotheses or to provide estimates of the impact of the full set of possible explanations.

This chapter uses evidence on the labor force activity of young persons across geographic areas (SMSAs) and across individuals to analyze the determinants of the market for young persons. The data on geographic areas provide a reasonably large sample of observations with considerable variation in both dependent and potential explanatory variables, variation that appears to provide a better "experiment" for testing various proposed causal forces for youth market problems than collinear time series. The major disadvantage of the geographic evidence is that variation across regions may reflect regional differences in "competitiveness"—the performance of one area versus another—that provide little insight into the possible causes of aggregate problems. Another potential problem is that correlations of factors across areas can give a misleading picture of the determinants of the position of individual (i.e., ecological

Any opinions expressed in this chapter are those of the author and not those of the National Bureau of Economic Research.

correlation bias). The data on individuals in the Survey of Income and Education provide a way around the ecological correlation problem and also cast light on several other aspects of the youth labor market position.[1]

I will begin with a brief review of several proposed causes of the youth labor market problem, and then analyze the differences in youth employment, unemployment, and labor force participation across geographic areas and among individuals.

There are four basic findings:

1. Geographic variation in the employment, unemployment, and labor force participation of young workers depends in large measure on identifiable supply and demand conditions in local labor markets, including the relative number of young persons, the percentage of homes below the poverty level, the rate of unemployment of prime-age men, the rate of growth of personal income, and the proportion of jobs in young-worker-intensive industries. While classification of explanatory variables such as supply or demand related is somewhat arbitrary, the evidence appears to support the notion that inadequate demand is a prime cause of the youth joblessness problem.

2. The employment and wages of young persons are differently affected by personal and background factors. Being black or coming from a family with certain socioeconomic problems affects the probability of employment but does *not* affect wages. The different effects of variables on employment and wages highlight the extent to which there is a distinct youth *employment* problem.

3. Because determinants of youth employment often have the same directional impact on labor force participation rates as on employment, they have little effect, or occasionally a contradictory effect, on unemployment rates. This suggests that analyses focusing on unemployment can give misleading impressions about the determinants of the youth labor market position.

4. Though cross-area models tell a roughly similar story about the determinants of the youth labor market as do comparable time series analyses, neither cross-section nor time series analyses explain the behavior of the youth labor market in the 1970s, when, with the marked exception of young blacks, employment to population rates held steady and labor participation rates rose, despite adverse changes in their putative determinants.

## 5.1 Causes of Youth Labor Market Problems

The factors that underly youth employment problems can be examined with standard partial equilibrium models of the job market, in which supply and demand determine equilibrium employment and wages and in which joblessness (above frictional levels) results from failure to attain market clearing wages, either because wages respond relatively slowly (for diverse reasons) to rapid changes in demand or supply or because of rigidities such as legislated minima. To illustrate the way in which dynamic shifts in demand or supply and sluggish wages adjustments can produce joblessness, consider the following simple model

(1)        Supply: $\ln S = \epsilon \ln W + Bt$

(2)        Demand: $\ln D = \eta \ln W + At$

(3)        Wage Adjustment: $\Delta \ln W = \psi (\ln D - \ln S)$

where $S$ = supply of labor, $D$ = demand for labor, $W$ = wage, $A$ = shift in demand per unit time, $B$ = shift in supply per unit time, $\epsilon$ = elasticity of supply, and $\eta$ = elasticity of demand, $\Delta$ = change over time.

Joblessness occurs in the system (1)–(3) because wages respond to disequilibrium with a lag. Since $\ln D - \ln S = -(\eta + \epsilon)\ln W + (A - B)t$, $\Delta(\ln D - \ln S) = -(\eta + \epsilon)\Delta \ln W + (A - B)$. Solving for the "equilibrium" level of unemployment by substituting (3) for $\Delta \ln W$ and setting $\Delta(\ln D - \ln S) = 0$, we get $\ln S - \ln D = (B - A)/(\eta + \epsilon)\Psi$. When supply increases more rapidly than demand $(B > A)$, the slow adjustment of wages produces unemployment in the relevant time period. Relatively slow movement in wages could result from the normal process of wage determination in an economy with long-term contracts and unexpected or uncertain shocks.

The analysis of *shifts* in the schedules directs attention to the factors that cause the supply of young workers to increase significantly or cause the demand for young workers to decrease significantly.

The major potential cause of increased supply is the sizable expansion of the youth population, which resulted from the baby boom of the fifties and sixties. Given noninfinite substitution elasticities among workers by age, the increase in supply could be expected to cause significant pressures on the youth market. If increased numbers are an important determinant of the problems of the seventies, the youth market should improve steadily in the 1980s when the number of young persons declines as a share of the total population.

Two basic types of shifts in demand are likely to contribute to the joblessness problem. The first are shifts due to changes in the overall level of economic activity, such as cyclical declines or a longer-run slowdown in the rate of growth. When aggregate demand declines or grows slowly, the reduction in hiring will have significant effects on the demand for the young. The second type of shifts involve structural changes in the mix of industries and occupations or in the supplies of workers who can substitute for the young, such as illegal aliens willing to undertake unpleasant tasks for low wages and/or adult women, who at existing wages may be preferred by employers for certain entry-level positions.

Failure of wages to attain market-clearing levels because of rigidities such as the minimum wage represents another potential cause of youth joblessness. In contrast to a failure to clear because of sluggish adjustment, failure to clear because of the minimum can produce joblessness even in periods of stable supply and demand if the minima are above the equilibrium rate.

In addition to shifts in demand and supply due to general market or demographic factors, the labor market for some groups of youths may be adversely affected by more complex social forces, the impact of which is difficult to measure with the type of data currently available. One such set of factors pertains to opportunities for work and earnings outside the mainline economy, ranging from casual street jobs to crime, which offer an alternative to normal labor force activity. Another set of factors relates to possible disparities between the skills of young persons from disadvantaged backgrounds and their aspirations and willingness to take "undesirable jobs." Yet another relates to the conditions of the individual's family or community: for diverse reasons, those from welfare homes or from communities with widespread welfare or poverty may have greater problems in obtaining jobs than other youngsters. Finally, for discriminatory or other reasons, it is well known that black youngsters face especially poor employment prospects. Under certain circumstances, moreover, the rise in the number of white youths could have adversely affected the position of black youths.

This chapter will focus largely on the contribution of differences in broad supply and demand forces to youth joblessness and touch only briefly on the more complex social factors mentioned above. The geographic data set is well suited to analyze the effect of broad market forces on youths because these forces vary substantively across areas and can be viewed as appropriate indicators of labor market conditions. The data set on individuals provides information to assess the incidence of joblessness among young persons with different characteristics but lacks the information on incentives, skills, attitudes, and employment practices that is needed to determine the *causal* forces behind many observed relations.

## 5.2    Geographic Variation in Youth Employment and Joblessness

The effect of some of the proposed explanatory factors on the youth labor market can be analyzed with information on the work activity of youths across SMSAs using data from the U.S. Census of Population of 1970 (see the data appendix for a detailed description). The Census has sufficiently large samples to provide information on the activity of youths by age, sex, and enrollment status in 125 SMSAs. More limited information on certain explanatory factors is available from 114 SMSAs.

The state of the youth labor market in each SMSA is measured by three related variables: the ratio of youth employment to the youth civilian population, which reflects the overall impact of supply and demand forces on the amount of work from the group; the civilian labor force participation rate of the young; and the rate of unemployment among the young. The employment to population ratio is given the greatest stress, as it is the clearest measure of objective behavior. The high mobility of young persons into and out of the work force (see Clark and Summers, chapter 7 of the present volume) and the possibility of significant encouraged/discouraged worker behavior makes the labor force and unemployment measures of activity looser and subject to greater potential error.

The analysis differentiates between males and females and among three age groups: 16–17 year olds, most of whom are in school; 18–19 year olds; and 20–24 year olds. Because of significant differences in work activity by school status, calculations relating to the total youth group always contain a variable for the proportion of the group enrolled in school. In addition, separate calculations are made for young persons out of and in school.

The three measures of youth labor market activity show considerable differences in employment and joblessness across SMSAs, providing the variation that is a prerequisite for fruitful analysis. As can be seen in line 1 of table 5.1, the standard deviation of the employment to population ratio across SMSAs for all young men range from .069 for 16–17 year olds to .059 for 20–24 year olds. The standard deviations of labor participation rates are similar while those for unemployment are lower, but with lower means.

Differences in the relative supply of young persons are measured by the ratio of the number of young civilians in a specified age-sex group to the number of civilian men 16 and over. Sizable differences in the distribution of young workers by age among industries and occupations suggest the value of separate analyses for each age-sex group.[2] The ratio of young persons to men 16 and over varies considerably across areas,[3] in part because of differing fertility, mortality, and migration patterns and in part, it should be noted, because the Census enumerates college students at their area of residence during college.

Differences in demand for young workers due to differences in the overall level of economic activity across SMSAs are measured by: the unemployment rate of 30–34 year old men and by the rate of growth of total personal income.[4] Areas with strong labor markets for adult workers or with significant growth in income over time are likely to have greater numbers of entry-level jobs for the young.

To take into account the likely impact of an SMSAs industrial mix on the demand for young workers, a fixed weight index of the favorableness of each SMSA's industrial composition to youth employment was estimated, using national figures on youth employment in industries (see Bowen and Finegan 1969 for a similar index). Specifically, let $\alpha_i$ equal the ratio of the number of young persons in a specified age-sex group working in industry $i$ to total employment in industry $i$ in the United States as a whole; Let $W_{ij}$ equal the share of employment in SMSA $j$ accounted by industry $i$; and let $\alpha$ equal the ratio of the number of young persons in the age-sex group employed in the United States to total employment. Then the index of industrial mix is defined by

(4)     $$I_j = \sum_i (\alpha_i / \alpha) W_{ij}$$

where $\alpha$ is used as a scaling factor.

The federal minimum, the market imperfection most likely to affect demand, does not, of course, vary across areas. Since the minimum might be expected to have a bigger impact on low-wage than high-wage SMSAs, average hourly earnings in industry in an area can be used as a crude proxy measure of the effect of the minimum: the higher the earnings, the less effective the minimum should be. Since earnings measure other characteristics of an area, however, this provides at most a weak test of the effect of the minimum.[5] State minimum wages do of course differ across areas but have low levels and are weakly enforced. A 0–1 dummy variable for the presence of a state minimum is entered in the calculations.

Unfortunately, given current survey data, it is difficult to measure behaviorally more complex determinants of youth market problems, such as motivation, skill, and social difficulties. At best one can include measures of area characteristics which may be associated with these factors. The following measures are examined: the proportion of one-parent/female-headed homes in the area; the proportion of homes in the SMSA that are below the official poverty line; the proportion of young persons in the SMSA who are black; and the number of AFDC recipients per person in the SMSA. The proportion of impoverished homes turns out to be the most important of this set of variables. Unfortunately, the causal effect of the variable is subject to several interpretations: it could be an indicator of inadequate demand in the area in which the individual resides; it could reflect inadequate work skills and "human capital" formation in disadvantaged homes; or it could reflect "community effects" on young persons in poverty areas, of the type stressed by Loury. Because of the difficulties of interpretation and because both poverty and youth unemployment may be *simultaneously determined* by other area characteristics, the variable is deleted from some calculations.

Since the welfare, one-parent female, poverty, and black variables measure *area* characteristics, interpretation of their coefficients is subject to the "ecological correlation" problem referred to earlier. Accordingly, their impact is also examined with the data set on individuals.

### 5.3   Empirical Analysis: Young Men 16–24

The effect of the explanatory variables described above on the employment to population rate, labor force participation rate, and rate of unemployment of young workers is examined with ordinary least squares (OLS) linear regressions of the following form:[6]

(5)         $Y_i = \Sigma a_i X_i + U_i$

where $Y_i$ equals the relevant measure of labor force activity, $X_i$ equals the explanatory variable, and $U_i$ equals the residual.

Table 5.1 contains the basic regression results for young men aged 16–17, 18–19, and 20–24. The regressions include eight region dummies and a measure of the size of the SMSA (number of persons), as well as the explanatory factors described earlier. Regional dummies are included to control for potential omitted factors that vary among major regions. The size of the SMSA is included to evaluate the possible concentration of youth joblessness in the larger areas. The figures in the odd-numbered columns show the results of regressions which exclude one of the key variables, the proportion of homes below the poverty level, while the figures in the even-numbered columns shows results with that variable included as an explanatory factor.

Let us consider first the equations that exclude the poverty level variable. While there are some peculiarities, the general story told by these calculations is clear: both the supply and demand forces have a substantial effect on the position of youths with, however, the demand factors apparently having a more important role in explaining differences in the position of youths in their twenties and supply factors being more important for those in their mid-teens.

On the demand side, the two measures of the level of economic activity in an SMSA, the rate of unemployment of prime-age (30–34 year old) men and the rate of growth of total personal income in an area, have powerful effects on the position of young workers in nearly all of the equations. The prime-age male unemployment rate significantly reduces the employment ratio and labor force participation rate in all three age groups and raises the unemployment rates of 18–19 and 20–24 year olds though not the unemployment rate of 16–17 year olds, for whom the reduction in participation is especially large. The rate of growth variables is also accorded generally significant nonnegligible coefficients, which suggest that growing areas tend to have more jobs for the young then declining areas. The measure of the favorableness of industry mix to youth employment also turns out to be a major determinant of the position of the young. The index is strongly related positively to the employment rate and participation rate.

On the supply side, the relative number of young people has a noticeable effect on the employment and participation rates of 16–17 and 18–19 year olds but *not* on that of 20–24 year olds. This differential impact by age probably reflects the fact that because of the minimum wage, the wages of the younger groups have less room for downward adjustment to supply increases.[7] Among 16–17 year olds, the reduction in the employment rate dominates the reduction in the participation rate so that unemployment increases; among 18–19 year olds, the change in employment and participation yield no effective change in the unemployment rate; while among 20–24 year olds, the greater reduction in participation than in employment in response to increased numbers of person actually *reduces* unemployment—which highlights possible misinterpretation from analyses that focus solely on unemployment rates.

In the absence of the poverty level variable, the percentage of homes headed by women in an SMSA also has a sizable impact on the position of young workers: youths in areas with a significant female-headed population do worse than other youths.

As for the other variables (whose coefficients are not reported in the table), the log of average hourly earnings in manufacturing and the dichotomous dummy variable for presence of a state minimum had no noticeable effect on any of the dependent variables. Neither did the size of city nor the AFDC recipients/population variable nor, more surprisingly, the percentage of blacks. Because these are measures of area characteristics rather than measures of individual characteristics, however, it should not be concluded that blacks or those from welfare homes are not especially hard hit by joblessness. By contrast the percentage in school reduced labor market activity noticeably, while the coefficients on the regional dummy variable indicate that the young tend to do better in the Midwest and New England and relatively worse in the Pacific, the South, and the North Atlantic.

The even-numbered equations, which include the percentage of families below the poverty level as an explanatory factor, tell a very different story about the determinants of the youth market. For when the proportion of families below the poverty is included, it dominates the calculations. The coefficients in the demand-side variable are reduced noticeably while those on supply factors—the relative number of young people—and social factors—the percentage of homes headed by females—generally drop to insignificance.

As noted earlier, the dominant effect of the percentage of impoverished families raises important issues of interpretation. The variable could reflect the impact of *individual* poverty, say, through inadequate human capital formation, lack of connections, or related social ills in the homes of those in poverty, or it could reflect the impact of *community* factors on either the demand or supply side.

The difference between these interpretations is significant, for, as Loury has stressed in his analysis of communal externalities, improving the economic position of the disadvantaged is significantly more difficult when individuals are affected by communal factors than when only family background influences them.

The most efficacious way to differentiate between "individual" and "community" effects is to analyze the employment of individuals themselves using a data tape that includes *both* the position of the individual's family and whether the family lives in a poverty tract. Such an analysis is given in tables 5.8 and 5.9, and suggests that while the bulk of the observed relations appears attributable to the individual effect, there is *a separate community effect* which provides some support for the existence of community externalities, as postulated by Loury.

Finally, it should be emphasized that in many of the calculations in table 5.1 explanatory variables have a stronger impact on employment to population rates than on unemployment rates. For example, the relative number of young persons significantly reduces the employment ratio of 18–19 year olds but has no effect on their rate of unemployment, while the prime-age male unemployment rate, the percent annual growth of personal income, and the index of industrial mix have more significant effects on employment ratios than on unemployment rates. The reason for this pattern is that variables which alter employment rates have comparable, sometimes larger and sometimes smaller, effects on participation rates because of "encouraged" or "discouraged" worker behavior and thus uncertain effects on unemployment.[8] The tendency for explanatory factors to affect employment and participation in the same way and mute their effect on unemployment raises serious doubts about the emphasis usually placed on unemployment as the key indicator of the youth market and as the main dependent variable with which to study the market effects of diverse supply and demand forces.

### 5.4   Labor Market Position by Enrollment Status

Thus far the analysis has used a single variable, the proportion of young persons in school, to differentiate between the behavior of persons enrolled in school and persons not enrolled in school. This assumes that the major difference between the two groups lies in the level of labor force activity rather than in the effect of explanatory factors. As the response of young persons to conditions may differ depending on enrollment status and as lack of work is presumably a more serious problem for those out of school, it is important to examine the determinants of the

**Table 5.1  Regression Coefficients and Standard Errors for the Effect of Explanatory Factors on the Labor Market Position of Young Men, 1970**

| Variables | Employment ratio 16–17 | Employment ratio 18–19 | Employment ratio 20–24 | Labor force participation rate 16–17 | Labor force participation rate 18–19 | Labor force participation rate 20–24 | Unemployment rate 16–17 | Unemployment rate 18–19 | Unemployment rate 20–24 |
|---|---|---|---|---|---|---|---|---|---|
| Means and standard deviations | .323 (.069) | .527 (.065) | .743 (.059) | .369 (.072) | .587 (.067) | .797 (.055) | .125 (.024) | .102 (.036) | .068 (.028) |
| Prime-age male | −1.01 (.50); −1.50 (.55) | −1.28 (.47); −1.06 (.45) | −2.01 (.37); −1.88 (.35) | −1.59 (.60); −1.04 (.53) | −.57 (.48); −.38 (.47) | −.65 (.36); −.55 (.35) | .28 (.31); .20 (.31) | 1.21 (.29); 1.11 (.28) | 1.70 (.16); 1.66 (.16) |
| Unemployment rate | .23 (.34); .62 (.37) | .77 (.31); 1.01 (.32) | .25 (.24); .40 (.25) | .18 (.53); .18 (.36) | .68 (.32); .88 (.33) | .23 (.35); .35 (.24) | −.14 (.21); −.20 (.21) | −.26 (.20); −.37 (.20) | −.07 (.11); −.11 (.11) |
| Percent annual growth | .77 (.34); .62 (.37) | 1.01 (.25); .88 (.24) | .40 (.24); .35 (.25) | .68 (.36); .88 (.33) | .18 (.32); .18 (.33) | .26 (.24); .25 (.24) | .04 (.21); .03 (.21) | −.06 (.20); −.07 (.20) | −.04 (.11); −.03 (.11) |
| Personal income (×100) | .21 (.14); .39 (.27) | .42 (.39); .26 (.27) | .26 (.27); .27 (.26) | .18 (.26); .41 (.25) | .39 (.41); .18 (.39) | .25 (.26); .26 (.25) | .04 (.05); .03 (.05) | −.06 (.07); −.07 (.08) | −.04 (.05); −.03 (.05) |
| Index of industrial mix | .21 (.09); .14 (.12) | .42 (.12); .39 (.11) | .26 (.12); .27 (.11) | .18 (.09); .41 (.13) | .39 (.12); .18 (.13) | .25 (.11); .26 (.12) | 1.52 (.05)?; 1.78 (.05) | −.19 (.07); −.12 (.08) | −.29 (.05); −.29 (.05) |
| Relative number of young people | −.82 (.75); −2.52 (.77) | −1.51 (.62); −1.36 (.59) | −.09 (.24); −.07 (.25) | −2.16 (.83); −1.73 (.80) | −1.60 (.62); −1.31 (.64) | −.31 (.25); −.33 (.24) | .46 (.33); .68 (.29) | .27 (.38); .67 (.38) | −.29 (.11); −.29 (.11) |
| Percent homes headed by females (×100) | −1.81 (.52); −.42 (.51) | −1.43 (.41); −.53 (.47) | −.82 (.31); −.07 (.37) | −1.73 (.55); −.18 (.56) | −1.17 (.42); −.41 (.49) | −.65 (.30); −.06 (.37) | .46 (.29)?; .68 (.33) | .27 (.25)?; .67 (.30) | .02 (.17); .26 (.14) |
| Percent families below low income level (×100) | — ; −1.61 (.30) | — ; −.84 (.24) | .65 (.20) ; — | −1.80 (.32) ; — | −.71 (.25) ; — | −.50 (.19) ; — | .24 (.19) ; — | .37 (.15) ; — | .21 (.09) ; — |
| **Additional controls** | | | | | | | | | |
| Log average hourly earnings in manufacturing | ✓ | ✓ | ✓ | ✓ | ✓ | ✓ | ✓ | ✓ | ✓ |
| AFDC recipients/population | ✓ | ✓ | ✓ | ✓ | ✓ | ✓ | ✓ | ✓ | ✓ |
| Dummy for state minimum wage | ✓ | ✓ | ✓ | ✓ | ✓ | ✓ | ✓ | ✓ | ✓ |
| Log of city size | ✓ | ✓ | ✓ | ✓ | ✓ | ✓ | ✓ | ✓ | ✓ |
| Percent black | ✓ | ✓ | ✓ | ✓ | ✓ | ✓ | ✓ | ✓ | ✓ |
| Percent in school | ✓ | ✓ | ✓ | ✓ | ✓ | ✓ | ✓ | ✓ | ✓ |
| Region dummies | 8 | 8 | 8 | 8 | 8 | 8 | 8 | 8 | 8 |
| Intercept | ✓ | ✓ | ✓ | ✓ | ✓ | ✓ | ✓ | ✓ | ✓ |
| **Summary statistic** | | | | | | | | | |
| $R^2$ | .71; .78 | .77; .80 | .84; .82 | .69; .77 | .76; .78 | .80; .82 | .62; .63 | .72; .71 | .85; .86 |

employment/population, labor force participation, and unemployment rates for the two groups separately. Accordingly, table 5.2 presents regressions in which the dependent variables relate solely to either out-of-school or in-school youths. The independent variables are identical to those used in table 5.1, except that the percentage of youths in school is deleted as an explanatory factor.

While selected coefficients differ, the results for the out-of-school and in-school youths are qualitatively similar, suggesting roughly comparable market processes at work. The ratio of young men to all men obtains negative coefficients on the employment and participation rates of all groups save 18–19 year olds out of school. As a set, the demand side variables obtain generally comparable regression coefficients, though particular variables have different effects. One noticeable difference is that the rate of unemployment of men 30–40 tends to have larger coefficients in the regressions for out-of-school than in-school youths, which runs counter to the notion that the latter are more "marginal." A similar result was obtained by Bowen and Finegan who explained it in terms of the effect of unemployment on the percentage in school and the composition of that group (Bowen and Finegan 1969, pp. 423–31). Specifically, they show that the greater response of the out-of-school group can be explained by the hypothesis that persons who leave school in response to better job opportunities have higher labor force activity rates than the "original" members of the out-of-school group. The same explanation may account for the effect here as well. Note, however, that one demand variable, growth of personal income, has a larger impact on the in-school than the out-of-school group.

## 5.5   The Effect of the Market on Those Youths in School

The preceding discussion naturally raises the question of the impact of our demand and supply variables on those youths in school.

Because the Census enumerates college students by their place of college residence (whose labor market conditions presumably do not influence enrollment decisions), this important question can be analyzed with published Census data only for 16–17 year olds who are unlikely to be in college. For that group, the labor market variables obtain reasonable coefficients: a larger relative number of young persons and higher average hourly earnings in the area (interpreted as reflecting the negative of the impact of the minimum wage, as discussed on page 120) raised the proportion in school while a faster rate of growth of personal income, a favorable industry mix, a larger rate of male unemployment and a larger proportion of homes with incomes below the poverty line reduce the proportion in school, as shown in table 5.3.

**Table 5.2** Regression Coefficients and Standard Errors for the Effect of Explanatory Factors on the Labor Market Position of Out-of-school and In-school Young Men, 1970

| | Out-of-school | | | | | | | | | In-school | | | | | | | | |
|---|---|---|---|---|---|---|---|---|---|---|---|---|---|---|---|---|---|---|
| | Employment ratio | | | Labor force Participation rate | | | Unemployment rate | | | Employment ratio | | | Labor force Participation rate | | | Unemployment rate | | |
| | 16-17 | 18-19 | 20-24 | 16-17 | 18-19 | 20-24 | 16-17 | 18-19 | 20-24 | 16-17 | 18-19 | 20-24 | 16-17 | 18-19 | 20-24 | 16-17 | 18-19 | 20-24 |
| Means and standard deviations | .438 (.094) | .700 (.074) | .830 (.051) | .555 (.092) | .804 (.054) | .895 (.034) | .214 (.070) | .131 (.053) | .073 (.032) | .310 (.071) | .429 (.074) | .532 (.083) | .347 (.075) | .464 (.079) | .559 (.087) | .115 (.034) | .087 (.030) | .055 (.022) |
| **Variables** | | | | | | | | | | | | | | | | | | |
| Prime-age male | -2.23 (1.00) | -1.99 (.57) | -2.22 (.35) | -1.42 (1.07) | -.69 (.47) | -.62 (.29) | 1.88 (.73) | 1.66 (.42) | 1.81 (.20) | -.93 (.46) | -.45 (.58) | -1.35 (.88) | -1.04 (.52) | -.14 (.63) | -.74 (.91) | .05 (.31) | .79 (.26) | 1.35 (.17) |
| Unemployment rate | -.22 | .01 | .12 (.24) | .18 | -.18 | -.01 (.20) | .84 (.49) | -.21 (.29) | -.16 (.13) | .37 (.33) | 1.41 (.40) | 1.37 (.60) | .26 (.35) | 1.29 (.43) | 1.36 (.62) | -.29 (.20) | -.39 (.18) | -.16 (.11) |
| Percent annual growth | .12 | .18 | -.01 | .35 | .48 | .27 | -.05 | -.12 | -.09 | .14 (.08) | .30 (.15) | .26 (.28) | .17 (.08) | .29 (.16) | .26 (.29) | .04 (.05) | -.07 (.07) | -.06 (.05) |
| Personal income (×100) | .35 (.17) | .54 (.14) | .33 (.11) | .35 (.17) | .48 (.12) | -.38 (.09) | -.05 (.12) | -.11 (.11) | -.05 (.06) | -.95 (.70) | -2.80 (.63) | -1.34 (.40) | -.48 (.76) | -2.77 (.68) | -1.33 (.41) | 1.45 (.44) | .36 (.28) | -.05 (.07) |
| Index of industrial mix | .32 (.16) | .54 (.14) | .33 (.11) | -.58 (1.55) | .87 (.57) | -.38 (.13) | 2.81 (.12) | -.17 (.11) | -.05 (.09) | -.25 (.51) | -.41 (.61) | .07 (.93) | -.02 (.55) | -.35 (.66) | -.04 (.96) | .47 (.44) | .29 (.28) | -.12 (.05) |
| Relative number of young people | -1.92 (1.45) | .88 (.57) | -.32 (.16) | -.58 (1.55) | .87 (.57) | -.38 (.13) | 2.81 (.42) | -.17 (.45) | -.05 (.09) | 1.45 (.44) | 1.45 (.44) | -1.34 (.40) | -1.85 (.30) | -.70 (.34) | -.67 (.51) | .47 (.44) | .36 (.28) | .17 (.07) |
| Percent homes headed by females (×100) | -2.00 (1.06) | -.84 (.60) | .01 (.36) | -1.71 (1.13) | -.57 (.49) | .00 (.31) | .36 (.77) | .36 (.44) | .00 (.21) | -.25 (.51) | -.41 (.61) | .07 (.93) | -.02 (.55) | -.35 (.66) | -.04 (.96) | .47 (.32) | .29 (.27) | -.12 (.17) |
| Percent families below low income level | -.36 (.58) | -.92 (.30) | -.52 (.19) | -.60 (.62) | -.70 (.25) | -.39 (.16) | .07 (.42) | .42 (.22) | .17 (.11) | -1.66 (.28) | -.71 (.32) | -.72 (.49) | -1.85 (.30) | -.70 (.34) | -.67 (.51) | .23 (.18) | .26 (.14) | .17 (.09) |
| **Additional controls** | | | | | | | | | | | | | | | | | | |
| Log average hourly earnings in manufacturing | √ | √ | √ | √ | √ | √ | √ | √ | √ | √ | √ | √ | √ | √ | √ | √ | √ | √ |
| AFDC recipients population | √ | √ | √ | √ | √ | √ | √ | √ | √ | √ | √ | √ | √ | √ | √ | √ | √ | √ |
| Dummy for state minimum wage | √ | √ | √ | √ | √ | √ | √ | √ | √ | √ | √ | √ | √ | √ | √ | √ | √ | √ |
| Log of city size | √ | √ | √ | √ | √ | √ | √ | √ | √ | √ | √ | √ | √ | √ | √ | √ | √ | √ |
| Percent black | √ | √ | √ | √ | √ | √ | √ | √ | √ | √ | √ | √ | √ | √ | √ | √ | √ | √ |
| Percent in school | √ | √ | √ | √ | √ | √ | √ | √ | √ | √ | √ | √ | √ | √ | √ | √ | √ | √ |
| Region dummies | 8 | 8 | 8 | 8 | 8 | 8 | 8 | 8 | 8 | 8 | 8 | 8 | 8 | 8 | 8 | 8 | 8 | 8 |
| Intercept | √ | √ | √ | √ | √ | √ | √ | √ | √ | √ | √ | √ | √ | √ | √ | √ | √ | √ |
| **Summary statistic** | | | | | | | | | | | | | | | | | | |

Table 5.3          **Estimated Effect of Variables on Percentage
in School, 16–17 Year Olds**[a]

|  | Coefficient | Standard Error |
|---|---|---|
| Relative number of young | 1.25 | .40 |
| Average hourly earnings | .04 | .02 |
| Growth of personal income | − .37 | .19 |
| Industry mix | − .08 | .04 |
| Percentage with incomes below poverty line | − .56 | .20 |
| Unemployment of 30–34 year old males | .29 | .28 |

[a]Includes all control variables used in table 5.2.

These results suggest that the proportion of young persons who drop out of school rises when the labor market is stronger. For 18–19 and 20–24 year olds, comparable regressions tell a similar story, with even larger coefficients on the labor market variables but, as noted, with less clear causal connections. I conclude that the same factors that influence the labor market for youths as a whole have roughly comparable effects on those out of school and those in school, which implies that inferences based on the entire youth population are reasonably likely to hold for either subgroup, and may also possibly affect the division between the two groups.[9]

## 5.6   Work Activity of Young Women

To see whether the labor market position of young women is influenced by the same factors that determine the position of young men, the employment to population rate, labor participation rate, and rate of unemployment of women age 16–17, 18–19, and 20–24 are regressed on essentially the same variables as in table 5.1 and 5.2, with two exceptions: the relative number of young persons is measured by the ratio of the number of young women in each group (rather than the number of young men) to the number of civilian men 16 and over, and the index of industrial mix is based on the ratio of young women to all workers in industry in the U.S. (rather than by the ratio of young men to all workers). For purposes of comparison, as well as issues of endogenity of family status, I have excluded measures of marital status from the calculations.

Table 5.4 summarized the results of the regressions for young women and presents comparable information from the regression for young men. The regressions reveal considerable similarities between the sexes in the labor market effects of most variables (the most noticeable exception being the relative number of young persons, which does not have as large an impact on 16–17 and 18–19 year old women as it does on 16–17 and 18–19 year old men). Most noticeably, the prime-age male unemployment rate has as sizable an impact on the employment/population, labor force participation, and unemployment rates of women as on those for

**Table 5.4**     Comparison of the Effects of Major Economic Variables on the Economic Position of Young Men and Women

| | Employment ratio | | Labor force participation rate | | Unemployment rate | |
|---|---|---|---|---|---|---|
| | Male | Female | Male | Female | Male | Female |
| **16–17** | | | | | | |
| Relative number | −.82 | −.17 | −.26 | −.07 | 1.52 | .26 |
| of young people | (.75) | (.79) | (.80) | (.85) | (.47) | (.58) |
| Prime-age male | −1.01 | −1.38 | −1.04 | −1.32 | .20 | .74 |
| unemployment rate | (.50) | (.53) | (.53) | (.57) | (.31) | (.39) |
| Percent growth of | .23 | .37 | .18 | .35 | −.14 | −.24 |
| personal income | (.34) | (.36) | (.36) | (.39) | (.21) | (.26) |
| Index of | .14 | .14 | .18 | .17 | .04 | .01 |
| industrial mix | (.08) | (.06) | (.08) | (.07) | (.05) | (.05) |
| Percent of female- | −.42 | −.10 | −.18 | −.07 | .46 | −.14 |
| headed households | (.52) | (.57) | (.56) | (.62) | (.33) | (.42) |
| Percent families below | −1.61 | −1.30 | −1.80 | −1.43 | .24 | .96 |
| low-income level | (.30) | (.33) | (.32) | (.35) | (.19) | (.24) |
| $R^2$ | .78 | .78 | .77 | .77 | .63 | .70 |
| **18–19** | | | | | | |
| Relative number | −1.36 | −.70 | −1.60 | −1.18 | −.19 | −.64 |
| of young people | (.59) | (.64) | (.62) | (.65) | (.38) | (.40) |
| Prime-age male | −1.06 | −.88 | −.38 | −.34 | 1.11 | 1.04 |
| unemployment rate | (.45) | (.50) | (.47) | (.51) | (.28) | (.31) |
| Percent growth of | .77 | .54 | .68 | .42 | −.26 | −.39 |
| personal income | (.31) | (.34) | (.32) | (.34) | (.20) | (.21) |
| Index of | .38 | .26 | .39 | .22 | −.06 | −.12 |
| industrial mix | (.12) | (.11) | (.12) | (.11) | (.07) | (.07) |
| Percent of female- | −.53 | .35 | −.41 | .52 | −.07 | −.16 |
| headed households | (.47) | (.54) | (.49) | (.54) | (.15) | (.17) |
| Percent families below | −.84 | −1.62 | −.71 | −1.51 | .27 | .02 |
| low-income level | (.24) | (.28) | (.25) | (.28) | (.30) | (.34) |
| $R^2$ | .80 | .81 | .78 | .79 | .72 | .76 |
| **20–24** | | | | | | |
| Relative number | −.09 | .16 | −.33 | .19 | −.29 | .05 |
| of young people | (.24) | (.21) | (.24) | (.19) | (.11) | (.09) |
| Prime-age male | −1.88 | −1.10 | −.55 | −.74 | 1.66 | .70 |
| unemployment rate | (.35) | (.42) | (.35) | (.39) | (.16) | (.18) |
| Percent growth of | .25 | .27 | .23 | .15 | −.07 | −.24 |
| personal income | (.24) | (.29) | (.24) | (.27) | (.11) | (.12) |
| Index of | .27 | .29 | .26 | .17 | .04 | −.21 |
| industrial mix | (.11) | (.14) | (.11) | (.13) | (.05) | (.06) |
| Percent of female- | −.07 | .86 | −.06 | .93 | .02 | .00 |
| headed households | (.37) | (.45) | (.37) | (.42) | (.17) | (.20) |
| Percent families below | −.65 | −1.55 | −.50 | −1.52 | .21 | .28 |
| low-income level | (.20) | (.23) | (.19) | (.22) | (.09) | (.10) |
| $R^2$ | .84 | .77 | .82 | .74 | .86 | .77 |

men. The growth of personal income, the index of individual mix, and the proportion of families below low-income level also have roughly comparable effects, while the proportion of one-parent/female homes has a somewhat smaller effect on the employment of 16–17 year old women than on 16–17 year old men, but comparable effects in the other age groups.

Although there are differences, the overall impression given by the table is that similar area factors are associated with geographic variation in the employment of young women as of young men.

### 5.6   Relevance to Changes over Time

The question naturally arises as to the relevance of the cross-sectional calculations to observed changes in youth labor force activity over time. Are the estimated effects of variables in the cross-section consistent with comparable estimates from time series data? Do the estimates help explain observed trends in the youth labor market?

To compare the effect of variables in cross-section and time series data, it is best to estimate their coefficients with identical controls. Since the time series has fewer observations and less information about some variables, a relatively simple set of comparable regressions was estimated for the SMSA data set and the time series. The employment to population rate, labor force participation rate, and rate of unemployment of young male workers aged 16–17, and 18–19, and 20–24 were regressed on three explanatory variables: the rate of total male unemployment (used because of differences in the age grouping in our SMSA and time series data sets); the ratio of the number of young men in each age group relative to the number of men 16 and over; and measures of the minimum wage, the inverse of the ln average earnings in private industry in the cross-section data and ln of the federal minimum divided by average earnings in private industry in the time series. The cross-section data are taken from the basic SMSA data set. The sources of the time series data are described in the data appendix. Because of the danger of mistaking similar trends in time series variables for causal relations, the time series regressions are estimated in two different specifications: without a time trend variable and with a trend variable included.

Table 5.5 presents the estimated coefficients from the time series and cross-SMSA regressions. While there are some differences in the estimated effect of variables, the general pattern is of broad similarity in the regression coefficients. On the demand side, the unemployment rate of men reduces the employment to population ratio and tends to raise the unemployment rate of all groups by similar magnitudes and has comparable effects on the labor force participation of 16–17 year olds (though not on that of 18–19 and 20–24 year olds). On the supply side, the relative

**Table 5.5**  Comparison of the Estimated Effect of Selected Variables on Youth Work Activity, 1948–77; Time Series Regressions vs. Cross-SMSA Regressions

| Variable | 16–17 year olds | | | 18–19 year olds | | | 20–24 year olds | | |
|---|---|---|---|---|---|---|---|---|---|
| | Cross-SMSA | time series | | Cross-SMSA | time series | | Cross-SMSA | time series | |
| **(A) Employment to population rate** | | | | | | | | | |
| Male unemployment rate | -2.25 (.60) | -2.05 (.36) | -2.44 (.36) | -2.28 (.52) | -1.94 (.51) | -1.72 (.54) | -3.41 (.42) | -1.49 (.32) | -1.51 (.25) |
| Rel. no. of young persons | -3.57 (.83) | -3.33 (.48) | -6.09 (1.12) | -3.38 (.58) | -3.18 (.64) | -1.27 (1.83) | -1.66 (.21) | -.94 (.20) | -.20 (.24) |
| "Minimum wage" proxy[1] | -.12 (.04) | -.09 (.03) | -.11 (.03) | -.15 (.04) | -.14 (.04) | -.10 (.05) | -.11 (.03) | -.01 (.03) | .06 (.03) |
| Time trend | — | — | .26 (.10) | — | — | -.18 (.17) | — | — | -.19 (.05) |
| $R^2$ | .25 | .75 | .80 | .33 | .60 | .62 | .49 | .65 | .79 |
| **(B) Labor force participation rate** | | | | | | | | | |
| Male unemployment rate | -2.03 (.63) | -1.07 (.46) | -1.69 (.41) | -1.08 (.53) | .13 (.51) | .21 (.55) | -1.70 (.41) | .56 (.24) | .55 (.22) |
| Rel. no. of young persons | -3.10 (.89) | -1.78 (.60) | -6.19 (1.28) | -3.43 (.59) | -2.18 (.64) | -1.45 (1.85) | -1.72 (.21) | -.61 (.15) | -.15 (.20) |

| | | | | | | | | | |
|---|---|---|---|---|---|---|---|---|---|
| "Minimum wage" proxy[1] | −.15 (.05) | −.09 (.04) | −.12 (.03) | −.18 (.04) | −.13 (.04) | −.12 (.05) | −.12 (.03) | .00 (.02) | .04 (.02) |
| Time trend | — | — | .41 (.11) | — | — | −.07 (.17) | — | — | −.11 (.04) |
| $R^2$ | .21 | .42 | .63 | .33 | .44 | .44 | .42 | .49 | .62 |

(C) Unemployment rate

| | | | | | | | | | |
|---|---|---|---|---|---|---|---|---|---|
| Male unemployment rate | 1.24 (.26) | 2.32 (.18) | 2.07 (.16) | 2.20 (.26) | 2.90 (.19) | 2.70 (.18) | 2.28 (.15) | 2.34 (.16) | 2.35 (.12) |
| Rel. no. of young persons | 2.41 (.37) | 3.65 (.24) | 1.88 (.49) | .48 (.29) | 1.72 (.24) | −.05 (.60) | .06 (.08) | .45 (.10) | .08 (.12) |
| "Minimum wage" proxy[1] | −.03 (.02) | .02 (.01) | .01 (.01) | −.02 (.02) | .03 (.02) | .00 (.02) | .00 (.01) | .01 (.01) | −.02 (.01) |
| Time trend | — | — | .17 (.04) | — | — | .17 (.04) | — | — | .09 (.02) |
| $R^2$ | .41 | .93 | .96 | .44 | .90 | .93 | .70 | .90 | .94 |

[1]The minimum wage variable in the cross-SMSA data set is the $ln$ of the inverse of average hourly earnings in the area. The minimum wage variable in the time series data set is the $ln$ of the ratio of the federal minimum to average hourly earnings.

SOURCE: Cross-SMSA figures based on regressions using 114 SMSA data set. Time series figures based on data described in data appendix.

number of young persons has a roughly similar qualitative impact on employment to population, labor participation and unemployment rates in the time series when trend is excluded as in the cross-section. However, inclusion of trend greatly alters the magnitude of the coefficient, a result that highlights the problem of inferring the effect of demographic factors from the time series data. The third explanatory factor, the minimum wage variable, obtains negative coefficients of comparable magnitude in the time series and cross-section regressions for 16–17 and 18–19 year olds, when it has significant effects on the employment to population and labor force participation rates, but not on the unemployment rate. The minimum wage does, however, obtain different coefficients for the 20–24 year olds in the cross-section and time series. Overall, despite these and other differences noted above, the coefficients from the two sets of regressions are roughly consistent, enhancing the believability of each.

While the cross-section and time series regressions yield roughly similar estimates, it is important to note that neither analysis explains developments in the youth labor market in the 1970s. As table 5.6 shows, from 1969 to 1977 the employment/population ratio of 16–17 year olds changed modestly while their labor force participation and unemployment rates rose. There was a marked divergence from 1969 to 1977 between actual changes in youth work activity and the changes predicted by either the cross-section or time series models. Because the adult male unemployment rate increased sharply while the relative number of young persons either changed only slightly (teenagers) or increased (20–24 year old workers), the cross section and time series regressions predict a marked decline in the employment/population and labor participation rates and a sizable increase in unemployment rates. In fact, employment/population ratios changed unevenly while labor participation rates rose sharply so that only the unemployment rates followed the predicted pattern. Despite concern over the inability of the labor market to generate jobs for youths, youth work activity, for reasons that are unclear, did not decline or decreased only slightly in the 1970s, despite adverse cyclical and other developments. While our time series and cross-section regressions yield comparable results, neither adequately tracks the performance of the youth market in the 1970s.[10]

## 5.7    The Impact of Supply and Demand Forces

The model presented in equations (1)–(3) suggested that the youth employment problem could be attributed, in part, to shifts in supply and demand schedules (coupled with sluggish wage adjustments). As the importance of supply and demand factors in the youth market problem has been subject to considerable debate, and since these factors imply

**Table 5.6**   Predicted and Actual Changes in Youth Work Activity, 1969–77

| | Actual value | | Actual change | Predicted changes, 1969–77 | | |
|---|---|---|---|---|---|---|
| | 1969 | 1977 | 1969–1977 | Using cross-section model | Using time series model without trend | Using time series model with trend |
| **Explanatory factor** | | | | | | |
| Rate of unemployment of adult men | .015 | .035 | .020 | | | |
| Relative no. of young persons | | | | | | |
|   16–17 year olds | .059 | .057 | −.002 | | | |
|   18–19 year olds | .051 | .053 | .002 | | | |
|   20–24 year olds | .101 | .124 | .023 | | | |
| Ln (Minimum wage/average wage) | −.734 | −.821 | −.087 | | | |
| Trend | 22 | 30 | 8 | | | |
| **Dependent variables** | | | | | | |
| Employment/population | | | | | | |
|   16–17 year olds | 40.8 | 40.5 | −.3 | −2.7 | −2.5 | −.04 |
|   18–19 year olds | 59.7 | 61.2 | 1.5 | −3.9 | −3.7 | −4.5 |
|   20–24 year olds | 78.6 | 76.5 | −2.1 | −9.7 | −5.1 | −5.4 |
| Labor force participation rate | | | | | | |
|   16–17 year olds | 47.3 | 50.3 | 3.0 | −2.1 | −0.9 | 2.4 |
|   18–19 year olds | 65.9 | 72.5 | 6.6 | −1.3 | 0.7 | 0.4 |
|   20–24 year olds | 82.8 | 85.7 | 2.9 | −6.3 | −0.3 | −0.4 |
| Unemployment rate | | | | | | |
|   16–17 year olds | 13.8 | 19.5 | 5.7 | 2.3 | 3.6 | 4.9 |
|   18–19 year olds | 9.4 | 15.6 | 6.2 | 4.7 | 6.0 | 6.8 |
|   20–24 year olds | 5.1 | 10.7 | 5.6 | 4.7 | 5.6 | 5.8 |

different policies remedies, it is important to determine the extent to which observed differences in youth joblessness across SMSAs are attributable to supply as opposed to demand factors.

One way of gauging the relative importance of factors is to examine the extent to which youth labor force activity is altered by changes in the explanatory factors. Table 5.7 presents such an analysis. It records the beta weights (regression coefficients adjusted to measure the effect of a standard deviation change in an independent variable on a standard deviation of the dependent variable). It also presents sums of the weights according to our classification of variables into demand and supply shift factors.

The columns labeled (a) are based on calculations which exclude the percentage of families below the poverty line from the analysis, while those labeled (b) include that variable. In the (a) calculations supply factors tend to be more important than demand factors for 16–17 year olds, about equally as important as demand for 18–19 year olds, and less important for 20–24 year olds. In the (b) calculations, the percentage of families below the poverty line dominates the regressions for the younger age groups, so that its inclusion as a demand or supply variable is critical in determining the relative importance of the two sets of factors. Even with the percentage below poverty variable, however, demand factors continue to be dominant factor for 20–24 year olds and remain more important than supply factors for 18–19 year olds as well. Perhaps the safest conclusion is that supply or background factors are relatively more important determinants of the position of teenagers while demand factors are more important for those in their early twenties.

## 5.8   Individual Variation

The analysis thus far has treated area data which, while well-suited for investigating the effects of broad market factors in the position of youths, provide only weak information on individual differences in youth participation or unemployment. To obtain a better understanding of the incidence of youth labor market problems among individuals and of the social characteristics of the individuals lacking employment, as well as to be able to differentiate the effect of area or communal factors from individual characteristics, it is necessary to analyze data on individuals rather than on SMSAs.

The Survey of Income and Education, conducted in the spring of 1976, provides an especially valuable sample for such an investigation. The survey contains about three times as many respondents as the standard Current Population Survey monthly samples and a variety of information on family background that is unavailable in most CPS months. Of particular importance, the SIE has data on wages and hours worked over a

**Table 5.7    Effect of One Standard Deviation Change in Supply and Demand Forces on Young Male Employment and Unemployment Rates**

| | Employment rate | | | | | | Unemployment rate | | | | | |
|---|---|---|---|---|---|---|---|---|---|---|---|---|
| | 16–17 year olds | | 18–19 year olds | | 20–24 year olds | | 16–17 year olds | | 18–19 year olds | | 20–24 year olds | |
| Measure of impact | (a) | (b) | (a) | (b) | (a) | (b) | (a) | (b) | (a) | (b) | (a) | (b) |
| Demand (sum of variables) | .52 | .32 | .67 | .56 | .61 | .55 | −.11 | −.05 | −.56 | −.49 | −.71 | −.68 |
| Prime-age male unemployment rate | (.22) | (.15) | (.20) | (.16) | (.35) | (.32) | (−.08) | (−.06) | (−.34) | (−.32) | (−.61) | (−.60) |
| Percent growth personal income | (.13) | (.05) | (.23) | (.17) | (.10) | (.06) | (−.09) | (−.06) | (−.15) | (−.11) | (−.06) | (−.03) |
| Index of industrial mix | (.17) | (.12) | (.24) | (.23) | (.16) | (.17) | (.06) | (.07) | (−.07) | (−.06) | (−.04) | (.05) |
| Supply (sum of variables) | −.72 | −.19 | −.53 | −.23 | −.22 | .00 | .54 | .37 | .28 | .07 | −.04 | −.20 |
| Relative no. of young people | (−.23) | (−.08) | (−.19) | (−.17) | (−.02) | (−.03) | (.33) | (.29) | (−.03) | (−.04) | (−.19) | (−.18) |
| AFDC recipients/pop. | (.00) | (.10) | (.05) | (.11) | (.07) | (.13) | (.02) | (−.02) | (.00) | (−.04) | (−.06) | (−.11) |
| Percent female-headed homes | (−.47) | (−.11) | (−.39) | (−.14) | (−.25) | (−.02) | (.36) | (.24) | (.33) | (.13) | (.16) | (.03) |
| Percent black | (−.02) | (−.10) | (.01) | (−.03) | (.02) | (−.08) | (−.17) | (−.14) | (−.02) | (.02) | (.05) | (.03) |
| Percent below poverty line | −.86 | | −.47 | | −.41 | | .27 | | .39 | | .23 | |

SOURCE:  Calculated from regressions, as in table 5.1, with percentage below poverty line excluded from column (a) and included in column (b) regressions. All calculations include control variables used in table 5.1 but not listed as reflecting demand or supply factors, i.e., region dummies.

year, as well as on employment status, which permits comparison of the effect of variables on rates of pay as opposed to the amount of work activity.

The SIE data are examined in two stages. First, a linear probability model is fit linking dichotomous dummy variables for employment and for unemployment in spring 1976 to various characteristics of the individual and his or her family. Since the linear model is additive, the effect of variables on the probability of labor force participation can be obtained by adding the coefficients on employment and unemployment. While the linear model is not entirely appropriate for analysis of 0–1 variables, the advantage of a more complex curvilinear form such as the logistic is likely to be modest. Second, ln earnings equations are estimated linking hourly and annual earnings in 1975 to the same set of measures of individual characteristics. The earnings equations provide information on the wage side of the youth labor market. Comparison of the effect of variables on hourly earnings and on the probability of employment or on annual earnings (which depends critically on the probability of employment over the year) can cast considerable light on the extent to which youth labor market problems are associated with joblessness as opposed to, or in conjunction with, low rates of pay.

The analysis treats separately young male workers 16–17, 18–19, and 20–24 and examines the impact of the following characteristics of individuals on their families:

—race, measured by a dichotomous variable ( = 1 when the individual is black);

—receipt of welfare by the household of residence, a dichotomous variable which takes the value 1 if the family obtained welfare in 1975;

—receipt of food stamps, a dichotomous variable which takes the value 1 if the family obtained food stamps in 1975;

—residence in public housing, a dichotomous variable which takes the value of 1 if the family was living in public housing when surveyed;

—residence in a one-parent/female home, a dichotomous variable which takes the value 1 if the individual's parental family contained a female head of household;

—years of education;

—school activity status, a dichotomous variable which takes the value 1 if the person's major activity at the time of the survey was attending school;

—other household income, a continuous measure of total family income in 1975 minus the individual's earnings in 1975;

—region of residence, consisting of seven dummy variables for region;

—urban status, a dichotomous variable which takes the value 1 if a person lived in an urban area in 1976;

—household income below the poverty line, a 0–1 variable which takes the value of 1 if the household income in 1975 fell below the official poverty line.

Since some of the respondents are no longer living with their parents or other adults, the measures of family background do not always relate to the position of the home in which they were brought up: for 16–17 and 18–19 year olds, of whom only 0.6% and 8% reside outside the home of their parent or other adult, the problem is not severe; for 20–24 year olds about half of whom are themselves heads of households and for many of those out of school, however, the family variables relate to parental homes for a significant proportion and to homes headed by the individual for a significant proportion, which confuses the interpretation. To deal with this problem, a dummy variable for those who are themselves heads of households was included in all of the calculations, and the variable was interacted with other family income. In addition, for 20–24 year olds, separate calculations for those residing in homes headed by others were estimated. The results are sufficiently similar to those reported in the table as to suggest that the head of household dummy variable suffices to deal with the problem.

To help understand the enormous impact of the percentage of impoverished families in the SMSA calculations earlier, we also examine a 0–1 dummy variable for whether the individual resides in a poverty tract, with poverty tract defined by the Census as an area with a poverty rate greater than or equal to 20%.

Not surprisingly, the calculations show that black youths, those with fewer years of schooling, and those whose major activity is school have excessively low rates of employment. The measures of family status—being in a female-headed home, family receipt of welfare or food stamps, residence in public housing, the income of the household exclusive of the young person himself, and whether the family is or is not below the poverty line—also have some effect, with a general pattern that those from more disadvantaged backgrounds have lower probabilities of employment and higher probabilities of unemployment than those from more advantaged backgrounds. The most noticeable exception to this generalization is that other household income is accorded little or no impact on employment or unemployment in the bulk of the calculations. Even with the poverty line variable omitted (not reported in table 5.8), household income appears to be essentially unrelated to labor market activity. The modest impact of being from a family below the poverty line suggests that any family income-unemployment of youth relation is decidedly nonlinear. Even so, the regressions suggest youth joblessness is concentrated among persons from disadvantaged homes and, with all other characteristics fixed, among blacks.

**Table 5.8  Linear Probability of Estimates of Determinants of the Employment of Young Men, 1976**

| Measure of background status | All 16-17 year olds | | | All 18-19 year olds | | | Out of school[a] 18-19 year olds | | | All 20-24 year olds | | | Out of school 20-24 year olds | | |
|---|---|---|---|---|---|---|---|---|---|---|---|---|---|---|---|
| | means | empl. | unemp. | means | empl. | unemp. | means | empl. | unemp. | means | empl. | unemp. | means | empl. | unemp. |
| **Individual status** | | | | | | | | | | | | | | | |
| black | .10 | −.21 | .07 | .09 | −.21 | .11 | .09 | −.21 | .13 | .08 | −.12 | .05 | .08 | −.10 | .05 |
| | | (.02) | (.01) | | (.02) | (.01) | | (.03) | (.02) | | (.01) | (.01) | | (.01) | (.01) |
| years of schooling | 10.0 | .045 | −.007 | 11.6 | .017 | −.01 | 11.1 | .034 | −.02 | 12.8 | .012 | −.005 | 12.2 | .014 | −.007 |
| | | (.005) | (.003) | | (.003) | (.002) | | (.005) | (.004) | | (.001) | (.001) | | (.002) | (.001) |
| major activity is in school | .67 | −.20 | −.10 | .36 | −.34 | −.08 | .00 | — | — | .00 | −.43 | −.05 | .00 | — | — |
| | | (.01) | (.01) | | (.01) | (.01) | | | | | (.01) | (.01) | | | |
| **Family status** | | | | | | | | | | | | | | | |
| female-headed home | .13 | −.03 | .01 | .11 | −.05 | .02 | .12 | −.03 | .02 | .06 | −.05 | .05 | .06 | −.05 | .05 |
| | | (.02) | (.01) | | (.02) | (.01) | | (.03) | (.02) | | (.01) | (.01) | | (.01) | (.01) |
| family receives welfare | .08 | −.05 | .08 | .06 | −.02 | −.01 | .08 | −.04 | −.00 | .04 | −.08 | .06 | .05 | −.08 | .06 |
| | | (.02) | (.01) | | (.02) | (.02) | | (.03) | (.03) | | (.02) | (.01) | | (.02) | (.01) |
| food stamps | .12 | −.03 | .01 | .10 | −.07 | .07 | .14 | −.08 | .10 | .10 | −.04 | .08 | .12 | −.06 | .07 |
| | | (.02) | (.01) | | (.02) | (.01) | | (.03) | (.02) | | (.01) | (.01) | | (.01) | (.01) |
| public housing | .02 | −.02 | .07 | .02 | −.11 | .09 | .02 | −.16 | .11 | .02 | −.11 | .00 | .02 | −.12 | −.00 |
| | | (.04) | (.02) | | (.03) | (.02) | | (.05) | (.04) | | (.02) | (.02) | | (.02) | (.02) |
| other family income (in thousands of $) | $18.90 | .046 | −.001 | 17.437 | −.001 | −.001 | 13.500 | .000 | −.001 | 11.973 | −.001 | .002 | 9.793 | −.001 | −.001 |
| | | (.026) | (.003) | | (.0004) | (.003) | | (.001) | (.0007) | | (.0003) | (.0007) | | (.005) | (.0004) |
| family below poverty line | .11 | −.05 | −.02 | .11 | −.07 | .01 | .14 | −.04 | .006 | .09 | −.09 | .03 | .08 | −.08 | .04 |
| | | (.02) | (.01) | | (.02) | (.01) | | (.02) | (.02) | | (.01) | (.01) | | (.01) | (.01) |
| Geographic status in poverty tract | .17 | −.02 | −.04 | .17 | −.03 | .01 | .19 | .01 | .01 | .14 | .01 | .00 | .19 | .03 | −.00 |
| | | (.01) | (.05) | | (.01) | (.01) | | (.02) | (.02) | | (.01) | (.01) | | (.01) | (.01) |

Other controls

| | | | | | | | | | |
|---|---|---|---|---|---|---|---|---|---|
| age | √ | √ | √ | √ | √ | √ | √ | √ | √ | √ |
| head of household | √ | √ | √ | √ | √ | √ | √ | √ | √ | √ |
| interaction: head of household and other household income | | | | | | | | | | |
| region | √ 8 | √ 8 | √ 8 | √ 8 | √ 8 | √ 8 | √ 8 | √ 8 | √ 8 | √ 8 |
| urban | √ | √ | √ | √ | √ | √ | √ | √ | √ | √ |
| subsidized rent | √ | √ | √ | √ | √ | √ | √ | √ | √ | √ |

Summary statistics

| | | | | | | | | | | |
|---|---|---|---|---|---|---|---|---|---|---|
| $R^2$ | .12 | .05 | .17 | .23 | .09 | .07 | .17 | .05 | .07 | .05 |
| n | 9297 | 9297 | 8476 | 8476 | 3185 | 3185 | 18,395 | 18,395 | 12,513 | 12,513 |

[a]The numbers in this column represent a smaller fraction of the youths than the proportion whose major activity is "in school." This is because a stricter definition of schooling is used. Persons out of school are *not* enrolled at all. Since some persons whose major activity is reported as other than being in school are enrolled, the numbers in the out-of-school columns represent a smaller fraction of the total than would be obtained from the major activity question.

SOURCE: Survey of Income and Education.

The results with the measure of poverty in the individual's communities of residence—whether or not he resides in a high poverty tract—are mixed. For 16–17 and 18–19 year olds, living in a poverty tract has a noticeable negative effect on employment and some impact on unemployment (to counteract the effect of lowered unemployment among 16–17 year olds). For the other groups, however, there is no strong effect, save for the odd positive impact of being in a poverty area on the employment of out-of-school 20–24 year olds. From these calculations it appears that the results with the poverty variable in tables 5.1 and 5.2 are due largely to individual factors rather than to area factors.

The ln hourly earnings in table 5.9 tell a very different story about the determinants of the wages of the young. First, *being black is not a major depressant of wages*. Among 16–17 year olds, being black is actually associated with higher wages, while in the other age groups blacks are estimated as having only a 3% disadvantage. Second, with the exception of the poverty line variable, the measures of family status also fail to evince the negative effects found in the employment and unemployment regressions. Being in school and years of schooling also have much smaller impacts on wage rates than on employment status. Since being below the poverty line is partially determined by wages, particularly for 20–24 year olds, making its strong effect on wages questionable in terms of the direction of causality,[12] the main conclusion is that the background factors that adversely affect employment changes have much diminished or in some cases opposite effects on wage rates.

Table 5.9 also yields results on residence in a poverty tract which differ greatly from those in table 5.8. In particular, residence in a poverty tract is substantially negatively related to hourly earnings and, with the exception of 16–17 year olds, to annual earnings as well. Since there is little reason a priori to expect residence in a poverty tract to affect individual wages through supply factors, this result suggests that there are substantial problems in such areas with respect to inadequate demand (possibly because of mix of industries).

Since the calculations in table 5.9 are limited to persons who worked and reported earnings in 1975 while those in table 5.8 refer to a larger sample which includes those who did not work, it is possible that some of the differential effects are attributable to differences in the samples. To check this possible bias, as well as to expand the analysis to a more continuous measure of time worked, the log of annual earnings was also regressed on the independent variables in the sample reporting earnings. Differences between the impact of variables on log of hourly and log of annual earnings reflect effects on annual hours worked. As can be seen in table 5.9, these calculations confirm the basic conclusion that rates of pay are largely unaffected or affected differently by the background factors under study than is time worked. Whereas, for example, being black reduces the log of hourly earnings of 18–19 year old blacks by .03 ln points, it reduces the log of annual earnings by .31, implying a .28 reduction in annual hours worked.

The divergent effect of race and background factors on time-worked and rates of earnings per hour (or week) highlights an important aspect of the youth labor market: striking differences between its employment and wage dimensions. The disadvantaged groups that bear the brunt of joblessness obtain roughly similar pay to other youngsters upon receipt of employment. While it may be argued that the concentration of jobless-ness among certain groups, whose pay is the same as that of others, could be alleviated by wage differentials (tying the employment and wage findings together), perhaps the safest conclusion is that the labor market problem for the disadvantaged is largely one of generating jobs. Once employed, blacks and other disadvantaged youths have roughly as high earnings as other young persons.

### 5.9  Summary of Findings

The results of my analysis of geographic and individual differences in youth employment, unemployment, and earnings can be summarized briefly. First, the employment of young workers across areas depends in a reasonably comprehensible way on demand and supply factors, notably the overall level of economic activity, as reflected in rates of unemploy-ment of prime-age men and growth of personal income, the industrial composition of employment, the number of young persons relative to the number of older persons (for teenagers only), and the poverty status of an area. Second, variables that influence employment often have compara-ble effects on labor participation, leading to smaller or even contrary effects on unemployment. Analyses that focus strictly on unemployment rates may, as a result, be highly misleading. Third, the cross-section calculations, while yielding results consistent with comparable time series regressions, do not provide an explanation of youth labor market de-velopments in the 1970s, when employment to population rates did *not* fall and participation rates increased in the face of adverse economic changes. Fourth, the correlates of youth joblessness are *not* the same as the correlates of low wages, with blacks and others from disadvantaged backgrounds having higher incidences of joblessness but obtaining wages similar to those of other workers. Fifth, there is some indication that residence in a poverty tract has an impact on youth earnings that goes beyond the effect of low household income itself.

**Table 5.9**   Regression Coefficient Estimates of the Background Determinants of the Ln of Hourly and Annual Earnings of Young Men, 1975

| Measure of background status | 16-17 year olds | | | | 18-19 year olds | | | | 20-24 year olds | | | |
|---|---|---|---|---|---|---|---|---|---|---|---|---|
| | mean | ln hourly earnings | ln annual earnings | implied ln annual hours worked | mean | ln hourly earnings | ln annual earnings | implied ln annual hours worked | mean | ln hourly earnings | ln annual earnings | implied ln annual hours worked |
| Individual status | | .53 | 6.37 | 5.84 | | .80 | 7.36 | 6.56 | | 1.16 | 8.29 | 7.16 |
| black | .07 | .17 (.04) | −.15 (.06) | −.33 | .07 | −.03 (.04) | −.31 (.05) | −.28 | .07 | −.03 (.02) | −.12 (.03) | −.09 |
| years of schooling | 10.2 | .03 (.01) | .09 (.02) | .06 | 11.7 | .02 (.01) | −.01 (.01) | −.03 | 12.8 | .006 (.002) | −.04 (.01) | −.03 |
| major activity is in school | .66 | −.01 (.02) | −.26 (.03) | −.25 | .34 | −.05 (.02) | −.50 (.03) | −.45 | .13 | −.08 (.01) | −.70 (.02) | −.62 |
| Family status | | | | | | | | | | | | |
| female-headed home | .13 | .08 (.03) | .01 (.05) | −.06 | .10 | .04 (.03) | −.08 (.04) | −.12 | .06 | −.00 (.02) | −.08 (.03) | −.08 |
| family receives welfare | .07 | .05 (.05) | −.12 (.07) | −.17 | .05 | .01 (.04) | −.10 (.06) | −.10 | .04 | −.06 (.03) | −.21 (.04) | −.16 |
| food stamps | .10 | .06 (.04) | .07 (.06) | .01 | .09 | .00 (.03) | −.08 (.05) | −.09 | | −.04 (.02) | −.24 (.02) | |
| public housing | .02 | .08 (.08) | .26 (.12) | .18 | .02 | .13 (.07) | .12 (.10) | −.02 | .02 | −.02 (.04) | −.04 (.05) | −.20 |

| | | | | | | | | | | | | |
|---|---|---|---|---|---|---|---|---|---|---|---|---|
| other household income (in thousands $) | $18.994 | .003 (.001) | .002 (.001) | −.001 | 17.815 | .002 (.001) | −.002 (.001) | −.004 | 11.924 | −.005 (.005) | −.008 (.001) | −.005 |
| family below 1975 poverty line | .08 | −.16 (.04) | −.43 (.06) | −.28 | .09 | −.37 (.03) | −.71 (.05) | −.25 | .07 | −.55 (.02) | −1.23 (.03) | −.79 |
| Geographic status in poverty tract | .15 | −.05 (.03) | .03 (.05) | .08 | .15 | −.08 (.03) | −.08 (.04) | .00 | .13 | −.09 (.01) | −.11 (.02) | −.02 |
| **Other controls** | | | | | | | | | | | | |
| age | | ✓ | ✓ | | | ✓ | ✓ | | | ✓ | ✓ | |
| head of household | | ✓ | ✓ | | | ✓ | ✓ | | | ✓ | ✓ | |
| interaction: head of household and other household income | | | ✓ | | | | ✓ | | | | ✓ | |
| region | | ✓ | ✓ | | | ✓ | ✓ | | | ✓ | ✓ | |
| urban | | ✓ | ✓ | | | ✓ | ✓ | | | ✓ | ✓ | |
| subsidized rent | | ✓ | ✓ | | | ✓ | ✓ | | | ✓ | ✓ | |
| **Summary statistic** | | | | | | | | | | | | |
| $R^2$ | | .03 | .10 | | | .06 | .20 | | | .13 | .34 | |
| n | | 5240 | 5240 | | | 6727 | 6727 | | | 15,430 | 15,430 | |

SOURCE: Survey of Income and Education.

# Data Appendix

*Cross-SMSA Data*

1. AFDC recipients.

Source: Bureau of the Census, *Statistical Abstract of the United States*, 1971, section 33: Metropolitan Area Statistics.

2. Average annual rate of growth of personal income, 1958–69.

Source: Bureau of the Census, *Statistical Abstract of the United States*, 1971, section 33: Metropolitan Area Statistics.

3. Average hourly earnings 1970 of production workers on manufacturing payrolls.

Source: Bureau of Labor Statistics, *Employment and Earnings States and Areas 1939–74*, Bulletin 1370–11.

4. Black population as percentage of total population.

Source: Bureau of the Census, 1970, Census of Population, *General Characteristics of Population*, 1970, table 24: Age by Race and Sex, for Areas and Places: 1970.

5. City size (population of central city).

Source: Bureau of the Census, *Statistical Abstract of the United States*, 1973, section 34: Metropolitan Area Statistics.

6. Demographic variables.

Source: Bureau of the Census, 1970, Census of Population, state volumes, *Detailed Characteristics*, 1970, table 164: Employment Status by Race, Sex, and Age: 1970.

Calculations: 16–17 year olds demographic variable = 16–17 year old male civilian population/total male civilian population. Demographic variables for 18–19 year olds and 20–24 year olds calculated in the same way.

7. Employment variables (employment rate, unemployment rate, labor force participation rate).

Source: Bureau of the Census, 1970 Census of Population, *Detailed Characteristics*, 1970, table 164: Employment Status by Race, Sex, and Age: 1970; for total group, table 166, Employment and Status and Hours Worked of Persons 14 to 34 year olds, by school enrollment, age, race, and sex: 1970; for persons not enrolled in school.

8. Female-headed households as percentage of all households.

Source: Bureau of the Census, *County and City Data Book*, 1972: Statistical Abstract Supplement, table 3: Standard Metropolitan Statistical Areas.

9. Industry indexes.

Sources: Percentages of civilian labor force employed in each industry, by SMSA: Bureau of the Census, *County and City Data Book*, 1972: Statistical Abstract Supplement, table 3: Standard Metropolitan Statistical Areas. Persons employed in each age group as percentage of total persons employed by industry: Bureau of the Census, 1970 Census of Population, Detailed Characteristics: United States Summary, table 239: Age of Employed Persons by Industry and Sex: 1970.

Calculations: Industry index for 16–17 year old males = $\sum_{\text{all industries}}$ (industry share of labor force in SMSA × fraction of industry labor force that is 16–17 years old)/fraction of total U.S. labor force that is 16–17 years old.

10. Percent of families below low-income level.)

Source: U.S. Bureau of the Census, *Statistical Abstract of the United States 1973*, Section 34: Metropolitan Area Statistics.

11. State minimum wage laws.

Source: Bureau of Labor Statistics, *Youth Unemployment and Minimum Wages*, Bulletin 1657, 1970, pp. 133–134, chapter IX, appendix B: Basic adult minimum wage rates and specified differential rates by state, June 1969.

*Time Series Data*

12. Time-series average hourly earnings of production workers on private payrolls.

Source: *Employment and Training Report of the President*, 1978, p. 265, table C-3, Gross Average Weekly Hours, Average Hourly Earnings, and Average Weekly Earnings of Production or Nonsupervisory Workers on private Payrolls, by Industry Division: Annual Averages, 1947–1977.

13. Time-series minimum wage.

Source: Bureau of Labor Statistics, *Youth Unemployment and Minimum Wages*, Bulletin 1657, 1970, p. 182, table 12.2: Proportion of earnings covered by the Federal minimum wage.

14. Time-series demographic variables

Source: *Employment and Training Report of the President*, 1978, p. 183, table A-3: Civilian Labor Force for Persons 16 Years and Over, by Sex, Race, and Age: Annual Averages, 1948–1977; p. 186 table A-4: Civilian Labor Force Participation Rates for Persons 16 Years and Over, by Race, Sex, and Age: Annual Averages, 1948–1977.

Calculation: Male civilian population for each age group and total number of persons in civilian labor force for cohort × 100/Civilian labor force participation rate for cohort.

— 16–17 year olds demographic variable = 16–17 year old male civilian population. Demographic variables for 18–19 year olds and 20–24 year olds calculated in the same way.

15. Time-series labor force participation rate.

Source: *Employment and Training Report of the President*, 1978, p. 186, table A-4: Civilian Labor Force Participation Rates for Persons 16

Years and Over, by Race, Sex, and Age: Annual Averages, 1948–77.
16. Time-series unemployment rate.

Source: *Employment and Training Report of the President*, 1978, p. 212, table A-19: Unemployed Persons 16 Years and Over and Unemployment Rates, by Sex and Age: Annual Averages, 1948–77.
17. Time-series employment ratio.

Calculations: Employment Ratio = (1 − unemployment rate/100) × labor force participation rate.

# Notes

1. The SMSA data set is described in the data appendix. For a detailed description of the SIE survey, see U.S. Department of Commerce and U.S. Department of Health Education and Welfare, "Assessment of the Accuracy of the Survey of Income and Education," A Report to Congress Mandated by the Education Amendment of 1974 (Jan. 1967).

2. See Freeman and Medoff, chapter 3 of this volume, table 3.6, where significant differences in the distribution of the 16–17, 18–19, and 20–24 year olds among industries and occupations are shown.

3. The coefficients of variation for the ratio of young men to men 16 and over are: 16–17 year olds, .113; 18–19 year olds, .16; 20–24 year olds, .17.

4. A more desirable measure would be the gross product in the area but that is not available on an SMSA basis. Note that the increase in personal income depends on changes in population as well as changes in income per person in the areas.

5. The information in the Census on the earnings of youth in an SMSA has too many problems to be helpful here. The available data do *not* provide figures for *hourly* pay.

6. The calculations use a linear form despite the fact that the dependent variables are ratios ranging from 0 to 1. Experiments with the variables in log odds ratio form yielded sufficiently similar results to those from the linear form to make the latter, which are easier to interpret directly, more desirable.

7. Another possible explanation is that 20–24 year olds migrate to areas with low rates of youth joblessness, which would mute or reverse any adverse effect of relative numbers on joblessness. By contrast, the bulk of teenagers reside with parents who are unlikely to migrate to areas where job opportunities are better for the young.

8. The algebra underlying different effects is direct. Let $u$ = unemployment rate; $\ell$ = labor participation rate; $e$ = employment rate (employment/population), then by definition: $u = 1 - e/\ell$
and $du/dx = e/\ell^2\ d\ell/dx - 1/\ell\ de/dx$ where $x$ is an explanatory variable.
Assuming $d\ell/dx$ and $de/dx$ have the same sign, then $du/dx$ will have the same sign as $de/dx$ when $e/\ell\ d\ell/dx > de/dx$.

9. Analysis of the in-school and out-of-school youths can be developed further through estimation of the structural supply and demand equations which presumably underlie the relations examined in the text. Such an analysis would seek to determine the degree of substitutability between in-school and out-of-school youths in the job market, among other things.

10. For a similar conclusion, see Burt Barnow, "Teenage Unemployment and Demographic Factors: A Survey of Recent Evidence" (U.S. Department of Labor, March 21, 1979). While there is obviously no way to deal with changes in coverage in the cross-section regressions, in the time-series regressions it is possible to measure the minimum wage

variable in a more complex way, taking account of coverage changes. Since coverage of the minimum *grew* in the period under study, using a more complex measure would not change my conclusion: the increased coverage presumably would reduce the employment/population ratio, which makes the puzzling stability of the employment/population ratio even more puzzling.

11. As described in the table note, persons in the out-of-school group are limited to those not enrolled in school and do not include enrolled persons who report their major activity as being other than in school.

12. Regressions with the poverty variable excluded, reported in an earlier version of this paper, yield results on other variables comparable to those in tables. Hence inclusion of the variable does not mar interpretation of the other regression coefficients.

# References

Barnow, Burt. 21 March 1979. Teenage unemployment and demographic factors: A survey of recent evidence. U.S. Department of Labor.

Bowen, W. G. and T. Aldrich Finegan, 1969. *The economics of labor force participation*. Princeton: Princeton University Press.

Clark, Kim B. and Lawrence H. Summers. The dynamics of youth unemployment. Chapter 7 of this volume.

Freeman, Richard B. and James Medoff. The youth labor market problem: An overview. Chapter 3 of this volume.

Loury, Glenn. May 1976. Essays in the theory of the distribution of income. Massachusetts Institute of Technology, Ph.D. dissertation.

U.S. Bureau of the Census, 1970. *Census of population: 1970, subject reports*, "General characteristics of population." Table 24. Washington, D.C.: Government Printing Office.

_____. 1970. *Census of population: 1970*, state volumes, "Detailed characteristics," Tables 164 and 166. Washington, D.C.: Government Printing Office.

_____. 1970. *Census of population: 1970*, "Detailed characteristics, United States summary." Table 239. Washington, D.C.: Government Printing Office.

_____. 1971. *Statistical abstract of the United States* Section 33: Metropolitan Area Statistics. Washington, D.C.: Government Printing Office.

_____. 1972. *County and city data book: 1972*, Statistical abstracts supplement. Table 3. Washington, D.C.: Government Printing Office.

_____. 1973. *Statistical abstract of the U.S.* Section 34: Metropolitan area statistics. Washington, D.C.: Government Printing Office.

U.S. Department of Commerce, Bureau of Labor Statistics, 1970. *Youth unemployment and minimum wages*. Bulletin 1657, pp. 133–34. Washington, D.C.: Government Printing Office.

_____. 1974. *Employment earnings states and areas 1939–74*. Bulletin 1370–11. Washington, D.C.: Government Printing Office.

U.S. Department of Commerce and U.S. Department of Health, Education and Welfare. 1976. Assessment of the accuracy of the survey of income and education. A Report to Congress Moderated by the Education Amendment of 1974. Washington, D.C.

———. 1978. *1978 employment and training report of the president*. P. 183, table A-3; p. 186, table A-4; p. 2.2, table A-19. Washington, D.C.: Government Printing Office.

## Comment    T. Aldrich Finegan

In this chapter Professor Freeman examines the socioeconomic factors affecting the labor force status and earnings of younger persons, specifically those 16 to 24 years old. To this end, three kinds of data are analyzed: (1) aggregated data for SMSAs from the 1970 Census of Population, (2) time series data (annual observations) from the Current Population Survey for 1948 through 1977, and (3) data for individuals and their families from the 1976 Survey of Income and Education (SIE). The intercity regressions seek to explain differences across SMSAs in the labor force participation rates, employment-population ratios, and unemployment rates of younger persons, classified by age, sex, and enrollment status (in the case of males). These regressions assess the role of several measures of local labor market conditions on the labor market status of the subject groups. The time-series regressions provide comparable estimates of the effects of three labor market indicators on the same dependent variables. The SIE data are harnessed to reveal associations between the labor market status and earnings of the young persons in the Survey and their own demographic characteristics along with selected socioeconomic characteristics of their families.

Reviewing a study of this scope is no easy task. The 89 regressions reported here contain a bumper crop of findings. Consequently, any discussion of particular results is bound to be highly selective, unbalanced, and perhaps even eccentric. Therefore, let me offer an overall assessment at the outset. Despite some puzzles and caveats, I believe that Freeman's paper makes an important contribution to our understanding of how labor market conditions and family characteristics shape the labor market experiences of younger persons. The empirical tests have been skillfully designed to illuminate the relationships at issue. While more effort could have been devoted to explaining and reconciling the results for different subsets, the main contours and implications of these findings have been highlighted by the author with admirable brevity.

T. Aldrich Finegan is professor of economics at Vanderbilt University.

I now turn to some of the particular results in Professor Freeman's chapter, beginning with his SMSA regressions.

First, while the labor market variables in tables 5.1 and 5.2 are generally well behaved, some results are puzzling. In table 5.1, for example, a large relative number of young people in the SMSA ($RP_y$) lowers the employment ratio of males 18–19 but has no effect on their unemployment rate. The prime-age male unemployment rate has similar asymmetrical effects in the case of males 16–17. More curious still, $RP_y$ is *inversely* related to the unemployment rate of males 20–24 but has no effect on their employment ratio. Yet the subset regressions in table 5.2 for enrolled and not-enrolled males aged 20–24 tell a very different story: here $RP_y$ is unrelated to group unemployment but negatively related to group employment. What accounts for such oddities?

Part of the answer, as Freeman points out, is that labor market variables usually affect employment ratios and labor force participation rates in the same direction (owing to the discouraged worker effect), thus reducing their impact on unemployment rates. I share his view that the employment effects deserve top billing. But I have trouble understanding a discouraged worker response so large that a group's labor force shrinks (or grows) by more than, or even as much as, its level of employment. When such results (or wrong signs) are observed, the labor market variable may be measuring more than labor market conditions (i.e., an omitted socioeconomic factor). Hence it pays to keep an eye on the unemployment coefficients for these variables in appraising the employment effects, and vice versa.

Second, some of the unexpected results for $RP_y$ may come from the fact that only the population of the subject age-sex group is included in the numerator of this ratio. Given substitution possibilities, the competition for jobs faced, say, by 18–19 year old males in an SMSA may also be affected by the number of 16–17 and 20–24 year olds living there. If so, broader age-interval population variables might be more appropriate.

Third, as Freeman shows, labor market conditions influence not only the labor market status of youngsters in and out of school but enrollment rates as well. In general, the enrollment rate tends to be lower in SMSAs where it is easier for youngsters to find jobs. Perhaps some of the anomalies in tables 5.1 and 5.2 can be attributed to this factor.[1] In any event, school enrollment really ought to be viewed as an endogenous variable.

This leads to a suggestion for further research. For nearly all 16–17 year old males, and for those older youngsters who are still living with their parents, what matters most is that they be in school (during the school year) or have a full-time job. Whether those in school also have a part-time job, and whether those not in school are reported as unemployed or out of the labor force, are questions of lesser importance. If we define a youngster as "active" when he is either in school or employed, an analysis of differences across SMSAs in the "activity rates" of younger males, classified by age and race, could be rewarding.[2] It would capture the most important joint effect of labor market conditions on enrollment decisions and labor market status, namely, how such conditions influence the fraction of school-age youngsters who are both out of work and out of school.[3]

My last comment on Freeman's SMSA regressions concerns the results for his poverty variable (the fraction of families in the SMSA falling below the official poverty line). As Freeman points out, this variable "could reflect the impact of *individual* poverty, say, through inadequate human capital formation, lack of connections, or related social ills in the homes of those in poverty, or it could reflect the impact of *community* factors on either the demand or supply side." Drawing on the findings of his SIE regressions, which show much larger negative employment effects from family income below the poverty line than from residence in a poverty tract, Freeman concludes that the SMSA variable appears to be measuring primarily the effects of individual poverty.

While Freeman's conclusion may be correct, I do not find his evidence entirely convincing. First, it is not obvious that area-wide community influences (whether of demand or supply) on youth employment are fully captured by comparing the employment ratios of a national sample of youngsters, classified by whether or not they live in poverty tracts; for this comparison cannot test the hypothesis that the employment ratios in *both* the poverty and nonpoverty areas of an SMSA are inversely related to the fraction of families in the SMSA living in poverty. Moreover, the sheer size of the regression coefficients for the SMSA poverty variable provides considerable support for this hypothesis. Of the nine negative coefficients for this variable in regressions explaining group employment ratios in tables 5.1 and 5.2, two are larger than $-1.0$, six fall between $-0.5$ and $-1.0$, and only one is smaller than $-0.5$. These coefficients tell us that, in eight cases out of nine, a one percentage point difference in an SMSA's poverty ratio was associated with more than a half-point difference (of opposite sign) in the all-SMSA employment ratio of the subject group. Given the small fraction of families below the poverty line in most SMSAs and the typical difference between the employment status of youngsters who live in poverty and those who do not, these variations in SMSA-wide employment ratios appear to be much too large to reflect mainly intercity differences in the extent or severity of individual poverty.

This brings me to the time-series regressions reported in table 5.5. It is a pleasant surprise to find that so many of the coefficients for the all-male unemployment rate in these regressions are similar in size to those in the comparable cross-SMSA tests. But the same thing cannot be said about the youth population variables, whose coefficients are often greatly increased or reduced in size when a linear time trend variable is added to the regression. The apparent collinearity between these variables clouds the interpretation of each.

Fortunately, the coefficients for the minimum wage proxy are much less sensitive to the inclusion or omission of a trend control, and they show that the employment and participation rates of male teenagers were significantly lower during periods in which the ratio of the FLSA minimum to average hourly earnings was unusually high. If I am interpreting the coefficients in table 5.5 correctly, a 10% rise in the minimum wage ratio reduced the employment of 16–17 year old males by about 2.5% and that of 18-19 year olds by about 2%.[4] Freeman's minimum wage measure presumably picks up only the short-run effects of such changes. A permanent increase in this ratio should have larger disemployment effects, since labor demand is more elastic in the long run. Besides, as Freeman points out, growth in the coverage of the federal minimum wage has probably further reduced the job opportunities for teenagers, although the magnitude of this loss is still unknown.

It is also noteworthy that some of the negative employment effects attributed to the growth of the relative number of young persons in the time series regressions are probably due to the presence of the minimum wage. If relative earnings of teenagers were wholly flexible downward, a rise in their relative numbers would lead to lower employment ratios only insofar as fewer teenagers wished to work at lower wage rates. In fact, as Freeman and Medoff have shown in chapter 3 of this volume (table 3.8), the relative earnings of younger persons have fallen substantially since 1967; but in the absence of minimum wage legislation they would probably have fallen more. It therefore seems likely that the time-series coefficients for the youth population in table 5.5 are larger than they would have been in the absence of the FLSA.

In table 5.6, Freeman compares the actual changes in employment, labor force, and unemployment rates of younger males between 1969 and 1977 with the changes predicted by his cross-section and time-series regressions. Interestingly, both models underpredict the rise in participation rates that actually occurred and project large drops in group employment ratios that did not occur.

First let me raise one procedural issue. Unless I am mistaken, the predicted changes for 1969 to 1977 are based on the time-series coefficients in table 5.5. But these coefficients are from regressions that *include* the years 1969 through 1977. Wouldn't it have been better to rerun the time-series tests for 1948 to 1969 and use those coefficients to predict the changes from 1969 to 1977?[5] Doing so would probably have strengthened the main conclusion of this analysis by increasing the gap between the actual and predicted changes in employment and labor force participation.

The intriguing question, of course, is what accounts for this gap. Surely part of the answer lies in two supply-side developments: the decline in the size of the armed forces and in the percentage of males 18–24 attending school.[6] Both caused the civilian participation and employment rates of young men to rise more (or fall less) during the 1970s than what earlier data would have predicted. One might also speculate whether the development of a "youth culture" and new consumer goods aimed especially at younger persons (e.g., skateboards and rock concerts) might help to account for the rising labor force participation of younger persons who are attending school.

At the same time, the results in Freeman's table 5.6 suggest that the *demand* for younger males also grew at a faster than projected rate during the 1970s. Had all (or nearly all) of the unexplained growth in employment and labor force participation been supply-push in origin, one would have expected the actual increases in group unemployment rates to exceed the predicted increases, given sluggish adjustment in relative wages. But that does not seem to have occurred except for 16–17 year olds. If one compares the actual increase in group unemployment rates with the mean of the two time-series projections in table 5.6, these two figures are very similar for males 18–19 and 20–24. In the case of males 16–17, however, the actual rise exceeds the predicted rise by 1.4 points. Thus only for 16–17 year old males does the unexplained growth in employment and labor force participation appear to have been dominated by supply-side forces.

The inferences drawn from table 5.6 for all younger males may not apply to black youths. Their employment ratios have declined relative to white youths in the 1970s, as Wachter and Kim have shown (see chapter 6 of this volume.) As a first step in trying to understand this on-going decline, it would be useful if time series tests similar to those in tables 5.5 and 5.6 could be run for black males.[7]

Finally, let me offer a few comments on Freeman's analysis of the SIE data. While most of the results in tables 5.8 and 5.9 are illuminating and believable, I would like to raise some questions about the income-related explanatory variables in these tests. In addition to other family income (total family income in 1975 minus the young person's earnings, if any), dummy variables have been included for whether or not the subject's family (1) received welfare (AFDC) payments in 1975, (2) received food stamps that year, (3) lived in public housing at the time of the survey (spring of 1976), or (4) had a level of total family income falling below the poverty line in 1975. Although most of these measures are highly significant in explaining employment, I am not sure what meaning should be attached to some of them. For example, after other family income (OFI) and poverty status have been held constant, what do the welfare and food stamps variables measure? Perhaps they measure the *fraction* of other family income from nonearnings sources, but why should that affect the employment or wages of younger persons? (Is receipt of welfare or food stamps a surrogate for greater unemployment of the head of the household?) And why does living in public housing discourage employment? (Do such persons have other handicaps, or are the available jobs simply further away?) Further research is needed to identify the underlying causes of these associations.

While Freeman is to be commended for trying to disentangle the effects of family poverty and living in a poverty neighborhood on the employment and earnings of youth, the simultaneous presence of a control for other family income (along with the trio of welfare variables mentioned earlier) makes it hard to interpret the results for the family poverty variable. The problem is not collinearity but what it means to vary one variable while holding the other constant. While one can imagine comparing families with different levels of OFI either above or below the poverty line, what really happens when we compare two families on different sides of that line but with the same OFI? Two possibilities occur to me: (1) the family below the poverty line may have more members, or (2) the subject youngster may have contributed less income to it. (Note that the poverty line variable depends on the *total* level of family income, among other things, not on OFI.) Both possibilities suggest that the comparative impact of family and residential poverty might have been sharper had OFI been omitted from these regressions.

At the same time, the large roster of income-related variables in these regressions serves to highlight one of Freeman's most noteworthy findings, namely, the large gap that remains, after all of these variables (and many others) have been held constant, between the employment ratios of white and black teenage males. The contrast between the growing relative disadvantage suffered by teenage blacks in finding work and their rough parity (or better) in hourly wages, as shown in table 5.9, could hardly be more striking. These results seem indicative of a labor market that does not clear, at least for minority groups—i.e., where background factors have a lot to do with which teenagers get jobs, and where blacks are increasingly being screened out. Finding the reasons for this disturbing trend should be high on the agenda for future research.

### Notes

1. When labor market conditions simultaneously affect both enrollment decisions and labor market status, the net effects of these conditions on group employment and unemployment rates are not fully captured by controlling for the percentage in school or by running separate regressions for enrolled and not-enrolled youngsters. The behavioral responses within each enrollment category may be different, and the results for each subset also reflect the effects of labor market conditions on the relative number and socioeconomic composition of the youngsters within it.

2. An earlier study cited by Freeman (Bowen and Finegan, 1969) examined inter-SMSA variations in a somewhat different activity measure, namely, the percentage of younger civilian males who were either enrolled in school or in the civilian labor force during the census week of 1960. Thus unemployed youngsters were included in this measure while those not in the labor force were excluded. Since the distinction between these two groups is of doubtful economic significance, I believe that the activity concept proposed in the text (being in school or *employed*) would be more fruitful.

3. The chapter by Wachter and Kim in this volume (6) contains an insightful analysis of time series changes in a somewhat narrower measure of inactivity, namely, the fraction of younger persons (classified by age, sex, and race) who were neither employed, unemployed, in the armed forces, nor enrolled in school.

4. I obtained these estimates by dividing the mean of the two regression coefficients for the minimum wage variable by the mean employment ratio for the subject group and then multiplied the quotient by 10 (for a 10% change).

It is worth noting that Freeman's minimum wage ratio is less subject to questions of interpretation than the relative wage measure (W/MW) used by Wachter and Kim. Whereas the denominator of Freeman's measure (average hourly earnings in all private industries) is relatively insensitive to changes in the youth labor market, the numerator in the Wachter-Kim measure (the average earnings of workers 16–24 years old) is quite sensitive to such changes. This is not a criticism of the latter variable, for it plays a somewhat different role in Wachter and Kim's analysis. The point is that variations in Freeman's variable are more clearly attributable to changes in the minimum wage.

5. A possible problem with this alternative procedure is that some independent variables may have changed more between 1969 and 1977 than during the two preceding decades. If so, to apply the regression coefficients from the earlier period to such changes would involve some extrapolation of these effects.

6. Between 1969 and 1977, the number of males 20–24 who were in the armed forces fell by almost 1.1 million. It is interesting that while the *civilian* labor force participation rate for these males rose by 2.9 points during this period, their *total* rate rose by only one-tenth of a point (source: 1979 *Employment and Training Report of the President*, tables A-2, A-3).

The enrollment rate for 18–19 year old males in the civilian noninstitutional population declined from 59% in October 1969 to 48% in October 1977, while the rate for males 20–24 fell from 32% to 26% (source: ibid., table B-6).

7. Time-series data for nonwhites in the Current Population Survey go back only to 1954 and contain greater sampling error. There are also conceptual issues in specifying the relevant labor market variables in time-series regressions for black youngsters. But these problems do not appear to be insurmountable.

# 6 Time Series Changes in Youth Joblessness

Michael L. Wachter and Choongsoo Kim

Youth unemployment has increased over the past two decades in absolute terms relative to prime-age male unemployment. More recently the unemployment rates for most youth groups have begun to level off and move in parallel with prime-age male unemployment rates. This is especially true for white males.

Explaining these developments in a statistical sense presents major problems. First, the underlying developments appear to be due to economic-demographic swings of intermediate-run duration. Hence the length of the time series data base is woefully short. Second, many of the most interesting and potentially important explanatory variables, such as government policy variables, present major measurement problems.

Our view stresses the role of "cohort overcrowding," which results from an imbalance between younger and older workers. The model is based on two central assumptions. The first is that younger and older workers are imperfect substitutes for each other. The main difference between them reflects their relative amounts of specific training. Given the "putty-clay" nature of physical and human capital and the transient nature of the cohort bulge, the economy's adjustment process may be slow and incomplete. In the short run, elasticities of substitution are relatively low so that large relative wage adjustments can occur.

The second is that aspiration levels or desired standards of living are formed when the younger workers are living with their parents. This is an endogenous taste or habit formation model in which past living standards

Michael L. Wachter is a professor of economics and management at the University of Pennsylvania. Choongsoo Kim is a senior research associate at the Center for Human Resource Research, the Ohio State University. The research was supported by grants from the General Electric Foundation, the National Institute of Child Health and Human Development, and the Twentieth Century Fund. The Bureau of Labor Statistics unpublished tabulations were kindly provided by Paul O. Flaim.

influence current desired standards. In addition, young families are assumed to treat their desired standard of living as a necessity. Hence, in the event of lower wage levels, families will increase the number of workers and/or hours worked. The increase in labor force participation rates of the young workers can thus be traced directly to the population demographics. In addition, the induced change in participation rates serves to aggravate the existing problem of oversupply of younger workers, thus further driving down relative wages.

As relative wages fall for the oversized cohort, institutional constraints, such as government transfer programs, minimum wage levels, etc., become relevant and cause an increase in unemployment rates as well as or instead of the increase in participation rates. If the unemployment effects are large enough, employment may actually decline.

Although some previous studies have attempted to isolate the effects of government programs, for example of minimum wage legislation and manpower programs, data problems make this task almost impossible. Besides the data problems, there are important conceptual problems as well. The government's social welfare package, whether intentional or not, is an integrated program. The parameters of the various programs tend to change together reflecting common political pressures. An example is the parallel increase in minimum wage coverage and government transfer payments (in relative terms) during the late 1960s. Since almost all studies concentrate on one government program at a time, they miss these crucial interrelationships and hence attribute too much to the single program under study. We also find that "relative wages" have some explanatory power, but cannot separate minimum wage from government transfer effects. In addition, attempts to include direct job creation effects invariably yield the wrong sign.

Our empirical work focuses on two approaches. The first attempts to measure unemployment in different ways by altering the numerator and/or the denominator of the unemployment rate term. For example, we argue that the variable which is closest to the traditional measure of unemployment would give school attendance equal status with employment. Hence the numerator would exclude those who were unemployed and whose primary activity was school and the denominator would include all of those who were in school. The second approach focuses on disaggregating youth activities into four categories: unemployment, employment, school, and a residual (all as a ratio to the population) for each of the age-sex-race groups. Equations are then estimated using the same explanatory variables and adding the constraint that the four ratios sum to unity.

Since black males pose a particular problem, we concentrate somewhat on the deterioration in the unemployment and employment ratios of this group relative to other youth groups. Why should this group suffer a deterioration in labor market position relative to other youth groups, including black females?

## 6.1 The Basic Model of Cohort Overcrowding

### 6.1.1 The Underlying Workings of the Model

In some earlier work by the authors and others, the youth unemployment problem was explained in the context of a broader economic-demographic model.[1] The basis of the model is a "cohort overcrowding" effect which results from an imbalance between younger and older workers. We shall utilize this approach to explore the developments in youth unemployment over the past fifteen years. It was during this period that the baby boom cohort was passing through the 16–24 age category.

This type of model can generate cyclical swings of intermediate length in unemployment rates. A fertility increase in generation $t$ causes a large cohort of entry level workers in $t + 1$. In the short run, elasticities of substitution are relatively low so that large relative wage adjustments occur. This deterioration in the income potential of young people causes a decline in fertility and family formation rates and an increase in the labor force participation rates of secondary workers. The increase in young workers' labor force participation rates can thus be traced directly to the population demographics. In addition, the induced change in participation rates serves to aggravate the existing oversupply problem of younger workers.[2]

As relative wages fall for the oversized cohort, institutional constraints become relevant and cause an increase in unemployment rates as well as or instead of the increase in participation rates. If the unemployment effects are large enough, employment may actually decline.

The institutional constraints that cause unemployment can exist on both the demand and supply sides of the market. For example, since minimum wage levels are informally indexed on average economy-wide wages, a decline in the relative wage for youths may cause the market clearing wage to fall below the minimum wage. Youths, of course, form a heterogeneous skill group with a wage distribution rather than a single wage. The decline of the relative wage, in this case, causes an adverse shift in the distribution of wages. That is, the probability of any youth having a skill and associated wage level that falls below the minimum wage is increased by the demographic overcrowding.

On the supply side, a different institutional factor is operating but with a similar potential result. In both neoclassical labor supply literature as well as institutional literature, workers are viewed as having a reservation wage; when market wages are below that reservation wage, individuals choose not to work. The neoclassical theory tends to specify a continuous trade-off between hours of work and wage rates. It is only at the corner of the indifference map that the wage rate is sufficiently low so that individuals will offer zero hours of work. The likelihood of a corner solution is increased by the existence of public assistance and government transfers in general. These programs have high implicit tax rates. Indeed, it is generally acknowledged that the eligible poverty population for these programs face higher implicit marginal tax rates than do the wealthiest individuals. The result of these programs is to considerably flatten the budget constraint.[3]

The likelihood of a corner solution is also determined by the mechanism through which individuals form their reservation wage. Specifically, individuals' attitudes toward an acceptable wage are determined by wages paid elsewhere in the economy. Of particular importance in defining the indifference map or "taste" for work is the minimum income level dictated by the government social welfare programs and minimum wage laws. These programs signal what constitutes an acceptable minimum wage to the voting public and policymakers. That is, government programs almost certainly influence the shape of the indifference map as they alter the budget constraint. A liberalization of benefits shifts both the indifference map and the budget constraint toward the corner solution of zero work.[4]

It should be noted that the fluctuations in unemployment discussed in this model are solely related to changes in the equilibrium rate of unemployment. Cyclical unemployment may be positive or negative in the short run, but the demographic cycle outlined above is an intermediate swing and averages out the peaks and troughs of the short-run business cycle.

### 6.1.2 A Simple Expositional Model[5]

The major factors that we use in our empirical work can be captured in a simple expositional model. The model is oriented toward the specific empirical factors involved in the demographic shift. To start, assume a production function that recognizes two different categories of labor: older workers who have accumulated specific training $(L_A)$ and younger workers who lack such training $(L_B)$. For our purposes we can view $L_A$ as skilled workers and $L_B$ as unskilled workers. In the long run, the production function can be written as:

$$(1) \qquad X^s = f^s (L_A{}^s, L_B{}^s, K)$$

where $K$ is the capital stock, $X$ is the level of output, and the superscript $s$ refers to supply. In the short run, there appear to be significant lags in achieving desired absolute and relative levels of factor inputs. The lags may arise for a number of reasons including adjustment and expectional factors. The literature on investment functions indicates that long lags are especially relevant to the capital input. If the capital stock is "putty-clay," the input coefficients are fixed as part of the capital endowment. These coefficients may vary for different vintages but, to the extent that they are empirically important, they impart a difficulty in substituting against scarce factors in the short run.

For our purposes, aggregate demand can be viewed as being controlled by monetary ($M$) and fiscal ($F$) policies, subject to unanticipated changes in demand from the private sector ($X_0$):

$$(2) \qquad X^d = f^d \, (M, \, F, \, X_0)$$

The derived demand for labor is constrained by either the level of the demand for or supply of output $X$ and by relative factor prices. For $B$ workers, the relevant own wage is either the minimum wage ($MW$) or a market wage, whichever is higher.

The labor supply for both $L_A$ and $L_B$ is a function of the population in each cohort and the factors that determined the labor force participation rates. For $A$ workers, we assume that the participation rate ($r_A$) is constant in the short run. Abstracting from influences such as school enrollment and fertility, the main forces determining participation for $B$ workers are the market wage rates for these workers ($W_B$), the government transfer payments for being unemployed ($T_g$), the effective minimum wage ($MW$), and some unspecified trend factors that capture changes in lifestyle. That is,

$$(3) \qquad L_A{}^s = L_A{}^s \, (r_A, \, POP_A)$$

and

$$(4) \qquad L_B{}^{s'} = L_B{}^{s'} \, (POP_B, \, TREND, \, g \, \{W_B, \, T_g, \, MW\}).$$

The relationship between $W_B$ and $T_g$ determines the cost of being unemployed. The level of government transfers depends upon unemployment compensation and public assistance. The supply of labor relevant to the production function, denoted $L_B{}^s$, is

$$(5) \qquad L_B{}^s = L_B{}^{s'} - g \, (W_B, \, T_g, \, MW)$$

That is, we distinguish between an observed labor supply, and $L_B{}^{s'}$, and an effective labor supply, $L_B{}^s$, which is available for employment. The discrepancy, measured by the $g$ function, is a type of structural unemployment.[6]

Equations (1) through (5) indicate a number of reasons for unemployment. The most obvious is cyclical unemployment which results from $X^s > X^d$. In addition, unemployment will vary with (1) the distribution of the labor force between $A$ and $B$ workers, (2) the cost of being unemployed and minimum wage effectiveness, and (3) the bottlenecks of either skilled workers or capital. Over the longer run, when coefficients of production are more flexible, bottlenecks gradually lose their importance as a cause of unemployment. On the other hand, traditional wage equations indicate another source of unemployment. As bottlenecks loosen, relative wages must adjust if the surplus of $B$ workers is to be absorbed. The evidence suggests, however, that the adjustment is very imperfect. Minimum wages prevent employers from moving down their demand curve for $B$ workers and/or altering the reservation wage of $B$ workers. In addition, government transfer programs help to maintain a high reservation wage (relative to their market wage) for the unskilled workers. These latter workers are in the labor force, but are not willing or able to work at the market clearing wage.

## 6.2   The Reduced Form Unemployment Equation

### 6.2.1   Basic Considerations

Estimating an unemployment function can be done in several ways given the basic building blocks of labor supply and employment functions. For our purposes it is useful to start by estimating a reduced form relative unemployment equation. In section 6.4 we shall estimate both unemployment and employment functions. In this case the unemployment equations serve the role of a labor supply equation. This approach is compatible with the theory outlined above and the fact that prime-age male unemployment is an independent variable. Specifically, it highlights our view that youth unemployment is largely structural in nature and dominated by fluctuations on the supply rather than demand side of the market. For reasons associated with government policy and the dynamics of the overcrowding model, supply side shifts do not induce adjustments in labor demand.

A reduced form relative unemployment equation can be obtained from equation (5) with the additional assumption that fluctuations in $L_B{}^{s'}$ are captured by a cyclical aggregate demand variable. For most of our calculations, we used the prime-age male unemployment rate.[7]

A large number of alternative proxies were attempted for the government policy variables. None were particularly satisfactory because of measurement errors; essentially, most of the data were simply not collected. Our various attempts at representing policy impact are described below. No single policy variable provided the best fit among the eighteen age-sex-race groups. Rather than use different policy variables in each equation, we adopted a compromise variable that performed as well as the others but could be viewed as representing several effects. The unemployment rate equations for the various age-sex groups are estimated in the general form:

(6)  $$U_i = a0 + a_i \{Si\} + a_2 \ln (U_{PM}) + a_3 \ln (RPy)$$
$$+ a_4 \ln (W/MW) + a_5 (\ln (AF/POP)) \text{ or } TREND$$

where $\{Si\}$ is a vector of seasonal dummies, $RPy$ is the proportion of the civilian population aged 16 to 24 to the population aged $16 +$, $AF/POP$ is the military/population ratio (added to the male equations), and $TREND$ is a time trend (added to the female equations).

The $RPy$ variable represents the cohort overcrowding referred to above. Several different specifications of the $RPy$ variable were tried, varying the treatment of the military, individuals over 65 years of age, and defining youth from the ages of 16 to 34. The results were largely unchanged. Given this inability to differentiate empirically, the choice of the $RPy$ variable was dictated by usage in earlier studies. It is important to note that this cohort variable assumes that young workers are substitutes for one another and define a distinct labor input. Needless to say, any age division of the labor market into two distinct components has to be arbitrary. The difference between a 24 and a 25 year old is not large. On the other hand, labor market attachment, employment patterns, unemployment rates, etc., differ considerably for a 20 year old compared with a 30 year old.

Some recent studies have used separate supply or cohort variables (denoted $RPy_i$) for each of the youth age-sex groups.[8] For example, the black male population aged 18–19 as a percentage of the population aged $16 +$ would be used to explain unemployment of the age-sex-race group. Our view is that this is too limiting a view of the degree of substitution across inputs. Labor market behavior over the past two decades shows more similarities than differences across youth age-sex-race groups. Where the $RPy_i$ variable has been successful, it was only capturing the worsening unemployment position of black youths relative to white youths.[9] As will be discussed below, however, black youths are not doing worse than comparable white groups by all economic yardsticks. Black school enrollment rates and relative wages, for example, show significant relative improvement. This suggests that $RPy_i$ will not provide a consistent answer to the changing white-black differential.

### 6.2.2  The Government Policy Variable

Although a properly specified unemployment equation should contain separate variables to represent transfer payments, direct job creation, and minimum wages, data and conceptual problems made this impossible. After considerable but largely unsuccessful experimentation with different proxies for the various programs, the actual government variable utilized in the equations is a "compromise variable" of the form $W/MW$ where $W$ is the average hourly earnings of workers 16–24 years of age and $MW$ is the minimum wage.[10]

Measurement problems are complicated by the fact that the social legislation programs including transfers, minimum wages, and direct job creation are not made independently of each other. That is, policy innovations in one program are likely to be reflected in others. Basically, political and social pressures do not become concentrated in one area. Rather, as was clearly the case during the 1960s and 1970s, the forces that can yield changes in one policy area are also likely to cause similar changes in other areas.

Most of the literature dealing with federal welfare initiatives investigates only one program at a time. There are studies on minimum wages, public assistance, direct job creation, etc., but few of these studies attempt to integrate the direct labor market impact of that single study into the overall package of programs. The limited range of individual studies is easily explainable given the data problems for each single study. The problem, however, in evaluating the overall effect of the various government programs on unemployment is that the programs interact. The sum of the impacts of the individual studies does not equal the overall effect of the variety of programs evaluated together.[11]

The data problems are due to the fact that the major change in the minimum wage is the change in coverage in 1967. Until the 1978 law, however, little other meaningful variation in that variable is evident. Many of the increases in coverage did not affect low wage workers and the staggered catch-up increase in the minimum wage created a saw-tooth pattern in the data with, if anything, a slightly declining trend of the $MW$ relative to $W$. That is, the time series minimum wage variable is largely a spike in 1967. This, of course, is difficult enough to represent using time series data. Suppose, however, as is likely, that firms adjusted with a lag to this sweeping change in coverage. One possibility is an exponential declining distributed lag response. Depending upon the speed of decay, this would move the mean of the response outward in time, probably to 1968 or 1969. Alternatively, firms may have responded very slowly at first. This may have included low levels of compliance or incomplete compliance in the year immediately after 1967. With a compliance lag and an employment response lag conditional on compliance, the distributed lag structure could resemble a parabola with a mean lag into 1970 or beyond.

Given these possible time profiles for $W/MW$, and the difficulty of isolating the best fit in the various equations, it is possible for $W/MW$ to move in near precision with transfer, supply-side variables. Moreover, as mentioned above, this multicollinearity may be a conceptual as well as a data problem. To the extent that individuals form their reservation wages as a function of $MW$ and transfer payments are adjusted to conform to the same underlying inflation and real income changes effects, the $MW$ construct may be a good approximation of the reservation wage. To the extent that the minimum wage helps to determine the reservation wage of low wage workers, the greater the difficulty in differentiating supply and demand effects.[12]

### 6.2.3 Empirical Results for the Reduced Form Unemployment Equation

Given a lack of agreement or data on the control variables, especially government policy variables, to be introduced into the unemployment equation, it is useful to start with the simplest equation. Shown in table 6.1, this equation only includes $RPy$, $U_{PM}$ and the seasonal dummies. As can be seen, the coefficients of $RPy$ are all positive and indicate higher elasticities for females and blacks.

Since the "cohort overcrowding" effect operates like a trend variable for half of the sample period, namely between 1958 and 1972, it is useful to see if $RPy$ is simply picking up a trend effect. Prior to 1958, $RPy$ is either stable or declining and after 1972 it remains largely unchanged. The question is whether youth unemployment, after controlling for $U_{PM}$, is best approximated by a $TREND$ or a cohort overcrowding variable. Of the eighteen age-sex-race groups, the equation with $RPy$ instead of a

**Table 6.1**    **Unemployment Equations with Demographic Overcrowding Variable 1954:1–1978:4**

| Age/race | Male | | | Female | | |
|---|---|---|---|---|---|---|
| | $RPy$ | $U_{PM}$ | $\bar{R}^2/DW$ | $RPy$ | $U_{PM}$ | $\bar{R}^2/DW$ |
| 16–17 | | | | | | |
| Total | 1.0424 | .3347 | .796/1.832 | 1.1466 | .2382 | .748/1.908 |
| | (14.82) | (12.37) | | (11.77) | (6.36) | |
| White | .8592 | .3528 | .760/1.808 | 1.0103 | .2667 | .707/2.078 |
| | (11.22) | (11.98) | | (9.34) | (6.41) | |
| Black | 2.2524 | .2879 | .728/1.478 | 2.0174 | .1515 | .658/1.490 |
| | (16.19) | (5.38) | | (13.37) | (2.61) | |
| 18–19 | | | | | | |
| Total | .4446 | .5576 | .843/1.337 | 1.2097 | .2881 | .743/1.188 |
| | (6.40) | (20.86) | | (14.24) | (8.82) | |
| White | .2386 | .5862 | .836/1.404 | 1.1605 | .3137 | .675/1.200 |
| | (3.13) | (19.97) | | (11.31) | (7.95) | |
| Black | 1.4952 | .4938 | .638/1.140 | 1.2334 | .2403 | .617/1.589 |
| | (10.99) | (9.43) | | (11.90) | (6.02) | |
| 20–24 | | | | | | |
| Total | .5090 | .8548 | .910/ .702 | 1.1347 | .5098 | .891/1.360 |
| | (6.68) | (29.16) | | (19.67) | (22.97) | |
| White | .4733 | .8629 | .893/ .728 | 1.2004 | .5158 | .874/1.388 |
| | (5.51) | (26.12) | | (18.43) | (20.59) | |
| Black | .7793 | .8352 | .760/ .879 | .9269 | .4782 | .652/1.101 |
| | (6.06) | (16.87) | | (8.77) | (11.76) | |

*TREND* yields a higher $\bar{R}^2$ in fifteen equations. This provides mild support for the *RPy* variable. Given their collinearity, it is not possible to distinguish between *RPy* and *TREND* to the desired extent. Beginning in the late 1970s, however, these two variables diverge sharply. The *RPy* variable tends to be strongest in female and white male equations and weakest in black male equations. This pattern will appear with consistency regardless of the exact specification and/or the sample period of the equation.

These results suggest that secular or intermediate swings in female and white youth unemployment rates do track well with *RPy*. The implication is that the unemployment rates of youth groups have largely peaked relative to prime-age male unemployment rates. Needless to say, we would be more comfortable with this conclusion if the data period were longer and included several complete intermediate swing cycles. The unemployment data by race, however, does not predate the 1950s, and the unemployment data by age and sex is only available after the late 1940s.

The black male 16–24 age groups are the major exceptions to the notion that youth unemployment rates may have peaked. Since their unemployment rates continue to rise, the *TREND* variable has a larger *t* statistic than *RPy* in the black male equations. A major problem is to explain this divergence between black male youth unemployment rates and those of other youth groups.[13]

### 6.3   Other Indicators of the Labor Market Status of Youths

Youth unemployment is a more complex phenomenon than unemployment for other age groups. Essentially, the unemployment rate construct is not attuned to the unique features of the youth labor market. Rather, it is based on the type of frictional and cyclical unemployment that is most relevant to prime-age males and, in general, to workers with a strong labor market attachment.

Youth unemployment, on the other hand, is much more difficult to categorize. The key difference is that prime-age males tend to be in the labor force year round, full time (either employed or unemployed), and youths are frequently moving among jobs or into and out of the labor force. Of the 4.24 million males aged 18–19, for example, only 2.37 million were in the labor force and not in school in 1978. Of the 4.23 million males aged 16–17, only 1.12 million were in the labor force and not in school. Furthermore, since these numbers are annual averages (and thus include the summer months when many youths are not in school), they overstate the number that is in the labor market and not in school for the remainder of the year.

Essentially, there are many options open to youths, besides being in the labor market, that fit into traditional roles. Young people, for example, can be in school, in the military, or at home beginning to raise their own families. In addition, they can combine these different activities; for example, a disproportionate number of youths who are in the labor market are part-time workers. An increasing percentage of these young people combine being full-time students and part-time workers. Moreover, the choice of activities shifts frequently over the years. Relatively few young people aged 16 to 19 work year round, full time. One traditional pattern for this group is to work full time only during the summer months. Yet even for those who are not in school, changes in status between being employed, unemployed, and out of the labor force can occur several times over the year.

Of importance for an evaluation of the unemployment issue is that, from society's perspective, working year round, full time is not necessarily the most desirable activity for a young person. Particularly for teenagers, attending school may be preferable to working. For some male youths, serving one's military obligation ranks above civilian employment. For young females, staying home and raising a family may be viewed as preferable to working.

Given this perspective, determining the youth unemployment rate presents four major problems. First, since many if not most youths are not in the labor force at any given time, the unemployment rate is a very incomplete measure of that group's economic position and well-being. Second, since youths move frequently among employment, unemployment, and various nonlabor market activities, and are disproportionately part-time workers when they work, their unemployment incidence should be higher than for other workers who have stronger attachments to their jobs. Third, since having a job is not necessarily the preferred activity and for some youth age groups is likely to be less desirable than schooling, changes in the unemployment rate may provide incorrect information as to the nature and extent of changes in the economic conditions in youth labor markets. Fourth, since many youths do not have a firm labor market attachment, the question of whether they are "actively" seeking work (and thus are unemployed by the BLS definition) is often a matter of opinion and this leads to a considerable measurement error.[14]

Our initial approach is to develop alternative unemployment rate indicators and to analyze how they vary over time. These new indicators for 1978 are shown in table 6.2. The point is not that one is better than the other, but rather that each provides a different and useful perspective on the problem. Our $U_1$ measure simply adds the military to the denominator of the unemployment rate. Including the military in the denominator

Table 6.2    Alternative Measures of Unemployment, 1978

|  | $U$ or BLS unemployment rate[a] | $U_1$ or unemployment divided by labor force + military[b] | $U_2$ or unemployment divided by labor force + school + military[c] | $U_3$ or unemployment of nonenrollees divided by labor force + school + military[d] |
|---|---|---|---|---|
| **Male** | | | | |
| White | | | | |
| 16–17 | 17.1 | 16.9 | 10.1 | 4.8 |
| 18–19 | 10.9 | 10.0 | 8.0 | 6.1 |
| 20–24 | 7.6 | 7.1 | 6.4 | 5.8 |
| Black | | | | |
| 16–17 | 40.7 | 39.9 | 15.4 | 7.8 |
| 18–19 | 30.9 | 26.3 | 18.5 | 14.2 |
| 20–24 | 20.1 | 17.3 | 15.2 | 13.6 |
| **Female** | | | | |
| White | | | | |
| 16–17 | 17.1 | 17.1 | 9.8 | 4.8 |
| 18–19 | 12.3 | 12.3 | 9.5 | 7.6 |
| 20–24 | 8.3 | 8.2 | 7.5 | 6.9 |
| Black | | | | |
| 16–17 | 41.9 | 41.9 | 14.8 | 8.7 |
| 18–19 | 36.8 | 36.4 | 23.8 | 18.4 |
| 20–24 | 21.6 | 21.3 | 18.6 | 16.8 |

[a]Measured as $U/L$ where $U$ is the number of unemployed and $L$ is the civilian labor force.
[b]Measured as $U/(L+M)$ where $M$ is the number in the military.
[c]Measured as $U/(L+M+S-(S \cap L))$ where $S$ is the number in school and $(S \cap L)$ indicates those who are both in school and in the civilian labor force.
[d]Measured as $(U-(U \cap S))/(L+M+S-(S \cap L))$.

of $U_1$ is an obvious addition since that construction is used by the Bureau of Labor Statistics and is referred to as the total (as distinct from civilian) labor force. Our $U_2$ measure is constructed by adding those in school and those in the military to the denominator of the unemployment rate; that is, $U_2 = U/(L + M + S - (S \cap L))$.[15] Including individuals in school (but not including these individuals in the labor force since they are already included in $L$) is controversial, but useful. Schooling can be viewed not only as a type of employment, involving general human capital training, but also as the preferred activity for many of the youth groups. Including schooling and military in the denominator, to yield an augumented labor force (ALF), helps to control for shifts among these activities which result in fluctuations in the unemployment rate that may be related to labor demand conditions.

The $U_3$ construct, also depicted in table 6.2, moves further toward treating schooling on a par with employment. Workers, specifically those who want to moonlight and work at more than one job, can be both employed at the first job and unemployed while looking for the second job. According to the definition of unemployment, however, such a worker is counted as employed but not counted as unemployed. The same issue arises when schooling is included. If individuals are in school, should they also be counted as unemployed if they are looking for a job as well? The $U_2$ measure does count them as unemployed. It is useful, however, to establish a $U_3$ measure which excludes this group from the unemployment pool. The $U_3$ variable is defined as $(U - (U \cap S))/(L + M + S - (S \cap L))$.

The justification for this is that individuals whose major activity is school are likely to be part-time workers with a relatively marginal attachment to a job. The fact that they are in school indicates that they will soon be looking for a different kind of job. Moreover, reporting errors for this group are especially large. What constitutes active job search for full-time students who are looking for part-time jobs?

Whether or not one agrees with this argument, $U_3$ is still an interesting measure of unemployment. Correctly interpreted, it is the nonenrolled unemployed youths as a percentage of the population that is in school, in the military, or in the labor force. The difference between $U$ and $U_3$ is even larger than that for $U$ and $U_2$. First, the unemployment rates are again reduced considerably, with the largest reductions affecting the youngest age group. For example, for white youths aged 16–17, the $U_3$ rate is 4.8%. If schooling is viewed as a job (an investment in human capital for future productivity), then this age group is nearly fully employed. Furthermore, one can make a good argument that the $U_3$ definition is closer to the meaning of unemployment for adults than is the BLS unemployment definition.

Essentially, white youths aged 16–17 are largely in school. The school enrollment rate for white males aged 16–17 as an annual average was 63.7% in 1978. But as mentioned above, teenage labor force statistics need to be inspected for the nonsummer period as well along with the annual average. For example, during the first quarter of 1978, the school enrollment rate for white males aged 16–17 was 81.4%. The $U_3$ rate in the first quarter of 1978 was 2.6% while the rate in the third quarter was 9.0%. That is, most of the 16–17 year old white males are in school in the winter and many of these are unemployed during the summer. The $U_3$ rate for white males aged 16–17 during the winter, however, is below the unemployment rate for white prime-age males.

Even for blacks aged 16–17, unemployment is largely a summer-time phenomenon. For black males aged 16–17, $U_3$ is only 7.8% compared with a BLS measured unemployment rate of 40.7%. Looking at the first quarter of 1978 instead of the annual data, the $U_3$ rate falls to 4.0%.

An important feature of table 6.2 is to show that black unemployment for the 18–24 age group remains a problem even after moving from a $U_2$ to a $U_3$ construct. Having narrowed the definition so that it only covers the nonenrolled unemployed as a percentage of the school and work forces, it is disturbing that the resulting $U_3$ measure is still approximately 15% for nonwhites. Moreover, the black $U_3$ rates for the 18–24 age groups are still more than double the white $U_3$ rates for comparable groups.

The basic equations containing $RPy$ and $U_{PM}$ as independent variables were estimated for the various unemployment constructs. Since the schooling data at the desired level of disaggregation are only available from 1962, the sample period is shortened to 1962:4 through 1978:4. For comparison purposes, the $U$ equations of table 6.1 are reestimated for the shorter time period.

The results support the notion that the alternative unemployment rate indicators, and especially $U_3$, may be a better cyclical indicator of youth unemployment than the BLS unemployment rate measure. For example, in all but one male equation, the coefficient of $U_{PM}$ is higher when $U_3$ rather than $U$ is the dependent variable. In the female equation, the coefficient of $U_{PM}$ is also larger for $U_3$ than $U$ for all the younger groups (where the school population is a significant percentage of the total). Only for the female groups aged 20–24 are the coefficients insignificantly different from one another.[16]

## 6.4   The Alternative Activity Equations: Employment, Unemployment, School, Residual

### 6.4.1   Background

Analyzing the labor market and general economic status of youths by focusing on unemployment presents severe problems. The Bureau of Labor Statistics divides the youth population into four categories on the basis of major activity. The categories are employment, unemployment, schooling, and residual (denoted $R$). Of these four divisions, the unemployment category is the smallest. Furthermore, the response error for unemployment is considerably larger than for employment and schooling. Especially for youths who may be either in school and looking for a part-time job or out of school for the summer and interested in working, the BLS question that refers to "actively" seeking work is ambiguous. Indeed, for most youth groups and particularly for teenagers, the notion of unemployment and hence labor force is sufficiently flawed and is a weak statistic for policy purposes.

To avoid concentrating solely on unemployment, we suggest a strategy of studying employment, unemployment, schooling, and the residual categories together. This allows for the observation of flows across categories. For example, it is useful to know whether a change in $U_{PM}$ causes a net increase in the schooling $(S)$ or residual $(R)$ categories.[17]

One problem with the alternative activity equation approach is that the residual category, $R$, includes both some of society's most advantaged and disadvantaged youths.[18] At one extreme, it includes high school dropouts who have such low skill levels that they cannot find a job, youths from welfare families who would cost their families their eligibility if they accepted a job, and youths who are in poor health. On the other hand, it also includes a large number of young females who are beginning to raise their families, teenagers who are taking the summer off, and relatively skilled youths who are pursuing other activities for a short period of time between jobs and/or school.

There is a tendency among some researchers to interpret an increase in $E/P$ as a positive development, especially if it does not parallel a decrease in $S/P$. The work ethic aside, there is little basis for this view. Although it would be an easier problem if $R$ only included problem nonworkers, our inspection of the data suggests that this is not the case.

In the equations, we disaggregate the age-sex-race youth population into four mutually exclusive categories. The categories are $U/P$, $(E + M)/P$, $(S - (S \cap L))/P$ and $R/P$. These dependent variables were regressed with the same set of independent variables, as indicated in equation (6), with the exceptions that the percentage in the military were included in the male equations and a time trend was included in the female equations.

By construction, the sum of the four dependent variables should be equal to one. The problem in estimating these dependent variables by single equation techniques is that the linear restriction across equations may not be satisfied. In order to estimate the coefficients of the explanatory variables for these four choices, subject to the linear constraint across equations, we used the logarithm of the pairwise odds as the dependent variables. To illustrate, denote the four youth categories as $P_i$, $0 < P_i < 1$, $i = 1, 2, 3, 4$, and $\sum_{i=1}^{4} P_i = 1$. The dependent variables are then $\ln (P_i/P_1)$, $i = 2, 3, 4$. The regressions determine the ratios of the probabilities. The absolute values can then be estimated using the condition that the sum of probabilities is equal to unity. The implicit coefficients of the respective independent variables can be obtained by numerical estimation. Based on the coefficients from the $P_i/P_1$ equations, the probabilities were computed by changing one specific right-hand side variable by 1%. These computed probabilities were compared with the corresponding original estimates to derive the implicit elasticities at a given period. These numerically derived elasticities for the third quarter of 1978 are reported in tables 6.3–6.6 by each variable.[19]

**Table 6.3**    Implicit Coefficients Derived From Constrained Equations: Implicit Coefficients of $RPy$, 1978:3

| | Male | | | | Female | | | |
|---|---|---|---|---|---|---|---|---|
| Age/ Race | $\dfrac{S-(S\cap L)}{P}$ P1 | $\dfrac{U}{P}$ P2 | $\dfrac{E}{P}$ P3 | $\dfrac{R}{P}$ P4 | $\dfrac{S-(S\cap L)}{P}$ P1 | $\dfrac{U}{P}$ P2 | $\dfrac{E}{P}$ P3 | $\dfrac{R}{P}$ P4 |
| **16–17** | | | | | | | | |
| Total | −.5909 | .8093 | .2441 | −.3843 | .8157 | .0371 | −.0525 | −.443 |
| White | −.9068 | 1.0256 | .4418 | −.7449 | .7697 | .2165 | −.0864 | −.380 |
| Black | 1.0749 | −.3633 | −1.5747 | .7839 | 1.6187 | −.6933 | −.3870 | −.755 |
| **18–19** | | | | | | | | |
| Total | .3485 | .3224 | −.4480 | 2.5670 | 1.7067 | .3337 | −.5336 | .448 |
| White | .1132 | .4435 | −.3748 | 2.5505 | 1.5159 | .4852 | −.4748 | .522 |
| Black | 1.5348 | −.5643 | −1.0509 | 3.1120 | 3.5698 | −.0459 | −1.6399 | .319 |
| **20–20** | | | | | | | | |
| Total | 1.4642 | .7323 | −.3295 | 2.6901 | 1.0297 | −.2925 | −.3222 | .69 |
| White | 1.1024 | .8918 | −.2889 | 2.7870 | .7907 | .5532 | −.4256 | .83 |
| Black | 5.4521 | −.1343 | −.6818 | 2.1400 | 2.8986 | −2.3216 | .2857 | .08 |

**Table 6.4**    Implicit Coefficients of $U_{PM}$, 1978:3

| | Male | | | | Female | | | |
|---|---|---|---|---|---|---|---|---|
| Age/ Race | $\dfrac{S-(S\cap L)}{P}$ P1 | $\dfrac{U}{P}$ P2 | $\dfrac{E}{P}$ P3 | $\dfrac{R}{P}$ P4 | $\dfrac{S-(S\cap L)}{P}$ P1 | $\dfrac{U}{P}$ P2 | $\dfrac{E}{P}$ P3 | $\dfrac{R}{P}$ P4 |
| **16–17** | | | | | | | | |
| Total | .1051 | .2411 | −.1001 | .0254 | .0160 | .2273 | −.0958 | .050 |
| White | .1093 | .3160 | −.0858 | −.0097 | .0271 | .2710 | −.0872 | .037 |
| Black | .0897 | −.1031 | −.1872 | .1631 | −.0369 | .0528 | −.1830 | .120 |
| **18–19** | | | | | | | | |
| Total | .0155 | .5534 | −.0963 | .1544 | −.0505 | .3350 | −.0819 | .080 |
| White | −.0074 | .6405 | −.0826 | .1137 | −.0790 | .3993 | −.0728 | .089 |
| Black | .1227 | .2558 | −.2043 | .3296 | .0835 | .1556 | −.1684 | .054 |
| **20–24** | | | | | | | | |
| Total | .0600 | .7820 | −.0824 | .1745 | −.0599 | .4918 | −.0618 | .017 |
| White | .0415 | .8370 | −.0736 | .1718 | −.0905 | .5376 | −.0440 | −.003 |
| Black | .2345 | .5909 | −.1527 | .2104 | .1207 | .3387 | −.1908 | .139 |

### 6.4.2 The Impact of $RPy$

For the constrained $U/P$ equations, six of the male and five of the female equations had the anticipated sign of $RPy$. It is interesting that the incorrect signs appeared in the black equations in all but one case. Does this suggest that the labor market position for black youths has improved with demographic overcrowding?

**Table 6.5**     **Implicit Coefficients of W/MW, 1978:3**

| | Male | | | | Female | | | |
|---|---|---|---|---|---|---|---|---|
| Age/Race | $\dfrac{S-(S\cap L)}{P}$ P1 | $\dfrac{U}{P}$ P2 | $\dfrac{E}{P}$ P3 | $\dfrac{R}{P}$ P4 | $\dfrac{S-(S\cap L)}{P}$ P1 | $\dfrac{U}{P}$ P2 | $\dfrac{E}{P}$ P3 | $\dfrac{R}{P}$ P4 |
| **16–17** | | | | | | | | |
| Total | −.4774 | −.2136 | .2570 | −.0707 | −.5827 | −.4211 | .2082 | .200 |
| White | −.4453 | −.4525 | .2851 | −.1431 | −.4966 | −.4343 | .1844 | .135 |
| Black | −.7215 | .6640 | .2238 | .1209 | −1.0165 | −.4865 | .9728 | .389 |
| **18–19** | | | | | | | | |
| Total | −.4771 | −.6632 | .1911 | −.2976 | −.6243 | −.2121 | −.1622 | −.03 |
| White | −.4762 | −.7328 | .1491 | −.1151 | −.5837 | −.1601 | .1303 | −.05 |
| Black | −.4218 | −.3860 | .4460 | −.7857 | −.8797 | −.2416 | .4702 | .010 |
| **20–24** | | | | | | | | |
| Total | −.5435 | −1.2411 | .1825 | −.6549 | −.0539 | −.1235 | .0831 | −.157 |
| White | −.4791 | −1.2867 | .1576 | −.6283 | .0216 | −.0401 | .1137 | −.291 |
| Black | −1.0187 | −.9860 | .3465 | −.6807 | −.5657 | −.3967 | −.1476 | .590 |

**Table 6.6**     **Implicit Coefficients of AF/POP, 1978:3**

| | Male | | | |
|---|---|---|---|---|
| | $\dfrac{S-(S\cap L)}{P}$ P1 | $\dfrac{U}{P}$ P2 | $\dfrac{E}{P}$ P3 | $\dfrac{R}{P}$ P4 |
| **16–17** | | | | |
| Total | .1535 | −.1499 | .0165 | −.0944 |
| White | .1979 | −.1134 | .0129 | −.1351 |
| Black | −.0022 | −.3133 | .1300 | .0347 |
| **18–19** | | | | |
| Total | .2845 | −.1509 | −.0441 | .1914 |
| White | .3158 | −.1082 | −.0534 | .2297 |
| Black | .1484 | −.2810 | .0060 | .1768 |
| **20–24** | | | | |
| Total | .2354 | −.3668 | .0185 | −.0174 |
| White | .2666 | −.3181 | .0035 | .0767 |
| Black | .0940 | −.4651 | .1108 | −.2696 |

To analyze this puzzling result, it is necessary to evaluate the other three activity equations. The equations indicate that the negative coefficients of $RPy$ in the $U$–$P$ equations do not indicate an improvement in blacks' labor market position. Of particular importance are the $E/P$ equations. For all but three of the eighteen equations, $E/P$ is negatively related to $RPy$. The only equation for blacks in which the coefficient is positive is with females aged 20–24. Moreover, the implied elasticities of

*RPy* in the E/P equations are considerably larger for blacks than for whites.

The public policy debate on youth unemployment invariably is in terms of the BLS unemployment rate variable, *U/L*. It is therefore useful to convert the *U–P* and *E/P* equations of tables 6.3–6.6 so that their implications for the more traditional unemployment rate variable can be analyzed. The results are shown in table 6.7. Column 1 of table 6.7 shows that the elasticity of *U/L* with respect to *RPy* has the anticipated positive sign in all but two equations (black females aged 16/17 and 20–24).

The results of tables 6.3–6.7 make it clear that both black and white youth labor market positions are adversely affected by demographic overcrowding. However, the response pattern of the two groups differs. For white youths, unemployment increases are large and are not offset by changes in labor force participation rates. For black youths, the unemployment response to *RPy* appears to be low, but this is mainly because of a sharp decline in participation rates.

Given the linear restriction across equations, an increase in one of the $P_i$'s requires a reduction in another. What happens to those workers who are not employed as a result of cohort overcrowding? The implicit coefficients of *RPy* in the $(S - (S \cap L))/P$ and *R/P* equations provide an answer.

Essentially, an increase in *RPy*, *ceteris paribus*, leads to an increase in *U/P*, a decrease in *E/P*, an increase in $(S - (S \cap L))/P$ and an increase in *Rl)P*. The displaced employed workers largely migrate to full-time school

Table 6.7    **Percent Change in Unemployment Rates[a] Due to One Percent Change in Respective Explanatory Variable in 1978:3, Derived from Constrained Equations**

| | Unemployment rates | | | | | | |
| Age/ | Male | | | | Female | | |
| Race | *RPy* | $U_{PM}$ | *AF/POP* | *W/MW* | *RPy* | $U_{PM}$ | *W/MW* |
|---|---|---|---|---|---|---|---|
| **16–17** | | | | | | | |
| Total | .4694 | .2844 | − .1387 | − .3916 | .0695 | .2567 | − .5133 |
| White | .4956 | .3430 | − .1078 | − .6284 | .2511 | .2879 | − .5268 |
| Black | .8095 | .0556 | − .2928 | .2896 | − .1867 | .1407 | − .8876 |
| **18–19** | | | | | | | |
| Total | .6835 | .5744 | − .0944 | − .7545 | .7408 | .3638 | − .3109 |
| White | .7403 | .6523 | − .0495 | − .7951 | .8408 | .4122 | − .2473 |
| Black | .3703 | .3472 | − .2166 | − .6260 | 1.0294 | .2070 | − .4498 |
| **20–24** | | | | | | | |
| Total | .9804 | .7962 | − .3548 | − 1.3103 | .0281 | .4964 | − .1873 |
| White | 1.1025 | .8486 | − .2998 | − 1.3451 | .9174 | .5505 | − .1262 |
| Black | .4660 | .6293 | − .4872 | − 1.1259 | − 2.0224 | .4125 | − .1907 |

[a]Unemployment rates $\equiv U/(E + U + M)$.

and/or to household activities. This is not, however, the complete story of the demographic overcrowding because of the *ceteris paribus* assumption. For example, government policy, responding to the effects of demographic overcrowding, may also affect the distribution of the youth population across the four activity categories. When the $AF/POP$ and $W/MW$ are removed from the schooling equation, the sign on $RPy$ becomes negative for white males. In addition, the $TREND$ term poses obvious problems in the female equations. Since the intermediate-run demographic swings are highly correlated with a trend variable over the short estimation period, it is likely that $TREND$ will capture some of these affects. That is, $RPy$ does not reflect the full effect of demographic overcrowding because changes in other variables should also be anticipated.

### 6.4.3   The Impact of $U_{PM}$

The cyclical variable, $U_{PM}$, produced the anticipated results. As illustrated in table 6.3–6.6, increases in $U_{PM}$ are associated with little change in schooling; an increase in $U/P$ with a decrease in $E/P$ and an increase in $R/P$.

The elasticities of $U/P$ with respect to $U_{PM}$ are the largest for white males. In addition, the elasticities tend to be larger for whites than for blacks, for males than for females, and for older than for younger workers. For all age-sex-race categories the elasticities are less than unity.

The overall results suggest a ranking of youth groups in terms of the cyclical versus structural sensitivity of their unemployment rates ($U/P$). In general, youths are more structurally than cyclically sensitive in comparison with adults. Females and the youngest youth groups are the most sensitive group to structural rather then cyclical swings in unemployment.

The ranking is also reflected in industry employment. For example, the older male groups have a high concentration of employment in the high-wage, cyclically sensitive industries such as mining, manufacturing, and construction. The younger and female groups are more heavily represented in the low wage, acyclical industries such as retail and service. Industry employment patterns, however, cannot be viewed simply as a causal factor in the unemployment behavior of these groups. Rather, the underlying structural features of these groups' labor market behavior is likely to determine their industry employment. For example, the 16–17 age group, looking for part-time, after-school work, is most suited for employment in the retail and service sectors. Training costs and work scheduling in industries such as manufacturing are not suitable for this group's casual labor market attachment.

The ranking of black and white groups, in terms of the cyclical versus structural issue, is more difficult than ranking age-sex groups. Although blacks have a lower elasticity of $U/P$ with respect to $U_{PM}$, it is necessary to inspect the $E/P$ as well as the $U/P$ equation. Of particular interest is that black youths have a considerably higher $E/P$ sensitivity to the business cycle than whites. That is, black youths have a lower $U/P$ but a higher $E/P$ elasticity with respect to $U_{PM}$. Since blacks and whites tend to be equally employed, in percentage terms, in the high- and low-wage industries, the cyclical nature of different industries cannot be a factor.

One possible explanation is that the black youth labor market response is more closely related to fluctuations in layoffs and hirings. On the other hand, changes in the labor market status for white youths, as reflected in reentrant and new entrant rates, may be relatively more important. In any case, the ranking across races is more complex than across age and sex groups.

### 6.4.4   The Impact of $W/MW$

The relative wage term exhibits the consistent and anticipated signs in the constrained equations.[20] For all but one demographic group changes in schooling, unemployment, and the residual category are inversely related, while changes in employment are directly related to movements in $W/MW$. In other words, an increase in the youth market wage, *ceteris paribus*, is related to a shift into employment and out of all other activities.

Of particular interest is the relationship between unemployment ($U/P$) and $W/MW$. As previously suggested, the youth unemployment rate depends upon the cost of being unemployed. Interpreting $MW$ as a proxy for the reservation wage, an increase in the market wage, $W$, leads to an increase in the cost of unemployment and hence a decrease in the unemployment rate. To the extent that $W/MW$ represents a minimum wage variable, however, the decrease in $U/P$, following an increase in $W/MW$, would be interpreted as a demand-side effect. These two views cannot be isolated on the basis of the time series data.

The one category that shows a mixed pattern with respect to $W/MW$ is the residual category, $R$. For the female equations, the three black groups and one white group are positively related, while the two white groups are negatively related to $W/MW$. Given the composition of $R$, a priori predictions of the signs of the coefficients are not obvious. One factor, however, is that the female $R$ category contains many more homeworkers who are raising families than the male $R$ category. The resulting sign pattern is thus compatible with a demographic overcrowding interpretation. In particular, a deterioration in $W/MW$ may reduce completed family size and lead to an exit from $R$ on the part of females. Since this household behavior response is not likely to be a factor in the male equations, the cost of unemployment argument should be dominant and explain the negative coefficient of $W/MW$.

### 6.4.5   The Impact of $AF/POP$

The armed forces variable plays an important role in distinguishing between the unemployment rate patterns for whites and blacks. First, this variable has had a large variance over the estimation period, rising sharply during the Vietnam War and then declining close to its prewar levels during the mid to late 1970s. Second, the black and white male groups respond differently to $AF/POP$. Unfortunately, given the data period, changes in $AF/POP$, especially its sharp increase to a peak value in the early 1970s, parallel changes in $RPy$. This may reduce the confidence that can be placed in interpreting separately these two quite different independent variables.

In the unemployment equations, the implicit coefficient of $AF/POP$ was negative in each of the nine male equations. The white and black equations, however, indicate a much greater sensitivity of black unemployment to military employment. This could conceivably explain the fact that black youth unemployment has increased since 1970 relative to that of white youths. Since both the percentage of the military that is black and the percentage of blacks in the military have increased since the change to the all-volunteer forces, the decline in $AF/POP$ cannot be a major factor in the black male unemployment trends.

The major differences in employment response also reflect the greater sensitivity of black labor market conditions to the level of military employment. For employment, the coefficient differences between whites and blacks are particularly large. Indeed, white employment in the 18–19 age group actually declines with increases in military employment. This is particularly surprising since $E/P$ includes $M$ as being employed. In other words, an increase in the military is associated with a decline in civilian employment for whites aged 18–19 that is larger than the number of whites who enter the military.

The differential white-black response pattern also holds for schooling. The increase in $AF/POP$ is associated with a much larger increase in white than in black schooling. This probably reflects behavior during the draft period when increases in $AF/POP$ encouraged youths to remain in or return to school to secure student deferments.

## 6.5   Considerations of the Deterioration of the Black Youth Labor Market

### 6.5.1   Unemployment and Labor Force Developments

Two basic factors suggest a deterioration in the labor market position for black relative to white youths during the 1970s. The first is that black youth unemployment increased throughout the 1970s. The second is that black youth $E/P$ ratios fell over most of the past decade while white $E/P$ ratios were increasing.[21]

Since increases in unemployment may be less of a problem if attributable to increases in participation rates, it is important to consider labor force and unemployment developments together. For black males, the participation rates decreased substantially for all age groups, while the rates for whites increased for all age groups. For females the situation is somewhat different. Both whites and blacks showed increasing participation rates during the period. However, the percentage growth in participation rates was much smaller for blacks than for whites for all female cohorts. In sum, these changes in unemployment and participation rates suggest a deterioration in labor market conditions for blacks, especially for black males (see table 6.8).

We have generally attributed the youth unemployment developments of the past decade to supply side factors. In the case of black males, however, the data on $U/L$ and $E/P$ may indicate a possibly different picture. Presumably, increases in $U/L$ combined with decreases in $L/P$ give at least the impression of a deterioration in demand conditions. To what extent has the demand for black males shifted adversely relative to whites and black females?

### 6.5.2    Trends in Secular Wages

Whereas the employment situation has worsened for blacks relative to whites, the relative wages for blacks have increased continuously during the last decade. The overall white median usual weekly earnings for full-time, wage, and salary workers increased by 6.7% per year between 1967 and 1977. However, the corresponding wage growth for blacks was 8.0% on average during the same period. The black-white wage ratios increased from 0.692 to 0.776 for males and from 0.797 to 0.936 for females during this period.

The full-time usual weekly earnings for youths whose major activities are other than school also show a similar pattern. Here again, the gap between black and white wage differentials has narrowed over time. Except for females aged 16–17, the wages of all black groups rose more than those of the comparable white groups. The black-white wage ratios increased from 0.832, 0.735, and 0.740 to 0.793, 0.799, and 0.868 for males aged 16–17, 18–19, and 20–24 groups respectively between 1967 and 1978. For females, the corresponding ratios changed from 1.125, 0.829, and 0.830 respectively to 0.914, 1.034, and 0.928. The puzzling development is that the groups with the most unfavorable unemployment-employment indicators enjoyed the best earnings growth.

### 6.5.3    Trends in Industry Employment

To explore further the issue of deteriorating $U/L$ and $E/P$ rates coupled with increasing relative wages for black youths, it is useful to explore the industry employment of black and white youths. For ease of analysis, we

**Table 6.8**        Unemployment Rates and Employment/Population Ratios by Age-Race-Sex

| | Unemployment rates[a] | | | Employment ratios[b] | | |
|---|---|---|---|---|---|---|
| | 1965 | 1972 | 1978 | 1965 | 1972 | 1978 |
| | | | Male | | | |
| White | | | | | | |
| 16–17 | 14.84 | 16.55 | 17.08 | 38.91 | 42.44 | 46.31 |
| 18–19 | 11.53 | 12.54 | 10.92 | 63.53 | 65.17 | 69.18 |
| 20–24 | 5.95 | 8.55 | 7.65 | 83.36 | 79.93 | 82.00 |
| Black | | | | | | |
| 16–17 | 27.78 | 36.66 | 40.71 | 28.97 | 22.52 | 20.47 |
| 18–19 | 20.13 | 26.40 | 30.90 | 56.87 | 48.61 | 46.59 |
| 20–24 | 9.29 | 14.79 | 20.13 | 83.38 | 72.81 | 66.29 |
| | | | Female | | | |
| White | | | | | | |
| 16–17 | 15.17 | 16.90 | 17.08 | 24.47 | 32.57 | 40.64 |
| 18–19 | 13.63 | 12.27 | 12.34 | 43.76 | 50.48 | 56.81 |
| 20–24 | 6.31 | 8.16 | 8.27 | 46.16 | 54.61 | 63.79 |
| Black | | | | | | |
| 16–17 | 39.67 | 35.56 | 41.87 | 12.55 | 13.23 | 16.03 |
| 18–19 | 28.01 | 38.64 | 36.81 | 28.88 | 27.01 | 31.41 |
| 20–24 | 13.79 | 17.44 | 21.56 | 47.71 | 47.04 | 49.81 |

[a]The unemployment rates are defined as $U/L$.
[b]The employment ratios are defined as $E/P$ where both $E$ and $P$ include the military.

use the percentage of each youth group which is employed in the retail and service sector compared with total employment of each demographic group. The retail and service sectors are the major employers of youths and are the lowest wage sectors. The data, presented in table 6.9, illustrate two overall developments. First, the percentage of black employment found in the lowest wage sectors is approximately equal to the percentage of white employment in these sectors. There are slightly more black males but many fewer black females (as a percentage), in comparison with white groups, in the low-wage sectors. Second, changes in the percentage of low-wage employment has worsened for black relative to white males, but improved for black relative to white females.

What is clear about these statistics is that they are not of great help in clarifying the puzzle. As a compositional issue, the improvement in black relative wages cannot be explained by the fact that their occupational status was unchanged. However, there is also no evidence of a significant deterioration in the employment status of black males that could explain their declining employment-population ratios and rising unemployment rates.

For those who believe that each age-sex-race group has its own $RPy_i$ variable as the proper cohort overcrowding variable, there is no problem

Table 6.9    Proportion of Each Group's Employment That Is in
Low-wage Industries (Service and Retail)

|  | Male | | | Female | | |
|---|---|---|---|---|---|---|
|  | 1968 | 1972 | 1978 | 1968 | 1972 | 1978 |
| **White** | | | | | | |
| 16–17 | .7270 | .7392 | .7290 | .8239 | .8422 | .8706 |
| 18–19 | .4763 | .5298 | .5105 | .5440 | .6554 | .6810 |
| 20–24 | .3232 | .3787 | .3804 | .5287 | .5975 | .6148 |
| 16–21 (out of school) | .3650 | .4657 | .4446 | .4914 | .6129 | .6399 |
| 16–21 (in school) | .7765 | .7833 | .7929 | .8881 | .8967 | .9051 |
| 16+ | .3037 | .3317 | .3449 | .5755 | .6124 | .6200 |
| **Black** | | | | | | |
| 16–17 | .6617 | .7013 | .7435 | .8291 | .7655 | .8315 |
| 18–19 | .4583 | .4393 | .5429 | .5738 | .6126 | .6514 |
| 20–24 | .3012 | .3500 | .3816 | .5453 | .5267 | .5536 |
| 16–21 (out of school) | .3519 | .4220 | .4583 | .5277 | .5519 | .6150 |
| 16–21 (in school) | .7603 | .7831 | .8167 | .8537 | .8511 | .8513 |
| 16+ | .3256 | .3307 | .3457 | .6429 | .6350 | .6121 |

in explaining the declining black male employment ratios. Specifically, the ratio of black youth employment to white youth employment (where employment includes the military) has been virtually unchanged since 1965. According to the "$RPy_i$" model, the entire deterioration in $E/P$ ratios for black males can thus be associated with their increasing percentage in the youth population. Since we believe that overcrowding is better defined over youths as a single group, we do not find this result a compelling explanation. Moreover, the puzzle of declining $E/P$ ratios for black males combined with increasing relative wage rates cannot be attributed to the higher growth rate of the black youth population.

6.5.4    Trends in School Enrollment

One of the main distinctive features between white and black groups over the last decade is that the school enrollment rates for all black groups increased substantially more than those for whites. Except for females aged 20–24, the enrollment rates for whites decreased for all age-sex groups between 1965 and 1978. During the same period, the enrollment rates for blacks consistently increased. Furthermore, although the enrollment rates for all black age-sex groups were lower than those for the corresponding white groups in 1965, the situation was reversed by 1978. That is, by 1978 the enrollment rates for all black age-sex groups were higher than the comparable white groups.

Does the increase in school enrollment rates for black males equal the decline in their $E/\dot{P}$ rates? The answer can be seen by comparing tables 6.8 and 6.10. The increase in school enrollment captures almost all of the decline in $E/P$ for black males aged 16–17. For black males aged 18–19, it picks up 4 of the 10 percentage point decline. For the black male group aged 20–24, a 17 percentage point decline in $E/P$ is reduced to 10 percentage points when $S/P$ is added. Perhaps as important, is that the wide gap between $E/P$ rates for whites and blacks becomes a very narrow gap for most age-sex groups when $(E + (S \cap E))/P$ is used as an indicator of labor market position.

The nature of the problem depends upon how one evaluates schooling versus employment for youth. In level terms as of 1978, white youths enjoyed an advantage in the combined employment plus schooling ratio over comparable black youths. The trend is less obvious. The increase in white employment ratios is, in part, due to their declining school enrollment and increasing part-time work while in school. The decrease in black employment ratios is, in part, due to their increasing school enrollments. In addition, black enrollment has gained without a significant increase in after-school work (comparable to that found for white enrollees).

### 6.6 Summary

In this paper we have advanced the argument that the deterioration in the absolute and relative youth unemployment ratios is due primarily to a cohort overcrowding effect. Other variables that seem to play a role are the decline in the size of military service since the Vietnam War, the decline in the market wage for youths relative to some combination of minimum wages and government transfer programs, and a cyclical variable representing changes in demand. Since we control for the business cycle, which does not have a secular trend, the deterioration in the labor market position for youths over the past two decades can be attributed to labor supply factors. That is, the increasing unemployment rate of this group represents an increase in their equilibrium unemployment rate due to overcrowding and the effects of government labor market and social welfare programs.

The BLS measured unemployment rate is usually the main piece of evidence indicating the declining labor market position of youths. Although we agree that an important decline has taken place, the magnitude of the job decline is overstated by the BLS statistics. Indeed, we argue that the BLS youth unemployment rate is a very weak statistic for policy purposes. Other measures of unemployment and/or employment ratios show less decline than do the BLS measures. For example, the percentage of youths who are either employed or in school is only slightly down from the 1965 levels. We argue that this variable, or an unemploy-

Table 6.10

Employment + School[a]

Population,
1965 and 1978

|                | 1965 | 1978 |
|----------------|------|------|
| Male, white    |      |      |
| 16–17          | 88.0 | 87.6 |
| 18–19          | 91.0 | 90.0 |
| 20–24          | 94.0 | 91.1 |
| Male, black    |      |      |
| 16–17          | 83.2 | 82.0 |
| 18–19          | 83.0 | 77.0 |
| 20–24          | 88.9 | 78.5 |
| Female, white  |      |      |
| 16–17          | 80.0 | 83.1 |
| 18–19          | 71.0 | 77.6 |
| 20–24          | 52.7 | 71.2 |
| Female, black  |      |      |
| 16–17          | 74.0 | 77.0 |
| 18–19          | 56.9 | 61.4 |
| 20–24          | 52.5 | 59.5 |

[a]The specific measure is $\dfrac{E+M+S-(S\cap E)}{P}$.

ment rate construct which treats schooling as equivalent in status to employment, is more useful as an indicator of the labor market position of youths with respect to jobs.

Whereas the job decline is less serious than the BLS unemployment rate indicates, the decline in the relative wage of youths may be more central to the relevant issues. That is, the labor market problem of youths is more a problem of low skill and hence low wage levels than of a lack of jobs. The increasing employment-population ratios for most youth groups, in spite of the high increase in their population, is one source of evidence of the ability of the economy to create large numbers of youth jobs.

Black males are the one sex-race youth group that combines steadily deteriorating unemployment and employment ratios. There are problems, however, in determining to what extent the overall position of this group has declined. First, the relative wage for black youths, both males and females, has improved relative to white youths. Second, the decline in employment and increase in relative wages have not been matched by a significant change in the proportion of black males in the low-wage industries. The percentage of black male employment remains approximately the same as the percentage of white male employment in the low-wage sectors. Finally, school enrollment rates have been increasing for blacks and decreasing for whites. As a result, the ratios of those employed plus those in school, as a percentage of the relevant population, show less of a difference between black and white youths than the employment ratios alone. But, from a social welfare perspective, it is difficult to weigh the increase in joblessness against the increase in relative wages and school enrollment.

The increase in the percentage of black males who are both out of school and not employed implies that a component of the black male youth population has suffered a significant decline in their relative economic status. This suggests that for black males aged 16–24 there may be a growing divergence in labor market performance.

# Notes

1. See, for example, Wachter (1972; 1976b; 1977), and Kim (1979). This work builds upon Easterlin (1968). Several relevant studies and a detailed bibliography are contained in Espenshade and Serow (1978). More recent work which develops this approach includes Ehrenberg (1979), Welch (1979), and Reubens (1979).

2. For a detailed discussion of the endogenous taste model for explaining economic-demographic variables, see Easterlin, Pollak and Wachter (forthcoming). The relative income model is presented in Easterlin (1968) and Wachter (1972; 1976b).

3. See, for example, Cain and Watts (1973).

4. The statistical problems of measuring the youth labor force is stressed by Clark and Summers (1979).

5. This model is drawn from Wachter and Wachter (1978).

6. In equations (3) and (4) it is assumed that experience or skill can be acquired only with age. The result is that the number of $A$ workers only increases with the population and participation rates of $A$ workers. In fact, the rate of accumulation of skill can be increased by more intensive training. The cost for training is likely to be upward sloping and steeper in the short than in the long run. Consequently, the accumulation of human capital will be slowed as workers spread their training to avoid the higher short-run costs. (This factor of increasing short-run supply costs is also a factor in the lag of actual capital behind its optimal level.)

7. An alternative measure of labor market pressure, denoted $UGAP$, yielded similar results. The $U_{PM}$ variable was used instead of $UGAP$ because the latter contains the unemployment rate of youths. For a discussion of $UGAP$, see Wachter (1976a).

8. See, for example, Ragan (1977).

9. In this chapter, the terms blacks and nonwhites are used interchangeably.

10. An alternative variable, $W/MW^*C$, where $C$ is the coverage rate, did not perform as well across equations. Especially given the lack of success of the coverage variable, our $W/MW$ cannot be interpreted as a straight minimum wage effect. As indicated, it cannot be empirically differentiated, in most equations, from a supply-side variable that measures changes in government transfer programs.

11. For a detailed discussion of the problems with measuring government policy variables, see the original NBER discussion paper.

12. The impact of welfare programs has received relatively limited attention until recently. See Levitan et. al. (1972), Garfinkle and Orr (1974), Saks (1975), Williams (1975), Levy (1979) and the Studies in Public Welfare of the Joint Economic Committee (1973).

Major studies of minimum wage laws include Moore (1971), Kosters and Welch (1972), Goldfarb (1974), Gramlich (1976), Mincer (1976), Welch (1976), (1977), Ashenfelter and Smith (1979), and U.S. Department of Labor (1970).

For several relevant models on the impact of direct job creation see Killingsworth and Killingsworth (1978) and Palmer (1979).

13. Some of the relevant papers that provide an empirical framework for the youth unemployment problem include Kalachek (1969), Doeringer and Piore (1971), R. A. Gordon (1973), R. J. Gordon (1977), and Adams and Mangum (1978).

Recent empirical time series studies on youth unemployment which address this same phenomenon include Freeman and Medoff (1981), Ragan (1977), Thurow (1977), and the conference on Youth Unemployment (1978).

14. Conceptual problems with the definition of the unemployment rate for youths are stressed by R. A. Gordon (1973), Levitan and Taggart (1974), and Clark and Summers (1979).

15. The $\cap$ notation indicates the intersection of two variables. Hence $S \cap L$ indicates those who are in school and in the labor force.

16. The results were included in the original NBER working paper prepared for the conference.

17. Relevant studies on schooling include Freeman (1976) and the recent comment by Smith and Welch (1978). Kim (1979) investigates the complexities of the military and schooling relationship with the youth labor market. A very useful collection of essays is found in the NCMP volume (1976).

18. One of the major questions concerning the $R$ category involves the issue of discouraged workers. The view that the number of disadvantaged potential workers in the $R$ group is significant is stressed by Doeringer and Piore (1971) and Harrison (1972) among others.

19. For those who prefer to analyze estimated coefficients directly, the equations for the four activities, unconstrained by $\sum_{i=1}^{4} P_i = 1$ were presented in the original NBER working paper.

20. In the unconstrained equations, the pattern of the signs is unchanged, but the variable is only marginally significant.

21. Studies which focus on minority unemployment include Doeringer and Piore (1971), Harrison (1972), Wallace (1974), the Congressional Budget Office (1976), Adams and Mangum (1978), and Osterman (1978).

# References

Adams, A. V. and Mangum, G. 1978. *The lingering crisis of youth unemployment*, Kalamazoo, Michigan: W. E. Upjohn Institute.

Ashenfelter, O. and Smith, R. S. April 1979. Compliance with the minimum wage law. *Journal of Political Economy*: 333–50.

Cain, G. G. and Watts, H. W. eds. 1973. *Income maintenance and labor supply*. Institute for Research on Poverty Monograph Series. Rand McNally College Publishing Company, Chicago.

Clark, K. and Summers, L. 1:1979, forthcoming. "Labor market dynamics and unemployment: A reconsideration. *Brookings Papers on Economic Activity*.

Congressional Budget Office. 1976. *The teenage unemployment problem*: *What are the options?* Washington, D.C.: U.S. Government Printing Office.

Doeringer, P. B., and Piore, M. 1971. *Internal labor markets and manpower analysis*. Lexington, Mass.: D. C. Heath.

Easterlin, R. A. 1968. *Population, labor force and long swings in economic growth: The american experience*. Columbia University Press for the National Bureau of Economic Research.

Easterlin, R. A., Pollak, R. A., and Wachter, M. L. 1980. Toward a more general economic model of fertility determination: Endogenous preferences and natural fertility. In *Population and economic change in less developed countries*. Chicago: The University of Chicago Press.

Ehrenberg, R. G. 1979. The demographic structure of unemployment rates and labor market transition probabilities. Paper prepared for the National Commission for Manpower Policy.

Espenshade, T. J. and Serow, W. J., eds. 1978. *The economic consequences of slowing population growth*. Academic Press. New York

Freeman, R. B. 1976. *The overeducated american*. Academic Press. New York

————. 1979. The effect of demographic factors on the age-earnings profile in the U.S. *Journal of Human Resources* 14, no. 3: 289–318.

Freeman, R. B., and Medoff, J. L. May 16–17, 1979. The youth labor market problem in the united states: An overview. Chapter 3 of the present volume.

Garfinkel, I. and Orr, L. L. July 1974. Welfare policy and the employment rate of AFDC mothers. *National Tax Journal* 27:275–84.

Goldfarb, R. S. The policy content of qualitative minimum wage research. *IRRA 27th Annual Winter Proceedings*:261–68.

Gordon, R. A. 1973. Some macroeconomic aspects of manpower policy. In L. Ulman, ed., *Manpower programs in the policy mix*. Baltimore: Johns Hopkins Press.

Gordon, R. J. 1977. Structural unemployment and the productivity of women. *Carnegie-Rochester conference series on public policy: Stabilization of the domestic and international economy*. Karl Brunner and Allan Meltzer, eds. 181–229. Amsterdam: North-Holland.

Gramlich, E. M. 1976. Impact of minimum wages on other wages, employment, and family income. *Brookings Papers on Economic Activity* 2: 409–61. Washington, D.C.: The Brookings Institution.

Harrison, B. 1972. *Education, training, and the urban ghetto*. Baltimore, Md.: Johns Hopkins University Press.

Kalachek, E. 1969. Determinants of teen age unemployment. *Journal of Human Resources* 4, no. 1:3–21.

Killingsworth, C. C. and Killingsworth, M. R. 1978. Direct effects of employment and training programs on employment and unemployment: New estimates and implications for employment policy. In *Conference report on youth unemployment: Its measurement and meaning*. Washington, D.C.: U.S. Government Printing Office.

Kim, C. 1979. Unpublished manuscript. A study of the military labor market. University of Pennsylvania.

————. 1979. Unpublished manuscript. A study of the school enrollment rate: An empirical and theoretical investigation. University of Pennsylvania.

Kosters, M. and Welch, F. June 1972. The effects of minimum wages on the distribution of changes in aggregate employment. *American Economic Review* 62, no. 3:323–34.

Levita, S. A., Rein, M., and Marwich, D. 1972. *Work and welfare go together*. Baltimore, Md.: Johns Hopkins University Press.

Levitan, S. A. and Taggart, R. 1974. *Employment and earnings inadequacy: A new social indicator*. Baltimore, Johns Hopkins University Press.

Levy, F. 1979. The labor supply of female household heads, or AFDC work incentives don't work too well. *Journal of Human Resources* 14, no. 1:76–97.

Mincer, J. August 1976. Unemployment effects of minimum wages. *Journal of Political Economy*, part 2:S87–S104.

Moore, T. G. July/August 1971. The effect of minimum wages on teenage unemployment rates. *Journal of Political Economy* 79, no. 4:897–903.

National Commission for Manpower Policy. 1976. *From school to work: Improving the transition*. Washington, D.C.: U.S. Government Printing Office.

Osterman, P. 1978. Racial differentials in male youth unemployment. *Conference report on youth unemployment: Its measurement and meaning*. Washington, D.C.: U.S. Government Printing Office.

Palmer, J. L. 1978. *Creating jobs: Public employment programs and wage subsidies*. Washington, D.C.: The Brookings Institution.

Perry, C. R., Anderson, B. E., Rowan, R. L., and Northrup, H. R. 1975. *The impact of government manpower programs*. Philadelphia: Industrial Relations Unit, University of Pennsylvania.

Ragan, J. F. Jr. May 1977. Minimum wages and the youth labor market. *Review of Economics and Statistics* 59 no. 2:129–36.

Reubens, B. G. February 1979. *The measurement and interpretation of teenage unemployment in the United States and other countries*. U.S. Department of Labor, ASPER, NTIS PB284161/AS.

Saks, D. H. 1975. *Public assistance for mothers in urban labor market*. Princeton: Industrials Relations Section, Princeton University.

Smith, J. P. and Welch, F. November 1978. The overeducated American? A review article. *The Rand Paper Series*.

Studies in Public Welfare: Staff Studies Prepared for the Use of the Subcommittee on Fiscal Policy of the Joint Economic Committee Congress of the United States. Washington, D.C.: U.S. Government Printing Office.

Thurow, L. C. Fall 1977. Youth unemployment. New York: Rockefeller Foundation Working Paper.

U.S. Department of Labor. 1970. *Youth unemployment and minimum wages.* Bulletin 1657. Washington, D.C.: U.S. Government Printing Office.

Wachter, M. L. May 1972. A labor supply model for secondary workers. *Review of Economics and Statistics* 54, no. 2:141–51.

――――. 1:1976. The changing cyclical responsiveness of wage inflation over the postwar period. *Brookings Papers on Economic Activity,* 115–59[a].

――――. December 1976. The demographic impact on unemployment: Past experience and the outlook for the future. In *Demographic trends and full employment.* Washington, D.C.: National Commission for Manpower Policy, Special Report no. 12, 27–99[b].

――――. 2:1977. Intermediate swings in labor-force participation. *Brookings Papers on Economic Activity* 545–76.

Wachter, M. L. and Wachter, S. M. 1978. The fiscal policy dilemma: Cyclical swings dominated by supply-side constraints. In *The economic consequences of slowing population growth.* Edited by T. J. Espenshade and W. J. Serow. New York: Academic Press, Inc., 71–99.

Wallace, P. A. 1974. *Pathways to work-unemployment among black teenage females.* Lexington, Mass.: Heath Lexington Books.

Welch, F. 1977. Minimum wage legislation in the United States. In *Evaluating the labor-market effects of social programs.* Edited by O. Ashenfelter and J. Blum. Princeton: Industrial Relations Section, Princeton University.

――――. January 1979. Effects of cohort size on earnings: The baby boom babies' financial bust. *Journal of Political Economy* .87:565–97.

Williams, R. G. 1975. *Public assistance and work effort: The labor supply of low-income female heads of household.* Princeton: Industrial Relations Section, Princeton University.

## Comment     Edward Kalachek

During the 1960s youth unemployment rates deteriorated relative to those of adults. The relative unemployment performance of white youths stabilized in the early 1970s but deterioration continues among blacks. Despite the importance of this phenomenon, economists have been unable to develop statistically convincing explanations. The labor market

Edward Kalachek, formerly professor of economics at Washington University, died in December 1979.

models that explain rather well why young persons experience high unemployment have limited power in explaining why youth rates have risen so much relative to those of adults. Wachter and Kim approach this somewhat embarrassing problem with a supply-side explanation based on two constructs, demographic or cohort overcrowding and a socially determined minimum wage. The first construct, cohort overcrowding, assumes that younger and older workers are imperfect substitutes. Given the embodiment of human and physical capital, the short-run elasticity of substitution between youths and adults is quite low. Consequently, changes in relative cohort sizes will be reflected in disproportionate changes in relative wages. To make matters worse, the material aspirations of young married workers are formed while they are still living in their parents' homes. Faced with lower than expected relative wages, young families opt for fewer children and for more market hours.

The second construct, the socially determined minimum wage, emphasizes the supply rather than the demand implications of changes in the legally required minimum. Changes in the coverage or the level of the minimum wage are not likely to occur as isolated political acts, but rather reflect a social mood that will manifest itself through the liberalization of transfer payments and of other social welfare programs. More liberal welfare programs will shift the budget line and reduce the cost of nonemployment. Furthermore, the minimum wage establishes a wage below which it is not socially acceptable to work. Increases in the minimum wage will thus alter leisure-consumption goods trade-off. Workers will no longer be willing to provide market effort at wages which hitherto were acceptable. The effect of higher reservation wages on the supply side may be as or more important than the demand-side effect.

The two constructs can now be combined to generate the time series scenario. The relative size of the youth cohort did increase substantially during the 1960s, and given that production processes adjusted slowly, relative youth earnings dropped. For many youths the market clearing wage was driven below the rising social minimum. Youth employment rose substantially but so did youth unemployment. Here Wachter and Kim develop an important and frequently overlooked point. In a comparative static analysis of workers with constant taste and perfect knowledge of this taste, individuals with market wages below the social minimum would exist and remain out of the labor force. In the real world, slight changes in tastes, mood, need, or health will lead to labor markets entry, to brief spells of employment, and to frequent reported unemployment.

This chapter would have benefited from a formally developed labor supply model. The argument that economic tastes and aspirations are molded during the period one lives with one's parents implies a forward falling labor supply curve, at least for married workers and over some range. The social minimum wage concept implies that the labor supply schedule has been shifting inward at low relative wage levels. Between the two it is not clear whether more or less labor will be effectively supplied at lower relative wages, and the authors seem to want to have it both ways. Otherwise, this is a neat piece of political economy; that is to say, an imaginative use of economic reasoning to explain a bothersome real-world development. The authors are particularly to be commended for rescuing the social minimum wage from its subterranean existence in the informal conversations of labor economists and government officials and bringing it to the respectability of the published page. Stress on the social minimum wage is consistent with the finding reported elsewhere in this volume (chapter 2 and 7) that teenage unemployment is heavily concentrated among less than 10% of the population. It is also consistent with the experiences of those who have attempted to obtain youngsters for house or yard work. Indeed, both constructs are appealing, but difficult to demonstrate empirically. Hence it is not surprising that the empirical section provides at most rather modest support for the theory.

The paucity of appropriate data on transfer payments, job creation, and the minimum wage does inhibit empirical research. Still, it is not quite accurate to describe the time series minimum wage variable as largely a spike in 1967. Effective coverage and the relative size of the minimum both increased substantially in teenage intensive activities after 1967. Ragan[1] and others have already ably demonstrated the adverse impact of the minimum wage on teenage employment and unemployment. An analysis of Ragan's work suggests that Wachter and Kim would have obtained similarly strong findings but for their relative population variable. It is thus unfortunate that the estimating procedure does not allow a fair or reasonable test of demographic overcrowding. A current quarter correlation of relative youth population with measures of youth labor market performance is a test for instantaneous rather than for slow adjustment of production processes to cohort size. A test of a demographic overcrowding hypothesis requires a distributed lag on the relative youth population. As it is, results could be better interpreted if significance levels were shown. The strongest evidence for demographic overcrowding presented in this chapter is contained in table 6.8, which shows dramatic increases in teenage employment-population ratios between 1965 and 1972 and between 1972 and 1978. Further support is provided by the fact that a similar cohort bulge in Europe is also associated with higher youth unemployment rates.

In common with other scholars who have analyzed the youth labor market, Wachter and Kim express acute dissatisfaction with the appropriateness of the BLS concept of unemployment for this age group. They propose three supplementary measures: $U_1$, $U_2$ and $U_3$. $U_1$ is identical to the BLS measure except that military employment is included in the denominator, as well it should be. $U_2$ adds those school attenders who are currently neither counted as employed or as unemployed to the denominator of $U_1$, since school attendance can be regarded as a work activity and is a socially acceptable alternative to paid employment for youngsters. $U_3$ eliminates the unemployment of school attenders from the numerator of $U_2$. This is the logical next step once school attendance is accepted as the equivalent of work. Since employment dominates unemployment in the BLS classification system, workers with one job who are also hunting for another are classified as employed rather than as unemployed. The array of new unemployment measures is shown in table 6.2 for 1978, though unfortunately a time series for $U_1$, $U_2$, and $U_3$ is not generated. For 1978 the array of measures provides a more balanced and certainly a more sanguine view than is obtained by simple reliance on the BLS measure. Indeed, if $U_3$ were to be accepted as the best measure, high youth unemployment would become a problem of blacks rather than a general problem.

These new unemployment measures are a useful contribution. The BLS measure is institutionally and historically based rather than being well grounded in current theory. The distinction between market and nonmarket work is far more important to the Internal Revenue Service than it is to anyone else. School attendance past age 16 is presumably a voluntary activity and the empirical evidence indicates that it is a highly productive economic activity. If we are willing to go this far, though, we must proceed still further and treat all legitimate nonmarket work as employment whether it is performed by youths or adults. The most general derivation of the $U_3$ measure would include in the denominator and subtract if necessary from the numerator any person engaged in significant nonmarket work. Assuming for simplicity that it is the wife who normally specializes in housekeeping and child-raising, alternative measures are required for female as well as for youth unemployment. The $U_3$ measure for married women, spouse and children present, will of course always be zero. Although this seems to define the problem away, it may point in the right direction. Most persons primarily engaged in important nonmarket work activity are not unemployed by reasonable or standard criteria. Rather, they wish to work more hours per year than are available, and they wish to work these hours in rather than out of the marketplace. $U_3$ would then be an insightful measure of labor market performance, so long as it were supplemented by an appropriate measure of the discrepancy between actual and desired hours.

**Note**

1. Ragan, James F. Jr., "Minimum Wages and the Youth Labor Market," *Review of Economics and Statistics*, May 1977:129–36.

# Comment    Robert J. Gordon

There is much to applaud in the chapter by Wachter and Kim. Three appealing methodological features of the approach should be noted before we study the basic hypotheses and results:

1. Instead of providing us simply with regressions explaining youth unemployment, the authors study jointly four mutually exclusive youth activities: employment, unemployment, schooling, and "other." Since equations are presented as tetrads, when an exogenous variable causes an increase in youth unemployment we can look to the other three equations to find out whether the higher unemployment rate is balanced by a decline in employment, in schooling, in "other," or in all three.

2. The authors argue that for most youths, schooling and military service are alternatives to work and that the unemployment rate should correspondingly be redefined as the number of unemployed divided by the total number of youths engaged in employment, unemployment, school, and military service (adjusted to eliminate the double counting of the employed and unemployed who are also in school). Two new unemployment ratio concepts are introduced, with the same expanded denominator and a numerator composed of the conventional count of unemployed ($U_2$) and alternatively the unemployed not enrolled in school ($U_3$). The new concepts make an enormous difference, and, for instance, reduce the 1978 white unemployment rate from the 16–17 age group from the BLS figure of 17.1% to the $U_3$ figure of 4.8%. For blacks in that age group, the reduction is from 40.7% to 7.8%.

3. A general methodological feature of the chapter is a consistent and healthy skepticism as to whether the results are really what they seem. Is the relative share variable just picking up a time trend? Does the minimum wage variable just stand as a proxy for the influence of all government transfer programs? Can one discriminate in a meaningful way between demand and supply factors that impede relative wage flexibility? The authors fully recognize that their coefficients may be consistent with several interpretations, and their attention to potential ambiguity in their results should serve as a model for subsequent research.

## The Hypotheses

The point of departure for the paper is a pair of hypotheses. First, youth and adult workers are imperfect substitutes for each other, largely because young workers have a shorter expected tenure over which employers can expect to amortize the costs of specific training. Although the underlying cause of short youth tenure is left unexplained, presumably a

Robert J. Gordon is associated with Northwestern University and the National Bureau of Economic Research.

contributing factor must be experimentation with different career alternatives, as well as the freedom enjoyed by American youths (especially relative to British and European youths) in shifting at low cost back and forth between work and school.

A second component of the Wachter-Kim model is an endogenous model of the birth rate and of labor force participation. The central ingredient is a sticky reservation or aspiration income level. Thus when a temporary oversupply of young workers drives down the real hourly wage rate, the desired income level can be maintained only by an increase in hours of work, mainly through an increase in female participation achieved through a reduction in family size. Thus a generation of "baby boom" is automatically followed by a subsequent era of "baby bust." It should be noted that if the income aspiration level is completely constant, then the labor supply curve becomes a rectangular hyperbola, with shifts in the real wage generating equiproportionate changes in hours worked in the opposite direction.

The basic idea of imperfect substitution must be supplemented by additional assumptions if it is to predict a particular response of youth unemployment to an increase in the relative supply of youths following a baby boom. Since Wachter and Kim fail to provide any simple theoretical diagram to facilitate an exposition of their approach, I provide here figure C6.1, which aids in a consideration of some of the important issues. In figure C6.1 the vertical axis measures the log of the wage of youth workers relative to adults, and the horizontal axis measures the log of the number of youth workers relative to adults. The assumption of imperfect substitutability is embodied in the downward sloping relative demand curve ($d$). The initial situation, before the increase in relative supply, is depicted by the two left-hand upward sloping supply curves, the relative supply of youth manhours to labor force activity ($n_0$), and the supply of employed manhours ($s_0$). The horizontal distance between the two supply schedules represents the supply of "voluntary search man-hours," the outcome of the worker's rational balancing of the marginal benefits and costs of search. In the initial situation at point $A$, it is assumed that all unemployment is voluntary, and that the labor market is in equilibrium at the crossing point of the demand ($d$) and supply ($s_0$) schedules.

The two supply curves are drawn so that the percentage unemployment rate (for instance the ratio $AB$ at the initial relative wage $w_0$) depends inversely on the wage rate. A permanent wage reduction should cause a substitution away from market work toward the joint activity of "searching and waiting."[1] Now consider the effects of an increase in the relative supply of youth labor, shown as a shift to the new pair of supply curves, $s_1$ and $n_1$, drawn to exhibit the same voluntary unemployment rate at the initial relative wage ($DE = AB$). The outcome depends on the degree of flexibility of the relative wage. If the relative wage drops from $w_0$ to $w_1$,

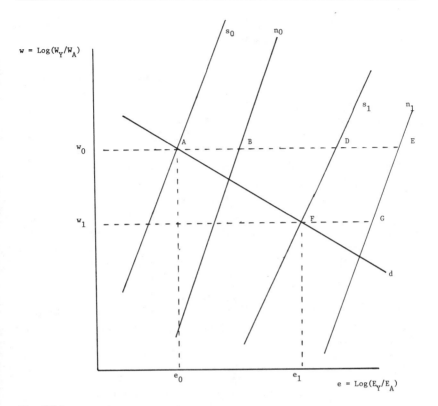

**Fig. C6.1**

the demand for employed manhours rises from $e_0$ to $e_1$, and the decline in the relative wage rate also induces an increase in the rate of voluntary unemployment $(FG > AB)$. The opposite possibility occurs if the relative wage is absolutely rigid, as would be caused by a minimum wage with universal coverage set by the legislature as a constant fraction of the adult wage rate. The relative demand for youth manhours would remain fixed at $e_0$, and the relative unemployment rate would rise from $AB$ to $AE$, of which $BE$ would be involuntary.

To determine whether the model of imperfect substitution is relevant, and whether the relative wage has been flexible in response to observed changes in relative supply, I have estimated two regression equations in which the observations are sixteen age-sex groups, and the variables are the logs of the ratios of 1974 to 1956 values of the group unemployment rates $(LRU_i)$, the group relative wage rates $(LRW_i)$, and the group labor-force shares $(LRS_i)$. The results show a strong positive statistical association between relative labor force shares and relative unemployment rates, and a strong negative statistical association between relative labor force shares and relative wage rates:

(1)    $LRU_i = .104 + .463\ LRS_i$    $R^2 = .412$
    [2.058]    [8.129]    $SEE = .194$

(2)    $LRW_i = -.088 - .355\ LRS_i$    $R^2 = .504$
    [-2.721]    [-3.768]    $SEE = .124$

Here the numbers in brackets are $t$-ratios. As an example, the labor force share of male youth aged 20–24 increased by 51.0% between 1956 and 1974. Equation (1) predicts an increase in the group unemployment rate by 23.6% as compared to the actual increase of 26.1%. Equation (2) predicts a decrease in the relative wage rate by 18.1% as compared to the actual decrease of 20.4% (from an actual ratio in 1956 of 71.2% of the wage paid to males 35–44 to 56.7% in 1974).[2]

The observed sensitivity of the relative wage to changes in relative supply is consistent both with the hypothesis of imperfect substitutability as well as with that of relative wage flexibility. Whether the relative wage was "perfectly" flexible or not cannot be determined from the results, since the observed increase in the relative unemployment rates of those groups in greater relative supply could have resulted either from the response of voluntary unemployment to the lower relative real wage or to involuntary unemployment caused by the incomplete adjustment of the relative wage.

The Time Series Results for Whites

While it contains no explicit estimates of the response of the relative youth wage to relative population shares, the Wachter-Kim chapter does present evidence that is broadly consistent with the simple cross-section regressions presented in equations (1) and (2). The higher population share of white youths has been associated with more unemployment, schooling, and "other" activity at the expense of less employment. By itself this conclusion does not tell us whether the increase in unemployment was voluntary or not, i.e., whether the observed higher level of unemployment corresponds to the interval $AE$ or $FG$ in figure C6.1. Our own evidence rules out $AE$ because of the strong downward response of the relative wage evident in equation (2). And Wachter and Kim appear to rule out $FG$ indirectly in their finding that unemployment has responded positively to the minimum wage, suggesting that minimum wage legislation may have interfered with the free downward movement in the relative youth wage required to clear the labor market. This minimum wage evidence is not as strong as would appear from the text of the chapter, however, because no measures of statistical significance are presented. (In the first draft of the chapter only one-third of the relative wage coefficients were both significant at the 5% level and had the anticipated sign.)

The time series results also indicate a very strong and significant effect on youth unemployment of the prime-age male unemployment rate, a proxy for aggregate demand. Thus an aggregate demand expansion can achieve a reduction in youth unemployment, yet the elasticity is below unity, implying that the demand expansion *raises* the unemployment rate of youths relative to prime-age men. This result confirms the earlier conclusion of Feldstein (1973) that high relative teenage unemployment rates cannot be reduced by expansive aggregate demand policy. Wachter and Kim also confirm Feldstein's finding that the relevant elasticities are higher for adults than for young teenagers, and for whites than for blacks. An important new result is that the black sensitivity is actually greater than that of whites but shows up in cyclical fluctuations of the employment-population ratio rather than in the conventional unemployment rate, confirming the conventional impression that blacks are victims of recessions because of their marginal job status, but that their job losses are translated into nonparticipation and "disguised unemployment" rather than fully into an increase in the official unemployment rate.

The Aspiration Hypothesis of Demographic Behavior

Much is made in the chapter of the hypothesis of an "echo effect" theory of demographic behavior, in which an oversupply of young people due to a baby boom in the previous generation creates a decline in the current generation's real wage relative to its aspiration level and an offsetting shift from child-raising to market labor force participation. Yet there is no evidence in the paper that is even relevant to the hypothesis, let alone any evidence that confirms it.

1. By and large an increase in the relative minimum wage in table 6.7 shifts young people from employment to unemployment, schooling, and the "other" category. But, as the authors recognize, this provides no evidence as to whether the response represents a conventional substitution effect on the demand side or a more indirect link between the minimum wage and the "aspiration wage" of youths.

2. The Wachter-Kim hypothesis interprets the declining birth rates and rising female labor force participation rates of the 1960s and 1970s as transitory phenomena that will be reversed when the current generation of "baby bust" children enters the labor force and finds its relative wage rising sufficiently by 1990 to send females back to the hearth to set about busily having four children apiece. An alternative hypothesis is that the recent behavior of the birth rate and female participation reflect permanent changes involving a changed perception of the social role of women. Not only do Wachter and Kim fail to provide any support for their interpretation that the recent behavior has been transitory rather than permanent, but they make no attempt to reconcile the rectangular hyper-

bolic shape of the labor supply curve required by their theory with the substantial body of evidence available that suggests a positively sloped labor supply curve for secondary workers.

3. A convincing demonstration of the cohort overcrowding theory of birthrate determination would require a much longer-term study. Even if Wachter and Kim had provided evidence on the birthrate issue, their sample period only contains one degree of freedom, the observed decline in birth rates between the 1950s and 1970s. Would their approach be able to explain the decline in birth rates between the 1920s and 1930s? My suspicion is that there was no problem of cohort overcrowding among young people at the end of the 1920s but rather the reverse because of the restrictive immigration legislation of 1924.

### The Black Youth Unemployment Puzzle

Wachter and Kim leave unresolved their anomalous results for black youths that pose the paradox of improving school attainment and wage rates relative to whites, set against a deterioration in relative unemployment rates and especially in employment/population ratios. Part of the decline in the $E/P$ ratio is, to be sure, a direct consequence of increased school attendance, but there is still a substantial problem evident in their table 6.10, which displays population shares engaged in schooling plus employment plus military service (minus the overlap involving working school enrollees). The deterioration in the black position is evident if we take the 1965–78 change in the white ratio and subtract the same change for blacks, as in table C6.1. Not only has the relative position of blacks deteriorated substantially between 1965 and 1978, but the absolute level of the ratio for the two older groups, both male and female, is between 12 and 16 percentage points lower for blacks than for whites in 1978.

The imperfect substitution framework used earlier in figure C6.1 is useful in sorting out hypotheses regarding the source of the black problem. In figure C6.2 the vertical axis is the log of the black wage rate relative to whites, and the horizontal axis is the log of black employment relative to whites. In contrast to figure C6.1, where the major event is a shift in the supply of young people relative to adults, I assume in figure C6.2 that the observed shift in the relative supply of black youths was relatively minor compared to a shift in relative demand. Starting from an initial situation at point $A$, with a relative wage of $w_0$ and relative employment of $e_0$, the new situation must be one with the higher relative black wage documented by Wachter and Kim. If there had been a simple shift in relative demand because of antidiscrimination legislation and the improved relative productivity of blacks resulting from their higher relative school attainment, the new situation would have occurred at point $C$, with a higher relative wage ($w_1$) and a higher employment/population ratio indicated by $e_1$. However, the deterioration in the black employ-

**Table C6.1**          **1965–78 Change in Ratio of Employment + School to Population**

|          | White | Black | Difference |
|----------|-------|-------|------------|
| Male     |       |       |            |
| 16–17    | −0.4  | −1.2  | 0.8        |
| 18–19    | −1.0  | −6.0  | 5.0        |
| 20–24    | −2.9  | −10.4 | 7.5        |
| Female   |       |       |            |
| 16–17    | 3.1   | 3.0   | 0.1        |
| 18–19    | 6.6   | 4.5   | 2.1        |
| 20–24    | 18.5  | 7.0   | 11.5       |

SOURCE: Wachter and Kim, table 6.10.

ment situation, even after the adjustment for schooling, suggests that instead the labor market has moved to a point like $F$, with an unemployment rate of $FG$ divided between conventionally measured and "disguised" unemployment.

The shift to point $F$ rather than to point $C$ is easily explained if antidiscrimination and minimum wage legislation have raised the actual relative wage paid to blacks faster than their relative productivity has increased. This is entirely consistent with the evidence provided by Wachter and Kim that "the groups with the most unfavorable unemployment-employment indicators enjoyed the best earnings growth," on the assumption that in the initial situation wage rates better reflected productivity differentials than in the new situation. The Wachter-Kim chapter contains no evidence on the relative roles of the minimum wage and antidiscrimination legislation in bringing about this compression of wage differentials, but since there was no important trend in the effective minimum wage over this period (only a sawtooth pattern), it would appear that antidiscrimination legislation may have been an important source both of the improved relative black wage and the deteriorating relative black unemployment-employment situation.[3]

Figure C6.2 is not the only possible interpretation of the black unemployment problem, because the implicit assumption that there has been an upward shift in the relative demand curve may not be valid. A new situation with a higher relative wage and lower relative employment could have been reached along the original relative demand curve ($d_0$), as well as along a lower demand curve, as long as there was an effective floor on the relative wage that forced blacks off of their relative supply curve. While increased education and urbanization may have improved the relative ability of blacks to compete for jobs, the ongoing shift of blue-collar jobs out of the central cities to the suburbs may have caused the net relative demand for young blacks, particularly males, to deteriorate. As one example, between 1970 and 1976 the number of jobs on Chicago's

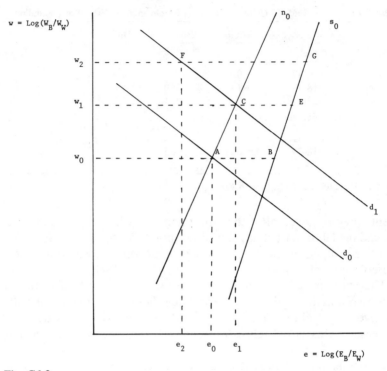

**Fig. C6.2**

black West Side dropped by 27.7% and by more than 10% on the South Side. In contrast, jobs in suburban northwestern Cook County increased by more than 30%, and by more than 60% in all-white suburban DuPage County. "In the 1960 and 1970 decades, most of the new jobs created in suburban Chicago were blue-collar jobs, whereas most new suburban homes were for upper-middle-class professional workers. As a result, there are now a lot more factory jobs in the suburbs than factory workers" (McManus, 1979).

At least partly as a result of this phenomenon, Chicago has the widest disparity of any major U. S. city between black and white unemployment rates (14.7% vs. 5.1% in 1976). To the extent that the problem is pervasive, if less extreme, in other cities, it would appear that the continuation of housing discrimination and segregation has aggravated the black employment problem and may have largely offset the favorable demand effects of antidiscrimination legislation in employment. The tendency of Chicago and other cities to generate new blue-collar jobs in the suburbs and new clerical jobs in the traditional central business district may also help to explain why the employment situation has deteriorated more for black males than for females (although table C6.1 indicates a substantial relative deterioration for black females aged 20–24).

There are other important causes of the growing geographical disparity between blue-collar jobs and blue-collar homes that are evident to anyone who travels between Europe and the United States. In Paris, Milan, and Rome, new suburban factory locations are interspersed with highrise apartment developments, many for working-class families, in contrast to the low-density middle-class subdivisions that continue to be built around U. S. cities. Among the American institutions that foster this inefficient and energy-wasting pattern of development are (1) a lack of metropolitan-wide land-use planning; (2) locally controlled restrictive zoning that keeps high-density residential developments out of the older inner suburbs; (3) the tax-deductibility of residential mortgages; (4) the Federal subsidy of interstate highways that have facilitated intrasuburban commuting; and (5) racial "steering" by local real estate agents.

Another uniquely American phenomenon is the deterioration and ultimate abandonment of vast amounts of inner-city real estate, in contrast to the continuing high density of land use within central European cities. Housing abandonment is both preceded and accompanied by the closing of commercial establishments in neighborhood shopping strips, thus eliminating a natural nearby source of employment for black youths and creating negative externalities for the remaining residents of the area. In turn, the problems of commercial flight and housing abandonment must be blamed primarily on a phenomenon which is pervasive in inner American cities but by contrast is almost unknown in most European cities: lower-class ghetto crime that simultaneously lowers the rate of return on commercial and residential investment and drives out many residents who can afford to move.

Thus at its heart the black employment problem is caused by a mixture of perverse local and Federal government policies that foster low-density middle-class suburban residential development, and the devastating impact of lower-class ghetto crime on the location of employment opportunities and on all other aspects of economic and social life in the central city. A new perspective is gained on the employment problem of U. S. blacks by contrasting their situation with that of disadvantaged lowerclass workers in other countries, and the inevitable conclusion is reached that the U. S. situation is unique, has no clear counterpart in other nations, and is more accurately classified as a social rather than an economic dilemma. In its analysis of the recent geographical shift of blue-collar employment opportunities in Chicago, a recent article concluded:

These shifts probably do not directly reflect the desire of industrialists and merchants to move their establishments as far as possible from Chicago's black South and West sides. Environmental deterioration and the fear of white workers to commute to black areas are probably more important explanations than racial discrimination. But the results of the shifts are the same. Factory jobs move to the northwest suburbs, but black workers cannot follow because of racial and economic segregation in housing. [McManus, 1979]

## Notes

1. See the expression for the marginal revenue from additional job search in Gordon (1973, p. 179, equation A-2). A reduction in the market wage relative to the shadow price of home time will raise marginal revenue relative to marginal cost, and thus extend the duration of job search. If this approach predicts correctly, a labor force group with an increasing share of supply should experience a higher duration of unemployment.

2. Data sources and further details are provided in Gordon (1977, pp. 199–206).

3. For an extended argument that Federal legislation prevents employers from paying blacks less to compensate for their lower productivity, see Williams (1979).

## References

Feldstein, M. S. 1973. *Lowering the permanent rate of unemployment.* A Joint Committee Print of the Joint Economic Committee. Washington, D.C.: Government Printing Office.

Gordon, R. J. 1973. The welfare cost of higher unemployment." *Brookings papers on economic activity.* Volume 4, no. 1, pp. 133–95.

———. 1977. Structural unemployment and the productivity of women." in K. Brunner and A. Meltzer, eds., *Stabilization of the domestic and international economy,* supplementary series to the *Journal of Monetary Economics.* Volume 5, pp. 181–229. North-Holland.

McManus, E. May 27, 1979. Blacks lose as jobs leave the city. *Chicago Tribune,* section 3, p. 6.

Williams, W. E. 1979. *Youth and minority unemployment.* Joint Economic Committee. Washington, D.C.: Government Printing Office.

# 7 The Dynamics of Youth Unemployment

Kim B. Clark and Lawrence H. Summers

At any given moment almost 2 million teenagers aged 16–19 are unemployed. Another 600,000 are out of school and neither working nor looking for work. Only about 60% of all teenagers and 25% of black youths who are out of school are employed. These high rates of joblessness have been a source of concern to both economists and policymakers. This chapter seeks to clarify the dimensions of the youth employment problem by analyzing the distribution of unemployment and related patterns of labor force mobility.

High rates of joblessness among young people have been explained in two quite different ways. The traditional view holds that the problem is one of job availability. A general shortage of openings makes it very difficult for some workers to find jobs. It takes the unemployed a long time to find a job. Much of the problem with the traditional view is traceable to a hardcore group who are out of work a large part of the time. The "new" view sees employment instability as the crux of the joblessness problem.[1] It treats the large flow into unemployment rather than the long length of unemployment spells as the crucial symptom of the problem. As Martin Feldstein, a leading exponent of the new view has written, "The picture of a hard core of unemployed persons unable to find jobs is an inaccurate description of our economy. . . . A more accurate description is an active labor market in which almost everyone who is out of work can find his usual type of job in a relatively short time. . . . The current structure of unemployment is not compatible with the traditional view of a hard core of unemployed who are unable to find

Kim B. Clark is associated with Harvard University and the National Bureau of Economic Research. Lawrence H. Summers is associated with the Massachusetts Institute of Technology and with the National Bureau of Economic Research. The authors are grateful to James Buchal, James Poterba, and Daniel Smith for their assistance with the computations.

jobs."[2] In particular, proponents of the new view emphatically reject the suggestion that the solution to the youth unemployment problem lies in job creation.

The results in this chapter strongly support the traditional view of the youth joblessness problem. They suggest that much of what appears to be evidence of dynamic labor market behavior is in fact a reflection of artifacts in the data. A large proportion of the measured flow into and out of unemployment is made up of quite spurious transitions into and out of the labor force. We also show that even though many unemployment spells are very short, their contribution to total unemployment is negligible. Most of the youth joblessness problem is attributable to a small group of young people who remain out of work a large portion of the time. Inability to find suitable work rather than pathological instability seems to be this group's main problem.

Section 7.1 of the paper presents raw data on labor market flows. Section 7.2 illustrates the long-term nature of "problem" youth unemployment. The role of job shortages and effects of aggregate demand are the subject of the section 7.3. A final section concludes the paper with a discussion of some implications of the findings and directions for future research.

## 7.1    Characteristics of the Teenage Labor Market

The central difference between the traditional and new views of youth unemployment lies in their conception of turnover. The former emphasizes the infrequency of job finding and the consequent lengthy duration of unemployment, while the latter focuses on the brevity and frequency of unemployment spells. Presentations of both views typically concentrate on flows between unemployment and employment. Less attention is devoted to movements into and out of the labor force. This section tries to present a fuller picture of the youth labor market by examining in a systematic way movements among all three labor market states (i.e., employment, unemployment, and not in the labor force [NILF]). We extend previous work on the dynamics of the youth labor market by focusing on the differences in behavior between young people who are in and out of school. After presenting the basic data characterizing the dynamics of youth labor markets, we examine the relative importance of transitions into and out of the labor force as well as the duration of completed spells in each of the labor market states.

### 7.1.1    The Basic Data

The dynamics of the youth labor market are examined in this section using the BLS gross changes data. Individuals included in the Current

Population Survey (CPS) are in the sample for four months, then out for eight months, and then in the sample for four months before leaving for good. The data in this study are derived from a special file which matches the March, April, May, and June Surveys taken in 1976. It is possible to follow one rotation group over the entire period and several rotation groups over shorter intervals. From these data it is possible to find the number of individuals who moved, for example, from unemployment to employment during the preceding month. Since there are three possible labor market states, nine monthly flows may be calculated.

We summarize the available information in a $3 \times 3$ matrix of transition probabilities and a vector of three stocks. Thus for each of several demographic groups we consider the matrix:

$$(1) \qquad P = \begin{vmatrix} P_{ee} & P_{eu} & P_{en} \\ P_{ue} & P_{uu} & P_{un} \\ P_{ne} & P_{nu} & P_{nn} \end{vmatrix}$$

where, for example, $P_{eu}$ represents the proportion of employed workers in a preceding month who are unemployed in the current month. Since a worker must always be in one of the three labor force states, the rows in $P$ sum to 1. Therefore, if any two of the transition probabilities out of a state are known, it is easy to compute the third. In order to calculate aggregate flows between states, we multiply the transition probabilities by appropriate initial stocks. This may be conveniently represented in matrix form as:

$$(2) \qquad \begin{vmatrix} F_{ee} & F_{eu} & F_{en} \\ F_{ue} & F_{uu} & F_{un} \\ F_{ne} & F_{nu} & F_{nn} \end{vmatrix} = \begin{vmatrix} S_e & O & O \\ O & S_u & O \\ O & O & S_n \end{vmatrix} P$$

where $F_{ij}$ represents the flow of workers into state $j$ from state $i$ and $S_e$, $S_u$, and $S_n$ refer to the stock of workers employed, unemployed, and not in labor force (NILF) respectively.

Since much of the emphasis in this study is on labor force transitions, it will be convenient to define a state $L$, for labor force, which includes both $E$ and $U$. It is clear that:

$$(3) \qquad \begin{aligned} F_{nL} &= F_{ne} + F_{nu} \\ F_{Ln} &= F_{en} + F_{un} \end{aligned}$$

The transition probabilities may then be represented as:

$$P_{nL} = P_{ne} + P_{nu}$$

(4) $$P_{Ln} = \frac{E_{t-1}}{L_{t-1}}P_{en} + \frac{U_{t-1}}{L_{t-1}}P_{un}$$

At the outset, it is crucial to acknowledge a major defect of the gross changes data. They are very sensitive to errors in reporting or recording labor force status. While such errors tend to cancel out in estimating stock-based statistics such as the unemployment rate, they cumulate in estimates of labor market flows. Several studies of CPS reinterviews have shown that there is substantial recall and recording error. Indeed, a recent census memorandum concluded that "the results for 1976 and 1977 indicate the gross change rate is at least two to three times as large as the adjusted estimate. . . . The gross change rate is greatly overstated due to simple response variance."[3] Below we suggest that much of what is called response variance is really a reflection of the arbitrariness of the official unemployment definition rather than recall error.[4] In any event, the estimates we report below using the flows data do characterize persons' actual reported movements in the CPS. It certainly does appear that they may overstate the dynamic character of the labor market. If so, the line of argument developed in section 7.2 is strengthened.

### 7.1.2   Transition Patterns

In table 7.1 we report average flow rates and transition probabilities for teenagers and mature adults as calculated from the March-April and the April-May CPS. Except for in-school youths it does not appear that the results are seasonally aberrant. For the total of male and female teenagers, the probabilities are consistent with average values for the 1968–76 period.[5]

An important feature of these data is the enormous magnitude of all the flows. For example, the results suggest that about 15% or 645,000 young men withdrew from the labor force within a month. At the same time about 20% of those outside the labor force entered the market.

The differences between persons who are in and out of school are particularly striking. Among young men who were in school, a very large proportion, almost half the unemployed, drop out of the labor force within a month. Slightly more than one-fifth find jobs. Almost one-third of the out-of-school group find jobs, while only 18% withdraw from the labor force. It is noteworthy that in the out-of-school group the job-finding probabilities of persons who are out of the labor force are quite close to those of the unemployed. While 32% of unemployed young men accept employment within a month, almost 22% of those outside the labor force find a job. Since the probability of exit from unemployment

**Table 7.1**     **Employment, Unemployment, and Labor Force Transitions March–May 1976**

| Demographic/schooling groups | en | eu | ue | un | nu | ne | nl | ln |
|---|---|---|---|---|---|---|---|---|
| **M1619 Total** | | | | | | | | |
| P | .105 | .042 | .272 | .307 | .074 | .129 | .203 | .147 |
| F | 350.3 | 147.0 | 237.3 | 294.6 | 253.8 | 450.5 | 704.4 | 644.5 |
| In school | | | | | | | | |
| P | .173 | .033 | .217 | .479 | .061 | .111 | .172 | .246 |
| F | 241.1 | 46.0 | 94.9 | 209.6 | 209.1 | 380.4 | 589.5 | 450.5 |
| Out of School | | | | | | | | |
| P | .053 | .049 | .310 | .185 | .134 | .210 | .344 | .077 |
| F | 109.2 | 101.0 | 142.4 | 85.0 | 44.7 | 70.1 | 114.9 | 194.0 |
| **F1619 Total** | | | | | | | | |
| P | .131 | .024 | .254 | .357 | .070 | .101 | .171 | .174 |
| F | 411.2 | 72.9 | 185.0 | 257.2 | 298.1 | 438.6 | 736.6 | 669.1 |
| In school | | | | | | | | |
| P | .209 | .023 | .163 | .515 | .057 | .090 | .147 | .272 |
| F | 265.5 | 29.2 | 54.3 | 171.6 | 201.3 | 317.8 | 519.1 | 437.8 |
| Out of school | | | | | | | | |
| P | .080 | .024 | .333 | .218 | .105 | .131 | .236 | .104 |
| F | 145.7 | 43.7 | 430.7 | 85.6 | 96.8 | 120.8 | 217.5 | 231.3 |
| **M2559 Total** | | | | | | | | |
| P | .009 | .010 | .323 | .081 | .053 | .082 | .135 | .013 |
| F | 332.3 | 369.1 | 685.1 | 171.8 | 162.6 | 251.6 | 414.2 | 504.0 |
| **W2559 Total** | | | | | | | | |
| P | .044 | .009 | .182 | .305 | .038 | .071 | .109 | .061 |
| F | 1033.8 | 211.5 | 293.0 | 491.1 | 767.3 | 1433.7 | 2201.0 | 1524.9 |

NOTE: $F$ indicates flow in thousands; $P$ indicates probability; $en$ indicates employment to not in labor force; $eu$ indicates employment to unemployment, and so forth.

SOURCE: Tabulations of the March–April–May–June 1976 CPS Match File. The flows have been adjusted to conform to the stock data. The probabilities are averages of the monthly probabilities for April and May.

declines quite sharply with duration, it appears that persons outside the labor force have as much chance of moving into employment as do persons unemployed for a significant period. As one would expect, the labor force distinction appears to be much more meaningful in the case of in-school youths; only 11.1% of the teenagers 16–19 find jobs within a month.

The differences between male and female transition probabilities are quite small. The largest difference is that young women appear to be much less likely to reenter the labor force than young men. When they leave employment they are also more likely to withdraw from the labor force rather than become unemployed. Not surprisingly, there are large differences between youth and adult transition probabilities. While the differences are much less pronounced for the out-of-school group, young people appear to be much more likely to enter and withdraw from the labor force. For example, 14.7% of male teenagers withdraw from the labor force each month compared to 1.3% of mature men. Similarly, 20.3% of teenagers outside enter the labor force contrasted with 13.5% for adults.

It is clear from table 7.1 that observed changes in the participation and unemployment of young people reflect a net of large gross movements into and out of the labor force. The importance of labor force entrance and exit in explaining youth employment and unemployment is documented in table 7.2. The data in line 1 illustrate the importance of flows from outside the labor force in changes in employment. Between 60 and 70% of all entrances into employment occur from outside the labor force. The second line indicates that most teenagers who leave employment leave the labor force rather than becoming unemployed. Among out-of-school women, this pattern is particularly pronounced: over 80% of those leaving employment withdraw from the labor force. Lines 3 and 4 indicate that labor force transitions are almost as important in determining flows into and out of unemployment. A large fraction of unemployment spells appear to begin and end outside the labor force.

These results indicate the artificiality of the not-in-labor-force unemployment distinction for young people. Given the frequency of movements between unemployment and not-in-labor-force, it is difficult to distinguish between these two states. Most of the newly employed did not search long enough to be recorded as unemployed. The evidence suggests the possibility that for many teenagers, job search is a passive process in which the main activity is waiting for a job opportunity to be presented. This conclusion is especially true of enrolled young people. Their extremely high withdrawal rate (80%) suggests that their job search is extremely casual. The ease with which most young people enter the labor force, documented in line 5 of the table, supports this view. While only about one-third of the unemployed find a job within a month, almost

Table 7.2    Relative Flows into and out of Not-in-labor-force, March–May 1976 Demographic/Schooling Groups

| Flow category | Males 16–19 | | | Females 16–19 | | | Males 25–59 | Females 25–59 |
|---|---|---|---|---|---|---|---|---|
| | Total | In school | Out of school | Total | In school | Out of school | | |
| 1. Proportion of flows into employment from NILF $(F_{ne}/(F_{ne}+F_{ue}))$ | .655 | .800 | .330 | .703 | .854 | .480 | .269 | .830 |
| 2. Proportion of flows out of employment into NILF $(F_{en}/F_{en}+F_{eu}))$ | .714 | .840 | .520 | .845 | .901 | .769 | .474 | .830 |
| 3. Proportion of flows out of unemployment into NILF $F_{un}/F_{un}+F_{ue}))$ | .530 | .688 | .374 | .584 | .760 | .396 | .200 | .626 |
| 4. Proportion of flows into unemployment from NILF $(F_{nu}/F_{nu}+F_{ue}))$ | .633 | .820 | .307 | .804 | .873 | .689 | .306 | .784 |
| 5. Proportion of flows into labor force which result in unemployment $(F_{ne}/F_{ne}+F_{nu}))$ | .635 | .645 | .610 | .591 | .612 | .555 | .607 | .651 |

SOURCE: See table 7.1.

two-thirds of labor force entrants are successful within a month. This strongly suggests that many people only enter the labor force when a job is presented.

The patterns of entrance suggest that the availability of jobs is an important element in determining movements into and out of the labor force. At the same time, the evidence indicating that most teenagers end spells of employment by withdrawing from the labor force provides some indication that teenage unemployment arises from voluntary turnover. Among unemployed teenagers, the quitting rate is about half the job loss rate. However, it seems reasonable to conjecture that a large proportion of those who withdraw from the labor force following employment are quitters. If, for example, it is assumed that 80% of this group is made up of quitters, it follows that about two-thirds of teenage employment spells end in quitting. The importance of considering labor force transitions is well illustrated by this calculation. Even if movements out of the labor force are in large part spurious, they nonetheless distort unemployment statistics.

## 7.1.3    Spell Durations

The results on flows and rates of transition in tables 7.1 and 7.2 underscore the dynamic character of the youth labor market. The tremendous volatility in the market behavior of young persons may also be conveyed by examining the mean duration of *completed spells* in each of the states. It should be emphasized that the estimates presented below differ from the mean duration of those *currently* in each state. As Kaitz (1970) has shown, the former concept will yield lower estimates than the latter. Table 7.3 presents estimates of mean duration of completed spells in each state. The brevity of mean durations for most groups is quite striking. Male teenagers, for example, have an average duration of a spell of employment of only about 6.5 months.

Out-of-school young people have longer durations in employment, about nine months, compared to about four months for enrolled teenagers. Since persons can remain employed but change jobs, these figures overstate the expected duration of a job. The only available evidence, from a 1961 BLS survey, suggests that about 54% of teenage job changes occur without intervening nonemployment. Adjusting for this flow yields the estimates of the mean duration of jobs shown in column 2. Young people do not appear to hold jobs for very long. The mean duration of a job for all male teenagers was three months. Even for out-of-school men the average job lasted a little over four months. In interpreting these figures, several factors should be recognized. First, the figures are based on exit probabilities calculated from March-April and April-May transi-

**Table 7.3    Labor Market Durations**

| Demographic/schooling groups | $D_e$ | $D_{job}$ | $D_n$ | $D_u$ |
|---|---|---|---|---|
| | | (mean duration in months) | | |
| M 16–19 | | | | |
| total | 6.80 | 3.00 | 4.93 | 1.73 |
| in school | 4.85 | 2.13 | 5.81 | 1.44 |
| out of school | 9.80 | 4.31 | 2.91 | 2.02 |
| F 16–19 | | | | |
| total | 6.45 | 2.84 | 5.85 | 1.64 |
| in school | 4.31 | 1.90 | 6.80 | 1.47 |
| out of school | 9.62 | 4.23 | 4.24 | 1.81 |
| M 25–29 | 52.6 | 24.1 | 7.41 | 2.48 |
| F 25–29 | 19.9 | 8.7 | 9.17 | 2.05 |

NOTE: $D$ indicates mean duration, $e$, $n$, $u$ represent employment, not-in-labor-force and unemployment. Mean duration for these states is defined as the reciprocal of the probability of leaving the state. $D$ is the duration in a job and is equal to $D_e(1-d)$, where $d$ is the fraction of job changes with no unemployment. The values of $d$ used here are the same for men and women. Estimates of $d$ are from Bancroft and Garfinkle, "Job Mobility in 1961," *Monthly Labor Review* (August 1973): 897–906.

tions. Hence they are unaffected by brief summer jobs. Moreover, the estimates may overstate the mean duration of jobs and employment because of the sampling interval. Individuals who are unemployed for less than a month may never appear as unemployed in the survey, so their employment may incorrectly appear unbroken. Similarly, very brief employment spells which would bring down the average may never be recorded. Second, spurious flows caused by reporting error as discussed above lead to an offsetting downward bias in all of the estimates in table 7.3

Columns 3 and 4 illustrate the brevity of unemployment and out-of-the-labor-force spells. Perhaps the most surprising result is the brevity of spells outside the labor force for out-of-school youths. The average NILF spell for this group lasts three months, which is only slightly longer than the average length spell of the unemployed. This is further evidence that these states are functionally almost indistinguishable. There appear to be relatively small differences between men and women, with somewhat more persistence in withdrawal among women. A striking feature of the results is that the mean duration of unemployment is not much different for teenagers and adults. This is in large part because of the high rate of labor force withdrawal among young people.[6]

### 7.1.4   Seasonal Variation in Labor Market Flows

Perhaps the most striking evidence of the success of the youth labor market in meeting the needs of most young people comes from evidence on seasonal fluctuations. In table 7.4 we examine the changes over the year in various key labor market rates for males 16–19. Seasonal patterns do not vary much among youth groups, and the male 16–19 group is fairly typical. The first line provides the unemployment rate for the summer months and the remainder of the year. No significant increase in the unemployment rate occurs during the summer months. Indeed, the rates in May, July, August, and September are actually lower than the rate over the rest of the year. Of course, the number of unemployed persons rises substantially because as the second row shows, the participation rate soars. The participation rate in July is amost 40% more than its annual average. As line 3 indicates, a parallel rise in the proportion employed also takes place. Not surprisingly, the vast majority of this increase in employment is due to summer-only workers. In the fourth line of the table, we present the proportion of the population who enter the labor force each month. In June, almost 21% of the male teenage population enters the labor force. This figure represents close to 50% of the NILF category. Another 12% of the population enter the labor force in July. Of course, a certain amount of labor force entrance occurs in all months, averaging about 7% of the population. Contrasting this figure with the

Table 7.4    Seasonal Variation in Labor Market Stocks and Flows
for Males 16–19, 1968–76

| Stock–flow category | May | June | July | August | September | Rest of year | Annual |
|---|---|---|---|---|---|---|---|
| | | | | | Average for: | | |
| 1. Unemployment rate | .129 | .182 | .152 | .122 | .149 | .160 | .155 |
| 2. Participation rate | .541 | .704 | .758 | .701 | .541 | .527 | .578 |
| 3. Employment ratio | .471 | .575 | .643 | .615 | .459 | .442 | .488 |
| 4. Labor force inflow as a percent of the population | .086 | .213 | .117 | .060 | .057 | .073 | .087 |
| 5. Labor force outflow as a percent of the population | .077 | .054 | .067 | .118 | .217 | .071 | .086 |
| 6. Probability of successful labor force entry ($P_{ns}$) | .711 | .655 | .670 | .676 | .630 | .622 | .641 |
| 7. Unemployment inflow as percent of population | .025 | .073 | .039 | .019 | .021 | .028 | .031 |
| 8. Probability of finding a job if unemployed ($P_{ue}$) | .269 | .332 | .386 | .312 | .280 | .249 | .277 |

Source: Unpublished tabulations by the Bureau of Labor Statistics, adjusted by the Urban Institute as described in J. E. Vanski, "Recession and the Employment of Demographic Groups: Adjustments to Gross Change Data," in Holt, C. C. et al., *Labor Markets, Inflation, and Manpower Policies*, Final Report to the Department of Labor (Washington, D.C.: The Urban Institute, May, 1975).

entry rates for May, June, and July, one finds that during the summer months about an extra 20% of the population enter the labor force. Note that this is a substantial underestimate of the extent of the increase in youths' labor supply, since many teenagers shift from desiring part-time to seeking full-time work during the summer months. Comparisons of the seasonality in teenage labor market behavior with the patterns observed for other demographic groups leads us to conclude that about three-quarters of summer entrances are due to school ending rather than to fluctuations in employment opportunities.

Not surprisingly, the rates of labor force entrance in June and July are mirrored by high rates of labor force exit in August and September. During these months, about 33% of the teenage population exits from the labor force. Since the rate of withdrawal in a typical month is about 7%, the extra labor force exits during August and September almost exactly offset the extra entrances in the early summer months. Thus both the flow and the stock data suggest that employment only during the summer months characterizes the behavior of about 20% of male teenagers.

The labor market appears to adapt very well to the surge in those seeking employment. In June, when the inflow is at its peak, about two-thirds of labor force entrants find jobs. This figure is actually greater by about 5% than the rate of successful entry during the remainder of the year. Those who do become unemployed during the summer months fare much better than the unemployed in other months, since the job finding rate $P_{ue}$ in May, June, and July far exceeds the rate in the nonsummer months. The fact that these flow rates are significantly higher during the summer months suggests that the additional members of the labor force may have an unemployment rate much lower than that of full-year workers. Clearly, the average unemployment rate over the summer months is lower than during the rest of the year. This suggests that the summer influx of teenagers actually reduces the average annual unemployment rate, since the additional workers appear to fare substantially better both as labor force entrants and as unemployed job seekers than do other teenagers. This quite striking fact bears further comment.

Undoubtedly, public employment and training policy affects the behavior of labor market flows during the summer months. Over the first six years of the period covered in table 7.4 (1868–73), the federal government provided about 600,000 summer jobs through the Neighborhood Youth Corps. The NYC was eliminated with the enactment of CETA in 1973, but summer jobs remain a component of the decentralized employment and training system. In 1976, for example, just over 820,000 jobs were provided in the CETA summer program. The great majority of participants were classified as economically disadvantaged (95.9%), drawn from the unemployed or from outside the labor force (98.7%), and were full-time students (87.8%).

A comparison of the size of the federal summer program with the average flow into the labor force reveals the relative importance of the summer jobs program. From 1968 to 1976, an average of 600,000 summer jobs were provided through NYC and CETA. The data in table 7.4 suggest that about 3 million teenagers left school and entered the labor market each summer. Given the estimated probability of entering with a job (about .6 of average), on the order of 1.2 million teenagers would have remained without employment if no adjustments had been made. Thus about 50% of this group were moved into employment through the federal jobs program. This calculation is likely to overstate, perhaps substantially, the contribution of public policy. We have assumed that the federal jobs constitute net job creation. It is likely however, that the federal program funds some jobs which would have existed anyway. This is more likely to be the case under CETA, where the program largely is run through state and local government units. Unfortunately, estimates of the net jobs created under the summer programs are not available.[7]

The ability of the labor market to deal with the large inflow of workers in the summer should lead one to question demographic explanations of recent increases in youth unemployment. As table 7.4 shows, the labor market is able to deal with a threefold increase in the proportion of the population newly seeking work without an appreciable increase in individual's difficulty in finding employment. It is improbable that the same labor market should be incapable of adapting to the easily foreseen, persistent, and much smaller increase in the labor force due to demographic shifts. Indeed, the adjustment should be much smoother because in the case of demographic shifts the time frame is much longer and there is no need to create very temporary jobs. While adaptations such as replacing vacationing workers and work scheduling are less feasible in this case, the longer run should permit much greater flexibility.

Taken together, the results in this section convey a picture of an enormously dynamic labor market. It is apparent that most teenagers move easily between labor market states. More than half of all job changes occur without intervening unemployment. Most labor force entrants find jobs without ever being measured as unemployed and incidents of unemployment are typically quite brief. There appears to be no evidence of a serious problem for most teenagers. Yet we did observe in March of 1976 that almost one-fifth of all young people who wanted jobs did not have them, and that an equal number were out of school and jobless, but had chosen not to search. The key question then is whether these average probabilities, which suggest that movement in all directions is quite easy, are relevant to a large part of nonemployment. The next section offers a negative answer to this question.

## 7.2 The Experience of the Nonemployed

There are at least three reasons why the picture of the labor market presented in the preceding section may be a misleading guide to the experience of the unemployed population at a given time. First, even if most unemployment spells are short, most unemployment may be contained in long spells. To see this, consider the following example. Suppose that each week twenty spells of unemployment begin lasting one week, and one begins with a duration of twenty weeks. This mean duration of a completed spell of unemployment would be 1.05 weeks, but half of all unemployment would be accounted for by spells lasting twenty weeks. Equivalently, in a steady state, the expectation of the length of time until a job is found among all those unemployed at any instant would be 9.5 weeks. Sole focus on the mean duration of a completed spell could clearly be quite misleading.

Second, as we have already emphasized, there is reason to doubt the salience of the distinction between unemployment and not-in-the-labor-force for young people. Unemployment durations appear to be short in large part because of high rates of labor force withdrawal. The brevity of many spells outside the labor force suggests that many of those who withdraw are in fact sensitive to labor market conditions. Indeed, it appears that our official statistics frequently record two brief spells of unemployment, broken by a period outside the labor force, when a single spell of joblessness would be more appropriate.

The third reason why it is necessary to go beyond the average transition probabilities is the need to study the incidence of multiple spells. As Richard Layard has emphasized in his contribution to this volume, one's view about the welfare consequences of youth nonemployment should depend on its concentration.[8] If the burden is quite evenly dispersed, individuals are unlikely to suffer greatly and the economy may even benefit from a better matching between workers and jobs. On the other hand, if the distribution of unemployment is very uneven, the welfare cost to individuals is likely to be greater, and the social benefit much more dubious.

In this section we shall try to deal with these three issues by studying the distributions of unemployment and nonemployment weeks. Basically, we seek to answer two questions. First, how long can we expect the teenagers who are unemployed at a given time to wait before entering employment? Second, how much unemployment and nonemployment can they expect to suffer within the year? It is crucial to realize that we seek to answer these two questions for all those *unemployed at a given time* rather than all those who flow into unemployment over some interval. This procedure gives more weight to long spells than to short ones, since persons suffering lengthy spells are more likely to appear in the sample at a given time. In assessing the nature of the unemployment problem, one wants to study the unemployed population, not the experience of persons flowing into unemployment. This key point is illustrated by the numerical example above in which much of unemployment was due to long spells even though the vast majority of spells were short.

## 7.2.1   How Long Does It Take to Find a Job?

In table 7.5 we present various estimates of how long it takes young people to find jobs. The first row displays the mean duration of completed unemployment spells. The durations of unemployment, as we have already noted, are fairly short. We have also pointed out that labor force withdrawal makes this figure a very misleading indicator of the ease of job finding. In line 2 we attempt to answer the more meaningful question of how long the unemployed must wait until a job is found. The calculation recognizes the possibility of labor force withdrawal and the attendant

Table 7.5    Alternative Measures of the Duration of Joblessness

| | Demographic groups | | | | | | Males 25–29 |
|---|---|---|---|---|---|---|---|
| | Males 16–19 | | | Females 16–19 | | | |
| Duration category | Total | In school | Out of school | Total | In school | Out of school | |
| 1. Mean duration of unemployment (months) $1/(P_{ue}+P_{un})$ | 1.7 | 1.4 | 2.0 | 1.6 | 1.5 | 1.8 | 2.5 |
| 2. Expected time until next employment spell for those currently unemployed[a] (months) | 5.4 | 7.2 | 3.0 | 6.6 | 9.4 | 4.2 | 4.3 |
| 3. Average months of unemployment to date | 2.9 | 2.4 | 3.4 | 2.4 | 2.0 | 2.7 | 5.3 |
| 4. Expected time between beginning of current spell of unemployment and next spell of employment for those currently unemployed[b] | 8.3 | 9.6 | 6.4 | 9.0 | 11.4 | 6.9 | 9.6 |
| 5. Mean duration of non-employment (months) $\left(\dfrac{U+N}{U\,P_{ue}+N\,P_{ne}}\right)$ | 6.4 | 8.1 | 3.7 | 8.2 | 10.4 | 5.2 | 5.5 |
| 6. Expected total weeks of nonemployment for those currently nonemployed[c] | — | — | 7.5 | — | — | 10.4 | 11.1 |

SOURCE: The probabilities underlying the calculations are taken from tables 7.1 and 7.2.

[a]This is equal to $\dfrac{D_u+P_{ex}D_n}{1-P_{ex}\,(1-P_{ns})}$ where $D_u$ and $D_n$ are durations in unemployment and nonemployment, $P_{ex}$ is the fraction of unemployment spells which end in labor force withdrawal, and $P_{ns}$ is the probability of entering the labor force with a job.

[b]Line 4 is line 2 plus line 3.

[c]Line 6 is line 5 multiplied by 2; this concept is only meaningful for the out of school group.

SOURCE: The probabilities underlying the calculations are taken from tables 7.1 and 7.2.

decline in the probability of finding a job. The possibility of subsequent labor force reentrance into unemployment is also taken into account. The average unemployed male teenager in March of 1976 could expect to wait 5.4 more months before finding a job. Line 3 notes that the average male 16–19 had been unemployed for 2.9 months. Hence the average unemployed person was in the midst of a spell of over eight months of joblessness. The notion that most of those currently unemployed can and·will find jobs quickly is simply false. Most are in the midst of lengthy spells without work.

Even the large estimates above may understate the difficulty of movement into jobs. We have argued that many persons who are out of the labor force behave in ways which are functionally equivalent to the unemployed. In line 5 we report the expected length of time until a job is found for currently nonemployed young people. Doubling this figure yields the mean total duration of joblessness for the nonemployed. The results indicate that it takes most persons a long time to find a job. The average nonemployed young man who is not in school will have been out of work for about 7.5 months before returning to employment. The corresponding figures for women are even larger, reflecting greater persistence of labor force withdrawal. All of the estimates in table 7.5 are conservative since they do not take account of the fact that continuation probabilities decline with duration.

### 7.2.2   How Extensive is Unemployment?

While the evidence suggests that joblessness is frequently prolonged, we have not yet considered multiple spells. The annual March Work Experience Survey asks all civilian noninstitutional respondents in the CPS to describe their work and unemployment experience in the preceding year. We have used the Work Experience data to calculate two measures of joblessness. The first is the official definition of unemployment as weeks looking for work or on layoff. This concept is referred to as "nonemployment." It is important to note that nonemployment excludes weeks out of the labor force for those citing illness, family responsibilities, or "other" as the principal reason for part-year work. For these individuals, nonemployment is defined as weeks of unemployment. In both calculations, persons who did not participate in the labor force are excluded from the sample.

The distribution of unemployment and nonemployment for selected demographic groups is shown in table 7.6. Of the approximately 6 million young people with labor force experience, about 1.7 million experience unemployment averaging about three months during the year. The average number of weeks is almost 50% greater for the out-of-school group. While the number of persons experiencing nonemployment is not different from the number with unemployment in this sample, weeks of joblessness are significantly greater when time out of the labor force is included. Out-of-school youths average six months of nonemployment per person becoming nonemployed.

In line 6 of the table we examine the experience of the unemployed population at a given time by focusing on the distribution of unemployment and nonemployment weeks. Because unemployment weeks are captured randomly by the survey, the statements that "$x$ percent of unemployment weeks are suffered by persons with $y$ weeks of unemployment during the year," and "$x$ percent of the currently unemployed will experience $y$ weeks of unemployment during the year" are equivalent. Both the unemployment and nonemployment distributions exhibit substantial concentration, with the preponderance of unemployment

**Table 7.6    The Concentration of Unemployment and Nonemployment for Teenagers, 1974**

|  | Demographic groups | | | | | | | |
|  | Males | | Females | | Nonwhite | | | |
|  | | | | | Males | | Females | |
|  | Total | Out of school | Total | Out of school | | Out of school | | Out of school |
| 1. Total with labor force experience (millions) | 5.99 | 2.82 | 5.27 | 2.44 | | .31 | | .30 |
| 2. Total with unemployment (millions) | 1.71 | .91 | 1.56 | .85 | | .14 | | .17 |
| 3. Average weeks of unemployment per person with unemployment | 12.7 | 18.6 | 10.4 | 14.9 | | 20.1 | | 16.4 |
| 4. Total with nonemployment (millions) | 1.71 | .91 | 1.56 | .85 | | .14 | | .17 |
| 5. Average weeks of nonemployment per person with nonemployment | 16.2 | 25.2 | 15.4 | 24.1 | | 29.0 | | 30.3 |

6. Distribution of in-
dividuals and weeks
by duration

| | $U$ | $NE$ | $U$ | $NE$ | $U$ | $NE$ | $U$ | $NE$ | $U$ | $NE$ | $U$ | $NE$ |
|---|---|---|---|---|---|---|---|---|---|---|---|---|
| **1–4 weeks** | | | | | | | | | | | | |
| % of labor force | 11.2 | 10.3 | 6.2 | 4.2 | 14.4 | 12.6 | 10.9 | 6.9 | 7.5 | 4.6 | 17.1 | 9.0 |
| % of total weeks | 6.2 | 4.4 | 2.1 | 1.0 | 9.4 | 5.5 | 4.2 | 1.6 | 1.6 | .7 | 3.7 | 1.0 |
| **5–14 weeks** | | | | | | | | | | | | |
| % of labor force | 9.0 | 7.9 | 9.7 | 7.3 | 8.3 | 7.2 | 9.9 | 7.7 | 16.5 | 11.3 | 17.5 | 8.0 |
| % of total weeks | 24.8 | 17.0 | 16.0 | 9.0 | 26.8 | 15.8 | 19.1 | 9.1 | 17.8 | 8.5 | 18.8 | 4.6 |
| **15–26 weeks** | | | | | | | | | | | | |
| % of labor force | 4.1 | 2.8 | 8.1 | 5.3 | 4.0 | 2.4 | 8.2 | 4.8 | 6.4 | 2.2 | 9.2 | 4.3 |
| % of total weeks | 23.8 | 12.7 | 28.2 | 13.7 | 27.1 | 11.0 | 33.2 | 12.0 | 14.6 | 3.4 | 20.8 | 5.3 |
| **40+ weeks** | | | | | | | | | | | | |
| % of labor force | 1.9 | 4.2 | 3.6 | 8.4 | 1.2 | 4.9 | 2.4 | 10.5 | 7.5 | 18.8 | 7.5 | 28.2 |
| % of total weeks | 24.0 | 41.3 | 27.6 | 47.4 | 17.1 | 49.4 | 21.5 | 57.2 | 37.3 | 65.0 | 37.0 | 75.1 |

attributable to persons out of work more than half the year. Among out-of-school male teenagers, 54% of unemployment and 76% of nonemployment were experienced by persons out of work more than six months. Among young black men who were not enrolled in school, 65.0% of nonemployment was accounted for by those out of work more than forty weeks during the year. As one would expect from these figures, individuals with brief, infrequent unemployment experience contribute only negligibly to overall unemployment. For example, persons out of work less than three months accounted for only 21% of nonemployment among young men who were out of school. While many teenagers experience short periods of unemployment in moving between jobs, these are of little consequence in explaining total weeks of nonemployment.

The statistics in tables 7.5 and 7.6 tell a consistent story. Youth unemployment is properly understood in terms of a fundamental failure of the labor market to meet the needs of some workers. A small portion of the population finds itself chronically unable to locate satisfactory work. They do not have the same ease of transition which characterizes the remainder of the population. Rather, they wait long periods between jobs. Moreover, they experience frequent unemployment because of the frequency with which they leave employment. Whether the source of the problem is a shortage of jobs or that the "hard core" group is unemployable can never be resolved conclusively. Some aspects of the problem are considered in section 7.3.

### 7.2.3    Racial Differences in Nonemployment Experience

The wide disparity between the unemployment rates of white and nonwhite teenagers has been the subject of considerable academic and public discussion. Research designed to explain racial unemployment differentials has emphasized differences in turnover and minimized the importance of long term joblessness. Writing in 1974, Barrett and Morgenstern stated this view quite clearly:

> The high unemployment rates of blacks and young people are attributable almost entirely to their higher turnover—that is, the frequency with which they become unemployed. The major unemployment problem among black Americans is not chronic long-duration unemployment, but frequent job changes and unemployed search. High turnover rates among young people are consistent with a search theoretic model in which frequent flows into unemployment represent a potentially efficient sampling of the job market.[9]

The importance of long-term unemployment, evident in tables 7.5 and 7.6, suggests the need to reexamine explanations of racial differences which rely on turnover and search associated with frequent job changes. Evidence on racial differences in transition probabilities and time to find a job is presented in table 7.7 for male and female teenagers not in school. A comparison of transition probabilities reveals three major differences between whites and nonwhites. Nonwhite teenagers are three times as likely to lose or quit their jobs and become unemployed as their white counterparts. Among young men, for example, the probability of leaving employment and entering unemployment is .042 for whites, while the comparable rate for nonwhites is .129. These differences may reflect a higher propensity of nonwhites to quit jobs, but they are also consistent with the view that nonwhites are more subject to layoff because of less seniority and because of discrimination. There are much smaller differences in the probability of employed teenagers leaving the labor force. Indeed, the racial differences in $P_{en}$ among young men are negligible.

One of the most striking differences in transition patterns is found in the probabilities of entering employment from unemployment and from outside the labor force. Young white men are three times as likely to find employment if unemployed than their nonwhite counterparts. Since the

| Table 7.7 | Differences in Unemployment Experience for Out-of-school Teenagers by Race, March–May 1976 | | | |
|---|---|---|---|---|
| | Demographic groups | | | |
| | Whites | | Nonwhites | |
| Category | Men 16–19 | Women 16–19 | Men 16–19 | Women 16–19 |
| 1. Transition probabilities | | | | |
| $P_{en}$ | .052 | .078 | .059 | .097 |
| $P_{eu}$ | .042 | .020 | .129 | .067 |
| $P_{ue}$ | .369 | .377 | .119 | .163 |
| $P_{un}$ | .184 | .225 | .187 | .193 |
| $P_{nu}$ | .118 | .107 | .194 | .100 |
| $P_{ne}$ | .240 | .153 | .102 | .048 |
| 2. Time to find a job | | | | |
| (a) Mean duration of unemployment (months) | 1.8 | 1.7 | 3.3 | 2.8 |
| (b) Expected months until next job (for the currently unemployed) | 3.1 | 3.7 | 8.9 | 10.2 |
| (c) Average months of unemployment to date | 3.2 | 2.7 | 4.0 | 3.0 |
| (d) Expected months of nonemployment from beginning of current spell of unemployment until next job | 6.3 | 6.4 | 12.9 | 13.2 |

NOTE: For definitions of the concepts in lines 2–5, see the note in table 7.5. The probabilities are taken from matched CPS files for March–April–May–June 1976. Additional details are contained in the note to table 7.1.

probability of dropping out of the labor force is identical for white and nonwhite teenage men, nonwhites are much more likely to remain unemployed. Similar patterns are found for young women, where unemployed whites are more than twice as likely to find work.

The apparent difficulty nonwhite teenagers have in finding work if unemployed is mirrored in the experience of those classified as outside the labor force. Using teenage women as an example, the probability of entering the labor force is .36 for whites and .15 for nonwhites. The probability of successful labor force entry (i.e., entering with a job) given by

$$(5) \qquad P_{ns} = \frac{P_{ne}}{P_{ne} + P_{nu}}$$

is two-thirds for whites but only one-third for nonwhites. Not only do young nonwhites experience more difficulty finding work if unemployed, they are much more likely to become unemployed upon entering the labor force. These calculations suggest that racial differences in unemployment rates are due largely to differences in the probability of entering employment. While differences in layoffs and quittings are important, the dominant explanation is found in the difficulty nonwhites have in locating work.

The implications of job-finding difficulty are examined in line 2 of table 7.7, which presents estimates of time needed to find a job for those currently unemployed. The differences between whites and nonwhites are quite striking. On average, unemployed white teenagers could expect to wait about three (men) or four (women) months before finding work, while nonwhites faced nine to ten months of further joblessness. Since nonwhites had already accumulated four months of unemployment, the data reveal that unemployed nonwhite teenagers were in the midst of very long spells without work. These calculations are undoubtedly influenced by the depressed state of the labor market in the spring of 1976. Yet even considerably reducing these estimates to account for the cycle would be unlikely to change the basic conclusion. It appears that nonwhite teenagers have much more difficulty finding work than their white counterparts, and that even when they find it, they are much more likely to be fired, laid off, or quit. As a result they spend extended periods out of work.

### 7.2.4 Employment Exit and Extensive Unemployment

Many observers regard the brevity of employment spells emphasized in section 7.1 as the root cause of the youth nonemployment problem. The results here call that interpretation into question. For most young people, frequent job change appears to be possible without extensive unemployment. The median length of unemployment spells is probably about three weeks. Half of all job changes occur without any unemployment at all. A person who held five jobs during the year and was unemployed during each change for the median length of time would suffer only twelve weeks of unemployment during the year. Persons with this little unemployment contribute less than one-fourth of all youth unemployment. It is therefore clear that without serious difficulty in job-finding even extreme employment instability could not account for observed patterns of concentrated joblessness.

A similar conclusion is obtained by examining in more detail the experience of young people reporting extensive joblessness. Among persons with over twenty-six weeks of nonemployment, who accounted for 76% of joblessness, the average number of unemployment spells was less than two. In many cases, these spells were separated by periods outside the labor force rather than by jobs. Hence this is an overstatement of the average number of employment spells during the year. Even neglecting this correction the average spell length of the extensively nonemployed appears to last close to five months.[10] Thus, for this group, with whom the real problem lies, the difficulty is prolonged unemployment rather than frequent joblessness.

Previous analyses of unemployment dynamics have emphasized the fact that the average flow into unemployment differs much more among demographic groups than does the average duration of unemployment. This has led them to conclude that the problem of high unemployment groups (e.g., teenagers) is excessive turnover, not difficulty in finding jobs. The results in this section show that this type of analysis can be very misleading. Group averages conceal wide variations. The vast majority of unemployment is experienced by a small minority of the population. Some groups are disproportionately represented in the "hardcore" population. The error is in tracing group differences to general turnover, rather than differences in the incidence of "hardcore" problems.

Nothing in the preceding paragraphs is inconsistent with the common observation that differences in demographic group unemployment rates are due largely to differences in the frequency of spells rather than their duration. The point here is that for the problem population it is very difficult to locate a suitable job. The demographic observation simply addresses the incidence of "problem" people in different subgroups of the population. Once it is recognized that nonemployment is largely a matter of a small minority of all demographic groups with serious job-finding problems, the fallacy of inferring the nature of individual problem unemployment from comparisons of demographic averages becomes clear.

## 7.3 Cyclical Variations in Employment

The cyclical behavior of youth employment and unemployment can shed light on the nature of the nonemployment problem. If extensive joblessness occurs only because some young people are essentially unemployable, one would expect changes in aggregate demand to have small effects. On the other hand, a finding that changes in aggregate demand had a large impact on young people would imply that at least some unemployment was due to a shortage of attractive opportunities. Of course, a finding that aggregate demand has a potent effect on the youth labor market need not imply the desirability of expansionary macroeconomic policy, which has other perhaps undesirable consequences.

### 7.3.1    Employment, Unemployment, and Participation

The cyclical sensitivity of unemployment is the reflection of two quite different phenomena. Unemployment can increase either because fewer jos are available or because more workers decide to seek the available jobs. These two sources of unemployment obviously have quite different welfare implications. While the former is almost certainly indicative of a worsening of labor market performance, the latter may reflect an improvement in conditions. Focusing only on unemployment rates is thus very likely to be misleading. Moreover, the results in section 7.1 suggest that the NILF-unemployed distinction is quite arbitrary. These considerations indicate the importance of examining the cyclical behavior of employment, unemployment, and participation.

These three measures summarize the labor market experience of a given demographic group. They are related by the following identity:

$$(6) \qquad \frac{E}{N^i} = \frac{L}{L^i} \frac{L}{N^i}$$

where $E$ is employment, $N$ is population, $L$ is labor force, and $i$ indexes demographic groups. Taking logs and differentiating yields:

$$(7) \qquad \text{dln} \left(\frac{E}{N}\right)_i = \text{dln} \left(\frac{E}{N}\right)_i + \text{dln} \left(\frac{L}{N}\right)_i$$

Thus changes in the employment ratio may be decomposed into changes in employment and participation rates. Since persons in the labor force are either employed or unemployed it is clear that

$$(8) \qquad \text{dln} \left(\frac{E}{N}\right)_i = \text{dln} \left(1 - UR\right)_i + \text{dln} \left(\frac{L}{N}\right)_i$$

where $UR$ is the unemployment rate. This decomposition provides the basis for our estimates of the effects of overall economic performance on youth employment.

### 7.3.2    A Simple Model

The cyclical responsiveness of youth employment is estimated using a quite simple model. For each group we postulate that the unemployment rate and participation rate are functions of aggregate demand, seasonal factors, and time. The time trends are included to reflect the impact of slowly changing social trends and other gradually moving variables omitted from the equation. Seasonal movements are captured with monthly dummies. The basic equations to be estimated are:

$$(9) \quad \ln(PR)_{it} = \beta_0 + \sum_{j=0}^{8} \beta_{t-j} \, UPRIME_{t-j} + \sum_{k=1}^{11} \Theta_k S_k$$
$$+ \delta_1 T + \delta_2 T67 + v_{it}$$

$$(10) \quad UR_{it} = \alpha_0 + \sum_{j=0}^{8} \alpha_{t-j} \, UPRIME_{t-j} + \sum_{k=1}^{11} \gamma_k S_k$$
$$+ \phi_1 T + \phi_2 T67 + u_{it}$$

where $UPRIME$ is the unemployment rate of men 35–44, $T$ is the time trend, $T67$ is a second time trend which begins in 1967, and $S_i$ are monthly dummies.

The specification of (9) is traditional in analyses of participation.[11] The prime-age male unemployment rate is assumed to measure variation in job opportunities and the ease of job finding. Since workers may respond to changes in the availability of jobs with a delay, lagged unemployment is also included in the equation. While equations of this sort have not been extensively used in studying the cyclical behavior of group unemployment rates, they are justified by essentially the same arguments.

The interpretation of the coefficients of the model is straightforward. For example, the cyclical responsiveness of the participation rate of the $i$th group is measured by $\gamma_{PR}^i = \Sigma \beta_{t-j}$. A value of $-1.0$ implies that a 1 percentage point decrease in $UPRIME$ (e.g., from 0.6 to 0.5) produces a 1% increase in the participation rate of the $i$th group (e.g., .430 to .434). Equations (9) and (10) have been estimated using both annual and monthly data for the period (1948–77) for various demographic groups. The identity (6) along with the properties of ordinary least squares insures that the relationship between the employment ratio, aggregate demand and time is given by:

$$(11) \quad \ln(EN)_{it} = \beta_0 - \alpha_0 + \Sigma(\beta_{t-j} - \alpha_{t-j}) \, UPRIME_{t-j}$$
$$+ \sum_{k=1}^{11} (\Theta_k - \gamma_k) S_k$$
$$+ (\delta_1 - \phi_1)t + (\delta_2 - \phi_2)T67 + e_i$$

It follows immediately that the equations presented here can be used to decompose cyclical movements in the employment ratio into unemployment and participation components since

$$(12) \quad \gamma_{EN}^i = \gamma_{PR}^i - \gamma_{UR}^i$$

In order to insure that this identity is exactly satisfied we have estimated all the equations using ordinary least squares without correcting for serial correlation. The results for individual equations, however, are not sensitive to this choice. The estimated equations are shown in table 7.8.

The principal conclusion that emerges is the tremendous responsiveness of youth employment to aggregate demand. For men 16–19, each one-point decrease in the prime-age male unemployment rate increases the employed proportion of the population by about 4.5%. About two-thirds of the response comes through unemployment, with the remainder due to increases in participation. For women 16–19, the cyclical respon-

**Table 7.8**     Cyclical Behavior of Unemployment, Participation, and Employment by Teenage Demographic Groups (Standard Errors in Parentheses)

| Demographic group/ dependent variable | CONS | UPRIME | T | T67 | $R^2$ | SEE | DW |
|---|---|---|---|---|---|---|---|
| | | | | $(12 \times 10^2)$ | | | |
| **1. Men 16–19: total** | | | | | | | |
| unemployment rate | .02 | 2.77 | .35 | −.15 | .84 | .018 | .85 |
| | (.005) | (.10) | (.02) | (.06) | | | |
| participation rate | −.47 | −1.87 | −1.11 | 2.82 | .95 | .035 | .73 |
| | (.01) | (.19) | (.04) | (.11) | | | |
| employment ratio | −.50 | −4.64 | −1.45 | 2.98 | .95 | .037 | .72 |
| | (.01) | (.20) | (.046) | (.12) | | | |
| **2. Men 16–19: nonwhite** | | | | | | | |
| unemployment rate | −.05 | 4.29 | 1.14 | −.21 | .69 | .051 | 1.32 |
| | (.03) | (.36) | (.12) | (.23) | | | |
| participation rate | −.35 | −1.99 | −2.12 | .84 | .90 | .064 | 1.13 |
| | (.03) | (.45) | (.14) | (.28) | | | |
| employment ratio | −.30 | −6.29 | −3.26 | 1.05 | .87 | .085 | 1.27 |
| | (.04) | (.59) | (.19) | (.37) | | | |
| **3. Women 16–19: total** | | | | | | | |
| unemployment rate | −.01 | 1.78 | .52 | −.36 | .82 | .021 | .94 |
| | (.007) | (.11) | (.03) | (.07) | | | |
| participation rate | −.83 | −2.29 | −.44 | 3.48 | .93 | .039 | .69 |
| | (.01) | (.22) | (.05) | (.12) | | | |
| employment ratio | −.81 | −4.07 | −.96 | 3.84 | .89 | .045 | .60 |
| | (.01) | (.24) | (.06) | (.14) | | | |
| **4. Women 16–19: nonwhite** | | | | | | | |
| employment rate | −.04 | 3.45 | 1.58 | −.99 | .58 | .070 | 1.44 |
| | (.04) | (.49) | (.16) | (.31) | | | |
| participation rate | −1.11 | −2.96 | −.22 | 1.02 | .75 | .105 | .82 |
| | (.05) | (.74) | (.24) | (.46) | | | |
| employment ratio | −1.07 | −6.41 | −1.80 | 2.00 | .65 | .131 | .93 |
| | (.07) | (.92) | (.29) | (.58) | | | |

NOTE: The coefficient on *UPRIME* is the sum of the coefficients obtained from a nine-month Almon lag (first degree, far restriction).

siveness estimates are comparable, with participation somewhat more responsive, and unemployment somewhat less responsive to aggregate demand. In line with the traditional view of disadvantaged youths as likely to be "last hired" and "first fired," black youth employment is even more cyclically sensitive than the total group. For black men 16–19, each point reduction in the unemployment rate raises the employment ratio by close to 6.3%. A comparable figure obtains for black women.

The substantial cyclical response to changes in aggregate demand suggest that a shortage of job opportunities characterizes the youth labor market. If there were not a dearth of attractive jobs, aggregate demand would not be expected to have a significant impact on youth employment. The very strong response of participation to unemployment confirms the importance of focusing on employment rather than unemployment in assessing labor market conditions. It also supports the argument of section 7.1 that much of the high rate of labor force withdrawal among the unemployed is attributable to discouragement.

It is instructive to consider the cyclical responsiveness of enrolled and nonenrolled young people separately.[12] This is done in table 7.9. The results display dramatic differences in the labor market behavior of enrolled and out-of-school youths. For young men and women enrolled in school almost all of the response of employment is due to movements in participation rather than unemployment. The opposite pattern characterizes youths who are out of school. Increases in employment for this group come almost entirely at the expense of unemployment. However, employment of out-of-school youths appears to be only about half as

**Table 7.9**    **Cyclical Response of Teenagers by Enrollment Status**

| Enrollment groups | | Employment ratio | Participation rate | Employment rate |
|---|---|---|---|---|
| In school | | | | |
| Men | 16–19 | 6.97 | 6.00 | .97 |
| | | (1.12) | (1.05) | (.40) |
| Women | 16–19 | 6.78 | 6.39 | .39 |
| | | (1.47) | (1.38) | (.51) |
| Out of school | | | | |
| Men | 16–19 | 2.80 | −.79 | 3.59 |
| | | ( .91) | ( .36) | ( .84) |
| Women | 16–19 | 3.38 | 1.00 | 2.38 |
| | | ( .85) | ( .72) | ( .45) |

SOURCE: These estimates are based on data taken from tables B6 and B7 of the *Employment and Training Report of the President*, 1978. The data are based on the October supplement of the CPS, and cover the period 1954–77. This table is reprinted from Clark and Summers, "Demographic Differences in Cyclical Employment Variation," *Journal of Human Resources* 16 (Winter, 1981).

sensitive to demand as that of enrolled young people. The reasons for these disparities are not clear. One possibility is that youths who are in school tend to await job offers passively. When offered an attractive job they accept and join the labor force; otherwise they remain out of the labor force. This would explain the observed pattern of participation and unemployment dynamics.

### 7.3.3   Evidence from Gross Flows

The strong response of employment and participation to aggregate demand reflects the large inflows and outflows described in section 7.1. The surges in employment and participation that accompany increases in aggregate demand may be due either to increased inflows or decreased outflows. That is, low unemployment may raise employment either by helping workers get jobs or by helping them hold jobs. In order to examine this issue we have estimated equations describing the time series movements in the monthly flow probabilities. In addition to trend, cycle, and seasonal variables, we also studied the effects of minimum wage legislation and federal youth employment programs. Since we were unable to isolate a significant effect of either of these measures on transition probabilities, the results of estimating the equations in which they were included are not reported here.

Table 7.10 summarizes the results of the flow probability equations. The first set of equations describes the probability of employment entrance. For men, the rate of entrance is very sensitive to demand. A one-point increase in the prime-age male unemployment rate reduces the probability of entry by .014, or about 9%. It is changes in entry rather than exit behavior which are the prime cause of employment fluctuations among young men. The probability of job entrance among women is much less affected by cyclical developments. The reasons for this difference are not clear. One possibility is that women are the first to be laid off in downturns. A more plausible explanation is that the entrance rate does not fall as unemployment rises because more women enter the labor force as their family income falls. The rate of exit does not appear to exhibit significant cyclical fluctuations.

The rates of labor force entry and exit also vary cyclically. The rate of exit falls during recessions largely because the probability of withdrawal is much greater for the unemployed than it is for those who are employed. For the male groups the probability of labor force entrance is strongly cyclical. It is much less cyclical for women because of the added worker behavior noted above.

On balance, the flow probability equations bear out the basic conclusions of this section. They demonstrate that both labor force entry and employment entry become significantly easier during peak periods. This is consistent with the findings about the responsiveness of nonemployment to the state of local labor markets, noted in section 7.30. Taken

**Table 7.10**      **Cyclical Behavior of Transition Probabilities 1968–76 (Standard Errors in Parentheses)**

| Transition probability/ demographic group | CONS | UPRIME | T $(12 \times 10^2)$ | $\bar{R}^2$ | SEE | ρ |
|---|---|---|---|---|---|---|
| **Dependent variable** | | | | | | |
| **1. Probability of employment entrance** | | | | | | |
| M1619 | .093 | −1.440 | −.185 | .937 | .019 | −.050 |
| | (.073) | (.257) | (.105) | | | (.105) |
| BM1619 | .172 | −1.420 | −.264 | .856 | .024 | .002 |
| | (.032) | (.357) | (.146) | | | (.105) |
| W1619 | .051 | −.273 | .169 | .930 | .010 | −.293 |
| | (.011) | (.110) | (.048) | | | (.100) |
| BW1619 | .110 | −.246 | −.206 | .796 | .017 | .029 |
| | (.023) | (.254) | (.104) | | | (.105) |
| **2. Probability of employment exit** | | | | | | |
| M1619 | .229 | .214 | −.377 | .946 | .015 | −.105 |
| | (.018) | (.194) | (.079) | | | (.104) |
| BM1619 | .134 | −.696 | .216 | .839 | .038 | .002 |
| | (.051) | (.557) | (.218) | | | (.104) |
| W1619 | .250 | .591 | −.535 | .940 | .015 | −.154 |
| | (.017) | (.184) | (.075) | | | (.104) |
| BW1619 | .364 | −.493 | −.714 | .793 | .048 | −.080 |
| | (.059) | (.642) | (.262) | | | (.104) |
| **3. Probability of labor force entrance** | | | | | | |
| M1619 | .063 | −.760 | .378 | .961 | .020 | −.122 |
| | (.024) | (.266) | (.109) | | | (.104) |
| BM1619 | .170 | −1.148 | −.115 | .932 | .027 | .111 |
| | (.039) | (.435) | (.178) | | | (.104) |
| W1619 | .032 | −.036 | .324 | .959 | .012 | −.25 |
| | (.013) | (.142) | (.058) | | | (.101) |
| BW1619 | .104 | .291 | .064 | .385 | .023 | −.018 |
| | (.030) | (.377) | (.133) | | | (.105) |
| **Dependent variable** | | | | | | |
| **4. Probability of labor force exit** | | | | | | |
| M1619 | .255 | .578 | −.541 | .940 | .014 | −.041 |
| | (.017) | (.190) | (.077) | | | (.104) |
| BM1619 | .170 | .498 | .026 | .851 | .029 | .112 |
| | (.043) | (.478) | (.195) | | | (.104) |
| W1619 | .280 | .627 | −.592 | .920 | .014 | −.158 |
| | (.016) | (.173) | (.071) | | | (.104) |
| BW1619 | .238 | 1.23 | −.149 | .753 | .036 | −.004 |
| | (.047) | (.515) | (.211) | | | (.106) |

The header spans: Independent variables (covering CONS, UPRIME, T $(12 \times 10^2)$).

NOTE: The coefficient on *UPRIME* is the sum of nine-month Almon lag (first degree, far restriction); each regression was estimated with seasonal dummies, and a correction for first order autocorrelation.

together with the evidence that most unemployed teenagers have and will experience quite prolonged joblessness, these findings suggest that a shortage of attractive jobs is at least a partial source of the youth unemployment problem.

## 7.4 Conclusions and Implications

In this section we shall discuss the implications of our results for policies designed to combat youth unemployment. Our argument can be stated in quite bold terms. Expansionary aggregate demand policy is the only proven way of enlarging the employment opportunities for young people. A consistent effort to keep the unemployment rate near its full employment level would do more to help young people find jobs than almost any other conceivable governmental policy. Of course, other considerations might suggest that, on balance, such a policy is not workable. While certain structural policies might have salutary effects, it is highly unlikely that they could succeed except in a full-employment economy. After discussing the positive effects of a tight labor market, we shall turn to an examination of potential structural initiatives.

### 7.4.1   The Macroeconomy and the Youth Labor Market

As section 7.3 showed, both teenage unemployment and participation respond strongly to labor market conditions. A reduction of one point in the prime-age male unemployment rate raises the proportion of teenagers who are employed by about 4%, which is split about 2:1 between a reduction in unemployment and an increase in participation. For black youths the proportion rises about 6.5% split in a similar way. These figures imply that the 1975 recession cost young workers about 800,000 jobs. The growth in the economy during the late 1960s created close to 300,000 jobs for young workers. Evidence from cross-section data underscores the responsiveness of teenage unemployment to changes in demand. Freeman (1978) and Clark and Summers (1978) have shown that the youth employment ratio is much higher in strong than in weak labor labor markets.[13]

Expansion of aggregate demand is especially potent in making available opportunities for those who are most disadvantaged. Between 1969, when the aggregate unemployment rate was 3.6%, and 1976 when it was 7.7%, the proportion of 16–19 year olds suffering more than six months of unemployment rose fourfold. For black youths the same figure increased by almost six times. The tremendous impact of demand on the amount of long-term unemployment is particularly important in light of the results of section 7.1. The evidence presented there suggests that while most teenagers experience little difficulty in moving into and out of employment, most unemployment is concentrated among those who face serious difficulties in obtaining jobs. The teenage unemployment problem is not the lack of desire to hold jobs, but the inability to find work. A shortage of jobs appears to be the only explanation for the large responsiveness of employment to changes in demand. If unemployment were simply a matter of instability, there would be little reason to expect it to respond strongly to aggregate demand. We conclude that the existence of a job shortage must be the central reality dominating efforts to evaluate or design structural initiatives to improve the labor market for youths.

This conclusion is buttressed by evidence on job applications for surveys of low-wage employers who have placed "help wanted" ads in newspapers. In Noverber 1978, *Fortune* magazine reported on a survey of want ads in a small city in upstate New York. The investigators tracked down all want ads, but the results for jobs requiring little skill provide insight into the operation of low-wage markets. A focus on low-wage/low-skill markets is critical for the validity of this evidence. The existence of a long queue for good high-paying jobs is not evidence of an overall shortage, since low-paying, dead-end jobs could go unfilled while people searched in the high-wage sector. Yet for jobs requiring no skill or previous experience, the *Fortune* investigators found employers swamped with applications. Many employers offering jobs paying as low as $3 per hour had as many as seventy applicants within twenty-four hours of placing an ad. Interviews with employers revealed that many never placed want ads since they had huge files of applications even for low-paying jobs.

A similar finding was uncovered in a recent study of the hiring policies of one low-wage employer.[14] Analysis of personnel records revealed that vancancies were rarely advertised. When jobs opened, the employer simply called past job applicants. In most cases, previous applicants were still unemployed and eager for work. Other new hirings came from the friends and relatives of existing employees.

Further evidence on queues and vacancies has emerged in our continuing analysis of want ads in the Boston area. Focusing on the very worst jobs advertised in the Sunday paper, we have found an average of fifteen to twenty responses within two days of the ads' placement, with some employers receiving more than thirty appliers, over half of whom appeared in person. The available evidence suggests that employers have no difficulty in filling vacancies even for jobs requiring menial tasks that pay close to the minimum wage and have little prospect for improvement. These findings are not definitive, but they do suggest that the long queues characteristic of the high-wage sector may exist in the low-wage sector as well.

The existence of a job shortage is of fundamental importance in assessing the policy implications of the instability view of teenage unemployment. We have noted the allegation that high turnover is the principal culprit in high youth unemployment rates which yields policy prescriptions designed to improve school-to-work transitions and upgrade teenage workers. However, in the face of a job shortage, reduction of turnover will only redistribute the burden of unemployment. Without job vacancies to be filled, or an increase in the number of jobs, reduced instability would simply reduce the frequency and increase the duration of unemployment spells.

Before we turn to an evaluation of potential structural initiatives, it is useful to review the extent to which strong aggregate demand can achieve structural goals. A key objective of almost all structural programs is to aid youths in obtaining the skills and employment experience necessary to succeed in the adult world. These goals are accomplished to a large extent by expansionary macroeconomic policies. Between 1969 and 1976 the rate of job loss rose by about 75%, substantially reducing the ability of young people to accumulate experience. Cyclical decreases in the youth employment rate also cause reductions in on-the-job training. Standard estimates (e.g., those of Mincer) suggest that an extra year's experience raises earnings by about 2 to 3%. Ellwood's results in this volume (chapter 10) appear to be consistent with this figure. This figure suggests that the 1975–76 recession reduced by a significant amount the lifetime earnings of the youth cohort. Since each year of youth nonemployment costs about $20,000, the extra nonemployment had a present value cost of about 16 billion dollars. This calculation is a substantial underestimate of the true difference that cyclical conditions can make in human capital formation. It ignores the benefits of both worker upgrading and the likelihood that if labor were in short supply employers would compete, at least in part, by offering training. When these factors are considered, it is clear that expansionary macroeconomic policy can do a great deal to achieve structural goals.

### 7.4.2   The Role of Structural Policies

The results in section 7.3 bear out Feldstein and Wright's (1974) conclusion that even if the prime-age male unemployment rate were reduced to unprecedented levels, teenage unemployment rates would remain relatively high.[15] This fact has led many to conclude that only structural measures can make an effective dent in the youth unemployment problem. As we have argued elsewhere, this inference is misleading. Youth unemployment rates remain so high when aggregate demand increases in large part because of increases in participation. In Clark and Summers (1979) we show that if the mature male unemployment rate were driven down its 1969 level, and participation were not allowed to expand, the teenage unemployment rate would fall to close to 6%. The question remains as to what, if any, contribution structural measures can make. These policies may be divided into three broad categories: (1)

programs to aid workers in searching for jobs through job matching or improved information; (2) job training programs designed to provide workers with necessary skills; (3) job creation programs designed to make available special jobs for youth groups.

A detailed review of the evidence and discussion of the effectiveness of job matching, job training, and job creation programs is beyond the scope of this chapter. Our results, however, suggest the following observations. First, given a shortage of jobs, training and job matching programs offer little prospect for making a significant contribution to the solution of the youth unemployment problem. Aiding any single worker through training or improved transition to work will improve his chances at the expense of others. As long as there is only a fixed number of jobs, total employment cannot be increased by helping all workers augment skills or search more efficiently. Each worker's additional search, for example, detracts from the opportunities open to other workers and so generates a negative externality. Under these circumstances, belief in training and job matching reflects the fallacy of composition. Matching and training programs cannot have the desired effects unless coupled with an expansion in the number of jobs. If such an expansion is forthcoming, and employers experience difficulty in filling vacancies, training and market transition programs could prove useful.

Second, direct job creation through public employment or private sector subsidies appears to offer the most promising structural approach to the youth unemployment problem. Like training programs, the impact of policy can be focused on those groups who account for the bulk of teenage unemployment. Moreover, the policy is directed at the root of the problem: a shortage of jobs. The success of such programs, however, depends on the extent of net job creation and the provision of skills and experience useful to young persons over the longer term. The evidence presented in section 7.3 suggests that governmental efforts to provide seasonal jobs for disadvantaged in-school youths have met with some success. The effect of other governmental programs like the Youth Conservation Corps, the Job Corps, and Public Service Employment remains an open question in need of further research.

### 7.4.3    Conclusion

This chapter has presented evidence on the characteristics and sources of teenage unemployment. Our results underscore the apparent dynamic character of the youth labor market, but suggest that market dynamics cannot account for the bulk of youth joblessness. The job instability/ turnover view of unemployment is applicable to the majority of teenagers who experience little difficulty in moving into and out of the labor force. Most unemployment, however, is concentrated among those people who are unemployed for extended periods, and who face serious difficulty in obtaining employment. The results suggest that the problem of teenage unemployment arises from a shortage of jobs. The evidence in section 7.4 indicates that aggregate demand has a potent impact on the job prospects and market experience of teenagers.

# Notes

1. This view has been expressed in Robert E. Hall, "Turnover in the Labor Force," *Brookings Papers on Economic Activity* 3 (1972):709–56, and "Why Is the Unemployment Rate So High at Full Employment?" *BPEA* 3 (1970):369–402; George L. Perry, "Unemployment Flows in the U.S. Labor Market," *BPEA* 2 (1972):245–78; Ralph E. Smith, Jean E. Vanski, and Charles C. Holt, "Recession and the Employment of Demographic Groups," *BPEA* 3 (1974):737–58; Stephen T. Marston, "Employment Instability and High Unemployment Rates," *BPEA* 1 (1976):169–203; and Martin S. Feldstein, *Lowering the Permanent Rate of Unemployment*, a study prepared for the use of the Joint Economic Committee, 93rd Cong. 1st sess. (Washington, D.C.: Government Printing Office, 1973).

2. Martin S. Feldstein, *Lowering the Permanent Rate of Unemployment*, a study prepared for the use of the Joint Economic Committee, 93rd Cong. 1st sess. (Washington, D.C.: Government Printing Office, 1973), pp. 11, 16.

3. Henry Woltman and Irv Schreiner, memorandum on "Possible Effects of Response Variance on the Gross Changes from Month to Month in the Current Population Survey," Bureau of the Census, Washington, D.C.

4. This point is developed in Kim B. Clark and Lawrence H. Summers, "Labor Market Dynamics and Unemployment: A Reconsideration," *BPEA* 1 (1979):14–60.

5. These data are contained in Kim B. Clark and Lawrence H. Summers, "Labor Force Transitions and Unemployment" (National Bureau of Economic Research Working Paper 277).

6. Ibid.

7. Preliminary statistical analysis suggests that seasonal fluctuations in teenage unemployment have been lower since the inception of various jobs programs in 1965.

8. Richard Layard, "Youth Unemployment in Britain and the U.S. Compared," chapter 15 of the present volume.

9. Nancy Barret and Richard Morgenstern, "Why Do Blacks and Women Have High Unemployment Rates?" *J. Hum. Resources* 9 (Fall, 1974):456.

10. This figure is also an underestimate because of spells which are not completely contained in a year.

11. See, for example, William E. Bowen and T. Aldrich Finegan, *The Economics of Labor Force Participation* (Princeton: Princeton University Press, 1969), and George C. Perry, "Potential Output and Productivity" *BPEA* 1 (1973):207–52.

12. This section draws on Kim B. Clark and Lawrence H. Summers, "Demographic Differences in Cyclical Employment Variation," *Journal of Human Resources* 16 (Winter, 1981):61–79.

13. Richard Freeman, "Economic Determinants of the Geographic and Individual Variation in Labor Market Positions of Young Persons," and Kim B. Clark and Lawrence H. Summers, "Labor Force Participation: Timing vs. Persistence," ASPER, U.S. Department of Labor, (Technical Analysis Paper no. 60, 1978).

14. Jane Schmeisser, "Hiring in a Low Wage Labor Market," (unpublished senior honors thesis, Department of Economics, Harvard University, 1979).

15. Martin S. Feldstein and Brian Wright, "High Unemployment Groups in Tight Labor Markets," (Harvard Institute of Economic Research Discussion Paper no. 488, June 1976).

# Comment    George L. Perry

The available statistics about what's going on in the labor market are notoriously hard to interpret. They have led some observers to characterize youth unemployment as a product of normal turnover. Clark and Summers have done a careful job of analyzing data on the employment and unemployment of young people; and they make a convincing case that long-term joblessness is a serious problem in this age group and is the principal factor behind the high unemployment rates recorded for teenagers.

The association of youth unemployment with normal turnover arises because the mean duration of unemployment spells for teenagers are relatively short, and so is their mean job tenure. Clark and Summers find that highly concentrated joblessness lies behind these statistics. Their discussion of concentration has three main parts: they look at spell-lengths among the unemployed rather than among all those who enter unemployment; they examine the incidence of multiple spells; and they estimate spells without jobs rather than spells of official unemployment.

The average spell-length of those currently unemployed is much longer than the average for all spells because persons suffering long spells are more likely to appear in the unemployment count. Thus when they calculate average spell durations for those unemployed at any time, Clark and Summers are answering a different question from the one that is usually posed. Theirs' is the right answer if we want to know what experience today's unemployed can expect. It is not the right way to characterize the labor market experience of all workers. The authors are very clear on this point, but it is worth alerting the reader.

Going beyond the data from monthly unemployment surveys, Clark and Summers point out that many workers experience much more extensive unemployment than the data on individual spell-lengths would reveal because they suffer multiple spells of unemployment within a year. More than half of the total unemployment experienced by male teenage youths who are out of school is accounted for by those unemployed more than six months; for their female counterparts, the fraction is nearly half.

According to official definitions, unemployment spells often end by withdrawal from the work force. Some analysts take this as evidence that their interest in, or need for, work is marginal and their unemployment, consequently, is relatively unimportant. Clark and Summers stress, by contrast, that the often spurious distinction in the official statistics between being unemployed and being out of the labor force leads to an understatement of the difficulty that the unemployed experience in finding a job. They argue for focusing on spells without jobs—including

George L. Perry is a senior fellow at the Brookings Institution.

time officially recorded as out of the labor force as well as time unemployed—in analyzing the labor market for out-of-school youths. It is pointless to try to decide how badly people need a job from their place in the official statistics. But Clark and Summers are surely correct in stressing that ending a spell of unemployment by getting a job is a very different matter from ending one by withdrawing from the official labor force. And if we are serious about understanding the youth employment problem, it is surely right to inquire about periods without work for out-of-school youths rather than just periods when they fall into the official definition of unemployment.

The authors' calculations illustrate the considerable difficulty that many unemployed teenagers have in getting a job, and the even greater difficulty experienced by the subset of unemployed nonwhite teenagers. In 1976, the average unemployed white teenager would expect to be without a job for more than six months at a time. His black counterpart would expect to be without a job for a little more than a year.

The authors point out carefully that such results are not representative of the experience of most teenagers. For most, any unemployment spells are brief. But their experience bears little resemblance to the job-finding difficulties of the much smaller number of teenagers who account for most of the observed unemployment. Clark and Summers show convincingly that job availability makes a big difference for the employment problem that they identify. They find that aggregate demand matters a lot and that a tight overall labor market greatly improves the job prospects of those youths who have the greatest problems finding jobs. They also advocate youth employment programs as the most useful structural remedy. I agree with this emphasis on providing jobs. And if we are entering a period of high overall unemployment in pursuing an antiinflation strategy, the need for specific youth employment programs will be greater than ever.

## Comment    Robert I. Lerman

Clark and Summers conclude that youth unemployment is not so much a matter of high turnover as of inadequate job opportunities. This is the most important of several interesting conclusions. While I agree with most of their conclusions, I believe there are weaknesses in their analysis, most of which concern their use of CPS gross flow data.

It is the gross flow data that lead Clark and Summers to the conclusion that the distinction between unemployment ($U$) and not-in-the-labor-

Robert I. Lerman is an economist at the Heller School at Brandeis University.

force ($N$) is very tenuous. But, for some reason, they use this conclusion in some contexts but ignore it in other contexts. Clark and Summers argue that if $U$ and $N$ are indistinguishable, the duration of $U$ may be understated because reported moves from $U$ to $N$ to $U$ should often be recorded as one long period of $U$. But when attempting to show that the labor market works well for most youth, they go back to the $U$-$N$ distinction. They point out that two-thirds of teenage moves into the labor market (from $N$ to $U$ or to employment) occur without any measured unemployment. This statement should have little meaning. If $N$ and $U$ are essentially the same status, it should not matter whether the transition to employment ($E$) comes from $N$ or $U$. They cannot have it both ways. If the move from $N$ to $U$ or to $E$ does represent labor force entry (and the continuation in $N$ does not), then one must allow the move from $U$ or $E$ to $N$ to represent labor force exit.

Clark and Summers interpret the lack of a $U$-$N$ distinction as implying that conventional approaches hide much involuntary joblessness. They imply that a month to month pattern of $U$-$N$-$U$-$E$ is essentially like a $U$-$U$-$U$-$E$ pattern. Unfortunately, they provide no more evidence for their interpretation ($U$ to $E$) than for the alternative interpretation of one long spell outside the labor force ($N$ to $E$).

Is it discouragement or lack of sufficient interest in working that keeps youths from such minimal job search as required by the CPS definition of $U$? Clark and Summers state: "The evidence suggests the possibility that for many teenagers, job search is a passive process in which the main activity is waiting for a job opportunity to be presented." This viewpoint is consistent with data from a January 1973 CPS supplement, which revealed that only 18% of unemployed teenagers spent more than ten hours per week actually looking for work. While all this lends support to the idea of a tenuous distinction between $U$ and $N$, it does not lead to the conclusion that we should abandon the CPS requirements that $U$ represent job availability along with *active* job search. The Clark-Summers analysis forces us to confront normative questions, such as: Is joblessness associated with only passive job search a serious problem? Should it be treated as involuntary unemployment or as indifference about work? To guide our thinking about such questions, we should obtain detailed information about passive job seekers. But, in addition, we must decide on an appropriate way to measure a labor market problem. As it is, if the $U$-$N$ ambiguity were carried to its logical extreme, one could interpret long-term unemployment as long-term leisure or as a vacation between jobs.

Clark and Summers rely on gross flow data to help sort out these matters. Unfortunately, they give only passing attention to the unreliability of the gross flow data. It is unfortunate that the Woltman-Schreiner memo to which Clark and Summers refer appeared after Clark and

Summers virtually completed their paper. As noted, the memo shows that the reported gross flows are probably two to three times the actual flows. Clark and Summers seem unfazed by this conclusion. In fact, they suggest that the existence of the upward bias in gross flow data actually strengthens their findings. They interpret CPS reporting variance which leads to the gross flow bias as the result of the often arbitrary nature of CPS definitions of $U$ and $N$. Since the true flows are less than the reported flows, the high concentrations of unemployment pointed out by Clark and Summers actually understate the true concentrations of unemployment.

Although this last implication is correct, the bias in the gross flow data raises other problems which Clark and Summers do not confront. For example, they ignore the fact that reported flows in and out of $E$ are as overstated as flows between $N$ and $U$. Would they argue that the high flows between $E$ and $U$ resulting largely from response variance indicate that the CPS definition of $E$ is arbitrary? The unreliable nature of the data on $E$ flows also creates difficulties for their analysis of the share of youths entering jobs without any unemployment and for their treatment of cyclical patterns of job change. Clearly, any future analysis based on these data must deal with the biases in a thorough manner.

Two other points about the Clark-Summers data are worth noting. They present results covering in-school and out-of-school youths. Actually, they make use of a CPS question asking whether an individual's major activity is school or something other than school. Some youths who attend school report work as their major activity. Thus, the CPS out-of-school group includes some enrolled youths who have jobs. If these enrolled workers are more committed to the work force than other enrolled youths, the Clark-Summers results would understate the stability of employment patterns of in-school youths. The second item is the number Clark and Summers cite for the percentage of job changers who experience no unemployment between jobs. The number comes from 1961 data. Clark and Summers should be cautious about using a 1961 number in their overall description of current labor markets.

While I have focused on problems in the Clark-Summers analysis, I believe their paper contributes much to our understanding of youth labor force patterns. Most important is the abundant evidence they cite showing that youth unemployment is highly concentrated among a small subset of young workers and that short-term, turnover factors cannot account for most youth unemployment.

# 8 Labor Turnover and Youth Unemployment

Linda Leighton and Jacob Mincer

## 8.1 Introduction: The Youth Unemployment Problem

Public concern about youth employment problems in the U.S. derives from three facts: (1) the unemployment rate of young people is high in absolute numbers, both in relation to adult unemployment and in comparison with other countries; (2) unemployment rates of black youths are much higher and a large fraction of nonworking black youths does not even search for jobs: (3) youth unemployment rates have increased in recent years. The trend is not pronounced among whites, but the rate for black youths has risen from levels comparable to white rates in the 1950s to the present depressionlike levels.

In this chapter we do not address the problem of trends. It is an important question for assessing the plight of black youths and a smaller one for the white population beyond the adverse but temporary conjunction of the business and demographic cycles. Rather, our question refers to the more permanent fact of high youth unemployment. Why is it so high? Are there criteria by which we can judge that it is too high? Why does it decline with age in a particular fashion?

Recent developments in the economics of labor markets provide two complementary approaches to the understanding of differential unem-

Linda Leighton is associated with Fordham University and with the Center for the Social Sciences at Columbia University. Jacob Mincer is associated with Columbia University and with the National Bureau of Economic Research. This work is an outgrowth of Leighton's study of unemployment (1978) and of the Mincer-Jovanovic study of labor mobility (1978). We are grateful to the U.S. Department of Labor, the National Science Foundation, and to the Sloan Foundation for support of this work. We benefited from the comments of Alan Gustman, Kip Viscusi, Robert Shakotko, and from competent research assistance of Margaret Lennon, Frank Nothaft, and Stephen Zuckerman. We are grateful to Carl Rosenfeld of the BLS for the unpublished data in table 8.3. Any opinions expressed are those of the authors and not those of the National Bureau of Economic Research or of the Columbia University Center for the Social Sciences.

ployment. Search models are applicable, in principle, to the analysis of duration of unemployment, as they highlight the conditions under which job search terminates. On the other hand, episodes of unemployment originate in the context of job or interlabor force moves, so that models of labor turnover are most useful in understanding the incidence of unemployment. Since age differences in the incidence of unemployment are even larger than differences in unemployment rates, we emphasize labor turnover as the main framework for analyzing the relationship between age and unemployment. We also employ a search model which captures some relevant aspects of the age differentials in job separation and in the duration of unemployment.

Our data sets are the panels of men in the National Longitudinal Surveys (NLS) and in the Michigan Income Dynamics surveys (MID). The data lend themselves to several analyses with which we attempt to illuminate the structure of unemployment. In section 8.2 we decompose the "unemployment rate" observed in a period into incidence, or proportion of persons experiencing unemployment some time during the period, and average duration of unemployment during the period. This enables us to assess the relative importance of each component in creating unemployment differentials among age or any other population subgroups.

We observe the incidence and duration of unemployment in periods longer than a year in section 8.3. The rate at which incidence and duration increase as the period is lengthened indicates the degree of persistence of unemployment or its converse, the degree of turnover among the unemployed. The observed degree of persistence may be due to positive serial correlation in the probability of experiencing unemployment for given individuals, or to heterogeneity in this probability across individuals, or both. These categories cannot be distinguished by lengthening the period, but are explored in regression analyses (section 8.5).

In section 8.4 we relate current unemployment incidence $P(u)$ to current labor mobility, defined as the probability of job separation from the current employer $P(s)$. We compare $P(u)$ and $P(s)$ over the life-cycle and by length of job tenure. The apparent absence of "aging effects" on the incidence of unemployment is tested in comparisons of youths with migrants. According to the identity $P(u) = P(s) \cdot P(u \mid s)$, factors underlying labor mobility $P(s)$ ought to account for some of the patterns of incidence $P(u)$, especially when recall unemployment is excluded from $P(u)$. We explore the factors underlying the probabilities $P(s)$ and $P(u)$ in regression analyses in section 8.5.

Further insights into differences in conditional unemployment $P(u \mid s)$ and in duration of unemployment are obtained in a search model presented in section 8.6. This model also carries implication for quit/layoff behavior and for wage changes connected with separations and unemployment.

Section 8.7 is a replication of regression analyses on data for blacks and an analysis of the racial differentials.

## 8.2  Components of Unemployment

The same rate of unemployment is observed during a survey week when a certain proportion of the labor force is unemployed two months on average or when only one-third of that proportion is unemployed for a period of six months. The rate does not tell us whether a large number of those affected share a small burden or whether the opposite is the case. If the observation period is sufficiently long, the rate can be decomposed into incidence and duration of unemployment. Whether or not time spent in unemployment is to be interpreted as distress or as productive activity, we want to know whether it is incidence or duration which is mainly responsible for the differences in particular comparisons of population groups.

To do this we may define a personal unemployment rate during the period (e.g., a year) by the ratio of weeks spent in unemployment to weeks spent in the labor force:

(1) $$u_i = \frac{W_{ui}}{W_{Li}}$$

A simple average of $u_i$ would measure the group unemployment rate in an average week if each person spent the same number of weeks per year in the labor force. Otherwise the individual $u_i$ must be weighted by his time in the labor force $W_{Li}$ in averaging. As a result the group rate is obtained in:

(2) $$\bar{u} = \frac{\sum_i W_{Li} \left( \frac{W_{ui}}{W_{Li}} \right)}{\sum_i W_{Li}} = \frac{\sum_i W_{ui}}{\sum_i W_{Li}} = \frac{N}{L} \cdot \frac{\bar{W}_u}{\bar{W}_L} = \frac{N}{L} \cdot \bar{W}_u \cdot \frac{1}{1 - \bar{W}_o}$$

where $N$ is the number of persons unemployed some time during the period, $L$ the number of people in the labor force some time during the period. $N/L$ is the incidence of unemployment during the period. $\bar{W}_u$ is the average fraction of the period spent in unemployment by the unemployed, $\bar{W}_L$ the average fraction of the time period spent in the labor force by the labor force group, and $\bar{W}o = 1 - \bar{W}_L$.

Table 8.1 provides decompositions of unemployment experience by the NLS samples of young and mature men for the years 1969–71. The young men ranged in age between 17 and 27, the older men were 48 to 62 years old. The men are classified by school enrollment status, educational attainment, and race. Unemployment followed by a return to the same employer ("recall" or "temporary layoff") is excluded from table 8.1, but is included in appendix tables.[1] The left-hand panel shows the compo-

**Table 8.1**     Decomposition of Incidence, Duration, and Nonparticipation NLS, 1969–71 (Excludes Temporary Layoffs)

| | | Levels | | |
|---|---|---|---|---|
| | $U$ | $\dfrac{N}{L}$ | $\bar{W}_u$ | $\dfrac{1}{(1-\bar{W}_0)}$ |
| Young whites | .052 | .328 | .136 | 1.15 |
| $n$ | (2364) | | | |
| Students | .075 | .455 | .127 | 1.36 |
| $n$ | (850) | | | |
| Nonstudents | .041 | .257 | .151 | 1.06 |
| $n$ | (1514) | | | |
| Education | | | | |
| 0–11 | .056 | .327 | .156 | 1.10 |
| 12 | .043 | .261 | .154 | 1.06 |
| ≥13 | .025 | .181 | .135 | 1.04 |
| Young blacks | .089 | .458 | .165 | 1.18 |
| $n$ | (835) | | | |
| Students | .127 | .581 | .153 | 1.43 |
| $n$ | (217) | | | |
| Nonstudents | .079 | .414 | .172 | 1.11 |
| $n$ | (618) | | | |
| Mature whites | .018 | .090 | .194 | 1.06 |
| $n$ | (2167) | | | |
| Education | | | | |
| 0–11 | .022 | .099 | .209 | 1.07 |
| 12 | .013 | .080 | .160 | 1.03 |
| ≥13 | .016 | .081 | .189 | 1.04 |
| Mature blacks | .030 | .117 | .236 | 1.08 |
| $n$ | (967) | | | |

| | | Percent Differentials | | |
|---|---|---|---|---|
| | $U$ | $\dfrac{N}{L}$ | $\bar{W}_u$ | $\dfrac{1}{(1-\bar{W}_0)}$ |
| Young blacks minus young whites | .545 | .332 | .193 | .022 |
| Students | .525 | .243 | .229 | .052 |
| Nonstudents | .648 | .478 | .127 | .049 |
| Young whites minus mature whites | 1.02 | 1.29 | − .354 | .087 |
| Nonstudent young whites minus mature whites | .801 | 1.04 | − .250 | .006 |
| Young blacks minus mature blacks | 1.10 | 1.36 | − .356 | .091 |
| Nonstudent young blacks minus mature blacks | .976 | 1.26 | − .319 | .032 |
| Mature blacks minus mature whites | .473 | .257 | .195 | .019 |

**Table 8.1** (continued)

| | | Percent Differentials | | |
|---|---|---|---|---|
| | $U$ | $\dfrac{N}{L}$ | $\bar{W}_u$ | $\dfrac{1}{(1-\bar{W}_0)}$ |
| Education: | | | | |
| less than H.S. minus H.S. | | | | |
| Nonstudent whites | .273 | .226 | .011 | .032 |
| Mature whites | .515 | .209 | .264 | .039 |
| H.S. minus >H.S. | | | | |
| Nonstudent whites | .522 | .367 | .136 | .018 |
| Mature whites | −.192 | −.012 | −.166 | −.009 |

NOTE: $\bar{W}$ = proportion of time spent unemployed by unemployed.
$\bar{W}_0^u$ = proportion of time spent out of the labor force by labor force participants.
$\dfrac{N}{L}$ = incidence of unemployment.
$n$ = sample size.

nents of levels of unemployment. The nonparticipation component $1/ 1 - \bar{W}_o$ is the major one among students in the period 1966–69 though not in 1969–71.[2] It is followed in relative importance by incidence and duration. Among the young, incidence exceeds duration in producing the unemployment total, while the opposite is true with the older groups. Both incidence and duration are greater with blacks than whites and with the less educated youths compared to the more educated.[3] In the right-hand panel, percent differentials in the unemployment rate and its components are calculated for selected groups. Clearly, higher unemployment rates of the young are attributable to higher probabilities of unemployment; duration actually works in the opposite direction. While duration always increases with age in the white sample, the age differential for blacks is quite small for 1966–67 and 1967–69.

On average, almost 40% of all unemployed older men were on temporary layoffs and were recalled by the employer, while about 18% of the nonstudent young unemployed workers were recalled. Inclusion of recall unemployment shows a narrowing of the age differential in both the incidence and duration components of unemployment. This is because of the greater proportion of recall unemployment among older workers.

A comparison of decompositions for 1967–69 and 1969–71 provides information about cyclical changes. Going from the tight labor markets of 1967–69 to the recession years 1969–71 we find that duration of unemployment shows a greater increase (proportionately twice as large) than incidence of unemployment, and that the age differentials widen in incidence and narrow in duration. Both incidence and duration of unemployment are more cyclically sensitive in the young than in the old labor force. Whatever the cycle phase, we conclude higher incidence is the reason for higher youth unemployment. It is, therefore, the component of major interest for our study.

## 8.3   Short- and Long-run Unemployment Experience

The longitudinal data unable us to observe the incidence and the amount of time spent in unemployment over periods of several years. As indicated in table 8.2 the average incidence in a single year ($p$) in the 1966–69 period was 13.5% for young white nonstudents. Over the three-year period it was $P_3 = 27.9\%$. For the same group the average number of weeks spent in unemployment during a single year was 7.7. It was 11.3 over the three-year period. We may define "complete persistence" in unemployment experience when the same persons are unemployed in the three-year period as are in a single year. Then $P_3 = p$ and $W_3 = 3w$. "Complete turnover" is the opposite case, when those unemployed in one year are not unemployed in the other two years. Then $P_3 = 3p$ and $W_3 = w$. The actual figures are between the extremes, so that a significant degree of persistence coexists with a great deal of turnover.

**Table 8.2**      **Turnover and Persistence of Unemployment NLS, 1966–69**

|  | $p$ | $P_n$ | $\hat{P}_n$ | $N$ | $\lambda$ |
|---|---|---|---|---|---|
| Young whites |  |  |  |  |  |
| Students | .177 | .370 | .442 | 1023 | .727 |
| Nonstudents | .135 | .279 | .353 | 803 | .659 |
| Education |  |  |  |  |  |
| 0–8 | .220 | .458 | .526 | 118 | .776 |
| 9–11 | .177 | .357 | .442 | 196 | .679 |
| 12 | .104 | .215 | .281 | 377 | .624 |
| 13–15 | .113 | .235 | .301 | 68 | .650 |
| 16+ | .023 | .068 | .067 | 44 | 1.04 |
| Young blacks |  |  |  |  |  |
| Students | .296 | .619 | .650 | 291 | .910 |
| Nonstudents | .242 | .454 | .564 | 335 | .658 |
| Mature whites | .067 | .128 | .187 | 3459 | .506 |
| Education |  |  |  |  |  |
| 0–8 | .088 | .163 | .242 | 1274 | .488 |
| 9–11 | .064 | .119 | .180 | 708 | .471 |
| 12 | .055 | .109 | .157 | 872 | .526 |
| 13–15 | .058 | .124 | .168 | 298 | .618 |
| 16+ | .028 | .064 | .082 | 343 | .667 |
| Mature blacks | .095 | .176 | .258 | 1491 | .496 |

NOTE: $P_n$ = the observed probability of unemployment in an $n$-year period.
$p$ = an average of the $n$-year single probabilities.
$\hat{P}_n = 1 - (1 - p)^n$ assuming $p$ is an independent yearly probability.
$$\lambda = \frac{P_n - p}{\hat{P}_n - p}$$
$N$ = sample size.

There are two possible and not mutually exclusive reasons why the number of people experiencing unemployment sometime in an $n$-year period is less then $n$-times the number of unemployed in a single year. First, the experience of unemployment in one year increases the probability of becoming unemployed the next year. The events are dependent in probability because of time or *tenure dependence*: the longer a person stays in the job the less likely he is to separate, hence to become unemployed. The other possibility is independence in probability over time, but differences in sizes of probability across people in the group: those with higher probabilities are more likely to be found unemployed at any time than are others. Both possibilities give rise to the persistence in observed incidence, so that $P_n < np$ and $W_n > w$.

Let us consider the two cases separately.

1. The assumption of homogeneity, that is, $p_i = p$ for all individuals $i$, with time independent probabilities yields an upper limit for $P_n$ (it is clearly less than $np$, which would require a negative serial correlation). Denote the upper limit by $\hat{p}_n$, $\hat{p}_n = 1 - (1 - p)^n$. The observed $n$-year incidence is $P_n \leq \hat{P}_n$, and a natural measure[4] of the degree of persistence is $1 - \lambda$, where $\lambda = P_n - p / \hat{P}_n - p$. When $\lambda = 1$, there is no persistence in the unemployment experience.

2. Assume independence, but heterogeneity. Here the group consists of individuals whose $p_i$ differ. Define $p = E(p_i)$ and $q_i = 1 - p_i, q = E(q_i)$. Then $E(\hat{P}_{ni}) = E[1 - (1 - p_i)^n] < 1 - (1 - p)^n$, and $1 - E[(q_i)^n] < 1 - q^n$. The inequality holds because, as is well known, $E[(q_i)^n] > [E(q_i)]^n$. In other words, if homogeneity and independence obtained within each of the subgroups differing in $p_i$, the observed $p_n$ would be smaller than $\hat{P}_n$ expected on the assumption of homogeneity of the whole group.

In table 8.2, $\lambda = 65.9\%$ for young white nonstudents, so the degree of persistence for this group is 34.1%; it is 49.4% for old NLS whites. Racial differences in $\lambda$ are small but they are not standardized by education. Among the young, persistence is greater in groups with education levels above high school and it does not change with age. Among the less educated, persistence increases with age. Apparently, tenure dependence is weaker and/or heterogeneity smaller in the young less educated than in the more educated groups. According to our analysis in the next section, this is reasonable if the less educated acquire less firm specific skills on the job. Over time there is a differentiation in these groups into people who acquire job attachments and others who continue to drift. The result is a growth of tenure dependence and of heterogeneity with age.

Of course, the observed $P_n$ will be even smaller if time dependence (or heterogeneity) obtains within the subgroups. Consequently, $\lambda < 1$ may reflect heterogeneity or time dependence or both. The data in table 8.2 cannot distinguish whether it is heterogeneity or time dependence which produce a less than proportionate increase in incidence and in time spent in unemployment. Regression analyses described in section 8.5 explore these matters further and suggest that both factors are at work in producing the result.

### 8.4   Incidence of Unemployment and Labor Turnover: Experience and Tenure Profiles

Since it is incidence that is responsible for high levels of youth unemployment, we direct our attention primarily to the analysis of $P(u)$ and secondarily to the question why adult men experience longer spells of unemployment. Spells of unemployment occur, if at all, during job change or during movement between the nonmarket (household, school, the military) and the labor market. They also occur without job change in the case of recalled workers on temporary layoffs.

Unemployment incidence is definitionally related to labor turnover in the probability formula $P(u) = P(s) \cdot P(u|s)$ with recall unemployment excluded. For the sake of completeness, our findings include also recall unemployment (not shown in the text).

Published data classified by age show that the high rates of youth unemployment drop quite sharply to relatively low levels beyond the first half-decade of working life. Table 8.3 shows the age profiles of unem-

**Table 8.3**      **Job Mobility and Unemployment**

|  | Men, 1961 | | | | | |
|---|---|---|---|---|---|---|
| Employed in 1961 | 18–19 | 20–24 | 25–34 | 35–44 | 45–54 | 55–64 |
| Percent job changers (jc) | 23.5 | 24.4 | 14.9 | 10.2 | 7.1 | 4.0 |
| Percent of jc unemployed | 47.7 | 50.1 | 46.0 | 46.7 | 49.2 | 54.2 |
| Percent of jc laid off | 41.5 | 43.6 | 43.8 | 49.8 | 58.4 | 70.6 |
| Percent of jc who quit | 58.5 | 56.4 | 56.2 | 50.2 | 41.6 | 29.4 |

Source: BLS, Special Labor Force Report no. 35, *Job Mobility in 1961.*

|  | Men, 1977 | | | | | |
|---|---|---|---|---|---|---|
|  | 18–19 | 20–24 | 25–34 | 35–44 | 45–54 | 55–64 |
| Percent with job tenure less than a year in Jan. 1978[a] | 69.8 | 49.6 | 27.6 | 16.2 | 10.5 | 8.9 |
| Percent with unemployment during 1977[b] | 34.5 | 32.2 | 17.7 | 11.8 | 10.2 | 9.6 |

Sources: *Job Tenure of Workers, January 1978*, and *Work Experience of the Population in 1977*, unpublished, BLS.

Notes: [a]Employed in January 1978.

[b]In labor force some time during the year. Includes temporary layoff unemployment.

ployment in relation to labor mobility. The upper panel, based on a 1961 BLS survey (the last available survey of this kind), shows the incidence of unemployment among *job changers*. It suggests strongly that the age profile of unemployment is very much a reflection of the typical age-mobility profile. Almost half of the job changers became unemployed during the year, although this proportion increased somewhat with age. In the lower panel mobility is defined more broadly as the proportion of the labor force that has held the current job (with the current employer) less than a year in January 1978. Unemployment incidence among all men in the labor force and not merely among job changers is shown in the lower row of the lower panel. Here the age curve of incidence is also convex as is the mobility curve, but flatter, expecially beyond age 35. This is because (1) temporary layoff unemployment is included in the figures, which almost doubles the incidence at older ages, and (2), even when temporary layoffs are excluded, the quit/layoff ratios decline  with age (see rows 3 and 4 of the upper panel). Since the probability of unemployment is higher following layoffs than quitting, unemployment conditional on separations increases with age. In view of the relatively minor changes in conditional unemployment, the steep decline of youth unemployment in the early years of experience can be attributed to the convex shape of the age curve in labor mobility.

Mincer and Jovanovic (1979) show that the age decline in job separations is due primarily to the fact that the probability of separating declines with tenure in the current job, whether or not the separation is initiated by the worker or the employer. The theory underlying this relation is that the informational process of job matching and the accumulation of specific capital on the job create differences between worker productivity in the current job and elsewhere as well as differences between wages in current and alternative employments. The convexity of the tenure-mobility profile is due to the initially sharp decline in the probability of a separation following a successful job-matching ("probation") period, and an eventual leveling off of $P(s)$ following completion of specific capital accumulation in the firm. The experience (working-age) profile of mobility is easily derived from the tenure profile. Given $s = f(T, x)$ where $s$ is the mobility (separation) rate, $T$ length of tenure, and $x$ length of experience in the labor market,

$$(3) \qquad \frac{ds}{dx} = \frac{\partial s}{\partial T} \cdot \frac{dT}{dx} + \frac{\partial s}{\partial x}$$

The negative slope of the tenure curve (relation between tenure and separations) $\partial s / \partial T$ diminishes with $T$, and $dT/dx$ is positive and nonincreasing.[5] The convexity of the experience mobility curve $s(x)$ is thus due to the convexity of the tenure curve. The "aging effect" $\partial s/\partial x$ steepens the slope of the experience profile but does not affect its convexity. The aging effect represents declines of mobility with experience at fixed levels of tenure, and is pronounced in quits but not in layoffs (Mincer and Jovanovic, table 1).

The longer a worker stays in a firm the less likely he is to separate. Consequently, he is less likely to become unemployed, unless separations after a longer stay in the firm carry a sufficiently higher risk of unemployment. This may be true of "permanent" (not recalled) layoffs which are less expected by higher tenured employees, while the opposite ought to hold for quits since the opportunity cost of unemployment increases with tenure. These predictions are weakly confirmed in MID regressions, not shown here. The opposing signs of unemployment conditional on quitting, and layoff cancel in total separations so that $P(u|s)$ shows no clear pattern with tenure as is shown in table 8.4.

Consequently, the tenure profile of unemployment should reflect the profile of separation, and the analyses of the experience profile of unemployment incidence can be represented equivalently to equation (3) in:

$$(4) \qquad \frac{dp(u)}{dx} = \frac{\partial P(u)}{\partial T} \cdot \frac{dT}{dx} + \frac{\partial P(u)}{\partial x}$$

Decline and convexity of the experience profile of unemployment is thus due, as was true of separations, to the sharp decline and convexity of the tenure profile of incidence.

A comparison of tenure profiles of incidence and of separations is shown in table 8.4. Over the first few years of tenure, the decline in unemployment incidence appears to be somewhat more rapid than the decline in separations for both age and race groups. Aside from a first year decline, the probability of unemployment conditional on separation $P(u|s)$ does not change systematically. However, as we already noticed in table 8.3, $P(u|s)$ is higher at older ages.

Among blacks the age differential in $P(u|s)$ varies over the business cycle. It is observable for 1969–71, but not for 1967–69. As noted before, a similar cycle pattern was observed in age differentials in duration. The age increase in $P(u|s)$ arises mainly from the increase in the layoff/quit ratio (apparent in table 8.3), but also from an increase in the probability of unemployment conditional on layoff $P(u|L)$. However, $P(u|Q)$ decreases slightly with age.[6]

The age increase in the conditional probability $P(u|s)$ is the reason for the absence of an aging effect ($\partial P(u)/\partial x$ in equation [4]) in unemployment in the face of a significant aging effect in separations. At given levels of tenure the difference in $P(u)$ between the young and the old white men is small although the difference is evident among the blacks who show a stronger "aging effect" in separations (temporary layoffs excluded). The age differences also increase in the recession period 1969–71.

We check on the age effect with the MID data which covers the complete age range. The absence of an aging effect in the probability of

**Table 8.4    Incidence of Unemployment by Tenure NLS, 1967–69 (Excludes Temporary Layoffs and Students)**

| Tenure as of 1967 | Young white men | | | Young black men | | | Mature white men | | | Mature black men | | |
|---|---|---|---|---|---|---|---|---|---|---|---|---|
| | P(U) | P(S) | P(U\|S) | P(U) | P(S) | P(U\|S) | P(U) | P(S) | P(U\|S) | P(U) | P(S) | P(U\|S) |
| 0 | .262 | .686 | .381 | .448 | .753 | .594 | .244 | .472 | .491 | .264 | .472 | .560 |
| 1 | .134 | .444 | .303 | .216 | .581 | .372 | .090 | .285 | .317 | .121 | .258 | .471 |
| 2 | .107 | .393 | .271 | .128 | .282 | .454 | .083 | .208 | .300 | .300 | .367 | .818 |
| 3 | .067 | .278 | .240 | .231 | .577 | .400 | .053 | .187 | .286 | .167 | .208 | .800 |
| 4 | .069 | .327 | .294 | .091 | .546 | .167 | .092 | .277 | .333 | .119 | .190 | .625 |
| 5 | .077 | .462 | .167 | .167 | .333 | .500 | .050 | .117 | .429 | .161 | .355 | .454 |
| 6 | .059 | .118 | .500 | .000 | .333 | .000 | .051 | .136 | .375 | .154 | .231 | .667 |
| 7 | .125 | .250 | .500 | .000 | .500 | .000 | .046 | .197 | .231 | .050 | .100 | .500 |
| 8 | .000 | .400 | .000 | .000 | .333 | .000 | .052 | .121 | .429 | .069 | .103 | .667 |
| 9 | 1.000 | 1.000 | 1.000 | — | — | — | .050 | .175 | .286 | .059 | .176 | .333 |
| 10–14 | .500 | .500 | 1.000 | .500 | .500 | 1.000 | .028 | .089 | .320 | .046 | .110 | .417 |
| 15–19 | | | | | | | .029 | .089 | .292 | .028 | .042 | .500 |
| 20–24 | | | | | | | .044 | .064 | .625 | .050 | .115 | .438 |
| >25 | | | | | | | .024 | .081 | .235 | .032 | .105 | .231 |
| Total | .178 | .518 | .342 | .337 | .642 | .525 | .066 | .163 | .382 | .095 | .179 | .519 |
| n | (1065) | | (552) | (410) | | (263) | (2084) | | (340) | (892) | | (160) |

unemployment of whites is confirmed in the MID data even though the period covered (1975–76) was a period of high unemployment. A regression of $P(u)$ on experience $x$, defined as years spent in the labor force, yields the equation ($t$-ratios in parentheses):

(5) $$P(u) = .162 - .006x + .001x_2$$
$$(2.7) \quad (1.8)$$

When job tenure $T$ is included in the equation, the effect of $x$ vanishes. Tenure effects are strong: unemployment declines twice as rapidly over a year of tenure than over a year of experience.

(6) $$P(u) = .172 - .002x - .00004x^2 - .0132T + .0003T^2$$
$$(.9) \quad (.8) \quad (4.3) \quad (2.8)$$

Both the experience profile in (5) and the tenure profile in (6) are convex.[7] Clearly, $P(u)$ *does not depend on $x$, but on $T$.* In other words, unemployment declines with age not because of aging but because of the lengthening of tenure: $dT/dx > 0$ and $\partial P(u)/\partial x = 0$ in equation (4).

The conclusion must be that the short tenure level of the young is the main reason for the age differential in the incidence of unemployment. By definition, new or recent entrants and reentrants into the labor market have short levels of tenure. The fact that their unemployment incidence is not higher than the incidence of older men at comparable levels of tenure suggests that it is not behavior or circumstances peculiar to young people, but the dynamics of "job shopping" in the labor market which is largely independent of age.

Does the finding of similar incidence at comparable tenure levels of the young and the old mean that youth unemployment is not excessively high? Not necessarily. One may argue that turnover is excessively high, so that tenure is unduly short among the young. One may also argue that older job movers with whom we are comparing the early tenured young represent an adverse selection of unstable workers. There is some evidence that this suspicion is correct: older men with short tenure tend to be persistent movers whose wages and wage progress over their careers are lower than those of stayers, while such differences (between movers and stayers) are negligible among the young (Mincer and Jovanovic 1979, tables 5 and 6).

Is it excessive turnover or is it newness in the labor market that produces the high early unemployment of the young? It is possible that among workers of *comparable quality* a first encounter with the labor market produces more turnover and unemployment than at early levels of tenure on any subsequent job. Being new in a labor market is an experience not restricted to the young. We may, for instance, compare the young with international and internal migrants of all ages who also encounter a new labor market. Since migrants do not represent an adverse selection, indeed the opposite is argued and shown to be the case in migration studies (e.g., Chiswick 1978), their unemployment is not likely to reflect *excessive* turnover.

Table 8.5 presents comparisons between the unemployment experience of migrants (of all ages) and of young natives: while unemployment rates of young nonmigrants (aged 18–24) are over twice as high as the rates of adult men, the rates of men who arrived in the U.S. from abroad were twice as high as the youth rate in *all* age groups (panel A). The reason the immigrant rates are higher is because they had at most only a year of experience in the U.S. labor market, certainly less that the (18–24) youths had on average. Rates of the immigrants are comparable to the unemployment rates of men who entered or reentered the labor force during the year (panel B), and, indeed, are somewhat higher than the rates of young (18–24) men who have less than a year of experience in the labor market.

In panel C immigrants (regardless of age) are compared with natives of the same educational level (high school, the largest group) by *years of experience* in the U.S. labor market. During the first two years the unemployment rate of immigrants is somewhat higher than of the young natives but it declines more rapidly. Initial handicaps (perhaps language) in settling in a job are overcome more quickly by immigrants. The slower

**Table 8.5**        **Unemployment Rates of Men by Migration Status**

| (A) | Newly Arrived Migrants, March 1963 (migration after March 1962) | | | |
|---|---|---|---|---|
| | All | 18–24 | 25–44 | 45–64 |
| Nonmigrants | 5.5 | 11.2 | 4.8 | 4.8 |
| Migrants | 12.2 | 15.5 | 9.2 | 16.7 |
| Immigrants | 22.1 | 22.9 | 18.0 | 22.5 |

| (B) | Labor Force Entrants (not in labor force, March 1962; in labor force, March 1963) | | | |
|---|---|---|---|---|
| | All | 18–24 | 25–44 | 45–64 |
| Nonmigrants | 20.0 | 19.6 | 18.5 | 23.0 |
| Migrants | 18.6 | 21.5 | 15.0 | 22.4 |

Source: BLS, Special Labor Force Report no 44, *Geographic Mobility and Employment Status*.

| (C) | Immigrants and Natives by Experience 1970 Census Week | | | | |
|---|---|---|---|---|---|
| Experience | 0–2 | 2–4 | 4–6 | 6–8 | 8+ |
| Natives | 9.3 | 6.0 | 4.7 | 4.1 | 2.0 |
| Immigrants | 11.4 | 3.5 | 2.5 | 3.4 | 1.9 |

Source: DeFreitas (1979).

rate of decline among the young reflects the change from single to married status and from part-time, part-period to full-time, full-period work. Thus, although the high initial turnover and unemployment of the young men are no greater than those of immigrants, a group that is highly motivated and committed to the labor market, the decline in turnover and unemployment is slower. The growth of commitment to the labor market takes time in the transition from dependent member of parental household to head of own family, with the mix of school, leisure, and work shifting toward the latter in the allocation of time. The significance of these factors in affecting unemployment incidence is shown in regression analyses to be described in the next section.

Internal migrants represent a group which is intermediate in an informational and cultural sense between immigrants and native experienced (nonmigrant) workers. Their unemployment rates are lower than those of immigrants during the first year in the new location and comparable to the rate of young nonmigrants (row 2 of panel A). Again, this comparison is biased because the young nonmigrants have had more than one year of labor market experience, while the migrants have been only a year or less in the new location.

Table 8.6 drawn from the NLS data, compares the incidence of unemployment of migrants during the first four years in the new labor market with the unemployment of young men with at most four years of labor market experience in 1967. Migrants who were unemployed at origin just before migrating were eliminated from the sample so as to avoid a possible adverse selection which would bias upward the destination unemployment of migrants. Within-firm geographic transfers were also eliminated to avoid an opposite bias. Temporary layoffs were excluded, and the sample restricted to nonstudent, white men. The results are that incidence of adult married migrants was 14%, about the same as for the young married men, and 19% for the nonmarried adult migrants compared to 26% for young single men. Inclusion of temporary layoff unemployment raises the figures for the young somewhat more than for the older migrants, the reverse of the general case.

We think it is fair to conclude that the major circumstance responsible for high youth unemployment is newness in the labor market rather than young age and unstable behavior. This is not to say, however, that the frequency of unemployment among the young stands in an immutable ratio to that of adults. Increases in young cohorts consequent on the "baby boom" create larger proportions of young workers with short tenure. Similarly, longer schooling means that work experience and tenure are shorter at a given age (e.g., 18 years), so that unemployment of young nonstudents is more prevalent (relative to adult unemployment) in countries with higher educational attainment. Of course, the partial labor market commitment of youths in transition between school and

Table 8.6    Incidence of Unemployment NLS White Men, 1967–69

|  | All | Married | Not married |
|---|---|---|---|
| (excludes temporary layoffs) | | | |
| Mature men | | | |
| 0–4 years residence | | | |
| in 1967 | .148 | .141 | .187 |
| n | (859) | (786) | (73) |
| Young nonstudents | | | |
| experience 0–4 years | | | |
| in 1967 | .189 | .128 | .260 |
| n | (644) | (344) | (300) |
| (includes temporary layoffs) | | | |
| Mature men | | | |
| 0–4 years residence | .168 | .165 | .188 |
| Young nonstudents | | | |
| 0–4 years experience | .230 | .160 | .310 |

NOTE: Respondents with unemployment in place of origin are deleted.

family status is a factor in greater turnover as is the interruption of work experience by military service. Minimum wage legislation may also be important although its impact on employment and labor force participation is probably stronger than on unemployment or on turnover (Mincer 1976). Note that black youths were not included in our comparisons with migrants and we have already seen that their unemployment incidence exceeds not only that of whites but also that of black adults at comparable levels of tenure, especially in early tenure where most unemployment is concentrated.

## 8.5  Factors Affecting the Incidence of Unemployment

The apparently close relation between turnover and unemployment suggests that some or most of the variables that affect separations are factors which also affect unemployment. We ascertain these factors and the similarity of their effects in parallel regressions of separations and of unemployment incidence on the same set of independent variables.

As is well understood in the analysis of labor mobility, the observed reduction of separation probabilities as tenure lengthens may be a statistical illusion rather than a description of individual behavior. Suppose that individual propensities to move are not reduced by tenure but still differ among workers. In that case, the estimated tenure profile of mobility $S(T)$ observed across a sample of workers will have a downward slope and will be convex as well. Persons with high propensities to move separate at early levels of tenure while those with lower propensities stay on for longer periods. As only stayers remain in long tenure classes, the apparently declining tenure curve would level off at low separation rates in the long-tenured classes.

Much the same phenomenon may be expected to appear in the statistical treatment of umployment incidence. Unemployment risk may not be related to duration of job tenure, yet differences among individuals in the unemployment risk to which they are subject can create exactly the same spuriousness in the tenure profile, given the relation between separation and unemployment. Actually, heterogeneity and "tenure dependence" are not mutually exclusive hypotheses regarding labor mobility and unemployment incidence. Indeed, the theory of job sorting and of acquisition of specific human capital implies heterogeneity in levels and slopes of tenure profiles (Mincer and Jovanovic 1979). Therefore heterogeneity does not fabricate an unreal tenure curve: it merely steepens the slope of the real (average) tenure curve.

Differences in levels of tenure profiles can be indexed by observations on past mobility behavior. If so, their inclusion in the regression should reduce the bias in the tenure slope. Other measured factors represent heterogeneity not captured by the limited observations on past mobility. Their inclusion further reduces the tenure slope while increasing the explanatory power of the regressions.

A comparison of the separation and unemployment regressions shows that the probability of unemployment is, just as labor mobility, subject to tenure dependence and that individual characteristics, such as education, health, marital status, local unemployment rate, and job training, affect the probabilities of separation and of unemployment, given tenure. These regressions appear in tables 8.8 and 8.9 for NLS young white nonstudents (1969–71), in tables 8.10 and 8.11 for the MID (1976–76), and in tables 8.12 and 8.13 for mature NLS men (1969–71). For the NLS, the dependent variables are defined as number of separations and number of unemployment spells during the period; for the MID survey, as the probability of separation and the probability of unemployment respectively. Results are similar for both number and incidence of events; however, we refer to both as incidence of unemployment and separation. Temporary layoffs are excluded. Comparable regressions covering the period 1967–69 for NLS, and 1973–74 for MID both including and excluding recall unemployment are available in the appendix. With minor exceptions, inclusion of recall unemployment yields qualitatively similar results. Sample means of the independent variables appear in table 8.7. The following regression variables are used in the tables:

| | |
|---|---|
| $X$ | Number of years since beginning the first job after leaving full-time school. |
| $T$ | Duration of job held at beginning of interval. |
| $JTRAIN$ | One if respondent received any training while employed in the job held at beginning of interval. |

Table 8.7   **Sample Means for Separation and Unemployment Regressions**

| | NLS 1969–71 | | | | MID 1975–76 |
|---|---|---|---|---|---|
| | Young whites | Mature whites | Young blacks | Mature blacks | Whites |
| $X$ | 4.63 | 35.64 | 4.45 | 37.02 | 18.65 |
| $X^2$ | 33.31 | 1317.16 | 30.05 | 1424.30 | 515.59 |
| $T$ | 1.61 | 13.15 | 1.10 | 10.89 | 7.18 |
| $T^2$ | 6.95 | 313.83 | 4.84 | 236.73 | 112.13 |
| JTRAIN | .221 | — | .083 | — | — |
| PTRAIN | .369 | — | .228 | — | — |
| LOCRATE | 4.88 | 3.80 | 5.24 | 4.35 | 8.38 |
| PSEP | 3.81 | .496 | 4.19 | .570 | .093 |
| PCOND | .163 | .068 | .328 | .111 | .113 |
| EDUC | 12.21 | 10.53 | 10.35 | 7.31 | 12.65 |
| HLTH | .042 | .222 | .020 | .192 | .074 |
| GOV | .114 | .187 | .109 | .231 | .196 |
| UNION | .318 | .378 | .323 | .457 | .308 |
| MARRY | .626 | .912 | .448 | .800 | .908 |
| PTIME | .137 | .086 | .167 | .137 | .030 |
| OLF | .328 | .200 | .405 | .253 | .051 |
| SEP | .852 | .278 | 1.01 | .323 | — |
| $SEP^2$ | 2.63 | .541 | 2.73 | .589 | — |
| ENTRY | .472 | — | .601 | — | .153 |
| $n$ | 1351 | 1957 | 504 | 866 | 1562 |

PTRAIN        One if respondent received any training aside from regular school prior to job held at beginning of interval.

LOCRATE   Unemployment rate for labor market of current residence.

PSEP           Prior separations per year since 1966 (NLS); probability of separation per year since 1968 (MID).

PCOND        Ratio of prior unemployment spells to prior separations (NLS); prior unemployment incidence (MID).

EDUC          Completed years of education.

HLTH          One if health is poor.

GOV           One if public employee.

UNION        One if wages are set by collective bargaining.

MARRY       One if married, spouse present.

PTIME        One if 34 hour workweek or less.

OLF            One if incidence of nonparticipation in current period (NLS); one if incidence of nonparticipation in prior years (MID).

SEP            Number of job separations.

ENTRY        Number of spells of nonparticipation (NLS); one if incidence of nonparticipation (MID).

| Table 8.8 | | The Determinants of Separations for Young White Men, NLS 1969–71 | | | | |
|---|---|---|---|---|---|---|
| | β | t | β | t | β | t |
| | | (1) | | (2) | | (3) |
| CONST | 1.12 | | .749 | | 1.50 | |
| X | −.110 | 3.23 | .064 | 1.76 | .056 | 1.50 |
| $X^2$ | .007 | 2.61 | −.003 | 1.16 | −.003 | 1.06 |
| T | | | −.264 | 4.99 | −.188 | 4.70 |
| $T^2$ | | | .022 | 3.36 | .015 | 3.01 |
| JTRAIN | | | −.260 | 2.61 | −.150 | 1.55 |
| PTRAIN | | | −.001 | .00 | .053 | .92 |
| LOCRATE | | | .014 | .57 | .008 | .34 |
| PSEP | | | .040 | 4.66 | .036 | 4.41 |
| PCOND | | | .147 | 1.80 | .045 | .57 |
| EDUC | | | | | −.064 | 3.83 |
| HLTH | | | | | −.202 | 1.16 |
| GOV | | | | | −.101 | .99 |
| UNION | | | | | −.159 | 2.10 |
| MARRY | | | | | −.261 | 3.28 |
| PTIME | | | | | .283 | 2.78 |
| OLF | | | | | .613 | 7.96 |
| $R^2$ | .008 | | .102 | | .173 | |
| $\bar{Y}$ | .852 | | | | | |
| n | 1351 | | | | | |

NOTE: β = regression coefficient.
$\bar{Y}$ = mean of the dependent variable.

The first column of the separation and incidence regressions in tables 8.8–8.13 shows an experience profile which disappears once tenure is added. This means that within the observed age range (which is limited in the NLS), probabilities of both separation and unemployment are the same as given levels of tenure regardless of experience. In the complete age range (available in the MID data) the inclusion of tenure reduces but does not eliminate experience effects on separations. However, such "aging effects" are eliminated in the unemployment incidence equations.

Next, the inclusion of heterogeneity indices of past behavior and of heterogeneity factors (col. 3) reduces the tenure slope in both separations and in unemployment incidence. Most of the reduction is achieved when prior mobility indices are added to tenure. As an example which holds in all the regressions, compare column 2 in table 8.11 with equation (6) above. Both prior separations (per year) and prior unemployment (conditional on separations) were used as indices in NLS. Prior unemployment incidence is unconditional in MID. Tenure remains significant after all other variables are included.

Two training variables were used in the young NLS regressions: training on the current job and training prior to the current job. Of these only the first approaches statistical significance and, as would be expected on

**Table 8.9**  The Determinants of Spells of Unemployment for Young White Men, NLS 1969–71

| | (1) | | (2) | | (3) | | (4) | | (5) | | Spells among separators and entrants (6) | |
|---|---|---|---|---|---|---|---|---|---|---|---|---|
| | β | t | β | t | β | t | β | t | β | t | β | t |
| CONST | .642 | | .115 | | .650 | | .007 | | −.056 | | .337 | .35 |
| $X$ | −.068 | 2.61 | .039 | 1.39 | .035 | 1.20 | | | −.004 | .17 | .007 | .44 |
| $X^2$ | .004 | 1.79 | −.002 | 1.08 | −.002 | 1.13 | | | −.000 | .21 | −.001 | 1.26 |
| $T$ | | | −.163 | 3.97 | −.120 | 2.97 | | | −.032 | 1.06 | −.039 | .43 |
| $T^2$ | | | .013 | 2.62 | .010 | 1.95 | | | .002 | .69 | .002 | .84 |
| JTRAIN | | | −.078 | 1.01 | −.005 | .07 | | | −.381 | 1.14 | .054 | .46 |
| PTRAIN | | | −.045 | .74 | −.008 | .14 | | | | | −.018 | .88 |
| LOCRATE | | | .064 | 3.41 | .056 | 3.03 | | | .054 | 3.94 | .028 | 2.28 |
| PSEP | | | .023 | 3.56 | .021 | 3.31 | | | .002 | .51 | .005 | 1.21 |
| PCOND | | | .244 | 3.84 | .172 | 2.71 | | | .153 | 3.30 | .076 | 2.14 |
| EDUC | | | | | −.043 | 3.29 | | | −.011 | 1.17 | −.015 | 1.69 |
| HLTH | | | | | −.117 | .85 | | | .002 | .00 | .008 | .01 |
| GOV | | | | | −.095 | 1.07 | | | −.046 | .69 | −.073 | 1.04 |
| UNION | | | | | .081 | 1.32 | | | .151 | 3.43 | .105 | 2.58 |
| MARRY | | | | | −.239 | 3.87 | | | −.101 | 2.17 | −.061 | 1.45 |
| PTIME | | | | | .160 | 1.94 | | | .001 | .03 | −.022 | .41 |
| OLF | | | | | .350 | 5.75 | | | — | — | | |
| SEP | | | | | | | .434 | 14.79 | .408 | 13.53 | | |
| SEP² | | | | | | | .017 | 3.95 | .019 | 4.43 | | |
| ENTRY | | | | | | | .063 | 2.31 | .028 | 1.03 | | |
| $R^2$ | .007 | | .082 | | .133 | | .505 | | .521 | | .035 | |
| γ | .452 | | | | | | | | | | .315 | |
| n | 1351 | | | | | | | | | | 737 | |

Table 8.10    The Determinants of the Incidence of Separation
for White Men, MID, 1975–76

|  | β | t | β | t | β | t |
|---|---|---|---|---|---|---|
|  | (1) | | (2) | | (3) | |
| CONST | .266 | | .228 | | .452 | |
| X | −.010 | 3.92 | −.007 | 2.37 | −.007 | 2.42 |
| X² | .0002 | 2.58 | .0001 | 1.98 | .010 | 1.70 |
| T | | | −.010 | 2.51 | −.012 | 3.07 |
| T² | | | .0002 | 1.44 | .0003 | 1.95 |
| LOCRATE | | | .001 | .20 | .001 | .48 |
| PSEP | | | .166 | 3.02 | .136 | 2.44 |
| PCOND | | | .124 | 2.85 | .094 | 2.05 |
| EDUC | | | | | −.010 | 2.74 |
| HLTH | | | | | .090 | 2.64 |
| GOV | | | | | −.027 | 1.22 |
| UNION | | | | | −.024 | 1.18 |
| MARRY | | | | | −.073 | 2.38 |
| PTIME | | | | | −.122 | 2.24 |
| OLF | | | | | −.070 | 1.59 |
| R² | .024 | | .056 | | .075 | |
| $\bar{Y}$ | .149 | | | | | |
| n | 1562 | | | | | |

specific capital grounds, it reduces both separations and unemployment incidence.

Unemployment incidence is positively affected by the local level of unemployment which, however, does not affect separations. This finding appears in the NLS regressions for young men in both periods (1969–71 and 1967–69) and in MID regressions for 1973–74 and less strongly for 1975–76. We also find that the local rate is not related to quits but is positively related to layoffs. These findings suggest that differences in local unemployment reflect differences in local demand for labor somewhat more clearly than differences in turnover. It it were turnover only, local rates would be positively related to separations, which is not observed. If only labor demand differs, there would be no relation between the local unemployment rate and separations, a positive relation with layoffs, both of which are observed, and a negative relations with quits, which is not observed.

Both separations and unemployment incidence are negatively related to education and to marital status among the young. Short hours (part-time work) and nonparticipation some time during the year (or in prior years) are associated with higher probabilities of separation and of unemployment in the young NLS data and in the MID data for 1973–74. (In 1975–76 part-timers appear to have fewer separations and the effect of part-time work on unemployment incidence disappears.)

**Table 8.11    The Determinants of the Incidence of Unemployment for White Men, MID 1975-76**

| | (1) | | (2) | | (3) | | (4) | | (5) | | Incidence among separators and entrants (6) | |
|---|---|---|---|---|---|---|---|---|---|---|---|---|
| | $\beta$ | $t$ | $\beta$ | $t$ | $\beta$ | $t$ | $\beta$ | $t$ | $\beta$ | $t$ | $\beta$ | $t$ |
| CONST | .162 | 2.73 | .099 | 1.26 | .296 | .57 | .018 | | .090 | 1.28 | .769 | 1.17 |
| $X$ | −.006 | 1.74 | −.003 | 1.08 | −.001 | .00 | | | −.0001 | .98 | .013 | 1.28 |
| $X^2$ | .0001 | | .0001 | 2.58 | −.000 | 2.06 | | | .002 | .46 | −.0003 | .00 |
| $T$ | | | −.008 | 1.63 | −.007 | 1.32 | | | −.001 | .33 | −.0001 | .45 |
| $T^2$ | | | .0002 | 1.20 | .0001 | 1.60 | | | .000 | 1.62 | −.000 | 1.69 |
| LOCRATE | | | .003 | 2.10 | .004 | 2.52 | | | .003 | 1.40 | .020 | .47 |
| PSEP | | | .100 | 7.10 | .114 | 5.68 | | | .052 | 5.43 | .076 | 2.86 |
| PCOND | | | .246 | | .209 | 3.53 | | | .166 | 2.38 | .387 | 2.36 |
| EDUC | | | | | −.010 | 1.82 | | | −.006 | .42 | −.034 | .00 |
| HLTH | | | | | .050 | 2.37 | | | .010 | 2.04 | −.009 | .47 |
| GOV | | | | | −.043 | .94 | | | −.030 | .37 | −.042 | .69 |
| UNION | | | | | −.015 | 3.40 | | | −.005 | 2.49 | .051 | 2.20 |
| MARRY | | | | | −.084 | .76 | | | −.052 | 2.40 | −.204 | .46 |
| PTIME | | | | | .034 | 3.00 | | | .087 | 4.48 | −.125 | 1.33 |
| OLF | | | | | .105 | | | | .131 | 26.50 | .239 | |
| SEP | | | | | | | .475 | 28.08 | .451 | 1.10 | | |
| ENTRY | | | | | | | .034 | 2.01 | .018 | | | |
| $R^2$ | .012 | | .047 | | .103 | | .336 | | .383 | | .112 | |
| $\bar{Y}$ | .094 | | | | | | | | | | .498 | |
| $n$ | 1562 | | | | | | | | | | 231 | |

Table 8.12          The Determinants of Separations
                    for Mature White Men, NLS 1969–71

| | β | t | β | t | β | t |
|---|---|---|---|---|---|---|
| | | (1) | | (2) | | (3) |
| CONST | .478 | | .480 | | .294 | |
| X | −.019 | 1.71 | −.016 | 1.62 | −.005 | .56 |
| X² | .0004 | 2.19 | .000 | 1.89 | .000 | .47 |
| T | | | −.019 | 4.85 | −.014 | 3.97 |
| T² | | | .0004 | 4.08 | .0003 | 3.29 |
| LOCRATE | | | .003 | .35 | .004 | .43 |
| PSEP | | | .177 | 18.66 | .164 | 18.31 |
| PCOND | | | .080 | 2.32 | .021 | .62 |
| EDUC | | | | | .003 | .62 |
| HLTH | | | | | .042 | 1.35 |
| GOV | | | | | −.083 | 2.48 |
| UNION | | | | | −.000 | .00 |
| MARRY | | | | | −.064 | 1.41 |
| PTIME | | | | | .078 | 1.69 |
| OLF | | | | | .505 | 15.22 |
| R² | .004 | | .235 | | .326 | |
| Ȳ | .278 | | | | | |
| n | 1957 | | | | | |

Union membership reduces separations and has no significant effect on incidence, unless temporary layoff unemployment is included when the effect becomes positive. Employment in the government sector has a weak negative effect on separation and on unemployment in the young NLS, but both effects are stronger at older ages (MID and NLS).

Bad health has no clear effects on separations and a positive effect on unemployment incidence in 1967–69 in the young NLS sample. Both effects are positive in the MID but not clear in the older NLS samples.

The following conclusions may be drawn. Regression results strongly support the turnover hypothesis of unemployment incidence. To the extent that differences in job sorting and specific capital processes underlie variation in labor mobility across people, they are important in creating differential unemployment. Therefore both tenure dependence and heterogeneity are characteristic of unemployment incidence as they are of separations. Factors which account for the convex (decelerating) decline of the incidence of unemployment with age are lengthening of tenure with age, change from single to marital status, and the shift from part-time and part-period work activities to full-time work.

We should note the relevance of marital status, part-time work, and nonparticipation in understanding the comparison with migrants in table 8.5 (panel C). The transition from school to market and from parental to one's own household which is observed in a cross-section of young people is gradual. It results in a slower decline of separation (lengthening of

**Table 8.13   The Determinants of Spells of Unemployment for Mature White Men, NLS 1969–71**

| | (1) β | t | (2) β | t | (3) β | t | (4) β | t | (5) β | t | Spells among separators and entrants (6) β | t |
|---|---|---|---|---|---|---|---|---|---|---|---|---|
| CONST | .248 | | .245 | | .266 | | .000 | | .147 | | .383 | |
| X | −.011 | 1.41 | −.010 | 1.42 | −.088 | 1.26 | | | −.006 | 1.22 | .004 | .24 |
| X² | .0002 | 1.62 | .0002 | 1.51 | .0001 | 1.25 | | | .000 | 1.34 | −.000 | .24 |
| T | | | −.006 | 2.41 | −.005 | 1.99 | | | .000 | .03 | .008 | 1.01 |
| T² | | | .0001 | 1.63 | .0001 | 1.18 | | | −.000 | .64 | .000 | .01 |
| LOCRATE | | | .001 | .09 | .001 | .16 | | | −.001 | .27 | −.002 | .10 |
| PSEP | | | .098 | 14.74 | .096 | 14.34 | | | .014 | 2.54 | .010 | .98 |
| PCOND | | | .097 | 4.00 | .086 | 3.49 | | | .077 | 4.14 | .102 | 2.04 |
| EDUC | | | | | .002 | .60 | | | .001 | .34 | .010 | 1.30 |
| HLTH | | | | | −.015 | .63 | | | −.027 | 1.54 | −.102 | 1.77 |
| GOV | | | | | −.007 | 2.70 | | | −.029 | 1.56 | −.155 | 1.89 |
| UNION | | | | | .008 | .39 | | | −.003 | .17 | −.027 | .46 |
| MARRY | | | | | −.063 | 1.87 | | | −.036 | 1.41 | −.086 | 1.05 |
| PTIME | | | | | −.011 | .31 | | | −.043 | 1.66 | −.085 | 1.10 |
| OLF | | | | | .110 | 4.45 | | | −.089 | 4.37 | | |
| SEP | | | | | | | .286 | 13.77 | .302 | 13.05 | | |
| SEP² | | | | | | | .061 | 10.35 | .054 | 8.91 | | |
| R² | .001 | | .163 | | .174 | | .516 | | .528 | | .051 | |
| Ȳ | .112 | | | | | | | | | | .367 | |
| n | 1957 | | | | | | | | | | 391 | |

tenure) compared to the experience of largely adult migrants, whose work in the new labor market was the major reason for migration.

A comparison of unemployment $P(u)$ regressions with separation regressions leaves out questions about the conditional probability of unemployment. This probability $P(u|s)$ enters the product in $P(u) = P(s) \cdot P(u|s)$. It was shown to increase with age in contrast to both $P(s)$ and $P(u)$. What are the factors associated with $P(u|s)$ and why does it increase with age? We try to estimate factors affecting $P(u|s)$ in two ways. In "augmented regressions" we add separation variables to all the others (col. 5 of the tables) and study factors affecting unemployment given separations. The alternative procedure is to restrict the regressions to workers who moved, that is, to job separators as well as to entrants and reentrants (col. 6). These we call "restricted regressions."

In both kinds of regressions the variables that remain significant are the local unemployment rate, prior conditional unemployment, marital status, education, and, less clearly, part-time work. Union membership becomes positive and significant at least in the 1969–71 period. Similar results are found in MID regressions. The variables show higher $t$-scores in the restricted regressions (col. 6), but the bulk of "explanatory power" in the augmented regressions is due to the turnover variables. For example, in the 1969–71 NLS sample of young men these variables produce an $R^2 = .505$ which increases only to .521 when all the factors are added.

Table 8.3 suggested that both separations and unemployment are more heavily weighted by layoffs than by quits at older ages. Some of the variables that are significant in affecting conditional unemployment in the regressions are apparently more closely associated with layoff unemployment. This is true of the local unemployment rate, as already noted. Prior conditional unemployment must be weighted toward layoff, since unemployment conditional on layoffs is twice as high as unemployment conditional on quitting. The same holds for unemployment of union members. However, education, marital status, and short hours affect both quits and layoffs and so affect the conditional in each type of separation.

Altogether, the NLS regressions are not very helpful in explaining the age increases in conditional unemployment. Lower levels of education and of health and more frequent union membership among the old account for a part of it. The other variables have no or even opposite effects on age patterns. That the variables we were able to measure do not account for the growth of conditional unemployment with age is apparent in observing the effects of experience on incidence in the regressions restricted to job movers. The effect is positive in the older NLS (ages 48 and over), and less so in MID (average age near 40) before and after all other variables are included. There are no experience effects in the restricted regressions within the first decade of work experience (the young NLS sample). Evidently, the probability of unemployment, when separating, increases at adult ages within each of the classes (levels) of the variables we have measured.

## 8.6    Conditional Unemployment and Age Differences in the Duration of Unemployment: A Search Model

Although we are not able to ascribe much of the higher conditional unemployment at older ages to the factors we have measured, we know that it is largely associated with the increased layoff/quit ratio. Why does quitting decline more rapidly at older ages than do layoffs?

At given tenure levels a worker's incentives to quit decline as he ages because the payoff period to whatever benefit his quitting might produce is getting shorter. Furthermore, we suggest that potential job changers encounter a diminished probability of finding a job at older ages. There are several possible reasons for this. Short prospective tenure inhibits hiring by employers in the presence of hiring or training costs. A record of job mobility at older ages is a deterrent to hiring for the same reasons, insofar as it suggests a higher probability of further separation as it does in our findings. On the supply side, workers' human capital, even if not specific to the firm, becomes progressively more specialized to a narrower cluster of firms within an industry or occupation. The proportion of job changers who also change industry and occupation diminishes at older ages.[8]

In the terminology of search models, we argue that, on average, older workers who separate from jobs have a lesser probability of finding a job per unit of search time, not because they are holding out for a higher acceptance wage within the relevant wage offer distribution (though it is true of some), but because the probability of getting any offer, that is, the probability of finding a vacancy, is smaller. On this assumption we can show that older workers who separate will search longer when unemployed, and quit less frequently, while their acceptance wage will be relatively lower, so the wage gain will be smaller (or negative) for older job movers than for younger ones.

In the standard search model, the individual samples from his wage offer distribution $f(w)$ receiving one offer per unit of time. The worker decides on an optimal wage floor which equates the gain from an additional unit of search to the cost of it. The resulting rule is:

$$(7) \qquad P_a(\bar{W}_a - W_a) = c = W_a - z$$

where $W_a$ is the lowest acceptable wage, $P_a$ is the probability of getting an acceptable wage offer, that is, of $W \geq W_a$, $\bar{W}_a$ the mean of all acceptable wage offers; $c$ is the (marginal) cost of search which includes opportunity and other costs. The highest opportunity cost or foregone wage is $W_a$.

Income offsets $z$ which are contingent on continued search, such as unemployment compensation or the current wage when searching on the job, enter costs with a negative sign. Duration of search $D$ is inverse to $P_a$. In this model search is longer the higher the acceptance wage, which is higher the lower cost of search.

Now the probability of accepting a wage offer must be redefined given that the probability of finding any offer in a unit period can be less than 1. A lesser frequency of vacancies may be a result of depressed business conditions in general, or depressed markets for a particular type of labor, or a function of lesser efficiency or intensity of search. The optimum condition becomes:

$$(8) \qquad p \cdot P_a \, (\bar{W}_a - W_a) = c = W_a - z$$

Here $p$ is the probability of finding a job offer, $P_a$ the probability of finding an acceptable job conditional on finding a vacancy, and $p \cdot P_a$ is the probability of finding an acceptable job. $D$ is now the inverse of the product $p \cdot P_a$. As before, changes in $c$ produce a positive relation between $W_a$ and $D$. However, changes in $p$ over the business cycle or otherwise, or differences in $p$ across people, tend to produce a negative correlation between $W_a$ and $D$.

A reduction in $p$ leads to a downward revision of $W_a$, hence to an increase in $P_a$. The question is whether $p \cdot P_a$ will rise or fall in (8). No perfectly general answer can be given to this question, but a most plausible answer is that $(p \cdot P_a)$ will fall, hence the duration of search will lengthen even though $W_a$ is revised downward in consequence of a fall in $p$.[9] It is easy to see that the difference $(\bar{W}_a - W_a)$ increases as $W_a$ is lowered in a uniform or triangular wage offer distribution. When $W_a$ is reduced, $\bar{W}_a$ is reduced by a smaller amount, so that $p \cdot P_a$ must fall if $c$ is fixed or reduced. Actually, $c$ will be reduced since lowering of $W_a$ will lead to a fall in foregone wages when search is continued.

An increase in $(\bar{W}_a - W_a)$ implies an increase in the ratio $\bar{W}_a / W_a$ when $W_a$ is reduced. It can be shown that $d(\bar{W}_a / W_a)/d W_a \le 0$ for a wide class of functions. Consequently, our conclusions hold more generally since equation (8) can be rewritten in ratio form:

$$(9) \qquad p \cdot P_a \, (\frac{\bar{W}_a}{W_a} - 1) = 1 - \frac{z}{W_a}$$

Only an unusually high skew in the distribution, such as in the Pareto distribution, yields a fixed $\bar{W}_a / W_a$ whatever the position of $W_a$. Even then $p \cdot P_a$ will fall as does the right-hand expression.

The conclusion that a lower $p$ is very likely to produce longer search and lower acceptance wages holds both for unemployed and for employed searchers. In the latter case, $c = W_a - W_o$, where $W_o$ is the wage paid on the job. An increased duration of search on the job, of course, means a reduction in the frequency of quit.

In sum, workers facing fewer vacancies in their search may be expected to have a longer duration of search and a lesser wage gain when unemployed, and to inhibit their job change (quitting) when employed. These conclusions are consistent with worker behavior during the business cycle: duration of unemployment increases and quits decline while layoffs increase, partly because employment demand declined and partly to substitute for a decline in attrition (quits). Note that in contrast to other models this explanation of behavior during the business cycle does not assume myopia or lags in adjustment.[10]

Applying the same model to the life-cycle, we may argue that either $p$ or $c$ declines at older ages. A decline in $c$ is not plausible except very early when labor market entrants become eligible for unemployment compensation. A decline in $c$ would lead to increases in $W_a$ and in wage gains, but the opposite is implied by a fall in $p$ and is observed. The implications that older men have a longer duration of unemployment, a reduced $Q/L$ ratio, and a lower $W_a$ when changing jobs are strongly confirmed by the data in table 8.14. The shorter duration of unemployment of the young is also due partly to relatively frequent interlabor force mobility. Again, this is characteristic of very early labor force behavior and cannot account for the age-uptrend in duration of adult unemployment. Nor can this upturn be ascribed to the somewhat longer duration of layoff than of quit unemployment. Duration increases with age in both cases. Table 8.14 shows that a similar search interpretation can be given to unemployment differentials by race and, somewhat less clearly, by education. We elaborate on the race differentials in the next section.

Although we have no direct evidence on the reduction of $p$ at older ages, $P(u \mid L)$ may be a good index. It increases with age, is inverse to education, and is higher for blacks. The only exception is that $P(u \mid L)$ is

**Table 8.14**    Conditional Unemployment and Duration NLS, 1967–69 (excludes temporary layoffs and students)

|  | $P(U \mid S)$ | $P(U \mid L)$ | $Q/L$ | Average duration | $\Delta w$ |
|---|---|---|---|---|---|
| Young whites | .342 | .573 | 4.66 | 5.30 | .816 |
| Education |  |  |  |  |  |
| 0–11 | .423 | .641 | 4.26 | 5.74 | .827 |
| 12 | .329 | .546 | 4.78 | 5.20 | .842 |
| ⩾13 | .218 | .471 | 5.36 | 3.93 | .744 |
| Young blacks | .525 | .607 | 3.03 | 6.33 | .608 |
| Mature whites | .382 | .623 | 1.62 | 9.99 | .658 |
| Education |  |  |  |  |  |
| 0–11 | .443 | .655 | 1.25 | 9.90 | .543 |
| 12 | .313 | .640 | 2.20 | 10.29 | .322 |
| ⩾13 | .268 | .385 | 3.00 | 10.03 | 1.830 |
| Mature blacks | .519 | .725 | 1.17 | 11.35 | .414 |

NOTE: $\Delta w$ = wage gain from job change.

less for the older, more educated whites compared to young whites in the same category.

In sum, as large as they are, age differentials in unemployment rates are attenuated by the longer duration of unemployment and higher probability of unemployment of older movers. Both the longer duration and the higher conditional probability of unemployment of older men can be ascribed to the decline in the probability of finding vacancies at older ages. Young white job changers face, on average, a more favorable environment in this respect.

### 8.7 Black/White Differences in Youth Unemployment

Black youth unemployment has grown relative to white youth unemployment over the past two decades or longer. A fuller understanding of the present differential, therefore, requires an analysis of this trend. This is beyond the scope of our present work. We did, however, replicate the statistical analyses on black data, and report some of the findings.

The salient features in the racial unemployment differentials are higher incidence, longer duration, and greater nonparticipation among black youths as shown in table 8.1. Those differences hold for both students and nonstudents. Age comparisons in 1966–67 and 1967–69 show that the duration of black youth unemployment is not much shorter than the duration of unemployment of older blacks. Since the race differential in duration of older men's unemployment is small, it is not clear whether our NLS sample of older blacks understates their adverse position or whether our findings about the young are, indeed, an indication of deterioration of labor market conditions in present cohorts of black youths. But these inferences are not mutually exclusive.

The longer duration of black youth unemployment compared with that of white youths is mirrored in table 8.4 in higher conditional unemployment at each level of tenure. The higher incidence of unemployment of black youths is due both to the higher separation rates and to higher conditional unemployment at fixed levels of tenure. The result is that while the black separation rates are 20% higher than the white rates, the black incidence of unemployment is twice as high as the white.

Table 8.14 shows also that the black conditional unemployment $P(u|s)$ is higher than the white largely because $Q/L$, the quit/layoff ratio is lower, and also because both conditional $P(u|L)$ and $P(u|Q)$ are higher.[11] Using the search model argument of the preceding section, we may conclude that because blacks face a lower probability of finding vacancies than do whites, their duration of unemployment is longer, wage gain smaller, and quit/layoff ratio lower. It has been noted that black quit rates are not higher than rates of whites.[12] In our interpretation, this does not suggest an equally stable work experience: total separations of blacks are higher, but quits are inhibited because of an adverse labor market, and some of the excess layoff is in part a substitution for reduced quitting.

Some of the factors that appear to influence the higher black separation rates and their slower decline with experience are suggested in comparisons of black and white regressions in tables 8.15 and 8.16. The effects of experience on separations and on unemployment incidence of blacks are not significant in the MID sample and are positive in the young NLS sample. These findings may not be inconsistent, since the quadratic experience term in the NLS black regression has a negative coefficient and implies that the positive effect vanishes within less than a decade (the MID sample is over a decade older). Similarly, tenure is not significant in the black MID sample, though it is negative and significant in the NLS sample of young blacks. The tenure effects are somewhat weaker, and the effect of training on the current job is, if anything, positive rather than negative in the black sample. This suggests that blacks receive not only less training, but also a lesser specific component of it. Marital status, which reduces separations of whites, has little effect on separations of blacks in NLS and MID and on unemployment of blacks in MID. Education reduces unemployment of blacks for 1973–74 but not for 1975–76 in the MID sample. At the same time, prior unemployment conditional on separation predicts future separations more sharply among blacks than

| Table 8.15 | The Determinants of Separations for Young Black Men, NLS 1969–71 | | | | | |
|---|---|---|---|---|---|---|
| | $\beta$ | $t$ | $\beta$ | $t$ | $\beta$ | $t$ |
| | (1) | | (2) | | (3) | |
| CONST | 1.32 | | .482 | | .432 | |
| X | −.072 | 1.24 | .138 | 2.17 | .166 | 2.65 |
| $X^2$ | .000 | .00 | −.012 | 2.50 | −.015 | 3.00 |
| T | | | −.231 | 3.59 | −.180 | 2.90 |
| $T^2$ | | | .019 | 3.04 | .015 | 2.48 |
| JTRAIN | | | .059 | .28 | .315 | 1.50 |
| PTRAIN | | | −.041 | .03 | .038 | .30 |
| LOCRATE | | | .012 | .38 | .005 | .16 |
| PSEP | | | .070 | 4.71 | .074 | 5.21 |
| PCOND | | | .267 | 2.66 | .239 | 2.46 |
| EDUC | | | | | −.012 | .58 |
| HLTH | | | | | −.264 | .68 |
| GOV | | | | | −.332 | 1.85 |
| UNION | | | | | −.479 | 4.07 |
| MARRY | | | | | −.015 | .13 |
| PTIME | | | | | .368 | 2.53 |
| OLF | | | | | .537 | 4.82 |
| $R^2$ | .023 | | .126 | | .203 | |
| $\bar{Y}$ | 1.01 | | | | | |
| n | 504 | | | | | |

**Table 8.16    The Determinants of Spells of Unemployment for Young Black Men, NLS 1969–71**

| | (1) | | (2) | | (3) | | (4) | | (5) | | Spells among separators and entrants (6) | |
|---|---|---|---|---|---|---|---|---|---|---|---|---|
| | β | t | β | t | β | t | β | t | β | t | β | t |
| CONST | .931 | | .264 | | −.182 | 3.07 | .038 | | −.397 | 1.77 | .040 | 2.11 |
| X | −.045 | .86 | .119 | 2.09 | .172 | 3.15 | | | .079 | 1.75 | .089 | 2.32 |
| X² | −.001 | .19 | −.011 | 2.44 | −.014 | 3.09 | | | −.006 | 1.39 | −.009 | 3.60 |
| T | | | −.208 | 3.58 | −.173 | 2.89 | | | −.071 | 1.59 | −.144 | 3.33 |
| T² | | | .017 | 3.14 | .016 | 1.87 | | | .007 | 1.01 | .014 | 1.49 |
| JTRAIN | | | .195 | 1.04 | .354 | .62 | | | .157 | .65 | .204 | .17 |
| PTRAIN | | | .071 | .59 | .072 | .75 | | | .062 | .89 | .013 | 1.30 |
| LOCRATE | | | .016 | .55 | .020 | 3.96 | | | .020 | 1.11 | .023 | .90 |
| PSEP | | | .046 | 3.40 | .051 | 2.07 | | | .012 | .66 | .007 | .14 |
| PCOND | | | .265 | 2.94 | .185 | 2.07 | | | .049 | 1.34 | .008 | 1.22 |
| EDUC | | | | | .014 | .71 | | | .021 | .66 | .016 | 3.27 |
| HLTH | | | | | .868 | 2.50 | | | .986 | 3.47 | .664 | .20 |
| GOV | | | | | −.158 | .99 | | | .010 | .17 | .025 | .14 |
| UNION | | | | | −.185 | 1.75 | | | .090 | 1.04 | .010 | 1.79 |
| MARRY | | | | | −.242 | 2.30 | | | −.244 | 2.98 | −.120 | .93 |
| PTIME | | | | | .220 | 1.69 | | | .019 | .17 | −.074 | |
| OLF | | | | | .534 | 5.26 | .673 | 9.85 | — | | | |
| SEP | | | | | | | −.026 | 1.93 | .622 | 8.83 | | |
| SEP² | | | | | | | | | −.020 | 1.50 | | |
| ENTRY | | | | | | | .313 | 2.04 | .082 | 1.69 | | |
| R² | .018 | | .102 | | .179 | | .435 | | .458 | | .065 | |
| Ȳ | .708 | | | | | | | | | | .443 | |
| n | 504 | | | | | | | | | | 328 | |

among whites; that is, black movers who encounter unemployment are more likely to separate from jobs than are those who move without unemployment and more than comparable whites. Taken together, these effects may also explain why over the early years of experience the decline in separations and in unemployment incidence is not pronounced among nonstudent blacks when it is for whites.

So much for the differential regression effects as estimated in the regression coefficients. Differential characteristics of black youths also contribute to the higher unemployment. On average, black youths had less tenure, less training, lower education, fewer marriages, and more part-time and intermittent work.

In our regression, which was designed to spot factors influencing conditional unemployment, the clues that might explain why such unemployment is higher for blacks are sparse. Education has no effect on blacks while it is negative for whites. Again, the likely conclusion is that the conditional unemployment of blacks is higher because their quit/layoff ratio is lower at all levels of the factors.

Our findings convey some impressions of greater job instability of blacks which is partly due to less training, to fewer specific components of job experience, to greater nonparticipation, and to weaker effects of education and of family status. Greater difficulties in job finding are consistent with longer duration of unemployment, inhibition of quits, and augmentation of layoffs. We do not know, however, how much of the difficulties are matters of discrimination, of perception of potential productivities by employers, or of informational efficiency of job search. In contrast to the whites, unemployment of young blacks is higher than unemployment of older blacks at fixed tenure levels as we noted in table 8.4. Also, the race differential in duration is larger at younger than at older ages. Both of these findings may be a reflection of the deterioration in labor market conditions of recent cohorts of young blacks.

### 8.7.1   Plus ça change . . . ?

A 1969 survey of research on youth labor markets concluded that "the normally high level of teenage unemployment is due primarily to the fact that so many teenagers are labor market entrants or reentrants rather than to their deficiency or instability as employees."[13] We amend this conclusion by interposing a continuum of job experience and showing how it translates into a decelerating age decline in the incidence of unemployment.

Our evidence is based on far richer data than were available to the researchers in the 1960s. But we do face a question of data comparability: the NLS shows lower unemployment rates for young nonstudents, consequently a smaller age differential than does the CPS. Yet our finding no "aging effects" is also reproduced in the MID data, apart from being consistent with the spirit of the conclusion reached a decade ago on the basis of fragmentary, cross-sectional CPS aggregates.

## Notes

1. Appendix tables available on request.
2. When not shown in text tables, the findings appear in appendix tables.
3. The educational differences are stronger in the 1966–69 period.
4. This measure has sampling properties akin to the likelihood ratio, according to R. Shakotko. We do not explore these issues.
5. $dT/dx = (1 - s) - Ts > 0$, and $d^2T/dx^2 < 0$. For argument and evidence see Mincer and Jovanovic (1979).
6. White nonstudent job quitters report a probability of unemployment of .313 for 1967–69 compared with .213 for mature men. For blacks these figures are .503 and .333 respectively.
7. Equation (6) is an intermediate step between col. (1) and (2) in table 8.11.
8. Unpublished work of Bartel and Mincer.
9. The same conclusion was reached independently by S. Nickell (1978).
10. See Alchian in the Phelps (1970) volume.
11. See n. 6.
12. Flanagan (1978).
13. Kalachek (1969), p. 2. Although the quotation refers to all teenagers as a group, the special problems of black youths were noted by Kalachek as well.

## References

Alchian, A. 1970. Information costs, pricing and resource unemployment. In Phelps, E. S. et al., *Microeconomic foundations of employment and inflation theory*. New York: W. W. Norton & Co.

Bancroft, G. and Garfinkle, S. 1963. Job mobility in 1961. BLS, Special Labor Force Report no. 35.

Chiswick, B. 1978. The Americanization of earnings. *Journal of Political Economy* 86:897–921.

DeFreitas, G. 1979. The earnings of immigrants in the American Labor Market. Ph.D. dissertation, Columbia University.

Flanagan, R. J. 1978. Discrimination theory, labor turnover, and racial unemployment differentials. *Journal of Human Resources* 13:187–207.

Jovanovic, B. and Mincer, J. 1979. Labor mobility and wages. National Bureau of Economic Research. Working Paper no. 357. New York: National Bureau of Economic Research.

Kalachek, E. 1969. *The youth labor market*. Policy papers in Human Resources and Industrial Relations no. 12. Ann Arbor, Mich.: The Institute of Labor and Industrial Relations, University of Michigan and Wayne State University.

Leighton, L. 1978. Unemployment over the work history. Ph.D. dissertation, Columbia University.

Mincer, J. 1976. Unemployment effects of minimum wages. *Journal of Political Economy* 84, part 2:S87–104.

Nickell, S. 1978. Estimating the probability of leaving unemployment. Center for Labor Economics, Discussion Paper no. 7, London School of Economics.

Saben, S. 1964. Geographic mobility and employment status, March 1962–March 1973. BLS, Special Labor Force Report no. 44.

# Comment    Alan L. Gustman

The major concern of this chapter is the question of why youth unemployment declines from the relatively high levels observed for male teenagers not enrolled in school to the lower levels experienced by adults. To provide an answer, the authors disaggregate unemployment into definitional components and relate these to explanatory variables which themselves are related to age. Closely interweaving theoretical and empirical considerations, they extend the human capital approach and apply it to analyze the unemployment-age relation. In so doing, Professors Leighton and Mincer provide needed emphasis on theory in an area that has been characterized mainly by empirical inquiry with little theoretical grounding.

While there are a number of findings, the basic conclusion is that the decline with age in unemployment, rapid at first and then decelerating, stems from a similarly shaped decline in the probability of a separation with tenure on the youth's last job. Thus high youth unemployment is attributed to short tenure on a particular job rather than to the youth's age or limited overall labor market experience. The process of matching employers and employees, and the subsequent arrangement to share the costs and benefit of specific training if the match is successful, play the central theoretical role. They suggest that "it is not the behavior or circumstances peculiar to the young, but the dynamics of 'experience search' in the labor market which is *largely independent of age* [that is responsible for their high unemployment incidence]." High youth unemployment, at least among white youths, is not the result of unemployment being high at any given level of tenure, reflecting "young age and unstable behavior," but is a result of low youth tenure.

The conclusion that age and overall market experience do not play a very important role is an empirical one. Nothing in the theory excludes

Alan L. Gustman is professor of economics at Dartmouth College and is a research associate with the National Bureau of Economic Research.

the possibility that young age and overall inexperience might account for an important part of high youth unemployment. For example, one could well integrate screening on the part of employers based on age and experience into the discussion. A finding that age and experience played an important independent role would square with the impression about employer attitudes created by past interview data. From these it appears that some firms in some industries are reluctant to hire young people, let alone to train them (e.g., see Lester 1954, pp. 53–6 and Barton 1976). Young people may be viewed as accident-prone, not trustworthy with expensive equipment, and likely to let their attention wander. As a result, they may be less likely to secure a position which offers an extensive amount of specific training. The authors' finding of lower separations and unemployment for married people reflects the more stable behavior of married young people and perhaps also the response of employers which makes positions offering opportunities for specific training more available to those who are married. But again, despite the fact that age or experience would be a good screen for unstable behavior and thus may have affected the availability of opportunities for accumulating specific training, according to Professors Leighton and Mincer's findings, past turnover and tenure constant, age or experience do not play a strong, independent role reducing the likelihood of separations and unemployment within the younger NLS group.

Some of the empirical evidence supporting the conclusions that age and experience do not reduce separations and unemployment may be subject to question. In particular, the regressions fitted for black youths based on data from the NLS raise the most serious doubts. The results indicate not that general experience has a significant negative impact, but that, tenure and other factors constant, black youths have a significantly *higher* probability of separation and of unemployment the *higher* the level of general labor market experience (see tables 8.15 and 8.16). To give an idea of the size of these effects, the sum of the products of the coefficients of the experience variables times their means exceeds the comparable sum for the tenure variables with their means. Similar but less severe problems arise in the identical regressions for white youths. There, too, the sign on the basic experience variable is *positive* in the separation equation, with a $t$-statistic above 1.4 for the linear experience term (table 8.8). In the analogous unemployment equation, the coefficient of the linear experience variable is also positive, with a $t$-statistic below 1 (table 8.9). In contrast to these findings, in regressions for white males of all ages using data from the Michigan Income Dynamics Survey, the linear experience term has, more plausibly, a negative effect on the probability of a separation (table 8.10). This effect is significant. Using the same data, the sign on the linear term is found to be negative in the analogous equations explaining the incidence of unemployment, but the coefficient estimates are not significant. None of these tables indicates a significant effect of experience on the probability of unemployment conditional on a separation.

Let me mention a possible reason for the counterintuitive results obtained in analyzing the NLS youth sample. Between 1966 and 1971, many young people were in the armed forces and were not sampled, and others who were sampled either were not eligible for the draft or may have altered their behavior expecting to be drafted. As a result, a disproportionate number of those with long experience may have been those who were turned down for military service. If this is so, it means that the Parnes data for young men, covering as they do a period when labor market activities were interrupted for selected individuals, may not be as useful as they might for tracing the process of integrating young workers into the labor force during more normal times. Another question concerns what accounts for the differences between the findings for black and white youths. As the authors note, some of the differences may reflect differences in the specific training received by each group, even at similar levels of tenure. A part of the explanation may also arise from differences in the way the draft affected individuals in each group.

Suppose the authors' findings that job tenure importantly influences youth unemployment, but age and overall labor market experience do not, is supported by further evidence. If this is so, I believe the implications for policy makers may be quite severe. Consider the finding that tenure plays a dominant role and that young people respond no differently from others with similar characteristics who are also new to the market. To reduce youth unemployment, at least that associated with permanent separations, one may have to improve the basic sorting process or, if possible, find a way to make employers take on the risk of increasing specific investment in younger workers beyond what they normally do, perhaps by providing a more reliable signal about new workers than is currently available. This is a difficult task.

A finding that market experience is not significant, tenure and past turnover constant, would not be very encouraging either. There is no reason to believe that general training *per se* reduces turnover. But one might think that the costs of specific investment can be reduced and search made more efficient by increasing the information the youth has about the nature of the labor market before he or she engages in serious job search. Aside from their direct training content, such programs as career education, cooperative vocational education, and other programs designed to provide work experience might be expected to increase a young person's knowledge of the market and of work. As a result, the youth may be less likely to find that a job he or she has chosen to sample is very different from what was expected, and may thus not be disappointed and quit. If early quttings were reduced by these programs, new employees who had completed the programs would constitute a less risky investment prospect for the firm. Once firms became aware of this, these young people would have a greater probability of finding specific training opportunities that ultimately reduce turnover. But one who strongly believed that these programs do improve the matching process would, in all probability, also expect that, turnover behavior constant, market experience informs the youth of what the labor market is like and makes the individual a better risk for specific investment. While one cannot infer from a finding that past experience will facilitate specific training that other labor market information programs will have a similar result, an advocate of programs promoting early labor market experience might be troubled justifiably by the finding that past labor market experience does not, tenure and past turnover behavior constant, reduce separations and unemployment.

An additional point should be made. In further attempts to test the author's model with a more suitable sample, it would be of interest to see the effect of measuring experience by something like total time at work in a civilian job, or both civilian and military employment, rather than the number of years since beginning the first job after leaving full-time school, the measure used by the authors. It is important to be sure the findings with respect to the role of experience are not sensitive to the definition of the experience variable.

In closing, let me note again that the chapter by Professors Leighton and Mincer contributes importantly to our understanding of the working of the youth labor market. It also provides a fruitful framework for analyzing policy. While scattered theoretical and empirical pieces and folk wisdom have been available, the extensive analysis contained in this paper provides a "critical mass" which can form the basis for much of our future work.

### References

Barton, P. E. 1976. Youth transition to work: The problem and federal policy setting. In National Commission for Manpower Policy, *From School to Work: Improving the Transition*. Washington, D.C.: U.S. Government Printing Office.

Lester, R. A. 1954. *Hiring practices and labor competition*. Princeton: Industrial Relations Section, Department of Economics and Sociology.

# Comment    W. Kip Viscusi

Several recent analyses have documented the effects of age and firm-specific experience on worker turnover and unemployment. The principal contribution of the Leighton-Mincer chapter is that it greatly extends our knowledge of both the direction and convexity of these relationships. With the exception of some aberrant age-separation results,[1] the empirical patterns of interest are established quite firmly.

What is less clear is how one should interpret these findings. Most particularly, the age-related decline in worker separations is due largely to the increase in firm-specific experience (tenure) with age, which in turn diminishes turnover. Although the econometric effects are clear-cut, age nevertheless may be important. Workers who are older may be more mature, better motivated, and better matched to appropriate jobs. Even though tenure *per se* may have no substantive impact, these age-related effects would diminish worker turnover, increase the value of the tenure variable, and generate the observed relationship. Indeed, it is impossible to construct any model with age affecting turnover in which tenure also doesn't increase, since lower turnover increases one's firm-specific experience.

The substantive impact of the pivotal tenure variable is difficult to assess. However, as I will note later, excessive attention to this issue may lead one to ignore the primary insight provided by the human capital literature regarding worker turnover.

## Search, Experience, and Age

One of the more intriguing findings is the lengthening of the duration of unemployment for older workers. Although this effect may be attributable in part to an adverse selection problem, it may also reflect an important aspect of the employment process. Considerable recent attention has been devoted to job search among alternative wage offers. In reality, workers are choosing among jobs with uncertain implications, such as the likelihood of promotion or being injured. Here I will sketch a simple model which is the first analysis to incorporate both job search among lotteries and adaptive worker behavior once on the job.[2] A major implication of this framework is that workers may substitute labor market search for on-the-job experimentation as they age. This behavior would generate both the observed relationship between age and the duration of unemployment as well as the higher turnover by youths.

W. Kip Viscusi is IBM Research Professor of Business Administration at Duke University and is a research associate at the National Bureau of Economic Research. This discussion draws on the results of the author's broader study of youth unemployment sponsored by the Rockefeller Foundation.

Consider the following model with three periods and two types of jobs. In each period the worker can choose to remain on his job or search for an alternative job. Search takes one period, is associated with a cost of $-c$ (where $c$ may be negative if the value of leisure exceeds direct search costs), and offers a probability $q$ that a type 1 job will be found and $1-q$ that a type 2 job will be found.

In every period, each job offers some probability of a successful job outcome with wage $w$ and a probability of an unsuccessful outcome with wage $w'$, where $w > w'$. Job 2 is preferred since it offers a prior probability of success $p_2$, which exceeds the comparable value $p_1$ for type 1 jobs.[3] These independent priors are updated in Bayesian fashion based on experiences with that type of job. Let $\gamma_i$ be a measure of the worker's prior information for job $i$. For probabilities belonging to the beta family, the posterior probability of success $p_i(m, n)$ after $m$ successful outcomes and $n$ unsuccessful outcomes on that job type is given by

$$p_i(m, n) = \frac{\gamma_i p_i + m}{\gamma_i + m + n}$$

so that

$$\frac{\partial p_i(1, 0)}{\partial \gamma_i} < 0 \text{ and } \frac{\partial p_i(0, 1)}{\partial \gamma_i} > 0$$

The final bit of notation is that ß is the discount factor.

Several features of the optimal strategy should be noted at the outset.[4] First, one never leaves an uncertain job after a favorable job outcome. Workers will be motivated to quit and undertake a job search only after unfavorable experiences. Second, since search takes a period of time, it will never be optimal to search in period 3. Searchers in period 2 will accept whatever job is generated by their search in that period since continued search will be unattractive. Third, workers will never leave a job because of an adverse experience after period 1. The period required by search makes quitting followed by subsequent search unproductive after the initial period. In short, search may be optimal in periods 1 and 2, whereas on-the-job experimentation may only be optimal in period 1. Time horizon effects create a bias toward search as opposed to on-the-job experimentation as the worker ages. The analysis below will focus on other age-related effects that reinforce this pattern.

Suppose the worker has the option of choosing between job 1 or job search with three periods remaining. Utilizing the above results regarding the nature of behavior, the value $V'$ of job 1 is given below.

$$V' = [p_1 w + (1 - p_1)w'] + ßp_1[p_1(1, 0)w$$
$$+ (1 - p_1(1, 0))w'](1 + ß)$$
$$+ (1 - p_1)ß \text{ } Max \text{ } \{[p_1(0, 1)w$$

$$+ (1 - p_1(1, 0))w'](1 + \text{\ss}),$$
$$- c + q\text{\ss}[p_1(0, 1)w + (1 - p_1(0, 1))w']$$

where the first bracketed expression is the expected first period reward, the second is the discounted expected reward in periods 2 and 3 following a successful period 1 outcome, and the final term represents the only subsequent decision facing the worker who starts on job 1. Following an unfavorable outcome, the worker must choose whether he will remain on job 1 thereafter or search for an alternative job in period 2. The condition for undertaking a job search simplifies to

(1) $$p_2 w + (1 - p_2)w' > \frac{c + p_1(0, 1)w + (1 - p_1(0, 1))w'}{\text{\ss}(1 - q)}$$
$$+ p_1(0, 1)w + (1 - p_1(0, 1))w'$$

If the worker chooses instead to begin period 1 by searching, the discounted expected value $V^s$ of his choice is given by

$$V^s = - c + \text{\ss}(1 - q)[p_2 w + (1 - p_2)w'](1 + b)$$
$$+ \text{\ss}q \; Max\{ - c + q\text{\ss}[p_1 w + (1 - p_1)w']$$
$$+ (1 - q)\text{\ss}[p_2 w + (1 - p_2)w'], \; [p_1 w$$
$$+ (1 - p_1)w'](1 + \text{\ss})\}$$

where the worker incurs a search cost $c$, has a probability $(1 - q)$ of finding a job of type 2 for work in periods 2 and 3, and a probability $q$ of finding a type 1 job that he either accepts or rejects in favor of continued search. The unsuccessful searcher will continue his search in period 2 if

(2) $$p_2 w + (1 - p_2)w' > \frac{c + p_1 w + (1 - p_1)w'}{\text{\ss}(1 - q)}$$
$$+ p_1 w + (1 - p_1)w'$$

Consider the search decision in period 2. Since $p_1(0, 1) < p_1$, the worker is more likely to search after an unfavorable job experience than after search in period 1, as comparison of equations 1 and 2 indicates. Work on the job provides a motivation for additional job search.

A particularly striking feature of equations 1 and 2 is that $V^s$ is independent of the sharpness $\gamma_i$ of either prior probability, whereas $V_1$ is independent of $\gamma_i$ only if the worker will never find it optimal to leave his job, as one can verify by substituting for the beta values of $p_1(0, 1)$ and $p_1(1, 0)$. If job search is preferred to remaining on job 1 after an unfavorable job 1 outcome, then $\partial V^1 / \partial \gamma_1 < 0$. The attractiveness of work on job 1 declines with the precision of the worker's prior beliefs. To the extent that the worker's experiences lead to a sharpening of $\gamma_i$ with age, the attractiveness of on-the-job experimentation $V^1$ will be diminished. Abstracting from the change in one's time horizon with age, there will be an age-related experience effect that diminishes the value of on-the-job experimentation and has no effect on the value of search, so that search will become a relatively more attractive mechanism for finding an optimal job match.

Both the high turnover of youths and the greater longevity of search by older workers are consistent with a hybrid model of search and adaptive behavior. The shortening time horizon with age will diminish the attractiveness of on-the-job experimentation before it makes search unattractive. Moreover, independent of any time horizon effect is the role of worker learning, which enhances the relative value of search as a form of information acquisition and labor market sorting.

### Toward a General Theory of Turnover

Leighton and Mincer are quite eclectic in their discussion of the theoretical underpinnings of turnover, utilizing diverse insights from human capital theory, search theory, and sorting and matching theories. A central issue in any analysis is the substantive effect of the tenure variable on separations. Consider two extreme models. In a standard human capital framework, the tenure variable would reflect specific training that enhanced the worker's firm-specific productivity. In a pure sorting model, the worker's productivity may not have been altered with experience, but he is more likely to be matched optimally to a job as his on-the-job experience increases.[5] Workers who discover that the job match is inappropriate have left the enterprise, and the optimally matched individuals remain.

Although these theories differ sharply in the process generating the tenure effect (training versus a lottery outcome), they share a common feature. Let us define "specific information" as experiences that affect one's probabilistic beliefs, only regarding the attractiveness of work at the firm, while "general information" also affects one's probabilistic beliefs about work elsewhere.[6] The learning in the adaptive model presented earlier was specific.

Specific information reduces the worker's incentive to quit since subsequent adverse experiences are less likely to diminish the job's attractiveness and lead him to quit. In contrast, general information has an ambiguous effect.[7] Even favorable experiences may lead to worker turnover since the relative attractiveness of work elsewhere may have increased. Moreover, worker turnover is always greater with general information than specific information. A firm's learning about the worker's productivity is quite similar. The firm is less likely to terminate an employment relationship if it has substantial knowledge about the worker's firm-specific capabilities, whereas knowledge concerning the worker's capabilities elsewhere is irrelevant. Information acquired regarding the productivity of other workers in the employment situation may lead to greater termination of the economic matchups by the firm. As with worker learning, turnover is negatively related to the specific information component.

These parallels suggest that the elusive search for a determination of the operative mechanism in the human capital theory may not be the appropriate focus. The theory's primary insight relating to turnover is the importance of specific as opposed to general learning. This distinction plays a pivotal role in pure sorting and adaptive behavior models as well as in analyses of actual training processes.

### Notes

1. See, for example, the findings for young black men in tables 8.15 and 8.16.

2. This model extends my earlier work in which a search process was not included as part of the job choice problem. See, for example, *Employment Hazards: An Investigation of Market Performance*, Harvard Economic Studies Series no. 148. Cambridge: Harvard University Press, 1979.

3. The precision of each prior is also assumed to be such that job 2 is preferred. As the discussion below indicates, in the case considered, only the precision $\gamma_1$ is of consequence.

4. Many of these properties are formalized in my earlier work cited in n. 2.

5. Sorting models may include specific human capital investment as part of the process, but they need not.

6. This analysis is developed more fully in my paper, "Specific Information, General Information, and Employment Matches under Uncertainty," NBER Working Paper no. 394 (1979).

7. This is the case of interdependent prior beliefs considered in chapter 4 of my *Employment Hazards* volume cited in n. 2.

# 9 High School Preparation and Early Labor Force Experience

Robert H. Meyer and David A. Wise

Many kinds of preparation and experience are presumed to prepare youths to find jobs, to perform them, and to keep them. At least three are often mentioned. One is general academic education: reading, writing, arithmetic. A second is vocational training intended to develop the skills necessary to perform particular tasks. A third is work experience itself, emphasized as the way to learn what it is like to work, to acquire the habits and attitudes that persons who work have, that draw one to want to work, and that those who hire want to find in those they pay. Motivated by these common hopes, we have investigated the relationships between early labor force experience and the three kinds of high school preparation that emphasize them. This chapter analyzes the relationship between high school curriculum, work experience, and academic achievement on the one hand and early labor force employment and wage rates on the other. We find that work experience acquired while in high school is strongly related to later employment. Academic performance in high school is also related to successful labor market experience. But we find no significant effect of current forms of high school vocational training on early labor force experience. Thus the weight of our evidence implies that programs that emphasize work experience for youths, together with general academic education, have the greatest chance of enhancing their subsequent labor force experiences.

Our analysis is based on male youths who graduated from high school. A large number of young persons enter the labor force immediately upon graduation from high school. Many receive no further formal education.

Robert H. Meyer is a graduate student at Harvard University. Elizabeth Philipp put together many summary tabulations for this chapter. The authors have benefited from the comments of Gary Chamberlain, David T. Ellwood, Richard B. Freeman, Zvi Griliches, Steven Venti, and other members of the NBER youth unemployment group.

For these youths, as well as those who continue their education, high school preparation is a potentially important determinant of early labor force experience. Because our study is limited to high school graduates, its implications for high school dropouts must be indirect. Among all groups of youths, high school dropouts, and in particular black school dropouts, have the poorest labor force experiences. Nonetheless, labor force statistics suggest a high youth unemployment rate, even among high school graduates. And our results for high school graduates, we think, have strong implications for future generations of persons who might contemplate dropping out of high school.

Our analysis is based on data collected by the National Center for Educational Statistics through the National Longitudinal Study of 1972 High School Seniors. The study collected a wide range of school, family background, and attitude and aspiration information from approximately 23,000 high school seniors in the spring of 1972. The 1972 base survey was based on a nationwide sample of high schools, stratified in such a way that schools in lower socioeconomic areas were somewhat oversampled. In addition to the base survey, the study included three follow-up surveys in 1973, 1974, and 1976. The follow-up surveys were used to obtain information on post-secondary school and work choices as well as labor force experiences.[1] Unlike most other data sources, this one allows us to follow a single cohort in their transition from school to work.

Most male youths in the years immediately after high school are either in the labor force or are attending a post-secondary school; some are in the labor force and going to school. Because the labor force aspirations of persons in school, their labor force behavior, their access to the labor market, and thus their realized experiences are likely to differ substantially from persons who are not in school, we have sought to obtain estimates that represent the experience that we would expect to find among persons not in school. To obtain such estimates, however, we must consider simultaneously both the decision to enter the labor force rather than go to school, and the expected experience of those who enter the labor force. In a strictly statistical sense, this may be thought of as correcting for sample selection bias. But in our case, the determinants of school attendance, as well as the determinants of labor force experience, are of considerable substantive interest. In fact, the decision to attend school may be expected to be determined in part by expected labor force experience. Although our primary emphasis will be on labor force experience, we will give some attention to the determinants of school attendance as well. The outline of the chapter is preceded by a summary of our major findings.

We have found a strong relationship between hours of work while in high school and weeks worked per year upon graduation. Persons who work while in high school also receive higher hourly wage rates than those who don't. The combined effect on earnings is very substantial. For example, with other individual characteristics equal to the average in the sample, persons who worked 16 to 20 hours per week in high school are estimated to earn annually about 12% more than those who didn't work at all in high school. Depending upon the amount of work in high school and estimated weeks worked based on other characteristics, the estimated "effect" on annual earnings of high school work could be as high as 30 or 35%. On the other hand, we find almost no relationship between any measure of high school vocational training and later weeks worked or wage rates. This has led us to raise the possibility that programs that emphasize work experience in high school may well have a greater impact on later labor market experience than programs that emphasize job skill training without work experience. Our evidence, however, establishes only a strong correspondence between work while in high school and later employment; it cannot be used to infer a cause-and-effect relationship of the same magnitude.

Traditional measures of academic achievement are also positively related to early success in the labor market. In particular, class rank is related to both weeks worked after graduation and to wage rates, after controlling for test scores reflecting a combination of aptitude and achievement. Combined with the results on hours worked in high school, this implies to us a substantial carry-over to the labor market of individual attributes associated with or developed through work effort in and out of school. Class rank may also measure general academic knowledge, and together with the positive estimated effect of test scores on both weeks worked and wage rates implies a significant effect of traditional measures of academic aptitude and achievement on labor market performance upon leaving school. Thus both high school academic performance and work experience seem to dominate specific vocational training as preparation for successful early experience in the labor market.

In contrast to the lasting relationship between high school work experience on weeks worked and wage rates over the next four years, there is little relationship between random—as distinct from individual specific—determinants of weeks worked in the first year after graduation and weeks worked four years later, and little relationship between random determinants of wage rates upon graduation and wage rates four years later. After controlling for individual specific characteristics, we find little lasting effect of unusually few weeks worked in the first year or two on weeks worked three or four years later. Similarly, after controlling for individual specific terms, we find little lasting effect of random fluctuations in initial wage rates on wages four years later. Whatever the determinants of wages and weeks worked, other than individual specific attributes, they do not lead to long-run persistence of initial experience. (On the other hand, wage rates increase with job experience so that weeks not working contribute to lower wage rates in the future.) And much if not most of work while in high school, which has a substantial positive relation to later labor market experience, must have been on jobs with limited direct relation to future job ladders, although our data do not provide any indication of the quality of high school jobs. Thus our findings suggest that the frequently expressed worry that poor initial jobs and initial jobs without a future should be avoided for fear that they will contribute to lasting poor labor force experience, may be misplaced. Our evidence on persons graduating from high school suggests, albeit indirectly, that this worry is unfounded and in fact should give way to policies to encourage early work experience, possibly without exaggerated initial concern for its relationship to a well-defined hierarchy of future jobs. We find no evidence that persons on average were hindered by the work experience they had in high school; on the contrary, the evidence suggests that they may well have been helped. And our evidence shows that low-wage jobs after graduation do not in themselves increase the likelihood of low-wage jobs a few years later.

We have distinguished weeks worked in the four years following high school by the year in which the experience was had. Thus after four years, for example, we know how much an individual worked in each of the three preceding years. As expected, we find that wage rates at any given date are determined in part by previous experience. Thus although there is no lasting effect of nonemployment in one year on employment in subsequent years, there is a cost associated with early nonemployment, namely, lower wages in future years. The effect of early labor force experience on subsequent wages is not obviously different in magnitude from the effect of work experience while in high school. But the effect of work experience while in high school does not decline over the first five years in the labor force, whereas there is some evidence that the effect of early labor force experience on subsequent wages may decline over time. Thus high school work experience may be capturing attributes that are in part at least distinct from those associated with later labor market experience. The pattern of the relationships between work while in high school and weeks worked in subsequent years in the labor force provides further evidence of this. Indeed, the latter finding suggests strongly that high school work experience is associated with individual attributes that persist over time.

The average wage rates of whites and nonwhites in the labor market are quite close, with whites earning a bit more per hour after the first year. But after controlling for other variables, nonwhites seem to earn a bit more per hour than whites. On the other hand, nonwhites work fewer weeks per year than whites on the average, but we find little difference between the two groups after controlling for other variables. After controlling for other variables, the probability that nonwhites are in school in each of the four years after high school is about 0.10 higher than the corresponding probability for whites.

In general, summary statistics based on the National Longitudinal Study do not suggest severe employment problems for these high school graduates. On the contrary, they suggest a group of persons moving rather smoothly into the labor force.

Finally, employment ratios of both white and nonwhite high school graduates based on these data are considerably higher than those calculated from Current Population Survey data, and unemployment rates much lower. Although employment ratios of nonwhites are lower than those of whites, and unemployment rates higher, four years after high school graduation they are close. The October 1976 white employment ratio was .909 and the nonwhite ratio .875; unemployment rates were .065 and .081 respectively. Very few persons in the sample were chronically out of school and unemployed.

The general outline of the chapter is as follows: section 9.1 contains some general descriptive statistics on the transition from school to work. Empirical estimates of weeks worked and wage equations are presented in section 9.2, and are accompanied by nonschool attendance equations. Section 9.3 is an analysis of the extent of persistence of individual experience over time. Concluding remarks are contained in section 9.4.

## 9.1    Some Descriptive Statistics on the Transition from School to Work

Through the National Longitudinal Study of 1972 High School Seniors, data were obtained on almost 23,000 persons from over 1,300 high schools. The high schools were a stratified sample of all public, private, and church-affiliated schools in the country. To increase the number of "disadvantaged" students in the sample, high schools located in low-income areas and schools with a high proportion of minority enrollment were sampled at approximately twice the sampling rate used for the other schools. The summary statistics reported below have not been adjusted to reflect population proportions. They are reported, however, separately for whites and nonwhites. Both groups probably reflect more persons from low-income families than would be found in a random sample of the population.

We will present summary statistics in three groups: the first on work and school status by year; the second on the likelihood of selected sequences of school and work status over time; and the third on weekly earnings and hours worked and annual employment and by year.

### 9.1.1    School and Work Status by Year

The distribution of white and nonwhite males in the survey sample by school and work status, together with some summary labor force statistics, is shown in table 9.1. (More detailed distributions by nine school and five work classifications are presented for five consecutive Octobers beginning in 1972 in tables available from the authors.) We will point out first some general findings based on an examination of table 9.1 and then indicate the kind of detail that can be found in the more detailed tables without presenting an extensive discussion of it.

The most striking statistics in table 9.1 are the comparatively low unemployment rates and high employment ratios, as compared with those based on Current Population Survey data (see Freeman and Medoff, chapter 3 of this volume). Although we cannot provide a direct comparison for each October, we can for 1972. In October of 1972, the Census Bureau conducted a special survey of spring 1972 high school graduates (see Bureau of Labor Statistics [1973], p. 27). A comparison of unemployment and other labor force statistics based on the two data sources is presented in the tabulation below (for persons not in school).

| Statistic | National Longitudinal Study | | Current Population Survey, October 1972 | |
|---|---|---|---|---|
| | White | Nonwhite | White | Nonwhite |
| Employment ratio | .880 | .784 | .815 | .680 |
| Labor force participation | .929 | .902 | .916 | .880 |
| Unemployment rate | .054 | .130 | .110 | .227 |

An investigation of the definitions used in the two surveys does not reveal any differences that would suggest such apparently contradictory results, although the survey questions are not identical. Although the NLS survey is weighted to oversample low income youths, this should tend to raise implied unemployment rates, not to lower them. The survey respondent, however, in the NLS survey is the individual youth, but is likely to be the mother or father of the youth in the CPS survey. The NLS data is collected through a mailed questionnaire (together with some mail and telephone reminders), while the CPS data is obtained by interview with a household member, often the female head. Freeman and Medoff find that a large portion of the difference between the CPS numbers and those based on the Parnes National Longitudinal Survey can be attributed to the different respondents.

The summary statistics also reveal several differences between white and nonwhite youths. The percentage of white youths in school full time is approximately 12 percentage points higher than the percentage of nonwhites until 1976, when many youths would have finished four years of college. Of those not in school, the percentage working full time is about 8 to 10 points higher for whites than for nonwhites. By 1976, the percentages were about 80 and 72 respectively. The proportions working

**Table 9.1**   Percentage of Male Youths in School and Work Categories and Labor Force Statistics, by Year and Race, October of Each Year

| | White | | | | | Nonwhite | | | | |
|---|---|---|---|---|---|---|---|---|---|---|
| | 1972 | 1973 | 1974 | 1975 | 1976 | 1972 | 1973 | 1974 | 1975 | 1976 |
| In school full time[a] | 53.6 | 43.3 | 38.2 | 35.2 | 22.1 | 42.3 | 30.3 | 26.5 | 23.3 | 17.7 |
| In school part time | 4.6 | 7.2 | 6.2 | 6.6 | 7.7 | 4.4 | 7.4 | 6.5 | 7.4 | 7.0 |
| Not in school, total | 42.4 | 49.5 | 55.7 | 58.2 | 70.2 | 53.3 | 62.3 | 67.1 | 69.4 | 75.3 |
| Working full time | 71.9 | 76.2 | 74.1 | 77.5 | 80.1 | 60.1 | 67.7 | 63.3 | 68.7 | 71.9 |
| Working part time | 9.2 | 5.1 | 4.9 | 4.2 | 4.1 | 11.4 | 6.2 | 5.1 | 5.2 | 5.1 |
| Military | 7.7 | 11.2 | 11.9 | 10.8 | 7.4 | 8.8 | 14.2 | 16.1 | 15.7 | 12.1 |
| Out of labor force | 6.6 | 4.5 | 2.3 | 2.7 | 2.7 | 9.0 | 6.2 | 2.9 | 3.1 | 4.1 |
| Looking for work | 4.6 | 2.8 | 6.7 | 4.7 | 5.7 | 10.7 | 5.8 | 12.6 | 7.3 | 6.9 |
| Labor force statistics:[b] | | | | | | | | | | |
| Employment ratio | .880 | .914 | .898 | .916 | .909 | .784 | .860 | .840 | .877 | .875 |
| Labor force participation | .929 | .946 | .974 | .969 | .972 | .902 | .928 | .965 | .964 | .953 |
| Unemployment ratio | .053 | .035 | .079 | .053 | .065 | .130 | .073 | .155 | .090 | .081 |

[a]Includes a small number of persons in graduate school in 1975 and 1976.

[b]For persons not in school and not in the military.

part time do not differ substantially in any of the years, although in each year the percentage for nonwhites is somewhat higher than for whites. It declines between 1972 and 1976 from 9.2 to 4.1 for whites and from 11.4 to 5.1 for nonwhites. A larger proportion of nonwhites than whites is in the military. In 1974, the year of highest military participation for both groups, about 12% of whites and 16% of nonwhites were in the armed forces.

More blacks than whites are out of the labor force, but the differences are not large. The proportion "looking for work," however, is about twice as high for nonwhites as for whites in 1972 through 1974. The differences decline in 1975 and 1976. The percentage of whites looking for work in 1976 was 5.7 versus 6.9 for nonwhites.

The labor force participation rates are high for both groups and do not differ substantially. Between 1972 and 1976 they moved from .93 to .97 for whites and .90 to .95 for nonwhites. The employment ratio is higher for whites than nonwhites in 1972, .88 versus .78; but by 1976 the two ratios were much closer, .91 versus .88. This closing of the gap between the two groups is reflected in the unemployment rate which was more than twice as high for nonwhites as for whites in 1972; but by 1976, the two rates were rather close, .065 versus .081.

In short, these numbers suggest a cohort of youths moving rather smoothly into the labor force. Although there are differences between the statistics for whites and nonwhites, they do not seem to us to be striking. In particular, the unemployment rates, although higher for nonwhites than whites, are not shocking to us for either group in any year. By 1976, somewhat more than four years after graduation from high school, labor force participation and employment ratios are high for both groups and the unemployment rates are modest for both groups. Youth unemployment does not appear from these data to be a severe problem for this group of high school graduates.

From the statistics in the tables available from the authors, one can find more detail within this more general picture. For example, it can be seen that most youths who are working part time are also in school full time, although the proportion is lower for nonwhites than for whites. Also, many persons looking for work are full-time students. They were not included in the unemployment statistics reported above.

### 9.1.2    Sequences of School and Work Status

The average statistics reported above do not reveal extremely high unemployment rates. But it could be that there are some youths who are often unemployed. As a worst case, we have lumped together the persons out of the labor force with those who are unemployed. Table 9.2 reports the percentage of persons not in school and not working (in either civilian or military jobs) for each possible number and sequence of time periods. For example, the sequence 10101 indicates not in school and not working

Table 9.2   Percent of Male Youths Not in School and Not Working, October 1972–76, by Sequence and Race[a]

| Sequence | All males | | White | | Nonwhite | |
|---|---|---|---|---|---|---|
| | Percentage of total | | | | | |
| 11111 | 0.1 | 0.1 | 0.1 | 0.1 | 0.1 | 0.1 |
| 11110 | | 0.1 | | 0.0 | | 0.3 |
| 11101 | | 0.0 | | 0.0 | | 0.1 |
| 11011 | 0.3 | 0.0 | 0.1 | 0.0 | 0.5 | 0.0 |
| 10111 | | 0.0 | | 0.0 | | 0.1 |
| 01111 | | 0.1 | | 0.1 | | 0.4 |
| 11100 | | 0.2 | | 0.1 | | 0.6 |
| 01110 | | 0.1 | | 0.1 | | 0.1 |
| 00111 | | 0.2 | | 0.2 | | 0.5 |
| 11010 | | 0.0 | | 0.0 | | 0.0 |
| 11001 | 1.0 | 0.1 | 0.8 | 0.1 | 2.0 | 0.3 |
| 01101 | | 0.0 | | 0.0 | | 0.0 |
| 10110 | | 0.1 | | 0.0 | | 0.2 |
| 10011 | | 0.1 | | 0.1 | | 0.3 |
| 01011 | | 0.1 | | 0.1 | | 0.1 |
| 10101 | | 0.0 | | 0.1 | | 0.0 |
| 11000 | | 0.6 | | 0.6 | | 1.0 |
| 01100 | | 0.5 | | 0.0 | | 1.0 |
| 00110 | | 0.5 | | 0.4 | | 0.9 |
| 00011 | | 0.5 | | 0.0 | | 0.7 |
| 10100 | | 0.3 | | 0.3 | | 0.4 |
| 01010 | 3.1 | 0.1 | 3.1 | 0.1 | 6.3 | 0.1 |
| 00101 | | 0.4 | | 0.3 | | 0.9 |
| 10010 | | 0.2 | | 0.1 | | 0.5 |
| 01001 | | 0.2 | | 0.2 | | 0.4 |
| 10001 | | 0.2 | | 0.2 | | 0.3 |
| 10000 | | 3.1 | | 2.3 | | 5.4 |
| 01000 | | 1.9 | | 1.8 | | 2.5 |
| 00100 | | 2.7 | | 2.5 | | 3.9 |
| 00010 | 14.1 | 2.5 | 13.2 | 2.3 | 18.6 | 3.2 |
| 00001 | | 3.9 | | 3.9 | | 3.7 |
| 00000 | 81.0 | 81.0 | 82.7 | 82.7 | 72.2 | 72.2 |
| Total | | 9115 | | 7639 | | 1475 |
| Missing | | 2052 | | 1448 | | 522 |

[a]The percentages have been rounded to the nearest tenth. Differences between the sum of the numbers in the groups and the group totals reported to the left in each column are due to rounding. A "1" indicates not in school and not working. The left digit pertains to October 1972.

in October 1972, October 1974, and October 1976, but not in this category in October 1973 or in October 1975. The left digit pertains to 1972.

Examination of table 9.2 reveals that 81% of the sample were *not* in this category in *any* of the five October periods (the data pertain to the first full week in October of each year). Only one-tenth of one percent were out of school and not working in all of the periods.[2] For whites and nonwhites together, this represents five persons out of 9115. Three-tenths of one percent were in this category four out of the five periods, and one-tenth of one percent in three out of the five. Only 14% were so classified in one of the five periods. We do not find a large group of chronically not in school and not working youths. More nonwhites than whites were in this status for one, two, three, and four periods; but over 72% of nonwhites were never out of school and without work in these October periods. These data do suggest, however, that some youths are much more likely to be in this category than others; there is heterogeneity among the group. For example, according to table 9.2 about 5 % of white youngsters are in this category in any year. If a person had a .05 probability of being in this category in any period and the probabilities were independent over time, the likelihood of being in this status three out of the five periods, for example, would be only .001, much less than the observed proportion of .008 for all white males.

Similarly defined sequences and associated percentages for full-time school and full-time work are reported in tables 9.3 and 9.4 respectively. Table 9.3 figures reveal that 36% of the sample were never in school full time, 35% for whites and 44% for nonwhites. (While these numbers suggest that whites are more often in school than nonwhites, the estimates below of the probability of attending school suggest a higher probability for nonwhites than whites after controlling for other relevant variables such as test scores and family background.)

Although there is some movement into and out of school, it is not the norm. Of persons who go to school at all, 69% begin in the first year after high school and attend only in consecutive years. Eighty-four percent of those who attend at all attend during the year immediately after high school. The in and out possibility that is sometimes emphasized, possibly more often for older persons, is not the norm among this group.

While 36% of the sample were never in school full time, only 24% worked full time in each of the five periods, as can be seen in table 9.4. As could be inferred from the school attendance figures, we see in table 9.4 that a relatively large number of persons work the last four, the last three, the last two, or the last year, but none of the prior years.

### 9.1.3 Weekly Earnings and Hours, Annual Employment and Unemployment, and Number of Employers

Average hourly wage rates, weekly earnings, and weekly hours worked for persons not in school and for those in school are shown in table 9.5.

**Table 9.3**  Percentage of Male Youths in School Full Time,
October 1972–76, by Sequence and Race[a]

| Sequence | Percentage of total | | |
| | All males | White | Nonwhite |
|---|---|---|---|
| 11111 | 11.7 | 12.4 | 8.1 |
| 11110 | 12.1 | 13.2 | 6.3 |
| 11101 | 1.3 | 1.3 | 1.2 |
| 11011 | 1.2 | 1.1 | 0.6 |
| 10111 | 1.2 | 1.2 | 1.3 |
| 01111 | 1.0 | 1.0 | 1.0 |
| 11100 | 3.8 | 3.9 | 3.3 |
| 01110 | 0.6 | 0.6 | 0.4 |
| 00111 | 0.5 | 0.5 | 0.5 |
| 11010 | 0.8 | 0.8 | 0.5 |
| 11001 | 0.4 | 0.5 | 0.3 |
| 01101 | 0.2 | 0.2 | 0.1 |
| 10110 | 1.1 | 1.1 | 0.9 |
| 10011 | 0.6 | 0.6 | 0.5 |
| 01011 | 0.2 | 0.2 | 0.1 |
| 10101 | 0.2 | 0.2 | 0.2 |
| 11000 | 7.1 | 7.0 | 7.3 |
| 01100 | 0.9 | 0.9 | 0.8 |
| 00110 | 0.5 | 0.5 | 0.7 |
| 00011 | 0.8 | 0.7 | 1.0 |
| 10100 | 1.2 | 1.1 | 1.2 |
| 01010 | 0.1 | 0.1 | 0.1 |
| 00101 | 0.1 | 0.1 | 0.1 |
| 10010 | 0.7 | 0.7 | 0.6 |
| 01001 | 0.1 | 0.1 | 0.1 |
| 10001 | 0.6 | 0.6 | 0.7 |
| 10000 | 9.5 | 9.2 | 11.2 |
| 01000 | 1.6 | 1.6 | 1.7 |
| 00100 | 1.5 | 1.4 | 1.9 |
| 00010 | 1.1 | 1.0 | 1.5 |
| 00001 | 1.3 | 1.2 | 2.0 |
| 00000 | 36.4 | 34.9 | 44.0 |
| Total | 9152 | 7659 | 1492 |
| Missing | 2052 | 1428 | 505 |

[a]The percentages have been rounded to the nearest tenth. Differences between the sum of the numbers in the groups and the group totals reported to the left in each column are due to rounding. A "1" indicates in school full time. The left digit pertains to October 1972.

**Table 9.4**          **Percentage of Male Youths Working Full Time,
October 1972–76, by Sequence and Race[a]**

| | Percentage of total | | |
| Sequence | All males | White | Nonwhite |
|---|---|---|---|
| 11111 | 23.7 | 23.7 | 24.1 |
| 11110 | 1.5 | 1.6 | 1.3 |
| 11101 | 1.2 | 1.1 | 1.5 |
| 11011 | 2.8 | 2.7 | 2.9 |
| 10111 | 2.9 | 2.9 | 3.2 |
| 01111 | 9.7 | 9.5 | 10.7 |
| 11100 | 1.0 | 0.9 | 1.5 |
| 01110 | 1.0 | 1.0 | 1.3 |
| 00111 | 7.6 | 7.2 | 9.7 |
| 11010 | 0.4 | 0.3 | 0.6 |
| 11001 | 0.8 | 0.8 | 0.9 |
| 01101 | 0.7 | 0.7 | 1.0 |
| 10110 | 0.5 | 0.4 | 0.9 |
| 10011 | 1.2 | 1.2 | 1.3 |
| 01011 | 1.8 | 1.7 | 2.1 |
| 10101 | 0.3 | 0.3 | 0.5 |
| 11000 | 1.0 | 0.9 | 1.2 |
| 01100 | 0.7 | 0.6 | 0.7 |
| 00110 | 1.3 | 1.3 | 1.2 |
| 00011 | 4.5 | 4.3 | 5.5 |
| 10100 | 0.4 | 0.4 | 0.3 |
| 01010 | 0.3 | 0.3 | 0.4 |
| 00101 | 1.4 | 1.4 | 1.4 |
| 10010 | 0.2 | 0.2 | 0.3 |
| 01001 | 0.9 | 0.9 | 0.9 |
| 10001 | 0.7 | 0.7 | 0.7 |
| 10000 | 1.2 | 1.2 | 1.3 |
| 01000 | 1.6 | 1.5 | 1.8 |
| 00100 | 1.6 | 1.6 | 1.4 |
| 00010 | 1.5 | 1.5 | 1.6 |
| 00001 | 9.9 | 10.6 | 6.5 |
| 00000 | 15.6 | 16.4 | 11.4 |
| Total | 9208 | 7689 | 1518 |
| Missing | 1959 | 1398 | 479 |

[a]The percentages have been rounded to the nearest tenth. Differences between the sum of the numbers in the groups and the group totals reported to the left in each column are due to rounding. A "1" indicates working full time. The left digit pertains to October 1972.

Table 9.5      **Average Hourly Wage Rates, Weekly Earnings, and Weekly Hours Worked for Persons Working in October, by School Status, Race, and Year[a]**

| Item and race | Out of school | | | | | In school | | | |
|---|---|---|---|---|---|---|---|---|---|
| | 1972 | 1973 | 1974 | 1975 | 1976 | 1973 | 1974 | 1975 | 1976 |
| **Hourly wage rate** | | | | | | | | | |
| All males | 2.67 | 3.18 | 3.69 | 4.14 | 4.56 | 2.66 | 3.06 | 3.49 | 4.04 |
| | (3040) | (3752) | (4199) | (4039) | (4950) | (2223) | (1892) | (1725) | (1347) |
| White | 2.68 | 3.22 | 3.73 | 4.17 | 4.61 | 2.65 | 3.00 | 3.47 | 4.06 |
| | (2471) | (3001) | (3403) | (3271) | (4097) | (1938) | (1625) | (1473) | (1162) |
| Nonwhite | 2.67 | 3.02 | 3.53 | 3.99 | 4.35 | 2.74 | 3.42 | 3.59 | 3.91 |
| | (550) | (731) | (796) | (753) | (841) | (273) | (267) | (248) | (181) |
| **Weekly earnings** | | | | | | | | | |
| All males | 108.68 | 133.61 | 154.21 | 173.48 | 192.15 | 74.34 | 89.25 | 103.77 | 130.80 |
| White | 110.32 | 137.04 | 157.41 | 176.47 | 195.52 | 73.43 | 86.94 | 101.47 | 129.74 |
| Nonwhite | 101.69 | 119.79 | 140.53 | 160.85 | 176.18 | 78.93 | 103.29 | 115.99 | 136.48 |
| **Weekly hours worked** | | | | | | | | | |
| All males | 41.50 | 42.79 | 42.47 | 42.53 | 42.63 | 27.47 | 27.95 | 28.88 | 31.45 |
| White | 41.90 | 43.21 | 42.80 | 42.86 | 42.95 | 27.24 | 27.58 | 28.39 | 31.06 |
| Nonwhite | 39.65 | 41.14 | 41.02 | 41.09 | 41.09 | 28.62 | 30.20 | 31.60 | 33.73 |

[a]The data pertain to the first full week in October of each year. The numbers reporting figures in each year are in parenthesis under the wage rates. They are the same for weekly earnings and weekly hours worked.

They cover all persons in the sample who were working in the first full week of October of the year indicated. Persons working full time or part time are included. For persons out of school, wage rates for the two groups are virtually identical right after graduation. After four years, whites earn about 6% more per hour than nonwhites, presumably, in part at least, because of the different schooling patterns of the two groups and post-high school work experience. Nonwhites also work about two hours per week less than whites in each of the time periods and thus have lower weekly earnings—about 8% in the first year and 10 or 11% in each of the subsequent years.

On the other hand, nonwhites who are in school work 1.5 to 3 hours per week more than whites, earn somewhat more per hour in all but the last period, and have higher weekly earnings in each of the periods between 5 and 19% depending on the period.

We also calculated the percentage of persons with wage rates below the federal minimum. The results of October of each year are shown in the tabulation below.

| Year | Minimum wage rate | Percentage below minimum | | |
|------|------|------|------|------|
| | | Total | White | Nonwhite |
| 1972 | $1.60 | 10.98 | 11.02 | 10.76 |
| 1973 | $1.60 | 5.89 | 5.93 | 5.59 |
| 1974 | $2.00 | 8.06 | 8.35 | 6.68 |
| 1975 | $2.10 | 8.14 | 8.14 | 7.99 |
| 1976 | $2.30 | 5.76 | 5.39 | 7.73 |

These numbers presumably reflect in large part wages of persons in jobs exempt from minimum wage legislation.

Average annual weeks worked, weeks looking, weeks out of the labor force, and number of employers, by school status, are shown in table 9.6. Among persons out of school, nonwhites work fewer weeks per year than whites, but the difference declines continuously over the four-year period. Nonwhites work 13% less in the first year, 10% in the second, 7% in the third, and 5% in the fourth. The differences are accounted for by both weeks looking for work and weeks out of the labor force. Differences among whites and nonwhites in school are somewhat less in general, although as among persons not in school nonwhites who are in school spend more weeks than whites looking for work.

## 9.2  High School Training and Labor Force Experience

Our goal is to estimate the effects of personal characteristics, particularly high school preparation, on labor force experiences in the years following high school graduation. The measures of labor force experience we shall use are weeks worked and wage rates. We have annual weeks worked for four years following high school graduation and wage rates for five consecutive October periods, as described above. We have estimated a weeks-worked equation separately for each of the four years and a separate wage equation for each of the five October periods. Jointly with each of the weeks-worked and wage equations we have estimated a "school nonattendance" equation, that is, the probability of being in the sample, and thus having recorded wage or weeks worked measures as defined below. We have followed this procedure in the first instance to correct for possible bias in the parameters of the weeks-worked and wage equations. But the school nonattendance equations have a behavioral interpretation in this case and the associated parameter estimates are of interest apart from their relationship to the weeks-worked and wage equation estimates. In addition, the procedure we have used to estimate weeks worked accounts for the upper limit of fifty-two weeks in a year. A large proportion of respondents report working a full fifty-two-week year. Parameter estimates obtained without recognizing this limit tend to underestimate the effects of explanatory variables on weeks worked. (An analogy would be the effect of knowledge about a subject on an examination score in that subject if the exam is very easy. After some level of knowledge, more doesn't help. You can't score above 100.) Thus we have combined a tobit specification for weeks worked with a probit school nonattendance specification. Finally, in section 9.3 we shall discuss the relationships between weeks worked and wage rates over time.

A more precise description of the approach we have followed to estimate weeks worked is presented in section 9.2.1 below. The variant of this procedure used to estimate wages is described in section 9.2.2. The results are then discussed in turn, beginning with estimates of the probability of school attendance, followed by parameter estimates for the weeks-worked and wage rate equations.

### 9.2.1   The Weeks Worked Estimation Procedure

Suppose that weeks worked in each of four years are indicated by $Y_1$ through $Y_4$. Assume also that in each period there are vectors of "exogenous" variables $X_1$ through $X_4$. In practice, these vectors will be composed largely of variables like test scores and family background that do not change over time, although some like schooling and work experience do. Let the relationships between weeks worked and the exogenous variables for individuals in the population, should they decide to work, be described by

$$
Y_{1i} = X_{1i}\beta_1 + \varepsilon_{1i},
$$
(1)
$$
Y_{2i} = X_{1i}\beta_2 + \varepsilon_{2i},
$$
$$
\vdots
$$
$$
Y_{4i} = X_{4i}\beta_4 + \varepsilon_{4i},
$$

Table 9.6    **Average Annual Weeks Worked, Weeks Looking for Work, Weeks out of the Labor Force, and Number of Employers for Male Youths, by School Status, Race, and Year[a]**

| Item and race | Out of school | | | | In school | | | |
|---|---|---|---|---|---|---|---|---|
| | 1972-73 | 1973-74 | 1974-75 | 1975-76 | 1972-73 | 1973-74 | 1974-75 | 1975-76 |
| **Weeks worked** | | | | | | | | |
| All males | 39.91 | 43.32 | 43.66 | 44.08 | 28.17 | 30.03 | 30.82 | 31.55 |
| | (4374) | (4214) | (5031) | (5470) | (5541) | (4253) | (3923) | (3708) |
| White | 41.05 | 44.18 | 44.26 | 44.52 | 28.55 | 30.22 | 30.86 | 31.54 |
| | (3433) | (3364) | (4087) | (4424) | (4742) | (3703) | (3432) | (3236) |
| Nonwhite | 35.77 | 39.91 | 41.05 | 42.14 | 25.70 | 28.78 | 30.58 | 31.60 |
| | (899) | (850) | (944) | (1030) | (779) | (549) | (490) | (463) |
| **Weeks looking for** | | | | | | | | |
| All males | 3.57 | 3.00 | 3.78 | 3.51 | 2.21 | 2.16 | 2.77 | 2.90 |
| | (3960) | (3941) | (5061) | (5470) | (5140) | (3987) | (3913) | (3730) |
| White | 3.06 | 2.77 | 3.60 | 3.42 | 1.98 | 1.99 | 2.59 | 2.75 |
| | (3112) | (3158) | (4091) | (4411) | (4438) | (3462) | (3418) | (3251) |
| Nonwhite | 5.55 | 3.93 | 4.54 | 3.88 | 3.70 | 3.25 | 4.03 | 3.92 |
| | (807) | (783) | (970) | (1042) | (683) | (524) | (494) | (470) |

Weeks out of the labor force

| | | | | | | | | |
|---|---|---|---|---|---|---|---|---|
| All males | 8.39 | 5.86 | 4.47 | 4.25 | 21.73 | 20.04 | 18.41 | 17.58 |
| | (3925) | (3899) | (4898) | (5313) | (5093) | (3948) | (3815) | (3646) |
| White | 7.72 | 5.17 | 4.02 | 3.89 | 21.59 | 20.00 | 18.59 | 17.71 |
| | (3089) | (3131) | (3980) | (4303) | (4408) | (3431) | (3339) | (3186) |
| Nonwhite | 10.79 | 8.66 | 6.39 | 5.84 | 22.84 | 20.32 | 17.09 | 16.63 |
| | (795) | (768) | (918) | (994) | (276) | (516) | (475) | (451) |

Number of employers

| | | | | | | | | |
|---|---|---|---|---|---|---|---|---|
| All males | 1.85 | 1.59 | 1.43 | 1.41 | 1.76 | 1.64 | 1.43 | 1.56 |
| | (4342) | (4409) | (5306) | (5732) | (5496) | (4399) | (4019) | (3837) |
| White | 1.89 | 1.60 | 1.43 | 1.41 | 1.78 | 1.67 | 1.43 | 1.57 |
| | (3418) | (3509) | (4290) | (4611) | (4726) | (3822) | (3503) | (3335) |
| Nonwhite | 1.72 | 1.55 | 1.43 | 1.41 | 1.66 | 1.46 | 1.43 | 1.47 |
| | (884) | (900) | (1016) | (1105) | (748) | (576) | (515) | (493) |

[a]The number of respondents is shown in parentheses under each average. The numbers for nonwhite and white may not add to the total because race is sometimes unknown.

where the $\varepsilon_{ti}$ are random terms and the $\beta_t$ vectors of parameters. It is important in our case that the $\beta_t$ be allowed to vary. We do not want to restrict the influence of variables like high school work experience to be constant over time. On the contrary, we would like to see if their effects change, and if so, how.

Two groups of individuals are distinguished: those who are in school and those who are not. Persons included in our out-of-school group were not in school in either the October beginning the year nor in the following October. Although one might well consider the determinants of weeks worked for persons in either group, we will concentrate on those not in school. We judged that the labor market behavior of the two groups would be quite different and we did not want estimates that confounded the decisions of both.[3] Each of the equations (1) is presumed to describe the work experience of persons in the population should they decide not to go to school in the year indicated by the subscripts 1 through 4.

Suppose that there are four unobserved variables $S_t$, one for each of the four time periods. Define them by

$$
\begin{aligned}
S_{1i} &= Z_{1i}\delta_1 + \eta_{1i}, \\
S_{2i} &= Z_{2i}\delta_2 + \eta_{2i}, \\
&\vdots \\
S_{4i} &= Z_{4i}\delta_4 + \eta_{4i},
\end{aligned}
$$

(2)

where the $Z_t$ are vectors of exogenous variables, the $\delta_t$ are vectors of parameters, and the $\eta_t$ are random terms. Let $s_{ti}$ be an indicator variable with $s_{ti} = 1$ if the $i^{\text{th}}$ individual is *not* in school in year $t$, and thus in the sample $s_{ti} = 0$ if he is. Also, let

$$
(3) \qquad s_{ti} = \begin{cases} 1 \text{ if } S_{ti} \geq 0 \\ 0 \text{ if } S_{ti} < 0 \end{cases}
$$

for $t$ equal to 1, 2, 3, or 4. Then the probability that the $i^{\text{th}}$ individual is not in school is given by $Pr(s_{ti} = 1) = Pr(S_{ti} = Z_{ti}\delta_t + \eta_{ti} \geq 0)$. And if $\eta_{ti}$ is assumed to be normally distributed, we have for each period a probit specification of the probability of not being in school:[4]

$$
\begin{aligned}
Pr\,(s_{1i} = 1) &= \Phi[Z_{1i}\delta_1] \\
Pr\,(s_{2i} = 1) &= \Phi[Z_{2i}\delta_2] \\
&\vdots \\
Pr\,(s_{4i} = 1) &= \Phi[Z_{4i}\delta_4]
\end{aligned}
$$

(4)

We know that estimation of any of the $Y_{ti}$ equations in (1), based only on persons not in school in year $t$, will yield biased coefficient estimates if $\varepsilon_{ti}$ and $\eta_{ti}$ are correlated.[5] We could correct for this potential bias by estimating jointly for each year the weeks-worked equation and the corresponding choice-of-status, or school attendance, equation.[6]

In our case, however, the upper limit on weeks worked has an important effect on the estimates of ß in equation (1) and thus on the interpretation of the relationship between preparation in high school and post-high school labor force experience. The percentage distribution of weeks worked for persons not in school by selected interval is shown for each of the four years in the tabulation below.

| Weeks worked interval | Percentage distribution | | | |
|---|---|---|---|---|
| | 1973 | 1974 | 1975 | 1976 |
| 0 to 10 | 5.2 | 5.3 | 4.6 | 4.6 |
| 11 to 20 | 4.8 | 3.1 | 3.6 | 3.5 |
| 21 to 30 | 8.0 | 5.9 | 5.7 | 5.5 |
| 31 to 40 | 12.5 | 12.0 | 9.9 | 10.2 |
| 41 to 51 | 30.3 | 32.3 | 24.2 | 24.7 |
| 52 | 39.2 | 41.4 | 52.0 | 51.5 |

The percentage reporting fifty-two weeks of work ranges from 39% in 1973 to 52% in 1976. It is apparently the case that many persons are prepared to work, and have work opportunities that exceed the time available constraint as measured in weeks.[7]

Thus we have changed the specification in equation (1), interpreting capital $Y_i$ as an unobserved "propensity" to work, with observed weeks worked given by

(5)
$$y_{1i} = \begin{cases} X_{1i}\beta_1 + \varepsilon_{1i} & \text{if } X_{1i}\beta_1 + \varepsilon_{1i} \leq 52, \\ 52 & \text{if } X_{1i}\beta_1 + \varepsilon_{1i} > 52, \end{cases}$$
$$\vdots$$
$$y_{4i} = \begin{cases} X_{4i}\beta_4 + \varepsilon_{4i} & \text{if } X_{4i}\beta_4 + \varepsilon_{4i} \leq 52, \\ 52 & \text{if } X_{4i}\beta_4 + \varepsilon_{4i} > 52. \end{cases}$$

The maximum likelihood procedure we have used estimates ß in (5) jointly with δ in (2), for each of the four years individually. It is explained in more detail in the appendix. The relationship between the expected value of $Y$ given by $X\beta$ and the expected value of weeks worked, $E(y)$, may be seen in figure 9.1, in which one right-hand variable is assumed. At low levels of $X\beta$, the estimated parameter ß represents the approximate effect of a change in $X$ on the expected number of weeks worked. As $X$ increases, its effect on weeks worked approaches zero.[8] For example, our results reported below suggest that ß is about twice as large as the derivative of $E(y)$ with respect to $X$, evaluated at $\bar{X}$. At the mean of the variables in our sample, the expected number of weeks worked is about forty-four, and the expected value of the unobserved $Y$ is somewhat

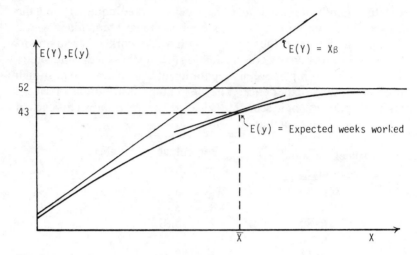

**Fig. 9.1**

greater than fifty-two. The derivative of $E(y)$ with respect to $X$ at $\bar{X}$ is approximately equal to the estimate of ß from a specification that does not distinguish employment at the limit of fifty-two weeks from observations below fifty-two.

There were also a few persons each year who did not work at all. We obtained some initial estimates that accounted for this by specifying weeks worked to be bounded at zero, as well as at fifty-two. It did not significantly affect our results and we did not incorporate it in the results presented below.

An alternative to separate estimates for each year is to divide the sample into two groups: one composed of persons who were never in school, and the other composed of everyone else. But for our purposes the procedure outlined above has at least two advantages over the alternative. First, it allows us to make use of as much of the data as possible.[9] Examination of table 9.3 shows that the number of persons out of school in all years is much smaller than the number in any single year.[10] Also, even if the group with weeks worked is defined in the alternative way, a sample selection correction must still be made to obtain unbiased estimates of the population parameters in the weeks-worked equations. This presumably would be done by estimating a probit equation pertaining to the probability of never being in school. Such an equation could be used to correct each of the weeks-worked equations for the sample selection bias.[11] But it is difficult to think of a behavioral interpretation for this sample selection equation, since in a given year one group includes persons who are in school as well as some who are not. Our status equations can be interpreted in each year as estimating the determinants of school attendance in that year.

### 9.2.2    The Wage Rate Estimation Procedure

Wage rate equations were also estimated jointly with school nonattendance equations. There are five wage equations, however, one for each of the October survey periods. But there is no limit problem as with weeks worked. Parameters in equations like (1) and (2) for weeks worked were estimated jointly, with the logarithm of the wage substituted for weeks worked.[12] There is, however, a complication that does not arise in the weeks-worked equation.

Wage rates are presumed to depend on years of schooling, as well as on other variables. For example, persons who were working in the fourth October period may have been in school during some or all of the previous periods, and their wage rates may be expected to depend on the amount of schooling. Suppose that the logarithm of the wage is given by

$$W_{4i} = X_{4i}\alpha_4 + a_1 A_{1i} + a_2 A_{2i} + a_3 A_{3i} + v_{4i}$$

where $A_1$ equals 1 if individual $i$ was in school during period 1 and zero if not, and similarly for $A_2$ and $A_3$. The potential bias resulting from the possibility that $E(v_{4i}|s_{4i} = 1)$ may not be zero is corrected for by estimating the equation jointly with the probability of school nonattendance. But if the $v_t$'s are correlated with the error in the school nonattendance equations, and the $\eta_t$'s or the $v_t$'s are correlated over time, then $A_1$ through $A_3$ may be correlated with the error $v_4$ in the wage equation. To overcome this problem, we experimented with an instrument for prior schooling.[13] In practice, we found that the use of an instrument for schooling did not substantially alter the character of our conclusions.[14] A similar problem may pertain to work experience that is also assumed to determine the wage rate. We did not attempt to correct for it. (In subsequent work we will estimate a more appropriate model for solving this problem. It will allow joint estimation of weeks worked, wage, schooling, and a sample selection equation.)

Finally, the sample selection equations estimated with the wage rate equations are not precisely school nonattendance equations, although in practice the two are almost interchangeable. The weeks-worked equation for a given year included all persons who were not in school during that year. Thus the status or sample selection equations are equivalent to school attendance equations. Students were also excluded from the wage equations. But we do not have wage rates for all persons who were not students. Some nonstudents were also not employed. To correct the wage equation for sample selection bias we need to consider all persons without a recorded wage rate, whatever the reason.[15]

The variables used in the analysis are defined below.

*Weeks worked*: Annual weeks worked, October to October.

*Wage rate*: Earnings divided by hours worked, first full week in October.

*Test scores total*: Sum of scores on six texts: vocabulary, reading, mathematics, picture-number, letter groups, mosaic comparisons.

*Class rank in high school*: Percentile ranking relative to other persons in individual's high school.

*Job training in high school*: One if the individual received in high school "any specialized training intended to prepare [him] for immediate employment upon leaving school (for example, auto mechanics, secretarial skills, or nurses aid)," zero otherwise.

*Hours worked during high school*: Response to the question, "On the average over the school year, how many hours per week do you work in a paid or unpaid job? (Exclude vacation.)" The response was by interval: 0, 1–5, 6–10, . . . , 26–30, over 30.

*Parents' income*: Annual income of parents, in thousands.

*Education of mother (father) less than high school*: One if the youth's mother (father) had less than a high school education and zero otherwise.

*Education of mother (father) college degree or more*: One if the youth's mother (father) had a college degree or more education, and zero otherwise. The excluded category is a high school degree but less than a college degree.

*Race*: One if nonwhite, zero otherwise.

*Dependents*: Number of persons dependent on the individual for income.

*School years*: Number of Octobers in which the individual said he was in school.

*On the job training*: Months of on-the-job training.

*Experience*: Work experience, in years. Excludes work while attending a post-secondary school. Experience is distinguished by the year in which it occurred.

*Part-time working*: One if the individual is working part time, zero otherwise.

*Rural, urban*: One if the individual's residence location corresponds to the one indicated, zero otherwise. The excluded category is suburban and town.

*West*: One if the person lives in the West, zero otherwise.

*State wage*: Annual average wage in manufacturing.

*State unemployment*: Average annual unemployment rate.

*Missing variable indicators*: For test scores, class rank, parents' income, experience. Each is one if the designated variable is missing and zero otherwise. The corresponding variable takes the value zero if it is missing and the recorded value if it is not.

The means and standard deviations of these variables are given in appendix table 9A.2.

### 9.2.3 School Attendance

Concomitant to the procedure used to estimate both the weeks worked and the wage equations, we estimated school attendance equations, or more precisely, the probability of not attending school. Before presenting results on the central questions of our analysis, we will summarize briefly the implications of the estimated attendance probability parameters.

School nonattendance equations estimated with the weeks worked-equations are presented in table 9.9; those estimated with the wage equations are shown in table 9.12. The two sets of parameter estimates are necessarily very similar. The discussion in this section is based on those estimated with weeks worked. Recall that the parameter estimates in table 9.9 are analogous to the parameters $\delta$ in equations (2) and (4). The variables used in the probability equations are easily identifiable by glancing at the table. They need no further explanation. The first two groups of variables pertain to school achievement and family background. All are measured with considerable precision, as shown in the table.

To get a better idea of the importance of the variables, however, we have calculated estimated differences in the probability of attending school for persons who have different values of a specified variable, but the same values for all the others. All other variables were assumed to have values equal to their respective means. The specified differences and the associated differences in estimated school attendance probabilities are shown in table 9.7.

Possibly the most notable finding is that the probability that nonwhites are in school, controlling for other variables, is considerably higher than for whites, at least .10 in each of the five years.[16] (Recall that the summary numbers in table 9.1 show that in each of the first four years following high school the percentage of nonwhites in school fulltime was between 11 and 13 percentage points less than the percentage for whites.) This could result from relatively fewer opportunities in the labor force. But as indicated in the wage equation estimates discussed below, after controlling for other variables, there is little difference between the wage rates of whites and nonwhites in the first three years; in the last two, nonwhites are estimated to earn about 4% more than whites.[17] And the weeks-worked equations indicate that after controlling for other variables nonwhites work about the same number of weeks per year as whites. This could also reflect higher returns to education for nonwhites than for whites, as discussed by Freeman (1976a, 1976b), for example.

The other academic and family background variables are all related in the expected way to school attendance, although the relative magnitudes may not be widely known. Parents' income seems to have much less effect

Table 9.7

| Difference in academic or social background | Associated differences in the probability of school attendance | | | | |
|---|---|---|---|---|---|
| | 1972–73 | 1973–74 | 1974–75 | 1975–76 | 1976[a] |
| Test scores one S.D. above the mean, versus one S.D. below | .242 | .254 | .247 | .230 | .181 |
| Class rank one S.D. above the mean, versus one S.D. below | .308 | .279 | .288 | .292 | .165 |
| Parents income one S.D. above the mean, versus one S.D. below | .112 | .104 | .096 | .104 | .059 |
| Education of Father and Mother college or more, versus less than h.s graduate | .341 | .247 | .319 | .323 | .230 |
| Nonwhite versus white | .103 | .097 | .091 | .109 | .136 |

[a]Based on the school nonattendance question estimated with the 1976 wage equation. See table 9.12.

on school attendance than either of the measures of academic achievement. Parents' income may be the least important of all the variables listed. Class rank seems somewhat more important than the test scores, although our comparison is only suggestive. Recall that the tests measure a range of abilities and achievements, some more academically oriented than others. Also, we have made no attempt to distinguish types of schools. The relative importance of academic ability is likely to increase with the quality of school.[18] Finally, there are large differences in expected probability of school attendance associated with extremes in parents' education.

In an alternative specification of the school attendance equations in table 9.9 we also included the number of hours worked per week in high school—measured as one of seven intervals, 1 to 5, 6 to 10, [. . .] over 30—and a variable indicating whether or not the individual had job training during high school. It is questionable whether the job training variable (and possibly hours worked in high school) should be included in a school attendance equation. The question arises because job training in high school may indicate a "noncollege trait" and thus a prior decision not to go to school—it may be more an indicator of post-secondary school attendance rather than a determinant of it. But because the relationship between these choices while in high school and later school attendance may be of interest we have reported the results when they are included. Their inclusion has a negligible effect on the other parameter estimates.[19]

Persons who work more than about 20 hours per week in high school are considerably less likely to be in school in any of the four years than those who work less, according to the estimates of the coefficients on hours worked in high school. The average effect on the probability of school attendance of working 21 to 25, 26 to 30, or more than 30 hours per week is about .10, with the probability evaluated at the means of the other variables. Persons who work less than 20 hours per week are also less likely to be in school during the first year after high school than those who don't work at all, but the relevant coefficients are not measured very precisely.[20] In the remaining three years, the estimates indicate little relationship between post-secondary school attendance and hours worked in high school until hours worked exceeds 20 hours per week approximately.

Recall that these are estimates after controlling for high school achievement and family background. We will show below that, with a few notable exceptions, the number of hours worked during high school is not strongly related to most measures of socioeconomic background nor to school achievement. It is largely an independent personal characteristic. Recall that only for persons who work many hours per week during high school is such work significantly related to later school attendance. There is a tendency for persons who work a lot to be less inclined to continue their formal schooling. Possibly some have made a prior decision to work rather than go to school. We will see, however, that hours worked in high school are strongly related to weeks worked per year after graduation. As expected, persons who get job training in high school are considerably less likely to go to school later than those who don't.

Only two of the other variables in table 9.12 need be mentioned; the others may be thought of simply as controls. One might suppose that school attendance would depend on expected wage, if the individual is not in school, and the ease of finding work; thus the state wage and unemployment variables have been included in the probability equations. They could be considered as rough instruments for individual wage and unemployment rates. Neither is significantly different from zero in most years, although the wage rate in each year is negatively related to school attendance and the unemployment rate positively related. The wage rate is significantly different from zero by standard criteria during the first two years. It could be that labor force opportunities are important determinants of school attendance right after high school, but that in the later years, once in school, persons don't drop out because of changes in the wage rate, and they are less likely to enter school having not attended previously. The marginal lifetime return to an additional year of school probably increases as one nears college graduation.

Finally, persons who go to rural high schools are less likely to be in school after graduation—the difference in probability is about .06 in the first two years and .12 and .13 respectively in the third and fourth years.

**Table 9.8**      **Estimates of Weeks Worked Equation Parameters by Year[a]**

| Variable | October 1972 to October 1973 | October 1973 to October 1974 | October 1974 to October 1975 | October 1975 to October 1976 |
|---|---|---|---|---|
| Hours worked during high school: | | | | |
| 1 to 5 | 0.1700 | 1.1246 | 0.9006 | 3.4239 |
| | (1.1629) | (1.6710) | (2.0376) | (1.9529) |
| 6 to 10 | 2.5027 | 2.2663 | 0.4056 | 3.0490 |
| | (1.1893) | (1.7883) | (1.9750) | (1.7620) |
| 11 to 15 | 7.3619 | 1.7668 | 4.0527 | 4.4541 |
| | (1.3896) | (1.9820) | (2.2907) | (1.9907) |
| 16 to 20 | 6.8180 | 4.2688 | 5.9215 | 6.5548 |
| | (1.1109) | (1.5694) | (1.9135) | (1.7884) |
| 21 to 25 | 7.8500 | 5.1503 | 4.2531 | 7.3057 |
| | (1.2329) | (1.7854) | (1.9096) | (1.7893) |
| 26 to 30 | 10.9685 | 6.1313 | 5.9604 | 7.1673 |
| | (1.3189) | (1.7165) | (1.9496) | (1.8737) |
| 31 or more | 12.5225 | 7.6769 | 8.9859 | 8.1603 |
| | (1.1273) | (1.5174) | (1.8231) | (1.6714) |
| Class rank in | 0.2323 | 0.2120 | 0.1914 | 0.2044 |
| high school | (0.0267) | (0.0276) | (0.0294) | (0.0270) |
| Test score total | 12.1144 | 10.8146 | 9.7233 | 6.7031 |
| | (1.4197) | (1.6811) | (1.7978) | (1.6649) |
| Job training during | −1.4376 | 1.4486 | 0.5983 | 3.0389 |
| high school | (0.7151) | (1.0539) | (1.2593) | (1.2358) |
| Race | −1.9184 | 0.1898 | 0.3935 | −0.9848 |
| | (1.3714) | (1.6311) | (1.7363) | (1.5666) |
| Parents' income | 0.6370 | 0.4868 | 0.5015 | 0.3137 |
| | (0.1168) | (0.1211) | (0.1401) | (0.1218) |
| Dependents | 4.2551 | 1.6987 | 1.3027 | 1.8420 |
| | (0.5997) | (0.7739) | (0.7485) | (0.6702) |
| On the job | | 0.6600 | 0.3335 | 0.3680 |
| training years | | (0.2667) | (0.1885) | (0.1653) |
| Rural | −2.5912 | 0.1617 | −2.7939 | 0.0897 |
| | (0.9628) | (1.3651) | (1.4721) | (1.3027) |
| Urban | −1.4913 | −2.2115 | −1.2479 | 0.3683 |
| | (0.8016) | (1.0583) | (1.2458) | (1.1566) |
| State wage | −2.1755 | −1.0422 | −1.9233 | −1.6065 |
| | (0.9391) | (1.1206) | (1.0218) | (0.8324) |
| State unemployment | −1.0645 | −0.4019 | −0.8878 | −0.7279 |
| | (0.4069) | (1.1206) | (0.4418) | (0.2826) |
| Test score missing | 33.0777 | 29.6297 | 26.4883 | 19.3229 |
| | (4.3147) | (5.1682) | (5.5833) | (5.1371) |
| Class rank missing | 10.1779 | 6.8823 | 6.6354 | 7.1726 |
| | (1.9191) | (2.2285) | (2.5529) | (2.2480) |
| Patents' income missing | 6.6426 | 6.8539 | 3.2212 | 2.2059 |
| | (1.7567) | (1.9804) | (2.2199) | (2.2028) |
| Constant | 27.2947 | 23.4604 | 36.8182 | 40.9972 |
| | (5.3019) | (6.3969) | (7.0262) | (6.5931) |

[a]Standard errors in parentheses.

**Table 9.9**    **Estimates of School Nonattendance Equation Parameters by Year (Estimated with Weeks-worked Equation)[a,b]**

| | October 1972 to October 1973 | October 1973 to October 1974 | October 1974 to October 1975 | October 1975 to October 1976 |
|---|---|---|---|---|
| Test scores total | −0.7411 | −0.7704 | −0.7180 | −0.6714 |
| | (0.0504) | (0.0684) | (0.0694) | (0.0674) |
| Class rank in high school | −0.0154 | −0.0133 | −0.0132 | −0.0136 |
| | (0.0008) | (0.0010) | (0.0010) | (0.0010) |
| Race | −0.2792 | −0.2509 | −0.2297 | −0.2726 |
| | (0.0519) | (0.0687) | (0.0696) | (0.0678) |
| Parents' income | −0.0284 | −0.0254 | −0.0228 | −0.0247 |
| | (0.0039) | (0.0051) | (0.0051) | (0.0049) |
| Education of mother | 0.1358 | 0.0509 | −0.0067 | 0.0372 |
| less than high school | (0.0275) | (0.0488) | (0.0511) | (0.0511) |
| Education of mother | −0.2534 | −0.1325 | −0.1540 | −0.1759 |
| college degree or more | (0.0449) | (0.0628) | (0.0703) | (0.0687) |
| Education of father | 0.2503 | 0.2808 | 0.2560 | 0.2295 |
| Less than high school | (0.0277) | (0.0466) | (0.0494) | (0.0504) |
| Education of father | −0.2890 | −0.1772 | −0.3991 | −0.3675 |
| college degree or more | (0.0377) | (0.0554) | (0.0631) | (0.0607) |
| Rural | 0.1708 | 0.1542 | 0.3022 | 0.3186 |
| | (0.0341) | (0.0529) | (0.0551) | (0.0554) |
| Urban | −0.0456 | −0.0174 | −0.0071 | −0.0387 |
| | (0.0278) | (0.0439) | (0.0475) | (0.0470) |
| State wage | 0.1444 | 0.0658 | 0.0063 | −0.0030 |
| | (0.0333) | (0.0437) | (0.0397) | (0.0339) |
| State unemployment | −0.0191 | −0.0156 | −0.0195 | 0.0008 |
| | (0.0141) | (0.0179) | (0.0167) | (0.0112) |
| Test score missing | −2.1016 | −2.1982 | −2.115 | −2.0005 |
| | (0.1597) | (0.2177) | (0.2237) | (0.2169) |
| Class rank missing | −0.5491 | −0.4709 | −0.5977 | −0.6305 |
| | (0.0704) | (0.0941) | (0.0980) | (0.0940) |
| Parents' income missing | −0.2979 | −0.3408 | −0.2796 | −0.3026 |
| | (0.0643) | (0.0845) | (0.0868) | (0.0836) |
| Constant | 2.5045 | 2.7335 | 3.0666 | 3.0571 |
| | (0.1903) | (0.2584) | (0.2675) | (0.2619) |
| Correlation with | −0.9276 | −0.9321 | −0.8680 | −0.8190 |
| weeks-worked equation | (0.0381) | (0.0248) | (0.0461) | (0.0543) |
| Standard error weeks- | 24.5215 | 23.3751 | 25.1452 | 24.0463 |
| worked equation | (0.7192) | (0.6595) | (0.8119) | (0.7394) |
| Likelihood value | −6243.7689 | −6435.9659 | −6598.4836 | −7607.7185 |
| Sample size total | 4100 | 3885 | 3864 | 4100 |
| Number with weeks worked | 1406 | 1545 | 1811 | 2150 |

[a]These equations pertain to the probability of *not* being in school in *both* the October beginning the year and the following October.

[b]Standard errors in parentheses.

### 9.2.4  Weeks Worked

Estimates of the parameters in the weeks-worked equations are shown in table 9.8. The most significant finding is that hours worked while in high school bear a substantial relationship to weeks worked per year in the years immediately following high school graduation. The estimated coefficients corresponding to hours-worked intervals in high school are reproduced in table 9.10 below. As can be seen in table 9.8, they are measured with considerable precision. Recall that they represent an upper bound on the effect of high school work. They are slightly larger than the estimated effect of high school hours worked on expected weeks worked, evaluated at $X\beta$ close to zero. As the expected value of $Y$ rises, and thus the expected value of weeks worked, the marginal effect of hours worked in high school falls. Indeed, as the expected number of weeks worked approaches fifty-two, the marginal effect of a change in any variable declines and must ultimately approach zero.

To give an idea of the magnitude of the decline, we have evaluated the estimated effects of high school work at two additional points. One is the expected value of weeks worked evaluated at the mean of $X$ for all persons in the sample, whether they were in fact in the labor force or in school. These values are shown in the second portion of table 9.10. In addition, the expected value of weeks worked is shown for each year, along with an "adjustment factor." The adjustment factor indicates the multiple by which the estimates in the first portion of the table must be multiplied to get the estimates in the second portion.[21] The other evaluation point is the mean of $X$ for persons who were in the labor force and is conditional on knowing that they were. The estimated effect on weeks worked over the four year period is shown in the last column.

Estimates of the $\beta$ coefficients on hours worked range from zero for hours between 1 and 5 to over 12 for hours greater than 30. Even in the fourth year, the estimated values of $\beta$ are very large, ranging from 3 for the fewest hours category to over 8 for the largest. It is notable that after four years the relationship of even a little work in high school to work after high school is substantial. Over the four-year period, the sum of the estimates ranges continuously upward from 6 weeks to 37 weeks.

Expected weeks worked per year evaluated at the mean of the right-hand variables averaged over all persons in the sample is about 47 weeks in each of the four years. Even at this level, the estimated relationship to work in high school is very large. The average over the four years of the effect of working between 16 and 20 hours per week is about 1.5 weeks per year. For persons who worked over 30 hours, the average of the estimated effects is almost 3 weeks per year. The sums of the effects for the four years range from 2 to 11 weeks.

Possibly the most intuitively meaningful results pertain to persons who did in fact choose to work rather than go to school. Expected weeks

**Table 9.10**

| Hours worked in high school | Estimated effect on weeks worked | | | | |
|---|---|---|---|---|---|
| | 1973 | 1974 | 1975 | 1976 | Total |
| | Effect at zero weeks worked (estimate of $\beta$) | | | | |
| 1 to 5 | 0.17 | 1.12 | 0.90 | 3.42 | 5.61 |
| 6 to 10 | 2.50 | 2.27 | 0.41 | 3.05 | 8.23 |
| 11 to 15 | 7.36 | 1.77 | 4.05 | 4.45 | 17.63 |
| 16 to 20 | 6.82 | 4.27 | 5.92 | 6.55 | 23.56 |
| 21 to 25 | 7.85 | 5.15 | 4.25 | 7.31 | 24.56 |
| 26 to 30 | 10.97 | 6.13 | 5.96 | 7.17 | 30.23 |
| over 30 | 12.52 | 7.68 | 8.99 | 8.16 | 37.35 |
| | Effect at mean of $X$ in total sample | | | | |
| Expected weeks | 47.20 | 47.26 | 47.36 | 47.04 | — |
| Adjustment factor | 0.270 | 0.287 | 0.270 | 0.297 | — |
| 1 to 5 | 0.06 | 0.32 | 0.24 | 1.02 | 1.64 |
| 6 to 10 | 0.68 | 0.65 | 0.11 | 0.91 | 2.35 |
| 11 to 15 | 1.99 | 0.51 | 1.09 | 1.32 | 4.91 |
| 16 to 20 | 1.84 | 1.22 | 1.60 | 1.95 | 6.61 |
| 21 to 25 | 2.12 | 1.48 | 1.15 | 2.17 | 6.92 |
| 26 to 30 | 2.96 | 1.76 | 1.61 | 2.13 | 8.46 |
| over 30 | 3.38 | 2.20 | 2.43 | 2.42 | 10.43 |
| | Effect at mean of $X$ for persons in labor force | | | | |
| Expected weeks | 44.17 | 43.26 | 44.42 | 44.41 | — |
| Adjustment factor | 0.484 | 0.567 | 0.461 | 0.458 | — |
| 1 to 5 | 0.08 | 0.64 | 0.41 | 1.57 | 2.70 |
| 6 to 10 | 1.21 | 1.29 | 0.19 | 1.40 | 4.09 |
| 11 to 15 | 3.56 | 1.00 | 1.87 | 2.04 | 8.47 |
| 16 to 20 | 3.30 | 2.42 | 2.73 | 3.00 | 11.45 |
| 21 to 25 | 3.80 | 2.92 | 1.96 | 3.35 | 12.03 |
| 26 to 30 | 5.31 | 3.48 | 2.75 | 3.28 | 14.82 |
| over 30 | 6.06 | 4.35 | 4.14 | 3.74 | 18.29 |

worked evaluated at the mean of $X$ over persons observed to be in the labor force is about 44 weeks in each of the four years. The sums of the effects over the four years range from almost 3 to close to 18 weeks. Sixteen to twenty hours of work in high school is associated with an average of almost 3 weeks per year in weeks worked during the four years after graduation.

Estimates of the marginal relationship between hours worked in high school and weeks worked, evaluated at any other expected value of weeks worked, can be obtained by multiplying the numbers in the top portion of table 9.10 by the appropriate adjustment factor. For example, the appropriate multiple when the expected value of weeks worked [$E(y)$] is thirty is approximately .86 in each of the four years.[22]

How to interpret this finding is open to question. It is possible that persons who work in high school *gain* skills and other attributes, through their work, that give them an advantage in the labor market after graduation. Demand may be greater for them than for persons who do not work. This is consistent with the finding that wage rates are also higher for persons who work in high school, although the relationship is not nearly as strong as that between weeks worked and work in high school. But we might expect such an advantage to diminish over time as post-high school experience becomes an increasingly larger proportion of total experience. And although the estimated effect declines somewhat, it is still very important four years after graduation. This suggests that working in high school may be an indication of personal characteristics not gained through work, but leading to work in high school as well as greater labor force participation following graduation. That is, it is not that the demand is greater for persons who work in high school, but that these persons have a greater propensity to work. That wage rates are not so greatly affected by high school work seems to add to the evidence for this interpretation.

Even this latter interpretation, however, would not rule out the possibility that work experience while in high school, for persons like those in our sample who did not work, would increase their employment after high school. Working may in fact enhance in these persons attributes that were associated with high school work of persons in our sample. And, as we shall see below, work experience while in high school may increase subsequent wage rates in much the same way that work experience upon graduation increases later wage rates in the labor market.

It is informative to consider these findings and the possible interpretations of them in conjunction with the relationship between work in high school and other school and family characteristics. We shall return to that after some discussion of some of the other results shown in table 9.8.

Class rank in high school is strongly related to weeks worked in *each* of the four post-high school years. The estimates indicate that a 50-point increase in class rank is associated with an increase of about 10 in the expected value of $Y$, or say 3 in the expected value of weeks worked, over the total sample. This result is based on holding constant the test score. The test score appears to measure a combination of aptitude and achievement. No matter what the interpretation of test score, conditional on holding it constant, class rank is likely to reflect effort directed to doing well in high school. Effort in school, like the characteristic reflected in high school work, is related to later labor force participation at least for the next four years. Both hours worked and class rank may capture what is sometimes referred to as the "work ethic." Those who work harder in high school also work more in subsequent years. Or, those who become accustomed to working at a young age maintain the habit. Or, if they have or develop early in life characteristics associated with working, they maintain them.

We also find that high test scores are associated with more employment after graduation, but the effect diminishes over the four years following graduation. An increase of one standard deviation—about .4—in the sum of the test scores is associated with a one-and-a-half-week increase in expected weeks worked in the first year and declines continuously to about one week in the fourth. It may be that persons with greater ability or achievement, as reflected in the test scores, have an advantage in the labor market, but as time goes on the skills that are associated with the test scores are in part compensated for by skills developed on the job or elsewhere. That their effect diminishes over time suggests that the reason is not entirely a permanent underlying individual characteristic. (The wage equation estimates suggest some advantage to higher test scores, but there is no distinct time pattern.)

We could find no measure of high school vocational or industrial training that was significantly related to employment or wage rates after graduation. The variable included in the results in table 9.8 is high school training for a particular job. We assumed that if any high school training mattered, this training should. It doesn't. We experimented with many other measures of job related training—semesters of various vocational courses, academic versus nonacademic tracking, and others. We found none that was related to subsequent employment. It could be that the least able are directed to vocational training courses or are self-selected into them. But our results are conditional on controlling for traditional measures of school performance: class rank and test scores. This cannot be interpreted to mean that no training matters; but it does indicate strongly that none of the training in current high school curriculums, or at least that training systematically measured in the survey, is related to later labor force participation after high school. We were not able to distinguish vocational high schools from others. In subsequent work we will. It is possible that the effect of training in a vocational high school is different from the effect of training received in schools whose curriculums are not primarily directed to job training.

Nonwhites are employed about the same number of weeks per year as whites during the first years following high school graduation. The differences between the expected value of weeks worked for nonwhites and whites, evaluated at the mean of $X$ in the sample, are $-.52$, $.05$, $.11$, and $-.29$ respectively in the first four years following high school graduation. None is significantly different from zero by standard criteria. Remember that these results are partial effects after controlling for other variables, unlike the summary statistics in the first section of the chapter. (The simple averages in table 9.6 indicate fewer weeks worked by nonwhites than whites during the first two years after high school, but little difference in the third and almost none in the last.) The wage estimates below indicate that after controlling for other variables, wage rates of whites and nonwhites are quite close in the first three October periods, and that in the last two that nonwhites earn about 4% more per hour than whites.

| Variable | Coefficient | Standard error |
|---|---|---|
| Test Score Total | −2.81 | (0.92) |
| Race | −5.33 | (0.87) |
| Parents' Income | 0.22 | (0.07) |
| Education of Mother | | |
| Less than High School | 0.49 | (0.69) |
| Education of Mother | | |
| College Degree or More | −0.85 | (1.51) |
| Education of Father | | |
| Less than High School | 0.36 | (0.68) |
| Education of Father | | |
| College Degree or More | −1.58 | (1.28) |
| Class Rank in High School | 0.01 | (0.01) |
| Job Training during | | |
| High School | 0.37 | (0.66) |
| Extracurricular Participation | | |
| in High School | 0.51 | (0.29) |

The averages in table 9.5 indicate whites and nonwhites who are not in school have very similar weekly earnings and hours worked as well as similar wages.

Parents' income bears a substantial positive relationship to weeks worked during each of the first four years after graduation. In the first year, an increase in parental income of $5,000—about a standard deviation—is associated with an increase in weeks worked of over three weeks. The relevant coefficient declines over time to about half of its original size by the fourth year. If children whose parents have higher-paying jobs have an advantage in finding work, the advantage apparently diminishes as the youth cohort gains labor market experience.

In sum, the most important determinants of weeks worked seemed to be characteristics associated with effort pursuant to succeeding in high school, as measured by class rank after controlling for ability, and to effort devoted to outside work while in high school, this last characteristic being particularly significant. It may be informative therefore to consider the relationship between hours of work while in high school and other personal and family characteristics.

For descriptive purposes, we have obtained coefficient estimates from a least-squares regression of hours worked per week on several variables. The coefficients and standard errors pertaining to the variables of most interest are listed above.[23] There are two groups of variables: one that can be interpreted as composed of predetermined personal and family characteristics, the second composed of measures of the individuals' high school experience other than hours worked while in high school. There does not seem to be a substantial trade-off between any of these latter measures and hours worked. For example, working does not seem to take the place of studying, as reflected in class rank after controlling for test scores. Comparable results were found by Griliches (1977).

Race is the only variable that stands out. Nonwhites work considerably less in high school than whites, given the measures of parents' income and education. This may result either from differences between the two groups in job opportunities, or from differences in work habits, or some combination of the two. Whatever the reason, five hours less work in high school is associated with a maximum of about 1.5 fewer weeks worked in the years following graduation, according to the weeks-worked results. Recall that after controlling for hours worked in high school as well as other variables, nonwhites work about the same number of weeks per year as whites.

In addition, persons with higher test scores work a bit less and those with higher parents' income a bit more. (The standard deviation of test scores is .4 and of parents' income is 5.7 in thousands.) The latter may result from more job possibilities if one's parents have better jobs, or it may reflect cultural differences related to income. Possibly persons with higher test scores, given class rank, foresee a greater probability of going to college and thus are somewhat less inclined to take jobs in high school. This is consistent with the school nonattendance results.

Thus we have in hours worked in high school a personal characteristic that is somewhat related to race, to test scores, and to parents' income.[24] But after controlling for these variables, hours worked in high school are strongly related to weeks worked after graduation. Hours worked capture an individual attribute that is not simply a reflection of other personal and family socioeconomic characteristics; they reflect a largely independent personal attribute that persists over time.

We shall mention briefly the effects of the remaining variables in table 9.9. The estimated effect of on-the-job training is always positive, but it declines over time. This result may be due to training agreements or employment expectations that lead to training for persons who expect to continue in the same job, or whom employers expect to continue. The effect might be expected to die out over time as persons are increasingly likely to have changed jobs.

Persons living in urban areas are employed less than others. According to our imprecise estimates, the maximum negative effect is 2.2 weeks; in the last year when a larger proportion of those working are college graduates the estimated urban effect is in fact positive, although not significantly different from zero. College graduates may have relatively greater work opportunities in urban areas. As expected, state unemployment is negatively related to the employment of youths. Roughly speaking, if the unemployment rate increases by a percentage point, expected weeks worked by these youths fall by about half a week, about one percent of the mean value of weeks worked. The higher the state wage as we have measured it, the lower the number of weeks worked by youths.[25]

Finally, for each year our procedure estimates the correlation between the random term in the weeks-worked equation and the random term in the probability of school nonattendance equation. They are reported for each year in the last section of table 9.9. Recall that a zero correlation coefficient indicates no sample selection bias. Our estimates (and standard errors) for the four consecutive years are $-.93$ (.03), $-.93$ (.02), $-.87$ (.05) and $-.82$ (.05). That is, in each year unmeasured determinants of college *attendance* bear a very strong positive relationship to unmeasured determinants of weeks worked. Holding constant the variables we have measured, persons who choose to go to school would work more if they are in the labor force than those who choose not to go to school after high school. The relationship is very striking. The results seem to indicate that the motivations or drives that characterize persons who continue their education are also attributes that are related to increased employment given school nonattendance. In practice, correction for sample selection by estimating jointly weeks worked and the probability of school nonattendance increases substantially the estimated coefficients on class rank, test scores, and parents' income, but yields coefficients on the other variables that are close to tobit results. For purposes of comparison, weeks-worked parameter estimates by method of estimation are presented in appendix table 9A.1.

We have not in this specification of weeks worked included a schooling variable. One might suppose, however, that if the probability of school attendance in a given year is positively related to the number of weeks a person would work if he were in the labor force, then the number of years of schooling prior to a given year would also be likely to affect weeks worked in that year if a person were in the labor force. When prior schooling is included in the weeks-worked equations, however, its effect is not significantly different from zero, even with prior schooling also included in the sample selection equation. This suggests that the large correlation between unmeasured determinants of school attendance and measured determinants of weeks worked reflects the difference between persons who attend school for several years after high school graduation—possibly long enough to obtain a degree—and those who don't. Apparently, persons who move in and out of school during the first four years after graduation are in this respect much like persons who don't attend school at all.

### 9.2.5   Wage Rates

The wage rate parameter estimates are reported in table 9.11. Some have been referred to already. Work experience in high school is positively related to post-high school wage rates as well as to weeks worked. In general, during the last four periods, persons who worked in high school earned roughly 5 to 9% more per hour than those who didn't. Thus not only are additional hours of work in high school associated with additional weeks worked after graduation, but with higher earnings per hour as well. But although there is an increasing relationship between the number of hours worked in high school and weeks worked later, given five or ten hours per week, additional hours in high school are not associated with increments in wage rates until high school hours exceed thirty per week.[26] For these reasons, we have used only three high school work intervals instead of the seven used in the weeks-worked equations.

To evaluate the relationship between hours worked in high school and annual earnings, we need to consider the association between high school work and both weeks worked and the wage rate. (We have not considered the possible effect on hours worked per week.) In addition, according to our specification, the marginal effect of any variable on weeks worked depends on the number of weeks worked at which the marginal effect is evaluated (see pages 295 and 305). Consider, for example, persons in the labor force who otherwise—if not for high school work experience—would have worked forty-four weeks per year. This is approximately the average number of weeks worked by persons who were in the labor force (see page 305). According to our estimates, those who worked between sixteen and twenty hours in high school earned about 12% more than those who didn't work at all in high school. Persons who worked over thirty hours earned about 18% more. The effect could be much greater for persons who would otherwise work less. For example, consider persons who would work only thirty weeks per year. Those who worked sixteen to twenty hours in high school would earn about 25% more than those who didn't work at all. Those who worked more than thirty hours would earn about 35% more. These latter figures should be considered only as suggestive because the estimates do not allow interactions among the variables and therefore imply substantial extrapolation based on estimated coefficients. Nonetheless, the relationship between earnings and work in high school is certainly large even for persons who are working most of the time and is probably much larger for persons who, based on other characteristics, would work much less.

As with weeks worked, it seems likely that at least part of the effect results from personal characteristics associated with or developed through high school work as distinct from later work. If higher wage rates were the result simply of the additional experience or associated acquired skills, one would expect both to be dominated eventually by post-high school work experience and the estimated effect to decline over time.[27] Note that the estimated coefficients on high school work do not simply reflect the fact that persons who work while in high school also are

**Table 9.11**      Estimates of Wage Equation Parameters by Year[a,b]

| Variable | October 1972 | October 1973 | October 1974 | October 1975 | October 1976 |
|---|---|---|---|---|---|
| Hours worked during high school | | | | | |
|   1 to 15 | 0.0446 | 0.0593 | 0.0627 | 0.0446 | 0.0610 |
| | (0.0297) | (0.0294) | (0.0255) | (0.0274) | (0.0238) |
|   16 to 30 | −0.0127 | 0.0407 | 0.0209 | 0.0637 | 0.0411 |
| | (0.0284) | (0.0252) | (0.0244) | (0.0250) | (0.0209) |
|   31 or more | 0.0202 | 0.0971 | 0.0541 | 0.0876 | 0.0904 |
| | (0.0342) | (0.0293) | (0.0284) | (0.0287) | (0.0251) |
| Class rank in | 0.0011 | 0.0013 | 0.0009 | 0.0007 | 0.0008 |
|   high school | (0.0009) | (0.0006) | (0.0006) | (0.0006) | (0.0004) |
| Test score total | 0.0294 | 0.1002 | 0.0363 | 0.0529 | 0.0996 |
| | (0.0358) | (0.0351) | (0.0300) | (0.0325) | (0.0271) |
| Job training during | −0.0272 | −0.0481 | −0.0152 | −0.0221 | 0.0196 |
|   high school | (0.0297) | (0.0266) | (0.0257) | (0.0236) | (0.0215) |
| Race | 0.0164 | 0.0160 | 0.0078 | 0.0479 | 0.0431 |
| | (0.0322) | (0.0287) | (0.0256) | (0.0297) | (0.0272) |
| Parents' income | 0.0095 | 0.0077 | 0.0113 | 0.0101 | 0.0083 |
| | (0.0026) | (0.0022) | (0.0021) | (0.0021) | (0.0019) |
| Dependents | 0.0221 | 0.0306 | 0.0336 | 0.0318 | 0.0326 |
| | (0.0143) | (0.0131) | (0.0109) | (0.0120) | (0.0091) |
| On-the-job | — | 0.0012 | 0.0021 | 0.0041 | 0.0060 |
|   training months | | (0.0041) | (0.0023) | (0.0026) | (0.0022) |
| School years | — | 0.0735 | 0.0547 | 0.0433 | 0.0166 |
| | | (0.0429) | (0.0247) | (0.0202) | (0.0082) |
| Experience: | | | | | |
|   First year | — | 0.1266 | 0.0997 | 0.0540 | 0.0385 |
|   (1972–73) | | (0.0471) | (0.0323) | (0.0307) | (0.0219) |
|   Second year | — | — | 0.0741 | 0.1055 | 0.0275 |
|   (1973–74) | | | (0.0345) | (0.0330) | (0.0231) |
|   Third year | — | — | — | 0.1168 | 0.0602 |
|   (1974–75) | | | | (0.0289) | (0.0239) |
|   Fourth year | — | — | — | — | 0.0513 |
|   (1975–76) | | | | | (0.0247) |
| Part-time working | −0.0141 | 0.0762 | −0.0961 | 0.0045 | −0.1456 |
| | (0.0242) | (0.0280) | (0.0344) | (0.0317) | (0.0305) |
| Rural | 0.0101 | −0.0287 | −0.0542 | −0.0029 | −0.0514 |
| | (0.0238) | (0.0208) | (0.0210) | (0.0220) | (0.0193) |
| West | −0.0153 | −0.0301 | −0.0014 | 0.0950 | 0.0814 |
| | (0.0242) | (0.0237) | (0.0218) | (0.0234) | (0.0213) |
| State wage | 0.0582 | 0.1218 | 0.0885 | 0.0855 | 0.0775 |
| | (0.0209) | (0.0174) | (0.0147) | (0.0145) | (0.0111) |
| Test score missing | 0.0713 | 0.2851 | 0.1144 | 0.2148 | 0.3366 |
| | (0.1072) | (0.1032) | (0.0887) | (0.1003) | (0.0856) |
| Class rank missing | 0.0106 | 0.0215 | 0.0181 | 0.0053 | 0.0361 |
| | (0.0438) | (0.0378) | (0.0383) | (0.0388) | (0.0326) |

**Table 9.11** (continued)

| Variable | October 1972 | October 1973 | October 1974 | October 1975 | October 1976 |
|---|---|---|---|---|---|
| Parents' income missing | 0.0896 | 0.0720 | 0.0891 | 0.1192 | 0.0786 |
| | (0.0399) | (0.0364) | (0.0331) | (0.0368) | (0.0305) |
| Experience missing | — | 0.0549 | 0.0408 | 0.0786 | 0.0275 |
| | | (0.0484) | (0.0335) | (0.0277) | (0.0204) |
| Constant | 0.5374 | 0.1421 | 0.5558 | 0.4187 | 0.4897 |
| | (0.1108) | (0.1165) | (0.1115) | (0.1288) | (0.0981) |

[a]The data pertain to the first full week in October of each year.
[b]Standard errors in parentheses.

employed more upon graduation and thus have higher wage rates because of more accumulated post-high school experience. The measured effect of high school experience is in addition to work experience after high school, also included in the equations.

Test scores and class rank are also positively related to wage rates. The effect of class rank seems to diminish somewhat with time, but the test score coefficients follow no apparent pattern. A standard deviation increase in the test scores total is associated with an average of estimated wage rate increases over the five periods of about 3%. The corresponding class rank effect is about 2 or 3%. The total effect of a standard deviation increase in both would be something like 5 or 6%. Together these measures may be assumed to represent some combination of academic aptitude, academic achievement, and academic success. Controlling for test score, class rank may also reflect effort in school comparable to hours worked as a measure of effort outside of school, as discussed in the section above on weeks worked. Any one of these attributes would presumably increase productivity per unit of time.

While traditional measures of academic success are positively related to wage rates, as are attributes associated with actual work experience in high school, high school training, which is presumably closely directed to the development of job skills, is not. The estimated coefficients on job training during high school are not significantly different from zero. This suggests that time taken from academic courses and devoted instead to job training has a negligible effect on future wage rates. If high school training contributes to the development of job-related skills, they are at least offset by the loss in traditional academic training related to job performance. It is also possible that persons who are relatively poor academic performers and would be relatively poor job performers are self-selected into job-training courses in high school. But, as mentioned above, our estimates are conditional on class rank and test scores, possibly the most common measures of high school performance.

One might suppose that the effect of high school training would be greater for persons who left school after high school graduation than for those who obtained further education. Vocational training, for example, may be more important in jobs filled by high school graduates than in those typically filled by college graduates. Our wage data for 1972 include only high school graduates; for that year the coefficient on high school training is negative but not statistically different from zero. In subsequent years, the sample with observed wage rates includes high school graduates as well as those with more education. Thus for 1974 and 1976 we reestimated the equations for high school graduates only; the coefficients on high school training were positive for each of these years but not statistically different from zero by standard criteria.[28]

While nonwhites worked about the same number of weeks as whites after controlling for other variables (table 9.8), the wage rates of nonwhites are a bit higher than those of whites, according to our estimates. The coefficient on race is positive in each of the five periods and significantly different from zero by standard criteria in the last two periods. In the fourth and fifth time periods, nonwhites are estimated to earn about 4% more per hour than whites. (The summary statistics in tables 9.5 and 9.6 show that the average wage rates of nonwhites were slightly lower than the white averages in all but the first period and that nonwhites worked somewhat fewer weeks per year than whites in each year, not controlling for other variables.)

Parents' income has a substantial effect on wage rates. An increase of $10,000 in parents' income is associated with an increase in wage rates of 8 to 12%. It may be that children of wealthier parents have different skills, values, or ambitions from those from poorer families. And, presumably, wealthier parents are able to find, or help to find, better paying jobs for their children. The preponderance of young persons say that their jobs were found through family contacts or through friends. The effect of this benefit as reflected in wage rates seems not to decline much over our five periods; the advantage is maintained for at least these first four years.[29] Recall that the positive relationship between parents' income and weeks worked declined over time.

Persons with dependents not only are employed more, but earn more per hour as well—approximately 3% per dependent in each period. This may result from greater pressure to find higher paying jobs, as well as to work more. Persons without dependents may be more willing to accept lower wages, at least temporarily, possibly while looking for another job.

On-the-job training does not yield appreciably higher wage rates during the first year or two after high school. But after that, when training has presumably paid off in better jobs, the effect shows up. By the fifth time period, the return to a year of on-the-job training is estimated to be

7.2%.[30] In the second, third, and fourth periods the estimated returns are 1.4, 2.5, and 6.1% respectively.

While the estimated effect of on-the-job training increases over time, our estimates suggest a decline over time in the return to years of post-secondary schooling. The estimates shown were obtained using nominal years of schooling.[31] As explained in section 9.2, these estimates should be expected to be biased. Indeed, the positive relationship between the unobserved determinants of wage rates and school attendance, together with the positive correlation among the wage disturbance (discussed in the next section), imply that the estimates are biased upward.[32] In the second, third, fourth, and fifth time periods—one, two, three, and four years after high school graduation—the schooling coefficients imply returns of 7.4, 5.5, 4.3 and 1.7% respectively. The results for the last period may be somewhat confounded because college graduates just entering the labor force are included in the sample. College graduates are likely to be in jobs with wage structures substantially different from persons without college degrees. There may not have been enough time for a college degree to pay off in terms of progression up the hierarchy associated with higher-level jobs.[33] In addition, the result may reflect declines in the return to college education.[34]

The estimated returns to experience are substantially greater than to schooling during these first years following high school graduation.[35] Unlike the effect of hours worked in high school, the effect of early experience on later wage rates declines according to this specification. For example, a year of experience during the first year after graduation is associated with a 13% increase in wage rates in the second time period (the second October after graduation). The effect declines to 10% by the third, 6% by the fourth, and 4% by the fifth period. In general, the effect on wage rates of recent experience is greater than the effect of earlier experience. Relative to the second, third, and fourth time periods—for which experience is relevant—the estimated effect of previous experience in the last time period is quite low, 4% for experience during the first two years and 5 or 6% for experience in the third and fourth years. Lest this pattern of results be taken too literally, we hasten to add two qualifications. The first is that the relative effect of experience across the time periods is dependent in part on changes in aggregate market conditions over the time period. Experience during the recession years is likely to have contributed less to earnings than experience in more expansive years. These results are of course determined in part by changes in aggregate market conditions over the 1972 to 1976 time period.[36]

Second, the specification as shown distinguishes experience by calendar year, but not by the number of years since leaving school. Thus, for example, experience in the "second year" may represent experience during the second year in the labor force for some persons, but during the first year in the labor force for others—those who went to school for one year after high school and then entered the labor force. We tried two other formulations to check the sensitivity of the results to changes in specification. For 1974 we distinguished a separate experience variable for each possible schooling/labor force sequence. Thus for persons who did not go to school after high school we allowed one experience variable for the first year in the labor force and another for experience in the second; these estimates (and standard errors) were .062 (.051) and .071 (.059) respectively. For persons who went to school the first year and entered the labor force the second, the coefficient on this first year of experience was .034 (.037). For those who were in the labor force the first year but went to school the second, the coefficient on the first year of experience was .042 (.059).

As mentioned above, for 1974 and 1976 we also estimated wage equations for persons with no post-secondary education. (Of course, persons in the sample in 1972 had no education past high school.) For this group, the estimated experience coefficients for 1974 were .116 (.057) and .134 (.074) respectively, as compared with .100 (.032) and .074 (.035) in table 9.11. For 1976, the coefficients were measured very imprecisely but tended to be somewhat larger than those shown in the table. Thus it seems clear that early experience affects later wage rates. The precise patterns of the effects shift with the sample and the specification although the differences are not statistically significant. Finally, we noted above that vocational training in high school was not significantly different from zero, even for persons with no post-secondary education. These estimates for 1974 and 1976 do reveal, however, that work experience in high school has a somewhat greater effect on wage rates for persons who got no further education than for the group as a whole.

The effect of experience as well as other variables is of course reflected in the small difference between the average wage rates of whites and nonwhites shown in table 9.5. For example, the average wage rate for whites is about 6% higher than for nonwhites in 1976. Our estimated coefficient on race for 1976 implies that nonwhites earn about 4% more than whites after controlling for other variables. But nonwhites work fewer weeks than whites in each year, as shown in table 9.6. Using these differences, the effect of fewer weeks worked per year on nonwhite wages would be about 1.3% in 1976, according to the estimated coefficients on experience in that year.

We also find that while part-time workers do not receive lower wages than full-time workers immediately after graduation, they do a few years later. By 1976, part-time workers were earning 15% less per hour than those working full time. It is likely that part-time jobs are less likely to be characterized by ladder movement and associated wage increases than full-time ones. This may not affect initial wage rates much, but would after some time when many full-time workers would have moved up the ladder.

We experimented with several regional and residential location variables. Only a rural indicator and an indicator for the western region are included in the specification shown. After controlling for an average state wage measure, none of the other controls for aggregate market conditions affected youth wages.

We will not comment on the "school nonattendance" estimates in table 9.12. They are essentially comparable to those in table 9.9 that were discussed above.

At the bottom of table 9.12, however, are shown the estimates of the correlations between the wage rate and school nonattendance disturbances. As in the weeks-worked results, we find a positive correlation between unmeasured determinants of school attendance and the disturbances in the wage rate equations, although the relevant correlations are much smaller. Thus, according to our results, persons who go to school, if they are working, earn more than those who in fact elect to work, even if the two groups of individuals have the same measured characteristics. The estimated correlation is .21 in 1972 and then rises to .36 in 1973. After that, they decline rather evenly to .19 in 1976. It is reasonable to expect them to decline as more and more persons enter the labor force after having been in school for one or more years.

### 9.3   The Persistence of Early Labor Force Experience

Early labor force experience may be related to later experience for at least four reasons: (1) Measured attributes of individuals are similar from period to period. For example, we have found that persons from wealthy families earn more per hour than those from poor families. And that persons with higher academic aptitude or measured achievement command higher wage rates than those with lower scores. (2) Some unmeasured attributes of individuals persist over time and are related to labor force experience. This reason is often referred to as heterogeneity. How much youths are helped by their families, for example, or difficult to define characteristics like motivation, may fall into this category. (3) Random factors that affect labor force experience, although not constant over time, may be related from one time period to the next. The fortunes or misfortunes of a large firm in a small town may be an example. (4) Finally, labor force experience due to random occurrences or shifts in exogenous variables in one period may affect outcomes in later periods. This possibility is often referred to as state dependence.[37]

The first of these reasons we have analyzed in section 9.2. The last three are the subject of this section, although we will not be able to distinguish each of them from all the others. Our analysis will concentrate on inferences that can be drawn from relationships among the distur-

**Table 9.12    Estimates of School Nonattendance Equation Parameters by Year (Estimated with Wage Equations)[a]**

| Variable | October 1972 | October 1973 | October 1974 | October 1975 | October 1976 |
|---|---|---|---|---|---|
| Test scores total | -0.4809 | -0.5913 | -0.6648 | -0.5853 | -0.5618 |
| | (0.0697) | (0.0757) | (0.0774) | (0.0790) | (0.0818) |
| Class rank in high school | -0.0160 | -0.0145 | -0.0136 | -0.0134 | -0.0083 |
| | (0.0011) | (0.0011) | (0.0011) | (0.0011) | (0.0011) |
| Race | -0.3242 | -0.2732 | -0.2534 | -0.3473 | -0.3863 |
| | (0.0705) | (0.0765) | (0.0797) | (0.0814) | (0.0831) |
| Parents' income | -0.0209 | -0.0201 | -0.0151 | -0.0201 | -0.0153 |
| | (0.0054) | (0.0057) | (0.0056) | (0.0057) | (0.0058) |
| Education of mother less than high school | 0.1406 | 0.2221 | -0.0123 | -0.0087 | -0.0019 |
| | (0.0563) | (0.0619) | (0.0641) | (0.0653) | (0.0690) |
| Education of mother college degree or more | -0.2725 | -0.0607 | -0.1357 | -0.2226 | -0.1247 |
| | (0.0911) | (0.0812) | (0.0840) | (0.0835) | (0.0808) |
| Education of father less than high school | 0.2712 | 0.2179 | 0.2848 | 0.3237 | 0.1985 |
| | (0.0549) | (0.0588) | (0.0621) | (0.0640) | (0.0670) |
| Education of father college degree or more | -0.2385 | -0.2521 | -0.3495 | -0.3798 | -0.3068 |
| | (0.0778) | (0.0735) | (0.0742) | (0.0742) | (0.0702) |
| Hours worked during high school | 0.1184 | 0.0998 | 0.1147 | 0.0786 | 0.0710 |
| | (0.0199) | (0.0209) | (0.0214) | (0.0220) | (0.0219) |
| Job training during high school | 0.4921 | 0.5072 | 0.4238 | 0.3498 | 0.1924 |
| | (0.0576) | (0.0655) | (0.0708) | (0.0721) | (0.0748) |

| | | | | |
|---|---|---|---|---|
| Rural | 0.1195 | 0.1157 | 0.3155 | 0.2781 | 0.3078 |
| | (0.0597) | (0.0632) | (0.0646) | (0.0676) | (0.0692) |
| Urban | −0.0605 | −0.0747 | 0.0450 | 0.0520 | −0.0817 |
| | (0.0551) | (0.0570) | (0.0576) | (0.0580) | (0.0582) |
| State wage | 0.1520 | 0.0815 | 0.0288 | −0.0311 | 0.0029 |
| | (0.0443) | (0.0447) | (0.0424) | (0.0388) | (0.0352) |
| Test score missing | −1.3909 | −1.7156 | −1.9021 | −1.7546 | −1.7570 |
| | (0.2196) | (0.2393) | (0.2499) | (0.2542) | (0.2666) |
| Class rank missing | −0.6499 | −0.4990 | −0.5336 | −0.5836 | −0.3744 |
| | (0.0960) | (0.1041) | (0.1043) | (0.1094) | (0.1133) |
| Parents' income missing | −0.2448 | −0.2928 | −0.2539 | −0.3713 | −0.2019 |
| | (0.0891) | (0.0944) | (0.0972) | (0.1021) | (0.1026) |
| Constant | 1.1362 | 1.9271 | 2.4743 | 2.7925 | 2.6646 |
| | (0.2678) | (0.2945) | (0.3024) | (0.3086) | (0.3146) |
| Correlation with wage equation | −0.2115 | −0.3610 | −0.3557 | −0.1932 | −0.1937 |
| | (0.1633) | (0.1414) | (0.1233) | (0.1416) | (0.1641) |
| Variance of wage error | 0.3542 | 0.3496 | 0.3509 | 0.3649 | 0.3482 |
| | (0.0100) | (0.0127) | (0.0102) | (0.0076) | (0.0070) |
| Likelihood value | −2538.7109 | −2321.7729 | −2354.3789 | −2441.3557 | −2444.0023 |
| Sample size total | 4000 | 3400 | 3300 | 3200 | 3100 |
| Number with wage | 1402 | 1489 | 1659 | 1728 | 2070 |

[a]Standard errors in parentheses.

bance terms in the wage equations and from relationships among nominal weeks worked, as well as disturbances from the weeks-worked equations. Because we have estimated weeks-worked and wage equations separately for each year, and because we have obtained wage equation estimates allowing for sample selection and weeks-worked equations allowing for both sample selection and a limit of fifty-two weeks, it is cumbersome to estimate unconditional correlations among the population disturbances, as specified in equations (1) and (5), for example. It is not straightforward to use the residuals because the independent variable is observed only for persons not in school and in the case of weeks worked because the independent variable is limited. For simplicity we will limit our discussion to the relationships over time, conditional on being in the labor force. This allows a rather straightforward variance components description of the structure of the correlations among the wage disturbances. We will consider them first. In addition to the variance components decomposition, we have used another method to describe the relationships among weeks worked over time. We will consider them second.[38]

For the wage rate disturbances we will be able to distinguish persistence over time due to heterogeneity from that caused by the last two reasons listed above. But we will not formally be able to distinguish the third from the fourth, that is, serial correlation from state dependence as they are interpreted here. What will show up as serial correlation in our analysis could result from what we would like to distinguish as state dependence. But we will be able to say something about the possible magnitude of a state-dependence effect. Because our analysis relies primarily on inferences based on the estimated correlations (or covariances) among the disturbances, we will not give much attention to the subsequent effects of changes in labor force experience due to shifts in exogenous variables in earlier periods (included under our fourth reason).[39]

Although subsequent analysis will use estimated covariance terms, it is informative to look first at estimates of the correlations between the disturbances in the wage equations.[40] They are reproduced below, together with a correlation matrix of the logarithm of nominal wages.[41]

Correlation Matrix of Disturbances
in the Wage Equations

| October '72 | 1 | | | | |
|---|---|---|---|---|---|
| October '73 | .538 | 1 | | | |
| October '74 | .304 | .505 | 1 | | |
| October '75 | .287 | .373 | .569 | 1 | |
| October '76 | .282 | .412 | .519 | .727 | 1 |

Correlation Matrix of the Logarithm
of Nominal Wages

October '72  1
October '73  .563     1
October '74  .342     .544    1
October '75  .323     .411    .590    1
October '76  .329     .458    .558    .752    1

The pattern of correlations suggests that unmeasured influences on wage rates are to a large degree temporary ones that do not persist from early to later years. The correlation between the first and the fifth wage disturbances is only .282. The correlations also suggest increasing consistency over time. For example, the correlation between the first and second disturbances is .538, but .727 between the fourth and the fifth. The correlations drop rapidly with increases in the time interval between periods. This can be seen by a glance at the last row of the correlation matrix, where the correlations between the last year's disturbance and those for prior years are recorded. Whatever the cause of the observed persistence, it declines rapidly over time to a floor of about .3. (As we will see in a moment, that can be attributed to persistent individual specific characteristics.) A casual comparison of the correlations suggests that the effect of individual specific characteristics on wage rates is dominated by random components that are serially correlated. We shall be more precise about that.

Suppose that the wage equation disturbances can be decomposed into individual specific and random terms. Let each disturbance be written as

$$\varepsilon_{ti} = u_i + e_{ti}$$

where $u$ is an individual specific term, presumed to persist over the period of our data, and $e$ is a random term. Suppose that the variance of $u$ over individuals is $\sigma_u^2$ and the variance of $e$, allowed to differ from period to period, is given by $\sigma_t^2$. Also, assume that the terms $e_{ti}$ follow a first order auto regressive process. Then the variances among the disturbances can be written as:

$$\sigma_{11} = \sigma_u^2 + \sigma_1^2$$
$$\sigma_{12} = \sigma_u^2 + \rho\sigma_1^2$$
$$\sigma_{13} = \sigma_u^2 + \rho^2\sigma_1^2$$
$$\sigma_{14} = \sigma_u^2 + \rho^3\sigma_1^2$$
$$\sigma_{22} = \sigma_u^2 + \sigma_2^2$$
$$\sigma_{23} = \sigma_u^2 + \rho\sigma_2^2$$
$$\sigma_{24} = \sigma_u^2 + \rho^2\sigma_2^2$$

$$\sigma_{33} = \sigma_u^2 + \sigma_3^2$$
$$\sigma_{34} = \sigma_u^2 + \rho\sigma_3^2$$
$$\sigma_{44} = \sigma_u^2 + \sigma_4^2$$

We have estimates of the $\sigma_{ij}$ based on residuals from the equations estimated above. Using a maximum likelihood procedure, we fitted these estimates to the specification just described. That is, we estimated $\sigma_u^2$, $\rho$, $\sigma_1^2, \ldots, \sigma_4^2$.[42] There are several special cases of this more general model. We shall mention two. One is obtained by supposing that the random components are not serially correlated, so that $\rho$ is zero. (This would of course rule out state dependence.) In this case, all the covariances would be equal. The corresponding correlations would be the same, except to the extent that the variances of the random terms differ. The second constrains $\sigma_u^2$ to be zero; it rules out heterogeneity. Then the correlations between disturbances one period apart are given by $\rho\sqrt{\sigma_t^2}/\sqrt{\sigma_{t+1}^2}$, and for two periods apart by $\rho^2\sqrt{\sigma_t^2}/\sqrt{\sigma_{t+2}^2}$, etc. If the random term variances are equal, the correlations become $\rho$, $\rho^2$, etc.

Estimates of the components of variance for the wage disturbances, based on the unconstrained model, are recorded below.

### Components of Variance Estimates and Standard Errors for the Wage Rate Covariance Structure[43]

| | | |
|---|---|---|
| Individual specific variance, $\sigma_u^2$ | 0.032 | (0.009) |
| Random variance, period 1, $\sigma_1^2$ | 0.089 | (0.013) |
| Random variance, period 2, $\sigma_2^2$ | 0.086 | (0.008) |
| Random variance, period 3, $\sigma_3^2$ | 0.093 | (0.013) |
| Random variance, period 4, $\sigma_4^2$ | 0.107 | (0.012) |
| Random variance, period 5, $\sigma_5^2$ | 0.090 | (0.013) |
| Serial correlation coefficient, $\rho$ | 0.454 | (0.082) |

We have also estimated a components of variance specification of the wage disturbances with the random component variances constrained to be equal. The results are as follows:

### Constrained Components of Variance Estimates and Standard Errors for the Wage Rate Covariance Structure

| | | |
|---|---|---|
| Individual specific variance | 0.034 | (0.009) |
| Random variance | 0.091 | (0.009) |
| Serial correlation coefficient, $\rho$ | 0.430 | (0.090) |

They suggest the same general conclusions as those based on the unconstrained model, although we reject the hypothesis of equal variances. It is clear that both individual specific and random terms are important determinants of variance. These estimates suggest that between 23 and 27% of the error variances can be ascribed to individual specific characteristics that persist over the five time periods. The bulk of the variance, however, remains in the additive random terms. Those random terms are correlated over time. The estimated serial correlation coefficient in the unconstrained model is .454. We conclude that whatever the cause of this correlation over time, its effect is not lasting. The estimated effect of serial correlation on the aggregate correlations in the matrix above declines rapidly. Ignoring differences in random term variances, without the individual specific terms the estimated correlations between the disturbances one, two, three, and four periods apart would be .454, .206, .094, and .042 respectively.[44]

Thus we conclude that whatever causal effect there may be of early wage rate experience on later wage rates, it does not last very long; it is essentially absent after four or five years.

The correlations among the weeks-worked disturbances for persons not in school are shown in the first tabulation below. The correlations among nominal weeks worked are shown in the second.[45]

Correlation Matrix of Weeks-
Worked Disturbances

| | | | | |
|---|---|---|---|---|
| October '72 to October '73 | 1 | | | |
| October '73 to October '74 | .351 | 1 | | |
| October '74 to October '75 | .240 | .333 | 1 | |
| October '75 to October '76 | .170 | .270 | .640 | 1 |

Correlation Matrix of Weeks Worked

| | | | | |
|---|---|---|---|---|
| October '72 to October '73 | 1 | | | |
| October '73 to October '74 | .394 | 1 | | |
| October '74 to October '75 | .285 | .373 | 1 | |
| October '75 to October '76 | .196 | .302 | .655 | 1 |

For comparison with the results for the wage disturbances, we fit the same variance components specification to the weeks worked residual covariance structure. The results are as follows:

Components of Variance Estimates and Standard
Errors for the Weeks Worked Covariance Structure

| | | |
|---|---|---|
| Individual specific variance, $\sigma_u^2$ | 26.19 | (19.14) |
| Random variance, period 1, $\sigma_1^2$ | 130.52 | (26.76) |
| Random variance, period 2, $\sigma_2^2$ | 125.52 | (16.84) |
| Random variance, period 3, $\sigma_3^2$ | 139.74 | (25.60) |
| Random variance, period 4, $\sigma_4^2$ | 128.04 | (26.48) |
| Serial correlation coefficient, $\rho$ | .343 | (.133) |

The estimates are quite similar to those pertaining to the wage disturbances, although the proportion of variance due to individual specific terms is smaller—between 16 and 18% depending on the year. As with the wage disturbances, without individual specific terms, the correlations among the errors would be quite small. Ignoring differences in random term variances, the implied correlations one, two, and three periods apart are .343, .118, and .040 respectively. Thus, whatever the reasons for the correlation over time—including a possible state dependence effect—it is not lasting. These results based on weeks worked residuals are similar to those obtained for wage disturbances.

But in this case, the disturbances, like nominal weeks worked, are limited by the upper bound on total weeks worked. In practice, the estimated correlations are not affected much by the truncation of weeks worked. Correlation matrices of nominal weeks worked, and of weeks worked disturbances, based only on observations with weeks worked less than fifty-two, are very close to those presented above. Nonetheless we found it more informative to describe relationships among weeks worked through a series of transition matrices, than to describe the relationship by an estimated components of variance structure. Our procedure was the following.

For each year we classified weeks worked into four intervals: 0 to 20, 21 to 40, 41 to 51, and 52. For each pair of years we calculated the transition probabilities of moving from an interval in the earlier year to each of the intervals in the second year. These are presented in figure 9.2 with the entries shown as percentages. For example, the matrix headed "1974–75" in the middle of the table says that 71% of the persons who worked 52 weeks in 1974 also worked 52 weeks in 1975; 4% worked between 0 and 20 weeks. The numbers below and to the left of each matrix are marginal proportions (percentages). All entries have been rounded to the nearest percentage.

The figure can also be used to calculate for each pair of years the joint probability of each of the interval combinations. For example, the matrix headed "1973–76" in the lower left of the figure says that 1% of the 892 persons who were not in school in both 1973 and 1976 worked less than 20 weeks in each of those years (13% of 8%).

Recall that some persistence over time is due to measured attributes of individuals that are similar from one period to the next. The slightly higher correlations among annual weeks worked than among the weeks-worked residuals reflects the effect of these variables. It can be seen from the matrices above, however, that this difference is small. Only a small proportion of the variance in weeks worked is explained by measured individual attributes. The transition matrices in figure 9.2 present a blowup of the information contained in the nominal weeks-worked correlation matrix. Thus persistence is somewhat higher than that due to unobserved components alone, but not much.

1973–74

```
30  24  23  24
11  35  33  21
 2  12  42  43
 4   8  26  62

 7  16  32  45
              N = 1045
```

| 1973–75 | 1974–75 | Weeks Worked Interval |

```
1973-75                          1974-75                      Weeks Worked
                                                              Interval
27  27  16  30           7   31  27  15  27                    0 to 20
 9  25  25  41          18   15  29  21  35                   21 to 40
 6  12  29  53          32    6  14  34  46                   41 to 51
 6   8  19  66          44    4   8  18  71                      52

 8  14  23  54               8  15  23  54
              N = 868                     N = 1164
```

```
1973-76                  1974-76                      1975-76

13  26  20  41     7   24  24  20  32      8    50  33   9   8
13  24  23  40    17   14  25  22  39     15    12  40  22  26
 4  15  29  53    32    5  15  35  46     25     3  13  61  23
 5   8  22  65    44    4   8  20  68     53     1   5  11  83

 7  15  24  54         7  14  25  53             7  14  24  54
              N = 892                N = 1093                  N = 1581
```

**Fig. 9.2** Transition Probabilities (Percentage) by Weeks-worked Interval for Each Two-year Combination, 1973–76

The transition matrices reveal several phenomena. The upper bound on weeks worked is reflected in the large probabilities of remaining in the fifty-two week "interval" from one period to the next, much larger than for any other interval. This is apparently because many persons who work fifty-two weeks are indeed constrained by this limit. Any who "would work" fifty-two weeks or more are observed to remain at the limit. Even persons observed to work fifty-two weeks in one year may still be at fifty-two weeks in the second even if their "unobserved propensity" to work declined between the two time periods. From the diagonal matrices it can be seen that those who remain at the limit for consecutive years increases from 62% between the first and the second to 83% between the third and the fourth.

Persistence in general increases over time, as can be seen from a comparison of the diagonal elements of the three diagonal matrices. For example, 30% of persons who are in the lowest interval in the first year are also in that interval in the second. But 50% of those who are in this interval in the third year are also there in the fourth. Apparently individual patterns become increasingly established.[46]

While experience in the fourth year seems strongly related to that in the third, the relationship between experience in the last year and earlier years declines rapidly with increasingly distant time periods. This pattern can be seen best by looking at the last row of matrices for 1976. Of persons in the four intervals in 1975; 50, 12, 3, and 1% respectively are in the lowest interval in 1976. Of persons in the four intervals in 1973, the corresponding percentages are 13, 13, 4, and 5. Whereas the likelihood that a person who was in the lowest interval in 1975 was also there in 1976 was 50 times as high as if he worked 52 weeks in 1975; if he were in the lowest interval in 1973, the likelihood of being in the lowest interval in 1976 was only about 2.5 times as high as if he had worked 52 weeks in 1973. These numbers are consistent with the simple correlations among weeks worked.

The numbers of persons who remain in the lowest intervals also can be inferred directly from figure 9.2. For example, 1% of persons who were not in school in both the first and the last year worked 20 weeks or less in each of the years.

We conclude, as with wage rates, that whatever the determinants of weeks worked, they do not for the most part persist over these four years. Recall that a small part of the relationship seen in the transition matrices is due to measured individual attributes. They are not distinguished in the matrices from unmeasured individual attributes, individual specific terms commonly referred to as representing heterogeneity. Both measured and unmeasured individual specific characteristics produce some persistence over time. (The proportion of the residual variance due to individual specific terms, implied by the "residual" covariance matrix, was presented above.) The remainder of the relationship over time may be due to a true state-dependence effect or to serial correlation induced by correlation over time of other factors that affect weeks worked. Whatever the reason, however, there seems to be very little room for a state dependence effect of labor force experience in the first year on experience in the last. Any effect there may be dies out rapidly.

As youngsters age their patterns of labor force experience become increasingly stable, as we might expect to find among persons moving from full-time school to full-time work, a process that is likely to involve considerable searching, job changing, and the like before settling into more or less permanent employment.[47]

Unmeasured determinants of wage rates in the early periods show little relationship to unmeasured determinants in later years. Unmeasured determinants of weeks worked in the earliest period show little relationship to those in the last. There is, however, a dependence between the two. As shown in table 9.11, experience in earlier years does affect wage rates in later years.[48]

## 9.4 Summary and Conclusion

We have used the National Longitudinal Study of 1972 High School Seniors to analyze the relationship between high school preparation and other personal characteristics on the one hand and early labor force experience on the other.

In general, the data do not suggest to us severe employment problems for this sample of high school graduates. There are very few persons who are chronically out of school and unemployed. Estimated unemployment rates are moderate and employment ratios high. The implications that we draw from these data are at variance with those based on the Current Population Survey data, which suggest substantially higher unemployment rates for high school graduates and considerably lower employment ratios.

Average wage rates of employed whites and nonwhites who are not in school are very similar. Wage equation estimates reveal that, after controlling for other variables, nonwhites earn slightly more per hour than whites. But average weeks worked per year are less for nonwhites than whites although annual weeks-worked equations that control for other variables indicate that nonwhites are employed about as many weeks per year as whites with similar characteristics. At the same time, nonwhites are more likely than whites to be in school; controlling for other variables, the probability of being in school is at least .10 higher for nonwhites in each of five periods covering four post-high school years.

Although traditional measures of academic success—standardized test scores and class rank—are related to employment and wage rates following high school, measures of vocational and industrial training are not. Training presumably directed toward job-related tasks does not enhance post-high school labor force experience, but attributes associated with traditional measures of academic success do.

Hours of work while in high school are very strongly related to weeks worked in particular and also to wage rates in each of the four years following graduation. An additional five hours of work per week in high school, at least up to 20, is associated with as much as 1.5 more weeks worked per year in each of the four post-high school years. The evidence suggests that this is due to individual attributes associated with working while in high school; these attributes may or may not be developed by this experience. Together with the effect on the hourly wage rate, the effect on earnings is quite substantial. This suggests to us that training only, without the attributes associated with work effort and or doing well in school, will not increase one's chances in the labor force. On the other hand, on-the-job training after high school is associated with higher wage rates. Possibly none of these findings should be especially surprising. They reinforce the frequently mentioned claim that ill-defined attributes associated with working hard and "doing well," perhaps the work ethic, are important determinants of labor force "success." This idea seems to come through strongly in our statistical results.

The results should not be interpreted to mean that vocational training will not help persons do jobs better. It seems to us more likely that the kinds of training in current high school curriculums do not. On-the-job training, for example, does have a significant effect on later wage rates. This is, of course, training combined with work. We were unable to distinguish training in vocational high schools from training in other high schools. Vocational high schools may provide better training and attract different kinds of students. More detailed investigation could reveal particular types of students for whom high school vocational training does enhance subsequent labor force experiences. We will pursue both of these possibilities in future research. It may also be that selection and tracking mechanisms in high school channel those least likely to succeed, either in or out of school, into nonacademic courses. Our results, however, are conditional on test scores and class rank, both common measures of high school performance.

Finally, we addressed the question of persistence over time of early labor force experience. An important question is whether or not early realized experience itself, after controlling for individual characteristics of persons, has an effect on later experience. Is there a "state dependence" effect? Our analysis suggests that if there is such an effect, it does not last long. There seems to be almost no relationship of this kind between weeks worked during the first year after high school graduation and weeks worked four years later. That is, we find no relationship other than that due to individual specific attributes. And random fluctuations in wage rates in the first year or two, resulting from nonindividual specific attributes, have almost no relationship to wages three or four years later. Thus our findings do not motivate or increase concern that there may be something intrinsically damaging about particular kinds of early labor force experience. After controlling for measured characteristics of individuals, we cannot identify a lasting effect of initial realized employment on later employment or of initial realized wage rates on later wage rates. We do find, however, that early weeks worked have an effect on wage rates; but even this effect may be rather small after four years.

Although early random fluctuations in weeks worked have little effect on later weeks worked and early random fluctuations in wages little effect on later wages, our results show a distinct trend of greater consistency between one year and the next as persons age. Employment patterns in the third year, for example, are much more likely to carry over to the fourth than are first-year patterns to carry over to the second. We find a concomitant increasing wage penalty associated with part-time work as persons age.

Along with the lasting relationship between high school work experience and later wage rates, as well as employment, we find that the effect of weeks worked in the first year after graduation has a substantial effect on wage rates in subsequent years, although the effect may decline over time.

There are three distinct findings here and we will put them all together. First, the estimated "effects" of high school work experience on weeks worked and wage rates after high school are about the same over the four post-high school years. Second, the effect of early post-high school weeks worked on wage rates in subsequent years is substantial but may decline over time, with weeks worked in the most recent year being more important than experience in earlier years in the determination of current wages. Third, we find no lasting effect of nonindividual specific random disturbances in early post-high school weeks worked on weeks worked in later years. And there is no lasting effect of nonindividual specific random disturbances in initial wage rates on later wages, although weeks worked in early years have an effect on later wage rates, as the second finding describes.

Thus our findings suggest, albeit indirectly, that to prepare persons for the labor force, programs that emphasize work experience for youths may be the most likely to succeed. Indirectly, they suggest that the concern that low-level or dead-end jobs will hinder subsequent labor market performance is likely to be misplaced. Even though we cannot be sure that the characteristics of those who now work in high school will be gained by those who don't, should future generations of them be got to work, the weight of our evidence is that it offers the best chance of enhancing future labor market experience. Certainly our evidence suggests that it should be given precedence over specific job training in high school. If there is a second priority, our evidence suggests that general academic preparation has a greater payoff than current high school vocational training.

## Appendix: Estimation

Consider the weeks-worked and the school nonattendance equations—given in equations (5) and (2) in the text—for any one of the four annual time periods:

$$y_i = \begin{cases} Y_i = X_i\beta + \varepsilon_i & \text{if } X_i\beta + \varepsilon_i \leq 52, \\ 52 & \text{if } X_i\beta + \varepsilon_i > 52, \end{cases}$$

$$S_i = Z_i\delta + \eta_i, \text{ with}$$

$$s_i = \begin{cases} 1 \text{ if } S_i \geq 0, \\ 0 \text{ if } S_i < 0, \text{ and} \end{cases}$$

$$\begin{bmatrix} Y_i \\ S_i \end{bmatrix} \sim N \left[ \begin{pmatrix} X_i\beta \\ Z_i\delta \end{pmatrix}, \begin{pmatrix} \sigma^2 & \rho\sigma \\ & 1 \end{pmatrix} \right]$$

where lower case $y_i$ is observed weeks worked and capital $Y_i$ is the unobserved propensity to work and $\rho$ is the correlation between $Y_i$ and $S_i$.

There are three possibilities: individual $i$ is in school so that $S_i < 0$; he is not in school and is working less than fifty-two weeks so that $S_i > 0$ and $y_i$ is observed with $y_i < 52$; he is not in school and is working fifty-two weeks so that $S_i > 0$ and $y_i = 52$. The probabilities of these outcomes, given $X_i$ and $Z_i$, are represented respectively by:

(1)    $$Pr(S_i < 0) = 1 - \Phi[Z_i\delta] = P_{1i}$$

(2)    $Pr(S_i > 0$ and $y_i$ observed, with $y_i < 52)$

$$= Pr(S_i > 0 | Y_i)f(Y_i)$$

$$= \Phi\left[\frac{Z_i\delta + \frac{\rho}{\sigma}(y_i - X_i\beta)}{\sqrt{1 - \rho^2}}\right] \cdot \frac{1}{\sigma}\phi\left(\frac{y_i - X_i\beta}{\sigma}\right),$$

$$= P_{2i}$$

(3)    $Pr(S_i > 0$ and $y_i = 52)$

$$= Pr(S_i > 0 \text{ and } Y_i > 52)$$

$$= Pr(\eta_i < Z_i\delta \text{ and } \varepsilon_i < X_i\beta - 52)$$

$$= \int_{-\infty}^{Z_i\delta} \int_{-\infty}^{X_i\beta - 52} f(\eta_i, \varepsilon_i)d\varepsilon_i d\eta_i$$

$$= \Phi[Z_i\delta, (X_i\beta - 52)/\sigma; \rho]$$

where $f$ is a bivariate normal density function and $\Phi$ must now be interpreted as a standardized bivariate normal distribution function with correlation parameter $\rho$. The log-likelihood function for the complete sample of observations is given by

$$L = \sum_i^{N1} \ln P_{1i} + \sum_i^{N2} \ln P_{2i} + \sum_i^{N3} \ln P_{3i}$$

where the three summations distinguish the groups corresponding to the three possible outcomes. This likelihood function is maximized to obtain estimates of $\beta$, $\delta$, $\sigma$, and $\rho$.

There are three expectations that it is useful to distinguish, together with the derivatives with respect to the variables $x$. They are given by:

(1)    $$E(Y | X) = X\beta$$

(2)    $$E(y | X) = Pr(Y \geq 52) \cdot 52 + Pr(Y < 52) \cdot E(Y | Y < 52)$$

$$= \left\{1 - \Phi\left[\frac{52 - X\beta}{\sigma}\right]\right\} \cdot 52$$

$$+ \Phi\left[\frac{52 - X\beta}{\sigma}\right] \cdot X\beta - \sigma\phi\left(\frac{52 - X\beta}{\sigma}\right)$$

(3)

$$E(y \mid X \text{ and } s = 1) = \frac{Pr(Y \geq 52, s = 1) \cdot 52}{Pr(s = 1)}$$

$$+ \frac{Pr(Y < 52, s = 1)}{Pr(s = 1)} \cdot E(Y \mid Y < 52, s = 1),$$

$$= \frac{\Phi[Zi\delta, (Xi\beta - 52)/\sigma; f]}{\Phi[Zi\delta]} \cdot 52$$

$$+ \frac{\Phi[Zi\delta, (52 - Xi\beta)/\sigma; -f]}{\Phi[Zi\delta]} \cdot E(Y \mid Y < 52, s = 1).$$

The derivatives of the expected values with respect to $X_j$ are given by:

(a)    $\partial E(Y \mid X)/\partial X_j = \beta_j$

(b)    $\partial E(y \mid X)/\partial X_j = \beta_j \cdot \Phi\left[\dfrac{52 - X\beta}{\sigma}\right]$

Recall that our maximum likelihood procedure estimates $\beta_j$. The derivative of the expected value of observed weeks worked is given by $\beta_j$ times the probability that $Y$ is less than 52. At $X\beta = 0$, this derivative is approximately equal to $\beta_j$ in our sample $\Phi[52/\sigma]$ is close to 1. It is informative to evaluate the derivative $b$ at say the mean of $X$. In our sample, $E(y \mid \bar{X})$ is about 43 weeks. Thus the derivative of $y$ at this point gives a reasonable indication of the effect of a change in an $X$ value when $y$ is approaching its maximum. Comparable adjustments can be made for persons who elect not to go to school.

The wage specification prescribes only two possible outcomes, analogous to the first two presented above for weeks worked. An individual is either not in the sample with a measured wage ("in school") so that $S_i < 0$ and $W_i$ is observed. These probabilities are given by:

(1)    $Pr(S_i < 0) = 1 - \Phi[Z_i\delta]$

(2)    $Pr(S_i > 0)$ and $W_i$ observed) $[= Pr(S_i > 0 \mid W_i) f(W_i)$

$$= \Phi\left[\frac{Z_i\delta + \frac{\rho}{\sigma}(W_i - X_i\beta)}{\sqrt{1 - \rho^2}}\right] \cdot \frac{1}{\sigma}\phi\left(\frac{W_i - X_i\beta}{\sigma}\right)$$

where $\sigma$ here is the standard deviation of $W_i$ given $X_i$ and $W_i$ represents the right-hand side variables in the wage equation, not all of which correspond to those in the weeks-worked equation. The likelihood function is formed as above. Maximization of its yields estimates of $\beta$, $\delta$, $\rho$, and $\sigma$.

**Table 9A.1**  **Estimates of Weeks-worked Equation Parameters for 1973 by Method of Estimation[a,b]**

| Variable | Tobit *with* sample selection, persons not in school[a] | Tobit *without* sample selection, persons not in school | Least squares, persons not in school | Least squares, persons in school |
|---|---|---|---|---|
| Hours worked during high school | | | | |
| 1 to 5 | 0.1700 | 0.4522 | 1.0774 | 4.3217 |
| | (1.1629) | (1.9881) | (1.2973) | (1.0991) |
| 6 to 10 | 2.5027 | 2.8743 | 2.8273 | 4.9857 |
| | (1.1893) | (2.0018) | (1.2663) | (1.1254) |
| 11 to 15 | 7.3619 | 7.6174 | 5.5637 | 9.1454 |
| | (1.3896) | (2.2155) | (1.3636) | (1.2168) |
| 16 to 20 | 6.8180 | 7.5513 | 5.8188 | 11.2879 |
| | (1.1109) | (1.8405) | (1.1591) | (1.0926) |
| 21 to 25 | 7.8500 | 8.1490 | 6.2343 | 11.1932 |
| | (1.2329) | (1.9460) | (1.1950) | (1.1718) |
| 26 to 30 | 10.9685 | 12.3107 | 8.9362 | 12.7374 |
| | (1.3189) | (2.0724) | (1.2203) | (1.3088) |
| 31 or more | 12.5225 | 13.8282 | 9.1276 | 13.4815 |
| | (1.1273) | (1.6996) | (1.0468) | (1.1888) |
| Class rank in high school | 0.2323 | 0.0205 | −0.0176 | −0.0709 |
| | (0.0267) | (0.0258) | (0.0151) | (0.0147) |
| Test score total | 12.1144 | 2.8301 | 2.4563 | −1.0417 |
| | (1.4197) | (1.5196) | (0.9271) | (1.0616) |
| Job training during high school | −1.4376 | 0.8732 | 1.3674 | 2.8242 |
| | (0.7151) | (1.1221) | (0.6967) | (1.0530) |
| Race | −1.9184 | −4.2791 | −3.4954 | −3.8434 |
| | (1.3714) | (1.3949) | (0.9061) | (1.0742) |
| Parents' income | 0.6370 | −0.0120 | −0.0615 | −0.3025 |
| | (0.1168) | (0.1179) | (0.0730) | (0.0673) |
| Dependents | 4.2551 | 2.8608 | 1.8077 | 3.1252 |
| | (0.5997) | (0.7401) | (0.5091) | (0.8161) |
| On-the-job training years | — | — | — | — |
| Rural | −2.5912 | −0.7243 | −0.3656 | 2.0630 |
| | (0.9628) | (1.3676) | (0.8149) | (1.0417) |
| Urban | −1.4913 | −2.1929 | −1.2437 | 0.5384 |
| | (0.8016) | (1.1968) | (0.7210) | (0.6827) |
| State wage | −2.1755 | −0.0931 | 0.1629 | 1.6083 |
| | (0.9391) | (1.0075) | (0.5938) | (0.6341) |
| State unemployment | −1.0645 | −1.4112 | −0.9576 | −0.0160 |
| | (0.4069) | (0.4399) | (0.2604) | (0.2551) |

**Table 9A.1** (continued)

| Variable | Tobit *with* sample selection, persons not in school[a] | Tobit *without* sample selection, persons not in school | Least squares, persons not in school | Least squares, persons in school |
|---|---|---|---|---|
| | | Method of estimation | | |
| Test score missing | 33.0777 | 6.6222 | 5.9033 | −3.3432 |
| | (4.3147) | (4.4468) | (2.8358) | (3.5306) |
| Class rank missing | 10.1779 | 1.9033 | −0.3888 | −2.4658 |
| | (1.9191) | (1.8276) | (1.2259) | (1.5017) |
| Parents' income missing | 6.6426 | 0.4868 | −0.7339 | −4.6648 |
| | (1.7567) | (1.7427) | (1.0865) | (1.2153) |
| Constant | 27.2947 | 40.2316 | — | — |
| | (5.3019) | (5.8471) | | |

[a]Reproduced from table 9.8, October 1972 to October 1973.
[b]Standard errors in parentheses.

**Table 9A.2**      **Means and Standard Deviations of Variables**

| Variable | Mean | Standard deviation | Sample[a] |
|---|---|---|---|
| Hours worked during high school: | | | |
| 1 to 5 | 0.088 | 0.2832 | A |
| 6 to 10 | 0.113 | 0.3161 | A |
| 11 to 15 | 0.083 | 0.2763 | A |
| 16 to 20 | 0.127 | 0.3335 | A |
| 21 to 25 | 0.127 | 0.3324 | A |
| 26 to 30 | 0.110 | 0.3132 | A |
| 31 or more | 0.191 | 0.3929 | A |
| Class rank in high school | 35.833 | 25.8589 | A |
| Test score total | 2.677 | 0.8367 | A |
| Job training during high school | 0.232 | 0.4219 | A |
| Race | 0.162 | 0.3683 | A |
| Parents' income | 8.846 | 5.8960 | A |
| Dependents | 0.604 | 0.7817 | A |
| On-the-job training weeks | 1.337 | 3.0180 | A |
| Rural | 0.266 | 0.4416 | A |
| Urban | 0.290 | 0.4539 | A |
| State wage | 4.814 | 0.6820 | A |
| State unemployment | 8.359 | 1.9841 | A |
| Education of mother less than high school | 0.259 | 0.4380 | B |
| Education of mother college degree or more | 0.117 | 0.3209 | B |
| Education of father less than high school | 0.325 | 0.4684 | B |
| Education of father college degree or more | 0.190 | 0.3923 | B |
| Experience: | | | |
| First year (1972–73) | 0.509 | 0.4532 | C |
| Second year (1973–74) | 0.584 | 0.4471 | C |
| Third year (1974–75) | 0.730 | 0.3852 | C |
| Fourth year (1975–76) | 0.830 | 0.3003 | C |

[a]The statistics in this table were calculated from the data used in estimating the 1975–76 weeks-worked model and the 1976 wage model. The particular sample used in calculating the mean and standard deviation of each variable is indicated by A, B, or C.

A: Persons working and used in estimation of the 1975–76 weeks-worked equation, 2150 observations.

B: Persons used in estimation of the school attendance equation estimated in conjunction with the 1975–76 weeks-worked equation, 3100 observations.

C: Persons used in estimation of the 1976 wage equation, 2070 observations.

# Notes

1. For more detail, see Levinsohn et al. (1978).
2. The number is in fact .068.
3. In appendix table 9A.1, we have presented an example of estimates for persons in school. For some parameter estimates, differences between the two groups are substantial.
4. We can give a behavioral interpretation to this model by supposing that in each year $t$ each individual attaches some value $U_{t0}$ to going to school and some value $U_{i1}$ to staying out of school. The values may depend, for example, on the expected effect of each of the choices on future earnings. Suppose that both $U_{t0}$ and $U_{t1}$ depend on individual characteristics $z_t$ and random terms $e$ so that $U_{t0} = z_t b_{t0} + e_{t0}$ and $U_{t1} = z_t b_{t1} + e_{t1}$. Then assume that the no-school alternative is chosen if $U_{t1} - U_{t0} = z_t(b_1 - b_0) + (e_{t1} - e_{t0})$ is greater than zero. If we define $S_t = U_{t1} - U_{t0}$, $Z_t = z_t$, $\delta_t = b_{t1} - b_{t0}$, and $\eta_t = e_{t1} - e_{t0}$, we can attach a random choice model interpretation to the specifications defined in equations (3), (4), and (5), with the individual profit specifications interpreted as yielding reduced form parameter estimates. This is similar to the more elaborate specification used by Willis and Rosen (1978).
5. See, for example, Hausman and Wise (1977). The expected value of $y_i$, given that individual $i$ is in the sample is given by:

$$E(Y_i | s_i = 1) = X_i\beta + \rho\sigma\frac{\phi(Z_i\delta)}{\Phi[Z_i\delta]}$$

6. A maximum likelihood method for doing this is laid out by Hausman and Wise (1977).
7. We have not considered hours worked per week.
8. The expected value of weeks worked is given by $E(y) = Pr(Y > 52) \cdot 52 + Pr(Y < 52) \cdot E(Y | Y < 52)$.
9. This could be done by estimating the four weeks-worked equations jointly with the four sample selection equations. Such a procedure would also yield estimates of the correlations among the random terms in equations (2) and (5), but it also presents substantial computational complexity.
10. Even though we have used only a subsample of the whole data set, to get a given number with "good" weeks-worked data, we have to have a much larger total sample size if only persons never in school are considered to have observations on the $y_t$.
11. By forming for example the appropriate inverse Mills ratio and entering it as a variable in each of the weeks-worked equations.
12. It may be technically inconsistent to use weeks worked while at the same time using the logarithm of wages, since earning is usually assumed to be lognormal. That is,

$$E = Y \cdot H \cdot W, \text{ and } \ln E = \ln Y + \ln H + \ln W$$

where $E$ is annual earnings, $H$ is hours per week, and $W$ is the hourly wage rate. But since our weeks-worked results suggest a slightly better fit using weeks rather than their logarithms, we have reported these results.
13. We predicted the conditional expectation of $S_1$, $S_2$, and $S_3$, given that a person was in the sample. We also predicted the sum of the schooling variables, conditional upon being in the sample.
14. Griliches, Hall, and Hausman (1978) found that corrections for the endogeneity of schooling increased the coefficient for schooling in their wage equation, even after correcting for sample selection. Our attempts to instrument schooling suggested, however, that the schooling coefficients in our model may be biased upward.
15. We experimented with two approaches. One was to include in the no-wage group all persons without a wage, whether they were students or unemployed nonstudents. The status equations in this case are simply sample selection equations; they cannot be interpreted as school attendance equations. The other approach was to eliminate altogether

from consideration nonstudents who were also unemployed in the October period being considered. The status equations may again be interpreted as school attendance equations, but the wage equation estimates are biased to the extent that they are affected by the elimination of unemployed nonstudents. In practice, the two procedures led to very similar wage equation estimates. (In fact, even the estimates in the status equations were affected very little by the selection procedure used.) The results reported below were based on the second method.

16. This is consistent with the findings of Freeman (1978) in a current NBER working paper.

17. The appropriate comparison may be the high school wage versus the wage with additional schooling—say a college degree. But the appropriate high school wage may be local, while the college wage may reflect a national market.

18. For a detailed discussion of the determinants of college going behavior, see Manski and Wise (1978), Radner and Miller (1975), or Kohn, Manski, and Mundell (1974). Work of Manski and Wise currently in progress suggests that blacks, once admitted to schools, are less likely than whites to choose four-year colleges, after controlling for SAT scores, parents' income, and other variables.

19. The estimated effects of hours worked in high school are somewhat lower with than without them and the estimated effects of high school training somewhat lower as well. The school attendance equations estimated with the wage rate equations as shown in table 9.12 include these two variables. Their inclusion in the wage sample selection equation has little effect on the wage equation parameters.

20. More precisely, the estimates indicate a substantial relationship if hours worked exceed 15.

21. For more details, see figure 9.1 and the text discussion of it, and the appendix.

22. $\Phi[52 - X\beta)/\sigma] = \Phi[(52 - 30)/20] = \Phi[1.1] = .8643$, if $X\beta$ is 30 and $\sigma$ is 20. Sigma is close to 20 in each of the four years. For more details see the appendix.

23. The other variables included in the regression are: Number of siblings 0.01 (0.01), State wage $- 1.62$ (0.90), State unemployment $- 0.03$ (0.38), Rural $- 1.87$ (1.03), Town $- 1.85$ (0.99), Urban $- 1.88$ (0.98), South $-0.19$ (1.25), East $- 1.32$ (1.19), West $- 0.55$ (1.38), Test score missing $- 9.37$ (2.76), Class rank missing 0.55 (1.18), and Parents' income missing 1.63 (1.05).

24. Griliches (1977), in an analysis of the Parnes National Longitudinal Survey, as well as National Longitudinal Study data, also found that work in high school was virtually unrelated to family socioeconomic variables.

25. At least in the first two years the estimates are not precisely measured. The state wage may be considered as an instrument for the individual wage. Possibly it is too weakly related to individual wages to pick up any labor supply effect that might be present. A more highly parameterized instrumental variables specification of the model might yield a different result. One interpretation of our results is that the higher the "going" wage the less likely are employers to be willing to fill jobs with youths.

26. Indeed, the estimates imply a relationship that is slightly U-shaped, with hours between 16 and 30 generally associated with slightly lower wage rates than high school hours of either more than 30 or greater than zero but less than 16.

27. Of course, high school work could enhance one's ability to learn from later work experience, and thus a decline in the effect would not necessarily be expected.

28. If the same specification as shown in table 9.11 is used, but with two high school training variables—one for persons with a high school degree only, and a second for persons with post-secondary education—the results are similar; the relevant coefficients are not significantly different from zero for either group.

29. We cannot rule out the possibility that family income captures individual attributes contributing to job performance and associated with income, although we think this is unlikely having controlled for school performance and other characteristics. Wise (1975a,

1975b) found that family background was not related to earnings or performance in a given corporate job setting after individual academic and nonacademic characteristics were controlled for.

30. This is consistent with other estimates of this type. See, for example, Griliches and Mason (1972) or Hausman and Wise (1972). A comparable monthly coefficient in Hausman and Wise, for example, is .0063 versus our estimate of .0060 in 1976.

31. In fact, the number of October time periods that the person was in school.

32. We experimented with the instrumental variable approach described in section 9.2 using the expected value of school in a given year, conditional on being in the labor force in that year. It did indeed yield lower estimates, but because we were not satisfied with the procedure in general, we have reported the uncorrected estimates. In subsequent work, we will set up a more highly specified simultaneous equations model that allows for the simultaneous determination of school and work experience, together with a sample selection equation. Such a system is cumbersome to apply over repeated years when the β parameters are estimated separately for each year. Because this was a primary concern of our analysis, we elected to work with a less complicated specification in this investigation.

33. The increase in salary with experience is generally higher for white collar workers than for blue collar workers.

34. See, for example, Freeman (1976a).

35. If there is an endogeneity bias with respect to experience, its sign is not clear. Because schooling is positively related to the error in the wage equation, and experience is accumulated only if a person is not in school, the estimates would tend to be biased downward. On the other hand, the error in weeks worked is positively related to school attendance. Experience may also be endogenous in that it may be determined in part by past wages and the wage disturbances are correlated over time.

36. And again, there may be some compounding of results because of the entry of recent college graduates in the last time period.

37. Although this terminology is intuitively appealing when there are discrete distinct states that are not artificial divisions of a continuous measure, it may be a misnomer here. Still we will stick with it.

38. A straightforward way to estimate the population covariance is to obtain joint maximum likelihood estimates of the parameters, including a covariance term, for each pair of years. This is expensive when different β parameters are allowed for each year. An easier and less expensive procedure is to use estimates for individual years (like ours) to obtain consistent estimates of the β parameters for each year, and then to use them in a second maximum likelihood stage to estimate covariances, assuming the means implied by the β's from the first stage. On the basis of preliminary analysis, however, we concluded that these alternatives would not change the conclusions that we reach on the basis of covariance estimates conditional on being in the labor force.

These same alternatives could be used to obtain population covariances among the weeks-worked disturbances, with the added complication of the upper limit on weeks. We will pursue this in subsequent work. But as with the wage disturbances, we concluded that the substance of our conclusions would not be changed by a more precise and detailed analysis.

39. For a more detailed analysis of state dependence following a somewhat different procedure, see Ellwood (chapter 10 of this volume). Related analysis is also contained in Brown (chapter 12 of this volume).

40. The correlation for any two periods is based on persons who were in the sample in both periods. The residuals are calculated conditional on being in the sample (not in school).

41. We also calculated a correlation matrix for the logarithm of nominal wages based on the sample of persons who had a recorded wage rate in each period (447 out of 3280 who worked in at least one of the five periods). The correlations are quite close to those shown

here, although the correlations between adjacent years are a bit larger in the later years—.811 between 1975 and 1976—indicating somewhat greater stability after four years than for the sample as a whole. The correlation between 1972 and 1976 is .319, slightly smaller than the one shown in the text.

42. Although our procedure is consistent, it is not efficient. A correct procedure would use a minimum modified $\chi^2$ procedure analogous to generalized least squares. Given our purpose and relatively large sample size, we did not pursue this approach.

43. These are asymptotic standard errors based on the maximum likelihood estimation procedure and the associated information matrix. They should be considered only as illustrative. A more efficient and consistent procedure would take account of the variance-covariance matrix of the initial covariance matrix estimates. Such a procedure is described in Hausman and Wise (1978). Because our original sample is so large, we suspect that the marginal gains from using this procedure would not be great.

44. Recall that if all variation were due to individual specific terms, correlations over time would be one; they would also be one if state dependence were extreme so that persons could not "change states".

45. The correlation matrix of weeks-worked disturbances is based on an earlier set of statistical results that are substantially the same as those reported in table 9.8. A correlation matrix based on nominal weeks worked for persons always in the sample—728 out of 2933 who were not in school in any of the years—reveals no systematic differences from those shown here.

46. These conclusions remain unchanged if the matrices are based only on persons who were not in school in any of the four years.

47. Relationships like those described in this section hold as well for persons who were in the labor force in each of the periods, who had no post-high school training.

48. See greater elaboration on this point in Ellwood (chapter 10 of this volume).

# References

Adams, A. V. and Mangum, G. L. 1978. *The lingering crisis of youth unemployment*. Kalamazoo, Michigan: The W. E. Upjohn Institute for Employment Research.

Brown, C. Dead-end jobs and youth unemployment. Chapter 12 of the present volume.

Bureau of Labor Statistics. 1973. Employment of high school graduates and dropouts October 1972: The high school class of 1972. Special Labor Force Report 155. Washington, D.C.: Bureau of Labor Statistics, Department of Labor.

Ellwood, D. T. Teenage unemployment: Permanent scars or temporary blemishes? Chapter 10 of the present volume.

Freeman, R. B. 1976a. *The overeducated American*. New York: Academic Press, Inc.

_____. 1976b. *Black elite, the new market for highly educated black Americans*. The Carnegie Commission on Higher Education. New York: McGraw-Hill Book Company.

_____. 1978. Black economic progress after 1964: who has gained and why. Cambridge, Massachusetts: National Bureau of Economic Research. Working Paper no. 282.

Freeman, R. B. and Medoff, J. L. Chapter 3 of this volume.

Griliches, Z. 1977. Schooling interruption, work while in school, and the return from schooling. Cambridge, Massachusetts: Harvard Institute of Economic Research, Discussion Paper no. 529.

Griliches, Z., Hall, B., and Hausman, J. A. 1978. Missing data and self-selection in large panels. *Annales de L'Insee* 30–31.

Griliches, Z. and Mason, W. M. 1972. Education, income, and ability. *Journal of Political Economy* 80:74–103.

Hausman, J. A. and Wise, D. A. 1978. AFDC participation: measured variables or unobserved characteristics, permanent or transitory. Working paper.

———. 1979. Attrition bias in experimental and panel data: The Gary income maintenance experiment. *Econometrica* 47, no. 2: 455–73.

Kohn, M., Manski, C., and Mundel, D. 1976. An empirical investigation of factors influencing college-going behavior. *Annals of Economic and Social Measurement*; also Rand Corporation Report, F-1470-NSF, 1974.

Levinsohn, J. R. et al. 1978. *National longitudinal study base year, first, second, and third follow-up data file users manual*, volumes 1 and 2, April 1978. Washington, D.C.: National Center for Education Statistics.

Manski, C. F. and Wise, D. A. 1978. *Experiences of recent high school graduates*. Lexington, Massachusetts: D. C. Heath and Co. Pp. 129–62.

Radner, R. and Miller, L. S. 1975. *Demand and supply in U. S. higher education*. Berkeley; The Carnegie Commission on Higher Education.

Wise, D. A. 1975. Academic achievement and job performance. *The American Economic Review*. June 1975: 350-66.

———. 1975. Personal attributes, job performance, and probability of promotion. *Econometrica* 43 (nos. 5–6):913-31.

## Comment    Frank Levy

I will begin by saying I enjoyed the Meyer and Wise chapter very much. In particular, the authors' presentation of their data and discussion of their methodology make the chapter a pleasure to read. It contains the clearest discussion of the self-selected sample problem I have seen to date. In what follows, I will criticize not so much what the authors did do but what they didn't or couldn't do. This technique—discussing the paper the authors should have written—is normally the height of bad form. It is necessary in this case because the chapter appears not in isolation but in a volume on teenage unemployment.

Frank Levy is a senior research associate at the Urban Institute.

The majority of chapters in this volume are directed to a common underlying question: How seriously should the country regard teenage unemployment rates? As evidenced by the Fedlstein and Elwood chapter (2), the question contains a red herring. Most teenagers are white and when one corrects for macroeconomic conditions, white teenagers, if anything, are doing better over time. Table C9.1 presents aggregate labor force statistics for black and white males and females, ages 16–19, for 1964 and 1978—two years that were roughly comparable in macroeconomic terms.[1] These data indicate that the correct underlying question should be: How seriously should the country regard black teenage unemployment rates? Because Meyer and Wise focus on males, I will do the same.

One's opinion of teenage unemployment depends upon a variety of factors. One of the most important is surely whether or not teenage unemployment indicates the presence of long run-problems. Meyer and Wise answer this question with a "Yes, but . . . " That is, hours worked in high school have a statistically significant and surprisingly long-lived impact on weeks of work in the years after graduation. But these differences take place in a context where levels of unemployment and, in particular, racial differences in those levels are smaller than one might imagine from the Current Population Survey. This context—the general lack of serious problems—is the bottom line of their story and so it bears some scrutiny.

Table C9.2 contrasts two sets of labor force statistics. The first are NLS statistics from Meyer and Wise's table 9.1 for 1975–76, the last year of the sample. In this year most of the NLS young men would have been about 21 years old. The second set of statistics are calculated for 20 and 21 year old young men from the March 1976 Current Population Survey. Both sets refer to young men who are out of school.

In contrast with the NLS, the CPS numbers suggest that things are not so rosy and that black/white differences are relatively large. There are, however, a number of ways to explain the differences.

The first is the exclusion from this NLS sample of persons who did not graduate from high school. The exclusion is important: CPS tabulations for 1976 indicate that among young black men out of school aged 20–24, 27% had less than a high school education. A second factor *may* be the geographic distribution of the NLS sample. Young black men differ from other young race-sex groups by historically showing particularly poor labor market experiences in central cities. In 1976, for example, the CPS shows out-of-school young black men aged 20–24 have an unemployment rate of .27 in central cities and .15 out of central cities. Despite these differences, lower black family incomes are still associated with rural areas and it may be that the NLS sample, in order to find more low income blacks, focused the sample in that direction.[2] Finally, part of the

**Table C9.1**

| | Black males | | | White males | | | Black females | | | White females | | |
|---|---|---|---|---|---|---|---|---|---|---|---|---|
| | *E/P* | *U* | *LFP* | *E/P* | *U* | *LFP* | *E/P* | *U* | *LFP* | *E/P* | *U* | *LFP* |
| 1964 | .33 | .23 | .43 | .38 | .17 | .46 | .16 | .35 | .25 | .30 | .12 | .34 |
| 1978 | .23 | .42 | .40 | .50 | .15 | .59 | .17 | .44 | .31 | .47 | .14 | .55 |

SOURCE: Current Population Survey for March 1964 and March 1978.

**Table C9.2    1976 Labor Force Statistics for Out-of-school Young Men from the NLS and the CPS**

| | NLS (HS graduate only) | | CPS (All men out of school aged 20–21 | |
|---|---|---|---|---|
| | Whites | Blacks | Whites | Blacks |
| *U* | .07 | .08 | .15 | .20 |
| *E/P* | .90 | .97 | .79 | .69 |
| *LFP* | .97 | .95 | .93 | .86 |

SOURCE: Meyer and Wise, table 9.6.

NLS/CPS difference may be accounted for by respondent misreporting (see Freeman and Medoff, chapter 4), but this explanation, to the extent that it is correct, seems more applicable to the level of labor market performance than to black/white differences. To summarize, Meyer and Wise's description of their data as a cohort, particularly for blacks, may not be representative. Correspondingly, smooth movement and serious employment problems can exist simultaneously, though among different subgroups.

The central finding of the Meyer-Wise chapter is the importance of work while in high school on subsequent labor market experience. This finding is surely correct. Analysis of the CPS data indicates that a young adult's labor market performance in a given year is strongly associated with his weeks of work in a preceding year even after his other characteristics are controlled. The question is: How does one interpret such a finding? Meyer and Wise offer two possible interpretations. First, the experience of working may actually impart useful skills to teenagers, general skills that may help teenagers in later market experiences. Alternatively, those who work in high school may be self-selected and have a relatively strong propensity to work even when all other variables are held constant. The first interpretation argues strongly for reorienting vocational programs toward cooperative education and other actual work experiences. The second interpretation weakens the first by assigning positive impact not to work but to the intrinsic (and unobserved) characteristics of persons who work.

In sorting through these competing interpretations, it is worth considering a third interpretation that lies somewhere between them. The hours worked in high school may say something about people who can get work; people who have not only the motivation, but the other attributes that permit them to become employed. Many of these attributes, while uncorrelated with motivation, may be equally unobservable in a typical data tape. As the labor market skews increasingly toward services, for example, a teenager's ability to deal with the public—his style—may become as important as any other factor in his employment prospects.

Trying to separate these hypotheses is important, particularly for young black men. The principal factor behind their deteriorating employment rates contained in table C9.1 is a rapid increase in the unemployment of young black men in school. In 1964, the in-school unemployment rate for young black men was .22, and roughly two out of every ten unemployed black young men aged 16–19 were in school. By 1978, their in-school unemployment rate had risen to .53 (.65 in central city schools), and six out of every ten unemployed young black men were in school. This increase was far in excess of any increases in black school enrollment and it occurred despite their constant level of in-school labor force participation. Changing attitudes and rising transfer payments undoubtedly played some part in these statistics, but common sense suggests the importance of falling demand. Casual discussion with high school pacement officers in Washington, D.C. and in the surrounding suburbs—placement officers who look for part time jobs for students—reinforce the idea that, with respect to job vacancies, the suburbs are a different world. All of this, then, argues in support of Meyer and Wise's principal policy conclusion that within vocational education, more emphasis should be put on finding people jobs. To say this, however, is only to begin the process. Within an inner city vocational education high school, most instructors will readily acknowledge that their courses—e.g., diesel mechanics—are substantially enhanced if the student can get a co-op placement in the same field. But finding such placements is very difficult and it is not clear to me what federal, state, or local government agencies can do to help.[3]

A quick reading of Meyer and Wise might suggest that I pose too hard a problem. They seem to argue strongly that what is important is work per se—bad jobs do not necessarily lead to bad jobs and so any first job will do, whether or not it is involved with the student's field of study. This conclusion cannot be taken too literally. In the first place, the period over which the NLS data was collected saw little federal provision of jobs for in-school youths. Thus most of the work experience recorded in the NLS tapes was private work experience. In the typical private organization, there is a greater tendency to think about costs and assign them to individuals. When a teenager messes up, everybody knows what is lost and the teenager's supervisor takes some heat. Correspondingly, there is a greater incentive for some discipline to be part of the workplace. Such discipline will be present in government projects only insofar as vocal people—people who can create a flap—care about the output that is being produced. Thus, Meyer and Wise's results probably refer to hours of actual work rather than hours of holding a job. Along the same lines, it should be noted that any student who worked an *average* of twenty hours or more per week during the school year was probably not working in just any job. The more menial the job, the more likely it is associated with high turnover and resultant unemployment, either because the employee quits or the employer fires him. These arguments suggest that while government policy should help create work for teenagers, purposeless work may be as bad or worse than no work at all.

While Meyer and Wise's findings on unemployment may be unrepresentative, their findings on wages seem to be correct. When other factors are held constant, racial factors per se exert relatively small influence on hourly earnings. In one sense this is cold comfort, because in life all other things are not held constant. Nonetheless, such results narrow the variables with which policy makers should be concerned.

What, then, is one to conclude? Seven years ago, Anthony Pascal and Leonard Rapping wrote a classic article testing for discrimination in organized baseball.[4] They chose the subject not only because (I assume) they were sports fans, but because baseball, more than most other team sports, is a sum of individual players in which each player has statistics—batting average, fielding average, etc.—that accurately reflect his product. They found that if a black man made it into the big leagues, his characteristics were paid for on the same basis as with white males. But they also found that holding constant all factors except race, a black was much less likely to make it into the big leagues. The labor market for black men today seems to resemble baseball writ large. If a black man finds work, he is likely to be paid on a par with white men with similar characteristics. But the chance that a black man will find work is less than the chances for a similar white and, if anything, seems to be marginally declining. Meyer and Wise have offered one important insight into how that process might be reversed. One can hope it will be utilized in future policy design.

# Notes

1. For example, in 1964 the unemployment rate for all men aged 25–54 was 3.2%. In 1978, the corresponding unemployment rate was 3.4%.

2. In fact, Meyer and Wise do find a negative impact on weeks worked for living in a city, particularly for the sample's early years. This impact arose from a single urban variable,

however, and was probably muted by the fact that whites do not seem to have such central-city problems. Had city residence been allowed to interact with race (or, more appropriately, had separate analyses been done for blacks and whites), a sharper picture would have emerged.

3. In fact, 1978 legislation created substantial federal tax incentives for the employment of low-income young adults, including both full time jobs and co-op placements. Unfortunately, these tax credits have not been widely publicized and so they seem to be known primarily to large-scale employers—e.g., McDonalds—who can afford to scan constantly new federal laws. By contrast, large numbers of small-scale employers, placement counselors, and youths themselves seem to be unaware of the credits.

4. Anthony H. Pascal and Leonard A. Rapping, "The Economics of Racial Discrimination in Organized Baseball" in *Racial Discrimination in Economic Life*, Lexington, 1972.

# Comment    Gary Chamberlain

This very informative chapter carefully presents a great deal of empirical detail. The concluding section of the chapter gives a concise statement of the authors' findings, only some of which will be referred to in my comments. The authors have been particularly aware of problems caused by sample selection bias, and my discussion will focus on the issues raised by their treatment of these problems.

The core of the model is a wage equation, a weeks-worked equation, and an equation for being out of school. The wage equation is estimated jointly with the out-of-school equation; the weeks equation is also (separately) estimated jointly with the out-of-school equation. This procedure is repeated for each of the five years.

The authors are concerned that the regression function for wages (or weeks) conditional on being out of school differs from the regression function that does not make this distinction. This latter regression function corresponds to imputing a wage to the in-school individuals, and then fitting a regression of wages on the current level of schooling and other characteristics for the entire sample. In thinking about this distinction, I found it useful to consider a third regression function, namely, wages on schooling and the other variables, once everyone has finished schooling. As we follow the sample, the authors' procedure will eventually, once everyone is out of school, give a least-squares estimate of this regression function. Then we shall be conditioning on the amount of schooling that the individual eventually attains; the selection of being out of school is roughly that this ultimate level of completed schooling is less than current age minus six. So if we are making inferences conditional on completed schooling and age, no additional conditioning is required; hence there is no sample selection bias.

Gary Chamberlain is associated with the University of Wisconsin at Madison.

For a variety of reasons we might consider schooling to be endogenous and use an instrumental variable estimator on the complete sample. There would then be a sample selection problem if we were to use this estimator on the out-of-school subsample, since an instrumental variable that satisfies orthogonality conditions in the full population will not satisfy them when we condition on schooling.

Similar arguments apply to the weeks equation except that schooling has been excluded from the weeks equation. An interpretation of the weeks equation as a reduced form labor supply schedule implies that all the variables in the wage equation should appear in the weeks equation. Schooling and experience, however, are excluded. The authors note that schooling is not significant when it is included; but if one argues that its regression coefficient is really zero, then there cannot be a sample selection bias from selecting on an irrelevant variable.

Nevertheless, the authors do find evidence for sample selection bias, particularly in the weeks equation in the first year. This is based on the estimated correlation between the disturbance in the weeks equation and the disturbance in the latent variable equation that generates the probit probability of being out of school. Alternatively, we can think of including a term (the inverse of Mill's ratio) in a regression for the out-of-school subsample. This term reflects the probability of being in the sample; a nonzero coefficient is evidence for sample selection bias. Note that this term is a nonlinear function of the variables in the probit equation. These are essentially the same variables that appear in the wage or weeks equation. So an alternative interpretation is that a nonlinearity has been found.

Now one might argue that it does not matter which interpretation we follow: a specification error has been detected and corrected. This is incorrect. Under the sample selection interpretation we would evaluate the effect of the explanatory variables by the linear term in the specification that includes the Mill's ratio. Under the functional form interpretation, we would evaluate the derivative of the nonlinear function at some average level of the explanatory variables; this often gives results similar to fitting a linear least-squares approximation. If the functional form interpretation is correct, then just looking at the linear term corresponds to measuring the effect of the explanatory variables at extreme (infinite) values; for only then is the truncated mean of the disturbance term independent of shifts in the truncation point.

I want to consider next some of the issues that arise when schooling is considered to be endogenous. Suppose that wages are affected by unobserved variables, which might correspond to different sorts of initial ability. The authors' procedure amounts to imputing a wage to those still in school, and then fitting, for the entire sample, a regression of wages on current schooling and on other variables. Consider the coefficient of schooling in this regression. In the second year, the schooling variable is an indicator for whether or not the individual went directly on to college after high school. The coefficient on this variable partly reflects a value added from that year of college, but it also reflects the mean ability differential between high school and college students. More precisely, in the first year of the sample, when everyone has the same amount of schooling, there is a differential between the mean wage of high school students and the (imputed) mean wage that the college students would have received had they not gone on to college. In subsequent years, the estimated coefficient of schooling will confound the value added of schooling with this mean wage differential.

This point is relevant for measuring the effect of vocational training. Suppose that people only get vocational training if they do not plan to attend college. Then the coefficient of vocational training in the full sample is partly measuring the imputed mean wage differential between high school and college students. If the mean wage of high school students is less than the imputed mean wage of college students in the first year of the sample, when everyone has the same amount of schooling, then the estimate of the vocational training effect is biased downward. A more appropriate measure might be based on comparing the measured wages of high school students with vocational training to the wages of high school students without it. There would still, of course, be the problem that the selection of high school students into vocational training programs is partly based on unmeasured differences in abilities.

Another sort of sample selection issue arises because each year new people enter the sample as they complete their schooling. The experience variable is specified by the year in which it occurred. So in the last year of the sample (1976), a year of experience in 1975 is assumed to have the same coefficient for a high school student, for whom it may be the fourth year of experience, and for a college graduate, for whom it is the first year of experience. Curvature in the profile, due to the investment content of a year of experience varying with the level of experience, is not permitted. The variables are freely interacted with time. Because of the changing sample composition, however, time and experience are not identical; yet at several points in the chapter, changes in the coefficients over time are interpreted as if the same group of people were being followed as the group accumulated experience. In particular, the patterns of change in test score coefficients and schooling coefficients are obscured by the continual entry of people with no experience.

These points have some relevance, I think, for the estimated effects of schooling, test scores, and experience, and the pattern of their changes over time. The policy implications of the paper, however, rest more on the lack of a vocational training effect and on the strong relationship between work in high school and subsequent weeks worked. I have commented on how the estimation procedure affects the measurement of a vocational training effect. An additional point, as the authors note, is that it would be useful to distinguish whether or not the training was given by a vocational high school. As for the relationship between work in high school and subsequent weeks worked, the authors point out that the correlation does not decline over time, whereas the correlation between weeks worked in different years after high school rapidly declines as the time interval between the years increases. This suggests that the relationship between work in high school and subsequent work may be due to unmeasured characteristics of the individual that are not affected by work in high school. In that case, the policy implications are not clear; but it certainly is an intriguing finding and an invitation for futher research to determine what work in high school is measuring.

# 10     Teenage Unemployment: Permanent Scars or Temporary Blemishes?

David T. Ellwood

Teenage unemployment poses a puzzle for economists. Its causes and consequences are not well understood becuase of conflicting economic analyses. The human capital model suggests that since investment should be quite heavy in the early years, teenage unemployment carries with it heavy costs. But search theory suggests that shopping around is a necessary and desirable activity, particularly for those with little information about opportunities in the labor market. There is also concern that early labor force attachment may be weak, raising the possibility that early unemployment may just represent consumption of leisure. This chapter focuses on the longer-term consequences of early spells out of work for male teenagers.

The fundamental problem in capturing the long-term effects of unemployment is separating differences in employment and wages which are causally related to early unemployment, from the differences due to unobserved personal characteristics correlated with early unemployment. Whereas elsewhere in economics researchers routinely assume homogeneity of tastes and preferences, heterogeneity lies at the very heart of the issue here. Separating the individual component is the primary challenge faced in this chapter.

This chapter is divided into three sections. The first simply describes the early labor market experience of the young men in this sample. Strangely, there is little published data tracing the experience of a complete cohort over four years. In most other work the high rates of attrition and reentrance into the sample over the period at least open the possibility of distorting the underlying pattern. The second section extends the

The author is extremely grateful for discussions with Richard B. Freeman, Gary Chamberlain, Robert H. Meyer, and David A. Wise, as well as for the helpful insights from participants in the Columbia University Labor Economics Seminar. Any opinions expressed are those of the author, not those of the National Bureau of Economic Research.

work of Heckman and Chamberlain to test the long-term effects of early employment on future employment. The final section uses a Sims-type causality model to measure the impact of work experience on wages.

I conclude that the effects of a period without work do not end with that spell. A teenager who spends time out of work in one year will probably spend less time working in the next than he would have had he worked the entire year. Furthermore, the lost work experience will also be reflected in lower wages. At the same time, my data provide no evidence that early unemployment sets off a vicious cycle of recurrent unemployment. The reduced employment effects die off very quickly. What appear to persist are effects of lost work experience on wages.

### Scars—In Theory and Practice

It is useful to begin by examining the implications of early unemployment according to several of the more common labor theories. Perhaps most prominent in its prediction of long-term effects is human capital theory. While the theory is not concerned with early unemployment inducing later unemployment, its emphasis on human investment early in the job career to explain the concave pattern of aggregate age-earnings profiles implicitly imposes heavy costs on the unfortunate young person who misses out on early investment opportunities. If no investment takes place during the period without employment, the entire profile is shifted back. Even if retirement is also delayed, the present value of the entire earnings streams must now be discounted over the lost time.

The dual labor market theorists paint an equally bleak picture. Poor work habits develop over the periods of discouragement, catalyzing weak labor force attachment and alienation. The result is a vicious cycle of unemployment followed by deterioration followed by more unemployment. Pervading the institutional literature is the related notion of tracking. Teenagers face only a limited number of entry-level jobs which lead to better jobs. Those who miss good jobs early are permanently tracked onto inferior ladders.

One troubling question is whether early unemployment is largely a result of a job shortage or of weak labor force attachment. Most theories that predict long-term impacts of unemployment emphasize the involuntary nature of early unemployment. If much of it is "voluntary," it still may be reasonable to consider whether there are long-term consequences. Teenage unemployment cannot be strictly voluntary since it is so strongly countercyclical. But it is possible that some portion of the problem is due to weak attachment. Young people may take jobs only when they are readily available. Early experience may quicken labor force attachment and reinforce desirable work skills. If it is considered socially desirable to hasten the assimilation process, then it would be desirable to make jobs readily available to the young.

A slightly more sophisticated argument emphasizes the severe informational problems of the young in the labor market. Teenagers and employers are involved in an elaborate game of mixing and matching skills and jobs, but there is relatively little information available to either party. The employers rely heavily on evidence of past work experience in making hiring decisions because they need to separate persons with poor work skills and weak attachments from those with superior work qualities. Employers avoid hiring workers who have been out of school for some time but have little experience, so those workers who were involuntarily unemployed are inappropriately typed as poor workers. The problems may be exacerbated in recessionary times. If employers are slow to adjust their expectations for experience from young applicants, cohorts entering a weak labor market will suffer. Of course, permanent damage need not occur at all. Early unemployment may simply be productive job search or simple consumption of leisure.

There is a small but rapidly growing literature testing the long-term effects of early spells of unemployment (see for example Becker and Hills [1978], Stevenson [1978]). These papers conclude that early unemployment has sizable long-term effects. The methodology usually involves regressions of wages or weeks worked of persons beyond their teens on duration and/or spells of teenage unemployment several years earlier. Although most pay lip service to the difficulty of controlling for individual differences, it is typical to include several background variables as a control in the equations. This methodology is troubling. If there is a true job shortage employers are likely to hire the highest quality workers first. If early unemployment is in part a reflection of weak attachment, then some persons with unemployment are also low-quality workers. In either case, early unemployment is certain to be highly correlated with aspects of worker quality. The findings of these studies document persistence very convincingly but serious questions remain about whether early experience has causal effects in later economic behavior.

I conclude that while long-term effects do exist, they may be a good deal smaller than the literature suggests.

## The Data

Current published data tends to obfuscate early patterns of market experience. Data from the Current Population Survey are currently published by age group and school enrollment status. Throughout this chapter, I will concentrate only on those persons out of school. I see many fewer possibilities for long-term effects of unemployment during school. The composition of the 16–19 year old out-of-school labor force is very different from that of the 20–24 age group. The 16–19 year old group includes early dropouts and high school graduates. The 20–24 year old group includes persons with little school but eight years of experience along with recent college graduates. To look across different age groups and to draw conclusions about the patterns of unemployment as persons age is to invite error.

Ideally, one should like to follow a cohort of persons permanently out of school over five or ten years. The National Longitudinal Survey of Young Men—the so-called "Parnes data"—allows such an examination. Some 5225 young men between the ages of 14 and 24 were interviewed in 1966. They were then reinterviewed annually through 1971, then again in 1973, and again in 1975. Typically, respondents were interviewed in November about their current labor force status and most recent wage as well as about their experience over the past year. The sample chosen for analysis here was a group of roughly 750 young men who left school "permanently" in 1965, 1966, or 1967 with less than fourteen years of education. Unfortunately, this period was the height of the Vietnam war. Thus slightly over half the sample is not observed in the four full years after they left school, primarily because of military service. The 364 young men who remain do appear to be somewhat less prone to unemployment and time out of the labor force. Persons who were observed in the first full year out of school but were not observed in some later year had a labor force participation rate of 84.1%, an unemployment rate of 7.1%, and an employment rate of 78.2%. Persons who remained in the sample had rates of 86.1%, 5.0%, and 81.8% respectively. This sample selection is an obvious source of potential bias and will be addressed in more detail later.

Another well-known "problem" with the Parnes data is that they show very different rates of employment and unemployment than do published statistics derived for the CPS.[1] The longitudinal data used here show much higher employment rates and lower unemployment rates than the CPS data. For a discussion of the likely reasons for these differences see Freeman and Medoff (chapter 4 of this volume). The sample selection and CPS comparison suggest that the NLS sample may miss some of the longer-term unemployed persons, for whom unemployment could have the most serious consequences. Thus the current sample could serve to underrepresent the long-term consequences of early labor market experience.

Few of the young men in the survey data leave school in November. In the year of leaving school, retrospective labor force figures cover both time in and out of school. After numerous attempts to adjust for the problem, I finally decided to simply omit the first part-year of experience. In later sections when I refer to the first year of experience, I refer to the first full survey year after graduation or dropping out.

## 10.1 The Early Labor Market Experience

The labor market position of young men improves dramatically during the first four years out of school. Table 10.1 shows that while an average

Table 10.1     Unemployment Rate, Employment Ratio, and Labor Force Participation Rate for Young Men during First Four Years after Leaving School in 1965, 1966, or 1967 with Less than Thirteen Years of Schooling

|  | Unemployment rate[a] | Employment rate[b] | Labor force participation rate[c] |
|---|---|---|---|
| Year 1 | 5.0 | 81.8 | 86.1 |
| Year 2 | 6.4 | 84.7 | 90.5 |
| Year 3 | 4.8 | 89.3 | 93.8 |
| Year 4 | 5.4 | 90.0 | 95.0 |

[a]Average weeks unemployed/average weeks in labor force.
[b]Average weeks employed/52.
[c]Average week in labor force/52.

of nearly 20% are without work in the first year, only 10% are not working three years later. Labor force participation rates rise precipitously, from 86% to 95%. The marked improvement is countercyclical in this case since for roughly two-thirds of the sample (those leaving school in 1966 and 1967) the fourth full year out of school comes during 1970 or 1971—recessionary years. Indeed, if the overall economic picture had remained stable over this period, even more rapid improvement would likely have occurred. Almost immediately, however, the unemployment rate shows up as a questionable indicator of labor market performance for this group. While the other statistics, most notably the employment ratio, show clear improvement over time, the unemployment rate follows no clear pattern. Although it is possible that the unemployment rate accurately captures the relative number of persons seeking work but unable to find it, it is also possible that the unchanging unemployment statistic misrepresents the trend in the labor market position of young men. In these retrospective figures, unemployment may well mean something different to persons one year out of school than to persons four years out. As the young men age, they may become increasingly reluctant to report themselves as out of the labor force even if they are not spending time in productive job search. Another alternative is that in later years only a hard core cannot find jobs. These persons become discouraged and drop out of the labor force. Either way the distinction between unemployment and time out of the labor force is blurred.

The steady improvement in the employment rate of the cohort masks remarkably dynamic labor force patterns. The initial years of employment experience are pocketed with spells of unemployment and time out of the labor force. Only 18% of all young men in this sample have four-year employment histories unmarred by a spell out of work. Table 10.2 shows that nearly 40% of all young men spend time out of the labor force in their first year, while just over one-quarter report unemploy-

**Table 10.2**    Probability of Unemployment, Time out of the Labor Force, and Time Not Employed during First Four Years after Leaving School

|  | Probability of unemployment | Probability of time out of labor force | Probability of time not employed |
|---|---|---|---|
| Year 1 | 26.9% | 40.1% | 56.6% |
| Year 2 | 27.5 | 31.9 | 51.1 |
| Year 3 | 23.0 | 23.6 | 40.9 |
| Year 4 | 21.9 | 24.1 | 38.2 |

ment. Overall, 57% of these young men spent some time out of work. The probabilities of adverse experiences decline substantially over the period. Yet even in the fourth year out of school when the overall employment ratio is 90%, almost 40% spend some time not employed. And while the labor force participation rate hovers at 95% in that fourth year, one-quarter spend some time neither working nor looking for work.

Perhaps the most dramatic result in these first few tables is the prominence of time out of the labor force. Nearly 40% of the sample self-report time spent neither working nor looking in the first years. These 40% report average spells of eighteen weeks—more than four months—during a period of very low unemployment. Perhaps these are discouraged workers. Yet three-quarters of them spent no time unemployed at all during that first year. Of course, some may have had severe unemployment problems in the part-year preceding the first survey year. Still, four months is a remarkably long time to be discouraged, particularly when one's peers are reporting a 5% unemployment rate. The sample selection rules, which appear to discriminate against the nonemployed, make the results seem even more dramatic. The rapid rise in labor force participation rates and employment rates during the downward swing of the business cycle must almost certainly indicate increasing labor force attachment.

One important concern is whether to regard reported unemployment as a separate experience from reported time out of the labor force. The evidence cited thus far suggests that retrospective unemployment figures do not appear to capture the essence of the employment situation. While the distinction between those actively seeking work and those who are not seems particularly important in this group, the line is poorly drawn using retrospective employment figures. Of course, few labor force statistics are derived from retrospective data. Still, the standard CPS question about whether the teenager has done anything to look for work in the past four weeks (a specific method must be listed) may not separate them too much more efficiently.

Unfortunately, if it is difficult to separate the truly unemployed from those with weak labor force attachment in surveys, it may be equally difficult for employers. Thus those persons who are seriously searching for work but have been unable to find it may suffer from guilt by association.

This brief section has painted a pattern of change and diversity. Early in their careers young men spend a great deal of time without work. By their fourth year, however, most workers are settling into a more stable and presumably permanent work situation. The next section shows that while the early years are periods of rapid improvement for the young men overall, adverse experiences persist.

### 10.1.1  The Persistent Pattern
of Adverse Labor Market Experiences

Early labor market experiences foretell future ones. Persons who escape unemployment early will likely escape it later. Figures 10.1, 10.2, and 10.3 are probability trees for unemployment, time out of the labor force, and time not employed for the four periods. Each branch corresponds to one period. A one indicates that unemployment or nonemployment was experienced in the period, a zero indicates that it was not. Above the line in any branch is the probability of being in that state *conditional* on being at the previous branch. Below the line in parentheses is the *unconditional* probability of being on that branch (or the proportion of all persons who are found on that branch). The bottom number is the average weeks of unemployment in that period by persons on that branch. Thus in figure 10.1, 53.1% of persons who had been unemployed in their first year were unemployed in their second year. Just over 14% of all persons had unemployment both periods and these persons averaged 14.2 weeks of unemployment in the second year.

All three figures demonstrate striking persistence in the labor force experiences. The probability of unemployment (nonemployment) in the second period conditional on first period spells is .531 (.631), while those who escaped early problems have only a .180 (.354) probability of unemployment (nonemployment). By the fourth period, boys with three straight years with unemployment are seven times more likely to become unemployed than those with three straight years without it.

This sort of probability tree is common in the literature (see Heckman and Willis [1977]; Heckman [1978a and 1978b]); however, the patterns can be misleading. If spells are long, say ten weeks, and if spells are distributed randomly throughout the year, then 20% of all the unemployed in one year will have spells which overlap into the next one. This would cause a much higher probability of unemployment in the second year conditional on having experienced it in the first, regardless of the underlying pattern. In this sort of table, there is no straightforward way of making an adjustment for this problem.

Happily, overlap problems do not affect probabilities of third or fourth period events conditional on the first period event. Table 10.3 reveals

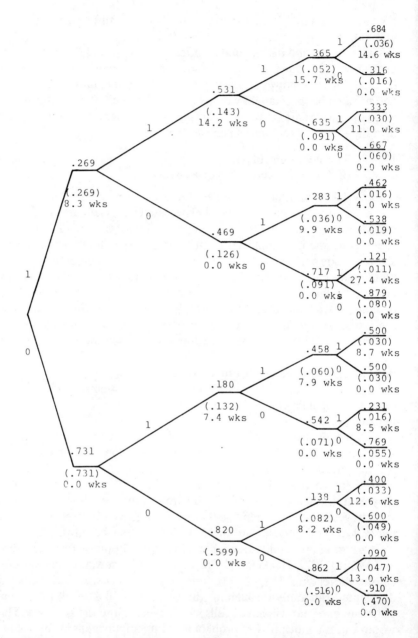

**Fig. 10.1**　　　Probability Tree of Weeks Unemployed in First Four Years out of School ($N = 364$)

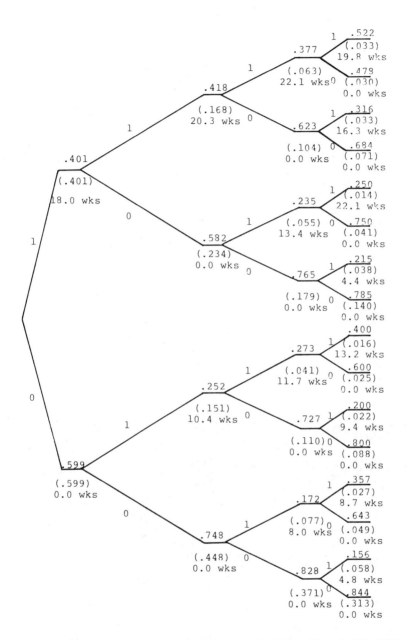

**Fig. 10.2**        Probability Tree of Weeks out of the Labor Force in First Four Years out of School ($N = 364$)

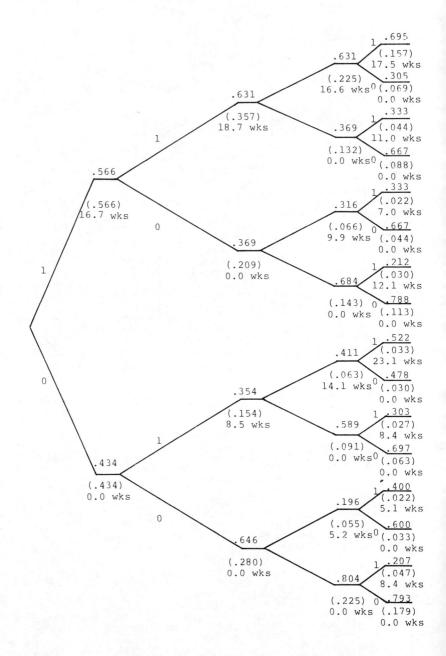

**Fig. 10.3**    Probability Tree of Weeks Not Employed in First Four Years out of School ($N = 364$)

that persons with poor first period records are likely to have poor records three or four years later. Persons who spent time out of work in the first period have a .447 probability of similar problems in the final year as contrasted to a .297 probability for those persons with uninterrupted work histories in the first year.

A somewhat more appealing measure of persistence is a simple correlation matrix. Table 10.4 provides the correlations for weeks of unemployment over the first four years and for the weeks not employed. Once again the persistence is prominent, but not quite so prominent as might be expected. Weeks not employed shows a one-year correlation of about .5, but it decays rapidly. Within two years the value falls to around .25. Remarkably, weeks unemployed show far less persistence and the pattern of decay is erratic. Adjacent year correlations ($\sigma_{12}$, $\sigma_{23}$, $\sigma_{34}$) show some stability, but hover at only about .3, a figure roughly comparable to the correlation between weeks not employed one or two years removed. The correlation between unemployment in the first and third years ($\sigma_{13}$) shows evidence of slight decay, but $\sigma_{24}$ shows no such evidence. Then, dramatically, $\sigma_{14}$ falls to .08. The unorthodox behavior of the unemployment figures once again reinforces the earlier concerns about the quality of unemployment measure (at least this retrospective measure) for this age group.

Both the unemployment and nonemployment correlations are more stable than would be generated by a first-order Markov process. The stability suggests that individual differences are an important part of the underlying process or that the process is of higher order. Unemployment and nonemployment are not events randomly distributed over this population of young men. If early unemployment or nonemployment is nothing more than search and matching of workers and jobs, then for

**Table 10.3**     **Probability of Adverse Market Experiences in Later Years Conditional on Early Experience**

|  | Unem- ployment | Time OLF | Time not employed |
|---|---|---|---|
| $P(1$ in year 2/ 1 in year 1) | .531 | .418 | .631 |
| $P(1$ in year 2/ 0 in year 1) | .180 | .252 | .354 |
| $P(1$ in year 3/ 1 in year 1) | .327 | .294 | .514 |
| $P(1$ in year 3/ 0 in year 1) | .194 | .197 | .272 |
| $P(1$ in year 4/ 1 in year 1) | .345 | .294 | .447 |
| $P(1$ in year 4/ 0 in year 1) | .172 | .205 | .297 |

**Table 10.4**    Correlation Matrix for Weeks Unemployed and Weeks Not Employed during the First Four Years out of School

| Weeks unemployed | Weeks unemployed | | | |
| --- | --- | --- | --- | --- |
| | Year 1 | Year 2 | Year 3 | Year 4 |
| Year 1 | 1.00 | .27 | .20 | .08 |
| Year 2 | | 1.00 | .27 | .26 |
| Year 3 | | | 1.00 | .39 |
| Year 4 | | | | 1.00 |

| Weeks not employed | Weeks not employed | | | |
| --- | --- | --- | --- | --- |
| | Year 1 | Year 2 | Year 3 | Year 4 |
| Year 1 | 1.00 | .54 | .34 | .25 |
| Year 2 | | 1.00 | .46 | .34 |
| Year 3 | | | 1.00 | .47 |
| Year 4 | | | | 1.00 |

some at least the process is quite protracted. Since adverse employment patterns are a problem of a subclass of youngsters, programs to aid them ought to be targeted to those with early problems.

The critical question of this chapter still remains: Is the persistence a reflection only of individual differences or is future employent causally related to past experience?

## 10.2    The Impact of Early Unemployment on Future Unemployment: Heterogeneity and State Dependence

Persistence of labor market behavior has been noted in numerous other settings, most notably in the labor force participation of married women. A newly developing literature seeks to separate the effects of individual differences in behavior (heterogeneity) from changes in behavior induced by a previous event (state dependence). The unique character of longitudinal data allows one to control for unobserved individual characteristics in a way that no strictly cross-sectional data set does. Although there are serious conceptual problems with this formulation, the following model is continuous time will help illustrate the methodology currently employed in the literature (the problems will be considered later):

$$Y_{it} = X_{it}\beta_t + \gamma_t Y_{it-1} + \delta_{it} + U_{it}$$

Here $Y_{it}$ is the time person $i$ was in a particular state during period $t$ (i.e., weeks worked), $X_{it}$ is a vector of exogenous variables, $\delta_{it}$ is an individual constant, $U_{it}$ is a random component. This is simply a model of a first-order Markov process with an individual component. In this example, $\delta_{it}$ is the control for heterogeneity, $\gamma_t$ is the test of state dependence. Such an equation cannot be estimated from cross-sectional data because there will be more parameters than observations since each individual is accorded his own intercept. Cross-sectional estimates made without the inclusion of $\delta_{it}$ will create upward bias in the state dependence coefficient unless that part of $\delta_{it}$ which is correlated with $Y_{it-1}$ is fully captured by a linear combination of the $X$s.

By imposing restrictions on $\delta_{it}$, one can estimate $\gamma_t$ from longitudinal data. The individual component can be controlled using data from previous years. The simplest assumption is to fix the individual component over time, $\delta_{it} = \delta_i$. To simplify the example further, assume $\beta_t = \beta$, $\gamma_t = \gamma$ and that $Cov\ (U_{it}, U_{it-1}) = 0$. Simple differencing eliminates the nuisance parameter $\delta_i$. Thus

$$Y_{it} - Y_{it-1} = (X_{it} - X_{it-1})\ \beta + \gamma(Y_{it-1} - Y_{it-2})$$
$$+ U_{it} - U_{it-1}$$

Of course all exogenous variables which are invariant over time are also eliminated with this approach. Since the focus here is with the state dependence parameter, $\gamma$, this is a source of no concern. The term $(Y_{it-1} - Y_{it-2})$ is now negatively correlated with the error term, so OLS results will be negatively biased. However, $Y_{it-2}$ and $X_{it-1}$ can be used as instruments for this term and consistent results will be generated. Note that absolutely no distributional restrictions are imposed on the $\delta_i$ across individuals since they are simply differenced away.

Heckman (1978a, 1978b) has developed an appealing and more general counterpart to this model for the discrete case. Heckman's model transforms the dichotomous variable into a continuous one by assuming the event occurs whenever a continuous latent variable ($Y^*_{it}$) crosses a threshold—here assumed to be zero. A dummy variable $d_{it}$ is assumed to be one when $Y^*_{it} > 0$ and zero otherwise. Exogenous variables $X_{it}$ are allowed. Using a variance components error structure in Heckman's model, we can allow each individual to have his own individual component, $\delta_{it}$, freely varying over time for the moment. One case of Heckman's somewhat more general model is then:

$$Y^*_{it} = X_{it}\ \beta_t + \sum_{j=1}^{k} \gamma_{it-j}\ d_{it-j} + \delta_{it} + \varepsilon_{it}$$

Setting $\gamma_{it-j} = \gamma_{t-j}$ and $\delta_{it} = \delta_i$ and assuming the $\delta_i$ and the $\varepsilon_{it}$ are IID normal provide for an estimable model. Heckman offers a heuristic proof of identifiability which relies on the ordering of unconditional probabilities. Suppose $t = 2$ and the $X$s are constant over time. Then conditional on $X_i$ and $\delta_i$, in the absence of state dependence, the probability of the sequence $(1, 0)$ (one in first period, zero in the second) is equal to the probability of the sequence $(0, 1)$. In the presence of state dependence, however, $P(1, 0) < P(0, 1)$. State dependence increases the likelihood that persons who experience the event in the first period will experience it again in the second. Therefore $P(1, 1)$ is increased and $P(1, 0)$ is reduced. $P(0, 1)$ on the other hand is unaffected since the event was not experienced in the first period. This relation holds for each individual; it must hold in aggregate. Thus simple run sequences alone allow testing for the presence of state dependence under particular functional form assumptions. Run sequences covering more time periods allow testing of less restrictive functional forms.

Heckman suggests this approach can be usefully applied to a variety of situations, including spells of unemployment. Several features of the Heckman model make its usefulness in this and related situations questionable. For purposes of this discussion, let us divide early job history into only two states: employed and not employed. The fundamental problem is that the model breaks a continuous time event into artificial periods. When the chosen interval is long relative to average length of stay in a state, there is inevitably an assymetry in the definition of states. Often periods are chosen to be one year long. A person is observationally reported to have been in a particular state for that period if and only if he or she experienced the state *at any time* during the period. In the current example persons who experience time out of work any time over a year receive ones, persons who do not receive zeros. Thus to be in a state, one need experience only one week of nonemployment, but to be out of the state one need experience fifty-two weeks of unemployment. If we simply redefine state 1 and having experienced any *employment*, a very different pattern of states emerges. Virtually everyone is always in state 1. The presence or absence of state dependence may depend on which state is accorded the special privilege of being designated as the 1.

On the other hand, if the periods are short relative to the spells, then state dependence exists almost by assumption. If spells tend to be longer than periods then the probability of being in the state conditional on having been in it in the previous period is high. Indeed, even if spells tend to be four or five times shorter than the periods, one can predict with certainty that at least 20 to 25% of persons who experience the event one period will experience it again in the next period simply because spells overlap.

The arbitrary designation of time periods and states means an observed data point $(1, 1)$ may represent a host of very different histories. One person may have been in the state continuously for two periods. Another may have been in it only a few days but those days happened to overlap two periods. Still a third person might have had several spells in the state in each period. These problems represent more than lost efficiency. They imply peculiar results. The problem of overlapping spells is particularly troubling in the current treatment. If spells last an average of thirteen weeks, then one-fourth of all spells in one year will overlap into another. This implies that even if the spell has no long-term effect, $P(1, 1)$ is increased. Since the $P(1|1) > P(1|0)$ there appears to be state dependence where there is none. Although these problems are particularly acute in the Heckman formulation using years as periods, they are also present to some degree in the continuous model presented earlier, as we shall see below.

One way to minimize these problems is to use point in time sampling. At the start of each time period persons are interviewed and their current state recorded. There is no asymmetry in the definition of states in this case. And if spells tend to be shorter than periods, overlap problems are less serious. Of course, there is great loss of information in this approach. More importantly, since spells of employment frequently last several years, the chosen periods may have to be quite long.

Obviously, the notion of state dependence is a confusing one. In the next few paragraphs I present a nontechnical discussion in an attempt to clarify some of the concepts. For a more technical treatment see Chamberlain (1978 and 1979).

A complete analysis of heterogeneity and state dependence would treat each event in continuous time with a particular starting and ending date. We must separate two distinct types of state dependence. Once a person has entered a particular state, say employment, there is a tendency to remain there for some period of time. The probability of remaining in some state is always higher than the probability of entering it from another if the time interval is short enough. Virtually all persons who work one minute will work the next, regardless of their underlying propensity to work over a month, year, or decade. Traditionally this inertia has been captured with a Markov model. Conditional on being in a state, a person has a certain escape probability over a given period of time *which may be quite independent of his past history of spells or states.*

For example, a young black male teenager who is unemployed this week could be far more likely to be unemployed next week than if he had been employed this week simply because it is hard for young blacks to find jobs. It could be that nothing about his work history or his duration of current unemployment influences his ability to get a job; yet being unemployed now indicates that he is less likely to be employed next week. Unemployment doesn't change the individual per se, it is just a difficult state for the teenager to escape. Heterogeneity must imply that each individual has his or her own escape probability from each state. Let us label this form of state dependence simple Markov-type persistence. The key notion is that it is what state one is in that counts, not his past history. This persistence is unquestionably present in all human endeavors to some degree.

If the force of escape from one or another state *is* influenced by previous experience, then the second form of state dependence—experience dependence—is present. Exit probabilities may rise or fall with time in the current spell. Work history may influence the likelihood of employment when a teenager is unemployed. Experience dependence corresponds most closely to the conception of state dependence described in the literature. A person is actually "changed" by a particular event. Models which postulate that the accumulation or depreciation of human capital or of information or even of signals of worker quality alters the likelihood of work all imply an altered force of escape from one state or another because of the individual's past experience. Ideally, it is this form of state dependence that we seek to capture.

Simple Markov-type persistence certainly is not uninteresting. The distribution of forces of excape will strongly influence the concentration of unemployment across individuals. Macroeconomic policies can alter escape rates and may provide great benefit to those with otherwise very low rates of escape from unemployment. But if experience dependence is not present, once a spell is over so is its impact.

Unfortunately, the current models capture both Markov-type persistence and experience dependence simultaneously. Markov persistence requires two heterogeneity parameters: the force of escape from each state. In the Heckman formulation this implies an individual intercept $\delta_i$ and an individual coefficient on the person's state last period. This can be modeled (omitting the $X$s):

$$Y^*_{it} = \delta_i + \psi_i d_{it-1} + \sum_{j=2}^{k} \gamma_{t-j} di_{t-j} + \varepsilon_{it}$$

If the time periods are quite short, then $\delta_i$ effectively captures the Markov-type probability of *entering* the 1 state; $\psi_i$, the probability of *remaining* in it. With short periods $d_{it-1}$ captures the persons most recent state—the "current state" while the state in "next period" is being determined. Markov persistence virtually guarantees that $\psi_i$ will be positive as the period shrinks. Experience dependence requires previous job history—not just that the current state alter the probability of entering or remaining in a state. Thus coefficients on $d_{it-2}, d_{it-3} \ldots$ are nonzero. The $\gamma_{t-j}$ here captures this experience dependence.[2]

Estimation of this model is complicated by the fact that the $\delta_i$ and $\psi_i$ are highly correlated with $d_{it-1}$ and the $d_{it-j}$ since high values of the individual components increase the likelihood that any $d_{ij} = 1$. Estimating the equation assuming $\psi_i = \Psi$ may substantially upward bias the $\gamma_{t-j}$ coefficients because the omitted term $(\psi_i - \Psi)d_{it-1}$ is positively correlated the $d_{it-j}$. Previous work using this model has overestimated experience dependence for two reasons. First, the coefficient on the once lagged $d_{it}$ inevitably reflects not only experience dependence but also Markov persistence. Second, because the coefficient on $d_{it-1}$ is constrained to equality across individuals, the $\gamma_{t-j}$ also captures some Markov-type persistence. Heterogeneity has simply not been properly controlled for.

The continuous model described at the beginning of this section also inadvertently captures some Markov-type persistence in the state dependence parameter. Suppose weeks worked is the dependent variable. Then it is tempting to regard $\delta_i$ as the expected weeks worked in year $t$ given an individual's two escape probabilities. However, even in the presence of Markov persistence alone, the individual's expected weeks worked will be greater if he begins the period working than if he enters without work. A preceding year's weeks worked help predict the person's state at the end of that year and therefore at the start of the current year. Anyone who worked fifty-two weeks in year $t + 1$ was working at the start of year $t$. He will certainly be expected to have more weeks worked in year $t$ than an identical individual who begins year $t$ out of work. Even conditional on $\delta_i$, weeks worked in one year are correlated with weeks worked in the next because they help predict the person's state at the start of the next period. The correct model is thus

$$Y_{it} = \delta_i + \psi_i b_{it} + \gamma Y_{it-1} + U_{it}$$

where $b_{it}$ is now a dummy variable capturing the person's state at the *beginning* of year $t$. In this model $\delta_i$ and $\psi_i$ are reflective of the two Markov escape probabilities and $\gamma$ is a measure of true experience dependence. Even if we know $\delta_i$ with certainty, we could not estimate this equation because $\psi_i$ varies with each individual and is highly correlated with $b_{it}$ and $Y_{it-1}$.

When we difference, however, the advantages of this continuous formulation become clearer:

$$Y_{it} - Y_{it-1} = \psi_i(b_{it} - b_{it-1}) + \gamma(Y_{it-1} - Y_{it-2})$$
$$+ U_{it} - U_{it-1}$$

There is only a bias problem for persons who change their beginning state from one period to the next. Otherwise $(b_{it} - b_{it-1}) = 0$ and $\psi_i$ vanishes. One cannot estimate the equation for these persons only because $b_{it}$ is correlated with $U_{it-1}$ and conditioning on it will introduce bias.[3] But in the present sample, nearly 90% of all persons are observed in the same state at the start of any two consecutive years, so the bias on $\gamma$ may be quite small.

Including $b_{it} - b_{it-1}$ (using $b_{it-1}$ as an instrument) will reduce the bias but will not fully eliminate it. At the same time $\gamma$ will not fully capture experience dependence because $\delta_i$ and $\psi_i$ are average yearly probabilities which will in part reflect some experience dependence if the underlying forces of escape are high. In the presence of these offsetting "biases," I regard $\gamma$ as a rough measure of experience dependence. Any better measures require complete work histories and present serious methodological problems.

In this continuous model, identification was achieved with the imposition of three important restrictions: $\delta_{it} = \delta_i$, $\psi_{it} = \psi_i$ and $Cov(U_{it}, U_{it-1}) = 0$. If any of these restrictions are false, spurious state dependence can be generated. Probably the most serious concern for this group is nonstationarity of the individual components $\delta_i$ and $\psi_i$. If weeks worked is the endogenous variable, $\delta_i$ and $\psi_i$ might be seen as that part of maturity, ability, or labor force attachment not captured by the $X$s. Since these may grow or decay over time, it seems desirable to free up the individual components. Although we cannot let the components decay or grow at different rates, a model allowing $\delta_{it} = \lambda_t\delta_i$ and $\psi_{it} = \lambda_t\psi_i$ can be estimated using four years of data. We solve for $\delta_i$ in the third year equations and substitute it into the fourth:

$$Y_{i3} = \lambda_3\delta_i + \lambda_3\psi_i b_{i3} + \gamma_3 Y_{i2} + X_{i3}\beta_3 + U_{i3}$$

So

$$\delta_i = -\psi_i b_{i3} + \frac{1}{\lambda_3}(Y_{i3} - \gamma_3 Y_{i2} - X_{i3}\beta_3 - U_{i3})$$

Substituting into the equation for $Y_{i4}$

$$Y_{i4} = \lambda_4\psi_i(b_{i4} - b_{i3}) + (\gamma_4 + \frac{\lambda_4}{\lambda_3})Y_{i3} - \frac{\lambda_4}{\lambda_3}\gamma_3 Y_{i2} +$$

$$X_{i4}\beta_4 - \frac{\lambda_4}{\lambda_3}X_{i3}\beta_3 + U_{i4} - \frac{\lambda_4}{\lambda_3}U_{i3}$$

The effects of the first term have been discussed earlier. The only other problem is that $Y_{i3}$ is correlated with the error term, $Y_{i1}$ is not however, and serves as a natural instrument for $Y_{i3}$. If we constrain $\gamma_4 = \gamma_3$ we can obtain estimates of $\gamma$ and $\lambda_4/\lambda_3$ although we cannot tell which is which since they enter the equation symmetrically.

The restriction $Cov(U_{it}, U_{it-1}) = 0$ helps to highlight an important distinction between state dependence and serial correlation. In the absence of strong $X$s which change over time, there is no meaningful empirical distinction between serial correlation and state dependence. However, in the presence of $X$s the distinction is important. State dependence implies that a change in $X$ will cause a change in $Y$ not only in the present period but in future periods as well, because the initial increase in $Y$ induces future increases in $Y$. If serial correlation is present, a change in $X$ will have its full force immediately, with no damped response into the future. In the case of unemployment, one might ask whether a weak labor market now induces more unemployment in the future even when the labor market regains its strength. If the answer is yes, then state dependence may be present. Otherwise, state dependence probably is not present. Unfortunately, it is likely to be virtually impossible to capture both serial correlation and a nonstationarity of individual specific constant. The only reasonable approach I can see is to assume that both serial correlation and nonstationarity are captured using a time specific coefficient on the individual effect. These models then were used to estimate the long-run effects of unemployment.

### 10.2.1 Empirical Results

Before performing the more complicated tests for state dependence described above, we might try to find "natural experiments" which would reveal it much more simply. Local unemployment rates vary dramatically over time and across locales. One natural experiment would be to test whether persons who enter a weak labor market which later turns strong fare less well than those who enter a strong market which remains strong. A unique feature of the "Parnes data" is the availability of an area unemployment rate for most persons in each year. The rate for small local areas about the size of an SMSA was derived from a twelve-month average of monthly local unemployment rates from the Current Population Survey. Presumably the area unemployment is only slightly correlated with individual effects, so with a few controls for individual characteristics, we might simply test the importance of lagged unemployment rate in equations with both current and lagged unemployment rates. If entering a weak labor market left long-term scars, then the lagged rate should be negative and significant. Unfortunately, the area rate behaved very poorly. Even in equations without the lagged rate, the coefficient on the current rate, though usually of the correct sign, was rarely significant and was highly unstable. When the lagged rate was included, the results were invariably insignificant and occasionally even the sign on the current rate was perverse.

Even though the area rates performed poorly on this data, this experiment should be performed on other samples if possible. Ultimately, a conclusion resting on such a simple methodology would be the most compelling test for the long-run effects of short-run macropolicy.[4]

The techniques described in the previous section were applied to weeks worked and to weeks unemployed. Weeks worked were chosen over weeks not worked only because they seem conceptually easier to deal with. Obviously since weeks not worked are simply fifty-two less weeks worked, the results would be identical except for the constant term and a sign change on the coefficients of the exogenous variables if the alternative variable was used. There were 298 observations in the final sample.

There is a purely statistical problem associated with the use of the various controls for heterogeneity in equations predicting weeks worked or weeks unemployed. Both are limited dependent variables; they cannot exceed fifty-two or fall below zero. The importance of the problem is most evident in the case of weeks worked. As weeks worked approach fifty-two the estimate of state dependence will approach zero if controls are made for heterogeneity. Statistically, the limited variable will induce an artifically negative correlation between once lagged weeks and the error term. The results follows from the fact that if lagged weeks are large, the positive end of the distribution of the error term is likely to be truncated. Intuitively, once weeks worked approach fifty-two, regardless of the true strength of state dependence, the next years' weeks cannot be pushed above fifty-two. This problem is of greater concern in later years when more and more of the young men approach fifty-two weeks employment. There are well-known methodologies to correct truncated dependent variables. These typically do not apply to situations where a lagged dependent variable is correlated with the error term for reasons other than truncation. Heterogeneity further complicates the problem. No attempt was made to develop the appropriate truncation corrections for these equations. If we view the solution to the truncation problem as the inclusion of a truncation correction variable, the problem is unlikely to be particularly acute in the difference equations. In these situations only the *change* in the truncation variable is omitted, and these changes will be relatively small, particularly as persons approach fifty-two weeks. Actually, persons who remain at fifty-two weeks in all three years impart no bias at all in the absence of exogenous variables. They simply provide no information since $y_{it} - y_{it-1} = 0$.[5]

The wage rate normally appears in labor supply equations. At the same time human capital theory suggests that work experience will be associated with higher wages as individuals invest in on-the-job training. To prevent the wage variable from capturing any effects of increased investment, the variable $LW_{it}$ reflects the wage at the beginning of period $t$ while $WW_t$ equals weeks worked during year $t$. To eliminate potential bias, the various equations (because weeks worked in year $t-1$ and therefore $U_{t-1}$ alters the wage in year $t$) the wage variables were always instrumented with $LW_{it-1}$ and $LW_{it-2}$ in equations controlling for heterogeneity. All strictly exogenous variables are measured at the beginning of each period.

Table 10.7 presents the results of regressions of weeks worked and weeks unemployed on the once lagged counterparts. The only correction for heterogeneity is the inclusion of a few personal characteristics like age, race, and level of schooling. As anticipated, lagged values of weeks worked and weeks unemployed have sizeable coefficients and small standard errors. As in previous examples in this paper the results for weeks worked are far more stable than those for weeks unemployed.

When all years are estimated as a system and the coefficient on lagged weeks unemployed is constrained to equality over all three years, the coefficient is .27; the coefficient on weeks worked, .39. The results again suggest substantial persistence of early experience. Still, even without controlling for heterogeneity, the coefficient on weeks unemployed is low. Even if this were the correct estimate of state dependence, a twenty-six-week spell of unemployment would induce just two extra weeks of unemployment two years later. An equal spell without work would induce a four-week spell two years later according to these results. With appropriate corrections for heterogeneity, state dependence estimates should fall to even lower levels.

One control for heterogeneity is differencing. This eliminates any stationary person effects. The second is to include the state at the beginning of each period. Difference equation results are displayed on tables 10.8 and 10.9. In equations (1) and (2), twice lagged weeks unemployed and weeks employed, and once lagged lag wage, and beginning state dummies, serve as the principle instruments to the lagged differences on weeks unemployed, weeks worked, lag wage, and beginning states re-

**Table 10.5**     **Definitions of Variables Used in Regressions**

| | |
|---|---|
| $AGE_t$ | Age at start of year $t$. |
| $AREA_t$ | Area unemployment rate at start of year $t$. |
| $BLACK$ | Race dummy (1 = nonwhite). |
| $EM_t$ | Employment dummy (1 = employed) at start of year $t$. |
| $LW_t$ | Log of wage at start of year $t$. |
| $MAR_t$ | Marriage dummy (1 = married) at start of year $t$. |
| $SCHOOL$ | Years of school completed. |
| $SMSA_t$ | SMSA dummy (1 = resides in SMSA) at start of year $t$. |
| $SOUTH_t$ | South dummy (1 = resides in South) at start of year $t$. |
| $UN_t$ | Unemployment dummy (1 = unemployed) at start of year $t$. |
| $WW_t$ | Weeks worked in year $t$. |
| $WUN_t$ | Weeks unemployed in year $t$. |
| $Dxxxx$ | Change in variable $xxxx$. |

**Table 10.6**     **Means and Standard Deviations for Variables Used in Regressions**

| | Mean | S.D. | | Mean | S.D. |
|---|---|---|---|---|---|
| AGE 2 | 18.8 | 1.98 | SMSA 3 | .664 | .473 |
| AREA 2 | 4.33 | 1.72 | SMSA 4 | .668 | .472 |
| AREA 3 | 4.22 | 1.85 | SOUTH 2 | .446 | .497 |
| AREA 4 | 4.59 | 1.93 | SOUTH 3 | .432 | .496 |
| BLACK | .383 | .487 | SOUTH 4 | .422 | .495 |
| EM 2 | .899 | .301 | UN 2 | .060 | .238 |
| EM 3 | .932 | .251 | UN 3 | .050 | .219 |
| EM 4 | .946 | .225 | UN 4 | .037 | .189 |
| LW 2 | .673 | .491 | WW 1 | 43.4 | 12.77 |
| LW 3 | .826 | .442 | WW 2 | 45.2 | 11.45 |
| LW 4 | .947 | .433 | WW 3 | 47.1 | 9.78 |
| MAR 2 | .292 | .455 | WW 4 | 47.2 | 10.64 |
| MAR 3 | .446 | .498 | WUN 1 | 2.53 | 6.28 |
| MAR 4 | .507 | .500 | WUN 2 | 2.88 | 7.27 |
| SCHOOL | 11.2 | 1.51 | WUN 3 | 2.33 | 6.33 |
| SMSA 2 | .634 | .482 | WUN 4 | 2.41 | 7.44 |

Table 10.7    Regressions of Weeks Worked and Weeks
              Unemployed on Once-lagged Values

| | Dependent Variables | | | | | |
| | Weeks worked | | | Weeks unemployed | | |
| | $WW_4$ ($t=4$) | $WW_3$ ($t=3$) | $WW_2$ ($t=2$) | $WUN_4$ ($t=4$) | $WUN_3$ ($t=3$) | $WUN_2$ ($t=2$) |
|---|---|---|---|---|---|---|
| BLACK | −.442 | .596 | −1.54 | .370 | .328 | 1.25 |
| | (1.31) | (1.16) | (1.40) | (.945) | (.847) | (.961) |
| SCHOOL | .348 | .239 | .541 | −.364 | −.497 | −.073 |
| | (.431) | (.384) | (.450) | (.310) | (.278) | (.306) |
| $AGE_2$ | .140 | .048 | .442 | −.154 | −.369 | .005 |
| | (.326) | (.293) | (.355) | (.235) | (.211) | (.242) |
| $SMSA_t$ | −2.55 | −1.78 | .910 | .824 | −.331 | 1.08 |
| | (1.33) | (1.19) | (1.37) | (.943) | (.867) | (.932) |
| $SOUTH_t$ | −.082 | .298 | 3.48 | −.768 | −1.01 | −2.23 |
| | (1.38) | (1.26) | (2.33) | (1.00) | (.914) | (1.03) |
| $MAR_t$ | 2.94 | .667 | 1.45 | −1.25 | −1.11 | −1.36 |
| | (1.22) | (1.09) | (1.43) | (.875) | (.789) | (.967) |
| $AREA_t$ | .193 | −.236 | −.464 | −.148 | .042 | .356 |
| | (.308) | (.291) | (.372) | (.222) | (.211) | (.255) |
| $LW_t$ | .686 | 2.54 | 1.31 | −.741 | 1.00 | −1.18 |
| | (1.64) | (1.54) | (1.49) | (1.16) | (1.12) | (1.01) |
| $WW_{t-1}$ | .378 | .399 | .354 | — | — | — |
| | (.062) | (.046) | (.049) | | | |
| $WUN_{t-1}$ | — | — | — | .359 | .163 | .300 |
| | | | | (.067) | (.051) | (.065) |
| SEE | 9.54 | 8.44 | 10.1 | 6.87 | 6.12 | 6.89 |
| $R^2$ | .23 | .28 | .25 | .18 | .10 | .13 |

spectively. The equations also include changes in residence, marital status, and area unemployment rate. The personal characteristic variables remain to capture any systematic changes in the dependent variables.

Efficiency can be gained, however, with the use of three stage least squares because both error terms contain the residuals from the third year. Equations (3) and (4) are the unconstrained three stage least squares results. For these equations weeks worked and weeks unemployed in the first year were used as the primary instruments. Finally, in equation (5) the coefficients on all variables shown were constrained to equality across the two years.

The results in the unemployment equations are quite striking. All evidence of state dependence is eliminated. The coefficients on the lagged change in weeks unemployed are rarely positive and never significant. Indeed, there is even a hint in the results of negative state dependence. Persons with unusually high unemployment one year will have unusually low unemployment the next. Note also the poor performance of the change in beginning state dummies, $DUN_t$. The standard errors are always quite high and in four of five cases the sign is incorrect. Very few persons change states, so $DUN_t$ is virtually always zero and its coefficient is derived using instrumental variables. These facts no doubt explain a large part of the perverse results. Nonetheless, there appears to be relatively little Markov persistence in unemployment not captured by $\delta_i$. Even without controlling for nonstationarity or serial correlation then, persistence of unemployment—as distinguished from nonemployment—can be entirely attributed to heterogeneity rather than state dependence.

The results for weeks worked are quite different. Although corrections for heterogeneity substantially reduce the coefficient on the lagged dependent variable, some experience dependence remains. The experience dependence parameter varies from .08 to .19 across years and specifications. In the constrained 3SLS equation its value is .13 and is nearly twice its standard error in spite of being derived using instrumental variables. Unless the results are due to serial correlation, this coefficient indicates that persons who work an extra thirty weeks one year will work an additional four during the next as a direct result of this extra employment.

There is also strong evidence for the presence of Markov persistence. On average, persons who are working at the beginning of a year are expected to work five weeks more in that year than if they are out of

**Table 10.8**     **Difference Equation Results for Weeks Unemployed**

| | Method and dependent variable | | | | |
| | IV[a] | | 3SLS[b] | | Constrained 3SLS[b] |
| | (1) | (2) | (3) | (4) | (5) |
| Variable | $DWUN_4$ | $DWUN_3$ | $DWUN_4$ | $DWUN_3$ | $DWUN_4$ $DWUN_3$ |
|---|---|---|---|---|---|
| $DSMSA_t$ | −4.51 | 0.28 | −4.41 | 0.48 | −1.89 |
| | (1.78) | (1.94) | (1.88) | (1.94) | (1.29) |
| $DSOUTH_t$ | −2.75 | 2.18 | −2.89 | 2.07 | −0.26 |
| | (4.99) | (4.61) | (4.91) | (4.59) | (3.32) |
| $DMAR_t$ | −0.43 | 1.30 | −0.78 | 1.33 | 0.69 |
| | (1.57) | (1.24) | (1.65) | (1.24) | (0.97) |
| $DAREA_t$ | −0.68 | 0.06 | −0.64 | 0.07 | −0.35 |
| | (0.36) | (0.46) | (0.38) | (0.46) | (0.28) |
| $DLW_t$ | 7.34 | 1.12 | 7.24 | 0.51 | 1.15 |
| | (3.07) | (2.20) | (5.15) | (1.99) | (1.77) |
| $DUN_t$ | 2.06 | −2.45 | −2.21 | −2.14 | −1.39 |
| | (2.67) | (2.20) | (6.99) | (2.20) | (2.04) |
| $DWUN_{t-1}$ | −0.05 | −0.002 | −0.09 | 0.001 | −0.04 |
| | (0.07) | (0.102) | (0.07) | (0.10) | (0.09) |

NOTE: Standard errors in parentheses. All equations include year dummies, $AGE2$, $BLACK$, and $SCHOOL$.
[a] Instruments include all past and future values of $WW_{t-2}$, $WUN_{t-2}$.
[b] Instruments include all past and future values of $SMSA$, $SOUTH$, $MAR$, $AREA$, $WW_1$, $WUN_1$.

**Table 10.9          Difference Equation Results for Weeks Worked**

| | Method and dependent variable | | | | |
|---|---|---|---|---|---|
| | IV[a] | | 3SLS[b] | | Constrained 3SLS[b] |
| | (1) | (2) | (3) | (4) | (5) |
| Variable | $DWW_4$ | $DWW_3$ | $DWW_4$ | $DWW_3$ | $DWW_4 \ DWW_3$ |
| $DSMSA_t$ | 4.36 | 4.54 | 5.61 | 3.77 | 3.97 |
| | (2.66) | (2.60) | (2.75) | (2.58) | (1.79) |
| $DSOUTH_t$ | 13.75 | 1.64 | 15.57 | 1.75 | 7.31 |
| | (7.50) | (6.17) | (7.18) | (6.10) | (4.56) |
| $DMAR_t$ | −0.69 | −1.75 | 0.76 | −1.59 | −1.22 |
| | (2.36) | (1.68) | (2.40) | (1.67) | (1.35) |
| $DAREA_t$ | 0.47 | −0.12 | 0.48 | −0.12 | 0.25 |
| | (0.53) | (0.62) | (0.54) | (0.62) | (0.39) |
| $DLW_t$ | 1.06 | −1.98 | −3.14 | −1.06 | −0.54 |
| | (4.54) | (2.68) | (7.72) | (2.65) | (2.39) |
| $DEM_t$ | 3.54 | 4.92 | 3.75 | 5.34 | 4.63 |
| | (3.18) | (2.40) | (7.35) | (2.39) | (2.22) |
| $DWW_{t-1}$ | 0.19 | 0.12 | 0.08 | 0.14 | 0.13 |
| | (0.10) | (0.08) | (0.25) | (0.08) | (0.07) |

NOTE: Standard errors in parentheses. All equations include year dummies, $AGE2$, $BLACK$, and $SCHOOL$.

[a]Instruments include all past and future values of $SMSA$, $SOUTH$, $MAR$, $AREA$, $WW_{t-2}$, $WUN_{t-2}$, $LW_{t-1}$, $EM_{t-1}$.

[b]Instruments include all past and future values of $SMSA$, $SOUTH$, $MAR$, $AREA$, $WW_1$, $WUN_1$, $LW_2$, $EM_2$.

work. Excluding this parameter does seriously upward bias the experience dependence parameter. In the constrained 3SLS equation with this omitted, the dependence parameter is 0.21.

In sharp contrast to the results for unemployment, then, controls for heterogeneity do not eliminate the experience dependence estimate and the beginning state variable performs well. This is perhaps the most conclusive evidence that the retrospective unemployment rates have little meaning. Unemployment as measured here does not beget unemployment. Nonemployment begets nonemployment. Or, even more convincingly, employment begets employment. The results suggest real gains from work.

One disappointment in the results is the poor showing of the exogenous variables. Most were insignificant in the constrained three-stage equations. The $SMSA$, $SOUTH$, and $MAR$ variables were not expected to perform well since few persons moved or got married. But the performance of the area variable was unanticipated. Its sign was often incorrect; its magnitude was usually low; and its standard error was always high. The lack of strong exogenous variables prevents certain isolation of serial correlation and state dependence. It is possible that the results are evidence only that shocks persist, not that a terminated spell has lasting effects. Corrections for nonstationarity, however, should capture much of the effects of serial correlation.

A second surprise was the very weak performance of the wage in all equations and specifications. Even in the equations that do not control for heterogeneity (table 10.7), the coefficients on $LW_t$ are quite small and never significant—at most a 10% increase in wage increases weeks worked by a trifling two days! In the difference equations, the standard errors are inevitably quite high and most signs are incorrect. Using the change in wage rather than the absolute level does little to improve the performance of this measure. Although perplexing, these results are strongly verified in the next section. *Measured* wage, of course, may be quite different from potential wage if the youngster is investing in on-the-job training.

Nonstationarity, because of some forms of serial correlation or changes in work attachment, might be a source of serious bias in the results. Sharply changing employment rates resulting from rising or decaying heterogeneity *unrelated* to employment could be spuriously picked up as experience dependence. Including age, race, marital status, and an intercept in the difference equations captures systematic changes and helps to minimize the problem. Corrections for nonstationarity require four years of data. Thus nonstationarity can only be tested between the third and fourth years.

Table 10.10 presents the results for weeks unemployed and weeks worked designed to isolate the effects of nonstationarity and state dependence. Once again the unemployment equation behaves badly, $WUN_3$ failing even to change sign. The weeks-worked equation, however, performs surprisingly well. Although the standard error in the twice lagged weeks worked is large, so too is its magnitude. The coefficients imply a nonstationarity parameter (ratio of the individual effects in years three and four) of 0.76 and a state dependence parameter of 0.11. (Although the specification allows either parameter to be 0.76 or 0.11, it is clear from context which is which.) The heterogeneity parameter does show some decay (capturing some serial correlation no doubt), but the experience dependence parameter is nearly identical to that derived in the constrained 3SLS specification.

This analysis illustrates the critical importance of controlling for heterogeneity. Controls eliminated all of the apparent state dependence in unemployment equations. They reduced by two-thirds the dependence parameter in the weeks-worked equations. Previous studies, which used only additional demographic variables to control for heterogeneity, have seriously overstated the true long-term impact of teenage unemployment on future labor market performance.

The conclusion then is that working does have some benefit beyond the current year. Someone working an extra thirty weeks in one year will

Table 10.10    Instrumental Variable Equations Allowing Nonstationarity of Individual Component

|  | Dependent variable | | | Dependent variable | |
|  | WW 4 | WUN 4 |  | WW 4 | WUN 4 |
|---|---|---|---|---|---|
| SMSA 4 | 4.42 | −4.03 | LW 4 | −7.13 | 11.96 |
|  | (2.71) | (2.08) |  | (6.67) | (5.23) |
| SMSA 3 | −5.67 | 4.70 | LW 3 | 1.65 | −7.08 |
|  | (2.59) | (1.99) |  | (4.34) | (3.45) |
| SOUTH 4 | 15.37 | −3.92 | DEM 4 | 3.64 | — |
|  | (6.65) | (4.96) |  | (3.01) |  |
| SOUTH 3 | −16.97 | 4.47 | WW 3 | 0.87 | — |
|  | (6.84) | (3.10) |  | (0.19) |  |
| MAR 4 | 2.01 | −2.76 | WW 2 | −0.084 | — |
|  | (2.42) | (1.75) |  | (0.098) |  |
| MAR 3 | 1.23 | 0.25 | DUN 4 | — | −0.04 |
|  | (2.29) | (1.66) |  |  | (3.03) |
| AREA 4 | 0.30 | 0.04 | WUN 3 | — | 0.43 |
|  | (0.50) | (0.39) |  |  | (0.20) |
| AREA 3 | 0.31 | 0.08 | WUN 2 | — | 0.081 |
|  | (0.54) | (0.39) |  |  | (0.072) |
|  |  |  | SEE | 10.5 | 7.84 |

NOTE: Equations also include $BLACK$, $SCHOOL$, $AGE$ 2. Instruments include $SMSA$ 4, $SMSA$ 3, $SOUTH$ 4, $SOUTH$ 3, $MAR$ 4, $MAR$ 3, $AREA$ 4, $AREA$ 3, $BLACK$, $SCHOOL$, $AGE_2$, $WW_2$, $WW_1$, $WUN_2$, $WUN_1$, $LW_3$, $LW_2$, $EM_3$, $EM_2$, $UN_3$, $UN_2$.

perhaps work an extra four in the next. This result does not distinguish between voluntary and involuntary time out of work. Work may improve skills, open new options for employment, or simply increase work attachment.

Nonetheless, in absolute terms, the long-run impact is relatively small. Even thirty weeks out of work have virtually no impact after one or two years. For this group of youngsters there is no evidence of a long-term cycle of recurring periods without employment induced by an early episode out of work—experience dependence yes, but a serious "permanent scar," no.

These estimates are not perfect. There are potential biases in both directions. Nevertheless, I find the evidence that teenage nonemployment exhibits short-term state dependence quite compelling. There are, however, three important caveats. First, this evidence is for a group of teenagers who entered the labor force in extremely favorable times. In this period it may have been the case that jobs were readily available for most youngsters. The seventies have brought a substantially worse job outlook. In this environment the effects of employment and the lack of it may be very different. Second, this is not a random sample of young persons. Some of the long term nonemployed may have been excluded from the sample. These persons may gain and lose more from being in or out of work. Finally, the sample here is too small to separate effects on specific groups. It may be that one can isolate stronger effects among blacks or low income persons.

These concerns notwithstanding, the current evidence is clear. Teenage nonemployment has real but short-lived adverse effects on teenage employment prospects.

## 10.3  The Impact of Work Experience on Wages

The second potential cost of being out of work is that the lost experience will translate into reduced wages. In the long run, reduced wages could be a far more important cost of unemployment. Lost experience could travel with the worker over his life. Each job may serve as a stepping stone to another. Lost experience at least delays the start of the young worker's climb. Worse, it may track the worker into a less desirable chain of jobs. This final section attempts to separate the cost of lost experience from differences in individual earning capacity correlated with work experience.

Assessing the true impact of work experience in a particular year apart from heterogeneity is a very complex problem. The triangular structure of wages whereby work experience influences wages which in turn influences future work experience, in combination with the direct experience dependence from work experience, creates a hopelessly tangled collection of heterogeneity terms with coefficients which vary over time.

The problems can best be understood by starting with a multiequation system. Let $LW_{it}$ be the natural log of wages of individual $i$ *at the start of* year $t$, $X_{it}$ a vector of exogenous variables, and $WW_{it}$ be weeks worked in year $t$. One model of wages and employment is:

$$(1) \qquad LW_{it} = X_{it}\beta_t + \sum_{j=1}^{t-1} \alpha_{tt-j} WW_{it-j} + \lambda_{it} + \varepsilon_{it}$$

$$(2) \qquad WW_{it} = X_{it}\beta_t + \gamma_t WW_{it-1} + \omega_t LW_{it} + \delta_{it} \\ + \Psi_{it}b_{it} + U_{it}$$

Here equation (1) is just a straightforward human capital-type wage equation; equation (2) is just the labor supply relation from the previous section. $\lambda_{it}$ is a heterogeneity term in the wage equation, $\delta_{it}$ and $\Psi_{it}$ are the individual components in the weeks-worked model. Note that $\alpha_{tt-j}$ is almost certainly not going to be constant across weeks worked in different years since the flattening profile suggests diminished investment over time.

Only lagged weeks worked appear in the wage equation. Thus the system is triangular and a reduced form equation can be derived in a straightforward fashion. If we assume $\lambda_{it} = \lambda_i$, $\delta_{it} = \delta_i$, and $\Psi_{it} = \Psi_i$ and if we condition on $WW_{i1}$, the reduced form equation will have the following form.

$$LW_{it} = \sum_{j=2}^{t} X_{ij}A_j + B_t WW_{i1} + C_t\delta_i + \sum_{j=2}^{t} D_t\Psi_i d_{it}$$
$$+ E_t\lambda_i + \sum_{j=2}^{t} F_t U_{it} + \sum_{j=2}^{t} G_t\varepsilon_{it}$$

The coefficient on $WW_{i1}$ in the correctly estimated reduced-form equation captures the full impact of early unemployment on the wage in year $t$. Previous authors have estimated equations of this type in the past but have included few controls for heterogeneity or Markov persistence.

The reduced-form equation helps point out the dual biases present in OLS estimation of this equation. Early experience may be correlated with the individual component in wages, $\lambda_i$ ("ability"), upward biasing the coefficient on $WW_{i1}$. This bias grows over time because $\lambda_i$ affects wages each year which alters future weeks worked which in turn influences future wages. At the same time, early experience is correlated with later experience in part because of the individual components of experience, $\delta_i$, $\Psi_i$ ("work attachment" and "ease of finding a job"). Since experience yields positive benefits, the coefficient on $WW_{i1}$ is further biased because early experience inappropriately captures some of the effects of later experience. This effect also grows over time; each year brings new experience correlated with first year's experience. (In practice, of course, most workers eventually hit roughly fifty-two weeks of employment each year so the correlation is not perpetual.) Thus previous estimates of the long-term impacts of early employment experience may be severely biased. One other feature of the equation should be noted. The equation includes *all* Xs between year 2 and year $t$. Exclusion of these is yet another source of potential bias.

Yet even this rather complicated model leaves much to be desired. Human capital theories suggest that persons may select differently shaped profiles. Persons with early unemployment and nonemployment may have flatter schedules. Blue-collar workers have slower wage growth than their white-collar counterparts. If the return to experience is systematically lower for persons lacking some early work experience, the coefficient will be further biased upward. Similarly, the individual components may not be stationary over time, introducing even more bias.

Even ignoring the inadequacies with the current model, however, it is virtually impossible to get consistent estimates of the coefficient on weeks worked in the first year. Simple differencing does not eliminate the heterogeneity components since the coefficients on all are changing over time. Equally troubling, $WW_{i1}$ is fixed over time. Differencing yields only the change in its coefficient, not its overall magnitude. The only hope for estimation is to find an instrument correlated with $WW_{i1}$ but partially uncorrelated with $\delta_i$, $\Psi_i$, or $\lambda_i$. One such instrument might be the area unemployment rate in year 1. It is not currently in the equations and the inclusion of race and residence dummies along with schooling may eliminate most of its correlation with the individual effects. Unfortunately, we have already seen that the area rate performed poorly in weeks-worked equations. Thus it is an unlikely instrument.

Although isolation of the full long-term impact of nonemployment in this data set is infeasible then, a more modest attempt can be made to isolate the impact of heterogeneity. Let us concentrate solely on equation (1), the regression of log wages on an individual constant and weeks worked in previous years. If we treat weeks worked in each year as exogenous, then simple differencing eliminates the nuisance parameter and leaves the last weeks-worked parameter intact. Thus

$$(1) \qquad LW_{it} = X_{it}\beta'_t + \sum_{j=1}^{t-1} \alpha_{t_i-j} WW_{i_{t-j}} + \lambda_i + \varepsilon_{it}$$

$$(1') \qquad LW_{it} - LW_{it-1} = X_{it}\beta'_t - X_{it-1}\beta'_{t-1}$$
$$+ \sum_{j=2}^{t-1} (\alpha_{ti-j} - \alpha_{t-1t-j}) WW_{it-j}$$
$$+ \alpha_{tt-1} WW_{it-1} + \varepsilon_{it} - \varepsilon_{it-1}$$

As long as the weeks worked are strictly exogenous, $\alpha_{tt-1}$, the coefficient on the weeks worked in year $t-1$ represents its impact in that year. One can also difference wages separated by two years. In that case, the coefficients on the last two years of experience could be captured.

The exogeneity assumption, however, is highly suspect. Even if we assume that $WW_{t-1}$ was uncorrelated with $\varepsilon_{it}$, the presence of $LW_{t-1}$ in the labor supply equation determining $WW_{t-1}$ guarantees that $Cov(WW_{it-1}, \varepsilon_{it-1}) > 0$. OLS estimates of the difference equation will then understate the true impact of $WW_t$ on wages. In the previous labor supply results the coefficient on $LW_{t-1}$ was often small, occasionally of wrong sign, and invariably insignificant. Still, without stronger evidence of exogeneity, we must be concerned that OLS estimates will be biased.

There are two reasonable approaches to this problem. First, Sims (1972) has suggested a very simple methodology to test for exogeneity: simply regress the dependent variable on all past and future values of the independent variable. Strict exogeneity in the absence of heterogeneity implies that the coefficient on future values will be zero; those on past values, nonzero. If causality is unidirectional, past values of the independent variable will influence the dependent variable, but the current dependent variable will not influence future values of the independent variables. Unfortunately, even if the independent variable is strictly exogenous, in the presence of heterogeneity the expectation of the future coefficients will be nonzero if the future values are correlated with any part of the heterogeneity not captured by other variables in the equation (see Chamberlain [1979]). The common-sense notion is that any variable partially correlated with an omitted stationary heterogeneity term will have a nonzero coefficient even in equations where the variable would otherwise have a zero coefficient, because it will be serving as a proxy for the omitted variable. If weeks worked in year 2 is capturing heterogeneity in the year 2 wage equation, it ought to capture the same heterogeneity in year 1. Essentially, Sims's is a test for true casuality as opposed to spurious correlation due to endogeneity or omitted variables.

If, as seems likely, the Sims test fails, we are forced to seek an instrument for $WW_{it-1}$ in equation (1'). If we assume that impact work experience in some year $j$ raises wages in years $t-1$ and $t$ by a equal amount, $\alpha_{tj} = \alpha_{t-1j}$ and we can withdraw $WW_{ij}$ from the equation and use it to instrument $WW_{it}$. $WW_{it-2}$ for instance, might serve as an effective instrument.

Many authors have previously sought to remove heterogeneity or "ability" bias from wage equations (see, for example, Chamberlain [1978a], Griliches and Mason [1972]). These efforts typically were not aimed at deriving the coefficient on work experience as distinct from age, nor did they focus particularly on the very early years of experience. Nonetheless it would be surprising in light of all the previous efforts if we did not find a substantial effect of work experience on wages.

### 10.3.1 Empirical Results in Wage Equations

To roughly replicate previous studies of the effects of unemployment on wages, wage equations were first estimated for 1975 and 1973 with no experience variables included other than weeks worked in the first year. The data base was the same sample of young men who left high school in 1965 to 1967. The results were similar to those reported by other authors. The coefficient on $WW_1$ was .00452 on 1975 and .00478 in 1973. Both coefficients were quite significant. If the values actually reflect the true effect of early nonemployment on future wages, the impact is staggering. Youngsters missing out on twenty-six weeks of employment experience in their first year out of school are left with 12% lower wages even ten years later. Accumulated over a lifetime, the cost could be enormous. These results are not purged of heterogeneity, of course. The large size of the possible losses thus makes the separation of the true impact quite important.

At the very least, the results do show dramatic persistence in wages for persons with early time not employed. Even if nonemployment had no important impact of its own, early unemployment can be used to single out persons who will do poorly in the future. They could be the recipients of special aid. The result is also important because it suggests that early experience could be used as a signal of "quality" or "ability" by employers. This is not to say that employers in 1975 would have looked at what happened in 1966, but employers in 1967 or 1968 might have, and employers in 1969 might have looked back to 1968, and so forth. In a market with great uncertainty, those persons who genuinely tried but failed to get work may be inadvertently classed as poor workers. It may take these workers some real time to recover from this early adverse signal.

The issue at hand, however, is whether this early experience or lack thereof actually has ill effects. The previous section described why the only possible hope of capturing the very long-term effects was with an effective instrument on $WW_1$. The area unemployment rate in year 1 was suggested. As expected, however, instrumental variable equations behaved poorly. The results were erratic; standard errors very high. Thus I chose to focus more narrowly on the effects of experience in the first four years of experience.

Table 10.11 presents regression results of wages at the end of each of the first four full years out of school as a function of weeks worked in previous years. These were estimated as seemingly unrelated equations

**Table 10.11     Wage Equations for the First Four Years out of School**

|  | Dependent variables | | | |
|---|---|---|---|---|
|  | $LWAGE_2$ $(t=2)$ | $LWAGE_3$ $(t=3)$ | $LWAGE_4$ $(t=4)$ | $LWAGE_5$ $(t=5)$ |
| SCHOOL | .040 | .051 | .046 | .060 |
|  | (.017) | (.014) | (.015) | (.014) |
| $AGE_2$ | .040 | .038 | .018 | .027 |
|  | (.017) | (.011) | (.012) | (.011) |
| BLACK | −.114 | −.125 | −.124 | −.070 |
|  | (.053) | (.045) | (.048) | (.045) |
| $SMSA_t$ | .135 | .145 | .171 | .138 |
|  | (.048) | (.039) | (.041) | (.038) |
| $SOUTH_t$ | −.275 | −.218 | −.197 | −.264 |
|  | (.055) | (.045) | (.047) | (.044) |
| $MAR_t$ | .078 | .105 | .078 | .085 |
|  | (.046) | (.033) | (.035) | (.034) |
| $AREA_t$ | .010 | .005 | −.003 | −.012 |
|  | (.013) | (.009) | (.008) | (.007) |
| $WW_1$ | .0030 | .0036 | .0034 | .0049 |
|  | (.0019) | (.0017) | (.0019) | (.0017) |
| $WW_2$ | — | .0028 | .0035 | .0010 |
|  |  | (.0018) | (.0021) | (.0020) |
| $WW_3$ | — | — | .0043 | .0019 |
|  |  |  | (.0020) | (.0022) |
| $WW_4$ | — | — | — | .0017 |
|  |  |  |  | (.0017) |
| INTERCEPT | −.675 | −.742 | −.433 | −.487 |
|  | (.258) | (.221) | (.237) | (.226) |

NOTE: All equations estimated as seemingly unrelated equations.

since the error terms will almost certainly be correlated. With only 271 observations, the results are plagued by rather high standard errors. Nonetheless, the coefficients on past weeks worked are quite sizable. Furthermore, the results seem quite stable until year 4 when collinearity seems to be excessive. The numbers suggest that each year of experience is associated with a 10 to 20% wage increase in these first four years. Although reserving some concern for the low significance of some estimates, I shall concentrate on determining whether these high point estimates appear to be the result of heterogeneity or state dependence.

The Sims test for true causality is to include future work experience in current wage equations. Strict exogeneity implies zero coefficients on future variables so that the coefficients on $WW_2$, $WW_3$, and $WW_4$ would be zero in the $LW_2$ regression; $WW_3$ and $WW_4$ in the $LW_3$ regression, and so forth. (Recall that $LW_t$ is wage at the beginning of year $t$ or end of year $t - 1$). Table 10.12 displays wage equations for years 2, 3, and 4, when weeks worked in years 1 to 4 are included in each regression. The results are striking. In spite of a high degree of multicollinearity, in each of the equations the coefficients on past experiences remain strongly positive. The coefficients on future experience tend to be small or of incorrect sign. Incredibly, neither endogeneity nor heterogeneity may seriously bias the coefficients on $WW_2$, $WW_3$ or $WW_4$. A likelihood ratio test that the coefficients on future values are zero is not rejected. Twice the natural log of the likelihood ratio is 7.7, while the critical value of $\chi^2$ (6) is 12.6. A similar test that the coefficients on past values are zero is overwhelmingly rejected (likelihood ratio = 126.3).

This evidence for the one-way causality of weeks worked on wages is quite surprising, although the very weak performance of the wage variables in the labor supply equation portended this exogeneity. The minimal bias resulting from heterogeneity is perhaps even more remarkable.

**Table 10.12**    **Wage Equations with Weeks Worked in First Four Years Included in All Regressions[a]**

| | Dependent variables | | |
| | $LWAGE_2$ ($t=2$) | $LWAGE_3$ ($t=3$) | $LWAGE_4$ ($t=4$) |
| --- | --- | --- | --- |
| WW1 | .0031 | .0036 | .0034 |
| | (.0021) | (.0018) | (.0019) |
| WW2 | − .0005 | .0025 | .0032 |
| | (.0026) | (.0022) | (.0023) |
| WW3 | .0014 | .0014 | .0047 |
| | (.0031) | (.0026) | (.0028) |
| WW4 | − .0019 | − .0015 | .0009 |
| | (.0026) | (.0022) | (.0024) |

[a]All equations include $SCHOOL$, $AGE_t$, $BLACK$, $SMSA_t$, $SOUTH_t$, $MAR_t$, $AREA_t$. All equations estimated as seemingly unrelated equations.

It should be remembered though, that these results in no way indicate that heterogeneity is absent. They show instead that the portion of heterogeneity correlated with $WW_2$, $WW_3$ and $WW_4$ is fully captured by $WW_1$, *SCHOOL, AGE,* and the other controls. The coefficients on these latter variables are presumably biased by the presence of heterogeneity.

The very powerful conclusion from this exercise is that, at least in these four years, the coefficients are a good reflection of the causal relationship between experience and wages. Not surprisingly, the difference results confirm these findings. Differencing eliminates any stationary effects correlated with weeks worked. If heterogeneity were a serious problem, we should expect the coefficients on work experience accumulated between the differenced years' wages to fall. At the same time, endogeneity would induce a negative correlation between this experience and the error term, thus causing a further fall.

Since the coefficients in year 4 showed that multicollinearity may be excessive, I will concentrate on the first three years' wage equations. (The results for year 4 are quite similar.) Table 10.13 presents the estimated coefficients in three difference equations. In the first column, first-year wages are subtracted from those of the second year. The second column presents results of the regressions on the difference in wages between years 2 and 3. The final column provides differences between years 3 and 1. Once again, the data strongly suggest that heterogeneity and endogeneity are relatively small parts of the measured association between experience and wages in the second and third years. The impact of weeks worked in year 1 is neutralized in all of the difference equations, as would be predicted, since the coefficient represents the difference in the effects of experience on wages in two future years. The coefficient on weeks worked in the second year is effectively zero in the second equation, again as predicted. However, the coefficients on weeks worked in the second and third years in equations where those effects were not differenced out remain quite large. The coefficients are much more stable across equations than they were in table 10.11. Their magnitude is, if anything, greater and their significance is increased. The results are thus highly supportive of a causal relationship between experience and wages. The increase in the significance is reassuring that the effects of experience are not purely spurious.

One possible problem may be that we have tested the wrong model. Jobs with the highest *wage growth* may have very stable employment requirements. This model would imply that if a Sims-type test were performed using the change in wages on the left hand side, future weeks worked enter significantly since workers would presumably remain with their jobs. Note also that past weeks worked would likely enter significantly since there is a good chance that persons with good jobs now, as measured by wage growth, had them in the previous year. Neither result

Table 10.13        Differenced Wage Equations[a]

| | $LWAGE_3 - LWAGE_2$ $(t_1=3, t_2=2)$ | Dependent variables $LWAGE_4 - LWAGE_3$ $(t_1=4, t_2=3)$ | $LWAGE_4 - LWAGE_2$ $(t_1=4, t_2=2)$ |
|---|---|---|---|
| $WW_1$ | .0002 | −.0001 | .0002 |
| | (.0019) | (.0016) | (.0020) |
| $WW_2$ | .0035 | .0006 | .0040 |
| | (.0022) | (.0020) | (.0025) |
| $WW_3$ | — | .0041 | .0040 |
| | | (.0021) | (.0021) |

[a]All equations include $SCHOOL$, $AGE_2$, $BLACK$, $SMSA_{t1}$, $SMSA_{t2}$, $SOUTH_{t1}$, $SOUTH_{t2}$, $MAR_{t1}$, $MAR_{t2}$, $AREA_{t1}$, $AREA_{t2}$. All equations estimated as seemingly unrelated equations.

was prominent in the data. Moreover, it is quite possible that the largest single year wage changes will be associated with job changes. Presumably, some young men find new jobs offering better pay. The movers probably have fewer weeks worked than the stayers. These persons bias the results downward.

The results presented here strongly suggest that in the first few years out of school, experience increases wages by as much as 10 to 20% per year. The biggest cost of being out of work therefore may well be the wages. These data do not reveal whether this is the result of the accumulation of general or specific human capital or even if they merely reflect signaling. Nor do they reveal what skills might be gained from early experience. They do reveal, however, that lost work experience really can be quite costly.

These data do not allow good tests for a catch-up effect. It is possible that the loss in wages due to previously lost experience is compensated for when the individual finally gets a steady job. Interaction terms simply make the results unstable. This is an important possibility which merits attention in future work.

The results here imply that early experience increases wages by 10 to 20%. I regard these wage equations as preliminary results requiring verification from other sources. Still, they provide surprisingly strong evidence that, at least in the short run, work experience really does make a difference. Just how long the effect persists requires another analyses. Ultimately, the final conclusion awaits the availability of a good area unemployment rate measure so that $WW_1$ can be properly instrumented.

## 10.4    Conclusion: Permanent Scars or Temporary Blemishes?

The first part of this paper examined the early pattern of labor market performance of young men. Several important conclusions were made.

• The early years of labor market experience are times of substantial change. Employment rates rise, as do participation rates. There is considerable evidence of weak labor force attachment early in many young men's careers.

• Although the distinction between time out of the labor force and time unemployed is conceptually appealing, the division is not accurately captured in these retrospective data. Unemployment rates behave erratically over time for this group. All of the results in this chapter suggest that time not employed is a far better measure of the labor market performance of young men.

• Even though there is a general improvement in employment rates for these young men over time, early labor market patterns persist. Young men with poor records early will typically have comparatively poor records later.

The next section revealed that much of the persistence in employment patterns could be directly attributed to heterogeneity.

• Controls for heterogeneity eliminate at least two-thirds of the observed persistence in employment, but evidence of experience dependence remains. That is, even controlling for individual differences in the propensity to work, experience dependence remains. However, the absolute magnitude of the effect is small. Even a six-month spell out of work tends to generate only an additional three to four weeks out of work one year later. There is no evidence in these data that time out of work sets off a long term cycle of recurring "nonemployment."

Finally, the effect of work experience on wages was examined. Apparently, neither heterogeneity nor endogeneity induce important biases in the estimated impact of work experience in the second, third, and fourth years out of school on the wages of youngsters in the first few years afterward. The impact of early experience on wages is quite large.

• Early work experience has a sizable impact on wages. Controlling for individual effects, experience in the second, third, or fourth year out of school tends to be associated with wage increases of between 10 and 20% a year.

The data did not allow testing for the possibility of catch-up, nor for testing how long these wage differentials persist.

There is a strong asymmetry in the problem of isolating the real effects of early labor market experience on future employment and wages from the differences in wages and employment that are the natural result of differences among people within the labor market. There are many reasons for expecting that unobserved differences among people will be correlated both with employment and wages. Thus a finding suggesting that early experience has real impact is always suspect. On the other hand, a finding of no impact is considered quite convincing since the deck was stacked against such a conclusion. The results in this chapter lead me to the former more suspect finding. Early experience really does seem to make a difference, particularly on wages. Even after rather elaborate controls for heterogeneity, both wages and labor supply seem to be directly related to past work experience in the short run, although the effects on labor supply are quite small.

As with all research, many caveats remain. This research was conducted on a small select sample in a period of tight labor markets, quite unlike the present situation. It may be that these findings are peculiar to this group or this era. No separate analysis has been done for the central city poor. The cleanest experiment—testing whether past unemployment rates predict future wages and employment—could not be performed. The ultimate answer to the question of the long-term impact must await these results. Until such time as high quality local unemployment data are available, we will have to rely on statistical methods of removing heterogeneity.

In this group of young men the heavy cost of time out of work was the impact of the lost work experience on wages. The data do not show whether working generates better work habits, or instills general or firm specific skills, or even just creates positive signals. Policy makers should keep in mind, however, that many forms of public employment may not generate the desirable human capital or worker quality signals. Employers may regard public employment quite differently from private employment. The challenge for public policy is to design aid programs which help young people accumulate the important labor experience, rather than simply provide programs which makes the government the last-resort employer.

# Notes

1. Meyer and Wise (chapter 9 of this volume) report similar results for the National Longitudinal Survey of the High School Class of 1972.

2. Actually, $\psi_i$ captures both the experience dependence from period $t-1$ plus the Markov type probability of remaining in state 1. This is of no serious concern if the periods are short. If periods are long, asymmetric definition of periods implies a serious loss of efficiency.

3. Actually, it can be proven that if we assume complete stationarity (exclude all $X$s), we can legitimately test the null hypothesis of no state dependence by conditioning on $b_{it-1} = b_{it} = b_{it+1}$.

4. For one analysis of the long-run performance of cohorts entering weak labor markets, see Plantes (1978).

5. See Meyer and Wise (chapter 9) for a treatment of the fifty-two-week truncation problem in the absence of heterogeneity. These authors do not use difference quations.

# References

Becker, E. and S. Hills. 1979. Teenage unemployment: Some evidence of the long run effects. *Journal of Human Resources*, forthcoming.

Chamberlain, G. 1978. Omitted variable bias in panel data: Estimating the returns to schooling. *Annales de l'INSEE* 30–31 (April–September 1978): 49–82.

————. 1979. Heterogeneity, omitted variable bias and duration dependence. HIER Discussion Paper no. 691.

Clark, K. and L. Summers. The dynamics of youth unemployment. Chapter 7 of this volume.

Grilliches, Z. and W. Mason. 1972. Education income and ability." *Journal of Political Economy* (80, no. 3):S74–S103.

Heckman, J. 1978a. Dummy endogenous variables in a simultaneous equation system. *Econometrica* (46, no. 4):931–59.

————. 1978b. Simple statistical models for discrete panel data developed and applied to test the hypothesis of true state dependence against the hypothesis of spurious state dependence. *Annales de l'INSEE* (30–31):227–70.

Heckman, J. and R. Willis. 1977. A beta-logistic model for the analysis of sequential labor force participation by married women. *Journal of Political Economy* (85):27–58.

Lillard, L. and R. Willis. 1977. Dynamic aspects of earning mobility. NBER Working Paper no. 150 (revised).

Meyer, R. and D. Wise. High school preparation and early labor force experience. Chapter 9 of this volume.

Plantes, M. K. 1978. *Work experience, economic activity and lifetime earnings: An intercohort analysis.* Ph.D. dissertation, Massachusetts Institute of Technology.

Sims, C. 1972. Money, income and casualty. *American Economic Review* (62):540–52.

Stevenson, W. 1978. The relationship between early work experience and future employability. In Adams, A. and G. Mangum, *The lingering crisis of youth unemployment.* Kalamazoo: Upjohn Institute for Empirical Research.

## Comment    Robert J. Willis

Is teenage unemployment a serious social problem? Despite high and rising levels of measured unemployment among teenagers, especially black teenagers, economists appear to have quite varied opinions about the seriousness of the problem. To a considerable degree, I suspect that those economists who are least alarmed about teenage unemployment tend to concentrate on short-run costs that are borne by the teenager. Here the magnitude of the welfare loss of the typical unemployed teenager appears to be modest because of the dominance of short spells, the likelihood of income protection from his family or from welfare programs, and the presumably positive value he attaches to his nonmarket time. Indeed, those who emphasize the supply-side determinants of unemployment might argue that teenage unemployment is high precisely because the costs to the teenager of unemployment are so low.

Of course, it is possible that the short-run social costs of teenage unemployment are much higher than those costs because of moral hazard caused by family or social insurance of the teenager's consumption against the risk of unemployment, or because the high private value of his nonmarket time is due to the gains from illegal activity. Even in these instances, however, it may be argued that teenage unemployment is more a symptom than a cause of social problems whose roots lie in the decline of the family as an agent of social control and the failure of other institutions to replace this function of the family as rapidly as they have replaced its protective functions. Unfortunately, there are as yet insufficient theory and data to judge how important these social welfare losses may be or whether the major part of the explanation for trends and levels of teenage unemployment should be sought in the functioning of the labor market or in changes in the broader social, economic, and institutional context of the society.

Even if teenage unemployment does not impose substantial short-run costs, it has been argued that it may have severe long-term consequences for an individual's labor market success. It is this "scar hypothesis" which is the subject of David T. Ellwood's interesting and important chapter. Previous researchers have found a fairly strong correlation between various measures of an individual's current labor force activity (e.g., unemployment, employment, or wage rate) and his teenage unemployment experience. Ellwood rightly argues that the major statistical issue to be resolved is to determine whether such a relationship represents the *causal* effect of early unemployment on the subsequent labor market success of a given individual or whether it simply reflects a correlation

Robert J. Willis is associated with the State University of New York at Stony Brook and with the National Bureau of Economic Research.

induced by persistent unmeasured differences (i.e., population heterogeneity) in labor supply parameters across individuals.

The distinction between correlation and causation is always difficult to establish in nonexperimental data, but is especially difficult in the current context because the dependent variable is the occupancy or duration of stay in a discrete state (e.g., unemployment) and the causal variable of interest is a lagged dependent variable (e.g., unemployment as a teenager). The econometric methodology to deal with such problems is just now being developed. It is to Ellwood's credit that he has not only provided a lucid description and critique of this literature but has also made an imaginative and thoughtful attempt to extend and apply this methodology to deal with an important issue.

In my judgment, Ellwood's work represents a significant advance over previous studies of the length of teenage unemployment, and his major finding that previous studies have substantially overstated these effects by neglecting unmeasured heterogeneity is quite plausible. Unfortunately, Ellwood is forced to use data which do not describe an individual's complete employment history (i.e., data on the dates and durations of each spell of employment, unemployment, and nonemployment since leaving school). In attempting to make his econometric model conform to data limitations, I believe that he may have introduced some confusion on two important issues—the definition of "true" state dependence and the distinction between continuous and discrete time models. I suspect that the model he employs is misspecified (relative to a model using ideal complete event history data), but it is beyond my competence to suggest what the best model specification might be given the available data or to guess what bias may inhere in the model he uses.

The causal effect Ellwood seeks to measure is the change in current employment behavior induced by a previous employment event such as the occurrence or nonoccurrence of teenage unemployment. Following the terminology in the emerging econometrics literature, he uses the term "state dependence" to denote such an effect. However, the two types of state dependence which Ellwood distinguishes in the paper, i.e., "simple Markovian dependence" and "true experience dependence" do not necessarily correspond to the type of state dependence implied by the scar hypothesis.

Simple Markovian dependence is designed to control for the inertia which leads an individual who is currently employed to be more likely than an unemployed individual to be employed a short time later. This control is necessary because, while the dependent variable is continuous (e.g., number of weeks worked during the year), the observation period is in discrete time units of a year. Thus it is misleading for Ellwood to characterize his model as continuous; in fact, I believe it suffers from many of the problems he raises concerning discrete time models applied to a continuous time process such as employment. True experience dependence (i.e., the $\gamma$ parameter) measures the effect of, for example, the number of weeks worked last year on the number of weeks worked this year, holding constant an unmeasured person-specific labor supply parameter. It is this form of state dependence that Ellwood hopes to measure in order to assess the importance of the scar effect.

I suspect that $\gamma$ measures a mixture of several "pure" forms of state dependence in the underlying continuous time process, not all of which correspond to the causal effects implied by the scar effect. One pure form of state dependence which has received considerable attention recently in the work of Chamberlain, Mincer, and Heckman is duration dependence. Roughly, duration dependence is present if the conditional probability of leaving a state (e.g., employment or unemployment) varies with the length of time spent in the state (i.e., the hazard function varies with duration). In the employment context, for example, Mincer suggests that the acquisition of firm-specific human capital would lead to a decrease in the probability of leaving a given employer as the length of job tenure increases. In this case, the hazard function for a given employment or job spell is said to be decreasing. If duration dependence is the only form of true state dependence, an individual's probability of exiting from a given spell of employment or unemployment is independent of his employment history prior to entering his current state. Clearly, the scar hypothesis suggests dependence on past history so that it is necessary to consider additional forms of true state dependence beyond pure duration dependence. For example, it may be reasonable to postulate that current probabilities of leaving employment (or unemployment) at given duration depend on the number and/or duration of previous jobs on unemployment spells as is suggested in a recent paper by Heckman and Borjas (1979) that was written after the Ellwood chapter.

The scar hypothesis should probably be elaborated in order to specify more precisely what types of state dependence one seeks to measure. For example, a past history of unemployment might be expected to influence both the level and slope of the hazard function pertaining to a given spell of employment because employers may be reluctant to make job-specific investments in "unreliable" individuals. If this is the case, past unemployment reduces the degree of duration dependence but increases the likelihood of turnover in employment at given duration. Because of data limitations which preclude the identification of separate spells of employment or unemployment, Ellwood's model is unable to distinguish between effects of duration in the current spell and effects of events that took place before the current spell began. His concept of true experience dependence probably captures a mixture of these effects. Despite these drawbacks, due largely to data limitations, Ellwood has written an important chapter, the findings of which deserve to be taken seriously.

**Reference**

Heckman, J. J. and G. J. Borjas. August 1979. Does unemployment cause future unemployment? Definitions, questions and answers from a continuous time model of heterogeneity and state dependence. Mimeo.

# Comment     Burt S. Barnow

David Ellwood's chapter provides a significant contribution to the literature on the long-term effects of teenage employment problems. Although the previous papers on this subject cited by Ellwood do a good job of documenting the persistence of employment problems, none does as thorough a job of exploring the causality of the persistence. My comments follow the organization of Ellwood's chapter, covering the data, the descriptive results, theory, and the analytical results.

The National Longitudinal Survey (NLS) of young men is useful for Ellwood's purpose, but it has several limitations. Because there are only 298 observations, small effects may not be detected with statistical significance; this problem is increased by the use of instrumental variable techniques. A more important limitation of the small sample size is that greatly different groups are constrained to have identical coefficients—it is questionable whether the same relationship can be expected to be appropriate for middle-class high school graduates and poor dropouts.

Although Ellwood is careful to point out the limitations of the sample, the reader should keep in mind the fact that the sample used is not representative of all youths. In addition to the omission of youths who attended college and other post-secondary schools, many youths of average intelligence and health were drafted. Thus Ellwood's sample over-represents those with low intelligence or poor health.

The presentation of the descriptive results, especially the probability trees, is very helpful in tracing the labor force experience of the sample. For example, although only 18% of the sample worked throughout the four years and only 39% were always employed in three or four of the years, we also find that 47% of the sample experienced no unemployment over the four years and 70% were unemployed in one or none of the four years. This suggests that unemployment and nonemployment are different phenomena. At several points Ellwood notes that unemployment appears to be a less stable variation than nonemployment. But it is worth noting from table 10.3 that unemployment status in year 1 is a better

Burt S. Barnow is acting director of the Office of Research and Development in the Employment and Training Administration of the U.S. Department of Labor.

predictor of unemployment status in year 4 than nonemployment status in year 1 is of nonemployment status in year 4.

Ellwood's theoretical section is excellent in its consideration of the concept of state dependence. The distinctions between what he refers to as Markov-type dependence and experience dependence are important from both a theoretical perspective and a policy perspective. What is troubling in the theory section is the lack of economic theory for identifying the variables and the functional forms of the models. For example, Ellwood uses the variable $\delta_{it}$ to represent unobservable individual variables. If $\delta_{it}$ represents I.Q., then the assumption $\delta_{it} = \delta_i$ is fine, but if $\delta_{it}$ represents motivation, then such an assumption is inappropriate. A possible extension of the model is to include interactions of the state dependence and $X$ or $\delta$ variables.

The emprical section of the paper contains some very interesting findings. The finding that an extended period of nonemployment has a small effect on future employment but a relatively large effect on wages is consistent with economic theory, but as Ellwood points out one cannot tell if the wage effects are due to human capital accumulation or signaling. However, it is important to note Ellwood's point that weeks worked is a truncated variable while the wage variable is not, and failure to correct for this will tend to understate the effects of the independent variables. Because of the complexity of Ellwood's models, a mechanism for correcting this potential bias would be extremely difficult to develop, but it is possible that bias in the estimates of the effects on weeks worked is present.

A second problem is that Ellwood's models require the use of many instrumental variables. Some of the instruments are lagged dependent variables, and if there is serial correlation of the error terms, the estimates of the coefficients will be inconsistent; note that in the Myer and Wise chapter in this volume (9), significant serial correlation for a similar data base was detected.

None of these comments is intended to detract from this fine chapter. Ellwood has taken a topic of great importance and applied some highly sophisticated techniques to isolate the parameters of interest. I am sure that this chapter will stimulate additional work in this area.

# 11    The Employment and Wage Consequences of Teenage Women's Nonemployment

Mary Corcoran

## Introduction

Teenage unemployment has risen dramatically in the last few years and has become an increasingly visible national problem, causing widespread concern. However, little is known about its causes and consequences. Some argue that being without work in what should be the early years of one's career does permanent harm by typing an individual as an unreliable worker, thus weakening labor force attachment and depriving him or her of valuable opportunities to invest in work skills. Search theory, on the other hand, suggests that teenage unemployment may be a necessary consequence of the process by which young workers look for the jobs most appropriate to their skills. Others argue that lack of employment in the teenage years is the result either of weak work attachment or (in the case of women) of rational and voluntary decisions to trade off wages and employment for family work.

I propose to examine the ways in which lack of employment during the teenage years affects the employment and wages of women in later years. I will concentrate on perhaps the most serious problem in capturing the consequences of not working, that of separating the differences in employment and wages which are causally related to teenage nonemployment from the differences due to unobserved personal characteristics correlated with it.[1]

Most analyses in this chapter do not separate unemployment time from time out of the labor force. This has the advantage of being comparable with Ellwood's analysis (chapter 10 of this volume). More importantly, while teenage women who are actively seeking work may differ in impor-

Mary Corcoran is assistant professor of political science at the University of Michigan, Ann Arbor.

tant ways from those who are not, it is not clear that either retrospective reports of unemployment or the standard CPS unemployment questions allow one to distinguish between these groups. Results reported by Clark and Summers (chapter 7 of this volume) and Ashenfelter (1978) suggest that unemployment statistics fail to capture the labor market activity of young workers adequately, and do not appear to distinguish nonworkers who are seeking work from those who are not. Moreover, unemployment forms a small part of teenage women's reported nonwork time. Understanding how nonwork in the teenage years affects women's later life changes is crucial, whether or not such nonwork is voluntary.

This chapter has three sections. First I describe teenage women's work activity in the years following high school completion. Next I investigate whether early nonemployment reduces women's chances of later employment once we adjust for individual differences that are stable over time and affect employment. Because of data restrictions, this section concentrates on short-run employment effects. In the last section, I estimate the long-run wages costs associated with early nonwork.

This chapter puts forward the following conclusions:

1. Young women's early labor market behavior is quite dynamic. Six out of seven women spent some time working and some time out of work in the four years following school completion.

2. In the four years following school completion, young women's employment rates and participation rates dropped, the duration of nonemployment increased, and the probability that a woman did not work at all doubled. This is the reverse of the pattern observed by Ellwood for young men.

3. Early labor market experiences persisted. Young women with poor early records typically had relatively poor records later. Heterogeneity accounted for a great deal of this persistence. The odds that a woman works given she worked last year were 14.8 times higher than if she did not work last year. Adjustments for heterogeneity halve these odds. Thus, even after controlling for individual differences in women's propensity to work, not working in one year is associated with a much lower probability of working in the next year.

4. There is also evidence that employment effects persist beyond adjacent years. Even given her current work status, a woman's past work history is significantly related to her future work. Because of data restrictions. I could not estimate the magnitude of this relationship or how soon it dies out.

5. Early nonwork involved considerable opportunity costs in the form of lower wages. Ten years after school completion, a woman who spent two years out of work in the years following school completion earned 3 to 5% less per hour than did an otherwise similar woman who had worked

continuously since leaving school. Moreover, for white women, the losses associated with nonwork are greater if that nonwork occurs at the beginning of their careers. This finding must be qualified in two ways. First, at least part of the cost of teenage nonemployment may result from individual differences which are correlated with early nonemployment and later wages. However, controls for differences in women's labor force attachment did not reduce the long-run wage costs associated with teenage nonemployment. Second, some women may be voluntarily electing these costs in order to pursue other goals. But whether voluntary or not, a prolonged period of nonemployment early in one's career is associated with considerably lower wages, even twenty years later. This pattern of long-term reductions in earnings potential is consistent with the results for young men reported by Ellwood and Meyer and Wise.

Nonemployment in women's teenage years is an important policy issue. A sizable proportion of young women reported extended periods of nonemployment in the years following school. Whether voluntary or not, this nonemployment had considerable opportunity costs. It was associated with a lower probability of employment in the short run and with lower wages throughout a woman's work career. Choices made about work and nonwork in the teenage years were clearly important to women's life chances.

## The Consequences of Early Nonwork: Theoretical Predictions

Patterns of teenage labor market activity in the years following school completion are quite dynamic, with the majority spending some time unemployed, out-of-the labor force, or both. This continual movement in and out of paid work is more striking for women than for men. Also, women's employment rates, unlike those of men, declined rather than grew in the years following school completion.

Opinions about the consequences of early nonwork vary considerably, with some claiming that it may seriously harm an individual's long-term economic prospects while others argue either that long-run effects are minor or that both any negative consequences associated with early nonwork and early nonwork itself merely reflect unobserved differences in worker quality or in workers' tastes for work. This latter argument has been applied to women in particular since some argue that many young women voluntarily decide to drop out of the labor force because of a preference for home versus market work. Others argue that such "preferences" may be conditioned or encouraged by sex discrimination, either perceived or actual, combined with a shortage of decent jobs.

Both human capital and crowding theories of women's labor market behavior lead to the conclusion that the long-term effects of an early lack of work may be less serious, on average, for women than for men. Human capital theorists stress the importance of early investments in on-the-job-training for men, but argue that a woman's optimal investment strategy may differ (see Mincer and Polachek 1974). Underlying this argument are two assumptions. The first is that many women will choose at some time to withdraw from the work force to meet family responsibilities; the second is that work skills depreciate during such withdrawals. If these assumptions hold, women might choose to defer investments in their future—such as on-the-job training—until after all their expected withdrawals have been completed. This might make the first few years of work less crucial for women than for men.

"Crowding" theorists argue that women tend to be segregated into "female" jobs and that these jobs provide few opportunities for on-the-job training (Bergmann 1971; Stevenson 1973). This job segregation need not be involuntary. Polachek (1975) argues that some women will choose jobs in which future movement into and out of the labor force will not be penalized. If women are disproportionately concentrated in jobs with few training opportunities, then delays in entering the labor market should have few permanent effects on women's careers since most women will not be missing out on valuable investment opportunities.

Even if we accept this reasoning, a number of factors may be operating to increase the harmful effects for women of not working in their early years. As women's participation in the labor force increases and fertility rates decrease, incentives to defer investment and/or to enter occupations which do not penalize them for frequent entries and exits should drop. This should also occur if younger women's perceptions of appropriate sex roles in the labor force and at home are less sex-stereotyped than those of previous generations. Similarly, if equal opportunity and affirmative action policies are widening the range of jobs available to women, then early work behavior might become a more important determinant of women's economic life chances.

Using Panel data, empirical researchers have estimated measures of persistence in the work participation of married women aged 30 to 50, which allow for individual differences (Heckman and Willis 1977; Heckman 1978b, d; Chamberlain 1978c). Cross-sectional analyses of wage determination suggest that periods of nonwork are associated with lower wages for married women aged 30 to 50 (Mincer and Polachek 1974; Corcoran 1979). But analysts have not made such a thorough investigation of the determinants and consequences of teenage nonemployment, particularly among teenage women. Yet economic theories suggest that the teenage years may be important decision years and that decisions about family and work are interrelated. Suppose, for instance, young women respond to a lack of decent jobs by getting married, bearing a child, or by staying home to raise a child; these decisions will in turn shape future work decisions.

Data and Samples

I examined the employment consequences of early nonwork for teenage girls using subsamples of the National Longitudinal Survey (NLS) of Young Women. This is a national sample of 5159 young women between the ages of 14 and 24 who were interviewed annually from 1968 to 1973, and then were interviewed again in 1975. Each year women reported on the past year's labor market experiences. I used this data to track employment experiences for a cohort of young women who left school in 1966, 1967, 1968 and remained out of school for at least four consecutive years. Women still in school were eliminated from analysis since nonwork during school may be less likely to have permanent effects on later employment or wages. Analysis was restricted to women with less than 14 years of schooling in order to avoid confounding the effects of age and education. The group of women aged 15 to 19 who were out of school included dropouts and high school graduates, while a group of women aged 20 to 24 and out of school included college graduates with little experience and high school dropouts with as much as eight years of experience. There is a potential selection bias here since education is a powerful predictor of women's labor supply. Finally, by including only women who reported their work behavior in each of the four years following school, the sample was reduced from 829 to 634 women. This may cause some selection bias problem since the 634 women who reported on their work behavior were apparently more likely to be employed and less likely to be out of the labor force (see table 11.1).

Thus my major sample consists of those 634 young women in the NLS who left school permanently in 1966, 1967, or 1968 with less than 14 years of education and who reported on their work behavior in each of the next four full years. Parallel analyses are also reported for those 401 women in this group who reported work behavior over five full years.

The NLS data show higher employment rates and lower unemployment rates than do the CPS data (see Ellwood and Meyer and Wise). Part of this difference probably reflects differences in respondents; in the NLS, the teenage reports on her work status; in the CPS, a parent reports on the child's work status. Freeman and Medoff (chapter 4 of this volume) show that if we compare reports of parents and teenagers in the same family, the teenagers' reports show more employment and less unemployment than do the parents' reports. However, part of the difference in NLS and CPS statistics could occur because the long-term unemployed are less likely to participate in or remain in longitudinal surveys.[2]

Both the sample selection procedures and the CPS comparison suggest that some women with long-term records of nonwork may be omitted from our sample of 634 women. Analysis performed on this sample may underestimate the long-run costs associated with nonemployment in the teenage years.

Table 11.1    Effects of Adjustments for Missing Data for Women Who Left School in 1966, 1967, or 1968 Who Had Less than 14 Years of Schooling

| | Respondents who reported their labor force status in years 1 to 4 at the time of the interview[a] | | | Respondents who reported their past year's work history for years 1 to 4 after school completion | | |
|---|---|---|---|---|---|---|
| Year | Percentage employed | Percentage unemployed | Percentage out of the labor force | Percentage employed | Percentage unemployed | Percentage out of the labor force |
| 1 | 58.5 | 8.3 | 33.2 | 65.0 | 8.2 | 26.8 |
| 2 | 56.6 | 8.2 | 35.3 | 63.1 | 7.7 | 29.1 |
| 3 | 56.6 | 6.5 | 36.9 | 63.1 | 6.1 | 30.8 |
| 4 | 52.4 | 6.1 | 41.5 | 57.7 | 6.1 | 36.2 |
| N | 770 | 770 | 770 | 634 | 634 | 634 |

[a]There are 829 women in the Parnes who left school in 1966, 1967, or 1968 and who had less than 14 years of school; 770 of these women reported their labor force status at the time of the interview in the next four years.

## 11.1    Women's Early Employment Patterns

Women's employment and labor force participation declined steadily in the first four years out of school. Women's participation and employment rates dropped from 68 and 64% in the first year to 60 and 57% by the fourth year (table 11.2). This is in marked contrast to young men whose employment and participation rates rose steadily over the same period to 90 and 95% by the fourth year (see Ellwood, table 10.1). The decreases in women's participation and employment rates were the result of increases in the amount of time women stayed out when they were employed. The average time spent out of the labor force by those with any such time increased from 27 to 34 weeks over the period, and the proportion of women who did not work at all in a given year almost doubled from 12% in the first year to 24% in the fourth year.

The diversity and change apparent in teenage women's labor force patterns is striking. Women move continually between work and non-work in the four years following school. Almost all women spend some time not employed (90%) and some time employed (96%) over this period. Even in a single year, at least three out of four women reported some work and six out of ten reported a period of nonwork (table 11.3).

Tracking the unemployment rate over time provides little information about changes in women's labor force activities. Although employment and participation rates decreased in the four years following school completion, there was no clear time trend in unemployment rates. Moreover, time unemployed formed less than one-seventh of women's total nonemployment time.

Women clearly spend a great deal of time not working in the years following school completion. Almost one-quarter of all women did not work at all in the fourth year following school and, in any given year, more than two-thirds reported some nonwork time. In addition, nonwork time per person out of work increased from an average of 27.4 weeks in the first year after school to an average of 32.3 in the fourth year. Given that the procedures for dealing with missing data and that NLS/CPS comparisons suggest that these data are likely to underrepresent nonwork time, these results are quite dramatic. Understanding the extent to which this nonwork time hinders women's future economic life chances is the central issue of this chapter.

### 11.1.1   The Persistence of Labor Market Experiences

Early labor market experiences predict later ones. This section documents the extent of this persistence in work experience. The next section will investigate whether or not this persistence is due to personal differences in worker characteristics or to a causal link between past and current employment.

Figures 11.1, 11.2, 11.3, and 11.4 are probability trees for unemployment, time out of the labor force, time not employed, and whether never employed over the four-year period. Each branch corresponds to one year. A one indicated that a woman was unemployed, spent time out of the labor force, was not employed, or was never employed in that year; a zero indicates the opposite. Above the line at a branch is the estimated

Table 11.2    **Unemployment Rate, Employment Rate, and Labor Force Participation Rate for Young Women during First Five Years[a] after Leaving School in 1966, 1967, or 1968 with Less than 14 Years of Schooling**

|  | Unemployment rate[d] | Employment rate[e] | Labor force participation rate[f] |
|---|---|---|---|
| Year 1[b] | 5.8 | 63.9 | 67.8 |
| Year 2[b] | 4.8 | 62.9 | 66.0 |
| Year 3[b] | 5.6 | 60.5 | 64.1 |
| Year 4[b] | 5.4 | 56.8 | 60.0 |
| Year 5[c] | 3.6 | 58.1 | 60.3 |

[a]A year here is not a single calendar year. Instead, the $n$th year represents the $n$th full year following school completion. Thus for women who left school in 1966, year 1 is 1967; while for women who left school in 1968, year 1 is 1969.

[b]$N = 634$.

[c]$N = 401$.

[d]Average weeks unemployed/average weeks in labor force.

[e]Average weeks employed/52.

[f]Average weeks in labor force/52.

probability of being in that state given one was at the previous branch. Below the line in parentheses is the proportion of all people who are found on that branch. The bottom number under a branch is the length of time spent in a particular state. Thus, in figure 11.1, 34.4% of women who were unemployed in their first year were also unemployed in the second year; 8.8% of all women were unemployed in both years, and these women averaged 9.3 weeks out of work.

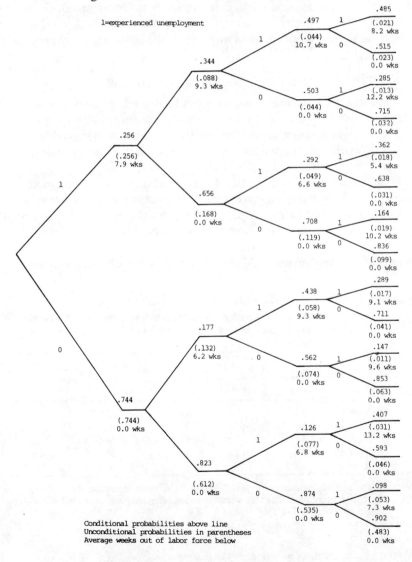

**Fig. 11.1**    Probability Tree of Weeks Unemployed in First Four Full Years out of School ($N = 634$)

There is considerable persistence in young women's labor market experiences. For instance, the estimated probability that a woman did not work at all in year 2 is .608 if she did not work in the previous year and .116 if she worked (see figure 11.4). By the fourth year after school completion, women who had never worked were eight times as likely not to work as were women who had worked in each of the previous years (.767 to .089).

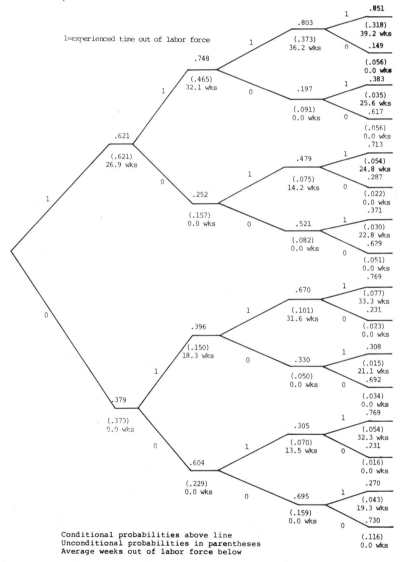

Conditional probabilities above line
Unconditional probabilities in parentheses
Average weeks out of labor force below

**Fig. 11.2**     Probability Tree of Weeks out of the Labor Force in First Four Full Years out of School ($N = 634$)

But such patterns can be misleading (see Ellwood). If spells of unemployment are long, say thirteen weeks, and are distributed randomly throughout the year, then one-quarter of all the unemployed in one year would have spells which overlap into the next one. Table 11.4 gives the estimated probabilities of being unemployed, out of the labor force, not employed, or never working in the third, fourth, and fifth years, given one's work experiences in year 1. Again, labor market behavior persists.

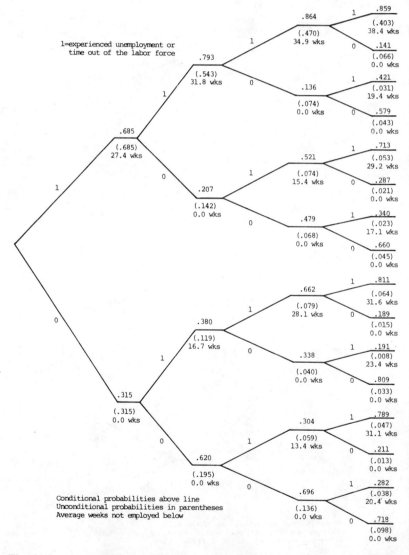

**Fig. 11.3**    Probability Tree of Weeks Not Employed in First Four Full Years out of School ($N = 634$)

Women who spent some time not employed in the first year were one and a half times as likely to miss some work in the fifth year as were women who had worked continuously in the first year. And women who did not work at all in year one were 1.8 times as likely not to work at all in the fifth year as were women who had worked in the first year.

Cross-year correlations for weeks not employed in the first four and five years following school completion also indicate that employment

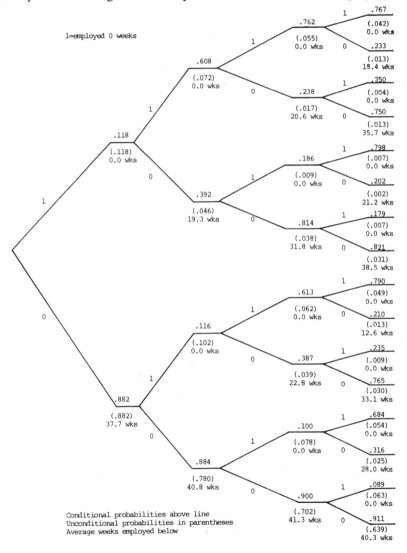

**Fig. 11.4**    Probability Tree of Zero Weeks Employed in First Four Full Years out of School ($N = 634$)

Table 11.3        Percentage of Women with Unemployment Time, Time out of Labor Force, and Time not Employed, and Who Never Worked during the First Four Years after Leaving School

|  | Percentage unemployed | Percentage with time out of labor force | Percentage with time not employed | Percentage who never worked in year $t$ |
|---|---|---|---|---|
| Year 1 | 25.6 | 62.1 | 68.5 | 11.8 |
| Year 2 | 22.0 | 61.5 | 66.3 | 17.2 |
| Year 3 | 22.8 | 61.8 | 68.2 | 20.4 |
| Year 4 | 18.2 | 62.6 | 66.7 | 23.9 |

NOTE: $N = 634$.

behavior persists (See table 11.5). Estimates of the one-year correlation range from .6 to .7 and the correlation between the first and fifth years is .26. Persistence in weeks not employed is stronger for young women than for young men (Ellwood). There is also a slight tendency for correlations to increase over time.

Women's weeks unemployed show far less persistence. Adjacent year correlations range from .12 to .35 and drop quickly. The correlations between weeks unemployed one year removed range from .05 to .21.

The cross-year correlations for weeks not employed are more stable than would be generated by a first-order Markov process. Individual differences could be an important part of the underlying process. The next section of this paper investigates whether persistence in employment merely reflects differences in workers' traits or whether future employment is causally related to past experience.

Table 11.4        Probability of Unemployment, Time out of Labor Force, Time Not Employed, and Never Working in Later Years Conditional on First Full Year out of School

|  | Unemployment | Time off | Time not employed | Never working |
|---|---|---|---|---|
| $P$(1 in year 2/1 in year 1)[a] | .344 | .748 | .786 | .608 |
| $P$(1 in year 2/0 in year 1)[a] | .177 | .396 | .370 | .116 |
| $P$(1 in year 3/1 in year 1)[a] | .362 | .721 | .793 | .542 |
| $P$(1 in year 3/0 in year 1)[a] | .182 | .449 | .440 | .159 |
| $P$(1 in year 4/1 in year 1)[a] | .278 | .702 | .744 | .508 |
| $P$(1 in year 4/0 in year 1)[a] | .150 | .499 | .499 | .198 |
| $P$(1 in year 5/1 in year 1)[b] | .242 | .719 | .758 | .408 |
| $P$(1 in year 5/0 in year 1)[b] | .187 | .519 | .485 | .221 |

[a] $N = 634$.
[b] $N = 401$.

**Table 11.5**          **Correlation Matrix for Weeks Not Working**
                          **during First Five Years out of School** ($N = 401$)

| Weeks not working | Year 1 | Year 2 | Weeks not working Year 3 | Year 4 | Year 5 |
|---|---|---|---|---|---|
| Year 1 | 1.00 | .57 | .46 | .32 | .26 |
| Year 2 | | 1.00 | .67 | .49 | .45 |
| Year 3 | | | 1.00 | .67 | .54 |
| Year 4 | | | | 1.00 | .74 |
| Year 5 | | | | | 1.00 |
| Weeks unem- ployed | Year 1 | Year 2 | Weeks unemployed Year 3 | Year 4 | Year 5 |
| Year 1 | 1.00 | .35 | .05 | .11 | .00 |
| Year 2 | | 1.00 | .15 | .15 | .03 |
| Year 3 | | | 1.00 | .12 | .21 |
| Year 4 | | | | 1.00 | .29 |
| Year 5 | | | | | 1.00 |

## 11.2 Sources of Persistence in Young Women's Employment Decisions

Past and current employment decisions show a positive and strong association, but several quite different processes could generate this association. It could be seen as a "mover-stayer" problem; unobserved differences in women's talents, motivatiðns, or preferences—"heterogeneity"—might be correlated with their past and present employment behavior (Heckman and Willis 1977). A second possibility is that women's past and present work behavior is affected by unobserved variables which are serially correlated over time. For instance, a woman may not work in two adjacent years because the local market is depressed both years. Finally, early work (or nonwork) may have a "real" effect on later work behavior—"state dependence." This could arise for several reasons. Women's preferences for market or home work may be altered as a result of early employment (or home production) activities; i.e., working may reinforce the desire to work. Similarly, women's work skills and hence their ability to find employment and/or demand high wages may grow as a result of employment (through investment in on-the-job training, accumulation of seniority, etc.) and depreciate during periods of nonwork (see Mincer and Polachek). Finally, even if worker skills and motivations are unaltered by early nonwork or employment experiences, employers may use past behavior as an indicator of future behavior when hiring.

Distinguishing heterogeneity from serial correlation and state dependence is not straightforward. Economists have routinely dealt with heterogeneity by assuming it away, i.e., by assuming that unmeasured tastes, preferences, and/or talents are uncorrelated with included independent variables (in this case with past work behavior). The ways in which panel data are collected further complicate this task. Apparent persistence in employment behavior over time could occur simply because a single employment spell spans two data collection periods.

### 11.2.1   Heterogeneity vs. State Dependence: Some Econometric Models

Heckman (1978b, 1978d) and Chamberlain (1978c) have developed models to explore persistence in behavior over time. I will use Chamberlain's autoregressive logistic model to investigate the extent to which a woman's work history influences her current work behavior. This model eliminates effects of unobserved person factors by comparing the likelihood that a woman works given she worked in the previous year to the likelihood that the *same* woman works given she did not work in the previous year.

The model is:

$$\text{Prob}(y_{it} = 1 \mid y_{i,\,t-1})$$

$$= \frac{\exp(\alpha_i + \gamma y_{i,\,t-1})}{1 + \exp(\alpha_i + \gamma y_{i,\,t-1})} \qquad \begin{aligned} &i = 1, \ldots, \text{N} \\ &t = 1, \ldots, \text{T} \end{aligned}$$

with $y_{it} = 1$ if person $i$ is employed anytime in period $t$, $= 0$ otherwise and $\alpha_i =$ unobserved personal characteristics which raise the $i$th person's propensity to work $i = 1 \ldots \text{N}$. In this model, the conditional probability that the $i$th woman works this year, given her last year's employment status depends on an individual-specific constant ($\alpha_i$) and on her employment status in the previous year. This model has $N + 1$ unknowns: $N$ individual-specific constants ($\alpha_i$) and $\gamma$, the coefficient on last year's employment status. If unmeasured person effects ($\alpha_i$) completely accounted for the observed association between past and present employment behavior then $\gamma$ should equal zero. We can test this by calculating a confidence interval for $\gamma$.

Note three characteristics of this model. First, the individual traits that influence a woman's probability of work ($\alpha_i$) do not vary over the time period considered (in this case over the five years following school completion). Second, this model assumes that $\gamma$ is constant over the time period considered; that is, the relationship between employment in two adjacent years does not change over time. Taken together, these two assumptions imply that the distributions of transitional employment probabilities should be similar across time. We can check this by seeing whether the estimated conditional employment probabilities change much over the five-year period. The estimated mean values of $p(1|0)$, the probability of working this year given one did not work last year, were quite similar across the five-year period, ranging from .106 to .120. But estimated values of $P(1|1)$, the conditional probability of employment this year given employment last year, increase over the five-year period from .549 in years 1 and 2 to .680 in years 4 and 5. This suggests that there may be a time trend in employment behavior. Third, there are no $X$s (exogenous predictors) in this model. Constant $X$s will be captured in $\alpha_i$, but the model cannot capture effects of changing $X$s. This means that we cannot differentiate serial correlation from state dependence with this model. In practice, this may not be such a serious limitation. I attempted to predict women's employment decisions using a number of demographic and demand variables which changed over time.[3] Only one of these consistently and significantly influenced women's probability of employment, "number of dependents." But if lack of early work reduces the probability of later work by increasing women's incentives to bear and raise children, then we should not control for family size when estimating state dependence.

If we allow each individual to have her own individual specific parameter ($\alpha_i$), maximizing the joint likelihood function over $\alpha_i$ and $\gamma$ will not in general provide a consistent estimator of $\gamma$. But Chamberlain shows that we can get a consistent estimator of $\gamma$ if we use a conditional likelihood function. The basic idea is that the number of years a women was employed over the period, $s_i = \sum_{t=1}^{T} (y_{it})$ and her employment status in the last year ($y_{iT}$) provide sufficient statistics for the omitted person factor, ($\alpha_i$). Holding fixed $s_i$ and $y_{iT}$, $\alpha_i$ drops from the likelihood function. Initial conditions are dealt with by conditioning a woman's employment status in the first full year following school completion ($y_{i1}$).[4] This gives:

$$\text{Prob}(y_{i1}, \ldots, y_{iT} | y_{i1}, \sum_{t=1}^{T} y_{it}, y_{iT})$$

$$= \frac{\exp(\gamma \sum_{t=2}^{T} y_{it} y_{it-1})}{\sum_{deB_i} \exp(\gamma \sum_{t=2}^{T} d_t d_{t-1})}$$

where $B_i = \{\underline{d} = (d_1, \ldots, d_T) | d_t = 0 \text{ or } 1,$

$d_1 = y_{i1}, \sum_t d_t = \sum_t y_{it}, d_T = y_{iT}\}$

Here, $S_{i11} = \sum_{t=2}^{\tilde{T}} y_{it} y_i, t-1$ is a sufficient statistic for $\gamma$.

For $T \geq 4$, there are conditional probabilities that depend upon $\gamma$. Since not all conditional probabilities will depend upon $\gamma$, this procedure uses only a subset of any given sample to estimate $\gamma$. For instance, when $T = 5$,

18 of the 31 possible sequences depend upon $\gamma$ (see Chamberlain 1978c for a more detailed discussion of this model).

Even if $\gamma$ were significantly different from zero we still cannot conclude that a woman's past work behavior is causally related to her current work behavior. Such persistence could also be due to unmeasured factors which influenced her chances of working and which were serially correlated over time (e.g., local demand conditions).[5] In addition, the measure $\gamma$ depends upon the period of observation. Even if women's past and current behavior were not causally related, we would expect $\gamma$ to be nonzero simply because a nomemployment spell may span two years. To see this, suppose our period of observation were one day; the probability that a person who worked yesterday would work today would be very close to one.

To describe completely a woman's work history we would want to know the length and timing of all spells of work and nonwork. If her past work history does not help us to predict her future, given her current state, then this is a Markov process. Chamberlain (1978c) calls deviations from the Markov property "duration dependence." He points out that duration independence would imply that a woman's employment history prior to the current spell should not affect the distribution of the length of the current spell, and the amount of time spent in the current spell should not affect the distribution of remaining time in that spell. This implies that the durations of the spells should be independent of each other and the distribution of time in a state should be exponential. If we assumed that all spells of employment have the same distribution, that all spells of nonwork have the same distribution, and that the exponential rate parameter for each of the states is the same for all spells, then we would have an alternating Poisson process. In this case, the stationary heterogeneity model implies that each woman is characterized by the two parameters of an alternating Poisson process. Departure from this model would be evidence of duration dependence at the individual level; i.e., even given her current state, a woman's past history helps predict her future.[6]

Chamberlain has developed tests for duration dependence based on binary employment sequences generated by questions such as "Did you work last year?" The basic idea underlying these tests is that stationary heterogeneity implies that a woman's probability of working in period $t$ depends upon the number of consecutive periods immediately preceding period $t$ in which she worked. The reasoning is as follows. If a woman is following an alternating Poisson process, then only her state at the end of the past year is relevant. If $y_{t-1} = 1$, we know only that she worked sometime last year. We do not know whether she worked at the end of the past year, and $y_{t-2}$ will affect the probability that she worked early in the year rather than late in the year. But if $y_{t-1} = 0$, then the woman *never* worked last year. Thus we know her state at the end of that year and $y_{t-2}$, $y_{t-3}$, etc. are irrelevant.

This gives

$$\text{Prob}(y_t = 1 \mid y_{t-1}, y_{t-2}, \ldots) = \text{Prob}(y_t = 1 \mid y_{t-1}$$
$$= \ldots = y_{t-J} = 1, y_{t, J-1} = 0) = \text{Prob}(y_t = 1 \mid J)$$

where $J$ = the number of consecutive preceding years that the woman was employed. That is, the probability that a woman works in year $t$ depends only on how many consecutive years she worked immediately preceding year $t$. This would give the following logistic model:

$$\text{Prob}(y_{it} = 1 \mid y_{i, t-1}, y_{i, t-2}, \ldots) = \frac{e^{A_i}}{1 + e^{A_i}}$$

where $A_i = \alpha_i + \sum_{k=1}^{\infty} \psi_{ik} \prod_{j=1}^{k} y_{i, t-j}$

Here, each woman has her own set of parameters $\alpha_i$ and $\Psi_{ik}$. Chamberlain extends this model to test for duration dependence as follows.

(2)     $\text{Prob}(y_{it} = 1 \mid y_{i, t-1}, y_{i, t-2}, \ldots)$

$$= \frac{\exp(A_i + \gamma_2 y_{i, t-2})}{1 + \exp(A_i + \gamma_2 y_{i, t-2})}$$

For $T \geq 6$ and large $N$, we can consistently estimate $\gamma_2$ using a conditional likelihood function. For $T = 5$, Chamberlain's model has some equality predictions for particular sets of conditional probabilities which enable us to tell whether or not $\gamma_2$ differs significantly from zero.

### 11.2.2   Empirical Results: Employment Effects of Early Nonwork

The techniques described in the previous section were used to analyze the persistence of employment. I looked at employment behavior rather than participation behavior because results of other studies (Ashenfelter, Summers and Clark) suggest that for young women time unemployed and time out of the labor force are not conceptually distinct.

I began by obtaining an estimate of first-order dependence that is based on Chamberlain's autoregressive logistic model, where each woman is assigned her own employment probability (equation 1). Chamberlain's conditional likelihood function on five-year employment sequences gives $\hat{\gamma} = 2.05$ with a standard error of .33. This estimate is based on the employment sequences of 80 women (19.9% of the five-year sample).[7]

A woman's employment behavior in one year is a good predictor of her employment behavior the next year—even after we allow each woman to have her own employment probability. The odds that the *same* woman works, given she worked in the previous year are $e^{2.05} = 7.8$ times higher than if she did not work last year. While high, these odds are only about half as large as the odds we would get if we ignored heterogeneity. Not allowing for unobserved person factors would increase these odds to 14.8.[8]

This estimate of adjacent year persistence in work behavior ($\hat{\gamma}$) assumes stationary heterogeneity, invariance of $\gamma$ over time, and does not control for changing $X$s. Yet the estimates of $P(1|1)$, the conditional probability of a woman being employed this year if she was employed last year, rise considerably in the five-year period following school from .549 for years 1 and 2 to .680 for years 4 and 5. This suggests employment transition probabilities may be increasing over time. Our estimate of persistence may pick up some of this time trend.

The following model suggested by Chamberlain (1979) allows us to include a time trend:

$$p(y_{it} = 1 | y_{i, t-1}) = \frac{\exp(\alpha_i + \beta X_t)}{1 + \exp(\alpha_i + \beta X_t)} + \gamma y_{i, t-1}$$

where $X_t = t - 1 \ t = 1, \ldots, T$

Here the term $\beta X_t$ allows us to pick up a time trend. Consistent estimates of $\hat{\beta}$ can be obtained using a conditional likelihood function. By comparing the value of $\gamma$ that obtains when we set $\beta = 0$ to the value of $\gamma$ that obtains when $\beta$ is estimated, we can get a rough idea of how much our estimate of adjacent-year persistence will drop if we allow for a time trend.

Not allowing for a time trend (i.e., setting $\beta = 0$) gives $\hat{\gamma} = .47$. This estimate is significant ($p < .05$). Not allowing for state dependence (setting $\gamma = 0$), gives $\hat{\beta} = .30$. This estimate is not very significant ($p = .25$). If we estimate both $\beta$ and $\gamma$, the estimate of $\gamma$ is still large, $\hat{\gamma} = .31$, but is not very significant ($p = .25$); the estimate of $\beta$ is quite small, $\hat{\beta} = .09$ and is quite insignificant ($p = .86$). Thus allowing for a time trend reduces estimates of adjacent year persistence ($\hat{\gamma}$) by about one-third.[9]

The NLS data did not provide strong predictors of the work decision, which also changed over time and which were not proxies for expectations. I tried area demand variables (whether South, whether lived in a city, and the local unemployment rate) and a measure of husband's income as predictors of the decision to work in the second, third, fourth, and fifth years following school completion. None of these consistently and significantly predicted the decision to work. Given this, I did not attempt to differentiate between serial correlation and state dependence on these analyses.

Recall that we would expect to observe some persistence in women's work behavior simply because of the way in which the NLS employment information is recorded. That is, past and current employment will be associated simply because a single work (or nonwork) spell may span two years. Instead of asking whether a woman's previous year's employment status helps to predict her current year's employment status we may want to ask whether, given her current employment status, her employment history enables us to predict her future. That is, does employment behavior follow a Markov process? Departures from this Markov property are evidence of duration dependence, i.e., evidence that given a woman's current employment status, her past employment history is informative about her future.

I tested for departures from this Markov property using Chamberlain's second-order autoregressive logistic model (equation 2). Chamberlain has shown that when $T = 5$, probabilities of certain binary employment sequences should be equally likely whenever there is no duration dependence. A likelihood ratio test comparing those probabilities which obtain under the assumption of no duration dependence ($\gamma_2 = 0$) to the probabilities in the data (unrestricted model) gives $\chi^2(5) = 10.9$, based on 30 women. This is significant at the .05 level, suggesting a departure from an alternating Poisson process. That is, we can not conclude that given a woman's current state, her past work history will not influence her future.

Taken together, these results strongly reject the notion that unexplained personal differences account entirely for the strong link between women's present and past employment behavior. The odds that a woman works given she worked last year are 7.8 times higher than if she did not work last year—even if we allow each woman to have her own employment probability. Furthermore, even after we adjust for data collection procedures, there is still a link between past and current employment. Given a woman's current employment status, her past work history still predicts her future. This finding was significant even though based on only a small number of cases.

Given the small number of cases, I could not estimate the magnitude of this duration dependence, nor could I estimate how quickly the predictive power of early employment dies out over time. Finally, it may be that women who do not work early in their careers "catch up" by working more later. Because of data restrictions I did not investigate this possibility.

These findings are not inconsistent with those reported by Ellwood and by Meyer and Wise. We all find employment behavior persists in the short run. Ellwood and Meyer and Wise further show that these employment effects diminish after several years; because of data restrictions I did not investigate this for women.

## 11.3 Long-Run Wage Losses Associated with Early Nonwork

The previous section documented and explored the persistence of employment in the short run. In the long run, lost wages may be a more serious cost of early nonemployment. Losing early work experience may impose costs in addition to delaying the start of a career. If employers evaluate a worker's potential by her past work behavior, women who spent considerable time out of work in the years following school completion may be permanently tracked into less desirable career ladders. If working (or not working) reinforces the tendency to work (or not to work) and/or if human capital depreciates during periods of nonwork, then women's expected lifetime earnings may be permanently lowered by extended periods of nonwork in their early careers. Even if much of the wage loss were "voluntary" (in the sense that women trade off wages for flexibility and/or time to engage in home work), it would still be useful to know the "opportunity costs" associated with early nonemployment.

I explore the long-run opportunity costs of early nonwork using a sample of 2,067 employed women aged 18 to 64 (1,326 whites and 741 blacks) from the 1976 wave of the Panel Study of Income Dynamics (PSID). In 1975, these women reported about their wages and current jobs and gave retrospective reports of their employment histories. Using these data, I constructed the experience and nonwork measures. (Elsewhere [Corcoran 1979] I describe in detail how these measures were constructed.) Note that these measures distinguish nonwork which occurs early in a woman's career and "number of years not employed in the period following school completion" from nonwork which occurs later in a woman's career and "other nonwork time." A large percentage of these women (29% of the whites and 42% of the blacks) experienced a year or more of nonwork early in their careers. And this nonwork was often quite extensive; the average duration was 9.6 years for white women and 7.2 years for black women.

This analysis involves seven pairs of equations. First I regress the natural logarithm of wages on experience and nonwork measures with controls for education, city size, and region for employed black and white women (table 11.6, columns 1 and 2). Some economists (Heckman 1974; Gronau 1974) have argued that restricting analysis to employed women could lead to selection bias if the independent variables in the wage equation influence a woman's market wage relative to her reservation wage. So next I reestimate the wage equation using a procedure described by Heckman (1977) which corrects parameter estimates for selection bias (table 11.6, columns 3 and 4).[10] This is followed by a modest attempt to control for heterogeneity by adjusting for individual differences in women' labor force attachments. The PSID provides four indicators of labor force attachment: absenteeism due to own illness; absenteeism due to others' illness; self-imposed restrictions on work hours and/or job location; and whether the respondent plans to leave work in the near future for reasons other than training. If women with less experience earn less than other women because low attachment to the labor force both decreases wages and leads to less work,[11] then controlling for attachment should reduce the observed effect of work and nonwork measures on wages. Columns 5 and 6 of table 11.6 present the results when these four indicators of attachment are added to the regression of experience and nonwork measures on wages. But to the extent that these measures of labor force attachment are subject to random measurement errors, use of OLS may still understate the influence of attachment on wages (Griliches and Mason 1973) and hence overstate the influence of experience and nonwork. To correct for this problem I use a two-stage procedure to get predicted values of the labor force attachment measures (table 11.6, colums 7 and 8).

Finally, work experience is not obviously an exogenous variable since a woman's expected market wage will presumably influence her decision to work. Table 11.7 compares results of three sets of equations. In the first (columns 1 and 2), experience is assumed exogenous; in the second (columns 3 and 4), experience is assumed to be endogenous; and in the third, experience is assumed endogenous and corrections are made for selection bias.[12]

Results were consistent across all sets of equations. Both black and white women's wages increased with experience; this increase was large for the first few years and then dropped off over time. In addition, not working for prolonged periods early in one's career lowered white women's expected wages by .7% for each of the nonworking years in addition to lowering wages indirectly by lowering total experience.[13] None of the observed influences of early nonwork and experience on wages was reduced when I adjusted for selection bias. This is consistent with other research (Heckman 1977a, Corcoran 1979). Similarly, treating experience as endogenous did not reduce the estimated effects of experience or early nonwork on wages. The magnitude of these influences also remained unchanged when controls were added for labor force attachment. But, of course, these procedures, which provide very crude adjustments for unmeasured personal traits, influence early experience and wages, so we may be overestimating the long-term wage costs that are causally associated with early nonwork.

Two kinds of opportunity are associated with early nonwork: foregone earnings and the reduction in later earnings that is associated with lower experience and extended nonwork. I estimated this latter cost by comparing the expected 1975 earnings of women who have worked continuously to those of otherwise similar women (in terms of education, age, race, residence, and on our measures of labor force attachment) who did not work for a year or more in the period immediately following school completion (see table 11.8). Note that these estimated costs are for nonwork which occurs in the years following school completion.[14] These costs are quite large even many years later. Ten years after school completion a two-year period of nonwork lowers white women's ex-

**Table 11.6**  Work Experience, Early Nonwork. and Wages for Employed Women Aged 18–64 Who Were Wives or Heads of Households in 1975 ($N = 1326$ Whites[a], 741 Blacks)

| Predictor Variables[b] | Dependent variable = ln (1975 hourly wage) | | | | | | | |
|---|---|---|---|---|---|---|---|---|
| | White | Black | White | Black | White | Black | White | Black |
| Education | .0855** | .0921** | .0859** | .0902** | .0842** | .0920** | .0831** | .0730** |
| | (.0053) | (.0070) | (.0055) | (.0073) | (.0054) | (.0073) | (.0057) | (.0091) |
| Total work experience | .0290* | .0251* | .0300* | .0284* | .0296* | .0242* | .0363* | .0264* |
| | (.0045) | (.0053) | (.0054) | (.0054) | (.0046) | (.0052) | (.0055) | (.0069) |
| Total work experience squared | −.0005* | −.0005* | −.0006* | −.0006* | −.0006* | −.0005* | −.0007* | −.0006* |
| | (.0001) | (.0001) | (.0001) | (.0001) | (.0001) | (.0001) | (.0001) | (.0001) |
| Number of years not employed following school completion[c] | −.0067* | .0016 | −.0073* | −.0018 | −.0066* | .0027 | −.0072* | .0018 |
| | (.0023) | (.0029) | (.0030) | (.0030) | (.0023) | (.0030) | (.0025) | (.0032) |
| Controls for labor force attachment measures[d] | | | | | — | — | | |
| Corrections for censoring[e] | | | — | — | | | | |
| Labor force attachment measures are instrumented[f] | | | | | | | — | — |

(*Notes appear on following page*)

**Table 11.7**    **Work Experiences and Wages: Corrections for Endogeneity for Employed Women Aged 18–64 Who Were Wives or Heads of Household in 1975 ($N = 1326$ Whites,[a] 741 Blacks)**

| Work experience measures[b] | Dependent variable = ln (1975 hourly wage) | | | | | |
| --- | --- | --- | --- | --- | --- | --- |
| | White | Black | White | Black | White | Black |
| Total work experience | .0271[e] | .0236[e] | .0292[e] | .0217[e] | .0301[e] | .0360[e] |
| | (.0047) | (.0052) | (.0056) | (.0073) | (.0056) | (.0085) |
| Total work | − .0005[e] | − .0055[e] | − .0007[e] | − .0006[e] | − .0008[e] | − .0010[e] |
| experience squared | (.0001) | (.0001) | (.0002) | (.0002) | (.0002) | (.0003) |
| Corrections for endogeneity | | | | | | |
| of experiences[c] | — | — | | | — | — |
| Corrections for censoring[d] | | | — | — | — | — |

NOTE: A dash indicates the procedure was followed.

[a]A white is defined as a nonblack.

[b]Controls were included for education, city size, and region.

[c]Experience as a fraction of time since leaving school was estimated as a function of education, family income exclusive of respondent's own earnings, marital status, and number and ages of children. Expected experience was estimated to be the product of this fraction and time since leaving school.

[d]This was done by estimating a probit analysis of the decision to work for all PSID wives and female heads using instrumented experience, education, city size, region, marital status, number and ages of children, and family income exclusive of the respondent's own earnings. I used this equation to construct the Mills ratio and included it in the regression.

[e]Significant at .05 level.

Table 11.6 notes

A dash indicates this variable was included.

[a]A white is defined as a nonblack.

[b]In all regressions, other nonwork time, city size, south and percentage of work experience that was full time were controlled. See Corcoran (1979) for details on how these variables were constructed.

[c]See Corcoran (1979) for details on how these measures were constructed.

[d]These measures include: days absent in 1975 because of own illness; days absent in 1975 for care for others; self-imposed restrictions on job hours or location; expect to leave work in the near future for nontraining reasons. See Coe (1979) for details on the absenteeism measure; Hill (1979) for details on the self-imposed restrictions measure, and Corcoran (1979) for details on the expect-to-leave-work measures.

[e]This was done by estimating a probit analysis of the decision to work for all PSID women using the work experience, and nonwork measures, education, city size, region, family income exclusive of the respondent's earnings, marital status, and the number of children less than 3 years, 3–6 years, 7–11 years, and 12–17 years. I used this equation to construct the Mills ratio and included it in my regression. See Heckman (1977) for a detailed description of this procedure.

[f]I instrumented the labor force attachment variables using a two-stage least squares routine. Instruments included the number and ages of children, marital status, family income exclusive of respondent's earnings, whether expect more children, own health problems, whether anyone in the family needed extra care, and fertility plans.

*Significant at .05 level.

Table 11.8    Expected Percentage Wage Differences between Women Who
Worked Continuously Since School Completion and Women Who
Experienced a Spell of Nonwork in the Period Immediately
Following School (White Women[a])

| Length of nonwork spell (in years) | Number of years since leaving school (maximum potential experience) | | | | |
|---|---|---|---|---|---|
| | 5 | 10 | 15 | 20 | 25 |
| 1 | 3.1 | 2.5 | 1.9 | 1.3 | .7 |
| 2 | 6.3 | 5.1 | 3.9 | 2.7 | 1.5 |
| 4 | 13.0 | 10.6 | 8.2 | 5.8 | 3.4 |
| 8 | — | 23.2 | 18.4 | 13.6 | 8.8 |
| 12 | — | — | 30.5 | 23.3 | 16.1 |
| 16 | — | — | — | 34.9 | 25.3 |

[a]These figures are estimated using the coefficients in table 11.6, column 5. This gives the effects of experience when education, city size, region, part-time work, self-imposed limits on jobs hours or location, days absent to care for oneself or others, and expectations about leaving work are held fixed.

pected wages by 5% and black women's expected wages by 3%. Even twenty years later, a four-year spell of nonwork lowers white women's wages by 5.8% and lowers black women's expected wages by 2.5%.

It might be more useful to estimate the expected wage reductions associated with an early spell of 9.6 years of nonwork for white women and a spell of 7.2 years of nonwork for black women (these are the average durations of early nonwork time for women with any such time). Twenty years after school completion, these expected wage reductions are 16.8% for white women and 5.6% for black women.

Given differences in sample populations and in methodology, it is difficult to compare these wage costs with those estimated by Ellwood and by Meyer and Wise. Nonetheless, the consistency across studies is quite remarkable. These authors also found that early nonwork was associated with significantly lower wages later on. Their estimates of men's wage losses were larger than those estimated for this sample of women.[15]

The wage losses associated with not working in the years following school completion are large and persist over time. I suspect, however, that a part of the wage costs associated with lower experience and early nonwork could be due to unobserved factors (e.g., "ability"; propensity to work) which differ across women and which are correlated with both employment behavior and wages, and which are inadequately captured by the included labor force attachment measures. In addition, even if all the observed wage losses were causally related to early nonwork, women may be voluntarily electing to trade off these wage gains for other desired goals. Nonetheless, it is evident from these data that women miss a great deal of nonwork early in their careers and that this loss of work is associated with lower lifetime earnings. Women forego earnings by not working, and early nonwork is associated with lower hourly wages throughout most of a woman's career.

### 11.3.1   Summary and Conclusions

Young women moved continuously in and out of employment in the four years following school. Almost all the young women in this sample spent some time not employed over this period, and it appears that these women's labor force attachment weakened somewhat over this period.

Many of these young women were not employed for a prolonged period. Descriptive results showed evidence of considerable persistence in women's employment behavior. Further analysis suggested that a part of this persistence was due to unmeasured individual differences which influenced a woman's propensity to work. Nonetheless, even allowing each woman to have her own employment probability, the odds that she worked given that she worked last year were 7.8 times higher than if she did not work in the previous year. Since the NLS data did not provide good exogenous predictors of employment behavior, I could not test whether this persistence was due to a causal relationship between past and present employment or to exogenous variables which were serially correlated over time.

Part of this persistence could, of course, be caused by the way the NLS collects and records employment behavior. That is, we would observe

**Table 11.9**     **Expected Percentage Wage Differences between Black Women Who Worked Continuously Since School Completion and Black Women Who Experienced a Spell of Nonwork in the Period Immediately Following School[a]**

| Length of nonwork spell (in years) | Number of years since leaving school | | | | |
|---|---|---|---|---|---|
| | 5 | 10 | 15 | 20 | 25 |
| 1 | 2.0 | 1.5 | 1.0 | .5 | 0 |
| 2 | 4.0 | 3.0 | 2.0 | 1.0 | 0 |
| 4 | 8.0 | 6.5 | 4.5 | 2.5 | .5 |
| 8 | | 14.6 | 10.6 | 6.6 | 2.6 |
| 12 | | | 18.2 | 12.2 | 6.2 |
| 16 | | | | 18.7 | 11.5 |

[a]These figures are estimated using the coefficients in table 11.6, column 6. This gives the effects of experience when education, city size, region, part-time work, self-imposed limits on jobs hours or location, days absent to care for oneself or others, and expectations about leaving work are held fixed.

some first-order serial correlation simply because a single employment spell may span two years. However, even given a woman's current employment status, her past work history is informative about her future. Because of the small sample size, I could not estimate the magnitude of this association.

Evidence also suggests that early nonemployment is associated with lower future wages—even as much as twenty years later. Moreover, for white women, the wage losses associated with prolonged nonwork are greatest when it occurs at the beginning of their careers. While part of these wage losses may result from individual differences which are correlated both with early nonwork and with wages, controls for a number of behavioral indicators of labor force attachment did not decrease the estimated long-run wage losses associated with early nonwork. Whether or not is is voluntary, not working for a prolonged period during the teenage years is associated with considerably lower wages later on.

Nonemployment is pervasive and prolonged among teenage women with less than fourteen years of schooling. It is associated with a lower probability of employment in the short run and with lower wages throughout women's work careers. Whether voluntary or not, early employment behavior apparently has lasting implications for women's future economic careers.

# Notes

1. This paper uses a set of techniques developed by Gary Chamberlain to examine employment persistence. Chamberlain has been extremely generous with both time and advice, and helped me plan an analysis strategy for examining employment persistence as well as providing useful assistance at every stage of the analysis. I am also grateful for discussions with Joan Brinser, Greg Duncan, David T. Ellwood, Elizabeth Phillips, and David A. Wise.

2. This does not appear to be the case for the NLS 74 (See Meyer and Wise).

3. I did this by estimating whether a woman worked in the $i^{th}$ year following school completion as a function of region, urban residence, local unemployment rate, husband's income, marital status, and number of dependents with controls for age, race, and schooling.

4. This affects the distribution of $\underset{\sim}{\alpha}$, but since we are conditioning on $\underset{\sim}{\alpha}$, no problems arise.

5. Theoretically, we can distinguish serial correlation from "true" state dependence when we have stong predictors ($X$s) of employment behavior which change over time. If all the remaining persistence in women's work behavior (after adjusting for heterogeneity) were due to exogenous factors that were serially correlated over time, then a change in $X$ should have its full effect on work behavior immediately with no damped response into the future. On the other hand, if past and present work behavior were causally related, then a change in $X$ should affect the probability of working now and should alter the probability of working in the future because the initial change in work behavior will induce future changes. To test this we need to introduce current and lagged values of predictors ($X$s) into a model which predicts the current decision to work, which omits the lagged decision to work, and which adjusts for heterogeneity.

6. This paragraph is a brief summary of a more elaborate argument developed by Chamberlain (1978b, 1978c).

7. Applying Chamberlain's model to four-year employment sequences gives much the same results. The estimate of first order dependence is large and significant ($\hat{\gamma} = 1.81$ with a standard error of .41), again suggesting that past employment is associated with significantly higher changes of future employment, even after adjustments for heterogeneity.

8. We may calculate these odds as follows. For each year after the first, calculate the probability that a woman works, given she worked in the previous year. The average of these probabilities over years 2 . . $T$ is equal to the average value of $P(1|1)$. Similarly calculate the average value of $P(1|0)$. For five years, these average values are .890 and .354. The odds are: $e^{\gamma} = (.890|.110)(.646|.354) = 14.8$. Here $\gamma$ would equal 2.84.

9. Chamberlain (1979), in response to a question about time trends, very generously developed this procedure and used the NLS four year sample as an example.

10. This procedure involves estimating a probit function of the decision to work for all women, employed and unemployed, calculating the Mills ratio for each employed woman using the probit estimates, and including this Mills ratio in the regression equation.

11. Note that this test will not allow us to distinguish between two quite different hypotheses. The first is that both work behavior and wages are causally related to attachment, but not to one another. The second is that work behavior alters attachment which, in turn, influences wages.

12. In order to treat work experience as endogenous, I assumed that fertility was exogenous. As Cain (1976) points out, this assumption is difficult to justify.

13. It should be noted that this result is consistent with many different hypotheses. This penalty associated with early nonwork could be due to the depreciation of human capital, to stereotyping by employers on the basis of early work behavior, or to reinforcement of "good" work attitudes by work and "bad" work attitudes by nonwork. I will not attempt to differentiate among these competing hypotheses, although each has quite different implications for our understanding of the wage determination process for women. Instead my purpose is in a more limited—to assess the opportunity costs associated with early nonwork.

14. It might also be useful to ask the question, Are labor force withdrawals which occur in the period following school completion more costly than labor force withdrawals which occur after beginning a career? This is true for white women but not for black women (see Corcoran 1979).

15. Ellwood attempted to remove heterogeneity from the relationship between experience and wages by differencing using the NLS data. To do this, he assumed that wages and experience were not simultaneously determined and that problems of selection bias could be ignored since almost all young men worked in both years 3 and 4. These assumptions become much more suspect if applied to women. Research on women's labor force participation typically assume that wages influence time worked. In the NLS four-year subsample of women, about 30% of the women did not work either in year 3 or in year 4 and so did not have wage measures for one or both years. Given problems of simultaneity and selection bias, I chose not to examine heterogeneity with the NLS data.

# References

Ashefelter, O. 1978. What do teenage employment statistics measure? In *Supplementary papers from the conference on youth unemployment: Its measurements and meaning*. Washington, D.C. U.S. Department of Labor.

Bergmann, B. R. 1971. Occupational segregaton, wages, and profits when employers discriminate by sex and race. College Park, Md.: Economics of discrimination project, University of Maryland. Mimeographed.

Cain, G. G. 1976. The challenge of segmented labor market theories to orthodox theory: A survey. *Journal of Economic Literature* 14:1215–57.

Chamberlain, G. 1978a. Omitted variable bias in panel data: Estimating the returns to schooling. *Annales de l'INSEE.*

———. 1978b. Analysis of covariance with qualitative data. Harvard University. Mimeographed.

———. 1978c. On the use of panel data. Harvard University. Mimeographed.

———. 1979. Unpublished communication on time trends in women's employment behavior.

Corcoran, M. 1979. Work experience, labor force withdrawals and women's wages. In Andrews, Gilroy and Lloyd, eds. *Women in the labor market.* Columbia University Press. Forthcoming.

Griliches, Z. and Mason, W. 1973. Education, income and ability. In Goldberger and Duncan eds., *Structural equation models in the social sciences.* New York: Seminar press.

Gronau, R. 1974. Wage comparisons—S selectivity bias. *Journal of Political Economy* 82:1119–43.

Heckman, J. A. 1977. Sample selection bias as a specification error. University of Chicago. Unpublished paper.

———. 1978a. A partial survey of recent research on the labor supply of women. *American Economic Review, Papers and Proceedings* (May):200–212.

———. 1978b. Heterogeneity and state dependence in dynamic models of labor supply. University of Chicago. Mimeographed.

———. 1978. Statistical models for discrete panel data developed and applied to test the hypothesis of true state dependence against the hypothesis of spurious state dependence. *Annales de l'INSEE.*

———. 1974. Shadow prices, market wages and labor supply. *Econometrica* 42:679–94.

Heckman, J. J., and Willis, R. 1977. A beta logistic model for analysis of sequential labor force participation by married women. *Journal of Economy* 85:27–58i (b).

Mincer, J. 1962. Labor force participation of married women: A study of labor supply. In Lewis, H. G. ed., *Aspects of labor economics.* Princeton: Princeton University Press.

Mincer, J. and Polachek, S. 1974. Family investments in human capital: Earnings of women. In Schultz, T. W. ed., *The economics of the family.* Chicago: University of Chicago press.

Polachek, S. 1975. Differences in expected post school investment as a determinant of market wage differentials. *International Economic Review* 16:451–70.

Stevenson, M. 1973. Women's wages and job segregation, *Politics and Society* (Fall):83–95.

## Comment    Solomon William Polachek

According to some schools of existential philosophy,[1] decisions may be interpreted as being based on the moment, and hence independent of one's past and future. Economists no longer adhere to such a philosophy concerning the decision process, and are hard at work integrating decisions made at a given time with aspects of one's past and future. The chapter by Mary Corcoran is an example of such an analysis. This chapter seeks to assess the impact of early teenage women's nonemployment on two aspects of future life: the first concerns the immediate future, and the second pertains to a long-run time horizon. With respect to the short run, Corcoran looks at the impact of nonemployment on a subsequent year's work prospects. That is, do teenage women (alike in observed and unobserved characteristics) have a higher probability of working in any year given that they were employed in the previous year? With respect to the long-run impact of nonwork, the chapter seeks to ascertain whether wages, even 20 to 25 years in the future, are affected by nonwork spells upon school completion.

Basically it is found (1) that past (non-) employment raises the probability of current (non-) employment (even when adjusting for individual differences in initial work probabilities), and (2) that future wages are affected greatly by spells of teenage unemployment. Thus, regardless of individual characteristics, the past, the present, and the future *are* related for all. This need not imply a heterogeneous population composed of workers and nonworkers, but instead that "state dependence" is important. In fact, even after adjusting for population heterogeneity, the odds of a woman working, given that she worked last year, are about seven times higher than if she did not work the previous year.

Qualitatively (with exceptions to be noted), these results appear intuitively reasonable and similar to the Elwood and Meyer-Wise chapters in this volume. Yet I see at least two problems of major concern to policy makers. First, policy prescriptions are not derived, and second (as the author readily admits) computed statistics are subject to biases inher-

Solomon William Polachek is associate professor of economics at the University of North Carolina at Chapel Hill and a fellow of the Carolina Population Center.

ent in restrictions innately embedded in the estimation techniques. My comments address this latter problem first and then move on to the former by proposing alternative estimation schemes.

Persistence is determined by a nonzero $\gamma$ parameter of Gary Chamberlain's "autoregressive logit model."[2] As Mary Corcoran aptly points out, three shortcomings exist: (1) that individual traits which influence work behavior are assumed not to vary over time; (2) that exogenous predictors are omitted; and (3) that the transitional probability ($\gamma$) is assumed to be stationary. It cannot be overemphasized that these restrictions can lead to serious biases. For example, if marital status or number of children (assumed constant in the model) in fact change, and if these variables determine work status (as is commonly found), then changes in labor force behavior will be observed, thereby appearing to lower the importance of state dependence when in fact marital status and children *could be* the sole determinants of work status, and state dependence could be absolute (true). Suffice it to say the other assumptions lead to more biases, but I think neglecting changing exogenous variables to be the most serious. Empirically, an illustration of this bias appears in different state dependencies observed by Mincer and Ofek (1978) and Heckman and Willis (1979) in their recent exchange.[3]

This bias and others can be corrected by applying slightly more sophisticated yet theoretically estimatable models. If one insists on a logit framework, the Chamberlain fixed effect logit augmented with an autoregressive structure could be used.[4] This too can be generalized by modifying the autoregressive structure so as to eliminate the necessity of a constant $\gamma$.

Even the long-term effects computed in tables 11.6 to 11.9 are subject to bias. These effects are computed essentially by OLS regressions of home-time on wages. Two-stage least-squares and adjustments for selectivity with respect to who is in the labor force at a given time do *not* alter results. Population heterogeneity (as adjusted for in computations on employment persistence) is not accounted for. Thus overestimates likely result since those with lower wages are most likely to face the most teenage nonemployment. The longitudinal nature of the data could be further exploited to alleviate the possibility of this potential bias. Two approaches are possible. One (that eliminates heterogeneity in a manner much like the autoregressive logit technique just used) would be to regress first differences of earnings with first differences in experience variables.[5] Another approach would be to apply pooled cross-section time-series techniques such as the variance of error components technique.[6]

Even if these possible biases prove to be inconsequential, one could ask how the estimates can be used by policy makers. It is to this end that I see some difficulty. Thus I wish to devote the remainder of my comments to this issue.

The major point of the chapter is that teenage unemployment is costly and therefore should be reduced. Yet no implication is given concerning what instruments are appropriate in achieving lower teenage unemployment rates. The reason for this omission stems from the fact that nonemployment is analyzed in a reduced form framework and hence taken as a "basic" measurement. Nonemployment causes more nonemployment, but the structural equations analyzing the real factors that cause nonemployment are treated as unobserved variables, and hence are omitted from the analysis. Thus, as a policy maker, I would not know whether decreases in nonemployment were more sensitive to unemployment insurance changes, antinatalist fertility policies, job training programs, minimum wage legislation, etc.[7] Furthermore, the decision to work may be innately tied to the wage equation, which is treated independently by Corcoran.

I thus propose an analysis of the structural equations of the system in a simultaneous equations context. As is well known, employment is related to the relationship between one's shadow value of time (a latent variable) and one's market earnings power. Fertility, too, may at least affect the value of one's home time. In short, both parts of the paper could be synthesized and studied within a unified framework.

Two approaches seem plausible. If one insists on treating employment as dichotomous, simultaneous equation probit techniques could be used. If one were to utilize more fully the per-period duration of employment status data, simultaneous tobit techniques could be adopted to perform panel estimates.

As an example of the former approach, let $d(i, t)$ depict individual $i$'s work status in period $t$. Generally, $d(i, t) = 1$ if one works and $d(i, t) = 0$ if one does not. Following the logic of Heckman (1974, 1978), work status is determined by whether one's market wage $w(i, t)$ exceeds one's shadow price of time $w^*(i, t)$. Thus

$$d(i, t) = 1 \text{ if } w(i, t) > w^*(i, t)$$

where

$$w(i, t) = Z_1 \beta_1 + \varepsilon_1$$
$$w^*(i, t) = Z_2 \beta_2 + \sum_{j=1}^{T} \gamma(i, t-j) \, d(i, t-j) + \varepsilon_2$$

Appropriate specifications of $Z_1$ and $Z_2$ (exogenous time dependent factors, both individual and market oriented) enable one to determine the individual and market characteristics most influential in determining labor force behavior. Distinguishing $\beta_1$ and $\beta_2$ disentangles which of these factors affects more greatly the shodow prices of time in the home as contrasted to the market wage level. Similarly, changes in exogenous factors that affect work status and are important to policy makers would be accounted for directly. Although I have neither written the likelihood function nor estimated this system, others have moved in this direction.[9] Thus such estimation is feasible.

To summarize, I believe Corcoran's chapter represents an excellent and careful piece of research which addresses a most important topic. Using the latest computer software, she finds strong short-run and long-run impacts of female teenage nonemployment on their future well-being. My comments are designed not to critize but instead to prod Corcoran and others into extending already existing panel data models to achieving innately less biased and more policy oriented parameters.

## Notes

1. For example, see Watts (1951) and Marcuse (1964).
2. See Chamberlain (October 1978), pp. 32–38.
3. Contrast the results of tables 2–3 of Mincer and Ofek (1979) with tables 1–4 of Heckman and Willis.
4. In this case,

$$\text{Prob } (y_{it} = 1 \,|\, \underline{x}_j, y_{i,\,t-1}) = \frac{e^{\alpha_i + \gamma y_{i,\,t-1}}}{e^{\alpha_i} + e^{-\underline{\beta}\,\underline{x}_{it}}}$$

where

$\underline{x}_i \equiv$ a vector of exogenous variables and the other variables are defined in the Corcoran chapter.

5. An example of this is Mincer and Polachek (1978).
6. An example of this technique is used in Lillard and Willis (1978) and Kniesner, Padilla, and Polachek (1980).
7. Also following Clark and Summers (chapter 7 of this volume), no distinction is made between being out of the labor force and in the labor force but not at work.
8. Dummy exogenous regressors could be used to indicate single work spells spanning two-year segments in an attempt to avoid possible first-order serial correlation.
9. For example see Waldman, "The Time Allocation of Young Men" (1979). In that application the joint decision of school and work status is modeled on the basis of wage and shadow wage equations.

## References

Chamberlain, G. 1978. On the use of panel data. Paper prepared for the Social Science Research Council Conference On Life Cycle Aspects of Employment and the Labor Market, Mount Kisco, New York.

Clark, K. and Summers, L. The dynamics of youth unemployment. Chapter 7 of the present volume.

Heckman, J. 1974. Shadow prices, market wages, and labor supply. *Econometrica* 42:679–94.

———. 1978. Dummy endogenous variables in a simultaneous equations system. *Econometrica.* 931–59

Heckman, J. and Willis, R. 1979. Reply to Mincer-Ofek. *Journal of Political Economy* 87:203–12.

Kniesner, T., Padilla, A. and Polachek, S. 1980. The rate of return to schooling and the business cycle: additional estimates. *Journal of Human Resources*:273–77.

Marcuse, H. 1964. *One dimensional man*. Boston: Beacon Press.

Mincer, J. and Ofek, H. 1979. The distribution of lifetime labor force participation of married women: A comment. *Journal of Political Economy* 87:197–202.

Mincer, J. and Polachek, S. 1978. Women's earnings reexamined. *Journal of Human Resources* (Winter):18–34.

Waldman, D. 1979. Time allocation of young men. Ph.D. dissertation, University of Wisconsin.

Watts, A. 1951. *The wisdom of insecurity*. New York: Pantheon Press.

# Comment   Isabel V. Sawhill

Mary Corcoran's chapter is the twin sister of David T. Ellwood's chapter (10). Both consider the so-called scarring effects of a lack of work experience in the years immediately following school, one for young women and the other for young men. In addition, both are first cousins of the chapter by Meyer and Wise (9) which examines the effects of high school work experience, vocational education, and academic achievement on later success in the labor market and post-secondary school attendance. It would have been helpful if these chapters could have been considered and discussed together. We should be trying to compare and contrast the findings to see if they vary because (1) different groups are being examined, (2) a slightly different question is being asked, or (3) different data sources or methodologies are being used. For example, it may be that scarring effects are different for men and women because the returns to female experience are smaller for the usual reasons identified in the human capital literature. Alternatively, these differences may reflect variations in data sources and methodologies across the two studies.

As an aid to those who are only interested in the bottom line, let me attempt to summarize the major findings of each of these papers without attempting to disentangle fully the reasons for any differences noted.

Meyer and Wise find that the relationship between work experience in high school and later employment and wages is large and permanent. However, the interpretaion of this finding is clouded, as the authors point out, because of the heterogeneity problem. As Chamberlain puts it, we

Isabel V. Sawhill is program director for Employment and Labor Policy at the Urban Institute.

don't know whether early labor market experience is doing something to a person or telling us something about the person. On the other hand, the authors find that after controlling for heterogeneity, work experience after high school is only weakly related to later employment, a conclusion that is consistent with both Ellwood and Corcoran.

Ellwood and Corcoran explain in detail the scarring hypothesis. Inability to control for individual heterogeneity has generated considerable skepticism about almost all past research which has purported to show a causal relationship between teenage joblessness and later success in the labor market.

Both Ellwood and Corcoran have adopted sophisticated methodological detours around this problem. As a result, their work represents a giant step forward in enabling us to document the longer-term consequences of early labor market experiences. To those who argue that youth unemployment is a nonproblem because it disappears with age and has no lingering effects, we can now say with some confidence, "You are wrong."

Specifically, Ellwood finds that the effects of early experience on the later employment of young men are not very significant but that the effects on wages are quite large and clear-cut. Corcoran finds that the employment effects for young women are larger than in the case of young men but that the wage effects are somewhat smaller. This latter finding is not too surprising when one realizes that it is based on historical data covering a period when women were tracked into jobs with flat age-earnings profiles. In fact, I was surprised that the wage effects were as significant and persistent as they were and am inclined to believe this is because heterogeneity was only crudely controlled for in these particular regressions.

I would now like to make some comments about remaining research gaps. First, we need to know why the relationship between early experience and later wages exists. It could be a simple human capital building effect or it could be a signalling or credentialling effect (reducing the power of age- or sex-based statistical discrimination). The policy implications of these different explanations vary. If human capital building is the key, then providing learning experiences or on-the-job training becomes critical. On the other hand, if labeling is what matters, then on-the-job training is not necessarily important, but providing private as opposed to subsidized public sector experience may be. In my own work, I am running into a lot of ancedotal evidence suggesting that employers discount the value of government work experience programs. Participants in these programs wear a "damaged goods" label.

A second research need is for more information on *noneconomic* consequences. Here there are some clear-cut sex differences in the predicted outcomes of teenage unemployment. We hypothesize that adolescent females who lack job opportunities will overinvest in *early* childbearing, which is known to have various adverse effects, including some which are intergenerational. For males, the expected outcome is a higher incidence of crime. In both cases, a relationship is known to exist, but the direction and extent of causation, if any, are not established. Yet documenting these effects is more important than in the case of economic outcomes because they involve greater externalities. This is precisely why they loom so large in popular discussions of youth unemployment.

As a final and related comment, I want to note that the justification for special intervention efforts on behalf of youths rests somewhat uneasily on the economic consequences alone. If the long-term opportunity costs (lower wages) are voluntarily paid because of young people's preferences for leisure or nonmarket work, then society should not intervene except perhaps to inform young people what the costs are so they can make more informed judgments. Unfortunately, there is still a lot of debate and uncertainty about how to distinguish between voluntary and involuntary joblessness, especially in the case of youths.

# 12 Dead-end Jobs and Youth Unemployment

Charles Brown

The hypothesis that one's job is related to one's chances of being unemployed is neither new nor very controversial. In every year since 1958, unemployment rates of craft workers have exceeded those of white-collar workers, while those of nonfarm laborers have been double those of craft workers. Moreover, a substantial fraction of these differences among broad occupational groups persists after controlling for differences in "personal" characteristics (age, sex, race, education, location) of the workers in them (Martson 1976, p. 196).

Recent analyses have emphasized "dead-end" jobs as an important factor in youth unemployment, even in relatively prosperous times. While the precise definition of a dead-end job is generally unstated, a recurring idea is that dead-end jobs do not offer opportunities for advancement and hence provide little incentive for stable, continuous employment. Feldstein argues that

> high turnover rates and voluntary unemployment are also a response to the unsatisfactory type of job that is available to many young workers. These are often dead-end jobs with neither opportunity for advancement within the firm nor training and experience that would be useful elsewhere. [1973, p. 14]

Similarly, a *Washington Post* report on unemployment among black teenagers in Washington, D.C. asserted that they

> sometimes refuse to take low level jobs as busboys, dishwashers, and janitors because they feel that these jobs cannot offer them money, status, or *an opportunity for advancement*. . . . [T]eenagers often stay at

Charles Brown is associated with the University of Maryland and with the National Bureau of Economic Research. The author is grateful to Nancy Lemrow for research assistance and to members of the NBER Project on Youth Unemployment for helpful comments on earlier drafts of this paper.

those jobs only long enough to buy a certain thing or qualify for unemployment [benefits]. [Italics added.]

The importance of the conceptual distinction between "low-wage" jobs and those that offer no chances for advancement is implicit in Hall's (1970, p. 395) assertion that "trainees in banks and workers in service stations receive about the same hourly wages, but the trainees have an incentive to work hard and steadily that is absent for the service station men."

To be sure, the long-run consequences of working in a dead-end job depend on the individual worker and his/her stage in the life cycle. Working in such a job during the summer before returning to college is unlikely to lead to later problems, but an out-of-school worker who bounces from one such a job to another may suffer permanent economic disadvantages. One would anticipate, however, that such jobs would generally be associated with more frequent quitting- and layoff-related unemployment in the short run, because neither the individual nor the employer stands to lose very much from such separations.

While the relationship between wages and unemployment has received considerable attention, the independent impact of opportunities for advancement has received less attention. Two factors appear to be responsible for this omission. First, while the notion that disadvantaged workers may end up in jobs with low wages and little prospect of advancement is present in the writings of human capital theorists (e.g., Rosen 1972, p. 338), it has received much greater emphasis in dual labor market theories (Piore 1971; Gordon 1972, chapter 4). Because both attributes are seen as common to the "secondary" labor market, the dichotomy between low-wage, no-advancement jobs and high-wage jobs with opportunities for advancement has been stressed, to the exclusion of separate analysis of each component. Second, existing occupational indices—e.g., the Duncan index, the Dictionary of Occupational Titles' General Educational Development and Specific Vocational Preparation scales—measure current position rather than opportunities for advancement. "Apprentice" classifications receive low ratings because they measure what a job requires, not what it promises.[1]

These observations suggest alternative strategies for further research on occupational differences in unemployment: (1) improving the controls for differences in personal characteristics by using more such variables or more sophisticated statistical techniques; and (2) attempting to characterize occupations in a parsimonious way which gives some clues as to why such differences exist. This chapter follows the second strategy. It focuses on young males; young people because their unemployment rates are so high, males to reduce complications which those not in the labor force introduce. The data—occupational characteristics based on the 1970 Census and labor-force status and personal characteristics of individuals from the Current Population Survey—are described in section 12.1. Characteristics related to opportunities for advancement are emphasized. In section 12.2, the hypothesized relationship between these characteristics and youth unemployment is explored. Some support for the dead-end job hypothesis is found, but several puzzles also emerge. Conclusions are offered in section 12.3.


## 12.1   Data

The 1970 Census ascertained each worker's occupation and industry in 1965 as well as in 1970, making it a unique source of data on the (realized) prospects for advancement in each occupation. The aspect of dead-end jobs emphasized in the introduction was the lack of orderly career advancement. This suggests that, whatever the average wage which such occupations pay, those who are in them can't expect future wages to be much higher.

Let $W_i(t, t_0, j)$ be the period $t$ wage of those who are/were in occupation $i$, with $j$ periods of experience, in period $t_0$. Thus $i$ and $j$ are occupation and experience level in period $t_0$. Ideally, a measure of realized opportunities for advancement in occupation $i$ would involve a comparison of $W_i$ (1965, 1965, $j$) and $W_i$ (1970, 1965, $j$).[2] Given $W_i$ (1965, 1965, $j$), an occupation which provided greater advancement opportunities would have a larger value of $W_i$ (1970, 1965, $j$) than those which did not provide such opportunities. While $W_i$ (1970, 1965, $j$) was determined directly by the Census, $W_i$(1965, 1965, $j$) was not (the Census did not ask individuals how much they earned five years ago). However, if wages grew uniformly at rate $g$ *within* each occupation-experience cell from 1965 to 1970,

$$W_i \ (1965, \ 1965, \ j) = (1 + g)^{-1} \ W_i \ (1970, \ 1970, \ j)$$

Thus the 1970 wage of those in occupation $i$ with $j$ periods of experience in 1970 is used to reflect the 1965 wage of those in that same occupation with $j$ periods of experience in 1965. To simplify later notation, let $W_i = W_i$ (1970, 1970, $j$) and $W_i' = W_i$ (1970, 1965, $j$). Opportunities for advancement are then inferred from large values of $W_i'$ given $W_i$.

$W_i$ and $W_i'$ were tabulated by three-digit occupation from the 1/100 Public Use File for out-of-school men with less than ten years of labor market experience.[3] Average weekly wages were calculated as the ratio of total earnings to total weeks worked in the year preceeding the Census.[4] Average hourly wages were calculated as total earnings divided by total hours worked, the latter being approximated by weeks worked last year times hours worked in the week preceding the Census. These averages were based on roughly 200 out-of-school men with less than ten years experience per occupational cell—a sample size unattainable with any other data source.

Having calculated $W_i$ and $W_i'$ one can ask which occupations provide the best prospects for $W_i'$ *given the level of* $W_i$. A simple answer is provided by regressing $\ln(W_i')$ on $\ln(W_i)$ and calculating the residuals.[5] Dead-end occupations are expected to have substantial negative residuals, while those in occupations which promise advancement should have positive residuals. Table 12.1 lists the sixty largest occupations by this criterion using hourly wage data. The list is restricted to "large" occupations in order to minimize the importance of sampling variation.

It is not clear which occupations should be rated high or low on such an index on a priori grounds. My own a priori candidates for high-advancement jobs (apprentice categories) do not appear in table 12.1 because no apprentice category achieved sufficient cell size. Other ways of generating table 12.1 (using weekly wages or a nonlogarithmic estimating function) produced similar, though certainly not identical, rankings.

One striking feature of table 12.1 is the high rating given to a few occupations which seem doubtful as sources of training or other avenues of advancement (farm laborers, gas station attendants). A plausible explanation for these "outliers" is that initial wages are so low in these occupations that the individual is likely to advance subsequently simply by leaving them.[6] Thus, if some occupations have substantial negative transitory effects (low $W_i$) they might show substantial positive "advancement" $(\ln W_i' - \ln W_i)$, but one would not expect such "advancement" to be reflected in low unemployment rates. This possibility should be kept in mind when considering the results in section 12.2.

A second, somewhat more tentative index can also be constructed. To the extent that what is "learned" on the job is industry-specific, those who are on career paths should remain in the same industry, even if they change occupational title or accept a position with a different employer. Those in jobs where such learning is absent have no particular incentive to find a new job in the same industry. Thus a plausible index of advancement opportunities expected by workers in an occupation is the probability that a worker in that occupation will be in the same *industry* at some point (five years) in the future. This probability was computed directly from the 1970 Census 1/100 File, using three-digit industries.

Table 12.2 presents the sixty largest occupations according to this index. The rankings seem to me more plausible than those in table 12.1, but that may be due largely to the fact that this index is not constructed to be uncorrelated with $\ln (W_i)$, so that low-wage occupations are more prominently represented among the "worst" occupations according to this index. However, $\ln (W_i)$ is held constant in the regressions in section 12.2.

Three other occupational characteristics were taken from published 1970 Census data: median years of schooling, percent female, and percent black (U.S. Census Bureau, 1973, tables 1 and 38). They may be

**Table 12.1    Occupations by Wage-Growth Residual**

| 3-digit Code | Occupation | Residual | N | 3-digit Code | Occupation | Residual | N |
|---|---|---|---|---|---|---|---|
| 65 | Physicians: med., osteo. | .1678 | 554. | 410 | Brickmasons, stonemasons | -.0057 | 283. |
| 305 | Bookkeepers | .1422 | 274. | 694 | Misc. operat. | -.0074 | 857. |
| 552 | Phone inst., repairmen | .1023 | 438. | 680 | Welders, flamecutters | -.0092 | 804. |
| 822 | Farm labor., wage work. | .0968 | 1052. | 643 | Packers, wrappers: x meat, produce | -.0103 | 267. |
| 623 | Garage work., gas station attend. | .0942 | 606. | 11 | Civil eng. | -.0105 | 322. |
| 31 | Lawyers | .0865 | 586. | 231 | Sales mgr., dept. heads: retail | -.0106 | 291. |
| 233 | Sales mgr., x retail | .0775 | 315. | 522 | Plumbers, pipefitters | -.0118 | 555. |
| 265 | Ins. agents, brokers, underwriters | .0744 | 870. | 23 | Eng., nec | -.0129 | 357. |
| 1 | Accountants | .0601 | 978. | 610 | Checkers, examiners, inspec.: manu. | -.0131 | 529. |
| 374 | Shipping, receiving clerks | .0524 | 620. | 715 | Truck drivers | -.0160 | 2474. |
| 430 | Electricians | .0495 | 727. | 395 | Not spec. clerical work. | -.0221 | 599. |
| 153 | Elec., electronic eng. technic. | .0460 | 349. | 602 | Assemblers | -.0223 | 1120. |
| 152 | Draftsmen | .0433 | 652. | 751 | Const. labor.: x carpenters' helpers | -.0230 | 1091. |
| 801 | Farmers: owners, tenants | .0324 | 1254. | 481 | Heavy equip. mech., incl. diesel | -.0265 | 612. |
| 202 | Bank officers, finan. mgr. | .0313 | 525. | 12 | Elec., electronic eng. | -.0293 | 589. |
| 640 | Mine operat., nec | .0197 | 323. | 144 | Sec. sch. teach. | -.0331 | 788. |
| 140 | Teach., coll., univ. | .0169 | 275. | 142 | Elem. sch. teach. | -.0358 | 797. |
| 510 | Painters: const., maint. | .0167 | 406. | 690 | Mach. operat.: misc., spec. | -.0382 | 1243. |
| 903 | Janitors, sextons | .0154 | 682. | 415 | Carpenters | -.0390 | 1103. |
| 935 | Barbers | .0106 | 269. | 441 | Foremen, nec | -.0399 | 1459. |
| 705 | Deliverymen, routemen | .0095 | 821. | 692 | Mach. operat.: not spec. | -.0437 | 908. |
| 912 | Cooks: x pri. hhold. | .0091 | 413. | 964 | Policemen, detectives | -.0459 | 632. |
| 245 | Mgr., admin., nec | .0079 | 3735. | 695 | Not spec. operat. | -.0498 | 727. |
| 473 | Auto mech. | .0033 | 1492. | 14 | Mechanical eng. | -.0508 | 318. |
| 631 | Meat cutters, butchers: x manu. | .0020 | 325. | 706 | Fork lift, tow motor operat. | -.0563 | 329. |
| 381 | Stock clerks, storekeepers | .0011 | 463. | 461 | Machinists | -.0567 | 752. |
| 162 | Eng., science technic., nec | .0006 | 306. | 436 | Excavating, grading, road mach. oper. | -.0635 | 358. |
| 785 | Not spec. labor. | .0005 | 882. | 753 | Freight, material handlers | -.0667 | 605. |
| 762 | Stock handlers | -.0030 | 475. | 755 | Gardeners, groundskeepers: x farm | -.0673 | 294. |
| 422 | Compositors, typesetters | -.0048 | 298. | 86 | Clergymen | -.0972 | 388. |

**Table 12.2    Occupations by Industry-Retention Rates**

| 3-digit Code | Occupation | Retention | N | 3-digit Code | Occupation | Retention | N |
|---|---|---|---|---|---|---|---|
| 140 | Teach., coll., univ. | .8444 | 315. | 1 | Accountants | .6020 | 1098. |
| 86 | Clergymen | .8404 | 445. | 231 | Sales mgr., dept. heads: retail | .5927 | 329. |
| 144 | Sec. sch. teach. | .8373 | 922. | 706 | Fork lift, tow motor operat. | .5914 | 394. |
| 552 | Phone inst., repairmen | .8350 | 509. | 610 | Checkers, examiners, inspec.: manu. | .5892 | 628. |
| 31 | Lawyers | .8258 | 666. | 415 | Carpenters | .5836 | 1388. |
| 142 | Elem. sch. teach. | .8149 | 929. | 280 | Salesmen, sales clerks, nec | .5777 | 4326. |
| 65 | Physicians: med., osteo. | .8148 | 637. | 690 | Mach. operat.: misc., spec. | .5630 | 1460. |
| 14 | Mechanical eng. | .7808 | 365. | 473 | Auto. mech. | .5628 | 1759. |
| 964 | Policemen, detectives | .7790 | 751. | 381 | Stock clerks, storekeepers | .5562 | 543. |
| 12 | Elec., electronic eng. | .7712 | 660. | 461 | Machinists | .5455 | 836. |
| 11 | Civil eng. | .7655 | 371. | 640 | Mine operat., nec | .5448 | 402. |
| 522 | Plumbers, pipefitters | .7432 | 662. | 680 | Welders, flamecutters | .5433 | 935. |
| 233 | Sales mgr., x retail | .7413 | 375. | 395 | Not spec. clerical work. | .5378 | 662. |
| 631 | Meat cutters, butchers: x manu. | .7247 | 385. | 692 | Mach. operat.: not spec. | .5330 | 1062. |
| 935 | Barbers | .7178 | 326. | 715 | Truck drivers | .5330 | 3013. |
| 801 | Farmers: owners, tenants | .7156 | 1575. | 694 | Misc. operat. | .5224 | 1005. |
| 202 | Bank officers, finan. mgr. | .7074 | 605. | 753 | Freight, material handlers | .5217 | 715. |
| 481 | Heavy equip. mech., incl. diesel | .6972 | 710. | 602 | Assemblers | .5201 | 1296. |
| 23 | Eng., nec | .6969 | 386. | 912 | Cooks: x pri. hhold. | .5172 | 522. |
| 430 | Electricians | .6845 | 862. | 374 | Shipping, receiving clerks | .5158 | 698. |
| 441 | Foremen, nec | .6795 | 1747. | 903 | Janitors, sextons | .5074 | 816. |
| 245 | Mgr., admin., nec | .6694 | 4374. | 822 | Farm labor., wage work. | .5071 | 1331. |
| 422 | Compositors, typesetters | .6638 | 348. | 762 | Stock handlers | .4927 | 548. |
| 153 | Elec., electronic eng. technic. | .6634 | 407. | 755 | Gardeners, groundskeepers: x farm | .4751 | 362. |
| 510 | Painters: const., maint. | .6623 | 539. | 785 | Not spec. labor | .4638 | 1022. |
| 265 | Ins. agents, brokers, underwriters | .6437 | 1002. | 705 | Deliverymen, routemen | .4626 | 936. |
| 152 | Draftsmen | .6412 | 694. | 643 | Packers, wrappers: x meat, produce | .4618 | 314. |
| 410 | Brickmasons, stonemasons | .6236 | 364. | 695 | Not spec. operat. | .4203 | 847. |
| 162 | Eng., science technic., nec | .6221 | 344. | 751 | Const. labor.: x carpenters' helpers | .3942 | 1380. |

interpreted as measures of the labor market disadvantage of the members of each occupation. They may also reflect the relative opportunities for advancement in occupations, to the extent that blacks, women, and those with less education choose low-training occupations (Rosen, 1972, p. 338) or are crowded into them (Bergmann 1971).

These occupational characteristics were matched to the 1973–75 May Current Population Survey according to the individual's three-digit occupation code. Apart from the restrictions noted above (male, not in school, less than 10 years of experience), the matching process imposes the additional requirement that the individual report an occupation. This excludes (1) all those who have never worked, whether they are unemployed or out of the labor force at the time of survey; and (2) most of those not in the labor force.[8] The first exclusion is inherent in the study of "occupation effects"; the second leads to the exclusion of all those not in the labor force from the regressions presented below.[9]

In addition to whether the individual was unemployed at time of survey, the CPS determined the reason for unemployment. Those who report they "have a job or business from which [they were] . . . on layoff last week" are counted as having "lost" their last job. Those who reported they started looking for work because they "lost or quit a job at that time" are counted as "lost" or "quit," respectively. Consequently, those who dropped out of the labor force between quitting or losing their previous job and beginning their current spell of unemployment probably aren't captured in either the "lost" or "quit" categories, though they are counted as unemployed.

Finally, the CPS files provided several potentially important individual characteristics: race, education, age (and hence experience), location, and marital and veteran statuses. Moreover, hourly earnings and union membership were determined for those who were working, who had a job but were absent or on layoff, or who had worked in the last three months.

## 12.2  Results

Equations in which personal and job characteristics are used to explain unemployment are presented in table 12.3. The dependent variable in each equation is a dummy variable indicating a state of being unemployed at time of survey multiplied by 100. Thus each regression coefficient can be interpreted as that variable's "effect" on the unemployment rate, measured as a percentage. The number in parentheses below each coefficient is the standard error. The number in brackets is the product of the regression coefficient and the variable's standard deviation. It reflects the impact of a one-standard deviation change in the independent variable on the unemployment rate and can, in that sense, be compared across variables.

Table 12.3    Unemployment Equations (Males Less than Ten Years after School-leaving)

| Variable | Mean (S.D.) | (1) | (2) | (3) | (4) | (5) |
|---|---|---|---|---|---|---|
| Constant | | 28.706* ( 1.213) | 34.814* ( 1.365) | 28.581* ( 1.895) | 30.632* ( 1.918) | 26.774* ( 2.738) |
| Region = north central | .284 ( .451) | -.308 ( .449) [ -.139] | -.288 ( .448) [ -.130] | -.324 ( .449) [ -.146] | -.243 ( .448) [ -.109] | -.291 ( .449) [ -.131] |
| Region = south | .308 ( .462) | -3.070* ( .459) [ -1.418] | -3.061* ( .458) [ -1.414] | -2.974* ( .457) [ -1.375] | -2.977* ( .458) [ -1.375] | -2.919* ( .458) [ -1.349] |
| Region = west | .184 ( .388) | -.155 ( .499) [ -.060] | -.310 ( .498) [ -.120] | -.307 ( .498) [ -.119] | -.337 ( .498) [ -.131] | -.295 ( .498) [ -.114] |
| Lives in SMSA | .697 ( .459) | .845* ( .379) [ .388] | .716 ( .380) [ .329] | .640 ( .382) [ .294] | .753 ( .380) [ .346] | .666 ( .382) [ .306] |
| Percent poor in area | 11.300 (10.800) | .075* ( .018) [ .805] | .079* ( .018) [ .848] | .082* ( .018) [ .889] | .077* ( .018) [ .828] | .080* ( .018) [ .868] |
| Race = white | .895 ( .306) | -4.600* ( .548) [ -1.408] | -4.301* ( .548) [ -1.316] | -3.995* ( .551) [ -1.223] | -3.914* ( .552) [ -1.198] | -3.793* ( .553) [ -1.161] |
| Married, spouse present | .640 ( .480) | -4.831* ( .363) [ -2.319] | -4.679* ( .364) [ -2.246] | -4.643* ( .365) [ -2.228] | -4.589* ( .364) [ -2.203] | -4.620* ( .365) [ -2.218] |
| Veteran | .351 ( .477) | .863* ( .352) [ .412] | .839* ( .351) [ .400] | .677 ( .352) [ .323] | .742* ( .351) [ .354] | .662 ( .352) [ .316] |

| | | | | | |
|---|---|---|---|---|---|
| Schooling | 13.000 (2.590) | −1.098* (.066) [−2.843] | −.895* (.082) [−2.317] | −.699* (.088) [−1.811] | −.747* (.089) [−1.934] | −.648* (.090) [−1.677] |
| Experience | 4.150 (2.870) | −.289 (.279) [−.829] | −.212 (.279) [−.608] | −.166 (.278) [−.478] | −.245 (.278) [−.704] | −.209 (.279) [−.601] |
| Max (0, Experience − 2) | 2.510 (2.440) | −.057 (.324) [−.138] | −.087 (.323) [−.213] | −.104 (.323) [−.254] | −.030 (.323) [−.073] | −.051 (.323) [−.124] |
| $\ln(W_f)$ | 1.160 (.299) | | 14.012* (2.190) [4.190] | 9.684* (2.575) [2.895] | 11.930* (2.257) [3.567] | 7.742* (2.628) [2.315] |
| $\ln(W_i)$ | 1.380 (.293) | | −10.166* (2.244) [−2.979] | −3.345 (2.530) [−.980] | −3.882 (2.426) [−1.137] | −.069 (2.634) [−.020] |
| Occ's retention rate | .612 (.125) | | −18.896* (1.778) [−2.362] | −15.134* (2.116) [−1.892] | −14.167* (1.901) [−1.771] | −13.467* (2.231) [−1.683] |
| Occ's median yrs school | 12.300 (2.110) | | | | −.709* (.166) [−1.496] | −.407 (.219) [−.859] |
| Occ's percent female | 17.800 (20.600) | | | | .012 (.009) [.238] | .002 (.010) [.046] |
| Occ's percent black | 8.640 (7.030) | | | | .148* (.032) [1.043] | .140* (.043) [.982] |
| 10 Occupation dummy variables | | No | No | Yes | No | Yes |
| $R^2$ | | .039 | .044 | .048 | .046 | .048 |
| Number of observations | 23714 | | | | | |

The equation in column 1 of table 12.3 includes only "personal" characteristics as independent variables. There are few surprises. The coefficients of the three regional variables show that unemployment is considerably lower in the South than elsewhere, but there is very little difference among the three other regions (Northeast, North Central, and West). Living in an SMSA or a poverty area is associated with a higher unemployment rate, and a standard deviation difference in the area poverty rate has a considerable impact. Even with other personal characteristics controlled, whites have an unemployment rate nearly five percentage points lower than nonwhites. Married men with spouses present enjoy considerably lower unemployment, while veterans' unemployment rate is almost one percentage point higher than others'. Schooling has a considerable impact, with the unemployment rate declining one point per year of schooling. Perhaps the strongest surprise is the failure of the two experience variables to achieve "significance." Experience was defined as years since estimated departure from school, following Mincer (1974, p. 48). The two experience variables allow the experience-unemployment relationship to have a different slope in the first two years than later on, in light of Ornstein's (1971, p. 417) finding that young workers appear to spend roughly two years finding their place in the labor market. The standard errors of these variables' coefficients may be increased by the sample selection, which limits the range of experience, and the estimated effect in the first two years is probably reduced by eliminating those without work experience.

Columns 2–5 reflect the addition of various occupational characteristics to the equation. The coefficients of the personal characteristics, taken as a group, are not greatly affected by the additional variables. Even granting the crudeness of the occupation variables, the small change in the coefficients of the poverty area and race coefficients is striking. Schooling does lose up to 40% of its estimated effect (column 5 vs. column 1), suggesting that a nonnegligible fraction of the advantage of those with more schooling comes from access to "better" occupations.

In column 2, the two wage variables ln $(W_i)$ and $(W_i')$ and the three-digit retention rate are added to the equation. Each is highly significant. A higher occupation wage $(W_i)$ is associated with a higher unemployment rate (when personal characteristics are held constant).[10] However, if only this wage is added to the personal characteristics, its coefficient is .166 (.864). The wage variable intended to capture advancement, $W_i'$, has an almost equally large negative coefficient. While the size of this coefficient relative to those of the personal characteristics is, of course, sensitive to scaling, the impact of a one-standard deviation difference (three percentage points) *is* quite large. Finally, the effect of occupation's "retention rate" is negative and significant: individuals in occupations in which industry-switching is less common (higher retention rate) have lower unemployment rates.

A sterner test of the three occupational characteristics is presented in column 3, where ten dummy variables for Census broad occupation groups (e.g., "clerical workers") are added to the equation. The occupation wage ($W_i$) and retention rate are not significantly affected, but the coefficient of $W_i$ falls to one-third its previous value and is no longer "significant" at conventional levels. The ten dummy variables are jointly significant at the 1% level.

Three additional occupational characteristics are added, with and without the broad-occupation dummies, in columns 4 and 5. Once again, the effects of the occupation wage and retention rate are not dramatically affected, but the coefficient of $W_i'$ is considerably reduced (column 4 vs. column 2) or eliminated (column 5). The standard error of $W_i'$ rises with the addition of the other occupation variables, but the increase is not very large. Two of the three new variables (the occupation's median years of schooling and the fraction of its workers who are black) have substantial effects on the unemployment rate, while the fraction that is female does not.

Modest experimentation with the specification produced similar results. Deletion of the retention rate reduced the impact of $W_i$ (though it remained positive and generally "significant") but had little impact on the other occupation characteristics' coefficients. The effect of $W_i$ was significantly positive when weekly wages replaced hourly wages, or when $W_i'$ was deleted. An industry retention rate based on about twenty broad industries produced similar, slightly weaker results. Median years of schooling, percent female, and percent black were little affected by these experiments.

The relationship between occupational characteristics and unemployment that emerges from these regressions is a good deal more complicated than the discussions cited in the introduction imply. The three major findings are as follows. (1) A consistent relationship between three occupational characteristics (retention rate, median schooling, and racial composition) and unemployment is evident. Whether this reflects the current position or future opportunities provided by the occupation is unclear, since quite plausible a priori arguments can be made for either. (2) The coefficient of $W_i'$, the wage variable intended to measure opportunities for advancement, was quite sensitive to the other occupational characteristics included, ranging from being a quite important factor to a thoroughly negligible one. The measurement difficulties noted in section 12.1 may help to explain its demise as other, correlated variables are added, but this remains a matter of conjecture until these difficulties can be overcome. (3) The broad-occupation dummies were consistently significant when added to any of the equations. This suggests that significant occupation differences in unemployment exist, independent of the variables discussed above. With service workers as the omitted category, white-collar and farm workers have uniformly lower unemployment.

Among blue-collar workers, craft workers and transport operatives had consistently lower unemployment rates, while unemployment among other operatives and nonfarm laborers was similar to that of service workers.

Table 12.4 decomposes unemployment by reason for leaving last job. Columns 1, 4, and 7 reproduce columns 1, 2, and 5 from table 12.3, and relate to total unemployment. The remaining columns relate to unemployment due to losing or quitting one's previous job. Thus, in column 2, the dependent variables was one (times the scaling factor 100) if the individual was unemployed through losing his previous job, and zero otherwise (including other types of unemployment). The difficulties in defining such categories of unemployment in these CPS data should be recalled (see p. 433) when interpreting the results.

Given that less than half of the unemployed fall into either the lost or quit category, one expects estimated coefficients to be smaller than in column 1. Indeed, the effect of each variable on "other" unemployment can be obtained by subtracting columns 2 and 3 from column 1. In general, the variables which had substantial effects on overall unemployment have substantial effects of this residual category.

Among the personal variables (columns 2 and 3), Southern and Western locations are associated with lower "lost" unemployment, but have negligible effects on the "quit" component. Living a poverty area has little effect on either component. The large overall advantage of whites does not appear to be attributable to differences in either the "lost" or "quit" components. Being married substantially reduces the "quit" component, but has much less effect on the "lost" component. Schooling remains a significant, negative determinant of both components.

The coefficients of the occupational characteristics vary with the type of unemployment (columns 5, 6, 8, and 9). The positive effect of the occupation wage ($W_i$) is concentrated on the "lost" category of unemployment, consistent with an equalizing difference interpretation. The lack of impact of occupation wage on quitting unemployment is surprising.[11] A higher value of $W_i'$ is associated with lower "lost" unemployment, "significantly" in column 5 and nearly so in column 8. This is consistent with the notion that jobs which offer advancement for the worker are also those which involve investing in the worker by the firm. However, it has no impact on quitting unemployment, and a mildly positive impact on nonlayoff unemployment (columns 7–8). Thus there is no evidence that $W_i'$ has a significant impact on the more "voluntary" components of unemployment. At the very least this contradicts the emphasis of the "opportunities for advancement" hypothesis on quitting. The occupation's industry retention rate was significant and negative for both components of unemployment. Median schooling has a modest coefficient in the "lost" unemployment equation, and the racial composition of the occupation is related to both components. Deletion of the retention rate once again had little effect on the other coefficients.

The individuals in tables 12.3 and 12.4 are "young" in the sense of having limited labor market experience, but they are not necessarily young in the more usual sense. A high school graduate with nine years of experience or a college graduate with four years of experience would each be twenty-seven years old—beyond that age the bounds the "youth unemployment problem." Consequently, equations identical to those in table 12.4 were estimated for a sample restricted to those who are most likely to be part of "the problem": those with no more than twelve years of schooling and less than five years of post-school experience.

Comparison of these equations (not shown) with those reported in table 12.4 revealed frequently larger coefficients and much larger standard errors (because of a smaller sample and less variation in independent variables). The most striking differences were the reduced impact of living in a poverty area, the almost complete concentration of the racial effect in the residual unemployment category, and the lack of any effect of $W_i'$ in the last three equations. In general, however, the earlier findings—both expected and anomalous—remain.

A final experiment concerned the relationship between unionization and unemployment. Union sector jobs are often regarded as among the better blue-collar jobs, so that the relationship between unionization and unemployment is of some interest. For about 80% of those in tables 12.3 and 12.4, union membership and individual's hourly wage rate were available in the CPS file.[12] Adding these variables to the equations shown in table 12.4 produced a fairly consistent pattern: union membership was associated with greater "lost" unemployment, less "quit" unemployment, and had no statistically significant relationship to overall unemployment. (The individual's hourly wage showed a similar pattern.) Thus, while unionization may be associated with several "good job" characteristics, it does not seem to be a source of lower unemployment rates for young workers.

## 12.3 Conclusions

Occupational characteristics did prove significantly related to the unemployment of young workers with given personal characteristics. This result is not very surprising, given previous research and the limited range of personal characteristics in the CPS. The more interesting question is the more narrow one: Is there evidence of a relationship between lack of opportunities for advancement and youth unemployment? Unfortunately, the results presented above are too weak to justify either a confident yes or a confident no.

**Table 12.4**      Unemployment Equations, by Type of Unemployment (Males Less than Ten Years after School-leaving)

| Variable | Mean (S.D.) | (1) All | (2) Lost | (3) Quit |
|---|---|---|---|---|
| Constant | | 28.706* | 8.336* | 3.781* |
| | | ( 1.213) | ( .694) | ( .490) |
| Region = north central | .284 | − .308 | .350 | .008 |
| | ( .451) | ( .449) | ( .257) | ( .181) |
| | | [ − .139] | [ .158] | [ .004] |
| Region = south | .308 | − 3.070* | − 1.113* | − .262 |
| | ( .462) | ( .459) | ( .262) | ( .185) |
| | | [ −1.418] | [ − .514] | [ − .121] |
| Region = west | .184 | − .155 | − .594* | − .237 |
| | ( .388) | ( .499) | ( .285) | ( .201) |
| | | [ − .060] | [ − .231] | [ − .092] |
| Lives in SMSA | .697 | .845* | − .348 | .299 |
| | ( .459) | ( .379) | ( .217) | ( .153) |
| | | [ .388] | [ − .160] | [ .137] |
| Percent poor in area | 11.300 | .075* | − .014 | .012 |
| | (10.800) | ( .018) | ( .010) | ( .007) |
| | | [ .805] | [ − .147] | [ .133] |
| Race = white | .895 | − 4.600* | − .677* | − .012 |
| | ( .306) | ( .548) | ( .314) | ( .221) |
| | | [ −1.408] | [ − .207] | [ − .004] |
| Married, spouse present | .640 | − 4.831* | − .329 | − 1.129* |
| | ( .480) | ( .363) | ( .208) | ( .147) |
| | | [ −2.319] | [ − .158] | [ − .542] |
| Veteran | .351 | .863* | − .007 | .107 |
| | ( .477) | ( .352) | ( .201) | ( .142) |
| | | [ .412] | [ − .003] | [ .051] |
| Schooling | 13.000 | − 1.098* | − .340* | − .192* |
| | ( 2.590) | ( .066) | ( .038) | ( .027) |
| | | [ −2.843] | [ − .880] | [ − .498] |
| Experience | 4.150 | − .289 | − .163 | .194 |
| | ( 2.870) | ( .279) | ( .160) | ( .113) |
| | | [ − .829] | [ − .467] | [ .558] |
| Max (0, experience − 2) | 2.510 | − .057 | .120 | − .256 |
| | ( 2.440) | ( .324) | ( .185) | ( .131) |
| | | [ − .138] | [ .293] | [ − .626] |
| $\ln(W_i)$ | 1.160 | | | |
| | ( .299) | | | |
| $\ln(W_i')$ | 1.380 | | | |
| | ( .293) | | | |
| Occ's retention rate | .612 | | | |
| | ( .125) | | | |
| Occ's median yrs school | 12.300 | | | |
| | ( 2.110) | | | |
| Occ's percent female | 17.800 | | | |
| | (20.600) | | | |
| Occ's percent black | 8.640 | | | |
| | ( 7.030) | | | |
| 10 occupation dummy variables | | No | No | No |
| $R^2$ | | .039 | .007 | .008 |
| Number of observations | 23714 | | | |

| (4) All | (5) Lost | (6) Quit | (7) All | (8) Lost | (9) Quit |
| --- | --- | --- | --- | --- | --- |
| 34.814* | 10.987* | 4.156* | 26.774* | 5.155* | 2.655* |
| ( 1.365) | ( .782) | ( .553) | ( 2.738) | ( 1.569) | ( 1.110) |
| −.288 | .343 | .018 | −.291 | .237 | .029 |
| ( .448) | ( .257) | ( .181) | ( .449) | ( .257) | ( .182) |
| [ −.130] | [ .155] | [ .008] | [ −.131] | [ .107] | [ .013] |
| −3.061* | −1.109* | −.266 | −2.919* | −1.040* | −.230 |
| ( .458) | ( .262) | ( .185) | ( .458) | ( .262) | ( .186) |
| [−1.414] | [ −.512] | [−.123] | [−1.349] | [ −.480] | [−.106] |
| −.310 | −.649* | −.247 | −.295 | −.668* | −.211 |
| ( .498) | ( .285) | ( .202) | ( .498) | ( .285) | ( .202) |
| [ −.120] | [ −.252] | [−.096] | [ −.114] | [ −.259] | [−.082] |
| .716 | −.364 | .270 | .666 | −.310 | .217 |
| ( .380) | ( .218) | ( .154) | ( .382) | ( .219) | ( .155) |
| [ .329] | [ −.167] | [ .124] | [ .306] | [ −.142] | [ .100] |
| .079* | −.013 | .013 | .080* | −.015 | .013 |
| ( .018) | ( .010) | ( .007) | ( .018) | ( .010) | ( .007) |
| [ .848] | [ −.138] | [ .142] | [ .868] | [ −.164] | [ .143] |
| −4.301* | −.593 | .018 | −3.793* | −.450 | .110 |
| ( .548) | ( .314) | ( .222) | ( .553) | ( .317) | ( .224) |
| [−1.316] | [ −.181] | [ .006] | [−1.161] | [ −.138] | [ .034] |
| −4.679* | −.325 | −1.102* | −4.620* | −.382 | −1.108* |
| ( .364) | ( .208) | ( .147) | ( .365) | ( .209) | ( .148) |
| [−2.246] | [ −.156] | [ −.529] | [−2.218] | [ −.183] | [ −.532] |
| .839* | −.001 | .101 | .662 | −.122 | .098 |
| ( .351) | ( .201) | ( .142) | ( .352) | ( .202) | ( .143) |
| [ .400] | [ −.000] | [ .048] | [ .316] | [ −.058] | [ .047] |
| −.895* | −.280* | −.178* | −.648* | −.148* | −.185* |
| ( .082) | ( .047) | ( .033) | ( .090) | ( .052) | ( .037) |
| [−2.317] | [ −.725] | [ −.461] | [−1.677] | [ −.384] | [ −.478] |
| −.212 | −.155 | .205 | −.209 | −.146 | .191 |
| ( .279) | ( .160) | ( .113) | ( .279) | ( .160) | ( .113) |
| [ −.608] | [ −.445] | [ .589] | [ −.601] | [ −.418] | [ .548] |
| −.087 | .124 | −.262* | −.051 | .132 | −.248 |
| ( .323) | ( .185) | ( .131) | ( .323) | ( .185) | ( .131) |
| [ −.213] | [ .303] | [−.640] | [ −.124] | [ .322] | [−.605] |
| 14.012* | 8.398* | .228 | 7.742* | 5.653* | −.058 |
| ( 2.190) | ( 1.255) | ( .887) | ( 2.628) | ( 1.506) | ( 1.066) |
| [ 4.190] | [ 2.511] | [ .068] | [ 2.315] | [ 1.690] | [−.017] |
| −10.166* | −7.498* | .437 | −.069 | −2.565 | .802 |
| ( 2.244) | ( 1.286) | ( .909) | ( 2.634) | ( 1.509) | ( 1.068) |
| [−2.979] | [−2.197] | [ .128] | [ −.020] | [−.752] | [ .235] |
| −18.896* | −4.859* | −2.429* | −13.467* | −2.715* | −2.533* |
| ( 1.778) | ( 1.019) | ( .720) | ( 2.231) | ( 1.279) | ( .905) |
| [−2.362] | [ −.607] | [−.304] | [−1.683] | [−.339] | [−.317] |
| | | | −.407 | −.147 | .081 |
| | | | ( .219) | ( .125) | ( .089) |
| | | | [ −.859] | [−.311] | [ .171] |
| | | | .002 | −.003 | .004 |
| | | | ( .010) | ( .006) | ( .004) |
| | | | [ .046] | [−.060] | [ .089] |
| | | | .140* | .050* | .052* |
| | | | ( .043) | ( .025) | ( .017) |
| | | | [ .982] | [ .351] | [ .369] |
| No | No | No | Yes | Yes | Yes |
| .044 | .009 | .008 | .048 | .013 | .009 |

One fairly straightforward way to measure opportunities for advancement is from the wage gains that different occupations provide. The main reservation about this approach is that if transitory variation in earnings is occupation-related—as seems almost certain—individuals in some occupations will have "low" initial earnings because of these transitory influences, while others will have "low" initial earnings because they are "buying" opportunities for advancement. This measurement problem clearly tends to obscure the effect of opportunities for advancement on unemployment, if they exist. When we turn to the data, we find that the wage variable designed to capture these opportunities exhibits a nontrivial relationship to unemployment, but it is not very sturdy in the presence of other occupational characteristics and is confined to unemployment of job losers. (The bias noted above might be expected to be stronger for quitters than for job losers, since those with low earnings due to transitory factors would have an incentive to quit.)

An alternative strategy is to assume (plausibly, I believe) that opportunities for advancement should lead, in most cases, to an individual remaining in his current industry. Industry-retention rates of occupations did prove consistently (negatively) related to unemployment, controlling both for personal characteristics and average wages of young workers in the occupation. The problem here is that an occupation's industry-retention rate is influenced by other factors besides opportunities for advancement. Indeed, any desirable job characteristic (apart from the wage, which is included separately) would be likely (other things equal) to reduce quitting, quitting-related unemployment, and industry-switching; whatever it is that reduces layoffs would also be likely to reduce layoff-related unemployment and layoff-induced industry switching.[13] One should not overstate the "automatic-ness" of these relationships, however: turnover and unemployment are not synonymous, and lack of opportunities for advancement would increase the likelihood that one would leave one job without having another lined up.

To end on a more positive note, two conclusions do seem warranted: (1) The industry retention rate is clearly measuring *something* that wages in the occupation and broad-occupation dummy variables do not. (2) While jobs in unionized firms may be desirable jobs for young workers for other reasons, improving access to these jobs is an unpromising approach to solving youth unemployment. Their greater layoff rates compensate for their lower quitting rates.

# Notes

1. In the NLS Young Men's file, SVP scores range from 0 to 9 years; apprentice occupations are coded 2 months. For the Duncan index (100-point scale), the median score for apprentice occupations was 33.

2. Knowing the *previous* occupation of each individual is critical when occupation-changing is common. Without such information, one is forced to infer opportunities for advancement from a purely cross-sectional wage-experience profile (e.g., Landes 1977, p. 529). But this compares, for example, apprentice carpenters five years out of school with apprentice carpenters ten years out of school, missing the fact that much of the return to being an apprentice carpenter depends on *not* being an apprentice carpenter (i.e., being a "regular" carpenter) five years later. In the sixty most common occupations (i.e., those in table 12.1), occupation-changing was quite important for those with less than ten years of experience. The fraction of those in an occupation in 1965 who were in the same occupation in 1970 ranged from 17 to 96%, the median being only 54%.

3. Labor market experience since leaving school is measured by age minus estimated age upon leaving school. Ages upon leaving school for each level of schooling are from Mincer (1974, p. 38).

4. The actual calculation was sightly more complicated. $W$ was calculated separately by occupation for those with 0–4 and 5–9 years of experience. The "final" $W$ was computed as a weeks-weighted average of the two experience groups, corrected for differences in experience composition.

5. Occupations were included in the regression if $W'_i$ and $W_i$ were each based on at least ten observations; occupations were weighted according to number of individuals used in calculating $W'_i$.

6. An analysis of the occupational transitions made by those initially in these occupations was consistent with this interpretation. Less than half of the workers in these two occupations were in the same occupation five years later, and there was little evidence of systematic movement to related occupations. (In general, the occupational transitions revealed only two patterns: remaining in one's prior occupation was the most frequent single outcome, and some workers in most occupations moved to supervisory [foreman, managers, n.e.c.] positions. Movements to skill-related occupations seemed surprisingly infrequent.)

7. Regressing $W_i$ on the characteristics of those in each occupation is *not* a helpful first step in solving this problem, since negative residuals would be expected for both high-training and negative-transistory occupations.

8. Those in "rotation groups" 4 and 8 who had worked in the last five years are asked their occupation by the CPS.

9. Those in "small" occupations—those in which published characteristics were unavailable or with less than ten individuals in the 1/100 file—were also deleted.

10. Marston (1976, p. 192) found the probability of becoming unemployed positvely related to the individual's wage; Bartel and Borjas (1977, table 10) found a negative relationship between wage and probability of separation (quit or layoff) for those with "long" tenure, and a non-significant positive relationship for those with short tenure in the NLS Mature Men sample.

11. Related previous research has used the individual wage as the independent variable: Marston (1976, table 7: positive, nonsignificant relationship to probability of becoming unemployed because of layoff and negative, nonsignificant relationship to becoming unemployed by quitting); Bartel and Borjas (1977, tables 7 and 4: positive, nonsignificant relationship to probability of layoff and significant negative relationship to quitting); Leighton (1978, table 16: positive, significant relationship to probability of layoff); Feldstein (1978, table 2: positive, sometimes significant relationship to probability of being on temporary layoff unemployment).

12. As noted earlier (p. 433), the availability of these variables was not random—those unemployed who hadn't "lost" their last job were overrepresented among those for whom these variables weren't available. Consequently, the conclusions in the text need to be read with some caution because of possible sample-selection biases.

13. One piece of information which supports this interpretation is the fact that a very high percentage of industry stayers are also firm stayers. Among out-of-school NLS young men, the percentage of industry stayers who were also firm stayers were 81.9% (1971 vs. 1966) and 86.3% (1973 vs. 1968).

# References

Bartel, A. P. and Borjas, G. J. 1977. Middle-age job mobility: Its determinants and consequences. In Seymour L. Wolfbein, ed., *Men in the pre-retirement years*. Philadelphia: Temple University School of Business Administration.

Bergmann, B. 1971. The effect on white incomes of discrimination in employment. *Journal of Political Economy* 79:294–313.

Feldstein, M. 1973. The economics of the new unemployment. *Public Interest* 33:3–42.

——. 1978. The effect of unemployment insurance on temporary layoff unemployment. *American Economic Review* 68:834–45.

Gordon, D. 1972. *Theories of poverty and underemployment*. Lexington, Mass.: Lexington Books.

Hall, R. E. 1970. Why is the unemployment rate so high at full employment. *Brookings Papers on Economic Activity* 1970/3:396–410.

Landes, E. M. 1977. Sex differences in wages and employment: A test of the specific capital hypothesis. *Economic Inquiry* 15:523–38.

Leighton, L. 1978. Unemployment over the work history: Structure, determinants, and consequences. Ph.D. dissertation, Columbia University.

Marston, S. T. 1976. Employment instability and high unemployment. *Brookings Papers on Economic Activity* 1976/1:169–210.

Mincer, J. 1974. *Schooling, experience, and earnings*. New York: National Bureau of Economic Research.

Ornstein, M. 1971. *Entry into the american labor force*. Baltimore: Center for Social Organization of Schools.

Piore, M. 1971. The dual labor market: Theory and implications. In David Gordon, ed., *Problems in political economy: An urban perspective*. Lexington, Mass.: Lexington Books.

Rosen, S. 1972. Learning and experience in the labor market. *Journal of Human Resources* 7:326–42.

U.S. Census Bureau. 1973. *1970 census of population*: Occupational characteristics. Washington, D.C.: Government Printing Office.

# Comment    Paul Osterman

The purpose of Brown's chapter is to determine if a particular character-istic of jobs—whether or not they offer opportunities for advancement—has an effect upon unemployment. The chapter develops two indices of the future possibility of jobs and enters these in linear probability models of unemployment. The results are mixed. One measure, a wage growth variable, performs quite poorly, losing significance when other occupa-tional controls are introduced. The other variable, the industry retention rate, does better but with some apparently anomalous results, especially its insignificance in quit equations.

These results seem weak, although it should be noted that some of the control variables—especially the racial and sexual composition of occupations—are probably collinear with "dead-endedness." In any case, Brown is to be commended for this effort because it represents one of the few serious attempts to examine the importance of the institutional characteristics of jobs upon youth unemployment. Most of the problems in the chapter stem from the quality of the data rather than from errors by the author and the results are sufficiently encouraging to suggest that further work along these lines would be useful.

My comments are directed toward three categories: (1) the theory underlying the analysis; (2) the definition of the variables measuring opportunities for advancement; and (3) the sample selection. I will argue that a correctly specified theory would in fact imply weak effects for the variables at issue and that problems of variable definition and sample selection raise difficulties for the interpretation of the results.

Brown introduces his chapter with several quotations which speak to the effect of dead-end jobs. However, it is not clear that these quotations in fact imply a consistent story. Feldstein suggests that if a youth had an opportunity to hold a job with a future he or she would take it and presumably not quit. I think that this comes closest to what Brown means, but an important assumption, which I will return to, is that youths want these jobs. The argument implied by the *Washington Post* quotation is quite different. The implication here is that there are certain categories of jobs which black youths find racially insulting, largely because those jobs have been traditionally associated with labor market discrimination. This implies a racial difference in the behavior of black and white youths, a hypothesis which is not tested by Brown. A further implication, re-levant to both racial differences and to the point I will make below about youth attitudes, is that behavior with respect to dead-end jobs will vary depending on whether the youth views the job as a temporary expedient

Paul Osterman is assistant professor of economics at Boston University.

or rather as emblematic of future treatment and prospects. Brown's data are not longitudinal and thus this issue cannot be addressed.

Why should a youth holding a dead-end job have a higher probability of experiencing subsequent unemployment than a youth holding a job with a future? One possibility is layoffs: firms which invest in screening, hiring, and training will be inclined to hoard labor, and these firms are also more likely to offer jobs with a future. Dead-end jobs should thus entail higher layoff rates and hence we should expect to see, and we do observe, an index perform well in a layoff equation. However, much of the burden of the argument seems to rest on quitting (as in the Feldstein passage) and here the argument is less clear. I would argue that much teenage labor market behavior is supply-driven in that most youths *want* to work only for spending money. They are target earners.[1] Thus there will be a tendency to leave jobs regardless of the jobs' characteristics and therefore I would not expect the index to perform well in the quit equation; in fact it does not.

Another issue is the definition of the indices. Brown is clearly unhappy with both and his approach was dictated by the data. However, it is important to emphasize two points. First, the wage growth index is not conceptually correct. It measures wage growth for both those who leave the occupation (or firm) and those who stay. But the unemployment question is whether low wage growth prospects lead people to leave firms. Many youths prefer working in low-paying casual jobs during the period in which they are target earners and they subsequently settle down into a different kind of work. The proper measure for the purposes of this chapter is the firm specific age-earnings profile of those who remain in the firm. This would capture the structure of opportunities for those who stay. The industry index comes closer, but it presents another problem. If an occupation—for any reason—has a low unemployment rate associated with it, then that occupation will score high on the index since a large source of industry leaving is reduced or eliminated. Thus the observed negative correlation between the index and unemployment is in some part the result of the construction of the variable.

Finally, the sample selection raises problems. The dependent variable takes on the value of one if the individual is currently experiencing unemployment, yet in samples of this sort the sampling procedure is such that currently unemployed indivuduals are likely to have longer than average durations of unemployment.[2] However, long durations are not characteristic of the youth labor market—the more common pattern is frequent spells and short durations. Thus it is not clear to what extent the paper addresses "typical" youth unemployment. A similar problem is raised by the exclusion of youths currently out of the labor force since movement in and out of the labor force is common in this age range.

As I said earlier, these problems are almost all the result of inadequate data. This paper is sufficiently promising to emphasize the need for good labor market data on individuals which will capture many more institutional characteristics of the firms in which they work than do the data commonly available. Most data sets now contain nothing beyond industry and occupation codes and perhaps a union variable. As a result, interesting questions such as the one raised by this chapter cannot adequately be addressed.

### Notes

1. For a discussion of this argument see Paul Osterman, *Getting Started*; *Youth Labor Market*, Cambridge: MIT Press, 1980.
2. For a demonstration of this point see Stephen Marston, "The Impact of Unemployment Insurance on Job Search," *Brookings Papers on Economic Activity* 1/1975:13–60.

## Comment    Ronald G. Ehrenberg

Charles Brown has very ambitiously attempted to analyze whether the existence of "dead-end jobs" contributes to the youth unemployment problem. He assumes that the average rate of wage growth of individuals initially employed in an occupation and the proportion of these individuals who remain employed in the same industry for five years are both inversely related to the probability that individuals initially employed in the occupation find themselves in dead end-jobs. His basic methodological approach involves using data from the 1/100 sample of the 1970 Census of Population to calculate both of these variables for each three-digit occupation, merging these occupation-specific data into individual records from the 1973–75 Current Population Surveys, and then estimating equations in which the probability that an individual is unemployed at the CPS survey date is a function of the individual's personal characteristics and these occupation-specific variables. Conclusions are then drawn about the extent to which these occupation-specific variables influence young men's probabilities of being unemployed, of having voluntarily left their last job, and of having been laid off. The paper clearly represents a large commitment of time and effort and Brown should be commended for having undertaken it.

My major concern about Brown's approach is that it may not be possible to infer information about the characteristics of an occupation from either data on average wage growth of individuals initially in the

Ronald G. Ehrenberg is professor of economics and labor economics at Cornell University.

occupation or data on the proportion of these individuals who remain employed in the same industry over a five-year period. Rather, what we may be observing is information about the characteristics of individuals who choose the occupation.

To illustrate this point, suppose there are two types of individuals: "peaches" who always choose or are selected into occupation 1, and "lemons" who always choose or are selected into occupation 2. Whether an individual is a peach or a lemon can be ascertained readily by employers, but the information used to make this judgment is *not* contained in the CPS survey. True to their names, lemons are "lemons," and as a result will exhibit lower rates of wage growth and higher probabilities of unemployment, which may also result in lower probabilities of their remaining in the same industry. In this situation, if one were to calculate measures of wage growth and industry retention rates for individuals initially in an occupation, and then find after controlling for *measured* personal characteristics, that these variables were correlated in the CPS data with the probability of an individual's being unemployed, one could not conclude that it was the occupational characteristic per se that caused this relationship. Rather, it may simply be that individuals in occupations classified as being "dead-end" ones, on average are lemons (even though we cannot observe this fact in the CPS data). Put another way, we cannot ascertain from Brown's analyses whether it is the characteristics of jobs or the characteristics of workers in those jobs that he has identified. This is a classic example of the problem of trying to distinguish between heterogeneity of individuals and state dependence (see Heckman 1978 for an example).

One might think that this problem could be solved if one could use occupational data that reflected specific technical job characteristics. For example, in some work that I am doing for the National Commission for Employment Policy, I am attempting to ascertain if the probability that an employed teenager becomes unemployed is related to the occupational characteristic data that are found in the *Dictionary of Occupational Titles*. These data have been used with some success by Quinn (1979) and Lucas (1977) in previous work on other subjects. The data include information for each three-digit occupation on a variety of job characteristics such as whether individuals in the occupation have a variety of responsibilities, find themselves in situations which involve repetitive operations carried out according to set procedures, have jobs that allow little or no room for independent action or judgment, are required to control directly or plan an entire activity or the activities of others, are required to perform adequately under stress, are required to have physical strength, and are required to work under poor working conditions (e.g., under extremes of cold, heat, or temperature change, wetness or humidity, noise and vibration, hazards, fumes, odors, toxic conditions, dust, or poor ventilation). It seems plausible that may of these job characteristics are associated with dead-end jobs.

If in my own work I ultimately observe a correlation between these characteristics and the probability that an employed worker voluntarily leaves or loses his job, one might be tempted to conclude that occupational job characteristics do affect turnover. However, the problem of unobservable individual characteristics still is present. That is, if lemons are sorted (by themselves or employers) into jobs with poor characteristics, it is difficult to determine whether it is the characteristics of the job or the characteristics of the employees which are "causing" the high probabilities of unemployment. To resolve this problem, one must use a methodology which allows one to distinguish between heterogeneity and state dependence. This requires a longitudinal data base that contains a number of observations for each individual; the cross-section data used by Brown is inadequate for this purpose.

Setting this major conceptual issue aside, let me now turn to a discussion of some of the specifics of Brown's work. Brown focuses on young males; young people because their unemployment rates are so high, males to reduce complications which those not in the labor force introduce. In fact, because of the nature of the CPS data, his empirical work excludes individuals not currently in the labor force from the sample. This exclusion has the potential to bias his results substantially since individuals who have dropped out of the labor force may be those who are the most likely to have been in dead-end jobs. Moreover, the fraction of younger males who move from employment to out of labor force status each month is not insubstantial. For example, in Ehrenberg (1980) I show that the gross-flow data from the CPS indicate that during the 1967–77 period approximately 11% of the white males and 14% of black males aged 16–19 who were employed one month were *not* in the labor force the next month. These percentages drop to about 3.5% for males aged 20–24; however, these numbers should be contrasted with the less than .3% rate for white males aged 25–59. The magnitude of these labor force exit rates suggests that exclusion of individuals currently not in the labor force is unwarranted. This is another serious weakness of the CPS data and it again suggests the need to use a longitudinal data source such as the National Longitudinal Surveys or the Michigan Income Dynamics data when one attempts to analyze this question.

Brown's initial discussion suggests that the five-year average growth rate of earnings of individuals initially employed in an occupation is a reasonable measure of whether the occupation consists of dead-end jobs. Somewhat surprisingly, in his empirical research the average beginning wage rate in the occupation and the average wage rate that the individuals obtain five years later are entered as separate independent variables, rather than the growth rate of earnings per se being entered. If his initial discussion was correct, some measure of the percentage or absolute change in wages in an occupation would be the relevant variable to include. This suggests that the coefficients of the current and future wage variables in his equations should bear certain relationships. In particular, if the percentage change is the correct variable in his equations, the coefficients of the logarithms of the current and future wages should be equal and opposite in sign. While this appears to occur in many cases, Brown does not formally test this implication himself.

Of course, one might question whether the relative wage growth of individuals initially employed in an occupation really does measure the extent to which the occupation is a dead-end job. Brown tabulates wage growth by occupation in table 12.1. Among the fifteen occupations with the lowest rates of wage growth we find clergymen, elementary school teachers, and secondary school teachers (but, fortunately, not college professors or economists). I doubt that one would really want to argue that being a clergyman is a dead-end job (especially if one considers the very long run). It seems clear that the wage growth measure must be capturing other factors, including nonpecuniary characteristics of jobs.

Brown's second proxy variable for the existence of dead-end jobs is the proportion of individuals in an occupation who remain in their initial industry of employment five years later. Estimates of this variable are found in table 12.2 for sixty large occupational groups. While this variable is capturing something in the empirical work, it is again not clear that it is capturing whether jobs are dead end. To draw such a conclusion first requires us to assume that skills learned in an occupation are industry- rather than occupation-specific. Furthermore, all of the eleven highest occupations in this ranking, save for police and telephone installers and repairmen (which is a highly industry-specific occupation since the vast majority of its members are employed by the Bell System), require individuals to have college degrees and are high-skill jobs. In contrast, the ten lowest-rated occupations are primarily low-skill jobs, with little formal educational or training requirements. Brown's industry retention rate variable, therefore, is very highly correlated with the skill level or educational requirements of occupations; it is not surprising then that he finds that unemployment probabilities are correlated with this variable. In my view, a much more interesting variable would be industry retention rates by occupation that standardize for the skill composition of occupations. The relevant question is not whether occupations in which college graduates wind up have lower turnover than those in which elementary and high school graduates are sorted, but rather if among the range of occupations open to elementary and high school graduates there are some dead-end and some non-dead-end jobs.

Brown's sample restrictions are also not always the ones I would have made. Restricting his sample to individuals who are not in school eliminates most teenagers from the sample. Furthermore, it prevents us from learning how initial part-time employment of enrolled youths influences their subsequent labor market success. I have already commented on the effects of his exclusion of individuals currently not in the labor force. Finally, his classification of unemployed individuals into those who were laid off or lost their last job, those who quit, and those who could not be identified (e.g., those who dropped out of the labor force and then reentered) ignores the distinction between permanent and temporary layoffs. While one might expect that high skill level jobs would have a low probability of permanent layoff, to my knowledge nothing in the theory or empirical evidence on temporary layoffs suggests that the probability of temporary layoff is small for this group. Unfortunately, he cannot make this distinction with the CPS data. Again, a true longitudinal data base is required.

Rather than rehashing his results, let me summarize the main message of my comments. First, longitudinal data are required and an attempt must be made to distinguish between unobservable heterogeneity of workers and state dependence. Occupational characteristic variables used in the analysis which are truly characteristics of the job (such as the *Dictionary of Occupational Titles* data) rather than the characteristics of the individuals who inhabit the positions will help but not solve the problem. Third, it is important to include those people temporarily out of the labor force in the sample, to consider the part-time employment experience of individuals enrolled in school, and to distinguish between temporary and permanent layoffs. While Brown must be commended for undertaking his ambitious, creative, and time-consuming study, it is clear, as he notes in his conclusion, that the results in the paper are too weak to justify either a confident yes or no answer to the question, "Is there evidence of a relationship between lack of opportunity for advancement and youth unemployment?" It is my hope, and I am certain his, that future research on this subject will provide more precise answers to this question.

### References

Ehrenberg, R. G. 1980. The demographic structure of unemployment rates and labor market transition probabilities. *Research in Labor Economics* 3, 1980.

Heckman, J. 1978. Heterogeneity and state dependence in dynamic models of labor supply. Revised version, May 1978. Mimeo.

Lucas, R. E. B. 1977. Hedonic wage equations and psychic wages in the returns to schooling. *American Economic Review* 67:549–58.

Quinn, J. 1979. Wage differentials among older workers in the public and private sectors. *Journal of Human Resources* 14:41–62.

# 13 Family Effects in Youth Employment

Albert Rees and Wayne Gray

## 13.1 Introduction

Youth unemployment can be divided into two principal components. One of these arises from the high turnover among young people. As Baily and Tobin have written: "Much teenage unemployment, it is often observed, comes from dissatisfaction with the available job options, a gap between expectations or aspirations and the realities of low wages and poor working conditions. One consequence is high turnover. Even when jobs are available, therefore, unemployment is high."[1]

The second component arises from the shortage of jobs. As Clark and Summers point out, "the substantial cyclic response to changes in aggregate demand suggest that a shortage of job opportunities characterizes the youth labor market."[2] This second component is, of course, larger during recessions. The data used in this study, described in the next section, refer to 1975 and the early part of 1976, when unemployment was still quite high. The unemployment rate for the whole civilian labor force was above 7% throughout this period and rates for young workers (16 to 19 years old) were above 18%. The component representing demand deficiency at current wage rates, rather than turnover, must therefore have been substantial.

The existence of demand deficiency unemployment of youths has an implication that we seek to test: If there is a shortage of jobs for young

Albert Rees is president of the Alfred P. Sloan Foundation. Wayne Gray is associated with Harvard University and the National Bureau of Economic Research. The authors are indebted to Richard B. Freeman and T. Aldrich Finegan for helpful comments and suggestions. The research reported here is part of the NBER's research program in labor studies. Any opinions expressed are those of the authors and not those of the National Bureau of Economic Research. This research was supported by the Alfred P. Sloan Foundation.

workers at prevailing wages, then there must be one or more nonprice rationing mechanisms that determine which young people get the available jobs. Our special hypothesis is that the family of the young person furnishes such a mechanism: those young people get jobs whose parents or siblings have jobs, particularly jobs in which they can influence hiring decisions. Some support for this view can be found in earlier studies of the labor force participation of young people. Bowen and Finegan, who found that after controlling for other factors the labor force participation of married women falls with husbands' incomes, were surprised to find that the adjusted labor force participation rate of males 14 to 17 in school in urban areas in 1960 *rose* through the range of other family income between $4,000 and $11,000. In seeking to explain this, they wrote: "We suspect that part of the explanation turns on the comparative advantage that youngsters in these families have in finding part-time jobs. For one thing, their parents are more frequently able to help, mainly as a result of their business and social contacts."[3] Robert Lerman found significant effects of parents' occupations on the employment of youths, using dummy variables for broad occupational categories. In particular, he found that having a parent who is a white-collar worker, either salaried or self-employed, or a farm manager, significantly increases the probability of employment relative to having one who is a low-level blue-collar worker.[4]

It should be noted that giving assistance in finding work is clearly not the only way in which family members can influence the employment prospects of young people. Much education takes place in the home so that youths who have well-educated parents and who have been exposed to books and to serious discussion while growing up may have advantages in finding and holding jobs over other youths with the same amount of formal schooling. Moreover, families have expectations about how their members should behave. Young people whose families expect them to go to work for whatever reason (cultural, religious, or economic) are more likely to be employed than young people whose families do not have this expectation. We shall refer to such expectations as a work ethic.

It follows that a variety of variables measuring different aspects of the family and its members might have some discernible effect on estimates of employment probabilities. In addition to family income, these could include education, occupation, and location. (The work ethic might be stronger in some areas than in others.)

We set out to test the hypothesis that parental contacts assist youths in finding jobs. Our results show no significant effects of parental characteristics on youth employment. We do, however, find significant effects of the employment status of siblings, which indicates the presence of some sort of intrafamily interactions.

## 13.2   The Data Set

The results presented in this paper are from the cross-sectional data set called the "Survey of Income and Education" collected in the spring of 1976 (April through July). The full sample is a national stratified probability sample of households in which 151,000 households were interviewed. This makes the sample roughly three times the size of the Current Population Survey. The interview includes most of the information available from CPS interviews, plus a good deal of additional detail on sources of 1975 income and on education.

We have analyzed data for men and women aged 17 to 20 living in nonfarm households where they are the children of the head. This excludes those young people who have moved out of their parents' household to live by themselves or establish their own families. The group that was 17 to 20 in 1976 was 16 to 19 in 1975, and one of our dependent variables measures work experience in 1975. Using the ages 17 to 20 in 1976 rather than 16 to 19 also gives us a less unequal division of the sample between those in school and those not in school.

The distinction made here between those in school and those not in school is based on whether or not the person had attended school since February 1976. The alternative of using major activity in the survey reference week is only viable for those observations collected in April and May, since many June and July observations were collected during school vacations.

The regressions presented in the next section are based on a data file we have created that merges observations on the young person with observations on household income and individual data on other members of the household 16 years of age and older. These individual data include sex, age, schooling status, employment status, and relationship to the young person. Additional data are used on the head of household (one of the youth's parents), including industry, occupation, and years of education. These, it was felt, could help to measure the likelihood of the parent having contacts that would help the youth get a job.

## 13.3   Regression Results

We have been persuaded by the work of Clark and Summers, among others, that for young people the distinction between being unemployed and being out of the labor force is not always meaningful, since the boundary between these states is so blurred. Accordingly, we use several measures of employment as our dependent variables. The two measures shown here are: (1) estimated total hours worked last year (the product of weeks worked and usual hours per week) and (2) a dichotomous variable taking the value of one if the teenager was employed in the survey reference week. We also used weeks worked last year and a dichotomous variable indicating unemployment in the survey reference week as dependent variables, but the results are not presented here. The regressions using weeks worked give similar results to those using total hours worked but their explanatory power is not quite as great. The regressions using unemployment explain very little for in-school youths. For out-of-school youths all significant coefficients in the employment regression have the opposite sign in the unemployment regression, though the explanatory power is again low.

Each model was estimated separately for males and females in and out of school. We chose to treat the decision to attend school as given, rather than as jointly endogenous with the decision to work, in order to simplify estimation. The means for many variables differ substantially across the subsets, especially for the dependent variables. The differences are most striking between in-school and out-of-school youths, with out-of-school youths showing stronger ties to the labor force: over one-third more employment and unemployment and twice as many hours worked last year as in-school youths. The coefficients obtained in the separate estimations are also quite different for in-school and out-of-school youths, ruling out any attempt to capture the effects of school attendance with a dummy variable. The split between male and female shows less conclusive differences, although the effects of some of the control variables (notably marriage) do vary substantially between groups.

Table 13.1 gives the means and standard deviations of all variables for each of the four subsets used. Table 13.2 shows our estimates of the determinants of estimated hours worked last year. We used a tobit technique to allow for the presence of people who did not work in 1975 and hence have zero hours observed. Table 13.4 shows the corresponding estimates of the determinants of employment in the reference week, using a probit technique to allow for the dichotomous nature of the dependent variable. Tables 13.3 and 13.5 simply involve rescaling the tobit and probit coefficients to correspond to ordinary least-squares coefficients for easier interpretation.

In general, we get significant effects (at the 5% level) for variables measuring schooling, race, being in a female-headed household, and being in a poverty area. We also estimate significant effects for the employment status of siblings, but generally not for the employment status of the head.

## 13.3.1 Schooling

Since we are dealing with people whose schooling has often not been completed, we measure years of school completed relative to the mean for all people of the same age in the main SIE sample. The variable "education gap 1" measures the number of years above the overall mean

**Table 13.1**        **Characteristics of the Population, Youths 17–20**

| Independent variables | Means and standard deviations of variables | | | |
|---|---|---|---|---|
| | In school | | Not in school | |
| | Male | Female | Male | Female |
| Education gap 1 | .689 | .800 | .240 | .332 |
| | (.738) | (.771) | (.452) | (.517) |
| Education gap 2 | .253 | .194 | .752 | .571 |
| | (.807) | (.790) | (1.365) | (1.273) |
| Other family income $\times$ $10^4$ | 2.088 | 2.117 | 1.677 | 1.704 |
| | (1.281) | (1.299) | (1.032) | (1.023) |
| Black | .092 | .098 | .106 | .126 |
| | (.290) | (.297) | (.308) | (.332) |
| Spanish | .032 | .035 | .045 | .040 |
| | (.175) | (.185) | (.207) | (.196) |
| Female head | .132 | .142 | .177 | .181 |
| | (.339) | (.349) | (.382) | (.385) |
| Male head self-employed | .101 | .103 | .090 | .082 |
| | (.302) | (.305) | (.287) | (.275) |
| Poverty area | .127 | .123 | .183 | .171 |
| | (.333) | (.329) | (.387) | (.377) |
| Older brother not employed | .093 | .093 | .065 | .060 |
| | (.291) | (.291) | (.247) | (.237) |
| Older brother employed | .160 | .162 | .140 | .154 |
| | (.366) | (.369) | (.347) | (.361) |
| Older sister not employed | .077 | .073 | .048 | .046 |
| | (.267) | (.260) | (.213) | (.209) |
| Older sister employed | .119 | .121 | .081 | .113 |
| | (.324) | (.326) | (.272) | (.317) |
| Younger brother not employed | .107 | .098 | .152 | .156 |
| | (.309) | (.297) | (.359) | (.362) |
| Younger brother employed | .091 | .086 | .143 | .126 |
| | (.288) | (.280) | (.350) | (.332) |
| Younger sister not employed | .117 | .114 | .157 | .153 |
| | (.321) | (.318) | (.364) | (.360) |
| Younger sister employed | .071 | .079 | .103 | .094 |
| | (.257) | (.270) | (.304) | (.293) |
| Dependent variables | | | | |
| Employment last week | .539 | .481 | .710 | .672 |
| | (.498) | (.500) | (.454) | (.470) |
| Total hours worked last year | 511.9 | 400.0 | 1064.2 | 925.8 |
| | (542.5) | (465.3) | (856.6) | (790.8) |
| Unemployment last week | .101 | .106 | .178 | .139 |
| | (.301) | (.307) | (.383) | (.346) |
| Number of observations | 9196 | 8385 | 3534 | 2604 |

**Table 13.2**      **Determinants of Total Hours Worked Last Year, Youths 17–20**

| Independent variables | Coefficients and $t$-ratios | | | |
|---|---|---|---|---|
| | In school | | Not in school | |
| | Male | Female | Male | Female |
| Education gap 1 | −22.9 | 14.0 | −165.2 | −81.4 |
| | (−2.20) | (1.46) | (−4.44) | (−2.17) |
| Education gap 2 | −127.2 | −90.5 | −85.6 | −122.8 |
| | (−11.99) | (−9.22) | (−7.40) | (−9.66) |
| Other family income $\times\ 10^{-4}$ | −13. | 8. | 46. | 61. |
| | (−2.00) | (1.22) | (2.64) | (2.95) |
| Black | −243.7 | −226.7 | −471.6 | −583.5 |
| | (−8.98) | (−8.70) | (−8.28) | (−9.62) |
| Spanish | −97.9 | −96.8 | −272.7 | −232.8 |
| | (−2.47) | (−2.66) | (−3.44) | (−2.66) |
| Female head | −47.6 | 1.9 | −82.5 | 35.1 |
| | (−2.14) | (0.10) | (−1.85) | (0.72) |
| Male head self-employed | 36.9 | −4.3 | 54.2 | 68.1 |
| | (1.69) | (−0.19) | (1.01) | (1.05) |
| Poverty area | −111.3 | −98.5 | −38.8 | −198.7 |
| | (−4.76) | (−4.19) | (−0.83) | (−3.71) |
| Older brother not employed | −129.3 | −64.1 | −207.5 | −42.9 |
| | (−5.27) | (−2.57) | (−3.36) | (−0.60) |
| Older brother employed | 35.0 | 19.7 | 123.1 | −58.9 |
| | (1.88) | (1.08) | (2.54) | (−1.18) |
| Older sister not employed | −87.9 | −59.4 | −148.4 | −144.7 |
| | (−3.32) | (−2.19) | (−2.10) | (−1.72) |
| Older sister employed | 43.3 | 17.6 | −5.4 | 115.1 |
| | (2.00) | (0.82) | (−0.09) | (1.95) |
| Younger brother not employed | −53.8 | −8.6 | −197.2 | −77.0 |
| | (−2.39) | (−0.37) | (−4.5) | (−1.58) |
| Younger brother employed | 168.6 | 128.0 | 207.8 | 24.9 |
| | (7.03) | (5.45) | (4.33) | (0.46) |
| Younger sister not employed | −49.9 | −65.0 | −107.5 | −33.1 |
| | (−2.32) | (−2.99) | (−2.52) | (−0.68) |
| Younger sister employed | 177.2 | 192.0 | 82.8 | 209.6 |
| | (6.65) | (7.32) | (1.54) | (3.00) |
| Controls for: | | | | |
|   Single years of age | 3 | 3 | 3 | 3 |
|   Health status | 2 | 2 | 2 | 2 |
|   Marriage | 1 | 1 | 1 | 1 |
|   Region | 8 | 8 | 8 | 8 |
| Number of observations | 9196 | 8385 | 3534 | 2604 |
| Number of uncensored | | | | |
|   observations | 7036 | 5806 | 2925 | 2032 |
| Log likelihood | −57101.3 | −47217.9 | −24670.9 | −17088.3 |
| Estimated sigma | 623.6 | 578.7 | 910.0 | 855.8 |
| Mean of dependent variable | | | | |
|   (for uncensored observations) | 669.0 | 577.7 | 1285.7 | 1186.5 |

**Table 13.3**        **Determinants of Total Hours Worked Last Year, Youths 17–20**

| Independent Variables | Standardized coefficients ("$DY/DX$") | | | |
|---|---|---|---|---|
| | In school | | Not in school | |
| | Male | Female | Male | Female |
| Education gap 1 | − 17.1 | 9.5 | − 141.6 | − 67.2 |
| Education gap 2 | − 94.9 | − 61.6 | − 73.4 | − 101.3 |
| Other family income × $10^{-4}$ | − 9. | 5. | 40. | 50. |
| Black | − 181.8 | − 154.3 | − 404.1 | − 481.1 |
| Spanish | − 73.0 | − 65.9 | − 233.6 | − 192.0 |
| Female head | − 35.5 | 1.3 | − 70.7 | 28.9 |
| Male head self-employed | 27.5 | − 2.9 | 46.5 | 56.2 |
| Poverty area | − 83.0 | − 67.1 | − 33.2 | − 163.8 |
| Older brother not employed | − 96.4 | − 43.6 | − 177.8 | −35.4 |
| Older brother employed | 26.1 | 13.4 | 105.5 | − 48.6 |
| Older sister not employed | − 65.5 | − 40.5 | − 127.1 | − 119.3 |
| Older sister employed | 32.3 | 12.0 | − 4.6 | 94.9 |
| Younger brother not employed | − 40.1 | − 5.9 | − 168.9 | − 63.5 |
| Younger brother employed | 125.7 | 87.1 | 178.1 | 20.5 |
| Younger sister not employed | − 37.2 | − 44.3 | − 92.1 | − 27.3 |
| Younger sister employed | 132.1 | 130.7 | 70.9 | 172.9 |

for those who are above. "Education gap 2" measures the number of years below the overall mean for those below. Having less education than the average of one's age group lowers employment significantly in all eight regressions.

The three negative signs on "education gap 1" in table 13.2 seem to be an anomaly arising because those people with more education than their age group had a greater than average probability of being in school in the preceding year. In table 13.4, where the schooling status and dependent variables both refer to the same year, the signs on "education gap 1" are all positive.

## 13.3.2   Income

A second set of variables measures family income. The one used here, "other family income," is the income of the household in 1975 minus the earnings of the young person whose behavior is being measured. This has no significant effect on employment in the reference week. For those in school its effect on total hours worked in the preceding year is mixed, while it is significantly positive for those who are not in school. In earlier work we used a number of additional variables indicating whether the household received income in 1975 from various kinds of transfer payments. At some stages of our work, a few of these variables showed significant negative effects on some measures of youth employment. However, they did not remain significant in the presence of the other variables included in the final model.

**Table 13.4**          **Determinants of Employment Last Week, Youths 17–20**

| Independent variables | Coefficients and $t$-ratios | | | |
|---|---|---|---|---|
| | In school | | Not in school | |
| | Male | Female | Male | Female |
| Education gap 1 | .057 | .019 | .046 | .335 |
| | (2.52) | (0.80) | (1.72) | (12.67) |
| Education gap 2 | −.128 | −0.88 | −.110 | −.160 |
| | (−7.50) | (−5.94) | (−5.85) | (−7.21) |
| Other family income × $10^{-4}$ | −.047 | −.013 | .023 | −.002 |
| | (−0.02) | (−0.01) | (0.01) | (−0.001) |
| Black | −.606 | −.492 | −.487 | −.686 |
| | (−63.68) | (−37.19) | (−33.39) | (−32.37) |
| Spanish | −.318 | −.231 | −.022 | −.210 |
| | (−16.28) | (−10.30) | (−0.60) | (−4.83) |
| Female head | −.189 | −.043 | −.166 | −.185 |
| | (−7.67) | (−1.74) | (−3.83) | (−3.75) |
| Male head self-employed | .004 | .015 | .156 | .250 |
| | (0.08) | (0.32) | (1.83) | (2.30) |
| Poverty area | −.244 | −.250 | −.067 | −.353 |
| | (−16.22) | (−16.24) | (−2.35) | (−9.74) |
| Older brother not employed | −.384 | −.187 | −.215 | −.179 |
| | (−85.98) | (−42.79) | (−23.51) | (−21.00) |
| Older brother employed | .100 | .047 | .074 | .084 |
| | (16.70) | (11.31) | (5.95) | (3.37) |
| Older sister not employed | −.214 | −.285 | −.199 | −.161 |
| | (−41.95) | (−123.14) | (−8.69) | (−14.60) |
| Older sister employed | .107 | .133 | .131 | .131 |
| | (22.65) | (29.82) | (6.89) | (7.84) |
| Younger brother not employed | −.220 | −.145 | −.220 | −.057 |
| | (−9.91) | (−7.06) | (−7.84) | (−1.83) |
| Younger brother employed | .334 | .385 | .217 | .152 |
| | (16.22) | (19.28) | (7.71) | (4.37) |
| Younger sister not employed | −.148 | −.204 | −.031 | .004 |
| | (−8.38) | (−10.36) | (−1.16) | (0.12) |
| Younger sister employed | .238 | .340 | .152 | .438 |
| | (11.47) | (16.61) | (6.56) | (16.04) |
| Controls: Same as in table 13.2 | | | | |
| Number of observations | 9196 | 8385 | 3534 | 2604 |
| Log likelihood | 874.7 | 624.8 | 372.7 | 606.5 |
| Mean of dependent variable | .539 | .481 | .710 | .672 |

### 13.3.3   Geographical Variables

A third set of variables deals with various geographic aspects of the labor market. The data set places observations in one of nine regions of the country. We have included a set of eight regional dummy variables in all regressions as control variables, and there are always some significant differences in youth employment by region. Variables indicating whether or not the household lived in an SMSA or in the central city of an SMSA

**Table 13.5**          **Determinants of Employment Last Week, Youths 17–20**

| Independent variables | Standardized coefficients ("DY/DX") | | | |
|---|---|---|---|---|
| | In school | | Not in school | |
| | Male | Female | Male | Female |
| Education gap 1 | 0.023 | 0.008 | 0.016 | 0.121 |
| Education gap 2 | −0.051 | −0.035 | −0.038 | −0.058 |
| Other family income × $10^{-4}$ | −0.019 | −0.005 | 0.008 | −0.001 |
| Black | −0.241 | −0.196 | −0.167 | −0.248 |
| Spanish | −0.126 | −0.092 | −0.008 | −0.076 |
| Female head | −0.075 | −0.017 | −0.057 | −0.067 |
| Male head self-employed | 0.002 | 0.006 | 0.053 | 0.091 |
| Poverty area | −0.096 | −0.100 | −0.023 | −0.128 |
| Older brother not employed | −0.152 | −0.074 | −0.074 | −0.065 |
| Older brother employed | 0.040 | 0.019 | 0.025 | 0.030 |
| Older sister not employed | −0.085 | −0.114 | −0.068 | −0.058 |
| Older sister employed | 0.042 | 0.053 | 0.045 | 0.047 |
| Younger brother not employed | −0.087 | −0.058 | −0.075 | −0.021 |
| Younger brother employed | 0.133 | 0.154 | 0.074 | 0.055 |
| Younger sister not employed | −0.059 | −0.081 | −0.011 | 0.001 |
| Younger sister employed | 0.094 | 0.136 | 0.052 | 0.159 |

were not significant. The final model includes a dummy variable taking the value of one if the household lives in an area designated by the Census Bureau as a poverty area. In our sample, 12 to 13% of youths in school and 17 to 18% of youths not in school lived in such areas. This variable has an effect that is consistently negative and usually clearly significant. For youths in school of both sexes, living in a poverty area reduces the probability of employment by 10%, other things equal. Since other family income and race appear in the regressions, this should probably be interpreted as measuring the availability of job opportunities in the locality.[5]

We also tried using a variable measuring the total unemployment rate in the SMSA for SMSAs that could be identified in the data set. The unemployment rate was taken from a published external source (Department of Labor estimates for May 1976) and merged into the data set. Only about one-third of our observations were in areas for which we could use this information. The variable did not have a significant effect even in regressions confined to observations for which the variable could be used. We might have gotten better results by generating unemployment rates by area for spring 1976 from our own data set. However, this would have required processing data on all households; we have used only households including youths.

### 13.3.4   Race

We have used two variables to identify youth by race, dummy variables identifying blacks and Hispanics. Both are consistently negative and usually significant with the effect of being black being generally substantially larger than that of being Hispanic. For regressions whose dependent variable is "employed last week," being black lowers the probability of employment by 17 to 25% even after controlling for schooling, other family income, and location in a poverty area. For youths not in school, in table 13.2, negative coefficients on the variable identifying blacks are about one-half the size of the mean of the dependent variable. With other measured variables equal, we estimate that black youths not in school worked half as many hours in 1975 as white youths. We also duplicated our analysis with regressions run using only observations on blacks. The results (not reported here) tend to be similar, with less consistency of coefficients between subsamples and lower significance levels, probably because of the large reduction in sample size.

We have tried using a variable measuring whether or not the principal language spoken in the household is English; this is less successful than the variable identifying Hispanics.

### 13.3.5  Family Influences

When we started our research, we expected to find powerful influences of the position of the head of the household on the employment status of youths living at home. The effects we find are much weaker than we expected. Living in a household with a female head has a negative effect in seven of eight regressions, and a significant one in four. Living in a household with a self-employed male head generally has a positive effect, but this is significant only once at the 5% level and twice at the 10% level for employment and hours worked last year. The effect of unemployment is consistently negative and generally significant.

Sets of dummy variables identifying male heads who were not employed and the major industry or occupation of the employed male heads performed very poorly. So did an index of three-digit occupations scaled by median income in the occupation in 1969. Education of the male head was tried and entered with a negative sign; that is, it acted as an index of permanent income rather than a measure of access to jobs.

Our second set of variables measuring family effects identifies the employment status of siblings between the ages of 16 and 24 who are in the household, using a set of eight dummy variables. Within this large set, there are four subsets, for older brother, older sister, younger brother, and younger sister.[6] In each of these subsets, there are two dummy variables, e.g., "older brother not employed" and "older brother employed"; the base or omitted variable of the subset is "no older brother living at home." If the person to whom the independent variable refers has more than one sibling between the ages of 16 and 24 living at home, there may be entries of one rather than zero in more than one of these dummy categories. For a person with two older brothers, for example, one employed and one not employed, both dummies in the older brother subset take the value one.

Employment decisions within the household are presumably made simultaneously, and our single equation model does not permit us to analyze the simultaneity. If we have an observation on a youth named John who is employed and he has an older brother named Fred who is also employed, we detect the associations, but we cannot tell whether John found Fred a job, Fred found John a job, or whether both were subject to some common parental or environmental influence that increased the probability of their being employed. It should also be noted that if both of them are between 17 and 20, observations for both will appear somewhere in our regressions with many (though not all) of the independent variables being identical. However, the scheme should permit us to separate the effects of job contacts and the family's work ethic from income effects by examining the signs of the coefficients. The income effect of Fred's working on the probability that John will work is presumably negative.

As shown in tables 13.2 and 13.4, the positive association of employment status among siblings is very strong. For males in school, having an employed sibling significantly increases the dependent variable in seven of eight cases in the two tables. Having a sibling not employed significantly decreases the dependent variable in all eight cases. For females and males not in school the effects are not always significant, though the signs are almost always the same. Some of the effects for females are also quite large. For example, other measured variables held constant, having a younger brother employed increases the chances of a female in school being employed by 15% or increases her estimated hours worked last year by 87 relative to a mean of 400.

The differences in coefficients for siblings of different sexes may support the interpretation that the sibling variables, rather than local job availability or parental influence, reflect information networks in the labor market. Because many occupations or industries still employ workers predominantly of one sex, a youth may be better able to help a sibling of the same sex find work. The differences in coefficients may also arise from stronger demonstration effects or closer personal relationships between siblings of the same sex.

The pattern of differences in coefficients is clearest for youths not in school in table 13.2. For a female, having a younger sister employed increases estimated hours in the preceding year by 173 hours, but the effect of a younger brother employed is only 21. For a male, having a younger brother employed increases estimated hours in the preceding year by 178, but the effect of a younger sister employed is only 80. In both cases the larger figure is clearly significant at the 5% level and the smaller is not.

One further refinement of the sibling dummies was used: splitting each dummy into two dummies for the sibling being in or out of school. Besides giving an unwieldy number of coefficients to interpret, the expanded set of dummies showed few differences in coefficients based on school status. Thus we chose to use only those sibling dummies presented here in the final model.

As mentioned above, these results can only be viewed as suggestive because the family's work ethic is not distinguishable from its job contacts. One possible area for future research would involve comparing the detailed occupation and industry of each youth with those of his parents or siblings. A high correlation could indicate the presence of helpful contacts made by relatives on the job. Another approach could be to examine some other data sets to check for consistency of the basic results and to add further explanatory variables, such as the presence of reading materials during childhood, that could capture more of the unobserved part of family background. In this regard one could consult data sets that ask how the respondent found his job (or why he in particular was hired after applying).

One final alternate approach requires a different estimation technique, one presented by Gary Chamberlain.[7] This would use analysis of covariance, with each set of siblings representing a different group for comparing the within-group to the between-group variation. Some complications result from the differing numbers of observations across groups and the need to use nonlinear estimation, but it would allow one to control for unobserved family characteristics.

Any of these approaches would shed more light on what role, if any, the family plays in the employment of youths.

# Notes

1. Martin Neil Baily and James Tobin, "Inflation-Unemployment Consequences of Job Creation Policies," in John L. Palmer, ed., *Creating Jobs: Public Employment Programs and Wage Subsidies* (Washington: Brookings, 1978), p. 61.

2. Kim B. Clark and Lawrence H. Summers, chapter 7 of this volume.

3. William G. Bowen and T. Aldrich Finegan, *The Economics of Labor Force Participation* (Princeton, N.J.: Princeton University Press, 1969), p. 387.

4. Robert Lerman, "Analysis of Youth Labor Force Participation, School Activity and Employment Rate," unpublished Ph.D. thesis, Massachusetts Institute of Technology, 1970.

5. An alternative explanation for this result lies in environmental characteristics common to poverty areas other than lack of jobs, such as low quality education and limited motivation.

6. This scheme of classifying siblings by sex and birth-order was suggested by the work of Claudia Goldin on the employment of youths in Philadelphia in 1880.

7. Gary Chamberlain, "Analysis of Covariance with Qualitative Data," National Bureau of Economic Research Working Paper no. 325, March 1979.

# Comment    Christopher Winship

Rees and Gray have carried out an important exploratory analysis of the effects of family background on youth employment behavior. Three of their findings are of particular note. These are: (1) that the usual measures of family background have little if any effect on employment behavior of youths: (2) that receipt of government transfers (welfare, social security, etc.) has little if any effect on employment behavior; (3) that there is a large correlation between the employment behavior of siblings even after observed variables measuring family background and local labor market conditions have been controlled for. It is this last finding that I want to discuss in more detail.

The strong relationship between the employment status of siblings may have a number of sources. It may be due to the effects of unobserved family characteristics, local labor market conditions, or, as Rees and Gray suggest, the fact that siblings are able to help each other find jobs. An unnoticed finding in Rees and Gray's analysis is the distinct pattern of the effects. The effect of younger sibling's employment status is almost always greater than that of the older sibling in real, not absolute, value (an observation made by Robert Mare). This relationship holds for 29 of the 32 possible comparisons that can be made for the regressions using present employment status and hours worked during the year. Thus the fact that a younger sibling is employed has a greater effect on a respondent's employment than the fact that an older sibling is employed. Conversely, the fact that an older sibling is not employed has a greater effect, in absolute value, on one's employment (note that the effects are negative rather than positive in this case) than the fact that a younger sibling is not employed. To put it another way, knowing that a younger sibling is employed tells us more about the respondent's probable employment status than knowing that an older sibling is employed. Conversely, knowing that an older sibling is not employed tells us more about the respondent's employment status than knowing that a younger sibling is not employed. This pattern holds net of the effects of age, educational attainment, and other variables that we would expect to produce this difference.

This pattern cannot be explained by the mechanism that Rees and Gray have suggested, namely, that siblings help each other find jobs. If we assume that this was the major explanation for the correlation between sibling employment status, then we would expect to find either no pattern in the effects or that the pattern was just the opposite: an older sibling being employed should have a greater effect on an individual's

Christopher Winship is associated with the National Opinion Research Center at the University of Chicago.

employment status than a younger sibling. This latter conclusion follows from the assumption that older siblings are more likely to be able to provide jobs for younger ones since, presumably, they would have higher status jobs and thus have access to better jobs. Younger siblings would be likely only to have access to jobs that their older siblings would find undesirable.

This finding (that older siblings, net of age, education, and other variables, are more likely to be employed), suggests a number of alternative explanations. I shall discuss three briefly. First, it may be the case that job rationing goes on within families on an oldest-first basis. This would be particularly likely if parental personal contacts were an important source of jobs for youths. Second, there may be a normative structure within households that imposes an obligation on older youths to obtain employment before their younger siblings do. Third, and not inconsistent with either of the first two explanations, there may be a definite structure to intrafamilial labor supply in terms of the age of different siblings.

Having discussed Rees and Gray's analysis briefly, I want to turn to a discussion of the major hypothesis that they propose in their chapter. Rees and Gray propose that jobs in the youth labor market are rationed by means of parental personal contacts. They contend that they find no support in their analysis for this hypothesis. This contention is based on their finding that the traditional measures of family background and parental status have no effect on a youth's employment status.

The question I want to ask is whether this finding provides an adequate test of the proposed hypothesis. Let us break down the reasoning implicit in Rees and Gray's argument into its three constituent parts: (1) that jobs are rationed in the labor market by means of personal contacts; (2) that it is parental contacts that are critical for youths in finding jobs; (3) that parents with higher socioeconomic status should have more effective contacts in terms of their ability to find their children jobs. In order for their hypothesis to be true, statements 1 and 2 would have to be correct. Rees and Gray's test, however, relies on all three statements being true. Clearly, there is no reason that subhypotheses 1 and 2 might hold whereas subhypothesis 3 might not. In fact, one could argue that parents with lower socioeconomic status might be in a better situation to provide their children with jobs since the type of jobs they have and the places where they are employed would be closer to the type that their children would have the necessary qualifications to work in.

Table C13.1 provides more direct evidence for subhypotheses 1 and 2. The data are taken from the January 1973 Current Population Survey and its supplement.

The table indicates that personal contacts are an important mechanism for finding jobs for individuals of all age groups. Personal contacts are

**Table C13.1**         **Method of Finding a Job by Age**

|  |  | Age | | |
|---|---|---|---|---|
| Method | | 16–19 | 20–24 | over 24 |
| Direct | % | 33.5 | 34.1 | 35.9 |
| application | f | 399 | 501 | 821 |
| Relatives | % | 13.3 | 9.4 | 5.4 |
| | f | 155 | 138 | 134 |
| Other personal | % | 28.0 | 18.5 | 18.4 |
| contacts | f | 331 | 273 | 425 |
| Formal and | % | 25.2 | 38.0 | 40.3 |
| other | f | 299 | 566 | 924 |

NOTE: Weighted percentages for individuals who searched for a job and found one in 1972. Data taken from the January 1973 CPS. Frequencies are the unweighted counts.

particularly important for teenagers, for whom a full 41.3% of the jobs found are found through personal contacts. This evidence supports the hypothesis that personal contacts are an important rationing mechanism, especially for youths.

Second, the table indicates that jobs are found more often through contacts involving persons other than relatives. This is consistent with Granovetter's (1974) finding that it is usually distant and weak contacts that are most effective in helping individuals find jobs. The table does, however, indicate that contacts with relatives are more important for youths than for adults. For youths, approximately one-third of the jobs found through personal contacts are found through relatives, whereas for adults the number is less than a quarter. Thus we find only weak support for subhypothesis 2.

I have no direct evidence on the relationship between family background and the use of personal contacts. Becker (1979), however, has done some preliminary analysis on differences by race. If we recompute his figures so they are comparable to those in table C13.1, his findings indicate that, using the same January 1973 Current Population Survey data, white youths (aged 16–24) are more likely to have found a job through personal contacts than black youths (33.6 versus 30.7%), but that of those using personal contacts blacks are more likely than whites to use relatives (47.5 versus 32.6%). Under the assumption that blacks in the survey come from families with lower socioeconomic status than whites, this finding is consistent with the argument made above that there is no necessary reason to suspect that there is a positive relationship between the effectiveness of parental contacts and socioeconomic background.

In summary, we can say that we have found evidence to support subhypothesis 1, weaker evidence to support subhypothesis 2, and no evidence to support subhypothesis 3. Clearly, however, our discussion of the importance of personal contacts has at best been suggestive. More work needs to be done to assess the importance of personal contacts as a mechanism by which people find jobs.

The analysis by Rees and Gray is also suggestive. Perhaps their contribution lies not so much in what they have told us about the importance or lack of importance of personal contacts, but rather in the suggestion that there are potentially rich analyses to be done on the nature of intrafamilial labor supply and employment behavior. This has been an active area with respect to husband and wives. Rees and Gray's analysis, however, suggests that there is much to be done with regard to the interdependencies among siblings. In this, their chapter has suggested important new directions for research.

**References**

Becker, H. J. 1979. Personal networks of opportunity in obtaining jobs: Racial differences and effects of segregation. Report no. 281, Center for Social Organization of Schools, John Hopkins University.

Granovetter, M. S. 1974. *Getting a job: A study of contacts and careers.* Cambridge, Massachusetts: Harvard University press.

# Comment     George Farkas and Ernst W. Stromsdorfer

Economists analyzing youth employment or labor supply with microdata have usually been content to estimate income and substitution effects, with little regard for intrafamily (supply-side) tastes and decision-making mechanisms or labor market (demand-side) distortions which might bias their results. Rees and Gray's chapter is thus particularly valuable in that it explicitly introduces "family work ethic" and "family job contacts" as variables which might play these roles. The authors make no attempt to separate these supply and demand side effects, and their test of the empirical importance of the resulting combined effect is only indirect, but they do produce findings which suggest that something beyond the usual income effect is occurring in their data.

As the authors note, the unexpected finding of a positive association between family income and youth labor force participation goes back at least to Bowen and Finegan (1969), who attributed it to a positive association between family income and job contacts. More recently, Gustman and Steinmeier (1979) have replicated this result; Boskin

George Farkas and Ernst W. Stromsdorfer are economists at Abt Associates, Inc., Cambridge, Massachusetts.

(1973), Hall (1973), and Ehrenberg and Marcus (1979) find little systematic effect of family income on youth employment; and both Masters and Garfinkel (1977) and McDonald and Stephenson (1979) find the expected negative effect of income. These studies differ according to data sources, age of the youth population, range of family incomes for the youth population, empirical specification (including approaches to coping with the endogeneity of schooling), and statistical methodology, among other issues, but the wide range of results suggests great uncertainty in our knowledge of family effects on youth employment.

Attempts to incorporate intrafamily taste variables into the usual offered-wage/asking-wage model of labor supply (Heckman 1974) present fewer problems of empirical implementation than do attempts to incorporate either fixed costs of working or demand-side distortions (such as minimum wages) which lead to the rationing of jobs. In the former case (intrafamily tastes), measures of taste differences can be taken as explicit determinants of the youth's reservation wage. In the latter case, the simple reservation wage theory is invalidated, since either fixed costs of working or demand deficiency at the prevailing wage cause youths to behave as though confronted with a nonconvex budget set. That is, the tobit model in which the probability of employment and the hours worked by those employed are determined by a single index (the difference between the wage offer and the asking wage), is replaced by a model in which this is no longer the case. As a result (and assuming that net wage offers are independent of the number of hours worked), estimation with tobit can be replaced by a strategy in which a truncated normal distribution is fit for the hours of those employed and a separate probit is fit for the probability of being employed. (For further discussion of these and related issues see Hausman 1979; Olsen 1977; Farkas, Stromsdorfer, and Olsen 1979.)

In this situation, the truncated normal for hours worked can still be taken to reveal the youth's "value of time at zero hours," and this can be used, in conjunction with the probit equation estimates, to identify a "disemployment index" measuring the extent to which employment probabilities inferred from the wage offer and "values of time at zero hours" of the truncated normal hours equation differ from those actually observed. This disemployment index subsumes both fixed costs of working and demand deficiencies, and its significance indicates whether the simpler tobit specification should be rejected. More formally, we write

(1)     $\text{Hours} = B_0\ (W^0 - W^*) + u\ ; H > 0$

(2)     $\text{Prob (Employment)} = \text{Prob}(W^0 > W^* + DI)$

where $W^0$ = the wage offer, $W^*$ = the value of time at zero hours, and $DI$ = the disemployment index, each of which is taken to be a function of exogeneous variables. If measures of family work ethic were introduced among the determinants of $W^*$, and measures of family job contacts were introduced among the determinants of $DI$, the effects of interest to Rees and Gray could be explicitly estimated.

The authors estimate instead two sets of reduced-form regressions, a tobit for hours worked and a probit for the probability of employment. They include no measure of the youth's own wage rate, but they do include other family income, and (their principle innovation) measures of whether the youth's siblings were employed. Their results for the effect of family income are as equivocal as those of others—the only significant effect is a positive one for the total hours worked by out-of-school youths. However, Rees and Gray's results for the effects of siblings' employment are new and quite suggestive—it appears that, other things being equal, the employment of siblings is strongly and positively associated. As the authors note, this may be because youths' jobs are rationed by parents' contacts rather than by price; because siblings are exposed to identical work-ethic climates; because both effects are operative; or because some other family characteristic is at work.

Further information on the determinants of youth employment is provided by estimating equations (1) and (2), above, along with a wage offer equation. This we have done with preprogram data collected for the evaluation of the Youth Incentive Entitlement Pilot Projects (see Barclay et al., 1979, for a discussion of the program, data, and evaluation design). Table C13.2 presents the results for 5,462 youths aged 14–17 from low-income households during the summer of 1977 and residing in one of the eight study sites. (We focus on summer labor supply in order to avoid complications associated with the endogeneity of schooling.)

We find that the youth's own wage exerts a powerful positive effect on total hours, but that other family income exerts no significant effect on the youth's value of time at zero hours. Wage offers (estimated with a maximum likelihood correction for possible selection bias and nonnormal residuals) are generally quite far in excess of estimated values of time at zero hours, yet only 36% of the sample is employed, suggesting that fixed costs of working or demand-side distortions are quite powerful. This situation is evidenced by the large constant term for the disemployment index (a finding which also demonstrates the inappropriateness of the simple tobit model). The relatively large positive coefficients associated with the effect of a youth's own child on his disemployment index suggests the existence of fixed costs associated with child care, but more important for Rees and Gray's concerns are the relatively insignificant effects of the other variables, including other family income. It appears that demand deficiency *is* present, but that, at least for this low-income youth population, during the summer of 1977 (when subsidized summer jobs programs for low-income youths were operating at relatively high

**Table C13.2** **Coefficient Estimates for the Wage Offer, Value of Time at Zero Hours, and Disemployment Index, Model of Equations (1) and (2); t-statistics in Parentheses**

| | Dependent variable[a] | | |
| | LnWage | W* | DI |
|---|---|---|---|
| Constant | .7484 (90.9) | .2497 (43.8) | .4633 (19.8) |
| White male | .0000 ( − ) | | .0000 ( − ) |
| Black male | − .0677 (2.19) | | − .0531 (1.53) |
| Hispanic male | − .0543 (1.31) | | − .0311 (0.65) |
| White female | − .1588 (3.66) | | − .0943 (1.28) |
| Black female | − .0772 (2.39) | | − .0251 (0.43) |
| Hispanic female | − .0899 (2.05) | | − .0392 (0.61) |
| Age (in months, by date of birth; 1 = December 1963) | .0021 (1.14) | | |
| Young (age < 28) | − .0253 (0.77) | .0181 (0.77) | − .0396 (0.66) |
| Very young (age < 17) | − .0422 (1.20) | − .0234 (0.62) | − .0077 (0.88) |
| Family earned income (minus that due to the youth) ÷ $10^4$ | | − .0089 (0.43) | .0122 (0.61) |
| Family welfare income (minus that due to the youth) ÷ $10^4$ | | .0038 (0.09) | − .0244 (0.99) |
| Family size | | | .0003 (0.33) |
| Living with parents | | .0008 (0.02) | .0105 (0.78) |
| Male youth with own child | | − .2140 (1.42) | .2056 (1.82) |
| Female youth with own child | | − .0422 (0.95) | .1055 (1.10) |
| Denver | .0406 (1.28) | | − .0361 (0.47) |
| Phoenix | .0979 (2.59) | | .0308 (0.43) |
| Cincinnati | − .0196 (0.71) | | − .0449 (1.23) |
| Louisville | − .0235 (0.62) | | − .0140 (0.35) |
| Baltimore | .0000 ( − ) | | .0000 ( − ) |
| Cleveland | .0074 (0.23) | | − .0560 (0.84) |
| Mississippi pilot | .0203 (0.49) | | .2166 (1.15) |
| Mississippi control | − .0261 (0.67) | | .0973 (1.04) |
| Urban sites combined | | .0000 ( − ) | |
| Mississippi combined | | − .1422 (5.08) | |
| $B_0$ for LnWage in hours equation | | 482.7 (5.09) | |

[a]The wage offer equation is estimated jointly with the probit by a maximum likelihood technique which accounts both for possible selection and nonnormal residuals in the wage equation. W* is calculated from a truncated normal for hours, in which $B_0$, the estimated coefficient for LnWage, is used to deflate the coefficients for the exogenous variables determining W*. The standard error in the hours equation is 169.1. The coefficients for DI are calculated from the probit by using the coefficient for the exogenous variable identifying the wage offer to identify the standard error in the probit, and using this value and the (already calculated) estimates of the determinants of W* to solve for the determinants of DI. For the LnWage equation only, the coefficients are as estimated when the right hand side variables are expressed as deviations from their means (source: Farkas, Stromsdorfer, and Olsen, 1979).

levels), the available jobs were rationed in close to a random manner. Of course, our table C13.2 estimates do not test Rees and Gray's sibling employment variables, but they do corroborate the results of those who have found relatively little effect of family income on youth employment.

Youth labor markets are probably characterized by an excess of supply over demand at the prevailing wage. Accordingly, Rees and Gray's attention to nonprice mechanisms for rationing jobs represents a potentially important area for further development. We hazard a guess, however, that personal and family characteristics other than parents' job contacts are of greatest importance for the allocation of the available employment among youths from low-income households.

## References

Barclay, S. C. Bottom, G. Farkas, E. W. Stromsdorfer, and R. J. Olsen. 1979. *Schooling and work among youths from low-income households: A baseline report from the entitlement demonstration.* New York: Manpower Demonstration Research Corporation.

Boskin, M. 1973. The economics of labor supply. In G. Cain and H. Watts eds., *Income maintenance and labor supply.* Chicago: Markham.

Bowen, W. G. and T. A. Finegan. 1969. *The economics of labor force participation.* Princeton, N.J.: Princeton University Press.

Ehrenberg, R. G. and A. J. Marcus. 1979. A multinomial logit model of teenagers: School enrollment and employment outcomes. Presented at the December Meetings of the Econometric Society.

Farkas, G., E. W. Stromsdorfer, and R. J. Olsen. 1979. Youth labor supply during the summer: Evidence for youths from low-income households. Presented at the December Meetings of the Econometric Society. Expanded version to appear in R. Ehrenberg ed., *Research in labor economics* (1981).

Gustman, A. L. and T. L. Steinmeier. 1979. The impact of the market and the family on youth enrollment and labor supply. Working paper (January).

Hall, R. E. 1973. Wages, income, and hours of work in the U.S. labor force. In Glen Cain and Harold Watts, eds., *Income maintenance and labor supply.* Chicago: Markham.

Hausman, J. A. 1979. The effect of wages, taxes, and fixed costs on women's labor force participation. Presented at the December Meetings of the Econometric Society. To appear in *Journal of Public Economics* (1980).

Heckman, J. 1974. Shadow prices, market wages, and labor supply. *Econometrica* 42 (July).

Masters, S. and I. Garfinkel. 1977. *Estimating the labor supply effects of income-maintenance alternatives.* New York: Academic Press.

McDonald, J. F. and S. P. Stephenson. 1979. The effect of income maintenance on the school-enrollment and labor-supply decisions of teenagers. *Journal of Human Resources* 4.

Olsen, R. J. 1977. An econometric model of family labor supply. Ph.D. dissertation, University of Chicago.

# 14 The Minimum Wage and Job Turnover in Markets for Young Workers

Robert E. Hall

By the standard analysis, the minimum wage ought to create a shortage of jobs for young workers. The minimum sets a reward to work which draws the young into the labor market in numbers beyond the level of employment which employers are willing to provide. With large numbers of job-hunters looking for a small number of actual jobs, jobs become exceedingly hard to find, according to this view. The excessive effort required for young workers to find jobs in such a market is one of the important social costs of the minimum wage and is starkly evident in high unemployment rates for the young. This analysis exhibits one important discrepancy from the actual experiences of American youths: in fact, jobs paying the minimum wage are quite easy to find. Millions of jobs are filled every year by a never-ending stream of youths. The young take no longer than mature workers to find jobs, even though they are clearly differentially influenced by the minimum wage. It is by now firmly established that high unemployment among youths is associated with high *frequency* of unemployment, not long duration of unemployment. To put it another way, the problem of jobs for the young is not that they are hard to find, but that they do not last very long.

This chapter presents an alternative analysis of the effects of the minimum wage within a labor market where both job turnover and the availability of new jobs are determined through the interaction of the preferences of young workers, the costs of turnover and recruiting faced by employers, and the minimum wage set by the government. The essential hypothesis is that the arrangements observed in markets for the

Robert E. Hall is associated with the Department of Economics and the Hoover Institution at Stanford University and with the National Bureau of Economic Research. The research for this chapter was supported by the National Science Foundation through a grant to the NBER.

young are an adaptation that is as efficient as it can be in the face of the distortion imposed by the minimum wage. This chapter argues that the principal effect of the minimum wage is to increase job turnover rather than make it more difficult for the unemployed to find work. Through their recruiting and layoff policies, firms can push the market toward a point where the trade-off between turnover costs and job-finding benefits is efficient. This point involves roughly the same degree of job-finding effort no matter how far the minimum wage distorts the market, at least up to a certain level. The markets most seriously affected by the minimum wage will have the highest rate of turnover, but the participants in them will not think of them as markets where work is hard to find.

The analysis presented here should help to square the economic analysis of the effects of the minimum wage with the facts about the operation of modern labor markets for the young. It does not alter in any important way the criticisms emerging from the standard analysis about the economic inefficiency of the minimum wage. Excessive turnover caused by the minimum wage is a waste of resources. High unemployment brought about by the minimum wage is just as costly if it comes from high turnover as it is when the minimum creates difficulties in finding work.

## 14.1 Data on Turnover and Employment

Table 14.1 presents data from U.S. surveys comparing turnover and unemployment among teenagers and adults. These data strongly confirm that the important difference between the two groups is in their rates of job separation, not in their rates of job-finding. The first two lines measure two different aspects of the job-finding process; teenagers and adults are similar in both. The first line shows the proportion of job-changers who do not experience any unemployment between jobs. If jobs for teenagers were harder to find than jobs for adults, the proportion of job-changers without unemployment would be lower for teenagers, but, in fact, the proportions are slightly higher for teenagers (the survey upon which this finding is based is not tabulated by sex). The second line shows the percentage of the unemployed who take jobs each week. Again, if teenage markets were slacker, this percentage would be lower than that for adults, but in fact it is higher, especially among women. Note that the evidence from the first two lines of table 14.1 does not involve the mistake of trying to infer rates of job-finding from data on the duration of unemployment. As Marston (1976) and Clark and Summers (1979) have pointed out, much of the explanation of the brief duration of unemployment among teenagers comes from their high propensity to drop out of the labor force while unemployed. However, the correct comparison in terms of actual success in finding work shows that teenagers are on a par with adults.

**Table 14.1**    **Job-finding, Separation, and Unemployment Rates by Age and Sex, 1974**

|  | Male | | Female | |
|---|---|---|---|---|
|  | Teenage | Adult | Teenage | Adult |
| Proportion of job-changers with no unemployment (%)[a] | 56.0 | 54.2 | 56.0 | 54.2 |
| Weekly job-finding rate of the unemployed (%)[b] | 6.0 | 5.7 | 5.3 | 3.9 |
| Weekly separation rate (%)[c] | 8.3 | 3.3 | 8.9 | 2.8 |
| Actual unemployment rate (%)[d] | 15.5 | 3.8 | 16.5 | 5.5 |

NOTES AND SOURCES: [a]Based on data from Bancroft and Garfinkle (1963), quoted in Clark and Summers (1979).
[b]Estimated by Clark and Summers (1979) from CPS gross flows data. This is the observed monthly transition rate from unemployment to employment, divided by 3.3.
[c]Estimated by Clark and Summers (1979) by multiplying the observed transition rate from employment to nonemployment by the fraction of job changes made without intervening nonemployment (line [1]).
[d]Source: *Employment and Training Report of the President.*

The third line of table 14.1 presents data on the weekly rate of departure from jobs among the four age-sex groups. Between 8 and 9% of teenagers lose or quit their jobs each week, compared to about 3% of adults. Teenage jobs are brief—they last about twelve weeks on the average. The dramatic difference in separation rates stands in sharp contrast to the virtual equality of job-finding rates. The well-known large gap in unemployment rates, shown in the fourth line of table 14.1, is due largely to the difference in job separation rates. Table 14.1 does not attempt a full description of the dynamic process by which workers move in and out of the labor force, which would be necessary to give a complete account of the differences in unemployment between teenagers and adults. For such an account, see Marston (1976) and Clark and Summers (1979).

Investigation of possible causes of high separation rates among young workers is the main purpose of this chapter. Obviously, there are important normal influences toward brief jobs, including the fact that a fraction of employment takes the form of summer jobs. But the impression remains that much turnover is pathological. Consequently, this chapter spends a good deal of effort investigating the possible role of the minimum wage in stimulating excessive job turnover.

## 14.2 Determination of Turnover, Job-finding Rates, and Unemployment in the Presence of a Minimum Wage

The analysis presented in this section is closely related to an earlier paper of mine (Hall 1979), modified suitably to take the minimum wage into account. The discussion here is intended to stand on its own, however.

The first component of the model describes the mechanical operation of the recruiting and job-finding process. The unemployed are viewed simply as a group of people who have not yet found work, but are confident of finding work eventually. Each of the unemployed has the same chance of locating a job each week. All unemployment is "frictional"; nobody is permanently unemployable. The state of tightness or slackness of the market is described by a single variable, the job-finding rate, which I will call $f$. It is the weekly probability that an unemployed worker will find a job. Tighter markets have higher values of $f$ and are preferred by workers. On the other hand, slacker markets with lower values of $f$ are preferred by employers for the following reason: employers compete with each other for workers who are available. When an employer extends a job offer in a tighter market, it is less likely to be accepted because the worker may also receive an offer from another employer at the same time. In formal terms, this consideration is embodied in a recruiting cost function, $\rho(f)$, which gives the number of offers that need to be made, on the average, to hire one new worker. As $f$ approaches one, $\rho(f)$ approaches infinity—guaranteed instantaneous job-finding would make recruiting prohibitively expensive. In very slack markets with $f$ near zero, $\rho(f)$ will be only slightly more than one. In my earlier paper, I derived an exact form, $\rho(f) = -\log(1 + f)/f$, for the recruiting cost function, based on some further simple assumptions.

The job-finding rate is one of two major dimensions of conditions in the labor market; it does not by itself determine the unemployment rate. A very slack market, in which it is nearly impossible to find work, could have a low unemployment rate because few workers came to it to search. Similarly, a tight market could have a high unemployment rate because there was a large continuing flow of newly unemployed workers into it. The latter is a good description of markets for youths in the modern U.S. economy. Thus the other dimension of labor market conditions is the separation rate—the weekly probability that an employed worker will become unemployed. In stochastic equilibrium, where the flow of workers into the pool of unemployment through job separations balances the flow out of the pool through finding new jobs, the unemployment rate will be

$$u = \frac{s}{s + f/(1 - f)}$$

The job-finding rate, $f$, the separation rate, $s$, and the unemployment rate, $u$, are linked by this relation. Given the values of any two of these measures, the third is fully determined by it. In this chapter, the job-finding and separation rates are considered explicitly and the corresponding unemployment rate is then derived. Of course, it is also true that unemployment is the difference between the supply of labor and the demand for it. Further discussion of determination of unemployment will continue after the principles of the efficient combination of separation and job-finding rates are presented.

It has already been established that both parties to the employment contract are concerned about the job-finding rate. Workers favor high rates and employers low rates. It is equally true that both parties are concerned about the separation rate. The rate is the reciprocal of the duration of employment: high separation rates mean jobs are brief. Both very long and very short jobs are generally undesirable from the employer's point of view. If an employer promises virtually permanent jobs to workers, it will be difficult to adjust total employment downward in the event of an adverse shift in demand. Permanent commitments also limit the employer's power to retain ony the most productive of a group of new recruits. For these reasons, it is costly for employers to promise lengthy employment. On the other hand, very high turnover implies excessive recruiting and training costs. This second consideration has dominated most discussions of the economics of turnover. In markets for young workers, though, rather high turnover rates may actually be efficient, expecially in lines of work where training costs can be made low. In these markets employers profit from the flexibility they enjoy in adjusting employment to each minor fluctuation in demand. The occasional redundancy of labor that is typical under more or less permanent employment arrangements is unnecessary where separation rates are high.

The hypothesis pursued here is that employment terms adjust to mediate the conflicting attitudes of employers and workers about job-finding and separation rates. Specifically, the two parties should equalize their trade-offs between the two aspects of the arrangement. The minimum wage does not impose any limitations on these dimensions of the employment package. In a market unaffected by the minimum wage, the parties ought to equalize their trade-offs between cash wages and the separation or job-finding rates. The fully efficient outcome is described in my earlier paper. The influence of an effective minimum wage in the present analysis is to prevent employers from offering better duration terms to workers in exchange for lower cash wages.

In analytical terms, the efficient combination of separation rates and job-finding rates occurs at the point of tangency of an indifference curve and an isocost curve. The indifference curve describes the alternative combinations of separation and job-finding rates that achieve the same level of satisfaction, on the average, for workers. Presumably, it slopes upward, since workers will need to be rewarded with higher job-finding rates in order to induce them to accept higher turnover. The isocost curve embodies the considerations about the costs and benefits to employers mentioned earlier. Its slope is positive for low separation rates, where the added flexibility of higher turnover is a benefit, and then turns negative for high separation rates, where recruiting and training costs begin to dominate. All this can be summarized in figure 14.1.

The outcome of this analysis is an expansion path of alternative efficient combinations of separation rates and job-finding rates; call it $f = \theta(s)$. Different points on the path correspond to different levels of satisfaction achieved by workers and costs incurred by employers. If the market is operating at separation and job-finding rates that are not on this path, employers' costs can be reduced and workers' level of satisfaction improved by a suitable movement to a point on the path. Along the path, cost can be reduced only by making workers worse off by raising the separation rate.

The forces of supply and demand determine which of the efficient combinations of separation and job-finding rates will prevail in the market, and thus determine the unemployment rate. Since costs are sensitive to the separation and job-finding rates through recruiting and training costs, the total demand for labor in a market will be a function $L^D(w, s, f)$ of the hourly wage $w$, and the separation and job-finding rates $s$ and $f$. Higher wages and higher job-finding rates depress the demand for labor, while higher separation rates stimulate it, at least over the range of

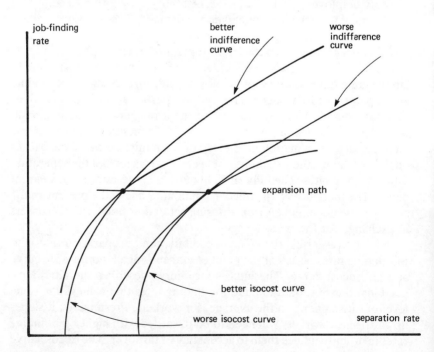

Fig. 14.1

variation that is considered here. Further implications of and justifications for the latter proposition are presented in the subsequent section of the paper.

The supply side of the market is a little more complex because the presence of unemployment even in equilibrium means that there are two different concepts of supply. The first, gross supply, corresponds to labor force participation—it consists of all the workers attracted to the market, including those looking for work who have not yet found it. Gross supply is a function $L^S(w, s, f)$ of the terms of employment offered by the market. The other concept is net supply, which does not count the unemployed. If $u$ is the unemployment rate implied by the separation and job-finding rates, net supply is $(1 - u)L^S(w, s, f)$. Recall that $u$ is a simple function of $s$ and $f$, so that another way to express net supply is

$$\frac{f}{(1 - f)s + f} L^S(w, s, f)$$

Equilibrium occurs in the market when demand and net supply are in balance:

$$L^D(w, s, f) = \frac{f}{(1 - f)s + f} L^S(w, s, f)$$

The equilibrium that concerns this chapter is the constrained one that occurs when the government sets the wage through an effective minimum wage at level $\bar{w}$. The wage itself cannot participate in the process of clearing the market, but variations in the separation and job-finding rates can bring about a constrained equilibrium in the market. I will assume that they move in tandem, so as to preserve the efficient combination of the two rates; that is, the job-finding rate is $\theta(s)$ and not a free variable. This condenses the market-clearing process to a single dimension, the separation rate:

$$L^D[\bar{w}, s, \theta(s)] = \frac{\theta(s)}{[1 - \theta(s)]s + \theta(s)} L^S[\bar{w}, s, \theta(s)]$$

This can be portrayed in the somewhat unconventional supply-and-demand diagram in figure 14.2.

The demand curve is shown as nearly vertical on the assumption that the benefits to the employer of higher turnover and the associated change in recruiting costs are not very large. On the other hand, gross labor supply may be reasonably sensitive to the separation rate—given the fixed wage rate, young workers will choose activities other than work in preference to the high unemployment rates that accompany high turnover rates. This is even more pronounced when supply is measured net of unemployment. Higher separation rates mean fewer workers are avail-

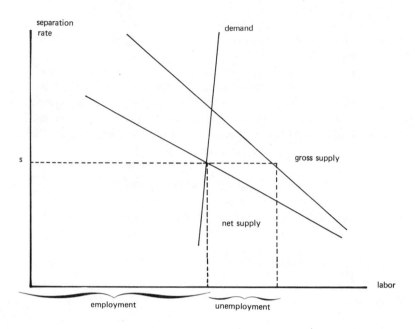

**Fig. 14.2**

able for work at any one time, both because the work is less attractive and because more of their time is spent finding new work.

When the wage is held fixed by minimum wage legislation, the separation rate assumes the role of clearing the market. Equality of supply and demand is achieved subject to the constraint of the minimum wage; in this sense, the market is in equilibrium. It is important to note, however, that this equilibrium is not efficient. Because the minimum wage does not try to peg either the separation rate or the job-finding rate, private economic arrangements yield an efficient trade-off between the two. However, the minimum wage does interfere with the trade-off between the separation rate and the cash wage rate. Separation rates (and therefore unemployment rates) are excessive under the minimum wage because employers are prohibited from offering a set of employment terms with lower wages and longer jobs, even though those terms would make workers better off and reduce employers' costs at the same time.

In a labor market unaffected by the minimum wage, the separation and job-finding rates are largely unaffected by shifts in supply or demand. Unemployment remains at a fixed "natural" rate when, say, demand increases. The wage rises to clear the market. This analysis of a free labor market is amplified in my earlier paper. In the presence of a minimum wage, the impact of an increase in demand is rather different. Because the wage cannot respond, the separation rate falls as demand rises, as shown in figure 14.3. The increase in employment, from $E$ to $E'$, is somewhat less than the amount of the rightward shift of the demand curve (just as it would be if the wage were permitted to rise). Unemployment, which is held above the natural rate by the minimum wage, falls toward the natural rate.

The same apparatus will help to explain the effect of an increase in the minimum wage itself. For a given separation rate, a higher minimum wage means lower labor demand and higher net supply, so the demand schedule shifts to the left and the net supply schedule to the right (figure 14.4). The combination brings about a decrease in employment from $E$ to $E'$ and an increase in the separation rate from $s$ to $s'$. Unemployment rises as well, as the figure 14.5 shows.

In the traditional analysis of the minimum wage, employment falls by the full amount of the downward shift in labor demand brought about by a higher minimum. Demand alone determines employment. The gap between supply and demand appears as unemployment. In the analysis presented here, the equilibrating role of the separation rate dampens the adverse effect of the minimum wage on employment. The rise in separations makes the labor market more attractive to employers and so helps to offset the disincentive of higher cash wages. A stricter minimum wage

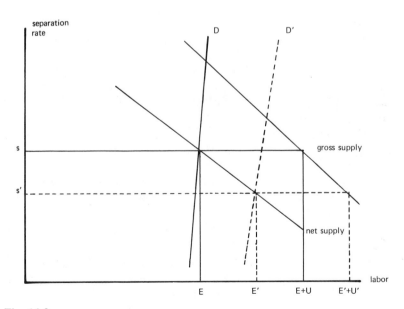

**Fig. 14.3**

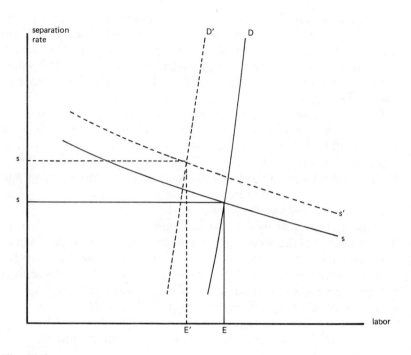

**Fig. 14.4**

must raise unemployment, however. Most, or perhaps all, of the increase comes from higher turnover rather than from lower job-finding rates and longer duration of unemployment.

This conclusion is rather different from one reached by Finis Welch (1976). In a brief discussion of the theory of the effect of the minimum wage on unemployment, he concludes that it is ambiguous because the shortage of jobs will decrease turnover among those lucky enough to find work. Implicit in Welch's discussion is the belief that jobs terminate at the initiative of workers, and that employers would prefer lower turnover. This situation would represent a failure of the market to achieve an efficient turnover rate where workers and employers have equalized their trade-offs between turnover and other aspects of the employment bargain. Under the hypothesis of an efficient trade-off, pursued here, it seems likely that turnover and unemployment are stimulated by a minimum wage.

Another discussion of the effect of the minimum wage on unemployment appears in Mincer (1976). In his analysis, the job turnover rate is taken as constant, unaffected by the minimum wage. He does consider the influence of unemployment on labor supply.

### 14.3  Turnover and Labor Costs

All of the novelty in section 14.2 rests on the hypothesis that employers can operate at lower costs when turnover rates are higher, given a fixed hourly cash wage. To see this, consider the opposite case where turnover above a certain critical level is undesirable from the point of view of the employer. Since turnover is assumed always to be undesirable to the worker, efficient arrangements will never involve a separation rate above the critical level. In this case, the efficient job-finding rate, $f = \theta(s)$, will rise rapidly as the separation rate approaches the critical level (say, $s^*$), as shown in figure 14.6.

The supply-and-demand diagram under a wage fixed by minimum wage legislation is shown in this case in figure 14.7. Here the net supply curve bends far to the left of the gross supply curve because the job-finding rate drops rapidly as the separation rate approaches $s^*$. If market equilibrium occurs at a separation rate near $s^*$, it will involve high rates of unemployment in the traditional sense of a stagnant market: the unemployed will consist of people who are having a great deal of trouble

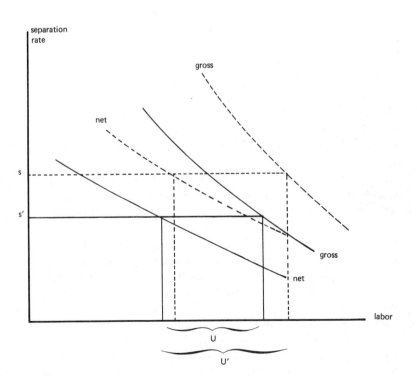

**Fig. 14.5**

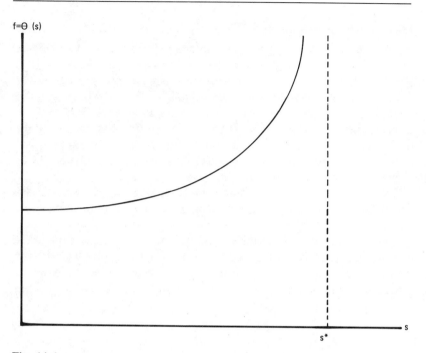

**Fig. 14.6**

finding jobs. The jobs they find eventually will last a reasonable length of time. This is the kind of influence of the minimum wage depicted in the standard analysis. To the extent that the minimum wage raises the wage above its full market-clearing level, it creates a shortage of jobs, and jobs are rationed among job-seekers by the increased difficulty in finding work.

My point here is the theoretical and practical possibility that a minimum wage operates in the opposite way, to stimulate job turnover rather than to depress job-finding. The most convincing part of the case favoring this hypothesis is the evidence presented earlier of very high job separation rates and rapid flows of workers into jobs in markets influenced by the minimum wage. This section gives some further reasons to think that the minimum wage exerts most of its effect in raising job turnover.

First, it may be useful to exhibit a class of utility functions and cost functions where the efficient job-finding rate is literally constant, independent of the minimum wage, and, indeed, independent of the supply and demand for labor generally. Within this class, workers' concerns about separation rates and job-finding operate through the unemployment rate. In other words, a worker is indifferent between two labor markets where wages and unemployment are the same, but one has higher separation and higher job-finding rates than the other. It is also necessary to say something about workers' willingness to trade off cash earnings against unemployment, which will depend on the level of public unemployment insurance and workers' attitudes about the value of time spent out of work. A reasonable approximation is that there is a constant, $\lambda$, equal to zero for workers who are indifferent between work and unemployment (either because of full unemployment insurance or high value of time in nonworking activities) and equal to one for workers for whom unemployment is a pure waste of time and who receive no unemployment insurance. Then a utility function capturing all of this is

$$w(1 - \lambda u)$$

or, in terms of separation and job-finding rates,

$$w\left[1 - \lambda \frac{s}{s + f/(1 - f)}\right]$$

The indifference curve along which workers achieve a certain level of satisfaction (say, $y$), can be written

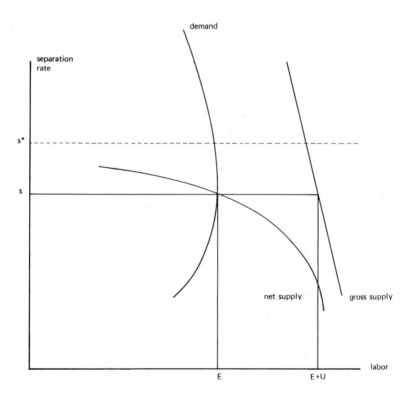

**Fig. 14.7**

$$s = \frac{f}{1-f} \frac{w-y}{y-(1-\lambda)}$$

On the cost side, it seems reasonable to approximate total cost as the sum of (1) costs not related to the type of labor under consideration, say, $A$; (2) regular hourly employment costs, say, $aw$; (3) recruiting costs, proportional to the rate at which jobs are filled, $s$, the effort required to fill one job, $\rho(f)$, and the hourly wage, $w$ less (4) the benefit, say, $bws$, of the flexibility associated with the separation rate, net of training costs. The resulting cost function has the form

$$C(w, s, f) = A + Bw[a + \rho(f)s - bs]$$

It is only a useful approximation over the range of separation rates where it is plausible that rising rates convey benefits to the firm, on net.

An efficient employment arrangement that yields a level of statisfaction $y$ to each worker can be described mathematically as the minimum of cost subject to the constraint that utility equal $y$:

$$\text{Min } A + Bw[a + \rho(f)s - bs]$$
$$s, f$$

$$\text{subject to } s = \frac{f}{1-f} \frac{w-y}{y-(1-\lambda)w}$$

The minimum wage prevents achievement of the fully efficient arrangement, where the minimum would be taken over the wage rate as well. Now the constraint can be substituted into the minimand to restate the problem as

$$\text{Min } A + Bw\left[a - [b - \rho(f)] \frac{f}{1-f} \frac{w-y}{y-(1-\lambda)w}\right]$$
$$f$$

But minimization of this over the job-finding rate, $f$, is equivalent to maximizing the expression

$$[b - \rho(f)] \frac{f}{1-f}$$

The maximum occurs somewhere between $f = 0$ and the critical job-finding rate, $f^*$, where the recruiting costs, $\rho(f)$, begin to outweigh the net benefits of turnover, $b$ (figure 14.8). The important point is that the efficient job-finding rate is determined by the narrow consideration of balancing the employer's benefits from turnover against the worker's costs. Both are proportional to the hourly wage, so *the efficient job-finding rate is independent of the level at which the government sets the minimum wage*. It is also independent of the level of satisfaction achieved by workers and so independent of the supply of and demand for labor.

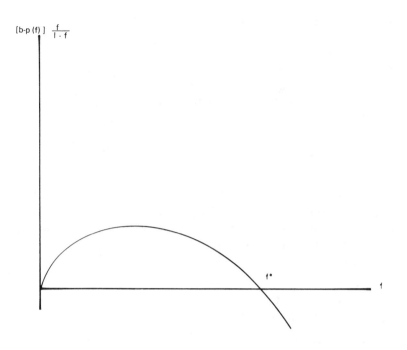

**Fig. 14.8**

It seems reasonable to expect that the efficient job-finding rate is fairly close to constant over a range of market conditions, even if the exact mathematical conditions set forth above do not hold. Obviously, the range includes only those separation rates where turnover has net benefits to employers. A sufficiently aggressive minimum wage will inevitably push the market close to the point where turnover becomes costly to employers, and the conventional analysis where the minimum creates a shortage of jobs will begin to apply. On the other hand, the effect of a minimum wage that pushes the cash wage only moderately above its equilibrium may well be to stimulate turnover rather than to depress job-finding.

The core of the argument that turnover can benefit employers, as I have emphasized earlier, is the flexibility that brief job commitments provide to employers. At the most basic level, the minimum wage induces turnover by inhibiting employers from holding overhead labor. Instead of paying a lower wage to long-term workers through thick or thin, employers subject to a minimum wage pay a high hourly wage to short-term workers who must finance themselves (at least partly) in times of slack. Only a tiny fraction of the fluctuations in demand that lie behind this process are aggregate—most affect just the firm itself. They are not necessarily purely random, either. A high-turnover employment policy makes it easier to accommodate seasonal swings in demand as well, for example.

Other adaptations to the minimum wage are more subtle and probably take longer to respond to changes in the minimum. The scope for taking advantage of a high-wage, high-turnover employment policy depends on the technical organization of work within a firm. Training costs must be low in order to benefit from high turnover. Jobs must be highly standardized. The fast-food industry, which is a major source of employment at the minimum wage, is the leading example of this kind of adaptation. Workers can be trained in a few hours. They need not even memorize the prices of items on the menu because each item has a separate button on the cash register. Job turnover is a way of life in this industry, and the industry has learned to profit from it. Though obviously many forces have contributed to the evolution of the high-turnover practices of the fast-food industry, my suggestion here is that the minimum wage is important among them.

## 14.4   Achievement of the Efficient Job-finding and Separation Rates within the Labor Market

The analysis in this chapter pictures employers and workers agreeing on three aspects of the employment arrangement: the cash hourly wage, the separation rate, and the job-finding rate. Only the first of these is considered in the conventional analysis of employment bargains. Is it meaningful to speak of an agreement about separation or job-finding rates?

Job separation is under the joint control of the two parties to an employment arrangement. Separations can occur unilaterally as quitting or layoffs. Alternatively, they may occur by prearrangement, as when a summer or other temporary job comes to an end. Evidence from the United States suggests that the latter case is particularly important for teenagers (Hall 1978). In cases where there is no advance agreement about the duration of the job, there are generally understandings about how the job will come to an end. It is fairly easy for workers to find out the past layoff rates of employers and reasonable to assume that these are guides to the future. Similarly, employers can inquire about the employment histories of potential workers to avoid those who have deviated from the norm for the market. Though neither party gives up the right to bring about a separation unilaterally in any one instance, both face penalties for systematic departures from the prevailing employment terms.

Agreement about job-finding rates is a harder issue. A very general argument can be made that a market operating at an inefficient job-finding rate will be displaced by one operating at the efficient rate. In the second market, everyone can be made better off than in the first. But this leaves the important question unanswered about how the market determines its job-finding rate. This point is discussed in my earlier paper. A market operating away from the efficient job-finding rate presents arbitrage opportunities for an intrepreneur willing to offer employment at alternative, efficient terms and to sell his workers' services to employers. Temporary employment firms could have exactly this function in clerical and other markets, though, of course, there are many other reasons for their existence as well. Alternatively, a market with an inefficient, high job-finding rate offers arbitrage profits to an employer who makes special efforts to advertise that jobs are readily available, but on terms favorable to the employer. As in the case of conventional supply-and-demand theory, the model presented here does not provide a fully worked-out story of how the market moves toward its equilibrium, but restricts its attention to the equilibrium itself.

While this discussion may lend some plausibility to the notion that the market does move eventually to the efficient equilibrium, it seems unlikely that the process is a speedy one. In particular, the prediction that the effect of a higher minimum wage is to stimulate turnover rather than to make jobs harder to find is a prediction for the long run. In the short run, the minimum wage seems likely to push the market into disequilibrium with an inefficiently low job-finding rate. The resulting lags are a potential complication in any empirical analysis of the effect of the minimum wage.

## 14.5  Conclusion

Jobs for young workers are readily available in the U.S. economy, in spite of minimum wage legislation that affects youths much more than any other segment of the labor force. Young workers find jobs just as fast as their older counterparts. The conventional analysis of the potential effects of a minimum wage suggests that it creates a shortage of jobs and so should make it more difficult for any one worker to find a job. Taken together, these constitute an apparent case against any important effect of the minimum wage. It seems that high unemployment rates of youths have to be blamed on something else.

This chapter has shown that a minimum wage can bring about high unemployment without causing a shortage of jobs or reducing the job-finding rate. Rather, in the long run, an effective minimum wage can induce the evolution of employment practices and arrangements that raise turnover. The minimum wage does not block the market from achieving an efficient degree of tightness, that is, an efficienctly high job-finding rate. In fact, under reasonable assumptions about turnover and recruiting costs, the efficient job-finding rate is a constant, unaffected by the minimum wage or the supply of and demand for labor. The adverse effects of the minimum wage are then concentrated in inefficiently high separation rates. The shockingly low average duration of jobs held by teenagers—less than three months—may be an important consequence of the minimum wage. If so, high unemployment among youths can be traced in part to the minimum wage, which makes them become unemployed too often even though it does not inhibit job-finding once they are unemployed.

# References

Bancroft, G. and S. Garfinkle. 1963. Job mobility in 1961. *Monthly Labor Review* 86:897–906.

Clark, K. and L. Summers. 1979. Labor market dynamics and unemployment: A reconsideration. *Brookings Papers on Economic Activity* 1/1979.

Hall, R. E. 1978. The nature and measurement of unemployment. NBER working paper no. 252.

Hall, R. E. 1979. A theory of the natural unemployment rate and the duration of employment. *Journal of Monetary Economics* 5:1–17.

Marston, S. 1976. Employment instability and high unemployment rates. *Brookings Papers on Economic Activity* 1/1976:169–203.

Mincer, J. 1976. Unemployment effects of minimum wages. *Journal of Political Economy* 84:87–104.

Welch, F. 1976. Minimum wage legislation in the united states. *In O. Ashenfelter and J. Blum, eds., Evaluating the labor market effects of social programs.* Industrial Relations Section, Princeton University, pp. 1–38.

## Comment    Christopher A. Sims

This chapter brings to bear on the youth unemployment problem a modern, abstractly interesting, theoretical apparatus. The operational implications of the analysis have not been pushed very far. The main one appears to be a refutation of the claim that, because job-finding rates for teenagers are not low relative to adult rates, the minimum wage must not be an important explanation for high youth unemployment rates. Hall is surely right that some of the impact of the minimum wage should be expected to show up in separation rates, as firms adapt and new firms enter exploiting the potential productivity gains from high unemployment (hence high employee-finding rates) and high separation rates.

Christopher A. Sims is associated with the Department of Economics at the University of Minnesota.

As the chapter makes clear, the relative importance of effects of the minimum on job-finding and on separation rates depends on the shapes of indifference curves and iso-cost functions about which there is essentially no information. If one presumed that in the absence of a minimum teenagers would have job-finding rates similar to adults and also that the minimum wage is a major explanatory factor for youth unemployment, then the facts that youth unemployment rates are high and job-finding rates for youths are not very different from adult rates would justify a conclusion that the minimum affects unemployment rates mainly through separation rates. Of course, in fact, it is quite plausible that youth job-finding rates would be much higher than adult job-finding rates in the absence of a minimum wage, so the question must remain open.

But the importance of this chapter lies less in its direct implications than in the promise of its style of analysis. The paper invokes the notion that labor market transactions involve implicit commitments about job duration on the part of both employers and employees. Hall follows most of the literature in this area in proceeding as if such implicit contracts work efficiently, but I think that in doing so he misses the main potential contribution of this kind of analysis to explaining the special character of youth job markets.

The labor market as a whole is rife with familiar externalities, most of which are regularly ignored in sophisticated theoretical work on equilibrium under uncertainty. Ignoring them may be justified for practical purposes as a first approximation, especially in developing aggregate conclusions. But some of the most important distinguishing features of the youth labor market are precisely that many of these externalities occur in magnified form there. Explicit long-term labor contracts are difficult to enforce legally, and raise moral hazard problems as well. Implicit contract theorists rely, as does Hall here, on the notion of "reputation" to enforce adherence to implicit contracts about duration. But youths who are taking their first few jobs have no reputation to guide their potential employers; furthermore, individual separations have very large impacts on their work histories. An employer who hires an inexperienced teenager and keeps him on twice the usual job tenure because he is reliable (or fires him quickly because he is unreliable) is performing a screening service for other employers for which he is not compensated. Job-finding rates matter to workers, and hiring rates matter to employers, but a worker's own employer's hiring rate (unlike the employer's separation rate) does not matter much to a worker. For older workers this externality is circumvented to some extent by seniority systems for layoffs and rehiring and by "internal labor markets." But these mechanisms are obviously much less important for youth labor markets.

An implicit contract theory framework which took account of these sources of externalities could be a valuable guide to empirical work with policy implications. As it is, casual meditation on the list of externalities in the preceding paragraph suggests the plausibility of a picture of the youth labor market very different from that Hall presents. One would think that in an unregulated market youths would place a socially inefficient premium on job stability (for fear that short tenure jobs, regardless of the reason for termination, would make their work history look unusually unstable). In addition, firms, having no way to get credit through the market for the contribution their hiring rates make to the job-finding rate, might put an inefficient premium on stability. A moderate minimum wage, by pushing the market in the direction of greater average turnover rates, may then make typical youths better off. Of course, as Summers and Clark emphasize in this volume (chapter 7), youths have diverse labor market experiences, and those who have low productivity may be made worse off by the minimum; this negative effect could operate mainly by decreasing the job-finding rate of the less productive group while preserving a high job-finding rate for the more productive majority and leaving an aggregate picture of a high job-finding rate.

This picture of the youth labor market and the minimum wage is put forth not as a firm conclusion, but as an indication of the range of reasonable views which remain consistent with a modern theoretical approach to the subject. Until more detailed theory is developed in tighter connection to empirical facts, Hall's picture of a youth labor market characterized by inefficiently high unemployment due to inefficiently high separation rates due in turn to the minimum wage remains in the category of stimulating speculation.

## Comment    Martin Neil Baily

Robert Hall has written an informative and elegant paper. Good theory is often uncomplicated; it focuses on the key relationships. The story comes through without a mess of algebra. Hall is following Mincer and others in incorporating turnover as an integral part of the analysis. This is the right way to go.

Trying to understand the nature of unemployment is like trying to put handcuffs on an octopus. You think you have it tied down and then another pair of tentacles get you round the throat. Hall presents a specific picture of teenage unemployment and it may very well be the correct one, but it is not the only one. Hall asserts that teenagers can find jobs easily, but that the minimum wage results in very short job tenure and excessive unemployment.

Martin Neil Baily is associated with the Brookings Institution.

There are, however, alternative scenarios consistent with observation. First, if the jobs open to teenagers do not match their job aspirations they may drift from job to job and in and out of the labor force of their own volition. Reducing the minimum wage would only reduce unemployment if it encouraged more low-wage but nevertheless attractive positions (like apprenticeships). It could have no impact at all.

Second, are jobs really easy to find? The evidence given for this view is that the average duration of unemployment spells is short and that the job-finding rate is similar for young persons and adults. The trouble is that words like "hard" and "easy" are not well defined. Consider a professional in his or her late thirties looking for a job. The job will be a major source of satisfaction or frustration and will probably be held for several years or perhaps for the remainder of the working life. Three months, six months, even longer is an appropriate time to spend searching or waiting for the right job to open up. On the other hand, consider the position of teenagers. Males 16 to 19 in 1974 spent nearly five months unemployed on average and then spent less than three months employed (see Clark and Summers, "Labor Market Dynamics and Unemployment," tables 4 and 8). Such a long wait for such a short job cannot possibly reflect productive search. Relative to the length of time they are held, jobs for teenagers appear hard to find. This point is important if one is predicting how a properly functioning youth labor market would work. It could be that young people want jobs that last only for short periods, either because of schooling or simply to sample several possible careers before settling down. If so, then an optimal pattern of unemployment would show teens with shorter spells of employment and very much shorter spells of unemployment than adults.

Third, since the incidence of unemployment is very unevenly distributed, the *average* rate of job finding or length of unemployment spell may not be relevant. Most of the unemployment problem and indeed most of the impact of the minimum wage may come from the minority of teenagers that have very great difficulty finding jobs.

However, while Hall's scenario is not obviously correct, it is not obviously incorrect either, so let me take it as given and consider his model on its own terms. The central variables in the analysis are the job-finding rate $f$ and the separation rate $s$. The discussion of the separation rate was a little confusing because it failed to distinguish between separations initiated or desired by a firm and those initiated by a worker. With due allowance for recruiting and training costs, firms will welcome quittings and initiate layoffs when the wage exceeds the value of the marginal product. The freedom to make layoffs is valued by firms. But during periods of high product demand, separations are unwelcome and firms will discourage them. Although the available data on quittings and layoffs do not provide perfect proxies for the two cases, the way these series move against each other over the cycle does suggest the importance of the distinction. I would have preferred "layoff rate" to "separation rate" as a description of the key parameter $s$ in the model.

My second misgiving concerns the ability of an unregulated labor market for teenagers to achieve the efficient solution described by Hall. In my own work on contract theory and temporary layoff models I assumed that everyone knew the true probability distributions. Firms with very variable employment patterns would have to compensate their workers fully for the resulting high probability of layoff. This assumption was made apologetically, but nowadays rational expectations are assumed routinely. I would echo Christopher Sim's view that in the case of teenagers the assumption is a very strong one. In 1978, 42% of those unemployed aged 16 to 19 had never worked before. It is hard to believe they knew the layoff probabilities for all their prospective jobs.

Is it necessary to use an implicit contract-type model to reconcile a minimum wage analysis with high turnover? Not really. All that is needed is a formulation incorporating frequent fluctuations in product demand. Suppose $\varepsilon_{it}$ is a shift parameter for the $i$th firm in period $t$. The shifts could come either in the product price for a competitive firm or in the position of the demand curve for a monopolistic firm. The value of the marginal product is then $V_i(L_{it}, \varepsilon_{it})$ where $L_{it}$ is employment. Firms equate $V_i$ to the minimum wage $\bar{W}$, giving labor demand $L_{it} = D_i(\bar{W}, \varepsilon_{it})$ at any instant. In a labor market made up of firms like firm $i$, aggregate employment will decrease with increases in the minimum wage and jobs are generally rationed. But there is quite possibly a great deal of turnover with vacancies opening up frequently and layoffs occurring frequently. It simply depends on the distributions of the $\varepsilon_i$.

Let me now finish with a few comments on the teenage unemployment problem (these comments are not addressed specifically to Hall's chapter).

1. I wonder about the magnitude of the impact of the minimum wage. When aggregate unemployment raises, the rate of wage inflation diminishes little and slowly. When the supply of teenage labor increases, would we expect the teenage relative wage to move quickly to a new equilibrium. Even in an unregulated market I would expect to see persistent high levels of unemployment as a result of the baby boom and the increase in labor-force participation.

Richard Freeman has been studying union wage behavior recently and he has observed that entry level wages are raised relative to the wages of senior workers. The legal minimum wage of $3.35 per hour hardly matters when the union entry wage is $5.00 per hour. Of course, unionized workers are in the minority, but unions are very influential in many of the industries and occupations that would be the best bet for young persons currently out of work.

Few if any of the existing studies of the impact of the minimum wage test alternative explanations of the persistent high level of teenage unemployment. If the minimum wage is the only possible explanation, presumably there is no need for econometrics. A high union entry wage gives an alternative. A model incorporating slow relative wage adjustment following shifts in supply or demand would be another.

2. Our inability to agree on the nature of youth unemployment suggest that there is no simple, single scenario that does justice to reality. Some teenagers are prevented from getting jobs by the minimum wage, some are prevented by other sources of wage stickiness and some could get jobs but aspire to become highly paid basketball players and will not accept them. Teenage unemployment probably has both voluntary and involuntary aspects to it.

3. It is legitimate to view joblessness among students somewhat differently from other unemployment. But simply to add employed youths to in-school youths to give a figure for those "productivly occupied" gives too rosy a picture. There is a crisis in our schools comparable to the problems in the labor market. Absenteeism and absence of real learning are common. There is a social problem afflicting a significant minority of our young people encompassing joblessness, crime, unwanted pregnancy, partial illiteracy, and lack of technical skills.

4. Migration has been a major factor in the labor market difficulties of young people, especially of blacks. In the early 1950s a much larger fraction of young blacks lived in rural areas than today. The decline of employment in agriculture has thrown a heavy burden of adjustment onto the low-skill urban labor market. New waves of low-skill immigrants and their children are perpetuating the problem.

5. The degree of inequality of opportunity between a suburban middle-class teenager and a lower-class ghetto youth is deeply disturbing. We must try to clarify the causes of the problem and do something about them, for we should not let the situation persist for generation after generation.

# 15 Youth Unemployment in Britain and the United States Compared

Richard Layard

British unemployment differs markedly from U.S. unemployment in two ways: (1) youth unemployment has been much lower relative to adult unemployment for decades; and (2) spells of unemployment last on average about twice as long (at a given point of the cycle), with the difference being greater for adults.

There are also two points of similarity: (1) in both countries youth unemployment rises relative to adult unemployment in slumps; and (2) in both countries the demand for young workers is very sensitive to wage levels. I shall examine these phenomena in turn, devoting one section to each.

Youth unemployment is relatively low in Britain, but why? It seems likely that both equilibrium and disequilibrium factors are involved (see section 15.1). An equilibrium approach to unemployment leads one to look mainly for supply-side factors which might affect the choice of whether to be "unemployed", rather than employed. I find good evidence that the higher relative youth unemployment in the U.S. reflects in part higher U.S. incomes, which also explain the remarkably low U.S. levels of labor force participation compared with Britain. Supply behavior is also influenced by price effects: income maintenance for adults is less generous in the U.S. than in Britain and this tends to reduce the relative unemployment of adults. Another price effect in supply comes from the rigidity of the British labor market, which refuses admission to

Richard Layard is professor of economics at the London School of Economics and head of the Centre for Labour Economics there. He is also associated with the National Bureau of Economic Research. The author is grateful to Tomoko Barker and Laura Nelson for excellent research assistance, and to John Abowd, Kim Clark, David Ellwood, Richard Freeman, Dan Hamermesh, Larry Lau, Peter Makeham and Beatrice Reubens for invaluable help and advice. A part of this work was financed by the U.K. Department of Employment.

apprenticeship programs to most people over the age of sixteen; this provides a strong incentive for youths to be employed.

I next explore whether differential disequilibrium can help to explain higher relative youth employment in the States. The obvious influence here is the minimum wage law, which does not exist in Britain. Though there is some noncompliance, it seems probable that the minimum wage has contributed to youth unemployment in the U.S. But the structure of age-wage profiles does not reveal any sharp differences between the countries.

Finally, there is an important difference in information. Almost every school-leaver in Britain is interviewed by the Careers Service before leaving school, and nearly a quarter find their first job through the Service. By contrast, in the U.S. the state plays little more role in the placement of youths than in the placement of adults. Unfortunately, I cannot say how important this factor is, nor could one estimate the influence of any of the factors that I document without analyzing data on many more countries. This should soon be feasible.

The next issue is the efficiency cost of the unemployment in each age group, and the impact of the unemployment upon the level of social inequality. To do this one needs to look at duration (see section 15.2). If unemployment arises from disequilibrium job-rationing, its cost (relative to the gross output lost) is approximately proportional to the average duration of the uncompleted spells. Taking all age groups at a given point in the cycle, average durations are about twice as high in Britain as in the U.S. And the average number of spells per year among those experiencing any unemployment has been about the same. Thus, even though average levels of unemployment have been higher in the U.S. than in Britain, the efficiency cost (relative to GNP) has been lower. Furthermore, annual unemployment has been more evenly distributed across people.

As between youths and adults, the higher relative rate of youth unemployment in the U.S. turns out to be mainly due to higher relative durations. Thus the share of youth unemployment in the total efficiency cost of unemployment may be higher in the U.S. On the other hand, the less generous scales of unemployment benefit may mean that adults suffer more when they are unemployed than youths do. Thus while the British worry particularly about youth unemployment (and now about long-term adult unemployment), the Americans may be right to worry particularly about adult male unemployment. The British experience, however, does suggest that a good case can be made for a Careers Service for youth. Feldstein argued some years ago that the U.S. should have such a service. Given the market failures that arise in the presence of asymmetrical information, there does seem to be a case for this proposal.

A further issue is the time-series behavior of youth unemployment rates (see section 15.3). In the late 1970s youth unemployment was much higher in Britain than ever before. This phenomenon has led to endless speculation about structural change. But in fact it is due almost entirely to cyclical factors. For in Britain, as in the U.S., the age structure of unemployment rates can be well explained by the state of the cycle, by relative youth earnings, and by demographic factors. In the 1970s the size of the youth cohort increased, as did relative youth earnings, so our equations tend, if anything, to overpredict recent levels of youth unemployment. There is no clear evidence that Britian has moved permanently toward the American pattern of high relative youth unemployment rates.

Across towns, the level of youth unemployment varies with the level of adult unemployment, in Britain as in America. The elasticity of youth unemployment with respect to adult unemployment is much less in the cross-section (0.6) than in the time series (1.4). This is what I would expect since over time youths are particularly strongly affected by cyclical variations in rates of hiring, and these cyclical effects are not present in the cross-section. American findings, however, do not in this respect mirror British experience.[1]

Finally, in section 15.4, I confirm that it is reasonable to find wage effects on youth unemployment by looking at the effect of wages on youth employment. I estimate the demand system derived from the trans-log cost function on time series data for British manufacturing (April and October 1949-69). Holding constant output and capital, the own-wage elasticity of demand is around $-1.3$ for youths, $-1.6$ for women, and $-0.3$ for girls and men. These effects are broadly consistent with the American evidence. Thus, if there must be minimum wages, the case for a separate youth rate seems overwhelming.

### 15.1   Why Is Relative Youth Unemployment Higher in the U.S.?

#### 15.1.1   The Puzzle

In the U.S., unemployment rates for young people are much higher relative to rates for adults than they are in Britain. There are various ways of looking at this. A crude way is to examine the unemployment rate of, say, all those under 25 relative to the unemployment rate of those over 25. This comparison is made in table 15.1, which is based on Census data since this is the source that is most truly comparable between the two countries, both in its questions and method of data collection.[2] It does not matter that it is rather out of date since I am mainly concerned with long-run differences between the countries. As the table shows, for males the rate for those under 25 is nearly twice as high (relative to the adult

Table 15.1    Age-specific Unemployment Rates for Nonstudents
in Britain (1971) and U.S. (1970)

|  | Percentage | | | |
|  | Males | | Females | |
|  | Britain | U.S. | Britain | U.S. |
| Under 25 | 6.6 | 9.6 | 5.1 | 8.2 |
| 25 + | 3.6 | 2.8 | 3.2 | 4.1 |
| Total | 4.2 | 3.6 | 3.7 | 4.9 |
| (Under 25 rate divided by 25 + rate) | (1.8) | (3.4) | (1.6) | (2.0) |

SOURCE AND NOTES: See appendix A.

rate) in the U.S. as in Britain.[3] There is less difference for women, but still some.

However, these differences could be misleading. For the U.S. labor force aged under 25 is much more recently out of school than the British labor force under 25; so one might *expect* that fewer of its members would have been absorbed into employment.[4] To deal with this problem one can compare the unemployment rates of people with similar periods of experience since leaving school. This comparison can be made in table 15.2.[5] For example, if one wants to compare British youths with U.S. whites [US($W$)], one notes that a half of 16 year olds in Britain were out of school, as were a half of 19 year old U.S. whites, and in each case about one-third had left school in the last year. If we now compare the unemployment rates of these groups for males, we find they were 8.8% in Britain and 11.2% for U.S. whites. By contrast, the adult unemployment rates (for those aged 30–34) were in the opposite order: 3.9% in Britain and only 2.6% for U.S. whites.

For women, the difference in age profiles between Britain and the U.S. is less striking. This may be because the concept of unemployment is more slippery for adult women than for any other group. In any case, there are no comprehensive data on female unemployment in Britain except at Census years, so I shall henceforth confine my remarks to men. For unemployed men the regular data come from registrations at employment offices, and these are quite comprehensive since most unemployed men register. The data show that at any point in the cycle the youth unemployment rates are lower relative to the adult rate than they are in the U.S. (see tables 15.3 and 15.4).

In passing, one should note the profound implications of this for the comparison of aggregate unemployment rates between Britain and the U.S. The normal assertion is that the British rate of registered unemployed needs to be raised by a fifth or less to allow for unregistered female unemployment and thus to get it onto a "survey basis" comparable with the U.S. rate.[6] This comparison always makes the U.S. rate look awfully high. For example, in 1976 the U.S. Bureau of Labor Statistics estimate that British unemployment adjusted to U.S. concepts was 6.4% compared with the published British figure of 5.6% and the U.S. figure of 7.7%. Thus the U.S. rate is still 1.3% higher. But at the same time the prime-age male rate (aged 25–54) was about 0.8% *lower* in the U.S. than in Britain.[7] In fact, it seems likely that in every year in the 1970s except 1976 the U.S. prime-age male rate was below the British. It is therefore well to remember how much the aggregate U.S. rate is boosted not only by the relatively high rate of female unemployment but also by the relatively high rate of youth unemployment.[8]

The question is why the youth rates should be so much higher (relative to adult rates) than in Britain. At least five possibilities come to mind.

### 15.1.2   Income Effects in Labor Supply

The U.S. is a richer society. To investigate the effects of income I shall begin by looking at labor force participation. Participation rates are

**Table 15.2**     **Schooling, Labor Force Participation and Unemployment in Britain (1971) and U.S. (1970)**

| Age | % of population who are nonstudents | | | % of nonstudents who are in labor force | | | % of nonstudents in civilian labor force who are unemployed | | |
|---|---|---|---|---|---|---|---|---|---|
| | Britain | US(W) | US(B) | Britain | US(W) | US(B) | Britain | US(W) | US(B) |
| | 1 | 2 | 3 | 4 | 5 | 6 | 7 | 8 | 9 |
| **Males** | | | | | | | | | |
| (15) | (31.4) | (4.4) | (7.6) | (87.3) | (32.5) | (26.5) | (21.7) | (16.0) | (20.6) |
| 16 | 52.3 | 7.9 | 11.8 | 97.1 | 48.6 | 34.7 | 8.8 | 21.6 | 27.0 |
| 17 | 71,0 | 13.3 | 20.5 | 97.9 | 65.3 | 48.0 | 6.7 | 19.0 | 27.1 |
| 18 | 78.8 | 30.2 | 45.0 | 98.1 | 82.8 | 71.8 | 7.2 | 12.9 | 20.8 |
| 19 | 83.6 | 48.2 | 61.6 | 98.0 | 86.4 | 71.8 | 7.1 | 11.2 | 18.6 |
| 20 | 85.5 | 59.8 | 77.8 | 97.8 | 88.3 | 76.0 | 6.9 | 9.6 | 14.6 |
| 21–24 | 92.8 | 75.8 | 87.5 | 98.2 | 92.4 | 82.1 | 5.4 | 6.4 | 10.4 |
| 25–29 | 98.2 | 89.5 | 93.3 | 98.3 | 95.6 | 87.3 | 4.2 | 3.3 | 6.0 |
| 30–34 | 99.2 | 94.7 | 95.3 | 98.2 | 96.2 | 89.1 | 3.9 | 2.6 | 4.7 |
| **Females** | | | | | | | | | |
| (15) | (31.7) | (5.0) | (8.4) | (87.0) | (19.5) | (16.7) | (14.9) | (15.9) | (25.4) |
| 16 | 52.0 | 8.5 | 13.1 | 94.1 | 26.5 | 20.7 | 6.8 | 21.9 | 33.0 |
| 17 | 69.7 | 15.0 | 22.2 | 91.6 | 35.2 | 29.2 | 5.3 | 19.3 | 31.1 |
| 18 | 79.6 | 38.9 | 46.9 | 86.5 | 59.6 | 44.4 | 5.0 | 11.7 | 24.4 |
| 19 | 85.2 | 54.9 | 63.6 | 80.9 | 63.1 | 50.6 | 4.8 | 9.3 | 21.0 |
| 20 | 87.2 | 67.6 | 79.5 | 74.4 | 62.4 | 55.3 | 4.5 | 7.8 | 15.9 |
| 21–24 | 95.9 | 85.6 | 89.8 | 61.1 | 56.9 | 58.9 | 4.1 | 5.7 | 11.8 |
| 25–29 | 99.2 | 95.4 | 95.5 | 43.1 | 43.1 | 58.3 | 4.3 | 4.9 | 8.5 |
| 30–34 | 99.4 | 96.6 | 96.3 | 44.8 | 41.8 | 59.1 | 4.2 | 4.6 | 7.0 |

Source and Notes: See appendix A.

Table 15.3    Male Unemployment Rates for Nonstudents: By Age (1976)

| Age | Britain (Jan.) | Britain (July) | U.S. (All year) |
|---|---|---|---|
| 16–17 | 12.4 | 26.8 | 28.4 |
| 18–19 | 11.1 | 10.6 | 17.3 |
| 20–24 | 10.0 | 9.3 | 11.0 |
| 25–34 | 6.6 | 6.2 | 6.2 |
| 35–44 | 5.5 | 5.2 | 4.1 |
| 45–54 | 4.6 | 4.5 | 4.0 |
| 55–59 | 4.9 | 4.9 | } 4.2 |
| 60–64 | } 9.5 | } 9.5 | |
| 65 + | | | 5.2 |
| Total | 6.9 | 7.3 | 7.0 |

SOURCE: *Department of Employment Gazette*, January 1979, p. 40. *Employment and Training Report of the President, 1978*, tables A3, A19 and B7.

NOTES: 1. U.S. data include persons in school if they were also in the labour force.

2. A fine age breakdown of youth unemployment is only available in the U.S. in October and in Britain quarterly (and till recently only in January and July). The first three U.S. figures relate to October, but other data show that for those aged 16–21 not in school the October rate is quite close to the annual average (Bureau of Labor Statistics, *Handbook of Labor Statistics* 1977 p. 57). There is surprisingly little month to month variation in the unemployment rate for such people. In Britain the youth unemployment rate is much higher in June/July than at any other time.

dramatically lower at all ages in the U.S. (except among the old). Table 15.2, gives the figures for those under 35, and the same is true for all age groups under 65. Whereas virtually all British males who are not incapacitated participate, the number of U.S. males not in the labor force is greater at every age than the number who are unemployed. (This has been true in most years, except for those aged 25–34 in a few recent years.)

If income accounts for this difference between the two countries, it should also have produced a decline in age-specific participation rates over time within the U.S., which we do indeed observe. It should also lead to lower participation rates in higher income groups, which we again observe for adults. But for youths, cross-sectional data may suggest the reverse pattern.[9] I believe that this can be explained by the role of job-rationing in the youth labor market. Suppose that family connections have an important effect on a teenager's ability to find a job, and thus in turn on his willingness to participate. If family connections can be represented by income relative to the mean $(y/\bar{y})$ then the probability of participation might be approximated by some function such as

$$p = f\left[y^{-\alpha}\left(\frac{y}{\bar{y}}\right)^{\beta}\right] \qquad \alpha, \beta, f' > 0$$

If $1 > \beta - \alpha > 0$, we should observe (1) that in a cross-section high-income youths participated more than low-income youths and (2) that over time and across countries, participation fell as average income rose.

Our main concern, however, is with the participation rate of youths relative to adults. This is much lower in America than in Britain (where it is roughly equal).[10] Can this be explained by income levels? It seems quite likely. For over time youth participation rates (of nonstudents) have fallen by a greater proportion than adult participation rates.[11] Thus it may

**Table 15.4**        **Unemployment Rates by Age**

| | Males | | | | Females | | | |
|---|---|---|---|---|---|---|---|---|
| | Britain | | U.S. | | Britain | | U.S. | |
| | Under 20* | All ages | 18–19 | All ages | Under 20* | All ages | 18–19 | All ages |
| 1959 | 1.6 | 2.2 | 15.1 | 5.3 | 0.8 | 1.5 | 13.1 | 5.9 |
| 1960 | 1.0 | 1.7 | 16.5 | 5.4 | 0.6 | 1.2 | 13.0 | 5.9 |
| 1961 | 0.8 | 1.5 | 15.2 | 6.4 | 0.5 | 1.0 | 14.5 | 7.2 |
| 1962 | 1.7 | 2.1 | 13.0 | 5.2 | 1.1 | 1.3 | 12.3 | 6.2 |
| 1963 | 1.9 | 2.6 | 14.8 | 5.2 | 1.4 | 1.5 | 14.9 | 6.5 |
| 1964 | 1.3 | 1.8 | 13.3 | 4.6 | 0.8 | 1.1 | 15.3 | 6.2 |
| 1965 | 1.1 | 1.6 | 10.4 | 4.0 | 0.7 | 0.9 | 13.7 | 5.5 |
| 1966 | 1.2 | 1.7 | 8.4 | 3.2 | 0.7 | 0.8 | 12.6 | 4.8 |
| 1967 | 2.6 | 2.8 | 10.7 | 3.1 | 1.3 | 1.1 | 16.1 | 5.2 |
| 1968 | 2.6 | 3.1 | 9.5 | 2.9 | 1.2 | 1.0 | 12.9 | 4.8 |
| 1969 | 2.7 | 3.1 | 8.9 | 2.8 | 1.1 | 0.9 | 11.0 | 4.7 |
| 1970 | 3.4 | 3.4 | 14.1 | 4.4 | 1.4 | 1.0 | 16.4 | 5.9 |
| 1971 | 5.4 | 4.5 | 14.6 | 5.3 | 2.4 | 1.3 | 16.7 | 6.9 |
| 1972 | 6.8 | 4.9 | 11.9 | 4.9 | 3.1 | 1.5 | 15.2 | 6.6 |
| 1973 | 3.3 | 3.5 | 9.9 | 4.1 | 2.0 | 1.1 | 13.8 | 6.0 |
| 1974 | 3.6 | 3.5 | 15.3 | 4.8 | 2.0 | 1.0 | 16.9 | 6.7 |
| 1975 | 7.4 | 5.2 | 18.6 | 7.9 | 5.3 | 1.9 | 19.0 | 9.3 |
| 1976 | 9.1 | 6.7 | 17.3 | 7.0 | 8.0 | 3.0 | 18.5 | 8.6 |
| 1977 | 9.6 | 7.0 | — | 6.2 | 9.4 | 3.8 | — | 8.2 |

SOURCE: British data kindly supplied by Peter Makeham of the Department of Employment from his forthcoming study of youth unemployment. For his basic findings see Department of Employment *Gazette*, August 1978. U.S.: *Employment and Training Report of the President, 1978*, tables B7 and A19.

NOTES: 1. *The British youth rates relate to July but exclude from the unemployed "unemployed school-leavers" (i.e., people under 18 who have never had a full-time job). This is to eliminate variation due to changes in school-leaving dates and dates of the unemployment count. If school-leavers are included the youth figures are males: 1959, 1.7; 1975, 9.8; females: 1959, 1.0; 1975, 7.4. Adult students are also excluded—there were very few of these till about 1975 when the National Union of Students began encouraging students to claim benefit (they are now no longer able to claim).

2. If British youth unemployment rates are measured in January (which is impossible for 1974 and 1975), they have similar year to year movements to this series but with the ratio of July to January rising secularly as the employment situation worsens.

3. U.S. rates are all-year rates.

Table 15.5     Average Hourly Earnings of Manual Workers within Each Age
Group as Percentage of Average Hourly Earnings of All Manual
Workers in the Same Column 1976–77

| | Britain | | | U.S. | |
| Age | Males | Females | Age | Males | Females |
| --- | --- | --- | --- | --- | --- |
| Under 18 | 51 | 68 | | | |
| 18–20 | 76 | 90 | 16–19 | 56 | 74 |
| 21–24 | 96 | 100 | 20–24 | 82 | 97 |

NOTE: U.S. data relate to workers paid at hourly rates (including part-timers and students) in May 1976. British data relate to full-time manual workers in April 1977.

SOURCE: Britain: Department of Employment, *New Earnings Survey 1977*, pp. A18 and A19. U.S.: U.S. Department of Labor, B.L.S. *Weekly and Hourly Earnings Data from the Current Population Survey*, Special Labor Force Report 195, 1977, table 4.

well be that higher income leads to disproportionate reduction in working-time at the beginning of life. Otherwise it is difficult to explain why so many American parents are willing to support children who are not even looking for work.[12] It is hard to imagine such a phenomenon occurring in a much poorer country.

Turning to unemployment, we again find that the unemployment rate of youths relative to adults has an upward trend in the U.S.[13] This is consistent with the notion that the U.S./British differences may be partly a function of the difference in income levels,[14] with leisure in youth being more luxurious than leisure in middle age. However, the story is much more complicated than this, and, while arguing that income effects are a part of the story, I now turn to other possible explanations.[15]

### 15.1.3   Price Effects in Labor Supply: Social Security

Does social security help to explain the lower relative unemployment of adults in the U.S.? Quite possibly. For adults, the key variable is net income out of work relative to net income in work. This is much lower in the U.S. than in Britain. In Britain the average male replacement ratio is .75 for all those currently unemployed and .69 for those currently employed.[16] In the U.S. the best data I can find are Feldstein's, which relate to individuals aged 25 to 55 excluding labor force entrants and reentrants.[17] Nearly all of these were entitled to UI, which would not be true of many younger people nor of many labor force entrants and reentrants. Yet even for the relatively "privileged" group the average replacement ratio was .59 for the unemployed and .55 for the population as a whole. Thus the U.S. system is less generous than the British system to the adult unemployed.[18]

But the U.S. system is also of course less generous to youths (see appendix B). However, for youths it is not the income replacement ratio that matters. What matters is the *consumption* "replacement ratio," and, given the indulgence of American parents, this may be quite high.[19]

Thus the lower adult income replacement ratios in the U.S. are probably an important reason for relatively high youth unemployment rates. But it is sometimes suggested that in addition Aid to Families with Dependent Children (AFDC) claimed by the family head raises relative youth rates. The argument is this. In Britain a child not in school is treated as an independent economic unit, even if living with the family. Thus the income received by a single parent mother with dependent children will be independent of the work behavior of the older child. The fact that she is subsidized will have an income effect on the youth's behavior, but that is all. In the U.S., however, a single-parent mother on AFDC has her AFDC income reduced (at a two-thirds marginal tax rate) for any income earned by a child who contributes to the family expenses. This would set up a substitution effect against the child working as well as an income effect. Moreover, if AFDC is lost because of excessive family earnings, the family also loses its Medicaid privileges. However, one would expect the mother would normally say the youth did not contribute to family expenses.[20] In this case AFDC sets up a substitution effect in favor of the child's working, since the parent's earnings are taxed, the child's are not, and the child's and parent's leisure must be substitutes.

In any case, the data show clearly that welfare is not a major part of the teenage unemployment story. For in families where the head is not on welfare the ratio of unemployment to employment is 97% of the overall ratio (including those on welfare); for blacks the comparable figure is 88%.[21] I conclude that AFDC does not explain the high relative youth unemployment rate, but the lower level of adult benefits may help to explain the low relative level of U.S. adult unemployment.

### 15.1.4    Price Effects in Labor Supply:
         Age Limits for Apprenticeship

Labor supply is affected not only by the cost of being unemployed, but by the returns to being employed. For many British teenagers these returns are very high. To become a skilled worker you will generally have to serve an apprenticeship, and most apprenticeships have to be entered at the age of 16. Thus the discounted cost of not getting a job at 16 can be quite high. This helps to explain low unemployment rates *and* high participation rates for young males. It does not apply to young women, few of whom become apprentices. This may explain why the U.S./British age profiles of unemployment differ more for men than for women (see table 15.1).

In the more flexible U.S. situation, the youth market is less separated and less institutionalized than in Britain. It may be disadvantageous to be in a somewhat separated market in the face of business cycle variations in demand, but it may be an advantage to be separated when it comes to the effect of exogenous increases in youth wages. This brings me to the question of the minimum wage.

### 15.1.5   Price Effects in Labor Demand

The U.S. has statutory minimum wages (identical for young and old) now covering most of the labor force. Britain only has statutory minimums in a few industries (mainly retailing and catering), though most other wages are covered by collective bargaining, which may also introduce rigidities into the structure.[22] However, in both statutory sectors and those covered by bargaining, youths and young women have special rates that are lower than those for adults.

It is difficult to draw any conclusions about the effects of minimum wages on relative youth unemployment by comparing the slope of British and American age-wage profiles, since so many *cetera* are not *para*. However, table 15.5 shows hourly earnings for manual workers of each age relative to the average for all ages. This does not suggest that on average American youths are relatively overpaid. As a further check, table 15.6 shows the average *weekly* earnings of youths relative to the all-age average. The median age of U.S. nonstudent workers aged under 25 is about 22, and British workers with comparable work experience are aged about 19. Again, it does not seem that young U.S. workers have higher relative pay than young British workers.[23]

But of course there is always the problem that we never observe the wage that would have been paid to those who do not get employed. The same problem arises when we look at the relation between the *distribution* of youth wages and the minimum wage. According to Ashenfelter and Smith, in the covered sector the proportion of workers aged 17–19 paid the federal minimum wage or less was only 8% in 1973 and 12% in

Table 15.6    Average Weekly Earnings within Each Age Group as Percentage of Average Weekly Earnings of Workers of All Ages in the Same Column 1976–77

|          | Britain | | U.S. | |
| Age | Males | Females | Males | Females |
| --- | --- | --- | --- | --- |
| Under 18 | 42 | 58 | | |
| 18–20 | 63 | 78 | 59 | 80 |
| 21–24 | 84 | 96 | 59 | 80 |
| 25–29 | 98 | 116 | 89 | 104 |

NOTE: U.S. data relate to annual earnings of year-round, full-time workers. British data relate to weekly earnings of full-time employees in the survey week or month.

SOURCE: Britain: Department of Employment, *New Earnings Survey 1977*, pp. A18 and A19. U.S.: Department of Commerce, Bureau of the Census, *Current Population Report*, Series P–60 no. 114., *Money Income in 1976 of Families and Persons in the U.S.* 1978 pp. 203–4.

1975.[24] The proportion in the uncovered sector was about one-half in 1973, but this sector was small. Thus the fraction of employed workers who would have been paid less than the minimum wage is not enormous; and, in addition, for employed workers the minimum wage is not paid in about a third of such cases. However, against this we have not allowed for the possible employment effects of the minimum wage, which could have ejected many low wage workers from the population being observed. It is therefore interesting to compare the shape of the British and U.S. wage distribution for young people, to see whether the U.S. distribution looks as though it is missing its lower tail. For males, the lower quartile was about 80% of the median for both U.S. whites aged 16–19 and for British youths aged under 18 and 18–20,[25] providing no evidence of a reduced lower tail in the U.S. Unfortunately, the published figures do not permit a similar calculation for U.S. blacks. Given the good time-series evidence for the effect of minimum wages on youth employment and unemployment,[26] I am inclined to conclude that minimum wages may contribute a little toward the higher rates of white youth unemployment in the U.S. and a lot to the higher still rates of black youth unemployment.

### 15.1.6   Information: The British Careers Service

Finally, we consider an important institutional feature of the British youth labor market: the Careers Service. About 97% of school-leavers register with the Careers Service.[27] Most of them are interviewed by a Careers Officer while they are in school and about a quarter get their first job through the Service. The state apparatus makes much more effort to find jobs for school-leavers than it does for adults.[28]

The following shows the process by which school-leavers find jobs. Each year over 650,000 youngsters leave school before the age of 18, most of them in June and July. The number who had still not found jobs is as follows (figures given in thousands):[29]

|           | 1974 | 1975 | 1976 | 1977 | 1978 |
|-----------|------|------|------|------|------|
| September | 33   | 118  | 142  | 166  | 131  |
| October   | 13   | 65   | 78   | 93   | 76   |
| November  | 8    | 40   | n.k. | 69   | 53   |
| December  | n.k. | 32   | 48   | 54   | 40   |

Since the school-leaving age was raised to 16 (with effect from 1973), the vast majority of all school-leavers have been leaving at the age of 16. Yet the unemployment rate has been hardly any higher for people aged 16–17 than for those aged 18–19 or 20–24 (see table 15.3). This suggests a relatively successful initial absorption of school-leavers, but considerable problems arising after the first job is over.

## 15.2 Duration as an Indicator of the Cost and Distribution of Unemployment

We have not so far compared the economic cost of unemployment in Britain and the U.S. To assess the economic cost of a given *stock* of unemployment one needs to know how long it has lasted. The key statistic is the distribution of those currently unemployed by the length of time they have been unemployed to date (i.e., the distribution of "interrupted spells"). Since this is not universally agreed, I should perhaps first justify this focus on interrupted spells.

It seems reasonable to suppose that the value of additional leisure varies with the amount of leisure already experienced. Thus if we want to cost the unemployment experienced in a particular week we look at the amount of unemployment already experienced by the unemployed. If a person could produce $W$ per week (gross) and values his $t^{th}$ week's leisure at $V_t$, then the economic cost of the $t^{th}$ week of unemployment is

$$C_t = W - V_t$$

Thus the total cost of unemployment per week is

$$(1) \qquad \sum_{t=1}^{\infty} N_t C_t = N \cdot \left( \sum_{t=1}^{\infty} \frac{N_t}{N} \cdot C_t \right)$$

where $N_t$ are the numbers with $t$ weeks unemployment experience and $N = \Sigma N_t$.[30] The significance of a given stock of unemployment ($N$) thus depends on the distribution of the interrupted durations ($N_t/N$).

This applies equally in a steady or a nonsteady state. However, for those who are naturally inclined to think of unemployment in terms of flows, there is of course an analogous expression which shows how in a steady state the significance of a given *flow* of unemployment ($F$) depends on the distribution of *completed* durations. Suppose $F$ is the flow per period of entrants whose completed duration will be $d$ periods, and $T_d$ is the total cost of a completed spell lasting $d$ weeks. Then the total cost per week in a steady state is

$$(2) \qquad \sum_{d=1}^{\infty} F_d T_d = F \cdot \left( \sum_{t=1}^{\infty} \frac{F_d}{F} \cdot T_d \right)$$

where $F = \Sigma F_d$. Most members of the public, however (and even most academics), have no idea what the flow into unemployment is, and it seems much better to focus on the average cost of the stock of unemployment rather than of the flow.[31]

To measure this average cost it is probably sufficient to concentrate on the mean spell length, at any rate on the assumption that unemployment is involuntary. For then, in the case of a person who has been unemployed so far for $t$ weeks and who is normally paid his marginal product[32]

$$C_t = W - V_t = \frac{t}{52\,\varepsilon}W$$

where $\varepsilon$ is the compensated elasticity of supply of annual weeks. The total cost relative to potential labor earnings is

$$u\frac{(\overline{tW})_U}{52\,\varepsilon}\frac{1}{\overline{W}_T}$$

where $u$ is the unemployment rate, $U$ relates to the unemployed, and $T$ to the total labor force. If duration and wages are independent, this reduces to

$$u\bar{t}\left(\frac{1}{52\,\varepsilon}\frac{\overline{W}_U}{\overline{W}_T}\right)$$

Thus assuming the term in brackets to be similar in the U.S. and Britain, $u\bar{t}$ is a good index of the cost of unemployment relative to potential earnings.[33]

This index is shown in table 15.7. Since duration in Britain is generally twice as large as in the U.S. (at a similar point in the cycle), the relative cost is higher even though the rates are generally lower. This is why people in Britain tend to worry more about unemployment.

Another possible reason for being interested in the mean uncompleted duration is that it is also equal to the mean time that those currently unemployed will remain unemployed from now on.[34] The length of the uncompleted duration may thus give some idea of the plausibility of viewing workers as engaged in search rather than (as we have hitherto assumed) as being rationed. There certainly appears to be more search unemployment in the U.S. than in Britain.

Of course, if a given stock of unemployment is associated with a longer duration, this means not only that it is more costly but also that it is more unequally distributed. Fewer people will be experiencing more unemployment (if we ignore for the time being the problem of repeated spells). Table 15.8 gives some relevant figures for all age groups combined.[35] We find for 1972–77 an average male *completed* duration of about 7 weeks in the U.S. and 13 weeks in Britain, with corresponding differences in probability of an individual's becoming unemployed. These differences are consistent with the picture of a more mobile society in which all durations are shorter (job tenure, housing tenure, marital tenure). For example, the monthly turnover rate in manufacturing in 1977 was 3.8 in the U.S. and 2.1 in Britain.[36] However, in addition the shorter duration may be due to the fact that UI normally expires after some months. Public assistance may then be available at a much lower rate. In Britain, social security is in effect paid indefinitely, though at a lower rate after the first 26 weeks and a slightly lower average rate after a year.

Table 15.7    Average Uncompleted Duration of Male Unemployment, and the Approximate Cost of Male Unemployment Relative to Potential Male Earnings

| Britain (July) | Average uncompleted duration (weeks) 1 | Unemployment rate (%) 2 | Approximate cost of unemployment relative to potential male earnings (index) 3 [= (2) × (1)] |
|---|---|---|---|
| 1971 | 23.4 | 4.5 | 105 |
| 1972 | 27.8 | 4.9 | 136 |
| 1973 | 30.8 | 3.5 | 107 |
| 1974 | 26.4 | 3.5 | 92 |
| 1975 | 22.3 | 5.2 | 116 |
| 1976 | 26.5 | 6.7 | 177 |
| 1977 | 28.1 | 7.0 | 196 |
| 1978 | 29.5 | 6.7 | 197 |
| U.S. (All year) | | | |
| 1971 | 11.3 | 5.3 | 60 |
| 1972 | 12.0 | 4.9 | 59 |
| 1973 | 10.0 | 4.1 | 41 |
| 1974 | 9.7 | 4.8 | 46 |
| 1975 | 14.1 | 7.9 | 112 |
| 1976 | 15.8 | 7.0 | 110 |
| 1977 | 14.3 | | |

SOURCE: Britain: Department of Employment *Gazette*, September 1978, p. 1049 and table 15.4 of this chapter. U.S.: G. Akerlof and B. Main, "Unemployment Spells and Unemployment Experience," Federal Reserve Board, Washington, D.C., Special Studies Paper no. 123, October 1978, and table 15.4 of this chapter.

NOTE: U.S. data assume duration to be the same for men as for men and women. This slightly understates duration (see table 15.12).

This reminds us that duration, though it may be the main determinant of the efficiency cost of a given unemployment rate, is not the only thing affecting the distributional consequences of unemployment. The social security system is probably more important. In the U.S., income out of work is lower relative to income in work than in Britain. Thus the disequalizing effect of unemployment is probably at least as high in the U.S. as in Britain. But it is relatively greater for adults than for youths, so far as consumption is concerned. Thus it is not obvious in the U.S. that there is any greater equity case for measures to relieve youth unemployment than adult unemployment. In fact, it is possible that the relative absence of measures to combat youth unemployment in the U.S., compared with Europe, can be explained by the comparatively low levels of income maintenance for adults in the U.S.

There is one obvious qualification, however, to be made to all of the preceding: the problem of repeated spells. If leisure in every week of one's life was a perfect substitute for leisure in every other period, the efficiency cost of unemployment would depend on the amount of unemployment that each individual had had so far over his whole life. And the fairness with which unemployment was distributed would depend on the distribution of lifetime unemployment. But leisure in more closely adjacent weeks is in fact more closely substitutable than leisure in weeks more widely separated. So we could think of the efficiency cost as depending on the distribution of unemployment accumulated over a year, and equity also as depending on the distribution of annual unemployment. A key statistic is therefore the amount of repetition. Are the short U.S. durations associated with more repetition? Apparently not. Unfortunately, the only British data are available for 1971–72 (the highest postwar unemployment year before the oil price rise). In that year the average number of spells per unemployed person was 1.8—almost the same as in the U.S. in 1975, 1976 and 1977 (see table 15.9).

Finally, we can return to the basic question of section 15.1 and ask whether the higher U.S. youth unemployment (relative to adults) is due to higher relative flow or to higher relative duration. In table 15.10 the British duration figures (for January) overstate the relative duration of teenagers on an all-year basis (see table 15.11). It follows that the

| Table 15.8 | Completed Duration of Unemployment (Weeks, Males) | | |
|---|---|---|---|
| Britain | Average completed duration (Weeks) 1 | Probability of entering unemployment (% per week) 2 | Unemployment rate (%) 3 |
| 1972 | 13 | 0.38 | 4.9 |
| 1973 | 10 | 0.35 | 3.5 |
| 1974 | 9 | 0.39 | 3.5 |
| 1975 | 14 | 0.37 | 5.2 |
| 1976 | 16 | 0.42 | 6.7 |
| 1977 | 17 | 0.41 | 7.0 |
| U.S. | | | |
| 1972 | 6.2 | 0.79 | 4.9 |
| 1973 | 7.0 | 0.59 | 4.1 |
| 1974 | 5.6 | 0.86 | 4.8 |
| 1975 | 9.1 | 0.87 | 7.9 |
| 1976 | 8.0 | 0.88 | 7.0 |
| 1977 | 7.2 | 0.86 | 6.2 |

SOURCE: Col. 1: 1. U.S. data from Akerlof and Main, (see table 15.8). They are got by applying the Salant method to the uncompleted durations. 2. The British data come from inflow data divided by stock data. *Department of Employment Gazette*, September 1978. They relate only to registered unemployment—most male unemployment is registered.

Col 3: Sources are *Employment and Training Report of the President* and Department of Employment *Gazette*.

Col 2: col. 3 divided by col. 1.

Table 15.9          Distribution of Males Unemployed Sometime during
                    a Twelve-month Period by Number of Spells

|                    | 1  | 2  | 3 | 4–9 | 10+ | All | Average number of spells |
|--------------------|----|----|---|-----|-----|-----|--------------------------|
| Britain June 71–72 | 66 | 20 | 7 | 5   | 2   | 100 | 1.8                      |
| U.S. Jan. 75–76    | 64 | 18 |   | 18  |     | 100 | 1.63                     |
| Jan. 76–77         | 61 | 19 |   | 20  |     | 100 | 1.67                     |
| Jan. 77–78         | 62 | 20 |   | 18  |     | 100 | 1.66                     |

SOURCE: Britain: DHSS study of claimants cited in D. Metcalf and S. Nickell, "The Plain Man's Guide to the Out of Work" in *Selected Evidence submitted to the Royal Commission for Report no. 6, Lower Incomes*, London, HMSO, pp. 310–29. The data are derived from social security records. Retrospective questions from the General Household Survey in 1975, 1976, and 1977 suggest fewer repeated spells for men aged 18–64 but the retrospective nature of the question casts doubt on the replies. For the record the results were (for men aged 18–64)

|      | 1  | 2  | 3+ | All | Av. cumulated weeks |
|------|----|----|----|-----|---------------------|
| 1975 | 85 | 10 | 5  | 100 | 19                  |
| 1976 | 87 | 9  | 3  | 100 | 24                  |
| 1977 | 83 | 13 | 3  | 100 | 23                  |

See Office of Population Censuses and Surveys, *General Household Survey, 1977*, London, HMSO, p. 57.

U.S.: Bureau of Labor Statistics, *Work Experience of the Population*, Special Tabulations. Data exclude students. The average figure is based on the assumption that average spells in the 3+ category are 3.5, as normally assumed by the Bureau of Labor Statistics.

durations of youths in the U.S. are definitely higher relative to adults than they are in Britain. And indeed, for people aged 20–24 differences of duration alone seem to explain the higher relative unemployment rate.[37] For teenagers there is in addition a disproportionately high inflow into unemployment in the U.S., but this must be largely due to the high proportion of teenagers who have recently left school.[38]

## 15.3    British Time-series and Cross-section Analysis of Youth Unemployment[39]

In Britian youth unemployment has risen much more sharply relative to adult unemployment than in the U.S. Present ratios of youth to adult unemployment are totally without postwar precedent. But so is the level of adult unemployment (see table 15.4 and figure 15.1).[40] By contrast, in the U.S. recent high levels of unemployment are less without precedent and have proved shorter-lived. However, it seems that similar mechanisms explain the time series (and cross-sectional) variation of youth unemployment in the two countries. Other things being equal, one would expect the youth unemployment rates to reflect (1) disequilibrium forces and (2) equilibrium forces, of the kinds discussed in section 15.1. Disequilibrium corresponds to the difference between effective supply and demand. One would expect that the demand for each type of labor would depend on output and on relative wages. Short-run changes in labor demand would not necessarily be proportional to changes in output. In fact, one would expect the demand for youths to be more responsive to the business cycle than the demand for adults, for two reasons. First, the simplest adjustment to a change in labor demand is to stop hiring, and hirings include a disproportionate number of youths. Second, the wages of youths include a higher fraction of capital expenditure than the wages of adults, and firms are averse to capital expenditure during slumps. Thus one could write the demand for youths relative to adults as

$$\frac{DY}{DA} = f(CYC, WY/WA)$$

where $CYC$ indicates the cycle and $WY/WA$ the wage of youths relative to adults. Building on this, one could approximate the unemployment rate of teenagers relative to adults (nonteenagers) by

**Table 15.10          Age Specific Indices (Male, Nonstudents; All Ages = 1.0)**

| Britain (Jan. 1978) | Average completed duration (weeks) 1 | Probability of entering unemployment (% per week) 2 | Unemployment rate (%) 3 |
|---|---|---|---|
| 16–17 | 0.53 | 3.38 | 1.79 |
| 18–19 | 0.70 | 2.11 | 1.48 |
| 20–24 | 0.80 | 1.71 | 1.37 |
| All ages | 1.00 | 1.00 | 1.00 |
| U.S. (1976) | | | |
| 16–17 | 0.75* | 5.41 | 4.06 |
| 18–19 | 0.75* | 3.29 | 2.47 |
| 20–24 | 1.06 | 1.48 | 1.57 |
| All ages | 1.00 | 1.00 | 1.00 |

SOURCE: U.S.: Col. 1: K. Clark and L. Summers, "Labor Force Transitions and Unemployment," table 3. They get very similar results for 1974—and also for 1968–76 in chapter 7 of this volume, table 7.3.
Col. 3: *Employment and Training Report of the President, 1977.*
Col. 2: col 3 divided by col. 1.
Britain: Col. 1: col. 3 divided by col. 2.
Col. 2: Department of Employment *Gazette*, February 1978, p. 205.
Col 3: Department of Employment *Gazette*, March 1979, p. 262.
NOTE: *Separate figures not available.

**Table 15.11    Uncompleted Duration of Unemployment (Weeks)**

| | Mean duration | | | | Percentage unemployed over 13 weeks (Britain) 15 weeks (U.S.) | | | |
| | Britain | | U.S. | | Britain | | U.S. | |
| | Jan. 1976 | July 1976 | Jan. 1976 | July 1976 | Jan. 1976 | July 1976 | Jan. 1976 | July 1976 |
|---|---|---|---|---|---|---|---|---|
| **Males** | | | | | | | | |
| Under 18 | 13.6 | 6.9 ⎫ | | | 41 | 11 ⎫ | | 11 |
| 18–19 | 16.6 | 18.0 ⎬ 10.3 | | 6.0 | 44 | 42 ⎭ 21 | | 11 |
| 20–24 | 19.5 | 22.5 | 14.9 | 10.0 | 48 | 51 | 30 | 29 |
| All ages | 25.4 | 26.5 | 15.9 | 12.3 | 56 | 54 | 32 | 29 |
| **Females** | | | | | | | | |
| Under 18 | 13.1 | 7.1 ⎫ | | | 41 | 12 ⎫ | | 10 |
| 18–19 | 15.2 | 16.1 ⎬ 9.5 | | 6.1 | 40 | 40 ⎭ 20 | | 10 |
| 20–24 | 16.1 | 18.1 | 10.9 | 8.1 | 42 | 45 | 20 | 16 |
| All ages | 18.0 | 16.7 | 12.6 | 9.5 | 45 | 38 | 25 | 21 |
| Aggregate unemployment rate | | | | | | | | |
| Males | 6.7 | | 6.2 | | | | | |
| Females | 3.0 | | 8.2 | | | | | |

SOURCE: Department of Employment, *British Labour Statistics Year Book*, 1976, table 113. Bureau of Labor Statistics, *Employment and Earnings*, July 1978, p. 32, and *Handbook of Labor Statistics*, 1977.

NOTES: 1. The British data relate to period registered at exchange; U.S. data relate to reported period looking for work.

2. U.S. data include students but other data suggest that, holding age constant, duration of students and nonstudents are similar.

$$(3) \qquad \ln\left(\frac{UY}{UA}\right) = a_0 + a_1\, CYC + a_2 \ln\left(\frac{WY}{WA}\right) + a_3 \ln\left(\frac{SY}{SA}\right)$$

where $SY/SA$ are the relative labor supplies.[41]

In addition, equilibrium forces should be at work. Relative income support levels for the two groups should be important, but the Supplementary Benefit for a youth relative to an adult rarely had a $t$-value above unity. Equation (3) is therefore our estimating equation. The analysis is confined to males, since the rate of registered unemployment of adult females is particularly difficult to interpret.

Before presenting the results, we discuss briefly the explanatory variables and their movement over time.

### 15.3.1   The Cycle ($VAC$ or $UA$)

This is probably best measured by the number of vacancies registered at employment offices ($VAC$). Alternatively, it can be measured by the

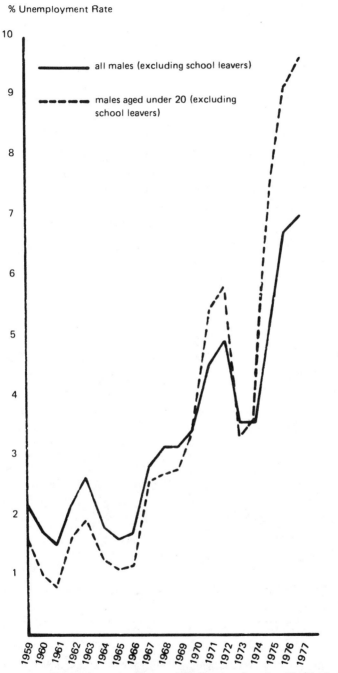

% Unemployment Rate

**Fig. 15.1**     Unemployment Rates of Males Aged under 20 (Excluding School Leavers) and All Males, 1959–76, July, Britain (Source: *Department of Employment Gazette*, August 1978)

adult male unemployment rate $(UA)$, but we are then explaining youth unemployment by adult unemployment, which is a highly trended variable whose significance has probably altered over time. Vacancies are relatively untrended but have almost indentical turning points to adult unemployment (up to 1976).

### 15.3.2    Relative Wage Rates $(RY/RA)$

The hourly earnings of men under 21 relative to those over 21 are shown in figure 15.2. Relative youth earnings rose steadily up until 1972. Then in 1973 they shot up and have continued shooting up since. The main explanation seems fairly clear. The compulsory minimum school-leaving age was raised from 15 to 16 for everyone becoming 15 after September 1972. About a half of all children were forced to stay an extra year at school. This had an immediate effect on the quality of the teenage

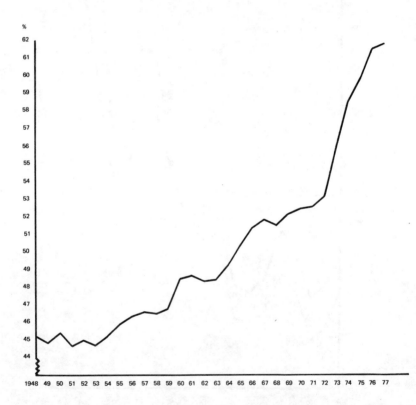

**Fig. 15.2**         Average Hourly Earnings of Youths and Boys Aged Under 21 as a Percentage of Adult Male Hourly Earnings 1948–76, Manual Workers, All Industries, Britain (Source: *Department of Employment Gazette*, October Earnings Survey)

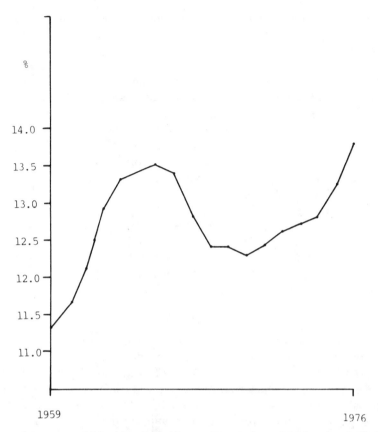

**Fig. 15.3**      Males Aged 15–19 as a Percentage of Males Aged 15–60, Britain (Source: Estimates Supplied by the Department of Employment)

workforce, but is unlikely to have raised its quality by more than 5% compared with the 16% wage increase that occured after 1972.[42]

So it is unclear why teenage earnings rose. If the earnings rise was due to changes in the balance of supply and demand, then one could hardly use it to explain movements in unemployment. This, however, does not seem to be the case. Let us begin with the period since 1972. Because of the raising of the school-leaving age there would of course have been a reduction in the number of teenage ergs at work (relative to adults) of perhaps 10%. However, as figure 15.3 shows, the teenage population rose between 1972 and 1976 by 10%—just enough by that date to offset the effect of the raised school-leaving age. And in any case a raised school-leaving age would not create much marked shortage of youths at existing wages if people in their early twenties were good substitutes for teenagers. So I am willing to accept the conventional view that youth wages have risen because of an unexplained tendency in collectively bargained wage agreements to start paying adult rates at ever younger ages.[43]

There is also the puzzle of the rise in relative youth earnings before 1972. Could this be due to quality improvement? During the period, the proportion of youngsters who stayed on rose continuously. This staying-on, if independent of ability levels, would raise quality whether the extra staying-on was voluntary or compulsory. However, the voluntary staying-on was in fact selective. So the average "natural ability" of the teenage work force declined as the abler people reduced the fraction of their teenage years spent in the labor force more rapidly than the less able people did. One cannot quantify this effect, but there seems no obvious reason to reject the null hypothesis that the quality of the teenage work force remained constant relative to the adult work force (which was itself improving in quality). Thus one would expect the series in figure 15.2 (including the dotted section) to help to explain relative teenage unemployment. Further confirmation of the power of this series to explain teenage employment is provided in section 15.4.

### 15.3.3   Relative Labor Supply ($POPY/POPA$)

There are two possible ways of measuring demographic movements: (1) the fraction of the total population aged 15–60 who are aged 15–19 ($POPY/POPA$), shown in figure 15.3; (2) the fraction of the total labor force aged 15–19.[44] The second of these appears to reflect more accurately the labor supply of teenagers, but is subject to two drawbacks. First, if teenage labor supply is reduced (for example by the raising of the school-leaving age) one would not necessarily expect less teenage unemployment if people in their early twenties are close substitutes for teenagers. In fact the youth labor market may be better considered as a market for people in their first five years of work experience. In such a case variable (1) is more relevant.[45] Second, labor supply may respond to unemployment, whereas population is exogenous. I therefore use variable (1).

One must of course remember that over time the teenage labor force (whose unemployment we are studying) has got increasingly close to the time when it left school. This means that its members have had less time for a successful job-search and job-matching. One might suppose this would have produced an upward trend in relative youth unemployment, but no such trend appears in the regressions. However, as table 15.3 shows, the youth unemployment problem is not primarily one of initial absorption, so this may not be an especially important aspect of the situation.

Turning to the results, these are estimated on annual data (males only). As table 15.12 shows, the effect of the cycle is transparent. The youth unemployment rate goes up relative to the adult unemployment rate

**Table 15.12**        **Time-series Regressions (All Variables in Logarithms), Britain**

| Dep. Var. | Period | VAC | UA | WY/WA | POPY/ POPA | Const. | $R^2$ | DW | SE |
|-----------|--------|-----|-----|-------|-----------|--------|-------|-----|-----|
| UY/UA | 59–72 | −.54 | | 4.62 | 1.29 | −18.7 | .96 | 2.63 | .048 |
| | | (.06) | | (.52) | (.40) | | | | |
| UY/UA | 59–74 | −.50 | | 5.01 | 1.43 | −20.7 | .96 | 2.55 | .046 |
| | | (.05) | | (.43) | (.40) | | | | |
| UY/UA | 59–76 | −.38 | | 4.07 | .42 | −15.1 | .93 | 1.49 | .071 |
| | | (.06) | | (.41) | (.43) | | | | |
| UY/UA | 59–72 | | .40 | 1.52 | 1.64 | −10.1 | .94 | 2.11 | .060 |
| | | | (.06) | (.88) | (.52) | | | | |
| UY/UA | 59–74 | | .43 | .60 | 1.46 | − 6.5 | .91 | 1.88 | .066 |
| | | | (.06) | (.70) | (.53) | | | | |
| UY/UA | 59–76 | | .38 | .71 | .96 | − 5.7 | .93 | 1.90 | .073 |
| | | | (.07) | (.69) | (.40) | | | | |

NOTE: Standard errors in brackets. All regressions estimated by Cochrane-Orcutt procedure; the Hildreth-Liu procedure gave very similar results.

during a slump. In fact, it rises 40% faster than the adult unemployment. Given that the youth unemployment rate is on average over the period close to the adult rate, it follows that youth employment falls in a slump faster than adult employment falls. The estimated effect is robust with respect to the other included variables, but falls as the sample period is extended forwards. This is because youth unemployment in 1976 was much lower than predicted by any equation. Since all our exploratory variables have high values in 1976, their estimated coefficients all fall when that year is included.

The estimated effect of relative wages seems to vary in addition according to how demand is specified, though it is always positive and reasonably significant. If, as I prefer, demand is measured by vacancies, the effect of relative wages is very large—with an elasticity of 4–5. In this case, relative wages are being made to explain most of the time trend in UY/UA. If, instead, adult unemployment is the explanatory variable, then it itself picks up a part of the time trend in UY/UA. By contrast, the effect of population size is unaffected by which demand variable is included.

One can therefore conclude that there is nothing surprising about recent high levels of youth unemployment. The world is still the same, except that we are in a protracted slump.

### 15.3.4    Cross-section of Towns

It is interesting to compare the time-series relation between youth and adult unemployment with the cross-sectional relation. In a cross-section of towns, one would expect the youth unemployment rate to vary positively with the adult unemployment rate. But one would also expect the elasticity of the youth rate with respect to the adult rate to be lower in the cross-section than in the time-series. For over time youths are not hired in a downturn, whereas in a "steady state" it is not obvious that a bad economic climate would affect youths more than adults. Indeed, since youths can more readily migrate, one might expect the youth rates (for the current work force) to vary less than the adult rate. One cannot of course claim that the 1971 data for 78 county boroughs (towns) represented a completely "steady state," however defined. Even so, the cross-sectional structure of unemployment rates has been fairly stable.

The data support our prediction: the cross-section elasticity of the youth rate with respect to the adult rate is only .6, compared with 1.4 for the time-series. The exact estimate is (s.e. in parentheses)

$$\ln UY = 1.19 + .61 \ln UA \qquad R^2 = 0.61$$
$$(.06)$$

where youths are teenage men as before and adults are men aged 25–59. Adding as a variable the relative supply of youths does not appear to add significantly to the explanatory power of the equation.

## 15.4  Time-series Analysis of the Demand for Labor by Age in British Manufacturing

Finally, we can examine whether wage movements are a plausible explanation of relative unemployment rates by looking at the effect of relative wages on the age composition of employment (rather than unemployment). The only available data on labor demand by age in Britain relate to manual workers in manufacturing, which I take to be a price-taking sector. I use data for April and October in the years 1949–69, on the man-hours of youths (males under 21), girls (females under 18), men, full-time women, and part-time women, together with associated hourly earnings.

The series are worth a brief description. Taking youths first, there was an increase in employment (relative to men) lasting into the 1960s, followed by a relative decline that began well before the raising of the school-leaving age in 1972. By contrast, the relative wage rose more or less continuously relative to men, as we have already seen. The number of girls employed (again relative to men) fell more or less continuously, indicating that the rise in the number of boys in the mid-sixties cannot be simply explained by the rise in the number of young people in the labor force resulting from the postwar baby boom. The relative wage of girls was more or less flat until it surged in the 1970s because of the forces already mentioned plus equal pay legislation for females. The relative employment of women has fallen more or less continuously, with the rise in part-time women-hours insufficient to compensate for the fall in full-time women-hours. Relative wages of women were more or less flat until a recent spurt, which was due partly to equal pay legislation.

To assess the effect of wages on labor demand requires a fully specified demand system. The most tractable general system is that derived from the translog cost function. In using this I shall not attempt to explain the pattern of investment and will therefore take the capital stock as a predetermined variable $(K)$ affecting labour costs (C). If $P_i$ is the price of the $i^{\text{th}}$ type of labour, $T$ is time, and $Y$ is output, the cost function is then

$$\ln C = a_0 + \Sigma g_i \ln P_i + g_K \ln K + g_T T + g_Y \ln Y$$
$$+ \tfrac{1}{2}\Sigma\Sigma d_{ij} \ln P_i \ln P_j + \tfrac{1}{2} d_{KK} (\ln K)^2$$
$$+ \tfrac{1}{2} d_{TT} T^2 + \tfrac{1}{2} d_{YY} (\ln Y)^2 + \Sigma d_{iK} \ln P_i \ln K$$
$$+ \Sigma d_{iT} \ln P_i. \, T + \Sigma d_{iY} \ln P_i \ln Y$$
$$+ d_{KT} \ln K. \, T + d_{KY} \ln K \ln Y + d_{TY} T \ln Y$$

where $d_{ij} = d_{ji}$ (assuming the function is thought of as a Taylor's series expansion of a general log-cost function).

If $x_i$ is the quantity of the $i^{\text{th}}$ type of labor,

$$\frac{\partial C}{\partial P_i} = x_i, \qquad \text{so that} \qquad \frac{\partial \ln C}{\partial \ln P_i} = \frac{x_i P_i}{C}$$

or the share of the $i^{\text{th}}$ factor in total labour cost (C). Hence differentiating $\ln C$ by $\ln P_i$ we find that

(4)
$$\frac{x_i P_i}{C} = g_i + \Sigma_j d_{ij} \ln P_j + d_{iK} \ln K + d_{iT} T + d_{iY} \ln Y$$
$$\ldots (i = 1, \ldots, n)$$

Since shares do not vary when all prices change by a common multiple,

(5)
$$\Sigma_j d_{ij} = 0 \qquad \text{(all } i)$$

Hence[46, 47]

(4')
$$\frac{x_i P_i}{C} = g_i + \Sigma_{j=1}^{n-1} d_{ij} (\ln P_j - \ln P_n) + d_{iK} \ln K$$
$$+ d_{iT} T + d_{iY} \ln Y \qquad (i = 1, \ldots, n)$$

where $n$ is some factor taken as numeraire. Moreover, since shares add to a constant (unity),

(6)
$$\Sigma_i d_{iK} = \Sigma_i d_{iT} = \Sigma_i d_{iY} = 0$$

Hence one need only estimate $(n-1)$ equations for $(n-1)$ shares. This is our estimating system, with the requirement that $d_{ij} = d_{ji}$ imposed upon it. The Allen elasticities of substitution are then evaluated as[48]

$$S_{ii} = \frac{d_{ii}}{A_i^2} + 1 - \frac{1}{A_i}$$

$$S_{ij} = \frac{d_{ij}}{A_i A_j} + 1 \qquad (i \neq j)$$

where $A_i = x_i P_i / C$ evaluated at the mean. The price elasticities of demand (with output and capital constant) are

$$e_{ij} = S_{ij} A_j$$

### 15.4.1 Estimates

System (4′) was estimated using the TSPs iterative version of Zellner's minimum distance estimator (LSQ) (see table 15.13).[49] The variables are defined in appendix C. Unfortunately, we have no data on nonmanual workers, so the assumption is that the relative demand for manual workers of different age and sex is independent of the number of nonmanual workers. Part-time women were amalgamated with full-timers in order to reduce the number of parameters.[50]

The results suggest a quite high short-run elasticity of demand for youths (1.25), and a smaller elasticity of demand for girls. There is quite high substitutability between categories of labor (except, rather oddly, between girls and women). Girls are very good substitutes for youths, and women are less good substitutes. As one would expect, youths and

**Table 15.13    Demand Elasticities and Elasticities of Substitution, Britain**

|          |        | Youths | Girls | Women | Men   |
|----------|--------|--------|-------|-------|-------|
| $e_{ij}$ | Youths | −1.25  | .29   | .50   | .47   |
|          | Girls  | .82    | −.31  | −.85  | .34   |
|          | Women  | .12    | −.07  | −1.59 | 1.55  |
|          | Men    | .02    | .01   | .32   | −.35  |
| $S_{ij}$ | Youths | −33.6  | 22.1  | 3.1   | .6    |
|          | Girls  | 22.1   | −23.5 | −5.3  | .4    |
|          | Women  | 3.1    | −5.3  | −9.9  | 2.0   |
|          | Men    | .6     | .4    | 2.0   | −.4   |
| $t$-ratio | Youths | 5.8    | 2.5   | 1.8   | 1.3   |
|          | Girls  | 2.5    | .9    | 2.0   | .7    |
|          | Women  | 1.8    | 2.0   | 10.5  | 9.5   |
|          | Men    | 1.3    | .7    | 9.5   | 9.2   |

NOTE: 1. The elasticities are for given capital and output. The $t$-ratios apply equally to $e_{ij}$ and $s_{ij}$.

2. In the equations for $A_Y$, $A_G$ and $A_W$ the implied values of $DW$ and $R^2$ were as follows:

|       | $A_Y$ | $A_G$ | $A_W$ |
|-------|-------|-------|-------|
| $R^2$ | .96   | .92   | .92   |
| $DW$  | 1.11  | 1.87  | .90   |

girls are not good substitutes for men, women being rather better substitutes. None of the effects of capital, output, or time were well-determined.

It is interesting to compare these findings with results obtained in the U.S. by Anderson and by Freeman.[51] Anderson used four factors in a translog production function for manufacturing: capital, and workers aged under 25 ($Y$), 25–55 ($M$), and over 55 ($O$). The implied price elasticities (with capital variable) were

|   | $Y$ | $M$ | $O$ |
|---|---|---|---|
| $Y$ | − 2.5 | 1.9 | .6 |
| $M$ | .3 | − 1.0 | .4 |
| $O$ | .3 | 1.7 | − 2.7 |

Freeman used four factors in a translog production function for the whole economy: capital, men 20–34 ($Y$), men 35–64 ($M$) and women 20–64 ($W$). The implied price elasticities (with capital variable) were

|   | $Y$ | $M$ | $W$ |
|---|---|---|---|
| $Y$ | − 2.1 | 1.6 | .2 |
| $M$ | .8 | − 1.2 | .3 |
| $W$ | .3 | .9 | − 1.3 |

Though the U.S. elasticities seem somewhat higher, any difference is probably due mainly to the fact that capital is variable and that definitions differ. Given the weight of evidence on price effects, one has some confidence in supposing that youth wages are highly relevant to the problem of youth unemployment.[52]

# Appendix A

### Sources to Tables 15.1 and 15.2

SOURCE: Britain: 1971 Census, Economic Activity, table 3.

U.S.: U.S. Department of Commerce, Bureau of the Census, 1970 Census of Population, Detailed Characteristics, Final Report, PC(1)-D1, U.S. Summary, table 217.

NOTES: 1. Britain relates to 24 April 1971; U.S. relates to 1 April 1970. U.S. ($W$) relates to whites and U.S. ($B$) to blacks.

2. Nonstudents in Britain include part-time students; in the U.S. they do not. In Britain a student is someone who will be studying in the following April/May term; in the U.S. a student is someone who has studied at all since 1 February.

3. The labor force is the employed (defined identically) plus the unemployed. The employed labor force includes those who worked at any time for pay or profit during the week (including unpaid family work) plus those temporarily away from their job because of holiday, sickness, or industrial dispute. In Britain, unlike the U.S., temporary layoffs are treated as employed, but the maximum number of such people since 1973 has been 34,000 and the usual number is under 10,000.

4. In Britain, the unemployed include those persons currently "seeking work or waiting to take up a job." In the U.S., the unemployed include all who have looked for work in the last 4 weeks *or* due to take up a job within a month, *or* on temporary layoff. The unemployed include those looking for part-time work, in both countries.

# Appendix B

## Income Maintenance for Young People

Income if unemployed as a fraction of income in full-time work is probably higher for youths relative to adults in Britain than in the U.S. A registered unemployed British youth, even if he or she has never worked and is living at home, can claim Supplementary Benefit. This is currently paid to someone living at home and aged 16 to 17 at a rate equal to about 30% of gross male weekly earnings at that age (and a higher percentage of net earnings). With a minimal work record an 18 or 19 year old can claim unemployment benefit equal to about 30% of the equivalent gross male earnings. About two-thirds of unemployed youths under 18 in Britain personally receive social security payments.[53]

In the U.S. it is more difficult for a youth to obtain benefit in his own right. Only 11% of those unemployed under twenty (out of school and looking for full-time work) were on U.I. in May 1976. In some states other youths would be receiving personal welfare payments, but there is no comprehensive information on the numbers.

# Appendix C

## Definitions of Variables in Section 15.4

$P$    Hourly earnings: from survey of Earnings and Hours of Manual Workers in Manufacturing in April and October (to 1969) and October (1970 onwards).

$X$     Manual manhours: from the same source.
$K$     Fixed assets in manufacturing. Gross value at constant prices (replacement cost). The series is rebased a number of times over the period and I have grafted one series onto the next.
$T$     Time (1 unit = 6 months; April 1948 = 1).
$Y$     Index of manufacturing production (this is a value-added measure).

# Notes

1. See Richard B. Freeman in this volume, table 5.6.
2. The General Household Survey is too small for disaggregated comparisons with the Current Population Survey; the EEC Labour Force Survey only occurs every two or three years.
3. The Census excludes full-time students in Britain, so students (including part-time students) have been excluded in the U.S. However, the age-specific unemployment rates of students in the U.S. are broadly similar to those of nonstudents.
4. A commonly used statistic in international comparisons is the percentage of the unemployed aged under 25. This is, however, very difficult to interpret since it reflects both the age pattern of leaving school and the demographic structure of the population, as well as the unemployment rates specific to given years since leaving school. The figures are:

|  | Men | | Women | |
| --- | --- | --- | --- | --- |
|  | Britain (1971) | U.S.A. (1970) | Britain (1971) | U.S.A. (1970) |
| % of unemployed aged under 25* | 31 | 30 | 34 | 31 |
| % of labor force aged under 25* | 20 | 11 | 25 | 19 |
| % of population aged 16–64 who are aged under 25 | 22 | 27 | 21 | 26 |

*Excluding students

5. One should ignore the figure for unemployed 15 year olds in Britain, since nearly all 15 year olds in the labor force had left school a month before the Census.
6. See U.S., Department of Labor, Bureau of Labor Statistics, *International Comparisons of Unemployment*, Bulletin 1979, 1978, p. 19.
7. A formula which would adjust the British aggregate rate so that in 1976 British aggregate adjusted rate − U.S. aggregate rate = British prime male rate − U.S. prime male rate would be to multiply the British aggregate rate by 1.5. The multiple would of course differ between years.
8. It is also "boosted" by the inclusion of unemployed students (some 14% of U.S. unemployed). Such people cannot be included when other countries are adjusted to U.S. concepts because of lack of data (and the absence of any large number of such people). Including them raises the U.S. rate by a multiple of between 1.05 and 1.10.
9. At any rate this is the broad effect of family income on *employment* reported in table 5.8 of Freeman's chapter in this volume and table 13.1 of the chapter by Rees and Gray. (Rees and Gray also report no effect of father's occupation holding constant family income.)
10. In addition in 1970/1 of *employed* males under 20 not in school 21% in the U.S. worked part-time (under 35 hours) compared with under 7% in Britain. (There were few differences here for women.) However some of the part-timers may have been looking for full-time jobs. (Source: Britain, 1971 Census Economic Activity table 23; U.S., as for table 15.2).

11. *Employment and Training Report of the President, 1978*, pp. 242 and 186–88.

12. C.P.S. analyses by D. Ellwood and M. Feldstein show that of males under 20 out of school and out of the labor force, only 37% say they would definitely like a job, and of these only 37% are not looking because they do not think they could find one. Of the whole group (males under 20 out of school and out of labor force) 28% say they will not look for work in the next 12 months (or their intentions are so reported).

13. See Freeman's paper in this volume, table 5.6.

14. I would explain the fact that individual youth unemployment is negatively correlated with income by the same type of expression as used to explain individual youth participation in the labor force.

15. Not all differences found in cross-sectional data for individuals are found repeated in a comparison of U.S. and Britain.

(a) The hours of work of full-time workers are not lower in the U.S. (1977): for men 43 hours in Britain and 45 in the U.S., and for women 38 hours in Britain and 40 in the U.S. (see Department of Employment, *New Earnings Survey*, 1977, p.A18–19 and Bureau of Labor Statistics, *Employment and Earnings*, July 1978, vol. 25, no. 7, p.39).

(b) Female participation is higher in Britain than the U.S.

16. R. Layard, D. Piachaud and M. Stewart, *The Causes of Poverty*, Royal Commission on the Distribution of Income and Wealth, Background Paper no. 5, London, HMSO, 1978, and S. J. Nickell, "The Effect of Unemployment and Related Benefits on the Duration of Unemployment," *Economic Journal*, March 1979.

17. M. Feldstein, "The Effect of Unemployment Insurance on Temporary Layoff Unemployment," *American Economic Review*, December 1978.

18. The previous comparison is complicated by two factors. First, Feldstein's figures include women but he also shows a figure of .54 for the subsample of (predominantly male) union members. Second, his figures are individual income replacement ratios and ours are family income replacement ratios. On average, women's earnings account for under one-fifth of family income so the British individual income replacement ratios for all males could not be as low as the U.S. ratios for "privileged" males. (Most international comparative statistics on unemployment relief fail to mention the British Supplementary Benefit system which determines the income maintenance levels of 50% of the unemployed, compared with 30% whose income maintenance is determined by National Insurance).

19. A youth in a family characterized by an altruistic head does not face the full cost of his actions. If he decides his own labor force behavior, he may make choices which do not maximize family income.

20. She is unlikely to say this if the youth is under 18, for if the youth is under 18, the AFDC entitlement includes a child allowance only payable (for a nonstudent) if the child is working or registered unemployed. This constitutes a strong pressure to participate (though not to take a job). But under a quarter of unemployed teenagers out of school are under 18.

21. 1975 Survey of Income and Education analysis by R. Freeman. Data relate to 18–19 year old males.

22. Seventy-five percent of men are covered.

23. Another approach is to look at the shape of estimated experience-earning profiles. If male annual earnings are regressed on schooling, experience and experience squared, earnings at the peak are 280% higher than starting earnings in Britain and 288% higher in the U.S. (G. Psacharopoulos and R. Layard, "Human Capital and Earnings: British Evidence and a Critique," *Review of Economic Studies*, 3 (1979):485–508; J. Mincer, *Schooling, Experience and Earnings*, 1974.)

24. O. Ashenfelter and R. Smith, "Compliance with the Minimum Wage Law," *Journal of Political Economy* 2 (1979):333–50.

25. Department of Employment, *New Earnings Survey*, 1977, table 126. For U.S., as in table 15.5.

26. See, for example, J. Mincer, "Unemployment Effects of Minimum Wages," *Journal of Political Economy* 4 (1976):S87–S104.

27. Formerly known as the Youth Employment Service, this is run by local education authorities and has primary responsibility for the placement of school leavers. Twenty-two percent of a random sample of 3,000 16 to 19 year olds interviewed in November 1976 said they got their first job through the Careers Service (Manpower Services Commission, *Young People and Work*, Manpower Studies no. 19781, 1978). Even for those who have already worked, the Careers Service remains the main public employment agency up to the age of 18. Even though they are entitled to use the Employment Services Agency, only 20% of the registered unemployed under 18 who had worked were registered with the E.S.A. (House of Commons Expenditure Committee: Social Services and Employment Sub-Committee Enquiry into Employment and Unemployment in the New Unemployment Situation. Second Memorandum Submitted by the Department of Employment, 1978. par. 27.)

28. For a useful comparison of placement services in Britain, U.S., and some other countries, see U.S. Department of Labor, Employment and Training Administration, *From Learning to Earning: A Transnational Comparison of Transition Services*, R and D. Monograph 63 (abridged version of a report by Beatrice G. Reubens).

29. Department of Émployment, *Gazette*, regular statistics. Relate to number of school-leavers registered as unemployed. A "school-leaver" is anyone under 18 who has never had a full-time job. From January 1961 to January 1975 the number of unemployed people under 18 who had not yet found a first job by January never rose above 10,000 in any year. In January 1976 it was 38,000.

30. I am assuming unemployment always lasts a whole number of weeks.

31. Expressions (1) and (2) are of course equivalent in a steady state since

$$\sum_{d=1}^{\infty} F_d T_d = \sum_{d=1}^{\infty} \left( F_d \sum_{t=1}^{d} C_t \right)$$
$$= (F_1 C_1 + F_2(C_1 + C_2) + F_3(C_1 + C_2 + C_3) + \ldots$$
$$= C_1(F_1 + F_2 + F_3 + \ldots) + C_2(F_2 + F_3 + \ldots)$$
$$+ C_3(F_3 + \ldots) + \ldots$$
$$= \Sigma C_t N_t$$

since $N_t = \sum_{d=t}^{\infty} F_d$

32. This assumes no repeated spells in a year. If a worker's annual weeks are held to $|\Delta H|$ below their equilibrium level, the compensated supply price falls from $W$ to $V$ where

$$W - V = \frac{dW}{dH} |\Delta H|$$

Hence
$$W - V = \frac{dW \cdot H}{dH \cdot W} \cdot \frac{|\Delta H| W}{H} = \frac{1}{\varepsilon} \frac{|\Delta H| W}{H}$$

The procedure also ignores the existence of income and product taxes (which means that the cost of unemployment is higher than we have measured it).

33. Since replacement ratios are higher in Britain than the U.S., $\varepsilon$ may also be higher. See R. Jackman and R. Layard, "The Efficiency Case for Long-Run Labour Market Policies," *Economica* 47 (1980):331–50.

34. See S. Salant, "Search Theory and Duration Data: A Theory of Sorts," *Quarterly Journal of Economics* 91 (1977):39–57.

35. The U.S. duration figures are taken from Akerlof and Main since Clark and Summers's figures do not reflect short spells beginning and ending between CPS interviews. (The Clark and Summers's figures are 9.4 for 1974, and 11.3 for 1976, see K. Clark and L.

Summers, "Labor Force Transitions and Unemployment," NBER., mimeo, April 1978). However, I rely on the Clark and Summers's finding of almost identical durations for men and women in assuming that Akerlof and Main's figures for both sexes also apply to men.

36. *Employment and Training Report of the President*, 1978, p. 275 and *Department of Employment Gazette*, May 1978, p. 577. It would be interesting to compare the distribution of establishments by their annual changes in employment, in order to see to what extent the labor turnover reflects demand-side as opposed to supply-side forces.

37. There is some evidence that in the U.S. and Britain the number of repeated spells is similar at all ages. For Britain the evidence comes from the Department of Health and Social Security Pilot Study on New Methods of Collecting Unemployment Statistics, 1971–72, unpublished. (See also, S. Owen, "Do the Faces in the Dole Queue Change?" University College, Cardiff, mimeo, summer 1978.) U.S. data are special tabulations relating to nonstudents and show average numbers of spells in 1971 of 1.83 for men aged 16–19 and 1.72 for men aged 20–24.

38. In both countries, of course, the inflow of youths into unemployment is much higher than of adults, though, perhaps interestingly, the difference in Britain seems rather less than the differential turnover rate. The percentage of employees who have been with their current employer for less than 12 months is (April 1976)

| | Under 18 | 18–20 | 21–24 | 25–29 | 30–39 | 40–49 | 50–59 | All |
|---|---|---|---|---|---|---|---|---|
| Males | 57 | 21 | 20 | 14 | 10 | 6 | 4 | 11 |
| Females | 60 | 25 | 21 | 16 | 15 | 9 | 5 | 16 |

(New Earnings Survey)

39. This whole section is based on data generously supplied by Peter Makeham of the Department of Employment from his forthcoming study of youth unemployment, summarized in Department of Employment Gazette, August 1978. Full details of the time-series sources are available in the Technical Annex to his article in the Department of Employment Gazette, August 1978, obtainable from the Department of Employment. The following definition is important. Unemployment rates are measured in July but exclude school-leavers in order to avoid problems to do with changes in school-leaving dates. Adult students are also excluded. The cross-section data are based on the 1971 Census table 18, unemployed rates being measured by total out of employment as percentage of all economically active.

40. The same has happened in France and Germany (see H. Gallis, "Youth Unemployment: A Statistical Analysis," EMP 47–1/WP 2, I.L.O. Oct. 1977).

41. Since $UY$ and $UA$ are small

$$\frac{UY}{UA} \simeq \ln\left(\frac{SY}{DY}\right) \bigg/ \ln\left(\frac{SA}{DA}\right)$$

But in addition, since $UY/UA$ is not far from unity

$$\ln\left(\frac{UY}{UA}\right) \simeq \frac{UY}{UA} \simeq \ln\left(\frac{DA}{DY}\right) + \ln\left(\frac{SY}{SA}\right) = f\left(\frac{WY}{WA}\right) + \ln\left(\frac{SY}{SA}\right)$$

with $f' > 0$.

42. The estimate of 5% is based on a simple calculation in which all teenage workers are assumed to have left at the minimum age but to experience a 10% increase in earnings for each year of work experience. An extra year of schooling is also assumed to add 10% to wages. Hence in a steady state the initial teenage work force has five age groups earning 1, 1.1, 1.2, 1.3, and 1.4 units respectively and the new teenage workforce has four age groups earning 1.1, 1.2, 1.3, and 1.4 respectively. This gives a 5% rise in earnings, which is too high since only a half a cohort were forced to stay on. Unfortunately, no more subtle exercise is worthwhile since there is no fine breakdown of teenage wages by age, let alone by age and education. The best data are in the source to table 15.5.

43. Insofar as unemployment affected pay, I assume the relationship has a lag so that current pay is predetermined.

44. See for example Department of Employment *Gazette*, April 1978, p. 427.

45. It might be better still to measure the fraction aged $(15 + D)$ to $(19 + D)$ where $D$ is unity from 1973 onwards and 0 before.

46. If there were no other factors of production, constant returns would require

$$d_{iK} + d_{iY} = 0$$

But, as we are omitting nonmanual workers from the demand system (for lack of information) there is no virtue in imposing this constraint.

47. A more complete system would include equations for $\partial \ln C / \partial T$, $\partial \ln C / \partial \ln K$ and $\partial \ln C / \partial \ln Y$ but there are no measures of these variables that do not require making very strong assumptions.

48. See H. Binswanger, "A Cost Function Approach to the Measurement of Elasticities of Factor Demand and Elasticities of Substitution," *American Journal of Agricultural Economics*, May 1974.

49. To reduce the autocorrelation of residuals, the system was estimated as follows:

$$A_i = g_i + \Sigma d_{ij}(\ln P_j - \ln Pn) + d_{iK} \ln K + d_{iT} \cdot T$$
$$- \rho(g_i + \Sigma d_{ij}(\ln P_{j, -1} - \ln P_{n, -1}) + d_{iK} \ln K_{-1}$$
$$+ d_{iT} \ln T_{-1} + \rho A_{i, -1}$$

Here $\rho$ is the autocorrelation coefficient in the equation

$$u_i = \rho u_{i, -1} + e_i$$

It has to be constrained to be the same for all $i$ in order to ensure that the factor shares add up to unity.

50. Up to 1956 I have to assume part-time woman-hours to be proportional to full-time, and part-time hourly earnings to be proportional to full-time.

51. J. M. Anderson, "Substitution among Age Groups in the U.S. Labor Force," Williams College, mimeo, December 1978; R. Freeman, "The Effect of Demographic Factors on Age-earnings Profiles," *Journal of Human Resources*, Fall 1979. For a full discussion of these and other related studies, see D. Hamermesh and J. Grant, "Econometric Studies of Labor-Labor Substitution and their Implications for Policy," Michigan State University, mimeo.

52. The model reported here includes no adjustment mechanism. But I have also estimated the model with $\ln P$ replaced by $.5 \ln P + .33 \ln P_{-1} + .17 \ln P_{-2}$. The estimated price elasticities were very similar. However, I am currently, with John Abowd and Stephen Nickell, estimating a fuller model which includes a fully specified adjustment mechanism and distinguishes between people and people-hours.

53. Department of Employment, *British Labour Statistics Year Book, 1976* table 119.

# Comment     Daniel S. Hamermesh

Clearly, the high points of Layard's chapter are the simple comparisons of the *outcomes* in the youth labor markets of the U.S. and Great Britain. He presents evidence corroborating the now familiar point that youth unemployment is relatively higher in the U.S. He then goes on, though,

Daniel S. Hamermesh is professor of economics at Michigan State University, and a research associate at the National Bureau of Economic Research.

to present new material bolstering this simple empirical fact. We learn, for example, that spells of unemployment among American youths, though shorter than those in the U.K., are longer relative to adult spells of unemployment. Thus part of the explanation of the higher relative youth unemployment rate in the U.S. is the relatively greater length of spells experienced by young people. He points out, too, using both cross-section and time-series data, that the relative youth unemployment rate in Britain rises as aggregate unemployment increases (or job vacancy rates decrease). Similarly, he shows convincingly that the demand for young workers is quite elastic.

The presentation of these facts alone more than justifies the chapter and makes it an important catalyst to our thinking about the nature of the labor market for youths. However, we should be careful attributing the causes Layard identifies to the outcomes he observes. There are two related areas where this is especially important. Layard stresses the role of demand forces far too much in his explanations, ignoring the induced effects on unemployment through discouraged worker and other supply phenomena. Simultaneously, and in part related, he underestimates the importance of the minimum wage's effect on the youth labor market. Let us consider each of these in its turn.

Layard's calculation of the relative welfare cost of unemployment in the two countries (section 15.2) understates his case, because it assumes that supply elasticities are equal. (Indeed, the footnote even suggests that the elasticity is greater in the U.K.) This is hardly likely to be correct, for (1) we have observed, as Layard notes, much greater secular changes in the participation patterns of adult males in the U.S. than in the U.K.; (2) the role of adult women, a group with a demonstrated high elasticity of supply, is greater in the U.S. labor force; and (3) the American youth labor force consists much more than its British counterpart of students interested in part-time employment. For all these reasons ε is likely to be higher here, implying that the welfare cost of unemployment in the U.S. is even lower compared to the U.K. than Layard suggests.

This emphasis on demand underlies the rationale for the time-series equation (3) and the interpretation of the parameter estimates. There is no reason why relative youth unemployment must necessarily vary negatively with the business cycle. Indeed, if the elasticity of youth labor supply is sufficiently high relative to that of adults, the relative decline in youth employment in a downturn, as employers reduce the hiring of youths disproportionately, will be outweighed by a reduction in participation among youths relative to adults. The net effect is unclear, but we should expect relative youth unemployment to be less countercyclical in the U.S. than in the U.K., given greater youth labor supply elasticities here. Thus the coefficient on adult male unemployment in a regression like (3) for the U.S. should be less positive, or perhaps even negative.

The minimum wage affects the youth labor market through the supply as well as the demand side. Surely Mincer's (1976) work stresses this, and the same is implied by a Harris-Todaro (1970) model of equlilibrium search unemployment. If the elasticity of supply of young labor is sufficiently high, the effect of the minimum wage is likely to be reflected mainly in changes in unemployment and labor-force participation, with relatively little effect on employment. This supply-side effect may help explain Layard's observation that the duration of unemployment is relatively high for American youths, reflecting, we can argue, added search unemployment in response to the potentially high rewards if the youth can find a job paying the minimum wage.

In the case of some U.S. labor market policies, supply-side inducements can be beneficial, as they offset the bias of the income tax system against market work.[1] This is not likely to be a valid justification of the minimum wage, for (1) induced labor-force entry reduces time available for investment in schooling, and (2) youths in the U.S. can earn a substantial amount through part-time or summer work without incurring any income-tax liability or adding to that of their parents—there is less of a problem with tax-induced biases against market work by youths. Without any offsetting beneficial supply-side effect, and with the demand-induced reductions in employment noted by Layard, there is no efficiency or equity basis for arguing against a youth subminimum wage.

To explore these ideas in the context of the labor market for youths in the United States, I will estimate a time-series equation modeled after Layard's equation (3). The logarithm of male youth unemployment compared to that of all males, $UY/UTOT$, is regressed on (1) the unemployment rate for men 35–44, in percent, a measure of cyclical activity (vacancy data are not available for the U.S. for a sufficiently long period); (2) the log of full-time earnings of youths relative to all male workers ($WY/WTOT$); (3) the log of the relative populations of young and all males ($POPY/POPTOT$); and (4) the effective minimum wage, computed by interpolating and deflating the series in Welch (1978, p. 29).[2] The regressions are on annual data, 1959–76, and are done separately for all youths 16–24 and for out-of-school youths 14–24.

The parameter estimates are presented in table C15.1. The importance of supply behavior in the youth labor market is underscored by the differences in the responses to adult male unemployment in the two equations. For all youths, whose labor supply is likely to be highly sensitive to the business cycle, I find that higher unemployment lowers their relative unemployment rate, in contradiction to Layard's findings for the U.K. However, when the sample is restricted to out-of-school youths, I observe the same positive relation that Layard found. This suggests that the problem of youth unemployment cannot be analyzed as a totality. Instead, we should distinguish between students and young

Table C15.1    Estimates of Equations for Log $(UY/UTOT)$, Males, 1959–76[a]

|  | All youths 16–24 | Out-of-school youths 14–24 |
|---|---|---|
| Constant | .683 | −.115 |
|  | (2.74) | (−.10) |
| Unemployment rate, men 35–44 | −.051 | .043 |
|  | (−5.11) | (1.36) |
| Log $(WY/WTOT)$ | .117 | .142 |
|  | (.56) | (.16) |
| Log $(POPY/POPTOT)$ | −.028 | .018 |
|  | (−.32) | (.05) |
| Effective minimum wage (100 = 1938–76 average) | .00222 | .00531 |
|  | (4.07) | (3.50) |
| $R^2$ | .92 | .53 |
| DW | 1.98 | 1.83 |

[a]$t$-statistics in parentheses.

people not in school, and recognize that comparisons to the U.K. are most relevant for the latter group.

The results on the minimum wage variable are in the expected direction and dwarf the coefficients on the relative wage variable, though these latter have the expected signs. That this occurs suggests the importance of the induced disemployment and search effects, and indicates too that noncompliance with minimum wage regulations may not be important enough to mitigate the program's detrimental effects on the labor market. Not only is this effect significant—the range of the minimum wage variable during this period is large enough to induce a 46% change in the unemployment rate of out-of-school youths and a 17% change for all youths. The rise in the minimum wage variable from 1959 to 1976, due mostly to extensions of coverage, is alone responsible for a 14% increase in the relative unemployment rate of out-of-school youths and a 6% increase in that of all youths. Finally, that the effects are greater for out-of-school youths is consistent with the observation that in-school youths have a more elastic labor supply and will leave the labor force as the increases in the level and coverage of the minimum wage restrict job opportunities.

Layard's translog cost function estimates of the elasticity of demand for youths are worthy of comment, as there are a number of reasons to suspect they are biased, most probably downward. The only possible reason for an upward bias is Layard's use of time-series data: one finds that cross-section translog estimates of multifactor production or cost functions generally produce lower values of the substitution parameters than do time-series estimates (see Hamermesh and Grant 1979). However, there are two reasons to expect the $e_{ij}$ for youths to be biased down

(1) because the capital stock is held constant, a rise in the wage rate of youths is constrained by Layard to have no effect on the capital stock. Assuming, as seems reasonable, and as is shown in three other studies, that youths and capital are substitutes, the gross elasticity presented by Layard is likely to be below the net elasticity that is relevant for policy.[3] (2) Hamermesh and Grant (1979) have shown that estimates of substitution parameters based on cost functions are generally below those based on production functions specified over the same time period and factor inputs. Which is correct depends of course on the factor markets under consideration, but there is good reason to expect that estimates of production functions, which treat factor quantities are exogenous, will produce better estimates than those of cost functions when the labor force is disaggregated by age and sex. This is especially likely to be true for data on the U.K., where supply elasticities are quite low and thus factor quantities still more likely to be exogenous than in the U.S. In sum, these criticisms suggest that the elasticity of demand for youths is higher than Layard's estimate of $-1.25$ and is probably closer to the estimates obtained in recent studies using the translog production function for the U.S. This underscores the importance of avoiding inducing wage rigidities in the labor market for youths.

Both one's priors and a comparison of my regression to Layard's suggest that great care must be taken in using explanations of British labor-market pathologies to explain those of our labor market. Most important, effects on labor supply among youths are far more important here. Aside from inducing substantial international differences in the cyclical responses of relative unemployment, and in our views of the seriousness of the welfare losses from unemployment, they also imply that fairly low earnings replacement rates in American transfer programs can have larger disincentive effects on effort than will foreign programs offering higher replacement. The international comparison of outcomes is essential, but the causes of those outcomes differ substantially.

## Notes

1. In my 1979 study I have demonstrated how the unemployment insurance system can, by reducing risk, induce increased labor force participation, and have shown that this entitlement effect increases employment and partly offsets the disincentive effect UI produces on the duration of unemployment spells.

2. *WY* and *WTOT* are earnings of year-round full-time male workers, from *Current Population Reports*, P-60 Series, various issues; the data on *POPY, POPTOT, UY,* and *UTOT* are from *Employment and Training Report of the President*, 1977; and the minimum wage variable is computed from Welch (1978, p. 29) by deflating using changes in the average manufacturing wage rate between the years for which Welch presents data on this measure. This series is available on request from the author.

3. Berndt and Wood (1977) discuss the distinction between gross and net elasticities and present conditions under which they will differ.

## References

Berndt, E. and Wood, D. 1977. Engineering and economic approaches to industrial energy conservation and capital formation. MIT Energy Laboratory. Mimeographed.

Hamermesh, D. S. 1979. Entitlement effects, unemployment insurance and employment decisions. *Economic Inquiry* 17:317–32.

Hamermesh, D. S. and Grant, J. H. 1979. Econometric studies of labor-labor substitution and their implications for policy. *Journal of Human Resources* 14:518–42.

Mincer, J. 1976. Unemployment effects of minimum wages. *Journal of Political Economy* 84:S87–104.

Harris, J. R. and Todaro, M. P. 1970. Migration, unemployment and development: A two-sector analysis. *American Economic Review* 60:126–42.

Welch, F. 1978. The rising impact of minimum wages. *Regulation* 2:28–37.

# Comment    Beatrice G. Reubens

In keeping with the purpose of the conference which this volume records, Richard Layard discusses American youth unemployment in light of British experience. He also draws some policy implications for the U.S., but not for Britain. Although Layard approaches some comparative issues with great depth and skill, on several subjects he deals only with Britain, thereby contributing new and valuable research and analysis, but omitting the necessary American data for comparison. On other issues, he ultiizes a limited selection from the body of American research.

As a special contribution to a volume on American youth unemployment, Layard's chapter is interesting and useful. But as an independent effort at comparative analysis, it is flawed not only by the imbalances noted above and the usual limitations of two-case studies, but also by an overly restricted choice of phenomena and explanatory factors, questionable choices in the basic data, and problems in the methods and content of the policy suggestions for the U.S.

The four points of comparison Layard selects as the main phenomena to be explained omit some important issues. Layard chooses intercountry differences in relative youth unemployment, that is, the youth to adult ratio rather than the level and trend in youth rates as the phenomenon. Within this framework, he does not discuss at least one relationship in

Beatrice G. Reubens is senior research associate at Conservation of Human Resources, Columbia University.

Britain which not only differs from American experience, but which American analysts usually reject as inherently unlikely to occur. As Layard's figure 15.1 indicates, British male teenagers had lower unemployment rates that all males through the 1960s, a time when the British postwar baby boom generation entered the labor market and, as figure 15.2 shows, hourly earnings of males under 21 rose rapidly in relation to those of adult males. A discussion of these relative phenomena in Britain and the contrast with the U.S., allowing for differences in data sources, would have dealt with an important comparative subject.

At least two other significant subjects for comparative purposes are not treated because the emphasis on relative youth to adult unemployment is not supplemented by consideration of comparative youth unemployment in the two countries. In section 15.1.6 Layard refers to the relatively successful initial absorption into the labor market of British school-leavers, but he does not present the relevant U.S. data, which show slower rates. Nor does he examine all of the factors that explain the British experience, which is most assuredly not the consequence solely of the differential placement rates in the two countries of such official sources as the Careers Service (Reubens 1977, ch. 7, 8, 9).

The second undiscussed subject is touched on in appendix B where Layard presents information indicating that unemployed British youths, including those who have never worked before, are entitled to welfare payments from age 16 in their own right. Since some U.S. analysts are persuaded that American youths are deterred from participating in the labor force or from holding jobs because of less direct and smaller transfer payments (some to the family rather than the individual), it would have been a prime interest to discover how the British youth benefits (running well over 30% of net weeky earnings for the age group) affect the desire to work. Layard's treatment of alternative income for unemployed youths entirely in relative age group terms neglects some of the issues which most closely affect U.S. policy decisions, especially because these tend to be made in terms of individual groups rather than as relationships between age groups. From many viewpoints, the direct comparison of British and American youths is of prime interest.

Turning from the choice of issues to the choice of explanatory factors, Layard's analytic framework of equilibrium and disequilibrium factors is sufficiently broad and well defined, but the specific elements discussed under each of these main readings is highly selective. Layard seems to have chosen single institutions as explanatory factors simply because the institution is not present in the other country. Thus apprenticeship, income transfers, the legal minimum wage, and the Careers Service are discussed without consideration of all the other relevant institutions and circumstances that might affect outcomes. These single institutions carry too heavy a weight in the discussion and conclusion.

The treatment of the British Careers Service offers an example of some of the shortcomings of the entire chapter. In his summary, Layard states, without documentation, that in the U.S. the government "plays little more role in the placement of youths than in the placement of adults." His discussion of Britain at that point, however, entirely concerns activities for youths. In section 15.1.6 of the text he makes no mention of the U.S. at all, but asserts that in Britain "the state apparatus makes much more effort to find jobs for school leavers than for adults." This statement is supported only by information on British youths (that 22% of a sample of school-leavers said in November 1976 that they obtained their first jobs through the Careers Service). However, the British adult employment service claimed a 23% placement rate in April-July 1977 (*Employment Gazette* June 1979, p. 560). Thus Layard's claim about relative placements in Britain is not documented or supported; no information is provided on the comparable situation in the U.S.; nothing is cited to prove that placements in the U.S. were lower than British for either age group; and no rationale is given for according such importance to this factor, especially to the relative ratio of youth to adult placements. As a conclusion to this unsatisfactory empirical presentation, Layard admits that he cannot say how important this factor is nor can he estimate its influence. Nevertheless, in another unrelated section of the summary, he declares that "the British experience does suggest that a good case can be made for a Careers Service for youths." He does not make clear whether he is recommending to the U.S. an organizational replica of the Careers Service, to which many objections might be raised, or whether he is simply urging better informational, guidance and job placement serivces for school-leavers in the U.S., an acceptable suggestion, but one requiring no comparative analysis and equally applicable to Britain.

Some factors are omitted from the comparative discussion that might have been expected to appear. The narrowing of British earnings differentials between youths and adults (figure 15.2) contrasts with the findings of a widening of differentials for the U.S. (Freeman 1979; Wachter 1977). The causes of this difference would be of high interest. Furthermore, although Layard takes account of the demographic changes in Britain in order to explan time-series changes in the level and ratios of British youth unemployment rates, he does not consider the influence on youth/adult unemployment rates of the differential demographic experience of Britain and the United States. In fact, the American baby boom was more intense and prolonged than the British. The proportion of American 15–19 year olds as a share of the 15–64 year-old population was 4 percentage points higher than the corresponding measure for Britain from the 1960s on; earlier the gap had been smaller. Moreover, teenage full-time educational enrollments, which remove young people from the labor market, grew at a much more rapid rate in

Britain than in the U.S. The growth of British educational enrollments was so rapid that the absolute size of the British teenage labor force actually declined from 1950 to 1975, but in the same period even the American nonenrolled teenage labor force grew and the enrolled teenage labor force grew enormously (Reubens, Harrisson, and Rupp 1981, ch. 2, 3, 4). Some effects on youth unemployment rates might be expected from such differences.

One of the persistent challenges to comparative research is the need for disaggregated data, the paucity of such information in many countries, and the noncomparability of available categories. Some of Layard's controversial explanations may arise from inadequate disaggregation. This may be the reason that Layard's job-rationing hypothesis is not upheld by the Rees-Gray chapter in this volume. Another result of inadequate dissegregation appears in the discussion of those who are neither in school nor in the labor force. Layard attributes this to general affluence and the indulgence of American parents, implying that the dropouts are mainly middle class when in fact the category is dispropor-tionately composed of poor and minority youths (Wachter 1980; Free-man 1980). Our study of youths who are out of school and out of the labor force in the industrialized countries shows that in the countries with a large proportion of youths in this category (namely, Italy, Canada and the United States) the chief common factor is persistently high youth unemployment rates (Reubens, Harrisson, and Rupp 1981).

Some of Layard's choices in regard to basic data are debatable. He completely excludes from his U.S. data, although not necessarily from American studies he cites, the sizable American in-school labor force on the ground that Britain does not count this category in its census. While this is true, it also should be borne in mind that the category is compara-tively small in Britain, partly because of differences in educational enroll-ment rates. For example, in 1960, 68.7% of teenage American boys (15–19 years) were in school against 18.5% in Britain, a difference of over 50 percentage points which has been falling over time but remains sub-stantial today.

It is questionable to exclude the U.S. student labor force, given the long average weekly work hours of older students during the school year, the relatively light demands of U.S. educational institutions on the time of young people, the reshaping of the youth labor market to accommo-date the student labor force, and the competition for jobs with out-of-school teenagers. Moreover, the relative size, labor force participation rates, skill composition, and unemployment rates of the American en-rolled and nonenrolled have varied considerably over time. Although current unemployment rates for enrolled and nonenrolled are similar, it has not always been the case, especially when statistics are separated by age and sex. Admittedly, it is unsatisfactory to count each in-school labor force participant as a full unit regardless of how few hours are worked, especially for cross-national comparisons. The adoption of a system of full-time equivalents might meet this problem. It would have been preferable to use U.S. data for each enrollment status separately, adjusted if necessary, rather than to exclude them entirely, as Layard did.

In focusing on teenagers, Layard has slighted comparisons for the 20–24 year old group which is likely increasingly to occupy the U.S. policy spotlight (Wachter, 1980; Winship 1979). Layard also excludes females from the analysis. Since this omission occurs frequently in cross-national studies, it may be timely to suggest that the use of adjusted and qualified data is preferable to exclusion of this significant part of the youth labor force. One specific effect of this omission is that Layard draws conclusions about income levels of the two societies in relation to participation rates based entirely on male rates and leaving out the offsetting influence of the faster-rising and higher U.S. female labor force participation rates.

Layard draws three policy implications for the U.S., of which the one on the Careers Service has already been discussed. Another concerns the minimum wage. He concludes that "if there must be minimum wages, the case for a separate youth rate seems overwhelming." As Layard himself suggests, his evidence for Britain, which has no legal minimum, and comparisons with U.S. age-wage information do not in themselves lead to his conclusion. He finds the age-wage profiles of youths in the two countries similar and does not find the expected truncation in the U.S. at the lower end as a result of the minimum wage. It may be that this subject cannot be decided by comparing countries which have and do not have a minimum wage law. In that case, should a conclusion be offered for U.S. policy as if it came from the comparative experience when in fact it appears to be mainly based on Layard's acceptance of an American analyst's findings?

The third conclusion for the U.S. is that "it is not obvious in the U.S. that there is any greater equity case for measures to relieve youth unemployment than adult unemployment." His discussion is not entirely about equity, however. He states immediately afterward, and without documentation, that there has been a "relative absence of measures to combat youth unemployment in the U.S. compared with Europe." While it is difficult to obtain precisely comparable records, it is likely that the number of youths on U.S. programs, relative to the youth population, and the amount spent per participant exceed the corresponding number and per participant expenditures in European countries (Anderson and Sawhill, eds. 1980, ch. 6, table 1; Reubens 1980, table 3). And there can be no doubt that American programs have been in effect for more years than European.

But leaving aside these facts, the argumentation by which Layard reaches his conclusion for U.S. policy seems complex and questionable. Layard acknowledges two ways in which American youths carry greater burdens of unemployment than adults compared to the British situation. First, Layard states in the summary that the share of youth unemployment in the total efficiency cost of unemployment may be higher in the U.S. than in Britain. Second, in appendix B, he states that income while unemployed as a percent of income in full-time work is probably lower for youths relative to adults in the U.S. than in Britain. These appear to be two strong grounds for U.S. policy to *favor* unemployed youths, on the dubious assumption that this type of national policy would be drawn from such comparative experience. But Layard introduces a third element (section 15.2). Overall, income out of work (mainly from unemployment compensation) is said to be lower relative to income in work in the U.S. than in Britain (unemployment insurance buttressed by means-tested Supplementary Benefits). Without discussing further the fine points of extended U.C. benefits in the U.S., which prolong it far beyond the 26 weeks offered in Britain, and the differences and similarities between welfare and Supplementary Benefits, it can be accepted that a lower income replacement ratio in the U.S. than in Britain would fall more heavily on adults with family responsibilities than on youths. But does it follow from this that the only course is to abandon the concern about reducing U.S. youth unemployment absolutely and relative to the adult rate? While continuing to give the reduction of youth unemployment a high priority, is it not possible to increase the adult income replacement ratio? Beyond the equity and efficiency issues, there are other reasons for a society to be concerned about high absolute or relative youth unemployment rates, especially if particular subgroups of youths with intensified employment problems are identified (American Assembly 1979).

If these comments have stressed the observed gaps or deficiencies in Layard's paper, it is because one hopes that his analytical skills will soon again address a comparative subject, preferably on a multicountry basis.

### References

American Assembly. 1979. *Report on youth employment.* New York.
Anderson, B. E. and Sawhill, I. V., eds. 1980. *Youth employment and public policy.* Englewood Cliffs: Prentice-Hall, Inc.
Freeman, R. B. 1979. The effect of demographic factors on age-earning profiles. Working Paper no. 316. Cambridge: National Bureau of Economic Research.
Freeman, R. B. 1980. Why is there a youth labor market problem? In Anderson, B. E. and Sawhill, I. V., eds., *Youth employment and public policy.* Englewood Cliffs: Prentice-Hall, Inc.
Great Britain. Department of Employment. June 1979. Market share of the general employment service. *Department of Employment Gazette* 87:558–63.

Reubens, B. G. 1977. *Bridges to work: International comparisons of transition services*. Montclair: Allenheld and Osmun.

———. 1980. Review of foreign experience. In Anderson, B. E. and Sawhill, I. V., eds., *Youth employment and public policy*. Englewood Cliffs: Prentice-Hall, Inc.

Reubens, B. G., Harrisson, J. A. C., and Rupp, Kalman, 1981. *The youth labor force 1945–1995: A cross-national analysis*. Monclair: Allenheld and Osmun.

Wachter, M. L. 1977. Intermediate swings in labor-force participation. *Brookings Paper on Economic Activity* 2/1977: 545–76.

———. 1980. The dimensions and complexities of the youth unemployment problem. In Anderson, B. E. and Sawhill, I. V., eds, *Youth employment and public policy*. Englewood Cliffs: Prentice-Hall, Inc.

Winship, C. 1979. Draft paper on youth labor force statistics. Unpublished.

# Contributors

Martin Neal Baily
Senior Fellow, The Brookings
    Institution
1775 Massachusetts Avenue, NW
Washington, DC 20036

Burt S. Barnow
Acting Director, Office of Research
    & Development
U.S. Department of Labor
Employment & Training
    Administration
601 D Street, NW, Rm 9100
Washington, DC 20213

Charles C. Brown
Department of Economics
University of Maryland
College Park, MD 20742

Gary Chamberlain
Department of Economics
Social Science Building
1180 Observatory Drive
University of Wisconsin
Madison, WI 53706

Kim B. Clark
Harvard University
Business School
Morgan 5—Soldiers Field
Boston, MA 02163

Mary Corcoran
Institute for Social Research
Room 3255
University of Michigan
Ann Arbor, MI 48104

Ronald G. Ehrenberg
Department of Labor Economics
Cornell University
P.O. Box 1000
Ithaca, NY 14853

David T. Ellwood
John F. Kennedy School of
    Government
79 Boylston Street
Cambridge, MA 02138

George Farkas
ABT Associates
55 Wheeler Street
Cambridge, MA 02138

Martin Feldstein
President, National Bureau of
    Economic Research
1050 Massachusetts Avenue
Cambridge, MA 02138

543

T. Aldrich Finegan
Vanderbilt University
Box 1526–B
Department of Economics and
 Business Administration
Nashville, TN 37235

Paul O. Flaim
Chief, Division of Labor Force
 Studies
Bureau of Labor Statistics
Washington, DC 20212

Richard B. Freeman
Department of Economics
Harvard University
Littauer Center, M-6
Cambridge, MA 02138

Robert J. Gordon
Department of Economics
Northwestern University
2003 Sheridan Road, Rm G-180
Evanston, IL 60201

Wayne Gray
National Bureau of Economic
 Research
1050 Massachusetts Avenue
Cambridge, MA 02138

Alan L. Gustman
Department of Economics
Dartmouth College
Hanover, NH 03755

Robert E. Hall
Herbert Hoover Memorial Bldg.
Stanford Univerity
Stanford, CA 94305

Daniel S. Hamermesh
Michigan State University
Department of Economics
Marshall Hall
East Lansing, MI 48824

Stephen M. Hills
Faculty of Labor and Human
 Resources
Ohio State University
1 Page Hall
1810 College Road
Columbus, OH 43201

Choongsoo Kim
Ohio State University
Center for Human Resource
 Research
5701 North High Street
Worthington, OH 43085

Richard Layard
London School of Economics
Houghton Street, Aldwych
London, WC2A 2AE
England

Linda Leighton
Columbia University
Center for Social Sciences
School of International Affairs
Social Science Center
8th Floor, Rm 816
New York, NY 10027

Robert I. Lerman
Heller School
Brandeis University
Waltham, MA 02254

Frank Levy
The Urban Institute
2100 M Street, NW
Washington, DC 20037

James L. Medoff
Department of Economics
Harvard University
Littauer Center, Rm 116
Cambridge, MA 02138

Robert H. Meyer
The Urban Institute
2100 M Street, NW
Washington, DC 20037

Jacob Mincer
Economics Department
International Affairs Bldg., Rm 8
Columbia University
New York, NY 10027

Paul Osterman
Department of Economics
Boston University
270 Bay State Road
Boston, MA 02215

George L. Perry
Brookings Institution
1775 Massachusetts Avenue, NW
Washington, DC 20036

Solomon William Polachek
Department of Economics
Gardner Hall
University of North Carolina
Chapel Hill, NC 27514

Albert Rees
Princeton University
Department of Economics
Princeton, NJ 08540

Beatrice G. Reubens
Senior Research Associate
Conservation of Human Resources
1125 Amsterdam Avenue
New York, NY 10025

Isabel V. Sawhill
Program Director, Employment &
    Labor Policy
The Urban Institute
2100 M Street, NW
Washington, DC 20037

Christopher A. Sims
Department of Economics
University of Minnesota
Minneapolis, MN 55455

Ernst W. Stromsdorfer
ABT Associates, Inc.
55 Wheeler Street
Cambridge, MA 02138

Lawrence H. Summers
Department of Economics
Massachusetts Institute of
    Technology
E52-274A
77 Massachusetts Avenue
Cambridge, MA 02139

W. Kip Viscusi
National Commission for
    Employment Policy
Suite 300
1522 K Street, NW
Washington, DC 20005

Michael Wachter
Department of Economics
3718 Locust Walk/CR
University of Pennsylvania
Philadelphia, PA 19104

Robert J. Willis
Department of Economics
State University of New York at
    Stony Brook
Stony Brook, NY 11790

Christopher Winship
National Opinion Research Center
University of Chicago
6030 South Ellis Ave.
Chicago, IL 60637

David Wise
John F. Kennedy School of
    Government
Harvard University
79 Boylston Street
Cambridge, MA 02138

# Author Index

# Subject Index